LAW AND THE LEGAL SYSTEM

EDITORIAL ADVISORY BOARD

Little, Brown and Company
Law Book Division

A. James Casner, *Chairman*
Austin Wakeman Scott Professor of Law, Emeritus
Harvard University

Francis A. Allen
Edson R. Sunderland Professor of Law
University of Michigan

Clark Byse
Byrne Professor of Administrative Law
Harvard University

Thomas Ehrlich
Provost and Professor of Law
University of Pennsylvania

Geoffrey C. Hazard, Jr.
John A. Garver Professor of Law
Yale University

Willis L. M. Reese
Charles Evans Hughes Professor of Law, Emeritus
Columbia University

Bernard Wolfman
Fessenden Professor of Law
Harvard University

LAW AND THE LEGAL SYSTEM

An Introduction

Second Edition

SAMUEL MERMIN
Emeritus Professor of Law
University of Wisconsin

Little, Brown and Company
Boston and Toronto

Copyright © 1982 by Samuel Mermin

All rights reserved. No part of this book may be reproduced in any form or by any electronic or mechanical means including information storage and retrieval systems without permission in writing from the publisher, except by a reviewer who may quote brief passages in a review.

Library of Congress Catalog Card No. 81-83102

Second Edition

Fourth Printing

ALP

Published simultaneously in Canada
by Little, Brown & Company (Canada) Limited

Printed in the United States of America

To the past, present, and future members of the Decagon, a society founded in New Haven in 1945 by Charles and Nechame Mermin's ten children, for their families and descendant families.

Summary of Contents

Contents

CHAPTER 3

Further Aspects of the Case: The Statute 237

CHAPTER 4

Further Aspects of the Case: The Precedents 281

Preface to the Second Edition

A word about how and why this book was born. As a beginning law student in the 1930s, I deplored the lack of any kind of orientation period. Hence, when after ten years as a government lawyer I went into teaching, one of the first courses I welcomed doing was an introduction-to-law course. I have taught such a course for more than two decades in a law school and several times in a political science department. I still believe there is great value in such a one-semester course.

The present book aims to fulfill the same need in a more abbreviated fashion. During these years of teaching, I have been asked for such an abbreviated text by a variety of people. They were: (1) college students considering the possibility of going to law school; (2) "prelaw advisors" in colleges; (3) parents (usually lawyers) desirous of having their college-age children exposed to what law study is about; (4) citizens desiring to gain a not too painful understanding of the functioning of our legal system; and (5) beginning law students. Some of them had seen books on "what every citizen should know" about leases, auto accidents, probate, etc., or surveys or exposés of the legal profession, or books of massive readings including cases and extracts from books and articles, or a civics book type of exposition that was either too dull and detailed or so simplified as to have substantial utility only for those (e.g., foreigners) quite unfamiliar with our legal institutions. These people were looking for something else.

They wanted a short expository analysis, giving some perspective on the system as a whole, couched in simple language, but not avoiding the difficult problems posed by the system. They wanted, I believe, a discussion of what the law is trying to do, what are some of its basic principles and techniques, what factors affect the success of its efforts, and the nature and interrelationships of the system's institutions.

And the beginning law students additionally wanted, before plunging into their case courses, a brief grounding in fundamentals and some tips on effective law study. The students wanted this assistance even if they were taking an introduction-to-law course (not offered, by the way, in all law schools), since some fundamentals to assist in coping with their other courses were needed at the outset rather than later.

I had been thinking of writing a book that would meet these varied demands, when it was recognized that the materials being used for a one-semester introduction course at my law school had become somewhat outdated; there was no time for a thorough revision, and a suitable substitute could not be agreed on. Thus was born the idea of filling the gap with the kind of book I had been contemplating — a short text that could be read by law students before regular classes began.

The experiment, which used a preliminary version of the present book in the fall of 1972, proved successful enough to warrant the book's publication. Although we used the book in an intensive week prior to regular classes and offered no introduction course, the book might also be used as a supplement to such a course. Alternatively, the student might be asked to read the book on his own, prior to commencement of regular classes or during the first few weeks or months of classes. Whatever system is used will, I think, be preferable to having the unoriented student embarked on law study, as he so often does today, in a climate of bewilderment and frustration.

The plan of the book is simple and readily explained. The long first chapter provides a jurisprudential perspective by discussing the law's interdependence with the social environment, the law's social functions, the social and moral limits on the law's efficacy, and the inescapable role of values in legal judgment. This part of the book also presents the law as a *system,* describing not only some salient characteristics and problems of each of the law's agencies (courts, legislatures, administrative and executive agencies) but also the functioning interrelationships and techniques of these agencies. Some of this chapter may seem elementary to you, but I have no way of knowing how much of my audience has more than the average college student's or college graduate's knowledge of our legal system.

In the succeeding chapters I deal with various aspects of a case involving the law of privacy that was litigated in the federal courts of South Carolina in the 1960s. It is a case in which a state criminal law prohibiting publication of the name of a rape victim was invoked in a privacy-invasion damage suit against a television broadcasting corporation by two rape victims (well-known performers in a traveling puppet show), claiming a television broadcast had named them, at least indirectly. I supplement various aspects of the case with Background Notes designed to canvass the problems raised by the case and to present relevant background information about our system.

Thus, the second chapter presents the pleadings, the trial court and appellate court opinions in the litigated case, and a glimpse of the lawyer's appellate briefs, together with a discussion of appellate advocacy. There is then a Background Note on mainly procedural materials to aid your understanding of how the court process works. The Note deals with organization and jurisdiction of courts; requirements for starting a lawsuit, including the difficult problem of "standing" to sue; why the case is in a federal court; some relations between state and federal courts; the significance of the "motion to dismiss" filed in the case; the nature of our "adversary system" of litigation; and aspects of criminal proceedings under the statute. A further Note provides a background in the tort law of privacy ("tort" being a name for conduct injuring certain interests that are noncontractual in nature, e.g., the interest in being free from the impact of another's negligence, or of his intentional conduct like assault, libellous injury to reputation, invasion of privacy, etc.).

The third chapter presents another aspect of the case — i.e., the court's treatment of the South Carolina statute — and discusses some basic issues of interpretation raised thereby. The Background Notes deal with further aspects of statutory interpretation and with the role of statutes in relation to common law.

Next come those aspects of the case involving the court's handling of case precedents. The text analysis of this process, together with the succeeding Background Note, treat some fundamental features of the Anglo-American precedent system.

The fifth chapter discusses (1) a constitutional issue the defendant might have raised but did not: whether the state statute violated the freedom of expression protected by the Fourteenth Amendment; and (2) the scope of the constitutional protection of privacy. The Background Note goes on to discuss four basic features of our constitutional jurisprudence.

Briefly treating some miscellaneous topics not previously discussed, the Postscript discusses the future of the legal profession, legal education, and law and other disciplines.

Appendix 1 deals with some bread-and-butter questions of the entering law student, such as: how to summarize an assigned case; how to prepare for class; what to do in class; and how to cope with law examinations. An examination question and a suggested answer are included, with footnoted references to pages of the text relevant to various parts of the answer.

Appendix 2 is concerned with Bill of Rights protections against government procedures in a criminal case.

Changes in this edition from the 1973 first edition are in part the result of student reaction to the first. I became aware that the first edition's relative neglect of the criminal law component in some of the procedural and constitutional areas covered was disappointing to the average reader — who tends, probably because of media influence, to think of law in terms of criminal law. This gap has been filled by the section in Chapter 2 on "aspects of criminal proceedings under the statute." The section includes procedural steps in a criminal case and the nature of corporate criminal liability. A third element in this section, Bill of Rights protections, proved so lengthy it was transferred to Appendix 2. The general reader and beginning student will probably have as great an interest in this handy summary reference to basic constitutional liberty protections as in any other topic.

A second reader reaction that I have taken into account is a dissatisfaction with generalizations not anchored to *specifics*. Specifics in the book — in the form of concrete situations, court decisions, and footnote documentation for further reference — have multiplied, both in the new criminal material and in other areas. This new emphasis is manifested particularly in the Postscript treatment of the future of the legal profession and legal education, and in the material on: statutory interpretation, interrelations of common law and statute, the precedent system, tort law of privacy, constitutional law of privacy, and law of "standing."

A third kind of change was necessitated by decisional, statutory, or developmental changes occurring since 1973 in some of the many substantive or procedural fields covered, particularly in federal jurisdiction; sovereign immunity; respective roles of legislative, executive, administrative, and judicial agencies; and the interrelations among agencies — including the movement for deregulation of business and stricter controls over administrative agencies.

The updating has been accompanied by attempts at improvement in analysis, coverage, and exposition throughout the book, while retaining for the most part the topical structure of the original. Because of new topics, and more thorough treatment of previous ones, the book is approximately one-third longer.

I am indebted to a number of my colleagues who were willing to read and make helpful comments on various portions of the manuscript (Willard Hurst, Abner Brodie, Gerald Thain, Stuart Gullickson, Walter Dickey, Frank Remington, Theodore Schneyer and Gordon Baldwin), and grateful for the monumental patience of Lora N. Mermin, who improved the entire manuscript by the critical eye of an intelligent nonlawyer, the "educated layperson" at whom the book is partly aimed. Quotations on p.262 from Llewelyn, "Remarks on the Theory of Appellate Decision," and on p.243 from Regina v. Ojibway were authorized by Vanderbilt Law Review and Canada Law Book Co., Aurora, Ontario, respectively. The job of typing and preparing the manuscript was superbly done by Sara Parisi.

S.M.

Madison, Wisconsin
July, 1981

LAW AND THE LEGAL SYSTEM

Chapter 1

Some General Observations on Law and the Legal System

A. The Law-in-Society Perspective

People specializing in a particular study area tend after a time to think of their area as being at the center of the universe. You have perhaps seen the humorous drawing of a New Yorker's view of the United States in which the eastern seaboard dominates the map, while the Midwest, mountain states, and Far West are an almost undifferentiated glob of shrunken territory off to the left. When your life is bound up with the law, you may tend to think of it as hovering over everything else, like some "brooding omnipresence in the sky."

But if you were a student of society as a whole, bent on assessing the roles of all factors in social life, law would assume a more subordinate role. You would tend to think of society as molding the law. You would tend to say that society shapes people's attitudes and ideals, while these in turn shape the kinds of conduct ("law-abiding" or otherwise) in which people engage and the kinds of courts, legislatures, and other legal institutions we have. If you were a Marxist sociologist you would lay particular stress on how legal and other aspects of the society are influenced by the "means of production" and economic class interest.

Even the non-Marxist, however, recognizes the vital role of economic interest and the material conditions of life in influencing the law. The Supreme Court itself can be cited on this point. In 1943, when the Court was dealing with a damage suit by an injured railroad worker who (the railroad argued) had "assumed" the risk of injury on the job, the Court discussed the development, in the preceding century, of this "assumption of risk" doctrine. Recognizing that the doctrine was based on a judicially *implied* provision in the employment contract, the Court said the doctrine was "a judicially created rule which was developed in response to the general impulse of common law courts at the beginning of this period to insulate the employer as much as possible from bearing the 'human overhead' which is an inevitable part of the cost — to someone — of the doing of industrialized business. The general purpose behind this development in the common law seems to have been to give maximum freedom to expanding industry."[1] Many have agreed with this assessment.[2]

Or consider the following history of judicial interpretation of an insurance policy clause. Not long after invention of the airplane, an exclusion clause under which the insurance company was not liable for injuries or death resulting from the policyholder's "participation in aeronautics" was often written into accident and life insurance policies. In the 1920s and early 1930s, court decisions upheld the inclusion of *passengers* within the exclusion clause; an individual had, by virtue of being a passenger, "participated" in aeronautics.[3] But a shift in judicial opinion to the opposite view occurred in the next two decades. Why? The courts were simply taking account of the enormously expanded role of aviation since the early cases, and the consequently broader social impact of adverse decisions on the status of passengers. A court in 1942 put it this way: " 'Participating in aeronautics' in 1913 is far different in its meaning than is 'participating in aeronautics' now or in 1929. . . . The law is a living thing that must keep [pace] with the people and conditions it regulates."[4]

On a broader scale, the fact that one "can plausibly correlate factors in the material environment in America with developments in American law, law enforcement, and public attitudes towards law"[5] is

1. Tiller v. Atlantic Coast Line RR. Co., 318 U.S. 54, 58-59 (1943).

2. Among those works suggesting a similar explanation of the "assumption of risk" doctrine — or of a subdoctrine, the "fellow servant rule" (under which the employee was said to have impliedly assumed the risk of injury by a fellow employee's negligence) — are Levy, The Law of the Commonwealth and Chief Justice Shaw 178-181 (1957); Bohlen, Voluntary Assumption of Risk, 20 Harv. L. Rev. 14, 31 (1906); Friedman & Ladinsky, Social Change and the Law of Industrial Accidents, 67 Colum. L. Rev. 50, 51-58 (1967). For opposing arguments see Pound, The Economic Interpretation of the Law of Torts, 53 Harv. L. Rev. 365, 373-380, 382 (1940); Burdick, Is Law the Expression of Class Selfishness? 25 Harv. L. Rev. 349, 354-371 (1912).

3. See, e.g., Bew v. Travelers' Ins. Co., 95 N.J.L. 533, 112 A. 859 (1921); Travelers' Ins. Co. v. Peake, 82 Fla. 128, 89 So. 418 (1921); Meredith v. Business Men's Accident Assn., 213 Mo. App. 688, 252 S.W. 976 (1923); Head v. New York Life Ins. Co., 43 F.2d 517 (10th Cir. 1930).

4. Wells v. Kansas City Life Ins. Co., 46 F. Supp. 754, 758 (D.N.D. 1942), aff'd, 133 F.2d 224 (8th Cir. 1943). For a summary of the development of the law in these insurance cases, see Annot., 45 A.L.R.2d 462 (1956).

5. Auerbach, Garrison, Hurst & Mermin, The Legal Process 85 (1961). The authors go on to say (at 85-86): "For instance, the fact of abundant land permitted a legal policy of liberal disposition of the public domain; led to habits of wasteful-

widely accepted. This social environment of law, however, actually comprehends far more than material conditions. Other influences are social institutions such as educational and religious institutions, the family unit, unions, corporations, trade associations, fraternal organizations, neighborhood associations, political parties, pressure groups, and lobbies of all kinds. Further, the power of tradition, habits, ideas, and ideals — a force often identified with a general contemporary "climate of opinion" — is a weighty aspect of law's environment. Such factors as human inertia,[6] greed, altruism, prejudice, and ignorance, and sheer accident also should not be ignored.

The significance of these ever-shifting social factors was epitomized in 1881 on the first page of Holmes's *The Common Law*. The book was one of the first attempts to create a unifying perspective on the mass of technical, seemingly inconsistent, and confusing doctrines in Anglo-American judge-made law. The often-quoted passage reads:

> The life of the law has not been logic: it has been experience. The felt necessities of the time, the prevalent moral and political theories, intuitions of public policy, avowed or unconscious, even the prejudices which judges share with their fellow-men, have had a good deal more to do than the syllogism in determining the rules by which men should be governed. The law embodies the story of a nation's development through many centuries, and it cannot be dealt with as if it contained only the axioms and corollaries of a book of mathematics.

Yet, after all this has been said, it remains true that the "law" blade of the law-society scissors must be reckoned with. Among other

---

ness, ultimately requiring legislation on conservation; and promoted an American tendency to thumb one's nose at legal authority (one could, if necessary, move on). A difference in the availability of water, as between the arid western states and the eastern states, correlates with clear differences in the legal doctrines governing the use of water in the various states. Although the Supreme Court held in 1825 that the federal admiralty and maritime jurisdiction extended only to tidewater, it overruled itself in 1851, recognizing explicitly that the effects of the invention of the steamboat and settlement of the Mississippi Valley upon commerce on navigable streams made it necessary that the federal jurisdiction apply to all navigable waters. Technological change in such fields as printing and telegraphy produced new legal problems, in areas of trademark and copyright, libel, and freedom of speech. Urbanization, the coming of the automobile, mass production, meant new problems for legal solution, and new doctrines in auto negligence law, legislation on health, safety, fair dealing, employer-employee relations, monopolies, and many other subjects. Technological change also affected law enforcement: it made enforcement in some ways more difficult (e.g., the auto provided a fast means of escape) but in many ways easier (officials had not only fast transport and quick communication, but many scientific weapons of crime detection)". For concise elaboration of the dependent aspect of the role of law, see Hurst, The Growth of American Law 3-19 (1950).

6. The factor of "drift and inertia," not as commonly noticed as the others listed here, has been emphasized by Hurst. See, e.g., Hurst, Law and Social Process

things,[7] pressures are exerted upon courts by the intellectual force of legal precedents and ideas, their logical implications and analogies, the traditional legal ways of approaching problems, and the traditional legal notions of justice.[8] These may not have been simply the product of social forces. And they may block or impede, temporarily at least, social forces pushing in an opposite direction (though this effect is mitigated by the ambiguities of principle and competition among principles, precedents, analogies, and maxims in the judicial arsenal).[9]

Furthermore, laws and judicial decisions — in spite of well-known exceptions — do have tangible social consequences that otherwise probably would not occur. It can hardly be denied that the Supreme Court decisions on abortion, school segregation, affirmative action, criminal procedure, and obscenity; or congressional statutes on welfare, labor relations, taxes, government spending or wage-price-rent controls; or executive decisions on such matters as the Vietnam War (coupled with court decisions not to interfere) have substantially affected people's lives.[10]

Thus a beginner in the study of law should recognize the significant impact of such decisions and statutes while at the same time understanding that the most common mistake made at that stage of study is to forget the social setting of the law — this interaction between society and law. Indeed, such forgetting has even been charged against

---

in United States History 63-75 (1960); Law and Social Order in the United States 63-67, 206-213 (1977).

7. Included in this "legal" world is the intellectual and charismatic force exerted by particular individuals — the "greats" among the judges, legislators, administrators, and advocates.

8. This is the sort of thing that Roscoe Pound discussed (sometimes, I think, in exaggerated fashion) in terms of "the tenacity of a taught tradition," "received ideals" of rightness and wrongness, and "received techniques" of utilizing "principles" to "bring about a body of logically interdependent precepts." See Pound, *supra* n.2.

9. For exposition of the point in the parenthesis, see Chap. 4 herein under **A.** The rest of the material in the paragraph reflects a familiar "cultural lag" idea: The ability of new social forces to supplant existing legal rules is diminished by the sticky persistence of the old rules, assisted by courts whose interpretations of common law, statute, or constitution are initially shaped more by the old order than the new. Also, the mere attainment of a legal change — even one that is relatively ineffective — has sometimes defused the social and political forces responsible for the change. See Tushnet, Commentary, Perspectives On the Development of American Law, 1977 Wis. L. Rev. 81, 102-105. And survival of some rules and traditions may be due not to their acceptability to dominant social groups but to their relation to other rules and traditions that do have such acceptability. Nelson, Legal History, Ann. Survey Am. L. 625, 639-640 (1973-1974).

10. For realistic details on the striking impact of a number of Burger Court rulings on personal rights (indigent misdemeanants' right to counsel; hearings with procedural safeguards for alleged probation and parole violators; severe limits on death penalty; limits on involuntary commitment of mentally ill; abortion rights), see Choper, Judicial Review and the National Political Process 108-122 (1980).

respected legal historians.[11] One mode of accommodating these interacting elements is to restrict to "short-term" periods any dominating role of the "law" element.[12] Another is to say that "the law . . . was acted upon by other social forces *more often* than acting upon them . . . its role has been much more to organize, channel, legitimize and, in a substantial measure to redirect, the course of changes that started outside the law" (emphasis added).[13]

B. Functions of Law

Let me now explore one general aspect of this relation: What does law *do* for people in our society — or, putting it in terms of what the legal agencies are supposed to do or are trying to do (sometimes successfully), what are the social functions of our law?

You probably think first about the *dispute-settling* function. We do tend to think about the courts and their business of settling disputes. These may be disputes between private parties, or between a private party and a government unit or official, or between different government units or officials. Many government administrative agencies also engage in adjudicative dispute-settling. But it is worth remembering that private individuals functioning in the area of labor arbitration and commercial arbitration already account for a larger number of dispute settlements per year than do all the courts of the nation. Here too, however, the courts play a role — they can be called on to enforce the arbitration award, and sometimes to enforce an agreement to arbitrate.

Another function we tend to think of right away is *maintaining*

11. Thus, Friedman, A History of American Law (1973) has been taken to task for its stated view of law (at 10) as a "mirror of society" or as "molded by economy and society." For criticism based on the book's relative neglect of social factors other than economic, of "autonomous" and "ideological" aspects of law, and of the reciprocal effects of law on society, see Tushnet, *supra* n.9. See also book reviews by Presser, 122 U. Pa. L. Rev. 217, 225-228 (1973), and White, 59 Va. L. Rev. 1130, 1134-1135, 1138-1141 (1973). The economic class emphasis in Horwitz, The Transformation of American Law, 1780-1860 (1977) has also been subjected to criticism for too narrow or doctrinaire a view of legal history. See reviews by Reid, 55 Tex. L. Rev. 1307, 1310-1321 (1977); McClain, 68 Calif. L. Rev. 382 (1980); Gilmore, 86 Yale L.J. 788, 793-797 (1977); Smith, 1977 Wis. L. Rev. 1253, 1263-1276; Bridwell, 53 Ind. L.J. 449 (1978). The "ruling class domination" hypothesis is further criticized in Hurst, Old and New Dimensions of Research In United States Legal History, 23 Am. J. Legal Hist. 1, 14-19 (1979); Pound, Interpretations of Legal History, chap. 5 (1923).

12. E.g., Tushnet, *supra* n.9 at 105; Pound, *supra* n.2 at 366.

13. Hurst, *supra* n.5 at 4, 9.

order, through the bulk of criminal law, against violence or aggravated harm to persons or property, by the threat of the penalties of imprisonment and/or fines. This of course includes the policing function as well as the court's role in trials and sentencing, and the operations of other officials such as prosecutors and parole and probation personnel. Maintaining order also involves protection (through sedition, treason, and related laws) against that extreme threat to order, the violent overthrow of government. Thus the law legitimates certain uses of force by government but not (save for exceptional circumstances, such as legitimate self-defense) by private parties.

But there is much more to our legal system than settling disputes and maintaining order. For one thing, the legal system constitutes a *framework within which certain common expectations about the transactions, relationships, planned happenings, and accidents of daily life can be met* (and this force for predictability and regularity can itself be viewed as a species of maintenance of order.)[14] We expect that our customary ways of behavior will be facilitated and not disrupted by law without strong reason; we expect that those who have suffered personal injuries — particularly those who were without fault — will be compensated for their injuries under the laws of tort; that those who have made promises will be held to their promises (or, if not, be required to make recompense) under the laws of contract; that those who own property can get the law to enforce their expectations that they have exclusive rights in it and are free to dispose of it as they wish. All of these expectations have to be somewhat qualified since the rights involved — especially those of property — have been subjected to conditions and exceptions. That is, the nature of the expectations is partly a product of conditioning by the legal system, thereby illustrating what I referred to before as the interaction of law and society.

In both constitution and statute there are functions of yet another sort: provisions aimed at *securing efficiency, harmony, and balance in the functioning of the government machinery.* Here I am thinking of the constitutional separation of powers by which specific kinds of power are allocated to specific branches of government with an attempt to avoid undue concentration in any one branch. And I think of other provisions for planning the affairs of government — statutes like the Full Employment Act and government reorganization acts — and the fiscal planning represented by budgets for the raising (taxation, borrowing) and spending of public money. I think of a different kind of

14. One of the ideas stressed by Professor Lon Fuller was that the law was simultaneously a means of social control and a means of facilitating human interaction and the realization of reciprocal expectancies. Fuller, Law as an Instrument of Social Control and Law as a Facilitation of Human Interaction, 1975 B.Y.U.L. Rev. 89.

planning, too, exemplified by zoning and other land use controls, conservation laws, and environmental protections. I think also — because the legal machinery requires maintaining legal skills for its maintenance — of provisions governing the qualifications of lawyers, judges, and other government officials for their respective vocations. There are, moreover, measures that build into the system agencies to make continuing assessments and proposals for improvement of the system — e.g., the state legislative councils and judicial councils, the commissioners on uniform state laws, the federal judicial conferences, and the Administrative Conference of the United States.

In the Constitution can be seen another vital function of our law: *protection of the citizen against excessive or unfair government power.* I refer mainly to the Bill of Rights — to such basic rights as freedom of speech, press, and religion, the right to privacy and against unreasonable searches and seizure, the privilege against self-incrimination, the right of jury trial for crime. Remember that the "due process" clause has been construed by the courts to assure both fair *procedure* and freedom from arbitrariness in the *substance* of government requirements. A standard of equality of treatment applies to the states through the equal protection clause of the Fourteenth Amendment and is, to some uncertain extent, applicable to the federal government through the due process clause of the Fifth Amendment. Remember also that included in the due process protection against both governments are property rights, as well as life and liberty.

Our legal system is concerned, too, with *protecting people against excessive or unfair private power.* In addition to antitrust law protection against private monopolistic power are a number of specialized protections. For example, an employer's power is curbed by laws like those compelling the payment of minimum wages, or prohibiting discrimination in employment, or compelling collective bargaining with unions; a corporation's power in the sale of its securities is curbed by SEC requirements. Analogous restrictions apply through a host of regulatory laws and administrative commissions on both federal and state levels.

Somewhat overlapping in function with these laws are some that are aimed at *assuring people an opportunity to enjoy the minimum decencies of life* by protecting their economic and health status. These functions have been more prominent in the later history of our society. I have in mind laws on unemployment insurance, social security, Medicare, public housing, welfare, and antipoverty programs, as well as older statutes like those on bankruptcy and garnishment. I would also include measures for psychic health, by which I mean not only government services for the poor who are mentally ill, but also measures attempting to eliminate various external sources of psychic distress.

These include laws and decisions discouraging discrimination, giving redress for injuries to reputation and invasions of privacy, enlarging opportunities for recreation, and reducing the pollution of air, water, and landscape.

One other point: Is there any sense in which it is true that law has an *ethical or moral function?* The answer, I think, is definitely yes. Most of the functions already mentioned have a clear ethical dimension. Thus, in settling disputes, the law aims at a result that is fair and socially desirable. A good deal of criminal law carries out ethical precepts of conduct — many of which are in the Ten Commandments. In tort law, many of the principles concerning either negligent or intentional infliction of injury may be traced to the Golden Rule. The obligation to keep one's promises is an ethical obligation. Similarly, the agencies I mentioned as being concerned with improving the legal system have had as goals not only increased efficiency but also more socially desirable results. Ethical or humanitarian motivation has been at least one of the sources of the mentioned legislation aimed at raising the standard of living of the disadvantaged and legislation protecting people against unfair exercise of public or private power. Much legislation and general legal principle uses explicitly ethical terms in laying down standards of conduct — phrases like "good faith," "not profiting by one's own wrong," "fair and equitable," "unjust enrichment." The Constitution itself, as we have seen, speaks in terms of equality and (as a judicial interpretation of "due process") fairness. Hence it is altogether misleading to say, as some have said, that legal duties have nothing to do with moral duties.

One might, it is true, find certain dissimilarities between legal and moral rules, e.g., in the different "levels" of morality sometimes embodied in them,[15] or in various other respects.[16] There are certainly situations in which, it is said, a moral duty but not a legal duty exists. For example, a blind stranger is starting to cross the street. You are beside him and without harm to yourself can avoid his walking into an automobile by simply grabbing his arm. You don't do so, and he is injured. Generally in America the law says you are not liable for damages. Your inaction in this circumstance was, legally, not "negligence." The court might say: You had an ethical or moral duty but not a legal duty. But this does not mean that the law is here indifferent to ethical or moral duties. It means that the law here chooses a different ethical duty from that which some moralists might choose, and does so on the assumption that its choice will better serve the public welfare.

15. See discussion in Fuller, The Morality of Law, chap. 1 (rev. ed., 1969); Cahn, The Moral Decision 38-43 (1955).

16. Cahn, *id.* at 43-49; Hart, The Concept of Law 163-176 (1961).

Thus, the judges are in effect saying: One ought not to have to respond to damages here, because one ought not to have legal obligations that (1) strongly limit our basic ideal of individual freedom of action (including our freedom to do nothing) by requiring affirmative action in an emergency situation where it is not clear that the average man would so act, especially in the absence of a known requirement to do so; (2) are very difficult to administer because of the vagueness of the rule and because of the difficulty arising from there being more than one spectator on hand, i.e., which one has the duty? and if all have, won't they get in each other's way? (3) apply in the kind of emergency situations where people tend to freeze or panic. In short, the judges are saying in this situation — and in others that could be cited[17] — that it is *unfair* or too violative of other values to impose a legal duty here. You may disagree with the reasoning, but you cannot say the law is being indifferent to ethical or moral duties. In its concern with standards of conduct, the law is honeycombed with "ought" propositions that purport to be rationally based. After all, the law is not an end in itself; it is a means for the achievement of social ends. Even the Sabbath, we are told, was made for man, not man for the Sabbath.

Perhaps you tend to think of a judge's decision as value-free, i.e., as flowing strictly and logically from the unequivocal requirements of

17. Even the duty toward truth may, in some circumstances, be rationally sacrificed in the light of other values. In criminal cases, concern for the defendant (who, except in minor cases, is in peril of deprivation of his liberty) has led our law to entitle the defendant to put the burden on the prosecution to prove its case beyond a reasonable doubt, even when he and his lawyer know he is guilty; i.e., the defendant is entitled to lie by pleading "not guilty." And after an acquittal, he cannot be subjected to double jeopardy by re-prosecution for the same crime — even if overwhelming new evidence has been discovered manifesting his guilt and the perjury of his testimony. He could be prosecuted for the separate crime of that perjury, but not on the basis of any part of the testimony "that related to the elements of the charge on which the acquittal was obtained. And in the civil area, most jurisdictions prohibit suits for libel, malicious prosecution, or similar torts where the foundation of the suit is the alleged commission of perjury by the [present] defendant in prior litigation which led to a judgment against the present plaintiff. The values of finality in litigation — and peace for those released by a judgment from entoilment in it — are in these instances thought to override the interest in finding the truth." Wolfram, Client Perjury: The Kutak Commission and the Association of Trial Lawyers on Lawyers, Lying Clients, and the Adversary System, 1980 Am. B. Foundation Research J. 964, 976.

Another illustration involves the controverted question whether a lawyer should, by disclosure to the court, breach his client's confidences about perjury committed or to be committed by the client. The argument for nondisclosure has been: "If an attorney were required (or, perhaps, even permitted) to reveal client perjury, this would unduly chill the willingness of too many clients to confide in their attorneys their knowledge of matters that, perhaps mistakenly, they might regard as embarrassing, illegal, dangerous, or irrelevant. Unless attorneys are able to assure their clients that nothing they reveal to them will be used against their interests, it is feared that much that should be revealed will remain unknown to the lawyer." *Id.* Further on this issue of lawyer disclosure, see Postscript herein at nn. 76-79.

statute or judicial precedent. This, as Chapter 4 tries to make clear, and as my earlier quotation from Holmes suggests, is a delusion. Of course, the requirements of logical and factual truth are not irrelevant to a judicial decision. The judge does want his facts to be substantiated and wants his decision to be logically consistent with a reasonable view of the requirements of constitution, statute, and judicial precedent. But notice that I speak of a *reasonable view* of the requirements, for they are not free from ambiguity. Within the range of freedom allowed for his choice of that reasonable view (and I suspect it is a larger range than you presently suppose), he is concerned — at least in difficult cases — with questions like fairness and social reasonableness of the result. This is why an astute legal scholar has said that judicial decisions are not true or false, but rather good or bad.[18]

C. *Limits of Law*

Given some such list of law's functions as I have set out — and other lists could be compiled, shorter or longer, or couched in different categories[19] — an interesting question is, how far can these functions go? What kinds of specific barriers have been encountered in the attempt to fulfill these functions? What, in other words, are the major "limits on effective legal action," to use the phrase of Roscoe Pound? By this I don't mean legal limits like those set by the Constitution. I am concerned rather with the important nonlegal or practical limits that are rooted, you might say, in the human condition — though I shall occasionally refer to the Constitution as well.

1. Social Conditioning

One outer limit, of course, arises from an already mentioned fact: the social conditioning of law. In other words, if basic socioeconomic conditions and interests have a shaping influence on the law, one cannot

18. Cohen, Ethical Systems and Legal Ideals 32-33 (1933; Cornell ed. 1959). A contrary and presently distinctly minority view is Dworkin's assertion that even in "hard cases," there is a single correct or right answer derivable from legal principles (rather than "policies"), including, in case of ambiguities or conflict of principle, more ultimate principles underlying the others and the legal system as a whole. See text of Chap. 4 herein at nn. 27-34.

19. Thus, Professor Hurst observes that within the limits of the ideal of "constitutionalism," law's functions in American history were (1) embodying the "legitimate monopoly of force" and claiming "as a corollary, the right to appraise the

expect the law to turn around and completely transcend those conditions and interests. No one, in a society with the kind of private property substructure that America now has, expects that Congress will in the foreseeable future pass a National Communization of Property Act destroying and replacing that substructure.

This is not to say that gradual legislative restrictions on private property rights have not occurred and will not occur. Some of these occurrences I have mentioned in discussing the function of law. They have occurred in spite of the fact that legislators' economic interest is generally viewed as closer to that of the "Establishment" than to the classes that were principal beneficiaries of the legislation. The same can be said of the role played by, and prior backgrounds of, the judges. Paul Freund reminded us in 1949 of Supreme Court justices who on the bench departed from views held, or probably held, in their pre-Court careers.[20] More recent examples also can be found.[21]

Yet when all such cautionary qualifications have been made, it remains true that "the business of a legal system is to make the postulates of a society work. It would be remarkable indeed if it could be so worked as to secure their fundamental transformation."[22] Thus one aspect of the social conditioning limit on law is that basic change in the socioeconomic structure is, to put it mildly, neither easily nor

legitimacy of all private forms of power," (2) emphasizing "regular and rational procedures," as well as "some level of rationality in the substance of public policy," (3) "allocat[ing] scarce economic resources . . . by taxing and by spending" and indirectly by "public borrowing and also by the standards by which it regulated behavior (as when by setting standards for marketing food, it required a certain level of capital investment by food dealers)." Hurst, Legal Elements in United States History, in Fleming & Bailyn, eds., Law in American History 3-6 (1971). Llewellyn thought that the "law-jobs" consisted of: "cleaning up . . . grievances and disputes"; "channeling conduct . . . so that, negatively grievances and disputes are avoided, and, positively, men's work is geared into team-play"; "re-channeling along new lines"; "allocation of that *say* which in case of doubt or trouble is to go, and . . . the procedures for making that say an official and binding say"; "producing a net organization and direction of the work of the whole group or society, and in a fashion which unleashes incentive"; "building and using techniques and skills for keeping the men and machinery of all the law-jobs on their jobs and up to the jobs." Llewellyn, On the Good, the True, the Beautiful in Law, 9 U. Chi. L. Rev. 224, 253 (1942); The Normative, the Legal, and the Law Jobs, 49 Yale L.J. 1355, 1373-1400 (1940). Summers and Howard recognize seven functions of law: helping to (1) promote human health, including a healthy environment, (2) reinforce the family and protect private life, (3) keep community peace, (4) protect basic freedoms, (5) secure equality of opportunity, (6) recognize and order private ownership, (7) exercise surveillance and control over persons in positions of power. Summers & Howard, Law, Its Nature, Functions and Limits 440 (2d ed. 1972). See also Raz, The Authority of Law 163-179 (1979).

20. Freund, On Understanding the Supreme Court 45-47 (1949). See also Croyle, Industrial Accident Liability Policy of the Early Twentieth Century, 7 J. Legal Stud. 279 (1978).

21. See Chap. 4 herein, text at nn. 74-82.

22. Laski, The State in Theory and Practice 177 (1935).

quickly achieved through legal agencies. This is as true (I think *more* true) of drastically different legal systems — Soviet, Chinese, or Cuban.

2. Popular Habits, Attitudes, Ideals

A second limit that comes quickly to mind is that the law dare not get too far away from popular attitudes, habits, and ideals in the various situations that arise in everyday life (this necessity can also be viewed as a form of social conditioning). A number of these habits, attitudes, and ideals will be dealt with below.

a. *Racial or Ethnic Prejudices*

The significance of the role of racial or ethnic prejudice in our society needs no elaboration.[23] The difficulties we have encountered in enforcing racial desegregation have stemmed largely from strongly entrenched popular attitudes or habits on the part of substantial segments of the population. It is possible — but far from easy — for the law to help change those racial or ethnic attitudes. I shall comment later on some basis for optimism in this respect.

b. *Opposition to Sumptuary Restraints*

Racial prejudice is of course not the only illustration of this second limit. Liquor prohibition was contrary to the entrenched attitudes of so many people that it led to widespread violation and big-time racketeering, and eventually had to be repealed. But remember, in comparing the law's retreat in the case of liquor prohibition with its relative lack of retreat in the case of prohibiting segregation, that the opposition to liquor prohibition was quite widespread rather than opposition to liquor prohibition was more widespread — not concentrated in one geographical region of the country. Moreover, it was not backed by the moral force of providing equality of opportunity for a long-suffering race. Experience with marijuana prohibition seems to be developing in a fashion somewhat resembling the experience with liquor prohibition: Penalties are being drastically reduced, and ultimate legalization is probable if new evidence of the drug's harmfulness, surfacing from time to time, proves unpersuasive.

23. See generally, 12 Intl. Encyc. Soc. Sci. 439-451; 13 *id.* at 277-282 (1968).

c. Opposition to Excessive Rigor: The Death Penalty

Consider another example, this time from further back in history. In eighteenth-century England, you may remember, the penalty imposed for various crimes — even the minor crimes like pickpocketing and other petty theft — was death. In the later eighteenth century and the early nineteenth century, as the opposition to the severity of these penalties developed more strongly, an interesting thing happened. Judges and juries started circumventing these penalties. The law had diverged too much from the general attitudes of the people. So judges interpreted the statutes in a very peculiar way in order to place a particular defendant out of the reach of the particular statute that, with a normal reading, would apply to him. The jury would also come in with strange verdicts, such as acquittals when the evidence seemed to indicate guilt. Sometimes the jury would merely postpone the day of reckoning. For instance, a well-known case involved a defendant charged with stealing a pair of trousers, an act to which the death penalty applied. The jury, while ultimately coming in with a verdict of manslaughter, knew that the judge would set aside the verdict as not making sense. A little time was gained, and this was augmented by the uncertainty of a second prosecution.[24]

In our day, we have seen a rather analogous inability of the death penalty to operate effectively — this time because a substantial segment of public sentiment was finding the penalty too cruel not merely for certain relatively minor offenses but for major offenses, typically murder. Witness the protracted delays in executions; the executive commutations to life sentences; the seemingly greater tendency of appellate courts in capital cases to find that reversible errors had been committed in the trial; a seemingly greater jury tendency in capital cases to convict of an offense less than the charged offense; the Supreme Court of California's 1972 decision that the death penalty violated the state constitution as a "cruel or unusual punishment"[25]; and the United States Supreme Court's decisions in the same decade.

The latter Court ruled that the death penalty was "cruel and unusual punishment" (1) when imposed for *rape* of an adult woman, in the absence of aggravating circumstances like excessive brutality or serious, lasting injury;[26] (2) when, as in the *Furman* case, sentencing provisions left so much room for unguided discretion that the death

24. Hall, Theft, Law and Society 138 (1935). For various instances of circumventions by judges, prosecutors, and juries, of death penalties for minor transgressions, see *id.* at 118-141.

25. California v. Anderson, 6 Cal. 3d 628, 493 P.2d 880, *cert. denied*, 406 U.S. 958 (1972).

26. Coker v. Georgia, 433 U.S. 584 (1977).

penalty could be administered in an arbitrary or capricious way.[27] The Court did uphold statutes thereafter enacted which supplanted wide discretion with various standards and safeguards, but invalidated others which rigidly made the death penalty mandatory for certain crimes without proper standards and safeguards.[28]

You will note I referred to "a substantial segment of public sentiment" being against the death penalty rather than ascribing such an opinion to the public as a whole. The Supreme Court's 1972 *Furman* decision represents the unusual instance of a strong legal change, in an area of controversial moral attitudes, being made by a court's invalidation of a legislative judgment even though popular sentiment for the change does not represent a strong majority.[29] The dissenters in the case argued strenuously that the Court's about-face in its constitutional interpretation of cruel and unusual punishment (limited though the decision was, as I have described above) was an inappropriate, "legislative" act — because it was in the face of recent as well as traditional state and federal legislative approval of the penalty and its administration through jury discretion, and in the face of sharply divided public opinion.

d. *Opposition to Excessive Rigor: Jury, Prosecutor, and Police Moderation*

Let me now expand on the role of the jury. The oft-noted observation that juries exert a moderating influence on the rigors of the law seems accurate, though exaggerated. Elaborate studies by the University of Chicago Law School show that in about 17 percent of criminal cases, the jury acquitted when the judge (who had been asked by the researchers to record his own attitude) would have convicted; and in convictions in capital cases, the discretion whether to assess the

27. Furman v. Georgia, 408 U.S. 238 (1972). Two of the majority of five took the absolute position that the death penalty itself was "cruel and unusual punishment." The other three based their position on the arbitrary or discriminatory choice in imposition of the penalty and its infrequent, hence nondeterrent, imposition.

28. The death penalty cases are treated in App. 2 herein at nn. 240-245.

29. Opinion polls on the subject have shown considerable fluctuation over the years, with a majority at the time of *Furman* (ranging from about 50 to 57%) apparently supporting capital punishment for murder. Vidmar & Ellsworth, Public Opinion and the Death Penalty, 26 Stan. L. Rev. 1245, 1249-1250 (1974). There are discrepancies in percentage of support when the questions are general, as against when they pinpoint specific circumstances; and also when different subpopulations are isolated. *Id.* at 1250-1255. Justice Marshall's concurrence in *Furman* observed that the public is ill informed about capital punishment, and that if informed of its purposes and liabilities, a majority would find it immoral. 408 U.S. at 362, 363.

death penalty was exercised against the death penalty slightly more by the jury than by the judge.[30]

In recent years, the controversy over the jury's moderating, or indeed "nullification," power in criminal cases has been most prominent in connection with prosecutions for politically motivated crimes — e.g., those stemming from opposition to the Vietnam War. Defendants' lawyers have asked judges to instruct juries that they have the power to acquit when they have strong reasons (of conscience, let us say) to depart from the law laid down by the other instructions. Current legal opinion seems strongly against such a nullification instruction,[31] though in the early years of the Republic the jury was legally the final arbiter of both the law and the facts.[32] The Chicago research figures previously cited suggest that the jury today in fact does exercise this nullification power occasionally.[33] The researchers assert that "the jury does not often consciously and explicitly" depart from the law.[34] One reason may be that, in the oft-expressed view of Judge Jerome Frank, juries often do not understand the instructions.[35]

30. Kalven & Zeisel, The American Jury 56, 62, 436 (1966). The figures are restated somewhat differently after "hung juries" (see *id.* at 57) are taken into account: Concerning jury trials in all criminal cases, the "jury is less lenient than the judge in 3% of the cases and more lenient than the judge in 19% of the cases. Thus, the jury trials show on balance a net leniency of 16%" (at 59).

31. See Sparf and Hansen v. U.S., 156 U.S. 51 (1895); Leventhal, J. for the majority in U.S. v. Dougherty, 473 F.2d 1113, 1130-1137 (D.C. Cir. 1972); State v. McClanahan, 212 Kan. 208, 510 P.2d 153 (1973); Simson, Jury Nullification in the American System: A Skeptical View, 54 Tex. L. Rev. 488 (1976); Christie, Lawful Departure From Legal Rules: "Jury Nullification" and Legitimated Disobedience, 62 Calif. L. Rev. 1289, 1296-1305, esp. 1302-1305 (1974). See also Kadish & Kadish, Discretion to Disobey 45-72, esp. 64-65 (1973).

For contrary views see Justice Gray's dissenting opinion in *Sparf, supra* at 110-177; Judge Bazelon's dissent in *Dougherty, supra* at 1138-1144; Scheflin & Van Dyke, Jury Nullification: The Contours of a Controversy, 43 L. & Contemp. Prob. 51 (1980); Sax, Conscience and Anarchy: The Prosecution of War Resistors, 57 Yale Rev. 481 (1968). Constitutional provisions in Indiana and Maryland are construed, within certain limits, to give the jury the right in criminal cases to determine law as well as facts and thereby depart from instructions on the law if it wishes to acquit, or to convict of a lesser offense. (See discussion in Scheflin & Van Dyke, *supra* at 79-85.)

32. See, e.g., Howe, Juries As Judges of Criminal Law, 52 Harv. L. Rev. 582 (1939).

33. Kalven & Zeisel, *supra* n.30, point to a number of reasons, not envisaged in the instructions, for jury verdicts disagreeing with what the presiding judge's verdict would have been. These include: unpopularity of the statute; and jury sentiments concerning proper boundaries of self-defense, significance of the victim's own fault, the suffering already experienced by the defendant, or the severity of the threatened punishment. Mainly, the jury "yields to sentiment in the apparent process of resolving doubts as to evidence. The jury . . . is able to conduct its revolt from the law within the etiquette of resolving issues of fact" (at 165).

34. *Id.* at 165.

35. Frank, Courts On Trial 116-118, 130 (1950). His general attack on the jury system (mainly in civil cases) is at 108-145. See also, on jury understanding of the instructions, Chap. 2 herein at nn. 173-175.

The Chicago studies also suggest the jury is a moderating force in civil cases. Take the usual personal injury case, e.g., involving an auto accident, where the rule is that the injured plaintiff has the burden of proving the negligence of the defendant. The Chicago studies suggest that the jury, in fact, in spite of this rule, tends to resolve the doubts it has about the defendant's negligence in favor of the injured plaintiff. I am assuming, of course, that it is a case of some doubt. It is true that the jury still brings in verdicts against the injured plaintiff in cases of clear absence of negligence on the part of the defendant. But it seems that the jury tends to resolve the doubts it has in the controversial, fairly evenly balanced cases in favor of the plaintiff, whereas this rule of the burden of proof seems to mean that it would have to resolve doubts in favor of the defendant. What we mean by saying that the plaintiff has the burden in this personal injury suit is that he has to prove and convince by a *preponderance* of the evidence. (In a criminal case, the plaintiff, i.e., the prosecution, has the burden of proving its case beyond a reasonable doubt.)

Other tendencies have been found to exist in the actual, as distinct from the theoretical, operation of juries in these personal injury cases. For example, there is a rule in most states to the effect that if the injured plaintiff was himself negligent (what the law terms "contributory negligence") and this negligence contributed substantially to the injury that he suffered, such a plaintiff is barred from recovery. His own contributory negligence prevents his recovery of damages, even though the defendant was negligent. That is a pretty harsh rule and it doesn't even take cognizance of the relative amount of negligence as between the plaintiff and the defendant. It simply says that if the plaintiff's negligence also contributed to the injury, he cannot recover. A growing number of states, following the example of Wisconsin, uphold a more enlightened attitude based on what we call the "comparative negligence" rule. But even in the other states the jury in fact *tends* to operate on a comparative negligence basis. That is to say, what the jury seems to be doing in a case where it feels that the plaintiff's own negligence contributed to his injury is this: It brings in a verdict with reduced damages for the plaintiff rather than a verdict for the defendant, as would have been proper under the judge's instructions. Here is another example of the "law in action" differing from the "law in books."

However, you should not assume that the moderating or nullifying role of juries in civil cases represents much greater sympathy for the plaintiff than would be shown by the judge if he were deciding the case. The Chicago studies show that in 80 percent of the personal injury cases, the judge agreed with the jury's determination as to who should win (the same percentage as in criminal cases). And "[t]he judge disagrees with the jury because he is more pro-plaintiff about as often as the jury disagrees with him because it is more pro-plaintiff." But looking "simply at the 44 percent of the cases where both decide for the plaintiff, we find considerable disagreement on the level of damages. In roughly 23 percent the jury gives the higher award, in 17 percent the judge gives the higher award and in the remaining 4 percent they are in approximate agreement. More important, however, is the fact that the jury awards average 20 percent higher than those of the judge."[36]

Sometimes, in criminal cases, instead of the jury the prosecutor takes the role of potential moderator or nullifier. He too is sensitive to popular attitudes, and he acts accordingly. Witness, for example, the well-known reluctance to prosecute sexual behavior that violates statutory prohibitions like those against adultery or fornication. But failure to prosecute, or to prosecute fully (e.g., engaging in "plea bargaining"), is a result of many other factors as well: inadequate prosecutorial and adjudicative resources, lack of cooperation from the victim, availability of effective non-criminal procedures, and the suspect's willingness to cooperate as an informant or witness.[37]

So, too, enforcement duties of police are moderated, generally for quite practical reasons.[38]

e. Desire for Government Noninterference with Privacy and with Conduct Not Injurious to Others; the "Mill Principle"

The above-mentioned fornication prohibitions (existing in less than a third of the states) and adultery prohibitions (existing in perhaps half of the states) may be expected to dwindle still further in the

36. Kalven, The Dignity of the Civil Jury, 50 Va. L. Rev. 1055, 1065 (1964).

37. Miller, Prosecution (1969); Newman, Conviction (1966) (Part III); 2 Davis, Administrative Law Treatise, §9:11 (2d ed. 1979); Miller, McDonald & Cramer, Plea Bargaining in the United States (1978) (chap. 2). The prosecutor's discretion is subject to abuse, which has usually been treated as judicially nonreviewable, though there are some decisions pointing in a contrary direction. 2 Davis, *supra*, §9:6. Some, like Kenneth Davis (*id.*, §§9:1-9:13; Davis, Discretionary Justice 188-214 (1969)) have argued for fuller recognition of reviewability, as well as (on the federal agency level, at least) for greater use of prosecutorial policy statements, findings, and reasons in making various kinds of prosecution decisions.

38. "Many persons whose conduct apparently violates the criminal law are not arrested. In some instances this can be explained by the fact that there is no legislative purpose to enforcing some statutes which are obsolete or drafted in overly general or ambiguous terms." There are other reasons, such as inadequacy of available enforcement resources, or the use of non-arrest as a reward for information. LaFave, Arrest 9-10 (1965). See *id.* at 63-82, 492-495; 2 Davis, *supra* n.37, §§9:14-9:22; Davis, Police Discretion (1975); Thomas & Fitch, The Exercise of Discretionary

future, in line with the position taken by the influential American Law Institute. Having sponsored research for some ten years on a Model Penal Code, which it approved in 1962, the Institution re-published the second part of the Code (Definition of Specific Crimes) with revised Commentaries in 1980. Though not generally adopted as such, the Code has influenced numerous state legislatures and courts on many topics, as well as affecting the pending revision of the federal criminal statutes.[39]

The Code omits any prohibition against fornication or adultery, a position which the Commentary explains in the following manner: The Code "does not place the coercive power of the penal law behind strictures of private morality or religious precept. . . . Punishing instances of private immorality can justly be regarded as an invasion of personal liberty. . . . The amount of money available for law enforcement is limited. It makes more sense to concentrate on conduct directly harmful to others than to divert attention and resources to instances of private immorality [requiring] enforcement techniques that could have serious implications for personal privacy." And to continue the prohibition *without* effective enforcement leads to various evils like discriminatory enforcement, official extortion, private blackmail, and weakening of respect for law. Finally the Commentary found specious the argument that the consensual sexual conduct in question does cause preventable harm to others.[40]

Similarly, under the Model Penal Code, "deviate" sexual intercourse (homosexual practices), regardless of the gender or marital status of the parties, "is not criminal where both parties consent, where each is of sufficient age and mental capacity to render consent effective and where they conduct relations in private and create no public nuisance."[41] The Code does, however, prohibit certain other sex-related offenses.[42]

Decisionmaking by the Police, 54 N.D.L. Rev. 61 (1977). Davis has argued for confinement of police discretion through police rulemaking, in public procedures. Davis, Discretionary Justice 80-96. See the interchanges between Davis and Allen on this, in 125 U. Pa. L. Rev. 62, 1167, 1172 (1976-1977).

39. See 1 ALI Model Penal Code and Commentaries, Part II, foreword, p.xi (1980).

40. *Id.* at 430-439.

41. *Id.* at 363.

42. This includes prostitution and related offenses, 3 *id.* at 453-473; certain lewd exposures or indecencies in public, 3 *id.* at 448-453; 1 *id.* at 405-411; loitering in a public place for the purpose of engaging in deviate sexual relations, 3 *id.* at 473-479; sexual relations involving force, fraud, or females underage or mentally incapable, 1 *id.* at 271-405; bigamy and polygamy, 2 *id.* at 368-397; incest, 2 *id.* at 397-424; and obscenity, 3 *id.* at 479-523. The abortion prohibition (see 2 *id.* at 424-444) went beyond the then existing (1962) state statutes by permitting abortion where there was substantial risk that continuance of the pregnancy would gravely impair the physical or mental health of the mother, that the child would be born with grave physical

This rather permissive attitude in the area of consensual sex conduct is a good illustration of a more encompassing attitude, strongly held by large numbers of people and in even larger proportion among young people. I have in mind the drawing of a circle around certain kinds of conduct as being "private" — conduct that the law should not stick its nose into in order to promote one view of morality, or further the defendant's own good, as distinguished from the purpose of protecting other people from harm. John Stuart Mill expressed this quite common attitude when he said in the first chapter of his essay "On Liberty": "The object of this essay is to assert one simple principle, as entitled to govern absolutely the dealings of society with the individual by way of compulsion and control, whether the means used be political force in the form of legal penalties, or the moral coercion of public opinion. That principle is that . . . the only purpose for which power can be rightfully exercised over any member of a civilized community, against his will, is to prevent harm to others. His own good, either physical or mental, or moral, is not a sufficient warrant."[43] (*Cf.* the play, "Hair," Act I: "Kids, be free. Be whatever you are, do whatever you want to do, just as long as you don't hurt anybody.")

Such a principle extends far beyond the field of sexual behavior. On the basis of this principle, for instance, it could be argued that a state could not compel a person to accept for his own good a life-preserving blood transfusion he did not want; or compel mental health treatment for the harmlessly insane; or compel participation in an air raid drill, or the wearing of seatbelts by autoists and helmets by motorcyclists; or prohibit euthanasia, or attempted suicide; or prohibit gambling, prostitution, or personal use or consumption (or possession for personal use or consumption) of alcohol, drugs (at least "soft" drugs, such as marijuana), or obscene material; or prohibit abortions, particularly early ones.

These positions *could* be argued. Whether such arguments would or should succeed in all instances is another question. The problem is that the ambiguities and exceptions in Mill's "simple principle"

---

or mental defects, or that the pregnancy resulted from rape, incest, or other felonious intercourse. Such a statute does not go far enough, in the light of the subsequent Supreme Court decisions in Roe v. Wade, 410 U.S. 113, and Doe v. Bolton, 410 U.S. 179 (1973) invalidating the then typical restrictive laws against abortion. The Court treated the decision to abort as a matter of the woman's constitutional "privacy" right which she is free to exercise in the first trimester of pregnancy in consultation with her physician. The Court did rule that the state may regulate abortion in the second trimester in ways reasonably related to maternal health; and the state may go so far as to prohibit abortion after viability of the fetus, except where the abortion is necessary to preserve the mother's life or health.

43. Mill, Utilitarianism, Liberty and Representative Government 72-73 (Everyman ed. 1910).

make its application anything but easy. For instance, what kind and what quantity of "harm" to others will qualify? Looking at the differences in the American Law Institute's treatment of various harms suggests that the Institute's application of the Mill principle has been based upon judgment, prediction, and weighing of freedom against other values rather than upon any self-evident inferences from the "simple principle."[44] Indeed, Mill himself seemed aware of some of the possible difficulties in applying the "harm" concept,[45] and recognized some actual exceptions to his principle, as did his critics.[46] Yet

44. In the case of homosexuality, the Institute had to consider the relevance of *psychological harm*, i.e., distress, caused to the opponents of sexual freedom from the mere knowledge that private homosexual conduct was occurring without legal hindrance. Furthermore, these opponents could argue (as Lord Devlin of England has argued) that there is potentially a strong threat of *social disintegration* created by removing criminal prohibitions from conduct believed by the average person to be immoral and disgusting. Alternatively, in the case of fornication and adultery, one might argue that these practices cause *indirect harm to the institution of marriage and the family*. Under the previously quoted philosophy of the American Law Institute, however, all these kinds of harms do not qualify — apparently because they are not viewed as sufficiently probable and substantial enough to justify (1) the invasion of human freedom and privacy involved in criminally punishing private consensual conduct, and (2) certain costs attendant upon attempted enforcement. But some other kinds of harm — even though involving consent and occurring in private — would qualify and thus fall in the realm of prohibition. For instance, the ALI has not suggested that our long-standing and relatively uncriticized prohibitions against assaults involving mutual consent (including sado-masochistic sex practices) should be removed from the books. Nor has it been willing to decriminalize prostitution, generally a consensual and private act.

45. Mill recognized that "the mischief which a person does to himself may seriously affect, both through their sympathies and their interests, those nearly connected with him and, in a minor degree, society at large," and that a judgment had to be made whether the conduct had produced "definite damage, or a definite risk of damage, either to an individual or to the public." Mill, *supra* n.43 at 137, 138. Interestingly, he could not make up his mind how to decide the issue of whether a legal system that did not punish fornication or gambling should punish the pimp and the keeper of a public gambling house. *Id.* at 154-155.

46. A recent critical discussion of the Mill principle, Grey, The Legal Enforcement of Morality 1-35 (ABA Commission on Undergraduate Education in Law and the Humanities, 1980), points to a few areas of law where we now have, and would want to retain, penal sanctions against mere psychological harm, i.e., distress — and argues that this undermines the Mill principle, construed as denigrating all such alleged harm. See for further critical discussion, Reynolds, The Enforcement of Morals and the Rule of Law, 11 Ga. L. Rev. 1325 (1977); Golding, Philosophy of Law 54-59 (1975); Devlin, The Enforcement of Morals (1965); Hart, Law, Liberty and Morality (1963); Schwartz, Morals Offenses and the Model Penal Code, 63 Colum. L. Rev. 669, 675-677 (1963).

In referring to Mill's own recognition of exceptions to his principle, I do not mean only his toleration of state paternal intervention to protect children, the feeble minded, and backward peoples. He thought the freedom to sell oneself into slavery was properly restrained by law — because his principle was designed to preserve freedom of choice, and this purpose would be defeated by conduct precluding future use of that freedom. Mill, *supra* n.43 at 157-158. This category of exception could be extended beyond slavery to situations in which the law curtails the freedom of an individual to commit a serious injury against himself, such as suicide or maim-

another problem is the ambiguity in the concept of "will" (in "against his will"),[47] as well as in the concept of "others" (in "harm to others") as exemplified in the abortion problem.[48]

Still, the Mill principle's thrust in the direction of an individual's private conduct being free from the state's moralistic strictures is an appealing one in our time. "For more than a decade there has been a Privacy Revolution underway in the United States. . . . [T]he American legal structure has reacted with relatively incredible speed to what ten years ago was an ill-defined anxiety about individual privacy. During this period, for example, Congress has enacted three major statutes primarily directed to matters of privacy and has included dozens of individual provisions relating to privacy in other statutes; the states also have enacted hundreds of privacy statutes during this period."[49] In the area of criminal law, although state legislatures have not shown as much impetus for change as the American Law Institute (in its omission of fornication, adultery, and homosexual practices), there has been a tendency to omit fornication and adultery as crimes from recent modifications and re-codifications of state penal codes,[50] abortion laws have followed the liberal line laid down by the Supreme Court, the severity of marijuana offenses has been lessened through lowering the level of offense and/or the penalties, and many motorcycle helmet laws have been repealed.

Turning from legislative judgments on desirable policy to judicial judgments on whether to strike down the legislative judgment as unconstitutional:[51] It is still true that state courts are finding a sufficient

---

ing — any action that would destroy or greatly impair subsequent freedom of choice. Motorcycle helmet laws or laws prohibiting suicide or attempted suicide fall into this category, but the limits of the category itself are ill defined. Should we, for instance, prohibit dangerous mountain climbing or cigarette smoking? See Hughes, The Conscience of the Court 87 (1975).

47. Might some situations, e.g., where an individual is contemplating suicide, be said to involve an impairment of "will" so that he is incapable of making the kind of *free* choice that Mill envisaged? See Hughes, *id.* at 85.

48. Is a non-viable fetus to be included in "others"? It would not, if the Supreme Court's 1973 abortion decisions were to be followed. See *supra* n.42.

49. Miller, The Privacy Revolution: A Report From the Barricades, 19 Washburn L.J. 1 (1979).

50. See 1 ALI, *supra* n.39 at 439.

51. It is important to understand the difference in the nature of the legislative as against the judicial judgment. A legislator might reasonably disagree with the ALI's version of the Mill or "liberty principle," viewing it as going too far in the direction of liberty or underestimating the "harm" from decriminalization. Another legislator might reasonably perceive the Code as not carrying the liberty principle far enough in some areas, or overestimating the harm from decriminalization in certain other areas, e.g., prostitution and abortion. But the judgment of a court reviewing a statute embodying such provisions is not in terms of what the court would rule if it were a legislator. The decision is based on whether the rights in the Constitution, such as privacy, stand in the way of the particular legislative judgment. A judge may answer that question in the affirmative even though he thinks the law

social harm-prevention basis to uphold motorcycle helmet laws, fornication and adultery laws, and statutes prohibiting possession and consumption of liquor and drugs (including marijuana). Persistent challenges have been occasionally successful, however: A 1977 New Jersey Supreme Court decision invalidated the fornication statute on grounds of privacy invasion and insufficient serving of alleged social harm-prevention purposes;[52] a 1975 Alaska Supreme Court decision held that a drug law as applied to possession of marijuana by adults at home for personal use violated the state constitution's privacy provision;[53] and a minority of motorcycle helmet cases find an inadequate relation of the law to the *public's* safety and health (as distinct from the individual motorcyclist's).[54]

The Supreme Court's decisions in the last two decades have supported such challenges by revitalizing a constitutional right of privacy, thus giving new life to the Mill principle. The decisions principally involved here are those *invalidating* laws against use of contraceptives by married persons,[55] laws imposing certain restraints on the distribution of contraceptives to unmarried persons, minors, and others,[56] laws against most abortions[57] (including some cases subsequent to the basic

---

represents desirable policy; and he may answer in the negative even though he disagrees with the legislative policy. The problem is complicated by the fact that the Court has evolved a tougher standard for review, under the due process clause, in the case of "fundamental" rights — i.e., in the case of such a right, the statutory invasion thereof would have to be *necessitated* by a *compelling* state interest. On standards for review under the due process clause, see Chap. 5 herein at nn. 63-68.

The problem for the legislature as distinct from the court (though the court's problem of constitutional interpretation under the tougher standard of review gets close to the legislature's problem) is often this: Should a humane democratic state impose the liberty-invading sanctions of criminal law upon allegedly immoral conduct that substantial segments of the public (in the case of abortion, approximately half or more of the public, at least as to first-trimester pregnancies) sincerely and reasonably believe to be insufficiently harmful to others and morally proper?

52. State v. Saunders, 75 N.J. 200, 381 A.2d 333 (1977); Notes, 27 Buffalo L. Rev. 395 (1978); 77 Mich. L. Rev. 252 (1978). But constitutional attacks on prostitution statutes on privacy grounds have failed. See Note, 58 Wash. U.L.Q. 439 (1980).

53. Ravin v. State, 537 P.2d 494 (Alaska, 1975). See Annot., 96 A.L.R.3d 225 (1980).

54. People v. Fries, 42 Ill. 2d 446, 250 N.E.2d 149 (1969); American Motorcycle Assn. v. Davids, 11 Mich. App. 351, 158 N.W.2d 72 (1968). The Michigan case also referred to the privacy idea. See Annot., 32 A.L.R.3d 1270 (1970). More generally, see Note, Limiting the State's Police Power: Judicial Reaction to John Stuart Mill, 37 U. Chi. L. Rev. 605 (1970).

55. Griswold v. Connecticut, 381 U.S. 479 (1965).

56. Eisenstadt v. Baird, 405 U.S. 438 (1972); Carey v. Population Services Intl., 431 U.S. 678 (1977).

57. Roe v. Wade, 409 U.S. 817 (1973). See *supra* n.42 for summary. There has been substantial criticism of the reasoning and evidence on which the abortion decision was based, though not necessarily of the result. See, e.g., Ely, The Wages of Crying Wolf: A Comment on Roe v. Wade, 82 Yale L.J. 920 (1973); Friendly, The Courts and Social Policy: Substance and Procedure, 33 U. Miami L. Rev. 21,

1973 decisions),[58] and laws against possession of obscene films, as applied to possession of films in the home, intended for viewing therein.[59]

32-39 (1978); Cox, The Role of the Supreme Court in American Government 113-114 (1976); Lusky, By What Right 15-17, 100 (1976). The companion case of Doe v. Bolton, 410 U.S. 179 (1973) among other things held unconstitutional a state law requiring (1) that all abortions be performed only in certain accredited hospitals, and that a hospital committee approve all abortions contemplated by the hospital's doctors, (2) that two other doctors must first concur in the decision to abort, and (3) that abortions be limited to the state's residents.

58. The case of Planned Parenthood of Mo. v. Danforth, 428 U.S. 52 (1976) *upheld* state provisions that (1) defined viability of the fetus (in a provision restricting abortions to those necessary for preserving the mother's life or health unless a doctor's certification of non-viability has been obtained) in terms of the stage of fetal development when life may be continued indefinitely outside the womb by natural or artificial support systems; (2) required that a woman prior to an abortion during the first 12 weeks must certify in writing her consent to the procedure, and that her consent is informed and freely given without coercion; (3) required certain record-keeping and reporting on the health facilities and physicians concerned, irrespective of the pregnancy stage involved. But the court held *unconstitutional,* provisions (1) requiring written consent of the spouse for abortion during the first 12 weeks unless a doctor certifies the abortion to be necessary to preserve the mother's life; (2) requiring any person performing or inducing an abortion at any stage of pregnancy to exercise, on pain of manslaughter penalty in case of the fetus's death, the same professional skill, care, and diligence to preserve the fetus's health as required to preserve the health of a fetus intended to be born and not aborted; (3) requiring, with respect to an abortion in the first 12 weeks of pregnancy of an unmarried woman under 18, the written consent of a parent or person in loco parentis, unless a doctor certifies the abortion to be necessary to preserve the mother's life; (4) prohibiting after the first 12 weeks of pregnancy an abortion technique whereby the amniotic fluid is withdrawn and a saline or other fluid is inserted into the amniotic sac.

However, in H.L. v. Matheson, 67 L. Ed. 2d 388 (1981), the Court upheld a state law requiring a doctor to "notify if possible" the parents of a minor upon whom he was to perform an abortion — as applied to an unemancipated, unmarried fifteen-year-old girl living with and dependent on her parents — even though the law did not provide for a mandatory period of delay after such notification or a description of what information the parents could supply the doctor, and allowed a pregnant minor to consent to other procedures without formal notice to her parents if she carried the child to term.

Finally, in Maher v. Roe, 432 U.S. 464 (1977), the Court ruled that a state that funded childbirth services for indigents could properly *exclude indigents' non-therapeutic abortions from public funding* and could require, for medically necessary abortions, the indigent woman's prior consent in writing and the state official's prior authorization of payment. And even where the exclusion of public funding applied to some *medically necessary* abortions (funding being restricted, under the most extreme version of the federal "Hyde amendment," to cases where childbirth would threaten the mother's life — thus excluding abortions that threatened her physical or mental health) the Court upheld the exclusion, in Harris v. McRae, 448 U.S. 297 (1980).

See generally, Symposium on the Law and Politics of Abortion, 77 Mich. L. Rev. 1569 (1979); Dembitz, The Supreme Court and a Minor's Abortion Decision, 80 Colum. L. Rev. 1251 (1980); Goldstein, A Critique of the Abortion Funding Decisions: On Private Rights in the Public Sector, 8 Hastings Const. L.Q. 313 (1981); Isaacs, Law of Fertility Regulation in U.S.: 1980 Review, 19 J. Fam. L. 65 (1980) (abortion, contraception, and sterilization).

59. Stanley v. Georgia, 394 U.S. 557 (1969).

(Certain other pro-privacy decisions might have been disapproved by Mill because they involved the *upholding of legal requirements* adopted to enhance a kind of privacy, as distinguished from decisions protecting privacy *against legal interference*.)[60]

It is true that the Supreme Court has steered a rather uncertain course in the constitutional law of privacy (as Chap. 5 herein shows[61]) and has frowned on the Mill principle as such.[62] But its concern, and that of other courts and legislatures, for maintaining an area of individual liberty free from legal interference reflects a public concern[63] that lawmaking must reckon with if it is to be effective. This public concern is one example of the limits I lumped together into my second category, namely, the "popular attitudes, habits, and ideals in the various situations that arise in everyday life."

f. Desire for Other Freedoms

Obviously, the desire for privacy is not the only kind of freedom urge that operates as a limit on law in our society. Nor is it the only

60. The Court upheld legal requirements designed (1) to permit a householder to be free from mailings of erotically arousing advertisements (Rowan v. Post Office Dept., 397 U.S. 728 (1960), and from uninvited house-to-house solicitation by magazine salesmen (Breard v. Alexandria, 341 U.S. 622 (1951), *cf.* Schaumberg v. Citizens for a Better Environment, 444 U.S. 620 (1980)), and from "dirty words" broadcasts (FCC v. Pacifica Foundation, 438 U.S. 726 (1978)); and (2) to permit anyone to be free from sound trucks' "loud and raucous noises," Kovacs v. Cooper, 336 U.S. 77 (1949), and from certain kinds of advertising on city bus cards, Lehman v. Shaker Heights, 418 U.S. 298 (1974).

61. See Chap. 5 between nn. 12 & 44. A notable pulling back on the right to privacy was the summary affirmance in 425 U.S. 901 (1976) of Doe v. Commonwealth's Attorney, 403 F. Supp. 1199 (E.D. Va. 1975), which had upheld the Virginia sodomy law as applied to private consensual conduct of male adults.

62. In a 1973 obscenity case, the Court showed no sympathy for the Mill principle (which in its view meant "that conduct involving consenting adults only is always beyond state regulation") when it said: (1) The state may prohibit conduct (even when it involves "consenting adults only") to further its legitimate interest in "order and morality," and "a decent society"; and to protect the "quality of life and the total community environment" and the privacies of others, from infringement by the allegedly private conduct. (2) The prohibition against exhibition of obscene films was not rendered unconstitutional by the absence of scientific data conclusively demonstrating that exposure to such films did harm adult men or women or their society. The legislature could "quite reasonably" make the "unprovable assumption" that "such a connection does or might exist." (3) "The state statute books are replete with constitutionally unchallenged laws against prostitution, suicide, voluntary self-mutilation, brutalizing 'bare fist' prize fights . . ."; and the Court cited language in prior Court opinions supporting legitimacy of laws against various other consensual activities, including fornication and adultery. Paris Adult Theatre I v. Slaton, 413 U.S. 49, 58-63, 68-69 (1973).

63. A 1968 Harris poll showed "a continued rise in public concern about individual privacy, and a belief in the existence of a threat to privacy, as well as a need for greater protection." Miller, *supra* n.50 at 1.

attitude that has been given constitutional protection. The Constitution protects, against undue governmental invasions, one's life, one's liberties, and one's property, as well as assuring equal protection of the laws. Should government press too far against such ideals as freedom and equality, it will be reminded through popular resistance, if not through court decision, that these ideals set limits to the law's possibilities. Unfortunately, it would unduly lengthen this book to explore, as I have done in the case of "privacy,"[64] some court attitudes on such limits.[65]

g. *Attitudes on Importance of "Fault" or "Blame"*

There are some additional attitudes or ideals that seem to me so pervasive as to necessarily put limits on the lawmaker, though they are so obvious as to perhaps escape attention. One is the general acceptance of the notion of "fault" or "blame," and the feeling that the innocent should be treated differently from those who are at fault or worthy of blame. This point may seem self-evident, but you will encounter many instances of difficulties arising from its neglect.

As one example, consider the proposals made by some responsible students of criminal law that the insanity defense should be abolished because of difficulties in interpreting and administering the defense. They point to the fact that psychiatrists are in disagreement on the issue of insanity, with many of these critics asserting that the psychiatrists are no better equipped than the layman to answer the kinds of questions put to them as witnesses in an insanity case; that some defendants take unfair advantage of the defense; that the defense is too ambiguous to justify sending Defendant A to an institution for treatment of mental illness and Defendant B, whose overt homicidal conduct was the same, to prison or the gas chamber. These critics urge that the trial should merely determine whether the defendant did what he is accused of doing. After a finding of guilt, his mental condition then and now would be considered, on the issue of proper "disposition," by getting answers to questions like: "Is he treatable? Is he dangerous? Is he deterrable?" Perhaps the chief obstacle to adopting this proposal is the sentiment that one who was incapable of avoiding the doing of what he did, or of knowing that what he did was wrong, should not be *blamed* for doing it. He should not be subjected to the same stigma of guilt through a criminal conviction as the person

64. I shall be saying more about privacy in Chap. 2 (tort law) and Chap. 5 (constitutional law).

65. But you can get a good idea of the nature of, and legal limits on, a variety of other freedoms or strong claims made by Americans, in Dorsen, ed., The Rights of Americans (1970).

who did have the capacity to control himself and appreciate the wrongfulness of his conduct.[66] Any such similar treatment would arouse a widely shared sense of injustice. Even a dog, Holmes reminded us, distinguishes between being kicked and being stumbled over.

The proposed reform encounters, therefore, one of law's powerful limits and is unlikely to receive any near future acceptance.

Much the same point is illustrated by the limits on the possibility of extending "strict liability" in criminal law. This needs a little explanation. The typical crime involves a certain culpable mental element, as for instance the intent to kill, the intent to take away another's property without his consent, or carelessness that is gross enough (in relation to the circumstances known by defendant) to amount to criminal negligence. The typical tort, too, involves culpability or fault, as for instance the intent to assault, the intent to defame, or negligence (by which is meant the failure to abide by the standard of conduct which would have been followed by a "reasonable man" in the circumstances involved).

In the tort field there have developed some areas of "strict liability," i.e., liability *without* fault. One example is the workmen's compensation system under which the worker injured on the job files his claim with an administrative agency and collects compensation on the basis of a governmentally prescribed schedule of benefits. He does not have to assert the employer's negligence, or his own freedom from contributory negligence. The financial structure varies, but a common system is for the compensation payments to be made by the insurance company with which the employer has insured himself. Another illustration of strict liability in tort is the field of "products liability." Suppose you were personally injured in an auto accident because your steering wheel had a defect which was unknown to you and which was there when the car left the factory. If you can prove these facts to the satisfaction of the jury, then under the developing law of recent years you would be able to recover damages from the manufacturer without proving negligence on his part.

In neither of these tort fields has there been very strong criticism of the fact that liability was being imposed in the absence of fault. We have, in recent decades, been increasingly sympathetic to the injured worker and injured consumer; the negligence standard in both fields has not worked out satisfactorily for plaintiffs; the employer and manufacturer defendants are in a better position to shoulder the loss, and can protect themselves by insurance. Moreover, under the strict

66. See Packer, The Limits of the Criminal Sanction 62-69, 131-135 (1968); Kadish, The Decline of Innocence, 26 Cambridge L.J. 273, 283 (1968). For a summary survey of the problems posed by the insanity reform proposals, see Monahan, Abolish the Insanity Defense? — Not Yet, 26 Rutgers L. Rev. 719 (1973).

liability standard they are not going to jail and are free from the stigma of a criminal conviction. "It's only money" they are paying out, in insurance premiums, and the added costs can probably be reflected in their selling prices.

There are similar practical reasons for the growing success of the movement for "no-fault" auto accident insurance — under which at least certain economic losses from accidents (medical expenses, loss of work income) would be recovered under the victim's own insurance policy, regardless of who was at fault. A mounting concern over the difficulties, delays, and inequities of the prevailing "fault" system has made people receptive to such an alternative system (of which there are many varieties) that promises to be cheaper and to make recoveries more rapid and certain.[67] There are even proposals now to extend the no-fault insurance approach beyond automobiles, i.e., to accidents involving other products and services as well.[68]

The situation is quite different when you are dealing with strict criminal liability. Criminal liability without fault has existed on the outer edge of criminal law but it has been a slightly growing edge, with a tendency of the laws to extend beyond such standard categories as food and drugs, liquor, conservation, and traffic regulation.[69] The sense of injustice that I earlier described with respect to the insanity defense operates here too, and is mirrored in the call by scholars for a halt to the spread of strict criminal liability, and in the willingness of courts to reject the idea that *imprisonment* can ever be imposed on a strict liability basis, and in the forthright position of the American Law Institute that: "Crime does and should mean condemnation and no court should have to pass that judgment unless it can declare that the defendant's act was wrong. This is too fundamental to be compromised. The law goes far enough if it permits the imposition of a monetary penalty in cases where strict liability has been imposed."[70]

67. ABA Special Commission on Automobile Insurance Legislation, Automobile No-Fault Insurance (1978); Epstein, Automobile No-Fault Plans: A Second Look at First Principles, 13 Creighton L. Rev. 769 (1980); O'Connell, The Injury Industry (1971); New York Insurance Department (report to Governor Rockefeller), Automobile Insurance . . . for Whose Benefit? (1970); U.S. Department of Transportation, Motor Vehicle Crash Losses and Their Compensation in the United States (1971); Kimball, Automobile Accident Compensation Systems — Objectives and Perspectives, 1967 U. Ill. L.F. 370.

68. See O'Connell, Ending Insult to Injury: No-fault Insurance for Products and Services (1975); O'Connell, The Lawsuit Lottery: Only the Lawyers Win (1979).

69. See ALI Model Penal Code, Commentary at 141-145 (Tent. Draft No. 4, 1955); Saltzman, Strict Criminal Liability and the United States Constitution: Substantive Criminal Law Due Process, 24 Wayne L. Rev. 1571 (1978); Note, 75 Colum. L. Rev. 1517 (1975).

70. ALI, *supra* n.69 at 140. See scholars cited therein after the quotation; see also Commonwealth v. Koczwara, 397 Pa. 575, 155 A.2d 825 (1959); Morisette v. U.S., 342 U.S. 246 (1952).

Even where a statute seems to permit imposition of criminal liability without fault (i.e., because it is silent on the required mental element; very rarely does a statute explicitly authorize imposition of criminal liability without fault) some studies show that the same feeling I have described about the necessity of a fault element strongly influences the actual administration and enforcement of the statute. Thus, a study of Wisconsin's food and drug regulations shows that "prosecution under them takes place *only when the defendant has demonstrated subjective fault* by showing a conscious intent to violate, or, at least, a wilful heedlessness in failing to respond to repeated warnings. However, the liability without fault character of these provisions is still of prime importance . . . because the necessity of proving guilty knowledge or intent to the satisfaction of a court or jury would in many instances present an insurmountable burden to the department and greatly hinder efforts at control and regulation. This would be true even in many cases of conscious and advertent violation."[71] (Emphasis added.)

Relevant also is the matter of sentencing policy: In modern times the rise of a "rehabilitation" ideal worked to soften the blameworthiness and deterrence approaches to punishment. But disillusionment in the 1970s and 1980s has increasingly been a catalyst for legislation making sentences less "indeterminate," sentencing guidelines less concerned with rehabilitation, and juvenile courts more similar to adult criminal courts. " . . . We have not yet reached a state, supposing we ever should, in which the infliction of punishments for crime may be divorced generally from the ideas of blameworthiness, recompense and proportionality."[72]

h. The "Rule of Reason" Ideal

The final attitude or ideal I wish to point to is something that underlies many of the points I have already made (and even some of those I shall make later). Looking back, for instance, at my examples of people resisting law that strikes them as *overly* severe, or *unduly* encroaching on people's "private" conduct, or *unreasonably* hampering the exercise of strong and pleasurable human drives: These bespeak a "rule of reason." That is, people generally expect legal standards to be reasonable. Laws and decisions that depart too far from this com-

71. Zick, Liability Without Fault in the Food and Drug Statutes, 1956 Wis. L. Rev. 641, 654-655.

72. From the sentencing memorandum of Judge Frankel in U.S. v. Bergman, 416 F. Supp. 496, 500 (S.D.N.Y. 1976). See also Allen, The Decline of the Rehabilitative Ideal (1980), and Chap. 2 herein at n.216.

mon expectation create enforcement problems and the danger of a spreading disrespect for law. Even in the most complex bodies of doctrine in any legal field, the lawmaker is constantly trying to avoid overstepping the boundaries of the rule of reason; remember that and you will have a good guide through many interpretation perplexities. "The main underlying purpose" of the law of contracts, said one of its most respected students, Arthur Corbin, is to attempt "the realization of reasonable expectations that have been induced by the making of a promise."[73] "The common thread woven into all torts," said the prominent torts scholar, William Prosser, "is the idea of unreasonable interference with the interests of others."[74] And when *official* unreasonableness becomes gross enough it runs afoul of barriers within the law itself, such as the Constitution's "due process" protection against arbitrariness.

3. Human Frailties in Emergencies

I come now to a third type of limit — one which is set by human frailties in moments of great stress.

1. For example, the law tends to deal rather leniently with some kinds of criminal conduct that are impelled by a sense of overwhelming necessity. You have no doubt heard of the famous American criminal case involving the lifeboat, adrift on rough seas, that was leaking and so overcrowded that the first mate thought it imperative to throw some people overboard in order to lighten the load and thereby save the lives of others, rather than lose the lives of all. This was a case in about mid-nineteenth century, in a lower federal court.[75] The ship *William Brown* with 65 passengers and a crew of 17 had hit an iceberg off Newfoundland. About half the passengers went down with the ship. And so perhaps did a noble maritime tradition: While the facts are not altogether clear, it seems that the captain and crew got out first. At least we know that all of them, together with the other half of the passengers, managed to get into a "long boat" and a "jolly boat." In the long boat, where the relevant action occurred, there were 9 crew members and 32 passengers. Acting pursuant to the first mate's orders to spare the women and not part husband from wife, the crew threw over most of the male adults. Next morning the long boat was sighted by a ship, and all on board were saved.

73. 1 Corbin, Contracts 2 (1963).

74. Prosser, Handbook of the Law of Torts 6 (4th ed. 1972).

75. U.S. v. Holmes, 26 F. Cas. 360 (No. 15,383) (C.C.E.D. Pa. 1842). Further on the Holmes situation, see Cahn, The Moral Decision 61-71 (1955); Hicks, Human Jettison (1927).

The sole defendant in the criminal prosecution was a crew member named Holmes; the first mate and the other participating crew members could not be located. The moderating influence on the law exerted by the fact that the situation was one of emergency stress is seen first in the fact that the grand jury refused to indict for murder, but rather charged manslaughter. Moreover, the trial jury which came in with a guilty verdict of manslaughter recommended mercy, and the prison sentence finally imposed by the judge on Holmes (who had already waited nine months in jail) was only six months. The judge's instructions to the jury had said that the law recognized a defense in terms of "necessity," applying to extreme situations as in defending oneself against mortal attack, where the "peril [is] instant, overwhelming, leaving no alternative but to lose our own life or to take the life of another person." But this defense would not apply where "the slayer" not only wasn't attacked by others but was "under . . . obligation to make his own safety secondary to the safety of others," as the defendant sailor was, said the judge, in relation to the passengers. Where action need not be instantaneous, the drawing of lots would be a fair procedure, the judge thought, among those "in equal relation"; the sailor's obligation to the passengers, however, would have made that alternative unavailing here. In a 1928 address, Supreme Court Justice Cardozo, then a New York Court of Appeals judge, discussed the *Holmes* case in his distinctively ornate style (which you will come to recognize instantly upon reading a court opinion authored by him):

> There is no rule of human jettison. Men there will often be who, when told that their going will be the salvation of the remnant, will choose the nobler part and make the plunge into the waters. In that supreme moment the darkness for them will be illumined by the thought that those behind will ride to safety. If none of such mold are found aboard the boat, or too few to save the others, the human freight must be left to meet the chances of the waters. Who shall choose in such an hour between the victims and the saved? Who shall know when masts and sails of rescue may emerge out of the fog?[76]

The issue in a case like this is profoundly troubling,[77] and so was the analogous issue in a famous English case involving cannibalism on

76. Hall, ed., Selected Writings of B. N. Cardozo 390 (1947).

77. Note how confounding are the questions that persist: What basis was there for the judge's finding an "obligation" in the sailor that would not, in this situation, reside in a passenger? How realistic was it to assume that for passengers (those in "equal relation") in so exigent a situation the drawing of lots should be required? How does the drawing of lots compare, in fairness, with sailor Holmes's order (described by his lawyer as "the clear dictate of humanity") to spare the women

the high seas.[78] There too, because of compassion for human frailties in situations of overwhelming stress, the letter of the law was moderated: A death sentence was commuted by the Crown to six months.[79]

There have been cannibalism cases in this country, not all of which were immortalized in court opinions. One involved the Donner party, trapped by early snow in what is now known as the Donner Pass in the high Sierras. Some survivors of the disaster fed on the bodies of some of the dead, as Bernard De Voto has vividly described.[80] Murder and subsequent cannibalism by a Utah gold hunter, Frank Packer, in Colorado in 1873 drew a sentence of hanging by Judge Gerry in 1883 — of which Gene Fowler contributes a memorable vignette:

> Although Judge Gerry delivered what was considered the most eloquent hanging speech in Western court history, an apocryphal sentence is the one that persists, and by which this scholarly gentleman's name still lives. . . . Larry Dolan, who had a grudge against Packer, attended every session of the trial. Between times, Larry filled himself to the larynx

---

and not to separate man and wife? Should Holmes's order have been different if the passengers included children, a dying man, male and female prisoners being transported to a place of execution, a world-famous male scientist or top political leader or Olympic record-holder? Is there a "natural law" principle (and if so, should the criminal law follow it here) that under no circumstances shall an "innocent" life be deliberately taken in order that another, or even a greater number, shall live? Should the kind of situation in the *Holmes* case be viewed as governed by the practices applicable in a "state of nature," i.e., outside the bounds of organized society, on the theory of Holmes's lawyer that "[a]ll became their own lawgivers. . . . Every man on board had a right to make law with his own right hand"?

78. Regina v. Dudley and Stephens, 14 Q.B. 273, 15 Cox Crim. Cas. 624 (1884). Four seamen were in an open boat on the high seas, 1600 miles from the Cape of Good Hope, having had to abandon a yacht in a storm. After drifting for eighteen days, and after seven days without food and six days without water, two of them agreed, with the third dissenting, that the fourth seaman — a youth of seventeen or eighteen who lay helpless, extremely weakened by famine and the drinking of seawater — should be killed for sustenance the next day if help hadn't yet arrived. And kill him they did, next day. All three of them fed on his body for four days before being picked up by a passing vessel. The two ringleaders were prosecuted for murder. The jury found that probably all would have died within the four days had not the three men fed on the body; that probably the youth would have died first anyway. The jury left it to the court to determine whether it was murder. The judge so held, rejecting the idea that "necessity" could justify taking an innocent human life. He referred to the "awful danger of admitting the principle which has been contended for." "Who is to be the judge of this sort of necessity? By what measure is the comparative value of lives to be measured?" For more detail on this case see Mallin, In Warm Blood: Some Historical and Procedural Aspects of Regina v. Dudley and Stephens, 34 U. Chi. L. Rev. 387 (1967).

79. Further on the type of situation presented in this English case, see McCormick, Blood on the Sea (1962); Gibson, The Boat (1953) (a World War II episode); Fuller, The Case of the Speluncean Explorers, 62 Harv. L. Rev. 616 (1949) (imaginary case and opinions).

80. DeVoto, The Year of Decision: 1846, at 386-387 (1943). Cannibalism following an Andes plane crash is described in Read, Alive (1974).

with "Taos Lightning". . . . Just as the fluent Judge Gerry began a classical pronouncement of doom, Larry let out a cheer and fell from a bench. Then he rose, and ran drunkenly to his favorite saloon, bellowing like ten Apis bulls of Egypt:

"Well, boys, ut's all over; Packer's to hang. The Judge, God bless him . . . p'intin' his tremblin' finger at Packer, so ragin' mad as he was, he said: "They was siven Dimmycrats in Hinsdale County, but you, yah voracious man-eatin' son of a bitch, yuh eat five of thim! I sintince ye t' be hanged by th' neck until y're dead, dead, dead; as a warnin' ag'n reducin' the Dimmycratic popalashun of th' State.' "[81]

I cannot resist telling one more tale, of the same macabre genre. The whaleship *Essex* was rammed and sunk in the Pacific in 1820 by an enormous whale, and this incident became the climax of Herman Melville's *Moby Dick*. What happened after the sinking — which Melville did not write about — was this: Of the three lifeboats that were launched, one was lost; on the other two, after lengthy ordeals of storm and famine, cannibalism was practised on the bodies of a few who had died. On one boat the men were also driven to kill one of their number, after drawing lots. The victim was the cabin boy, a nephew of the master of the *Essex,* Captain Pollard, who was in the same lifeboat. "There is a Nantucket legend that when a reporter from the mainland came out to the island to interview [Captain Pollard] on his last birthday, the reporter closed the interview with the personal remark that he was distantly related to one of the Essex' crew. 'You remember him, of course,' he added. 'Remember him,' the old man cackled. 'Hell, son, I et him!' "[82]

There was apparently no prosecution in this case. Where prosecution did occur in the other cases mentioned, we have seen that the courts typically refused to recognize a "necessity" defense as such, but punishment tended to be lenient. "The law falters and averts her face and sheathes her own sword when pronouncing judgment upon creatures of flesh and blood thus goaded by the Furies."[83] (Yes, that was Cardozo again.) Judge Gerry's treatment of Frank Packer does not fit this description, but not all the facts of the case are clear; and further data presented by Gene Fowler might suggest that the multiple killings were unnecessary and connected with a robbery motive.

Though the states today would rarely be found recognizing a necessity defense where the defendant had taken an innocent, human life (as distinct from, say, theft or destruction of another's property),

81. Fowler, Timber Line 37 (1933). After reversal and a second conviction, Packer received a life sentence, and was pardoned after 18 years. *Id.*, at 38.

82. Whipple, Three-Month Ordeal in Open Boats, Life, Nov. 10, 1952, at 156.

83. Hall, ed., *supra* n.75 at 390.

the American Law Institute's Model Penal Code is willing to go further by recognizing for all crimes a "choice of evils" provision. This recognizes as a defense the defendant's belief in the necessity of his conduct where "the harm or evil sought to be avoided by [the defendant's] conduct is greater than that sought to be prevented by the law defining the offense charged," unless this defense would be inconsistent with a legislative purpose appearing elsewhere in the state's statutes.[84]

2. Related to this necessity defense is a classic defense in terms of "duress" or coercion. The Model Penal Code, for instance, recognizes this defense where there was coercion against the defendant by use or threatened use of unlawful force against the person — force which a person of reasonable firmness in his situation would have been unable to resist.[85]

3. Some other related situations: You are doubtless familiar with the fact that some rather frequently occurring stressful circumstances will mitigate an intentional killing so as to prevent its classification as "murder." If the circumstances amount to "self-defense," there is a complete defense to the alleged crime. If the defendant were not acting in self-defense but his intentional killing can be shown to have been done "in the heat of passion" and upon "sufficient provocation," then under many homicide statutes these stressful circumstances would mitigate the crime from murder to "voluntary manslaughter."

4. A highly stressful situation of still a different sort is that of euthanasia or mercy-killing — involving, for example, the terminal cancer patient who is in great pain which cannot be relieved by drugs (or can be relieved only by a fatal dosage) and which impels the defendant to commit euthanasia. Here the letter of the law is still against the act, through a legislative prohibition either against murder or against assisting a suicide. But the letter of the law is being moderated by leniency in the administration of the law. There have been a number of cases in which a jury acquittal was based upon a defense in terms of temporary insanity, or a defense that the conduct of the defendant had not actually *caused* the death. You may remember the much-publicized English trial of Dr. John Bodkin Adams a good many years ago, skillfully described in Sybille Bedford's book.[86] The defense was in terms of causation — i.e., that his conduct had not caused the death. The reason why the jury was able to acquit on that ground was that the judge's instruction said: If the administration of the drug by the doctor merely had the effect of hastening the death so that it occurred

84. ALI Model Penal Code §3.02 (Proposed Official Draft 1962); *id.*, Commentary at 5-10 (Tent. Draft No. 8, 1958).

85. ALI Model Penal Code §2.09 (Proposed Official Draft 1962); *id.*, Commentary at 2-16 (Tent. Draft No. 10, 1960).

86. Bedford, The Trial of Dr. Adams (1958).

on Monday rather than on Tuesday, this could not be viewed as the *cause* of the death. That is a pretty lenient instruction on what constitutes cause. Here you have an illustration of a judge, not only a jury, showing compassion; and there have been other mercy-killing cases in which, after a jury verdict of guilty, the judge was lenient in the sentence. So, too, in some cases after a substantial sentence has been imposed, the executive has shown clemency by reducing it considerably.

There is an opinion in a euthanasia case, by the highly respected Judge Learned Hand of the federal Court of Appeals for the Second Circuit (which sits in New York), together with a dissenting opinion by the equally renowned Judge Jerome Frank, that is important enough to merit consideration at some length. Judge Hand set out the basic facts as follows:

> The District Attorney, on behalf of the Immigration and Naturalization Service has appealed from an order naturalizing the appellee, Repouille. The ground of the objection in the district court and here is that he did not show himself to have been a person of "good moral character" for the five years which preceded the filing of his petition. The facts were as follows: The petition was filed on September 22, 1944 and on October 12, 1939, he had deliberately put to death his son, a boy of thirteen, by means of chloroform. His reason for this tragic deed was that the child had "suffered from birth from a brain injury which destined him to be an idiot and a physical monstrosity malformed in all four limbs. The child was blind, mute and deformed. He had to be fed; the movements of his bladder and bowels were involuntary, and his entire life was spent in a small crib." Repouille had four other children at the time towards whom he has always been a dutiful and responsible parent; it may be assumed that his act was to help him in their nurture, which was being compromised by the burden imposed upon him in the care of the fifth. The family was altogether dependent upon his industry for its support. He was indicted for manslaughter in the first degree; but the jury brought in a verdict of manslaughter in the second degree with a recommendation of the "utmost clemency"; and the judge sentenced him to not less than five years nor more than ten, execution to be stayed, and the defendant to be placed on probation, from which he was discharged in December 1945. Concededly, except for this act he conducted himself as a person of "good moral character" during the five years before he filed his petition. Indeed, if he had waited before filing his petition from September 22, to October 14, 1944, he would have been admitted without question.[87]

Judge Hand went on to say that, under prior decisions of the court, the statutory "good moral character" requirement was to be

87. Repouille v. U.S., 165 F.2d 152 (2d Cir. 1947).

decided by the "generally accepted moral conventions current at the time." He acknowledged that ascertaining these conventions was extremely difficult "in the absence of some national inquisition, like a Gallup Poll." He thought many people would be willing, in some matters of deep personal conviction, to defy the law; "few of us exact of ourselves or of others the unflinching obedience of a Socrates." But he was unwilling to give decisive weight to the sympathetic attitude shown by the jury and judge in Repouille's criminal case, since "a similar offender in Massachusetts . . . although . . . not executed, was imprisoned for life." So on the basis of the best guess he could make about current moral conventions, he concluded that "only a minority of virtuous persons would deem the practise morally justifiable, while it remains in private hands, even when the provocation is as overwhelming as it was in this instance." Therefore, disagreeing with the trial judge, he ordered the petition for naturalization dismissed, but "without prejudice to the filing of a second petition."

The decision was concurred in by Augustus Hand (Learned's cousin), but Judge Jerome Frank dissented. He argued first that the statute contemplated as a standard not the opinions of the whole public but rather "the attitudes of ethical leaders." But since prior decisions had already ruled against that interpretation, he addressed himself to the ascertainment of public opinion by declaring that

> in any case such as this, where we lack the means of determining present-day public reactions, we should remand to the district judge with these directions: The judge should give the petitioner and the government the opportunity to bring to the judge's attention reliable information on the subject, which he may supplement in any appropriate way. All the data so obtained should be put on record. On the basis thereof, the judge should reconsider his decision and arrive at a conclusion.

Notice, first of all, that the treatment of Repouille by the criminal court and by this court does not represent an exception to the point I have been making. The criminal court did show leniency at every stage: The grand jury had indicted for manslaughter in the first degree instead of murder; the jury convicted of manslaughter in the second degree with a recommendation of utmost clemency; the judge's sentence of five to ten years was suspended and Repouille was merely put on probation. Moreover, in the naturalization case, the majority's decision was only superficially tough; they knew, and mentioned in the opinion, that Repouille's application after the decision would be successful because of expiration of the statutory five-year period. Nor did the Massachusetts case referred to by Judge Hand represent an exception to my point. In that case, the governor had gotten his executive council to approve a reduction of sentence from death to life imprisonment; and (a couple of years after the *Repouille* decision) a new governor got approval of his council, by a 6 to 3 vote, to reduce the sentence to six-years-to-life, thereby resulting in the prisoner's immediate parole.[88]

Notice also the difference in the attitudes of Judges Hand and Frank toward ascertaining public opinion on the "good moral character" issue. Hand was willing to depend on his best guess; Frank said actual evidence of public opinion should be taken. It so happened that just prior to the decision a Gallup "national inquisition" *had* occurred, in which the question, "When a person has incurable disease, should doctors be allowed to end his life painlessly if requested by patient and family?" was answered yes by 37 percent of those queried — with much variation on the basis of age, sex, economic status, and education.[89] A question put in terms of the *Repouille* situation would presumably have drawn an even smaller percentage of approval, so Hand probably guessed right.

But Frank's approach rides the wave of the future as far as poll evidence is concerned. Such evidence is relatively new and there are certain obstacles to be hurdled in the law of evidence, but a widening variety of such evidence is being accepted as valid, when the witness is a qualified expert who explains the method and theory of his polling procedures. Poll evidence is obviously pertinent when a defendant seeks a change of venue (place of trial) on the ground that community opinion is inflamed against him. An interesting use of poll evidence in a breach of contract case involving a question rather analogous to the "good moral character" issue in the *Repouille* case was this: A movie screenwriter had a contract with a Hollywood studio in which he agreed to conduct himself with due regard to public conventions and morals, and not do anything tending to bring himself into public disgrace, ill will, or ridicule. He thereafter refused, on the ground of his Fifth Amendment privilege against self-incrimination, to answer questions before the House Committee on Un-American Activities concerning his alleged affiliation with Communists. In the breach of contract suit, the court received in evidence an opinion poll conducted by an expert pollster in Muncie, Indiana, indicating that about 67 percent of those polled thought such a refusal to testify showed the witness to be a Communist or Communist sympathizer.[90]

88. Newsweek, Jan. 17, 1949, at 24-25.

89. See Note, Judicial Determination of Moral Conduct in Naturalization Hearings, 16 U. Chi. L. Rev. 138, 141-142 (1948); 11 Pub. Opinion Q. 477 (1947).

90. This case together with numerous others, in a striking variety of situations, is covered in Annot., Admissibility and Weight of Surveys or Polls of Public or Consumers' Opinion, Recognition, Preference, or the Like, 76 A.L.R.2d 619 (1961). There is a good discussion of problems encountered in the use of such evidence in Zeisel, The Uniqueness of Survey Evidence, 45 Cornell L.Q. 322 (1960).

A lawyer-sociologist team of Nebraska resarchers has laid in a stock of poll evidence with potential use by courts and legislatures, by assessing public opinion on a number of issues in the field of domestic relations: e.g., parents' right to transfer custody of the child without supervision, their right to control a child's earnings, the child's duty to support indigent parents, etc.[91] It is important to understand, however, that such an ascertainment of community values is not the final word on what the law ought to be. In the *Repouille* case, it was treated as the final word (as against the views of "ethical leaders" or the court's personal views) because the naturalization statute was construed to require just that. Congress was viewed as requiring the court to adopt the *public's* view of what constituted "good moral character." In the absence of such legislative direction, the wise court takes the public's view into account but does not necessarily reflect that view. Even a legislator (who is regarded as more directly responsible to a constituency than is a court) is ideally responsible to his own conscience when that conflicts with what his constituency desires, as President Kennedy (then senator) tried to remind us in his 1955 book *Profiles in Courage*.

I can illustrate the point in still another way: When the above-mentioned Nebraska researchers expressed the hope that out of their study would come "a more reliable method than is now in use for those who seek to narrow the distance between lawmakers and their subjects," and seemed to be criticizing the Model Penal Code drafters for not consulting community opinion, this drew a response from a principal drafter of the Code. The response was that the Code was not trying "to 'narrow the distance between lawmakers and their subjects'; i.e., to make 'popular' law. On the contrary the Institute is trying to narrow the distance between lawmakers and such 'unpopular' people as psychiatrists and sociologists. We are engaged in making rational, useful law which we hope can be popularized by education."[92]

The point, as I have already suggested, is even more pertinent to the operation of a court — though obviously a known preponderance of public opinion would weigh very heavily in the deliberations of both legislator and judge. You can see how the point that I have been making about stressful situations (out of which grew the discussion about the court's active or passive role in relation to public attitudes about those situations) dovetails with the earlier point about the law's

91. Cohen, Robson & Bates, Parental Authority: The Community and the Law (1958). Another example of such research oriented toward what the law should be, is in the field of public attitudes concerning desirable property distribution when people die without a will. See Fellows, Simon & Rau, Public Attitudes About Property Distribution at Death and Intestate Succession Laws in the United States, 1978 Am. B. Foundation Research J. 321.

92. Schwartz, Ascertaining the Moral Sense of the Community: A Comment, 8 J. Legal Educ. 319-320 (1955).

inability to get too far out of line with public attitudes. At the close of this section on limits of law, I shall have more to say, by way of summary, on the law's capacity to *effectively change* people's attitudes and behavior.

Returning then to the main point for which the euthanasia cases have been used here — the limits put by stressful situations upon the law's effectiveness — you may well ask: Well, then, why doesn't the law openly recognize a right of mercy-killing? Why does it cling to the principle that a defendant's worthy motives may be considered in mitigation of penalty but not as a complete defense? Apparently for the same reason that it does not condone the other types of conduct under stress that I have already noted: the fact that great practical difficulties and dangers would arise from even such a limited recognition of the right to kill.

4. Difficulties and Risks in Administration

The practical dangers mentioned above represent a fourth general limit on what the law can do, namely, the fact that difficulties and risks in the administration of an otherwise desirable right may make the granting of the right more harmful than beneficial. In the case of euthanasia, what are these risks and difficulties?

I am not concerned here with cases based on a patient's right to refuse ordinary medical treatment (e.g., blood transfusions and limb amputation) allegedly necessary to sustain life;[93] or the right of a terminally ill patient to refuse or discontinue extraordinary measures (e.g., life-support machines designed to forestall an otherwise imminent "natural" death) often pursuant to the terms of a "living will" authorized under a number of states' statutes.[94] Rather, I have in mind what is more accurately called euthanasia (though similar to the right of the terminally ill above): those situations in which a person takes the affirmative step of hastening nature's course by, for example, administering an intentionally fatal overdose of a drug, for benign motives and with consent of the victim — a consent which was lacking in the *Repouille* case.[95]

There are obvious risks and difficulties in allowing such a right to

93. See Annot., 93 A.L.R.3d 67 (1979).

94. See In re Quinlan, 70 N.J. 10, 355 A.2d 647 (1976), *cert. denied*, sub. nom. Garger & Gallagher v. New Jersey, 429 U.S. 922 (1976); Symposium on In re Quinlan, 30 Rutgers L. Rev. 243 (1977); Symposium, Mental Incompetents and the Right to Die, 11 Suffolk L. Rev. 919 (1977); Notes, 46 U. Cin. L. Rev. 192 (1977); 49 *id.* 228 (1980).

95. See Right-to-Die Groups Seek Another Right: To Aid In Suicide, Wall St. J., Sept. 4, 1980, at 1.

assist another in committing suicide — primarily the danger that the assister has less than benign motives and is lying about the victim's consent. Legislative safeguards have been proposed, e.g., allowing a doctor to administer euthanasia (1) after two other doctors have concurred in the diagnosis of the disease as fatal and incurable, and (2) in the presence of another doctor, lawyer, or nurse, upon the patient's consent, obtained in writing, and in the presence of two witnesses. Even allowing for these conditions, objections are voiced that a patient crazed with pain is not in a position to freely give consent; and if he were not in such an extremity, would he be likely to give consent? Also, should we not worry, it is asked, that a miraculous cure may be discovered shortly after the killing? And might this procedure be an entering wedge for other less defensible killings — for instance, of the senile or of the mentally deficient? Should the law ignore the strong moral and religious objections to suicide and to assisting in suicide? You may not find these considerations sufficiently weighty, but so far they have led the law to say "no" to euthanasia.[96]

In most instances of euthanasia, however, the two proposed legal safeguards mentioned above would probably prevent fraudulent abuse. The possibility of such abuse has been stronger in certain other areas where the law has been unwilling to recognize an otherwise desirable right. For instance, there has been a well-established rule (departed from in a few exceptional situations) that you cannot recover damages for nonintentional but negligent infliction of mental or emotional suffering in the absence of physical impact. The plaintiff who, for instance, suffered emotional shock as an eyewitness to injury done to another could not recover. What has underlain this impact rule? Principally it has been the fear that the right of recovery would be too readily subjected to fraudulent abuse. The suffering testified to by plaintiffs might be wholly imaginary but disproof would be difficult, and the partial safeguard provided by an identifiable physical injury would be lacking. Still, court attitudes have been shifting — particularly when physical injury can be shown to have resulted *from* the emotional stress, or when the plaintiff had been in the "zone of danger" at the time of incurring the stress.[97]

As is apparent from this shift in judicial attitudes, courts have sometimes changed their minds on whether the problem of proof and disproof presented too much difficulty. Another illustration is the

96. See Morris, Voluntary Euthanasia, 45 Wash. L. Rev. 239 (1970); Kamisar, Some Non-Religious Views Against Proposed Mercy-Killing Legislation, 42 Minn. L. Rev. 969 (1958); Williams, "Mercy-Killing" Legislation — A Rejoinder, 38 U. Colo. L. Rev. 178 (1966); Williams, The Sanctity of Life and the Criminal Law 311-350 (1957); Silving, Euthanasia: A Study in Comparative Criminal Law, 103 U. Pa. L. Rev. 350 (1954).

97. Morris on Torts 191-195 (2d ed. 1980); Prosser, *supra* n.73 at 328-333.

repudiation in one case after another since 1946 of the long-standing rule that a child cannot recover damages for injury suffered (while in the mother's womb) as the result of negligent injury inflicted on the mother.[98] So too, the New Jersey Supreme Court did not abide by its 1967 decision rejecting a claim by parents against a doctor for his negligent failure to inform them of the increased possibility, in their case, of a defective birth. The 1967 court thought it was an "impossible" task to evaluate "the intangible, unmeasurable, and complex human benefits of motherhood and fatherhood and weigh these against the alleged emotional and money injuries" from a defective child.[99] In 1979, however, the same court found this weighing process not impossible as far as the parents' claim for emotional injury is concerned. In denying the parents' claim for the money injury, i.e., the costs of rearing the defective child, the court pointed to some other difficulties: Recovery "would be wholly disproportionate to the culpability involved, and . . . [would] constitute a windfall to the parents and place too unreasonable a financial burden upon physicians."[100]

The question of unreasonable burdens on others raises problems similar to those in the blind man situation described in Section B of this chapter. That is, why has American law not yet recognized the right of an individual to recover against a stranger for failing to come to his rescue when the stranger could have done so without much risk of injury? Apparently, the fear still prevails that the burden imposed by such a right might be too heavy — particularly considering the

98. Morris, *id.* at 190-191; Prosser, *supra* at 335-338.

99. Gleitman v. Cosgrove, 49 N.J. 22, 29, 227 A.2d 689, 693 (1967).

100. Berman v. Allen, 80 N.J. 421, 432, 404 A.2d 8, 14 (1979). It is more common for courts in this type of case to recognize the economic rather than emotional injury claim (Comment, 8 Hofstra L. Rev. 257, 266 (1979)), and either allow all economic costs of raising the child (Becker v. Schwartz, 46 N.Y.2d 401, 412-415, 386 N.E.2d 807, 813-814 (1978)) or deal with the above quoted difficulties by requiring a *deduction* from the economic damages of an amount representing the "benefits" from having a child, though defective (see Troppi v. Scarf, 31 Mich. App. 240, 254-255, 187 N.W.2d 511, 517-519 (1st Div. 1971), which incidentally, did not separate the economic and emotional injury claims) or by compensating for the "economic burden related solely to the physical defects of the child" (Jacobs v. Theimer, 519 S.W.2d 846, 849 (Tex. 1975)).

The defective child's claim (of "wrongful life") was usually joined with the parents' claim (of "wrongful birth") in those cases but has generally not been recognized: The courts usually spoke of the impossibility, or unduly speculative character, of weighing the child's impaired life against non-life, or flatly expressed the conclusion that impaired life is more precious than non-life. (Comment, 8 Hofstra L. Rev. 257, 267-268 (1979); for criticism, see 269-272.) For the defective child situation and related situations, see generally Robertson, Toward Rational Boundaries of Tort Liability for Injury to the Unborn: Prenatal Injuries, Preconception Injuries, and Wrongful Life, 1978 Duke L.J. 1401 (1979); Annot., Tort Liability For Wrongfully Causing One To Be Born, 83 A.L.R.3d 15 (1978). A number of courts have recognized "wrongful birth" actions by parents claiming the doctor's negligent performance of an unsuccessful sterilization or abortion operation. Comment, 8 Hofstra L. Rev. 257 nn. 3 & 4.

understandable panic in such emergency situations, and the lack of clearly defined situations in which there will be such a duty to act. Our prevailing morality barely makes us our blood brother's "keeper"; it has not yet made us a stranger's keeper. I must point out, however, that there has been strong moral criticism of this position of the law. A judicial change of mind — like those changes described above — is likely to occur here.[101]

Still another influential consideration, sometimes mentioned in the cases already considered, was specifically stressed in a case involving this claim by a child: that he should recover damages against his unwed father who had induced the mother to engage in sexual relations by fraudulent promise of marriage, thereby depriving the child of a claimed "right to be a legitimate child, to have a normal home, to have a legal father, to inherit from his father, to inherit from his paternal ancestors, and for being stigmatized as a bastard." A main concern of the Illinois court rejecting the claim was that to recognize the alleged right would open wide the "doors of litigation" to all persons "born into the world under conditions they might regard as adverse."[102] This, then, is another practical difficulty that gives the courts concern: the feared swamping of the courts with litigation, and the opening up of "a field that has no sensible or just stopping place."[103]

5. "Internal" Disputes

I move to another category, but it is not wholly a separate one. It involves in part the kind of practical considerations already treated in the previous category, together with privacy considerations also involved in an earlier category. I am thinking of the situations involving the internal affairs of nonprofit associations, like families, fraternal societies, religious groups, and unions.

101. See Weinrib, The Case For A Duty to Rescue, 90 Yale L.J. 247 (1980); Notes, 47 Ind. L.J. 321 (1972), 55 *id.*, 551 (1980); Franklin, Vermont Requires Rescue: A Comment, 25 Stan. L. Rev. 51 (1973); Prosser, *supra* n.73 at 340-343.

102. Zepeda v. Zepeda, 41 Ill. App. 2d 240, 190 N.E.2d 849 (1963), *cert. denied*, 379 U.S. 945 (1963). See also Williams v. State, 18 N.Y.2d 481, 223 N.E.2d 343 (1966); Note, 66 Colum. L. Rev. 127 (1966). Compare a 1977 Illinois case recognizing a child's claim against a doctor and hospital for pre-conception negligence: i.e., a negligent blood transfusion to the child's mother over seven years before conception had caused mental and physical impairments of the child, apparent at birth. Renslow v. Mennonite Hosp., 67 Ill. 2d 348, 367 N.E.2d 1250 (1977), discussed in Note, 48 U. Colo. L. Rev. 62 (1977).

103. Rieck v. Medical Protective Co., 64 Wis. 2d 514, 219 N.W.2d 242, 245 (1974). This was a parents' action against the clinic and obstetrician for negligently failing to ascertain the mother's pregnancy in time to permit abortion.

You can see why the law in these situations tends to stay its hand. Not only are there constitutional restraints to worry about,[104] but a court's inquiry into, and interpretation of, a group's rules and practices "may lead it into what Professor Chafee has called the 'dismal swamp,' the area of its activity concerning which only the group can speak with competence."[105] The difficulties encountered when the court tries to provide appropriate remedies must also not be discounted. The family is a good example here since some family disputes are obviously not appropriate for resolution by a court.[106] The wife who complains, for instance, that her husband no longer exhibits affection, can hardly get a court to order her husband to exhibit affection, or even get a court to order her wayward husband to live under the same roof. The same goes for certain other family disputes — e.g., the proper schooling and upbringing of children.[107]

This is not to say that "internal" affairs of institutional groups are immune from legal intervention. "Thus, although we must respect the autonomy of the family, intervention against child abuse is nonetheless essential. And although we delegate great power to labor unions, we impose upon them obligations of fair representation. . . ."[108] As for churches, the Supreme Court in dealing with church property disputes arising out of church schisms once counseled deference to the judgment

104. For instance, the First Amendment's clauses on religious freedom and church-state separation represent a barrier to government intervention in the religious affairs of church institutions. And, "[s]ince the First Amendment and due process clauses appear to guarantee to individuals the right to associate freely, . . . intervention might be challenged on constitutional grounds as an interference with the protected sphere within which groups are free to act as they wish, and, in particular, to choose their own members." Note, 76 Harv. L. Rev. 983, 990-991 (1963).

105. *Id.* at 991.

106. For discussion of state intrusion in family affairs, see Note, 26 Stan. L. Rev. 1383 (1974).

107. For example, in 1959 the Supreme Court of Alabama considered a case in which a father was seeking a court injunction to restrain his wife, with whom he was living, from sending their child to a public rather than a parochial school. The court decided that it should not interfere at all. It pointed out that the case did not involve a question concerning custody of the child, incident to a separation or divorce, "but simply whether a court of equity should settle a difference of opinion between parents as to what is best for their minor child when the parents and the child are all living together as a family group." "It seems to us," said the court, that "if we should hold that equity has jurisdiction in this case, such holding will open wide the gates for settlement in equity of all sorts and varieties of intimate family disputes concerning the upbringing of children. The absence of cases dealing with the question indicates a reluctance of the courts to assume jurisdiction in disputes arising out of the intimate family circle. It does not take much imagination to envision the extent to which explosive differences of opinion between parents as to the proper upbringing of their children would be brought into court for attempted solution. . . . Considerations of policy and expediency forbid a resort to injunctive relief in such a case." Kilgrow v. Kilgrow, 268 Ala. 475, 479, 108 So. 2d 885, 888 (1959).

108. Tribe, Seven Pluralist Fallacies: In Defense of the Adversary Process — A Reply to Justice Rehnquist, 33 U. Miami L. Rev. 43, 49 (1978).

of church tribunals but has qualified that decision with exceptions in the case of fraud, arbitrariness, or collusiveness, provided no extensive inquiry into church doctrine is required. And most recently it approved a lower court's application of "neutral principles" of property law as a permissible alternative to deference to the church tribunal's decision.[109] Nonetheless, the courts remain mindful that sometimes "special weight to the institutional decision [of church, family, union]" should be given, "perhaps because adversary litigation of the propriety of those decisions would have more disadvantageous consequences in terms of diminishing the usefulness of the institution than would the ultimate resolution by the court of the claim of individual right."[110]

I have by now given you numerous instances, in the present category and the preceding one, in which the law has been unwilling to recognize certain rights because of its anticipation of adverse consequences. But sometimes hindsight as well as foresight is involved. Occasionally, after a right has been recognized, the abuses of it are discovered to be so acute as to call for the withdrawal of that right. This is what has happened in some states that have passed statutes abolishing a right to damages for so-called heart-balm — where there had been, for example, a breach of promise to marry. A New York statute more than 40 years ago declared in its introductory section as follows (and I think this explanation would stand for many other states that have passed similar statutes):

> The remedies heretofore provided by law for the enforcement of actions based upon alleged alienation of affections, criminal conversation, seduction and breach of contract to marry, having been subjected to grave abuses, causing extreme annoyance, embarrassment, humiliation and pecuniary damage to many persons wholly innocent and free of any wrongdoing, who were merely the victims of circumstances, and such remedies having been exercised by unscrupulous persons for their unjust enrichment, and such remedies having furnished vehicles for the commission or attempted commission of a crime and in many cases having resulted in the perpetration of frauds, it is hereby declared as the public policy of the state, that the best interests of the people of the state will be served by the abolition of such remedies. . . ."[111]

But you should bear in mind that legislative withdrawal of a right or obligation, or complete judicial abstention, is not the only possible

109. Jones v. Wolf, 443 U.S. 595 (1979). See Adams & Hanlon, *Jones v. Wolf*: Church Autonomy and the Religion Clauses of the First Amendment, 128 U. Pa. L. Rev. 1291 (1980); Note, 68 Geo. L.J. 1141 (1980); Ellman, Driven from the Tribunal: Judicial Resolution of Internal Church Disputes, 69 Calif. L. Rev. 1378 (1981).

110. Rehnquist, The Adversary Society, 33 U. Miami L. Rev. 1, 8 (1978).

111. N.Y. Laws 1935, chap. 263. See Feinsinger, Legislative Attack on "Heart Balm", 33 Mich. L. Rev. 979 (1935).

solution to the kind of problem described. Sometimes an alternative right or obligation or remedy can be substituted. Thus, while a court, as I said before, will abstain from ordering a man to exhibit love for his wife or live under the same roof with her, the law does give the wife certain other remedies — like divorce or support money. Considering the court remedies of injunction, damages, restitution, and declaratory judgment, there are many situations in which courts will allow one remedy though excluding all others. Legislatures have alternatives, too: Unsuccessful criminal legislation, instead of being simply repealed, can be replaced with alternative systems of control.[112]

6. The Problem of Knowledge

Now finally let me suggest another broad limit on what the law can accomplish: the limit that is imposed by the relative dearth of reliable scientific knowledge.

Reliable knowledge is of course important to legislators, administrators, or judges since they are interested in ascertaining the probable consequences of their enactments or decisions. Knowledge of this kind is notoriously limited.

What about the kind of scientific knowledge that would enable the *fact finder* in a dispute to accurately reconstruct the happenings that gave rise to the dispute? We are here dealing with what Max Radin once called one of the two "permanent problems of the law" (the other permanent problem being the determination, and the public's prophesying the determination, of the "just" decision).[113] Jerome Frank, in his popular book *Courts on Trial* (1950), vigorously demonstrated the many pitfalls that lie in the path of the fact finder, among them the uncertainty surrounding the credibility of witnesses. The law would *like* to have a surefire method of testing the truth of a witness's testimony; but lie-detector (polygraph) evidence is generally *inadmissible* in court, partly because of unreliability. In this instance,

112. It has been urged that the solution for the present failures of narcotics enforcement is not simply abolition of punishment but a system of distribution that uses doctors to dispense controlled doses to addicts while also attempting cures, requires record-keeping, and prohibits distribution through other channels. Others suggest that the present ineffective prohibitions against marijuana might be replaced by a system permitting sales through licensed dealers under a control system similar to that for liquor. The 1972 Report of the National Commission on Marijuana and Drug Abuse took a middle ground on marijuana: Production and distribution of the drug, as well as possession with intent to distribute commercially, would remain criminal; but personal use, and possession incident thereto, would be decriminalized. Further on the varieties of available legislative and judicial techniques, see the final section of this chapter.

113. Radin, The Permanent Problems of the Law, 15 Cornell L.Q. 1 (1929).

though, the main reason for inadmissibility may be not inherent unreliability but the fear that the trier of facts, whether judge or jury, will tend to give an infallibility to the evidence that it does not deserve.[114]

Still, in very recent years, some courts have moved in the direction of admissibility of polygraph evidence, particularly when the tests were taken "upon stipulation of the parties";[115] and some have started admitting (what had previously also been inadmissible) evidence obtained by hypnosis.[116] Other new techniques of scientific evidence have caused considerable movement in the field: "Neutron activation analysis, sound spectrometry (voiceprints), psycholinguistics, atomic absorption, remote electromagnetic sensing, and bitemark comparisons are but a sample of the kinds of scientific evidence inundating the courts."[117] Change has worked in the opposite direction, too; there are cases in which "[s]ome well-accepted scientific techniques, such as radar and certain drug-testing procedures, have been challenged successfully."[118]

The legal approach to admissibility of evidence in general has been that any "relevant" conclusions should be admissible, in the absence of factors like "dangers of prejudicing or misleading the jury, and undue consumption of time"; and this approach, according to Professor McCormick, should be applied to scientific evidence as well, when the conclusions are "supported by a qualified expert witness."[119] While some courts have taken this approach, the most popular standard, announced in 1923, makes admissibility of scientific evidence more difficult: The scientific principle or discovery from which an expert's testimony is deduced "must be sufficiently established to have gained general acceptance in the particular field in which it belongs."[120] The many problems encountered in applying this standard have provoked strong criticisms, and suggestions for alternative approaches[121] —

114. McCormick on Evidence, §207 (2d ed. 1972).

115. See Gianelli, The Admissibility of Novel Scientific Evidence: *Frye v. United States*, a Half-Century Later, 80 Colum. L. Rev. 1197, 1199 n.8 (1980); Notes, 14 Akron L. Rev. 133 (1980); 73 Colum. L. Rev. 1120 (1973).

116. Gianelli, *supra* n.115; McLaughlan, Hypnosis in Its Role and Current Admissibility in the Criminal Law, 17 Willamette L.J. 665 (1981); Diamond, Inherent Problems in the Use of Pre-Trial Hypnosis on a Prospective Witness, 68 Calif. L. Rev. 313 (1980); Natl. L.J., June 2, 1980, at 1, col. 4.

117. Gianelli, *id.* at 1198.

118. *Id.* at 1199 nn. 9 & 10.

119. McCormick on Evidence, §203 at 491 (2d ed. 1972). The Federal Rules of Evidence, effective in 1975 and adopted in many state jurisdictions, declare relevant evidence to be admissible (except as otherwise provided by the Rules, Federal Constitution or statute, or Supreme Court rules) and define relevant evidence as "evidence having any tendency to make the existence of any fact that is of consequence to the determination of the action more probable or less probable than it would be without the evidence" (Rules 401, 402).

120. Frye v. U.S., 293 F. 1013, 1014 (D.C. Cir. 1923).

121. See Gianelli, *supra* n.115; Note, 40 Ohio St. L.J. 757 (1979). It is not yet

including the above relevance standard or some modification thereof, or "the creation of independent bodies of experts who would be called upon to review novel scientific techniques before they could be used in court."[122] Under the latter approach, the use of a "Science Court" has been proposed for resolving scientific fact questions underlying public policy issues.[123]

Contrasting with polygraph evidence, which is close to the "inadmissible" end of the spectrum, is the kind of scientific evidence that is not only admissible but *conclusive* — e.g., negative blood test evidence in a paternity case. That is, if the blood types of the child and the alleged father are incompatible — for instance, the father is AB type and the child is O type — then science declares the alleged father *cannot* be the actual father. One judge put it this way: On the basis of the scientific evidence, the defendant could no more be the father of the child in question than a dog could be the father of a cat. That is how utterly conclusive this evidence is deemed to be. Such acceptance is not accorded to scientific evidence that establishes a man might *possibly* be the father. That kind of test evidence generally would not even be admissible (though newly developing techniques are beginning to produce a change in this rule).[124] But if the expert testimony is to the effect that a man *cannot* be the father because of blood types, then in most states that would be regarded as conclusive evidence, no matter what the testimony of the woman in the case.

It is interesting that even when this kind of virtually absolute scientific knowledge exists, some features of the legal system can serve to undermine the normal legal consequence of such knowledge. I am referring to the powerful role of the initial fact finder, whether jury or judge, and to the special consequence that statutes may have.

Consider, for example, why in 1946 Charlie Chaplin lost a paternity suit brought against him in California.[125] The jury chose to believe the girl's testimony rather than the blood test evidence which, according to the scientists, showed he could not have been the father. It happened that the California statutes had *not* laid down a mechanical rule that negative blood test evidence (as I have described it above) would absolve the defendant of a paternity charge.

---

clear whether the Federal Rules of Evidence were intended to reject the *Frye* standard for scientific evidence. See Gianelli, *supra* at 1228-1231.

122. *Id.* at 1231.

123. *Id.* at 1232; Martin, The Proposed "Science Court," 75 Mich. L. Rev. 1058 (1977).

124. See Ellmann & Kaye, Probabilities and Proof: Can HLA and Blood Group Testing Prove Paternity? 54 N.Y.U.L. Rev. 1131 (1979). See also the Terasaki article and replying article by Jaffee, in 16 J. Fam. L. 543 (1977-1978) and 17 *id.* at 457 (1978-1979).

125. Berry v. Chaplin, 74 Cal. App. 2d 652, 169 P.2d 442 (1946).

A rather similar case was similarly decided in Wisconsin in 1957. The statute, unlike the statute of some other states (which made the negative type of blood test evidence conclusive of non-paternity) simply said that such negative evidence "shall be receivable in evidence." And another Wisconsin statute — quite common in other states, too — declared that when a child is born to a *married* woman, "any party asserting the illegitimacy of the child . . . shall have the burden of proving beyond all reasonable doubt that the husband was not the father of the child." The trial judge thought the wife's testimony rendered the negative blood test evidence doubtful enough to prevent the husband from fulfilling his burden of proof beyond a reasonable doubt. Why could the appellate court not rule as a matter of law that negative paternity evidence was conclusive of non-paternity? The majority of the court thought that the statutes prevented such a decision and, in particular, concluded that a legislature that had "pointedly refrained" from adopting the conclusive evidence standard of other state statutes should be allowed to let the fact finder weigh the negative paternity evidence along with all other evidence, and to preserve the fact finder's primacy in weighing evidence and judging the credibility of witnesses. The dissent countered this reasoning,[126] but as previously mentioned, even where firm scientific knowledge exists, other special factors may prevail: here, the weight given to findings of the original fact finder and the special role that a statute may play.

Now to get back to the point about the scientific knowledge spectrum: On one end, you have lie detector evidence, which the courts usually do not even admit into evidence. On the other end, you have the negative blood test evidence for paternity, with the law tending to view such evidence as absolutely conclusive. In between lies a range of evidence. For instance, psychiatric testimony is, as you know, admitted in evidence, but its weight will depend on many factors, including the expert's qualifications and persuasiveness and how persuasive the psy-

126. Prochnow v. Prochnow, 274 Wis. 491, 502, 80 N.W.2d 278 (1957): "This court has frequently held that the testimony of a witness or finding of a jury which is contrary to unquestionable physical situations or common knowledge is of no weight in favor of the side it is invoked to support. . . . Thus, it is frequently held in negligence cases that testimony as to location, speed, and the like must give way to physical facts established by uncontradicted testimony. For instance, if verified skid marks show that a car traveled on the left side of the road when and after the brakes were applied sufficiently to slide the wheels, no weight can be given to testimony of the driver and his passengers that he was at all times in the right-hand traffic lane. . . . Courts should not shut their eyes to advances in science which conclusively establish a fact, by simply repeating the age-old maxim that the credibility of witnesses is for the trier of fact." The majority opinion is worth reading if only for its revelation that one who dons the judicial robes need not simultaneously shed his sense of humor and style.

chiatrist is on the other side (generally each side does have such an expert). Most expert or scientific evidence brought before the law falls, like psychiatric evidence, somewhere between the two extremes indicated.

This is true, for instance, of the opinion poll evidence referred to in connection with the *Repouille* euthanasia case. It is also true of the social psychologist evidence that figured in the 1954 Brown v. Board of Education school desegregation decision of the Supreme Court.[127] Because that decision is often referred to — and (I think) erroneously — as being *based* on sociological evidence, some space will be given here to its explication.

The courtroom testimony by psychologists for the plaintiff school children in the *Brown* case centered around some "doll tests." Sixteen black children — ages six to nine — had been asked these questions about the drawings of a white doll and a black doll, identical except for skin color: (a) Show me the doll you like best, or that you would like to play with (10 chose the white doll); (b) Show me the doll that looks bad (11 chose the black doll, 1 chose the white doll, the remaining 4 were silent); (c) Show me the nice doll (9 chose the white).

The witness-stand interpretation of these answers by psychologist Kenneth Clark for the plaintiffs was that the black child accepts a "negative stereotype" about himself.

However, Edmond Cahn has argued with considerable force that the questions asked were ambiguous. The child might select what he "likes," or "likes to play with," or the "nice" doll, on the basis of what he is accustomed to; and most dolls are white. "Bad" might have been interpreted similarly, i.e., as not a customary type of doll (or might have been considered as the doll who had been naughty and hence more fun to play with and rebuke; or might have been treated as referring to the remaining dolls, by process of elimination, after the preceding question had been answered).[128]

Again, psychologist Clark's interpretation could be disputed when he described as an "evasion of reality" the children's answers to the last of the following questions: (d) Give me the doll that looks like a white child (16 picked the white doll); (e) Give me the doll that looks like a colored child (16 picked the black doll); (f) Give me the doll that looks like you (7 picked the white doll). Cahn here again points to ambiguities: "looks like you" in what respect? The child might not have been thinking of color but of other likenesses — i.e., since they found the white dolls "nice," perhaps it was this niceness they were identifying with, not the color.

127. 347 U.S. 483 (1954).

128. Cahn, A Dangerous Myth in the School Segregation Cases, 30 N.Y.U.L. Rev. 150 (1955).

There are other difficulties. Not only was the sampling not shown to be adequate, but the tests did not purport to isolate the *effect of school segregation* on the children's answers. Indeed, another study by Kenneth Clark had shown that black children's preference for white dolls *decreased* as their ages went from four years to seven years, yet these latter years are those of school attendance.[129] And still another Clark study had shown northern black children even more pronounced in their preference for the white doll — apparently tending to refute the notion that school segregation causes this preference.[130]

Thus the psychological evidence presented in the *Brown* case was not strong. Remember, however, that the Supreme Court opinion did not rely on or even cite this evidence. Neither did it refer to a lengthy appendix to plaintiff's Supreme Court brief, entitled "The Effects of Segregation and the Consequences of Desegregation: A Social Science Statement," signed by more than thirty leading scholars, including sociologists, anthropologists, psychologists, and psychiatrists. What it did cite in its now famous footnote 11 were several articles and books (most of which had been included in the authorities cited in the above appendix) dealing with the opinions of social scientists on the effects of school segregation. These seemed not to be cited as the *basis* of the Court decision but rather as corroboration. That is, after stating that school segregation had a detrimental effect on school children, and after quoting the finding of the Kansas court (in one of the four cases being heard together by the Supreme Court) to the same effect, the Court stated, "Whatever may have been the extent of psychological knowledge at the time of Plessy v. Ferguson,[131] this finding is amply supported by modern authority." And footnote 11 was appended to this statement.

Cahn made a further argument, namely that the use of social science evidence in these cases was dangerous. However appropriate such evidence might be in cases of socioeconomic regulation, he asserted, it should not be the basis for determining the scope of our "fundamental" rights, such as equal protection of the laws. These rights, he argued, should not depend on whatever happens to be current fad among social scientists; future social scientists may have illiberal, "racist" notions.

But note that while there is some conflict in the standards applicable to admissibility of scientific evidence, the following seems roughly true: (1) Scientific evidence, whether the case involves economic regulation or civil liberties, *cannot be kept out* — if relevant to the issues, pre-

129. Garfinkel, Social Science Evidence and the School Segregation Cases, 21 J. Pol. 37 (1959).

130. *Id.* For an absorbing personal account of witness Clark and the doll tests see Kluger, Simple Justice 317-321, 353-356 (1975).

131. 163 U.S. 537 (1896).

sented by properly qualified experts, and regarded as not too unreliable or misleading to the trier of fact by its aura of scientific infallibility (*cf.* lie detector evidence). (2) How much *weight* is to be given the evidence will depend on the facts of each case: on how careful the analyses, experimentation, survey, or testing; how qualified and persuasive the expert; how widely accepted the assumptions. (3) This does not mean that the court's common sense evaluations of fundamental rights, e.g., of what is unequal protection of the laws, will be automatically eliminated. It means that when common sense does not speak strongly and unequivocally, the court will be *more inclined* to rely on carefully prepared scientific evidence. The Supreme Court in the *Brown* case was more inclined to cite what it called the "supporting authority" from social scientists because of the past difference of opinion on the basis of commonsense evaluation, regarding constitutionality of racial segregation.

In Plessy v. Ferguson (the precedent that had upheld racial segregation in transportation) the Court as a matter of common sense had not thought that segregation produced unequal protection. In fact the Court there made some assertions that made it almost imperative for the plaintiff's lawyers in *Brown* to introduce psychological material designed to refute them. Thus, the Court in *Plessy* had said that segregation *does not* stamp the colored race with a badge of inferiority; that the colored race has merely put that construction on it. It had also asserted that "social prejudice" and "racial instincts" *cannot* be overcome by legislation. The psychological testimony and the collected social science opinion in the appendix were directed at refuting these assertions — as well as showing that school segregation did not fulfill a reasonable educational purpose, and that under certain conditions, desegregation could be accomplished without undue conflict or violence.

I do not wish to underestimate the difficulties in obtaining reliable social science evidence. One indication of these problems is this observation by the editors of a 1978 comprehensive symposium on "School Desegregation: Lessons of the First Twenty-five Years": "Almost all of the social scientists writing for this symposium . . . note how little competent research has actually been done to date."[132] One contributor

132. Levin & Hawley, Foreword to the Symposium, 42 Law & Contemp. Prob., No. 3, 1,3 (1978). They went on to say that "much of the social science research that has been the far too narrow focus of the social, political and legal justifications for desegregation has used inadequate methodologies, inappropriate samples, varying definitions of critical variables such as desegregation or student outcomes and reached contradictory or ambiguous conclusions."

to the symposium, speaking of research on "children's self-images and racial self-identity" (e.g., the doll-test type of research previously described) showed why "this is an area beset with many methodological and conceptual problems that make it difficult to draw firm conclusions."[133] Such conclusions as had been drawn from social science research on school segregation and desegregation seemed to have been shifting. A lawyer contributor cited numerous studies for the proposition that "the near consensus among social scientists at the time of *Brown,* based upon the most feeble of policy research, that desegregation would work to the advantage of blacks, has given way to a myriad of more sophisticated and less conclusive research findings."[134]

He further observed that "federal courts frequently appear disinclined to give much credence to social science findings in school desegregation cases"[135] and he argued for caution and skepticism in dealing with such findings.[136] Social scientists, too, have been suggesting that the authoritativeness and superiority of knowledge arrived at by social science methods has been oversold, and that some social problems are better handled through "ordinary knowledge" or "interaction" of social groups.[137] The signers of the 1970 minority report of the Federal Commission on Obscenity and Pornography expressed their frustration at the fact that "conclusively proving causal relationships among social science type variables is extremely difficult if not impossible. Among adults whose life histories have included much exposure to pornography, it is nearly impossible to disentangle the literally hundreds of causal threads or chains that contributed to their later adjustment or maladjustment. Because of the extreme complexity of the problem and the uniqueness of the human experience it is doubtful that we will ever have absolutely convincing scientific proof that pornography is or isn't harmful. . . . "[138] Not surprisingly, the Supreme Court has shown some uncertainty and caution in its han-

133. Epps, The Impact of School Desegregation on the Self-Evaluation and Achievement Orientation of Minority Children, *id.* at 58.

134. Yudof, School Desegregation: Legal Realism, Reasoned Elaboration, and Social Science Research in the Supreme Court, *id.*, No. 4 at 61, & n.27. That the newer research may not be as negative as sometimes claimed, see Hawley, The New Mythology of School Desegregation, *id.*, No. 4, 214.

135. Yudof, *id.* at 62. See also Levin, *id.* at 1-2.

136. Yudof, *supra* at 70-77. See also Lermack, No Right Number? Social Science Research and the Jury-Size Cases, 54 N.Y.U.L. Rev. 951, 967-976 (1979).

137. Lindblom & Cohen, Usable Knowledge (1979), critically reviewed in Zeisel, Social Science Hubris?, 1981 Am. B. Foundation Research J. 273.

138. Report of Commissioners Hill & Link, concurred in by Commissioner Keating, in Report of the Commission on Obscenity and Pornography 489 (Bantam ed. 1970).

dling of social science evidence in school cases,[139] the jury-size cases,[140] and some other areas of constitutional decision.[141]

In spite of all the difficulties, it seems the part of wisdom not to ignore social science evidence, but rather to proceed cautiously, keeping pace with its reliability.[142] "We cannot turn back the clock. Social

139. Yudof, *supra* n.134 at 107-108.

140. The decision in Williams v. Florida, 399 U.S. 78 (1970), upholding constitutionality of a six-member jury in a state non-capital felony prosecution, rested in part on an inverted reliance on social science evidence; the Court said that neither the empirical studies (largely of civil juries) nor theory had shown six-member juries to be inferior to larger juries in fulfilling a jury's functions. In Ballew v. Georgia, 435 U.S. 223 (1978), invalidating a five-member jury in a state misdemeanor case, the majority of the Court seemed to be backing away from statistical studies. Justices Powell, Burger, and Rehnquist recognized that "the line between five- and six-member juries is difficult to justify but a line has to be drawn somewhere if the substance of jury trial is to be preserved"; and they questioned the wisdom and necessity of Justice Blackmun's "heavy reliance on numerology derived from statistical studies" (at 246). Justices Brennan, Stewart, and Marshall joined in the Blackmun opinion insofar as it "holds" that criminal juries must be larger than five; they too seemed to avoid endorsement of its reasoning, and so did the opinion of Justice White, who simply asserted that a jury of five would not be representative enough. (The Blackmun opinion, joined in by Stevens, had argued that post-Williams empirical studies supported the view that five-member juries would disadvantage the defendant; though the studies concerned juries of more than five, none showed the effect of a reduction from six to five, and if anything showed that the reduction from twelve to six in *Williams* should not have been approved. See critique in Lermack, *supra* n.136 at 962-966.)

141. In rejecting Oklahoma's statistics-oriented defense of its gender-based drinking law, Justice Brennan for the Court, after pointing to various difficulties and shortcomings in the research, said: "It is unrealistic to expect either members of the judiciary or state officials to be well versed in the rigors of experimental or statistical technique. But this merely illustrates that proving broad sociological propositions by statistics is a dubious business, and one that inevitably is in tension with the normative philosophy that underlies the Equal Protection Clause. . . ." Craig v. Boren, 429 U.S. 190, 204 (1976). In U.S. v. Janis, 428 U.S. 433, 450-451 (1976) after canvassing the many empirical studies focused on whether the "exclusionary rule" applicable to unconstitutionally seized evidence was fulfilling its function of deterring police misconduct, the Court found the studies inconclusive. The Court has also said that empirical data on the social harm done by pornography is not necessary in order to sustain a legislative ban on pornography, based on "unprovable assumptions." Paris Adult Theatre I v. Slaton, 413 U.S. 49, 60-63 (1973).

Kenneth Davis has argued that the Court in this case came to its conclusion too hastily; that "the crucial question of legislative fact was probably answerable with evidence"; that in general the Court should change its procedure as follows: "(1) The Court should recognize its affirmative responsibility to assure that reasonably available legislative facts that may affect its lawmaking are adequately developed. (2) When facts presented by the parties are inadequate, it should, unless it does its own research, either request factual briefs on designated questions or remand for factual development on those questions. (3) When extrarecord facts are crucial in its lawmaking, it should address the question whether procedural fairness requires that parties be given a pre-decision chance to challenge the facts it uses." Davis, Facts In Lawmaking, 80 Colum. L. Rev. 931, 939, 940 (1980). See also Horowitz, The Courts and Social Policy 274-284 (1977), for a discussion of courts' inadequate attention to, or erroneous assumptions about, relevant legislative facts. Generally on legislative facts in constitutional litigation see Karst, *infra* at n.259.

142. For some sober assessments of possible approaches to reliable sociolegal

scientists are with us for good, and are going to remain in the very midst of government. . . . Judges may and should become acquainted with the various non-legal disciplines. But because of the variety of these disciplines, and of the variety of their judicial tasks, they will always remain intelligent *laymen,* as far as these disciplines are concerned. And intelligent lay control . . . seems the best defense against the tyranny of experts. . . ."[143]

7. A Perspective on the Limits of Legal Effectiveness

Looking back now on the various limits that I have mentioned, the rather obvious moral is: It is silly to automatically respond to a social problem by saying "there oughta be a law" — without careful investigation into the limits that may apply.

On the other hand, it is just as silly to automatically respond by the slogans "you can't legislate morality" or "you can't change human nature by law" — because law does play an affirmative, a deterrent, and an educative role, getting people to act in a way that without the law they might not act, and to have attitudes that without the law they might not have.

Let me elaborate. Early in this chapter, I pointed out how the criminal law embodies moral precepts aimed at influencing people's attitudes and behavior. Can it really be argued that this attempted influence is ineffective; that when most of us respect and obey the criminal laws we are adopting attitudes and behavior that we would *all* adopt even in the absence of the promulgation and enforcement of those laws? Many years ago in Boston during a policemen's strike, the extensive looting of the stores in most cases was done by youths who had never done anything like that before. A clear inference is that the law had helped to keep them in line, and that once the policemen were removed they felt free to indulge in this activity.[144]

Andenaes[145] has pointed to a similar phenomenon during an English policemen's strike, and another during the period in 1944 when the Germans had arrested the Danish police force and substituted an unarmed watch corps. He has referred to instances in this country in

empirical and experimental research, see Lermack, *supra* n.136 at 967-976; Zeisel, Reflections on Experimental Techniques in the Law, 2 J. Legal Stud. 107 (1973); Kalven, The Quest For the Middle Range: Empirical Inquiry and Legal Policy, in Hazard, ed., Law In A Changing America 56-74 (1968).

143. Pekelis, The Case for a Jurisprudence of Welfare, Lawyers Guild Rev. 611, 625-626 (1946).

144. See M. R. Cohen, Reason and Law 49 (1950).

145. Andenaes, The General Preventive Effects of Punishment, 114 U. Pa. L. Rev. 949 (1966).

which criminal activity closely correlated with the degree of enforcement activity. And he reminds us that when the Norwegian drunken driving prohibition — the penalty for violation of which was an automatic year's revocation of driver's license and generally a minimum 21-day jail penalty — was strictly enforced, it seems to have changed people's habits and attitudes. I tried to show earlier that when penalties get too severe, obstacles may be created by prosecutors, juries, and judges. But within that outer limit, it seems true that the commission or noncommission of at least some kinds of conduct presently labeled criminal is closely related to the existence and degree of enforcement of legal prohibitions on that conduct, and sometimes to the severity of the known penalties. This is more likely to be true when the conduct is typically preceded by some rationalistic calculation of risks. But even in the case of less calculating conduct, the law is an important background factor, helping to shape moral inhibitions that exert some counterforce against the pressures for antisocial conduct.[146]

That is, the very fact that certain conduct is known to be prohibited by law exerts a morally inhibiting pressure — surely for some people and for some kinds of conduct, and perhaps for most people and most kinds of conduct. "Studies of public opinion show, says Hadley Cantril, that after the adoption of certain laws and policies there is a rise in public opinion favorable to these actions. Cantril offers as a 'law' of public opinion: 'When an opinion is held by a slight majority or when opinion is not solidly structured, an accomplished fact tends to shift opinion in the direction of acceptance.' "[147]

A 1964 study, comparing attitudes toward school desegregation existing in 1942 and in 1956 (the Supreme Court school desegregation decision having been in 1954) and then in 1964, reported substantial rises for both of the later years in the proportion of favorable attitudes; and the southern attitudes were found to "vary according to the degree of integration existing in a given area," with the official desegregation measures occurring before the change in attitude.[148] Involved in this

146. See Andenaes, General Prevention Revisited: Research and Policy Implications, 66 J. Crim. L. & Criminology 338, 358, 362-363 (1975); Andenaes, The Moral or Educative Influence of Criminal Law, 27 J. Soc. Issues 17 (1971); Andenaes, General Prevention — Illusion or Reality, 43 J. Crim. L.C. & P.S. 176, 179-180 (1952); Hawkins, Punishment and Deterrence: The Educative, Moralizing and Habituative Effects, 1969 Wis. L. Rev. 550; Berkowitz & Walker, Laws and Moral Judgments, 30 Sociometry 410 (1967), as reprinted in Friedman & Macaulay, Law and the Behavioral Sciences 200-201 (1969). On some complexities in the problem of the drinking driver, see Tomasic, Deterrence and the Drinking Driver (1977).

147. Berger, Equality by Statute 219 (rev. ed. 1967).

148. Hyman & Sheatsley, Attitudes Toward School Desegregation, 211 Scientific Am. 16-18, 19-23 (July 1964) as reprinted in Schwartz & Skolnick, Society and the Legal Order, esp. 487-488, 490-491 (1970). A Harris public opinion poll in August 1972 showed 42% of the American people favoring legalized abortions for pregnancies up to 3 months, as against 46% opposed; whereas the April 1973 poll (taken

example is a related phenomenon: The conforming *behavior* of others, especially those in one's own peer group, and even one's own conforming behavior, may tend to generate the appropriate approving *attitude*.[149] I am reminded here of an experiment reported in the memoirs of a British scientist, Sir Francis Galton. He had wondered why certain idols, in spite of being ugly and grotesque, were worshipped by primitive peoples, and whether he could induce such an attitude in himself. He selected a grotesque picture of Punch, set it up in a room of his house, and daily went through a ritual of obeisance and prayer before it. After several months he found to his surprise that he was experiencing a feeling of awe and reverence. He would catch himself turning toward the picture when he passed the room, with an impulse to bow and worship.

To get back to the study of desegregation attitudes: I am not saying that studies of attitudinal changes in relation to *other* laws and/or other circumstances are bound to come out the same way, or that law is the most significant variable affecting such changes. Rather, in the cautious words of a 1967 study: "There appears to be a comparatively small but nevertheless significant tendency for *some* people to alter their views of the morality of *some* actions in accord with laws specifying that these actions are legal or illegal. Knowledge of the existence of these laws, however, does not have as much effect in changing the moral judgments as knowledge of a consensus of opinions among one's peers."[150] (Emphasis added.)

Further on the racial problem, there are plenty of factors in addition to peer influence that can work *against* an accord between attitudes and legal requirements. For example, provocation from violent elements in the civil rights movement seems sometimes to have diminished favorable attitudes. So too, lack of positive support from prestigious sources can act as a negative factor — as when President Eisenhower declined to back the Supreme Court's 1954 decision with a strong moral stand. His position was that the decision was the law of the land and had to be enforced, but he pointedly declined to defend the court decision in moral terms. President Kennedy in the beginning of his administration had a similar attitude, though he changed eventually

---

after the Supreme Court decision legalizing such abortions) showed a jump to 52% in favor.

149. McConahay, in The Effects of School Desegregation Upon Students' Racial Attitudes and Behavior, 42 L. & Contemp. Prob., No. 3, 77, 105 (1978) says it is "now generally agreed" that by changing behavior we can change attitudes (and by changing attitudes we can change behavior); so, "[i]f in the desegregated school the students and teachers behave as though they respect and feel favorably toward one another, they can also come to feel that way after a while, regardless of their initial attitudes."

150. Berkowitz & Walker, *supra* n.146 at 209-210; see also 212-214.

to a more positive position. It was particularly important, I think, to get this national executive support for the decision at the crucial early stage when a drastic social change was being initiated by law. Its absence helped to fan the flames of resistance in the South even more than did President Nixon's go-slow position in the late 1960s and early 1970s.

So I repeat that the question of what limits apply to the law's accomplishment of desirable goals is not answered by mechanical application of any slogans, like "there oughta be a law" or "you can't change human nature by law." Each problem stands on its own feet. You have to investigate the significant facts in the particular problem and ask the questions relevant to the limits that may operate on the effectiveness of the proposed law or the proposed decision. Some relevant questions and considerations are:

(a) What is the strength of the values or attitudes or drives with which the law in question is inconsistent?[151] (Here, as with questions later on, we must ask whether there is reason to think that the strength varies with different individuals or classes of individuals.)[152] The problem is obviously greater, for instance, where human drives and widely enjoyed pleasures are involved, like sex, alcohol, and other drugs. The problem is also complicated by the fact that reinforcement of or opposition to attitudes, drives, etc. may be received: (1) from the rest of an individual's value system, including moral and religious values, his general tendency toward social conformity and toward conforming to the law (but if he has a strong proclivity both for the conduct prohibited and for conformity with law generally, then heaven help him); (2) from values and attitudes on the particular subject, of others in the society nationally, regionally, and locally, including molders of opinion such as newspapers, educators, clergy, the President, and those in his peer group; (3) from his belief that the prohibited conduct works no serious harm to others. Also pertinent, as we have seen, would be the question whether situations of great stress could be expected to occur to such an extent that the legal requirement could

151. This is related to the factor that is discussed in Zimring & Hawkins, The Legal Threat As An Instrument of Social Change, 27 J. Soc. Issues 33 (1971) as "variations in the nature of the custom." They discuss this factor in terms of the custom's "utilitarian and moral significance" to its adherents; extent of its popular support; visibility to enforcement agencies of the practice of the custom; extent to which the legal change alters one's expectations of others' nonconformity to the custom; extent to which the change meets current community needs. The two other factors discussed are: variations in the social characteristics of the individuals and groups adhering to the custom before it was forbidden; and variations in the way in which the threat of punishment is carried out.

152. "It is seductively easy to build elaborate theories of how groups will react, without regard to the complexity of human personality that psychological studies are beginning to uncover." Burman & Harrell-Bond, The Imposition of Law 6-7 (1979).

not be influential, and judges and juries could be expected to be lenient.

(b) What techniques would be used to establish and enforce the prohibition or requirement in question? (1) Legislatures, courts, executives, and administrative agencies do not all have the same prestige, though perhaps the ranking is different on different subjects and in different places. For instance, there are those who believe that a congressional statute, implementing the Fourteenth Amendment and requiring racial desegregation in the schools, would have had greater public acceptance than the Supreme Court's decision. (2) Is time allowed for a transition period, and does such allowance make acceptance more likely, or less so? The Supreme Court used this technique in the school segregation case by allowing the decision to be implemented by the policies of the local district courts, using "all deliberate speed." Some argue that the technique in this instance was less effective in gaining acceptance of the decision than the Court's issuance of its own plans for prompt desegregation would have been. (3) Would enforcement personnel be enthusiastic, well financed, and really committed, or are they likely to be tolerant, apathetic, corrupt, or starved for funds?[153] (4) Would enforcement be hampered for lack of complainants? This is a factor that, together with lack of enforcement enthusiasm, is important in the case of "crimes without victims," like prostitution, gambling, fornication, drugs, and consensual homosexuality. (5) Will there be a *perception* by potential violators, of the change in law or penalties, and also a perception of effective enforcement?[154] (6) Is it possible to point to "models" of compliance, e.g., communities where the legal change has worked successfully? (7) Would the law's expected benefits be outweighed by the costs, practical difficulties, and risks in administering it — such as possibilities of fraud or other abuse, difficulties of proof, a flood of litigation, and interference with internal affairs of private groups? In this connection, will the objections to one form of legal sanction be obviated by resorting to another form? Or to non-prohibitory techniques, such as subsidies or other rewards for compliance?

(c) To what extent do we have the knowledge necessary to answer not only (1) the fact questions relevant to the consequences and desirability of the proposed law, but also (2) all of the other questions? The more you study the law's problems, the more you will appreciate the significance of our relative lack of the necessary reliable knowledge. The law must continue to make impossible demands on a social science

153. On the importance of enforcement for effective reduction of drunk driving through higher penalties, see Andenaes, General Prevention Revisited, *supra* n.146 at 353.

154. See on this, *id.* at 354 et seq.

that too often is insufficiently developed to give clear and conclusive answers.

D. *Agencies and Techniques of Law*

By "agencies" I mean the judicial, legislative, executive, and administrative agencies that carry out the official business of law, and also the public. Consider first the nature of the judicial agency.

1. The Courts

a. Structure

I'll begin with the structure of the court system, and largely confine myself on this point to the state courts, since the structure of the federal court system will be developed in Chapter 2.

Each state has a triple-layered hierarchy of courts. On the bottom are those dealing with the petty cases in which small monetary amounts or minor criminal penalties are involved. In a nonurban area, the judge of such a court is likely to be called a justice of the peace, and his job might be only a part-time one. In the cities he is likely to be called a magistrate or a judge and might be attached to a specialized court like police court, traffic court, or small claims court. These petty or "inferior" courts are generally not "courts of record"; they make no detailed record of the proceedings beyond the identification of parties, lawyers, and disposition of the case. The procedure may be rather informal. The losing party may appeal to the next level of court, but not through what we usually mean by appeal, since typically a completely new trial is involved rather than appellate review of the record made in the lower court (there will usually have been no such record there).

This next level of court would be known as a "trial court of general jurisdiction," authorized to hear civil and criminal cases generally. Unlike the petty court, it is a court of record; its procedure is quite formal; it is not confined to, and indeed is usually prevented from entertaining, the petty cases. It is called perhaps most often a "district" court or "circuit" court, though in some places it has such other names as "superior court" or "court of common pleas." (New York State creates a special confusion by calling it the "supreme court" — which elsewhere of course means the highest appellate court — and recognizing both this trial part of its supreme court and an appellate part which is an intermediate court, the final appeals court being called the New

York Court of Appeals.) Besides the trial court of general jurisdiction — or, in some states, departments or divisions thereof — there are specialized courts like those handling probate matters, or divorce and other domestic relations issues, or juvenile problems.

The trial court of general jurisdiction, as I have indicated, exercises *some* appellate jurisdiction when it takes "appeals" from the petty courts. But I've said that those appeals are usually heard as completely new trials (trials "de novo"). To a limited extent, the trial court of general jurisdiction also exercises the more usual form of appellate jurisdiction — for instance, it may be authorized to review *administrative agency* decisions on the record made before the administrative agency, as distinguished from holding a trial *de novo*. In such a case the agency fact findings, while not conclusive, will be upheld by the court in the absence of arbitrariness.

Third and uppermost in the hierarchy are the appellate courts. In most states, there is only one appellate court, and that is the highest court of the state. It hears appeals from the judgments of the trial courts of general jurisdiction, and either affirms or reverses, or occasionally modifies, the judgment. There are some cases in which a litigant seeks to control the trial court's action not by waiting to take an appeal from its judgment but by seeking directly in the highest court an "extraordinary writ" directing the lower court to do something (e.g., grant a change in the venue or place of trial, or justify its order holding someone in allegedly illegal custody) or refrain from doing something (e.g., from continuing to exercise jurisdiction in a case).

In about a third of the states, there are intermediate appellate courts. Their role varies in the different states. A state may provide that the appeal from a trial court goes to this intermediate court, and that a further appeal is then permissible, after unfavorable judgment, to the highest court. The state may say that in some other classes of cases (deemed more serious) the losing party in the trial court can skip the intermediate court and appeal directly to the highest court. In still other cases, the appeal from the trial court may be allowed only to the intermediate court, and an additional appeal to the highest court is either not allowed or allowed only for special reasons, or is left to the discretion of the highest court to allow. This limited-review type of provision is being increasingly suggested as a means of coping with the overburdened dockets of the states' highest courts.

A prerequisite for review by the United States Supreme Court of the decisions of the highest state court that is empowered to decide a particular case is that the case comes within the "judicial power of the United States" as outlined in the Constitution. However, Congress in the exercise of its constitutional power to determine the appellate jurisdiction of the Supreme Court has made most such review discretionary — known as review by writ of certiorari. The Court's review of a state court decision can be demanded as a matter of *right,* according to Congress, only when the highest state court empowered to decide the case has held a federal law or treaty invalid, or upheld a state law against the claim that it violates the Federal Constitution, laws, or treaties.[155]

b. Selected Operational Features and Problems

Turning from the structure of the courts to aspects of their functioning, I'll confine myself to five such matters, though perforce dealing with them sketchily: (1) court delay, (2) selection and tenure of judges, (3) the limited role of the court itself in the disposition of litigation, (4) access to courts and other modes of dispute resolution, and (5) the courts' new administrative involvement in reforming public institutions.

(1) Court Delay

The problem we hear most about today is delay. It is not exactly a new problem. "Hammurabi denounced it; Shakespeare immortalized it: Hamlet, compiling his dolorous list of the burdens of men, sandwiched the 'law's delay' between the 'pangs of dispriz'd love' and the 'insolence of office.' English chancery delay made Bleak House one of the best known edifices in English literature and made Dickens a leading law reformer. Paradoxically, German court delay, scholars tell us, led Goethe to give up the law for letters."[156] But never before has there been such a pervasive concern over the problem, coupled with concerted efforts to find solutions.

One type of delay is caused not by the court system but by the lawyers: The court is ready for trial but the lawyers want postponement. Lawyers often feel unable to meet the date set for trial because of conflicting dates for other trials or other legal business. (This would be somewhat less of a problem if trial litigation were not such a specialty, concentrated in the hands of a fraction of the total bar.) Similarly, a Pittsburgh study showed that in more than half of the randomly picked cases, lawyers added more than a year to disposition of the case, by tardiness in filing papers. Although many cases are negotiated and settled by the parties after filing suit and long before

155. Federal court organization and jurisdiction is analyzed in Chap. 2 herein under **B, 3 & 4.**

156. Rosenberg, Court Congestion: Status, Causes and Proposed Remedies, in Jones, ed., The Courts, The Public and the Law Explosion 30 (1965).

possible trial, many others that could be so handled are delayed in settlement until close to trial or after the first day of trial, in order to put bargaining pressure on the other side — as well as, in some instances perhaps, in order for the lawyer to collect a fee for a day in court.[157]

The measures proposed for dealing with delay include tightening up the permission for postponements, and other devices aimed at lawyer-caused delay.[158] But principally, reforms are aimed at reducing court-system delay. One general approach is to reduce the volume of cases handled. For instance, it is said that eliminating federal diversity-of-citizenship jurisdiction (to be discussed in Chap. 2) would mean substantial relief to the federal courts and an easily borne increase in business for the "multiplicity of state forums available to absorb the cases."[159] A method of getting cases out of the courts altogether (on the trial level) is to shift some types of cases to administrative tribunals; what has already been done in the area of workmen's compensation has long been recommended for auto accident cases, which are in good part responsible for court congestion and delay.[160] A similar but broader proposal is for the creation of "new administrative tribunals of general jurisdiction that would address the repetitious factual issues inherent in the litigation of claims under a pool of specified regulatory and social service legislation."[161] Also aimed at reducing the flow of cases to the courts is the suggestion that proposed legislation should

157. In support of this paragraph, see *id.* at 35-37.

158. *Id.* at 45; Sipes et al., Managing to Reduce Delay 12-20 (National Center for State Courts, 1980). A growing number of courts are assessing court costs and attorney fees against parties who unreasonably prolong the proceedings through postponements or unnecessary use of "discovery" procedure (see Chap. 2 herein between nn. 186 & 187 and Postscript herein, n.18) or allowing even pre-judgment interest to be awarded to victorious plaintiffs, "in the hope of encouraging insurance companies and corporations to expedite their defense of damage suits." Natl. Law. J., Feb. 9, 1981, at 1.

159. Marcus, Judicial Overload: The Reasons and the Remedies, 28 Buffalo L. Rev. 111, 139 (1979). On federal diversity jurisdiction, see Chap. 2 herein between nn. 85 & 88.

160. Another kind of shift away from the courts for the auto cases is through the "no-fault" plans now gaining support, under which the major costs suffered in most auto accident cases would be compensated by insurance policies without the necessity of a court suit. See studies cited in n.67 *supra*.

161. Marcus, *supra* n.159 at 135-136. See *id.* at 121 for a listing of some fairly recent federal legislation that can be expected to generate substantial court litigation — the Mine Safety Act, for instance, being expected to generate more than 20,000 full jury trials each year. Even where administrative agencies already exist, the judicial review burden can sometimes be alleviated. Thus, it is argued that Congress could halve the National Labor Relations Board caseload in the courts of appeal by providing that the NLRB orders will be immediately enforceable unless the aggrieved party promptly initiates a review proceeding (instead of the present requirement that the Board petition the court to enforce its order). *Id.* at 140.

be accompanied by a "litigation impact statement" assessing the bill's effect on judicial administration.[162]

A second approach to court-system delay is to increase the man-hours spent in judging. Thus, proposals are being considered to increase the number of judges, and/or to make judges put in a longer workday, and with shorter vacations, and/or to use pseudojudges. By the latter I mean lawyers like the well-known "auditors" used in Massachusetts auto cases — and the "arbitrators" used in Pennsylvania small claims cases — their determinations being subject to possible (but in practice infrequent) review by a regular judge; or the use of that kind of non-judge personnel for handling pretrial conferences with the litigants.[163] An alternative system, in which the adjudicator need not be a lawyer, is that of "neighborhood justice" tribunals.[164]

Other approaches to a more efficient administration of judicial business have been suggested. They include shifting cases from overly busy courts to less busy ones; judicial appointment of impartial medical experts when the extent of the plaintiff's injuries is to be disputed by opposing experts — an appointment that often helps induce settlement; saving time by encouraging waivers of jury trial in civil cases, or by speeding up the process of jury selection, or getting the state to abolish the jury in state civil cases (University of Chicago studies suggest that a juryless trial is about "40% less time-consuming than a jury trial of the same case,"[165] or putting it the other way, a jury trial is one and two-thirds times as long);[166] using videotape;[167] employing modern managerial methods, including computers, to streamline the administration of the docket;[168] and two additional techniques,

162. Id. at 140-141; Hearing on Judicial Impact Statements, Before Subcomm. on Jurisprudence and Government Relations, Senate Judiciary Comm., 96 Cong., 1st Sess. (1980).

163. See Rosenberg, *supra* n.156 at 41-42, 51-54; Marcus, *supra* n.159 at 134. Johnson, Kantor & Schwartz, Outside the Courts: A Survey of Diversion Alternatives in Civil Cases (1977).

164. See Postscript herein at n. 16-17; Marcus, *supra* n.159 at 134, 135.

165. Kalven, The Dignity of the Civil Jury, 50 Va. L. Rev. 1055, 1059 (1964).

166. Kalven's translation of the first form of statement to the second gives him the mathematically erroneous figure of one and one-half rather than one and two-thirds. *Id.* at 1059-1060, n.12.

167. An Ohio court's use of videotape as a medium for prerecording testimony in civil cases and presenting the tape to a jury is said to reduce delay drastically. McCrystal & Maschari, Will Electric Technology Take the Witness Stand, 11 U. Tol. L. Rev. 239 (1980).

168. See Nagel, Neef & Manshaw, Bringing Management Science to the Courts to Reduce Delay, 62 Jud. 128 (1978); Sipes et al., *supra* n.158; Symposium, 4 Just. Sys. J. 131 (1978); LaBar, The Modernization of Court Functions: A Review of Court Management and Computer Technology, 5 Rutgers J. Computers & L. 97 (1975); Mermin, Computers, Law and Justice, 1967 Wis. L. Rev. 43, 50-51; Kozak, Foster & Lounder, Bibliography on Computer Use in Courts, 13 Law & Computer Tech. 65 (1980).

the advocacy of which has been somewhat dampened by recent studies: the greater use of pretrial conferences,[169] and the "split trial."[170]

What about delay in *criminal* cases? There is congestion in the criminal courts in spite of significant trial-eliminating factors, such as the fact that about three-quarters of the defendants plead guilty, and the fact most minor traffic offenses get disposed of by simple forfeiture of bail. One of the most tragic facts about criminal case delay is the impact on the indigent defendant, who waits in jail because he could not raise bail. Solutions involving a careful loosening of bail requirements are being experimented with.

169. The pretrial conference between the judge and the opposing lawyers has long been viewed as salutary. It is a preview of the case that helps clarify and simplify the issues. And it has been thought to shorten the trial and facilitate a settlement of the case without trial. The latter two effects are now subject to some doubt, as a result of empirical studies. The larger cases, in particular, resist settlement in spite of pretrial. Trials were found to be no shorter because of pretrial, yet the conferences do absorb an appreciable amount of the judge's time; so these would seem to be a negative contribution toward solving the problem of delay. To be weighed against this is the improved quality of the trial where there had been a pretrial conference — apparently because the conference had improved the lawyer's understanding of problems to be met and methods to be followed. Also to be pondered is the fact that plaintiff's recoveries were found to be higher when there had been a pretrial. After these facts had been revealed by the Columbia Project for Effective Justice in a study which had been requested by Chief Justice Weintraub of New Jersey, the New Jersey Supreme Court changed its rule requiring pretrial conferences in personal injury suits, and made the conference optional in auto accident cases. See, in support of this paragraph, Rosenberg, *supra* n.156 at 49-51. For a federal judge's call for strengthening pretrial procedures, see Peckham, The Federal Judge as a Case Manager: The New Role in Guiding a Case from Filing to Disposition, 69 Calif. L. Rev. 770 (1981).

170. In such a trial, instead of evidence being admitted on both the liability issue and the damage issue, there is no evidence admitted on damages until after there has been a determination of liability. This can save considerable time (some say about 20% of total trial time, some say "substantially less"), because (1) juries in personal injury suits bring in verdicts of *no* liability about 40% of the time, and (2) even after a verdict of liability, the split-trial system might save time that would normally be spent on evidence of damages, since in some cases the defendant chooses to settle after the liability verdict — i.e., no evidence is taken on damages. And here, as in the case of the pretrial conference technique, studies showed an unexpected substantive effect of the procedural change. This time the effect was to favor the defendant — i.e., in split trials, there were substantially more verdicts of nonliability (probably because of the absence of the emotional impact on the jury, on the liability issue, than one might expect from evidence on damage suffered by the plaintiff). Rosenberg, *supra* n.156 at 46-49.

In short, "there is no acceptable evidence that any remedy [for delay] so far devised has been efficacious to any substantial extent. Only a few of the new measures have worked even to a modest extent, and some of them have been positively counter-productive on the efficiency scale. More important, many of them have had unsuspected side effects in changing the outcome of appreciable numbers of law suits. A major lesson of this chronicle is that progress in coping with the old problem of court delay will have to come from marshalling relief measures in groups, not from a one-injection miracle cure. There is no such panacea." *Id.* at 55.

For an essay by the Director of the Federal Judicial Center on research related

But the delay problem in the criminal case is not so much the civil case problem of speeding up the court process between the time the initial papers are filed and the time the case is disposed of. Rather, one of the chief problems is how *more* time can be spent on the minor criminal cases that now may receive a minute or less of time per case in the assembly-line treatment of defendants who have pleaded guilty. An expansion in the number of minor criminal court judges seems imperative. It has been further suggested that some load can be removed from the criminal courts by (1) removing criminal penalties from some types of offenses and substituting other approaches such as civil monetary penalties; and (2) expansion of "medical, psychiatric and other treatment facilities so as to reduce by cure the volume of persons processed through the criminal courts because of addiction to alcohol or drugs."[171]

Finally, what can be done about congestion and delay in the appellate courts? Among the many suggestions that have been made, let me select a few for brief discussion. First is increasing the number of appellate judges. This could take the form of enlarging the highest court and/or creating or enlarging an intermediate appellate court (which most states still do not have). There are some limits here. Thus it has been observed that in California, "the number of intermediate appellate courts has been increased from three to five, and there has been an even greater increase in the number of judges sitting on those courts. To push the California development a few steps further, suppose that there were ten or fifteen intermediate appellate courts in that state ten years hence. In such circumstances, what were once authoritative appellate tribunals, subject to occasional review by the Supreme Court of California, would have been converted into a judicial Tower of Babel. The proliferation of utterances could divest any one of these courts of significant authority."[172]

Another suggestion is to make some classes of cases not appealable at all, or reviewable only at the discretion of the appellate court. This device is now used in some states with intermediate appellate courts when the appeal to the highest court, for at least some classes of cases, is precluded or else left discretionary with that court. But extending this, in states with no intermediate appellate courts, to cases of appeal

---

to delay and other aspects of judicial administration, see Levin, Research in Judicial Administration: The Federal Experience, 26 N.Y.L. Sch. L. Rev. 237 (1981).

171. Barrett, Criminal Justice: The Problem of Mass Production, in Jones, ed., *supra* n.156 at 121-123.

172. Hazard, After the Trial Court — The Realities of Appellate Review, in Jones, ed., *supra* n.156 at 81. See also Rosenberg, Contemporary Litigation in the United States, in Jones, ed., Legal Institutions Today: English and American Approaches Compared 174-175 (1977).

from the trial court to the highest state court, is going further than we presently seem prepared to go. It is not that the Constitution requires at least one appeal; it does not. But I think both the public and the profession do want a system of at least one appeal.[173] An additional objection centers around criteria for the class of case that would be excluded from appeal. If, for instance, the criterion were on the basis of how much money was at stake in the lawsuit, or on the particular subject matter involved (e.g., auto accidents), this might be attacked on the grounds that (1) importance of the legal points to be appealed has no necessary relation to money involved or subject matter, and (2) the criterion might be unconstitutionally discriminatory, denying to those excluded the "equal protection of the laws."

One further device presently used to cope with appellate congestion is the omission or attenuation of one or more of the usual steps in case disposition. Thus, a preliminary screening procedure may result in a "summary" disposition (without briefs and argument); judges may vote on some cases without a prior discussion; they may exclude or limit the opportunity for oral argument; they may issue decisions with no supporting opinions or only brief memorandum opinions. Such devices raise serious questions about the quality of appellate justice.[174]

At least some of the reasons[175] for court overload are likely to persist, and so are the techniques of coping with the problem, not all of which have been canvassed above.[176]

173. See Hazard, *supra* at 83. In the federal system, there is such an appeal as of right to the court of appeals, and the bulk of the Supreme Court's review is discretionary. Nonetheless the caseload of the Supreme Court is so great that proposals have been made for a new National Court of Appeals to screen cases for which Supreme Court review is sought. See Stern & Gressman, Supreme Court Practice, §1.16 (5th ed. 1978) and the articles cited therein for and against the proposal, and Chap. 2 below between nn. 48 & 51.

174. See Rosenberg, *supra* n.172 at 175; Carrington, Crowded Dockets and the Courts of Appeal, 82 Harv. L. Rev. 542, 558-561; 569-574 (1969). "Almost a third of the cases in the federal appellate courts are presently being decided without the opportunity for oral argument, and approximately the same percentage are delivered without opinion." Marcus, *supra* n.159 at 118. See also ABA Task Force on Appellate Procedure, Efficiency and Justice in Appeals: Methods and Selected Materials (1977) (loose-leaf); Reynolds & Richman, An Evaluation of Limited Publication in the Court of Appeals: The Price of Reform, 48 U. Chi. L. Rev. 573 (1981); McCree, Bureaucratic Justice: An Early Warning, 129 U. Pa. L. Rev. 777 (1981).

175. Marcus, *supra* n.174, argues that the reasons for judicial overload "include sociological factors such as the decline in traditional modes of social control and the growth of rights consciousness, legislative and judicial expansion of access to the courts, and economic incentives such as the award of attorneys' fees" (at 128). For a less confident treatment of reasons, see Carrington, *supra* at 543-547.

176. See for further approaches to appellate court congestion, Wasby, Marvell & Aikman, Volume and Delay in State Appellate Courts (1979); Rosenberg, Carrington & Meador, Justice on Appeal (1976); Symposium, Federal Appellate Justice in an Era of Growing Demand, 59 Cornell L. Rev. 571 (1974); Carrington, *supra* n.174.

(2) Selection and Tenure of Judges

American practice in the selection and tenure of judges falls into two groupings. The system for federal judges is *appointment* (by the President, with the advice and consent of the Senate) and *life tenure* (i.e., "during good behavior"). The system for state judges in a majority of the states[177] is *election* and *limited tenure* (for a fixed period such as six years). Even in the states the earliest preference was for appointed judges, but populist currents after the 1830s swung the practice toward the elective system.

The two systems are not as different as they seem. The appointment system is based indirectly on the elective process (election of the appointing executive and of the legislative representatives who must, in most of the appointive states, approve). Conversely, the system of electing judges can be viewed as a system of de facto appointment: (1) In practical effect, judicial elections are usually perfunctory ratifications of "appointments," i.e., nominations by party leaders, except when judges run without party labels. (2) A large proportion of elections come after a vacancy (due to death or retirement of an elected judge) had been filled by interim appointments by the governor — and this means, in view of the tradition favoring election of a sitting judge, that the governor's interim nominee is generally elected at the subsequent election.

But while there are elements of both election and nomination in the two systems, a combination of the elements in a different kind of mix has been adopted in some states and is steadily gaining ground. Often referred to as the "Missouri Plan," it has long been supported by the American Bar Association and by the American Judicature Society. Though there are variants of the plan, essentially it involves: (1) initial appointment by the governor (not merely for vacancies in an elected term) from a panel of names submitted by a commission composed of representatives of the bar, judiciary, and the public; (2) the incumbent judge's running for election, after expiration of a specified period, but on his own record — i.e., not against any rival. The plan would normally be instituted by legislative action, but it has also been done by executive order of the governor.[178]

Why the dissatisfaction with the purely elective system? There is,

177. For a succinct description of the numbers and varieties of state plans, see Adamany & Dubois, Electing State Judges, 1976 Wis. L. Rev. 731, 769.

178. In Missouri, the governor appoints three laypersons to the commission, which also has as members the chief justice and three lawyers elected by the state bar. The commission submits three names for the office and the governor must select one, for a term of one year, after which the judge runs for election without a rival candidate, for a full term. In the California Plan, the commission is composed of the chief justice, presiding judge of the district court of appeal, and attorney general. It submits the name of only one individual. If approved by the governor, the individual serves for one year, then stands for election on his record, as in

first of all, substantial opinion that the selection process does not pay primary attention to professional quality of the judges. Moreover, the public is thought not to cast an intelligent vote, in view of its limited knowledge of legal matters and of the qualifications of candidates. It is further argued that while in office the elected judge is more prone to allow improper political considerations to influence his judicial judgment, and as election time nears, feels the need to take time away from his judicial duties for campaigning or political fence-mending.

However, the elective system continues to have strong adherents, particularly among political scientists. They generally prefer the direct popular control associated with elections, to the indirect popular controls involved in gubernatorial appointments and the increased private bar influence[179] under the Missouri Plan. Their studies of alternatives like the Missouri Plan are claimed to show that ". . . selection systems themselves have little impact in guaranteeing that selection procedures will be free from partisan or interest group politics, or that decidedly superior judges will be selected for office."[180] Thus, studies are cited for the proposition that educational qualifications of state trial and appellate judges selected under various plans (appointed by governor or legislature, or selected under the Missouri Plan, or elected in partisan or nonpartisan elections) did not vary much with the type of plan;[181] nor did "the evidence . . . establish a close link between judicial selection and judges' voting."[182] As for reduction of political partisanship, "[e]ven in Missouri plan states, the selection commissions which submit lists of judicial candidates for gubernatorial consideration are usually dominated by members of the Chief Executive's party. Hence the Governor is ordinarily able to name one of his fellow partisans to the bench."[183] In addition, the political scientists tend to object to the denigration of political considerations. They point out that a

---

Missouri. If the governor rejects the name, or if the approved candidate fails in the election, the procedure is followed over again. Under both plans, the solo elections have been generally successful. Abraham, Justices and Presidents 13-14 (1974).

179. The opportunity for greater bar influence is not always fulfilled. See Glick, The Promise and the Performance of the Missouri Plan: Judicial Selection In the Fifty States, 32 U. Miami L. Rev. 509, 536-537, 539-540 (1978).

180. *Id.* at 539.

181. Adamany & Dubois, *supra* n.177 at 773. An interesting sidelight on the significance of educational qualifications and other measures of achievement is furnished by the responses of state trial judges, both new and experienced, to queries on the desirable attributes of a judge. They rated as low in importance such qualities as high law school record; high earnings in law practice; activity in civic, community, or professional affairs; or past honorable political activity. They rated the following as having the highest importance: moral courage, decisiveness, reputation for fairness and uprightness, patience, good health, and consideration for others. Rosenberg, The Qualities of Justices — Are They Strainable? 44 Tex. L. Rev. 1063, 1066-1072 (1966).

182. Glick, *supra* n.179 at 534. See *id.* at 531-539.

183. Adamany & Dubois, *supra* n.177 at 774. See also Glick, *supra* n.179 at 521-523.

judge's policy orientation is relevant; and an index of it, though not an unvarying one, is his party affiliation.[184] The latter has traditionally been thought to be relevant and legitimate in gubernatorial appointment of state judges and presidential appointment of federal judges, provided the candidate is otherwise "qualified."

The federal appointment system yields judges who, according to professional opinion, are of generally higher caliber than the state judges. This does not mean that no state judge measures up to the quality of the best federal judges. But it means that judges appointed to life-tenure judicial posts carrying substantially higher prestige and compensation, and screened by the President and the Senate with cooperation from an American Bar Association committee, are more likely to be quality judges than are state judges selected by currently orthodox methods.[185] Some poor ones do slip through the screen — but fortunately, not because of any acceptance of Senator Hruska's deathless remark in defending President Nixon's abortive Supreme Court nomination of Judge Carswell: that mediocrity, too, deserves representation on the Court. There have been not only some mediocre

184. Adamany & Dubois, *id.* at 761-768, 772; Nagel, Political Party Affiliation and Judges' Decisions, 55 Am. Pol. Sci. Rev. 843 (1961); Wormuth & Rich, Politics, the Bar, and the Selection of Judges, 3 Utah L. Rev. 459 (1953).

185. In the President's nomination of federal district and court of appeals judges, the three major influences have usually been those of (1) interested political leaders, especially the home-state Senators of the nominee's political party (their preferences would, by what is called "senatorial courtesy," be generally respected in the Senate); (2) ratings by the American Bar Association's Standing Committee on the Federal Judiciary, established in the mid-1940s and exercising substantial influence since the mid-1950s; (3) advice from sitting members of the bench. In the case of Supreme Court nominees, while these influences are present and he is advised by the Attorney General, the President feels more free to make an independent choice. Abraham, *supra* n.178 at 15-40 (1974).

Under President Carter, the 1978 Omnibus Judgeship Act (92 Stat. 1629) authorized the largest expansion of the federal judiciary in the nation's history, creating 117 new district judgeships and 35 additional court of appeals seats. The Carter policy favoring minority appointments resulted in his appointing more blacks, Hispanics, and women than any other President. Of *all* his nominees to the federal bench, 62.5% were rated by the ABA as either "exceptionally well-qualified" or "well-qualified" (the rest were "qualified"; none were in the fourth category, "not qualified"), a somewhat higher combined percentage than for Eisenhower or Kennedy, and substantially higher than for Johnson, Nixon, or Ford. Cong. Q., Oct. 27, 1979, at 2418. Under a Carter Executive Order, "all circuit [court of appeals] judgeships had to be filled from names submitted by nominating commissions" appointed by him and consisting of "a mix of lawyers and laymen. [See Berkson & Carbon, The U.S. Circuit Judge Nominating Commission (1980)]. Under pressure from both the president and the Attorney General . . . more than half the Senators set up similar nominating commissions for district judgeships." Nat. L.J., March 30, 1981, at 7.

In the Reagan administration, "there is no pressure on the senators to use merit selection screening panels, nor to affirmatively seek out women, minorities and lawyers outside the mainstream of corporate law practice. . . . Senate Republicans . . . insisted that the new system will be no more political than Mr. Carter's plan, under which nearly 98% of the more than 260 judges appointed were Democrats." *Id.*

but some actually corrupt federal judges. The most celebrated instance was that of Judge Manton of the Second Circuit Court of Appeals, who in 1939 was convicted of selling justice. It was he who argued, ingeniously and ingenuously, in his appeal to the Supreme Court, that "it serves no public policy for a high judicial officer to be convicted of a judicial crime. It tends to destroy the confidence of the people in the courts."[186] And it was he of whom Thomas Reed Powell observed that he was "the finest judge that money could buy." But as Hurst puts it, "over the years the instances in which even a substantial charge of corruption was raised against federal judges were trifling." And "when all the state *causes célèbres* were added together their total, like that in the federal courts, was trifling," though there was as yet no comprehensive study of corruption in the state judiciary.[187]

In addition to being criminally prosecuted for his derelictions, a judge may of course be removed from office. But the process for federal judges, and generally for state judges, is the cumbersome one of impeachment by the legislature. In recent years there has been much debate over the possibility of removal by other means, including exertion of pressure for resignation, through the medium of a judicial commission. In the federal sphere, the commentators have clashed over whether legislative impeachment is constitutionally the exclusive method of removal, and whether it is so even for misbehavior other than the constitutionally specified "high crimes and misdemeanors."[188] Persistent complaints about judicial neglect of duties, favoritism, drunkenness, arrogantly high-handed courtroom behavior, and the like have led the states, starting in the early 1960s, to adopt non-impeachment plans for control of judicial misconduct: Investigatory agencies can recommend sanctions, from censure up to removal, to a high state court or a special courts commission for final action.[189] Debate on the

186. Borkin, The Corrupt Judge 23 (1962).

187. Hurst, The Growth of American Law 142 (1950).

188. See e.g., Kaufman, The Essence of Judicial Independence, 80 Colum. L. Rev. 671 (1980); Kaufman, Chilling Judicial Independence, 88 Yale L.J. 681 (1979); Berger, Impeachment of Judges and Good Behavior Tenure, 79 Yale L.J. 1475 (1970); Kurland, The Constitution and the Tenure of Federal Judges: Some Notes From History, 36 U. Chi. L. Rev. 665 (1969); Stolz, Disciplining Federal Judges: Is Impeachment Hopeless? 57 Calif. L. Rev. 659 (1969).

189. Penn, More States Monitor Members of Judiciary for Improper Conduct, Wall St. J., Aug. 25, 1980, at 1. The California Commission on Judicial Performance, composed of lawyers, judges, and lay citizens, was created in 1960 by a state constitutional amendment to investigate judges suspected of incompetence or misconduct and to recommend removal, if appropriate. In 1979 there was a televised and otherwise publicized Commission hearing on whether some judges of the California Supreme Court had purposely delayed the court's issuance of a controversial decision (on constitutionality of a law making a prison term mandatory for anyone using a gun while committing a felony) until after the election, in order not to jeopardize the election chances of then Chief Justice Rose Bird. Under the California system, Governor Brown's prior appointment of Ms. Bird was subject to voter approval at

federal level finally resulted in a comparable federal law, effective October 1, 1981, authorizing judicial commission pressures and sanctions *short of removal*,[190] thereby making the constitutional issue less acute.

(3) Limited Role of the Court Itself in the Disposition of Litigation

Considering all the disputes that seem headed for resolution by courts (rather than by administrative agencies or arbitrators), to what extent is it the court's action that resolves those disputes? The smallness of the percentage the courts resolve is manifested by the following phenomena noted by Hurst as true of American courts since mid-twentieth century:[191] (1) In personal injury situations which might have produced claims in court, only about one-fifth resulted in court claims; of these claims, only 5 percent actually went to trial, and of those only about half ended in a decision by judge or jury.[192] (2) "Two-

---

the general election. The story of the controversy and the judicial testimony at the hearing, with its revealing details of decision making procedure by a leading state appellate court, are presented in Stolz, Judging Judges (1981).

190. The Judicial Councils Reform and Judicial Conduct and Disability Act of 1980 (94 Stat. 2035 (1980), 28 U.S.C. 372(c); for committee reports, see 4 U.S. Code Cong. & Ad. News 4315 et seq. (1980)) authorized anyone to lodge a complaint with the clerk of the court of appeals of the circuit alleging that a federal judge or magistrate "has engaged in conduct prejudicial to the effective and expeditious administration of the business of the courts" or "is unable to discharge all the duties of office by reason of mental or physical disability." A special committee of circuit and district judges investigates, with power of subpoena, and affords the judge or magistrate a full opportunity to be heard; then it reports to the judicial council of the circuit. The latter, in turn (after conducting any additional investigation it finds necessary) may choose among several alternatives, including: (1) requesting, after certifying a judge's disability, that the President appoint an additional judge (a previously existing remedy under 28 U.S.C. §372(b)); (2) requesting the judge to voluntarily retire; (3) ordering that for a specified period, no further cases be assigned to the judge; (4) issuing a censure or reprimand, either private or public; (5) following such other action as is deemed appropriate — but in no circumstances is a judge who was appointed to hold office during good behavior to be "removed" from office.

The judicial council is also authorized to refer the complaint to the Judicial Conference of the United States. It must so refer if the council determines that the conduct might be grounds for impeachment under the Constitution or "in the interest of justice is not amenable to resolution by the judicial council." The Judicial Conference (or a standing committee thereof appointed by the Chief Justice) can further investigate, with subpoena powers, and can choose among the above alternatives open to the council, or if it determines that impeachment is appropriate, shall transmit the proceedings and determination to the House of Representatives. The Court of Claims, Court of Customs and Patent Appeals, and Customs Court (now the Court of International Trade) are required to establish comparable procedures.

191. Hurst, The Functions of Courts in the United States, 1950-1980, 15 L. & Socy. Rev. 401, 428-435 (1980-1981).

192. A study of Michigan auto accidents showed the following: Of 86,100 cases

thirds of problems which consumers experienced with products they bought came to no action for redress; of matters which shaped up to some definition as disputes, very few came into even the first stages of handling by courts." (3) In civil cases where the court did enter judgment it often only "processed or approved outcomes to which parties had been able to agree or which they consented to accept." There has been a rise in proportion of uncontested judgments, as well as a decline in the number of cases brought to formal trial.[193] (4) In criminal matters, half of the reportable complaints were never reported to police. Of those that were, only 25 percent were labeled by the police as crimes, and only 5 percent involved arrest. The great majority of those arrested never came to trial. The percentage of all criminal court cases resolved by pleas of guilty without trial ranged up to 90 percent.[194]

The data for civil and criminal litigation in the federal courts present a generally comparable picture.[195]

---

of auto injuries in 1958, most of them (74,000) were not put in the hands of lawyers, i.e., 24,700 were settled by payment and in 49,300 the dispute was dropped, no payment being made. Of the 12,100 in which lawyers were hired, only 4,000 suits were filed in court (4,100 had been settled by payment, and in 4,000 the dispute was dropped, no payment being made). Of the 4,000 lawsuits, only 1,400 went to the pretrial stage (400 having been dropped and 2,200 having been settled by payment). Thereafter, only 500 went to trial (100 having been dropped and 800 having been settled by payment); and of these, 140 were terminated without payment, and 360 by settlement payment or pursuant to court judgment. There were only 80 appeals from judgments for or against liability. Conard, The Quantitative Analysis of Justice, 20 J. Legal Educ. 1, 3-5 (1967); Conard, Morgan, Pratt, Voltz & Bombaugh, Automobile Accident Costs and Payments 154-155 (1964).

193. As to subject matter, there was a rise in the proportion of tort filings (largely auto accident cases, usually settled before trial) and family law filings (largely uncontested divorce); and a decline in contract and property cases.

The authors of a study of courts in two California counties, which reveals the same trends already described, see "a general movement from dispute resolution to routine administration over the past century." The courts "are almost totally unused by ordinary individuals to resolve personal problems. The overwhelming majority of business disputes also avoid the courts. Citizen and businessmen alike either seek out some other agency, or make use of resources within the family, group, or trade association — or, as is frequently the case, handle the matter entirely on their own" (e.g., may resort to arbitration, or discontinue patronizing the other party, or simply "lumping it," i.e., doing nothing in response to the grievance). Friedman & Percival, A Tale of Two Courts: Litigation in Alameda and San Benito Counties, 10 Law & Socy. Rev. 267, 301 (1976). For a critique of this study, see Lempert, More Tales of Two Courts: Exploring Changes In The "Dispute Settlement Function" of Trial Courts, 13 Law & Socy. Rev. 91 (1978).

194. The attrition at each stage of the criminal proceeding is detailed in Chap. 2 herein under **B10c**.

195. According to Statistical Abstract of the United States (1979), for the year ended June 30, 1978, of the 138,770 federal civil cases commenced, only 7.4% reached trial. Of the criminal cases commenced in the same year, 80 or 90% pleaded guilty (see at 192, 193). The 1980 Report of the Director, Administrative Office of U.S. Courts reveals (at 97) that of the 36,560 criminal defendants whose cases were disposed of during the year ending June 30, 1980, 18% had their cases dismissed; and of the 78.2% who were convicted, more than 80% had pleaded guilty.

Moreover, the data show a limited role for appellate courts as well; and the cases that do go to an appellate court have a much better chance of success when the review granted has been within the court's discretion rather than as a matter of right.[196]

(4) Access to Modes of Dispute Settlement

Concern over insufficient "access" to the courts has flowed from two major sources. One is certain restrictive Supreme Court decisions on "standing" to sue (though on the whole the Court seems to have liberalized its standing requirement in recent years). This is a subject that is analyzed at length in Chapter 2.[197] The other is the high costs of litigation, particularly the high legal fees[198] and the inevitable court delay we have been discussing.

Inflationary pressures on legal fees are somewhat countered by certain downward pressures on costs. There is now more price competition within the profession — as a result of Supreme Court decisions banning concerted fee-fixing and permitting certain advertising by lawyers, and the existence of low-fee legal clinics[199] — as well as increased competition from outside the profession.[200] And there are efforts, still struggling, at reducing costs through a swifter, more efficient litigation process.[201]

For the poor, provision of free legal services has been greatly augmented in civil cases by federal funding (presently threatened, however, by the Reagan administration) of the National Legal Services

196. In state courts, appellate court judgments were "probably always much less than one percent of the total cases disposed of in all reporting trial courts" (the latter includes uncontested judgments as well, more precise figures on a comprehensive scale being unavailable). In federal courts in recent years, from civil "contested judgments" of trial courts there has been a 20 to 24% rate of appeal; in criminal cases the rate has been higher, perhaps largely because of the free legal services provided for indigents. The appeal made a difference in only a minority of the cases. In those state court appeals that could be had as of right, the reversal rate in the last few decades has been about 37% (and 50% for appeals heard at the appellate court's discretion). Appeals to federal courts of appeals in the same period have been about half as successful as in state appeals taken as of right. And "given the broad discretionary control of the U.S. Supreme Court over its review docket, and the peculiarly difficult issues usually brought to it, not surprisingly its rate of reversal consistently ran far higher. . . . Thus in 1956 the Supreme Court reversed in 61.1 percent of the cases it decided, in 1964 in 69.7 percent, and in 1974 in 59.8 percent." Hurst, *supra* n.191 at 424-428. See also Chap. 4 herein at n.25.

197. See the discussion in Chap. 2 under **B6.**

198. See Postscript herein at n.10.

199. *Id.* at nn. 11-13, 22-23.

200. *Id.* at nn. 14-16.

201. *Id.* at nn. 18-20.

Corporation. And free legal services are offered in criminal cases (except for certain minor ones) from the governmental unit affected.[202] Other than the poor, no one receives free legal services, except as they may be benefited by the legal activity of reformist organizations and "public interest law firms."[203] A broadened access to legal services is available, though, through the growth of plans charging more manageable fees, such as the monthly pre-payment "group legal service" plans or the reduced fee "legal clinics."[204] Litigation cost is also significantly affected by the opportunity, under new federal legislation, for judicial awards of attorney fees and expenses to prevailing parties in certain federal court suits and administrative proceedings.[205]

Non-court litigation of disputes — as by arbitration or by mediation and conciliation, applicable to poor and non-poor alike — is much cheaper but has not reached the bulk of the people yet, in spite of recent expansion; and it is generally limited to lesser disputes,[206] except for much of the commercial and labor arbitration.

Finally, a word on the scope of a constitutional right of access to courts is needed here. The Supreme Court thought such a constitutional right applied to a divorce action, viewed as the exercise of a constitutional right of freedom of choice in marital decisions — i.e., the Court invalidated a state's refusal to permit a divorce action by an indigent unable to pay certain court fees.[207] But the Court refused to extend the principle to $50 voluntary bankruptcy filing fees,[208] or to a $25 filing fee applicable to court appeals from state welfare agency decisions (made after administrative hearing) reducing old-age assistance and welfare payments.[209] Thus, there is no constitutional right of *free* access to a court in all types of cases, any more than there is a constitutional right to free counsel in all types of cases. In *criminal* cases, as discussed in Appendix 2, the indigent defendant has such a right of free counsel, with some exceptions. The Court has most often spoken of a constitutional "right of access" in certain cases involving prisoners — e.g., where prison officials have failed to afford law book facilities or other assistance to a prisoner seeking legal redress, or a court has

202. *Id.* at nn. 26-27.
203. *Id.* at nn. 28-30.
204. *Id.* at nn. 21-23.
205. *Id.* at nn. 31-32.
206. *Id.* at nn. 16-17; Marcus, *supra* n.159 at 134, 135.
207. Boddie v. Connecticut, 401 U.S. 371 (1971). On the related issue of an indigent's access to free services needed for his court case, the Court has held violative of due process a state's application of its paternity statute (which charged the cost of blood-grouping tests in a paternity suit to the requesting party) so as to deny free tests to the indigent putative father. Little v. Streater, 68 L. Ed. 2d 627 (1981).
208. U.S. v. Kras, 409 U.S. 434 (1973).
209. Ortwein v. Schwab, 410 U.S. 656 (1973).

failed to afford to an indigent prisoner desiring to appeal, a free copy of the trial transcript required for the appeal.[210]

Apart from the question of indigents' *free* access to a court, there is a broader issue: Under what circumstances may a legislature withhold a court remedy from *non*-indigents and leave the adjudication solely to an administrative agency hearing (permitting court review only of the *procedural* fairness of the agency hearing). Surprisingly, this question has thus far received fuzzy and incomplete answers from the Supreme Court.[211]

(5) The Courts' New Administrative Involvement in Remedying Public Institutions' Constitutional Violations

A striking development of the last couple of decades in the federal courts is the spectacle of federal judges as ultimate administrators in some states, for extended periods, of certain institutions like school systems, electoral district reapportionment systems, mental hospitals, and prisons. This has happened because the court found it necessary, as a means of remedying a violation of law (usually of the Constitution)[212] by the institution, to decree specific operational requirements and maintain long-term institutional administration or supervision[213] to insure compliance. In this type of case, the court usually cannot act on its own, and finds it necessary to appoint agents.[214]

In the burgeoning literature on this phenomenon,[215] one fre-

210. See Annot., 52 L. Ed. 2d 779 (1978). On this paragraph, see also Nowak et al., Constitutional Law 512-514 (1978).

211. Davis, Administrative Law Treatise, §§28.18, 28.19 (1st ed. 1958 and Supp.) (the relevant volume of the second edition has not yet appeared); Gellhorn, Byse & Strauss, Administrative Law, Cases and Comments 942-947 (7th ed. 1979); Davis, Administrative Law in the Seventies, §28.09 (1976) & 1980 Supp.; Jaffe, Judicial Control of Administrative Action 376-394 (1965).

212. Less frequently the violation is of statutes, like those on employment discrimination or housing (and here the nature and duration of court intrusion may be less extreme). See Special Project, The Remedial Process in Institutional Reform Litigation, 78 Colum. L. Rev. 784, 788 at nn. 4-6 (1978).

213. On problems concerning duration and termination of court involvement, see *id.* at 842-844.

214. They have been variously labeled (e.g., monitors, masters, mediators, administrators, ombudsmen, committees, receivers) and have performed varying functions. They may gather information and make recommendations as to formulation of the decree, or as to its proper implementation; or they may mediate disputes between plaintiff and defendant over interpretation of the decree and the pace of compliance, or may actively supplement the institution's management as administrators; or in the unusual case, they may even displace top management (as "receiver"). *Id.* at 823-837.

215. Eisenberg & Yeazell, The Ordinary and the Extraordinary in Institutional Litigation, 93 Harv. L. Rev. 465 (1980); Reynolds, The Mechanics of Institutional Reform Litigation, 8 Fordham Urb. L.J. 695 (1980); Note, 89 Yale L.J. 513 (1980);

quently encounters criticism to the effect that the functions here engaged in by the courts are executive or administrative rather than "judicial," and as a matter of separation-of-powers theory as well as democratic political theory should be avoided by courts; that in the cases involving state public institutions, state autonomy is being invaded; that courts lack the necessary expertise; that they act on a narrow record and lack the full investigative capacity of a legislative committee; that by not acting in terms of the "big picture" of a state's social and financial problems, they are oblivious to the possible adverse impact of a particular required funding increase — for instance, upon the funding in other areas that are equally or more in need; that the reforms tend to be the minimum necessary to remedy a violation of law, rather than the optimal ones that a reformist legislature and administrative agency might strive for; and that there are practical difficulties in the court's using compliance sanctions, primarily the contempt power.

On the other side, commentators acknowledge the shortcomings of judges in planning and administering social reforms, yet stress the judges' duty, upon the finding of law violation, to use their equitable powers to issue remedial decrees and to see that their decrees are effective. This judicial function conferred by the Constitution supersedes, it is thought, any prohibition against a judge's exercise of administrative functions — a prohibition to which the Supreme Court has lately given little recognition anyway.[216] Arguments are also offered to show that recent Supreme Court concern for preservation of state autonomy is inapplicable;[217] and that precedents are not lacking for judicial ordering of allocation or increase of state funding.[218] In addition, traditional judicial practice (in such fields as probate, trusts, and bankruptcy) is pointed to as having frequently involved administration of continuing enterprises, requirements of periodic accountings to a

---

Note, 52 U. Colo. L. Rev. 105 (1980); Fiss, The Supreme Court 1978 Term, Foreword, The Forms of Justice, 93 Harv. L. Rev. 1 (1979); Brakel, Special Masters in Institutional Litigation, 1979 Am. B. Foundation Research J. 543; Sarat & Cavanagh, Thinking About Courts: Traditional Expectations and Contemporary Challenges, at 66-79 (1979) (U. of Wis. Disputes Processing Research, Working Paper 1979-5); Mishkin, Federal Courts As State Reformers, 35 Wash. & Lee L. Rev. 949 (1978); Nagel, Separation of Powers and the Scope of Federal Equitable Remedies, 30 Stan. L. Rev. 661 (1978); Friendly, The Courts and Social Policy, 33 U. Miami L. Rev. 21, 40-42 (1978); Horowitz, The Courts and Social Policy (1977); Note, 91 Harv. L. Rev. 428 (1977); Chayes, The Role of the Judge in Public Law Litigation, 89 Harv. L. Rev. 1281 (1976).

216. On this prohibition, see Bator, Mishkin, Shapiro & Wechsler, The Federal Courts and the Federal System 237-238 (2d. ed. 1973). But see Gilligan v. Morgan, 413 U.S. 18 (1973), which is discussed along with the general separation-of-powers theory in Eisenberg & Yeazell, *supra* n.216 at 495-501.

217. Eisenberg & Yeazell, *supra* at 501-506.

218. *Id.* at 506-510.

court, and reorganization of large industrial and railroad corporations.[219] Finally, the pragmatic point is made that judicial relief may be a catalyst; it may, as, "in the civil rights field", help to "mobilize political action whose legislative consequences far transcended anything that judges were equipped to compel."[220]

The controversy is sure to continue. In Judge Friendly's words, "the risk of confrontation between a court, generally a federal court, and a financially hard-pressed city or state is fearsome, although perhaps inescapable."[221]

2. The Legislatures

An initial difference to observe between the powers of Congress and those of state legislatures is that Congress can exercise only the powers enumerated in the Constitution, occurring almost wholly in Article I,[222] whereas state legislatures are not confined to a specified list of powers. Under the Tenth Amendment, all powers that the Constitution does not assign to the federal government, and does not prohibit to the states, are reserved to the states. "For the purposes of federal law, state governments or their subsidiaries are not creatures of limited powers: they are recognized as having a general 'police power' — the inherent power to protect the health, safety, welfare or morals of persons within their jurisdiction."[223]

In their structure and mechanics of operation, Congress and the state legislatures manifest both similarities and differences. For instance, the states typically have a two-chamber legislature; and like Congress, one chamber has a shorter term, more numerous members, and a narrower geographical constituency than the other. But congressional sessions are almost continuous whereas state sessions are either every other year or, as the great majority have now come to be,

219. *Id.* at 481-485. Courts exercised these powers before any statutes specifically authorized them. *Id.* at 486-491.

220. Sarat & Cavanagh, *supra* n.215 at 77. For a similar point in the mental hospital field, see Note, 91 Harv. L. Rev. 428, 463 & n.178.

221. Friendly, *supra* n.215 at 40.

222. There are 18 enumerations in Article I, §8. Perhaps the powers that have had the most significant legal and social ramifications domestically have been the powers to regulate "commerce"; to tax and spend for the general welfare; and to "make all Laws which shall be necessary and proper for carrying into Execution the foregoing Powers, and all other Powers vested by this Constitution in the Government of the United States, or in any Department or Officer thereof" (known as the "necessary and proper clause"). There are sources of congressional power outside of Article I, too, such as the important power given by §5 of the Fourteenth Amendment to enforce the Amendment by appropriate legislation. For other sources see Nowak, Rotunda & Young, Constitutional Law 122-126 (1978).

223. *Id.* at 112.

annually, with unfortunately rigid limits on length of session.[224] Also, in the referral, screening, shaping, and passage of bills, the standing committees may play different roles on the state and federal level.[225]

Physical and technical facilities and perquisites of office have long been poorer on the state level. I refer not only to such matters as salaries, office, and staff assistance but to the fact that the states have lagged behind in supplying legislators with up-to-date information on the text, amendments, and calendar status of bills; have far less frequently held committee hearings; and done little or no printing of floor discussion, committee hearings, or committee reports[226] — among other deficiencies criticized by the 1971 Citizens' Conference on State Legislatures.[227] But the last decade or so has, in some ways, seen some substantial improvements.[228]

Can we also say that the substantive performance of state legislative functions has improved? The answer, on the whole, seems to be

224. This has an adverse effect on the legislature's ability to cope in a deliberative way with the mounting volume of business. Any substantial research and study has to be done largely between sessions. Commissions or special committees often undertake such work rather than (as professional opinion seems to prefer) the standing committees — though the number of states using standing committees for this purpose has been increasing. Rosenthal, Legislative Performance In the States 32-34 (1974).

225. In the states, in contrast to Congress, not every bill is first referred to a standing committee. When a congressional committee does receive a bill, the committee can kill it by simply not reporting it out. Most federal bills die in that way, though in a rare case Congress forces a bill out of committee. In some states, however, the committee must report out each bill, favorably or unfavorably. *Id.* at 20-21. State committees often report the bill in modified form, but not as often as in Congress. *Id.* at 25. On the federal as opposed to the state level, all reported bills are scheduled for floor consideration. *Id.* at 28-29. While few bills reported by congressional committees lose on the floor (though they are often amended), many state bills do not enjoy such success; and the rules in a particular state may discourage amendments. *Id.* at 30-31.

226. Wahlke, Organization and Procedure, in Heard, ed., State Legislatures in American Politics 131-132, 133-137 (1966). Fuller reporting would not only tend to make legislators act more responsibly and intelligently but would help courts in interpreting statutes. You will find, in reading Chapter 3, that a statute's "legislative history" (e.g., the various drafts of the bill, the committee hearings, the committee reports, what was said on the floor) when available often plays a significant role in its interpretation. Accordingly, the role of legislative history is much more important in interpreting federal statutes, since Congressional reporting is excellent.

227. Citizens' Conference on State Legislatures, The Sometime Governments (1971).

228. "Today legislatures are more likely to meet annually than biennially. They spend more time in session than before. Professional staff has increased. Research agencies nearly everywhere are larger, many of the standing committees have assistance, and leaders in more than half the states have full-time staff support. Facilities are better. Salaries are higher. Procedures have become more efficient and more public. Electronic data processing, in one form or another, is widespread. Legislative office is more attractive and larger numbers of able individuals are willing to make personal sacrifices in order to serve. Probably more than other American public institutions, state legislatures have recently undergone significant change." Rosenthal, *supra* n.224 at 2-3.

affirmative, whether we consider the function of (1) "service to constituents,"[229] (2) "policy and program formulation,"[230] or (3) "policy and program control" (i.e., evaluating the effects of state policies and programs, and "oversight" of administration).[231]

As for these functions on the federal level, probably some improvement has occurred in all three. Policy and program formulation has seen the least enhancement because the dominant policy making role of the President's OMB (Office of Management and Budget) has been only partially offset by Congress's reassertion of some budget controls in 1974.[232] These matters, as well as salient aspects of the third function, will be discussed later under the headings of "Legislature and

229. This and the two other quoted categories are those of Rosenthal, *id.* at 11-12. In terms of the first category, "toll-free telephone 'hot lines' now enable the ruled to contact their rulers directly; 'sunshine laws' obligate legislators to do their work in public, in full view of interested persons and the mass media; ethics codes, with financial disclosure requirements, make it more difficult for legislators so inclined to put private interests ahead of the commonweal." Rieselbach, Legislative Reform 1-2 (1978).

230. Independence in this function is hampered by the role of the governor and of political parties. While some reformers have urged a resurgence of legislative supremacy in policy making, and others on the opposite end have urged that legislatures should "accept subordination to the executive and his/her political party," current reforms seem to have been more moderate. They have "revolved around efforts to revive legislatures' status as coequal makers of public policy, as institutions able . . . to 'counterbalance' political executives." *Id.* at 2. See also Rosenthal, *supra* n.224 at 191.

231. "There are now 40 states where the audit function is part of the legislative branch. Legislative audit units which were traditionally financial in scope have been expanded to provide a broad program evaluation capability. . . . The evaluation function under sunset laws [these laws require, at fixed periods of years, legislative committee evaluations of regulatory laws and programs thereunder, and recommendations as to whether the laws should be allowed to expire] has been vested in audit or evaluation committees in many states. . . ." Council of State Government, Book of the States 1980-81, at 80 (1980); Rosenthal, *supra* n.224 at 66-83. Sunset legislation had been passed in 33 states by 1980. Council, *supra* at 81. Committees for the review of administrative rules had spread to 38 states by 1980. *Id.* at 80.

In addition, the "state budget process remains one of the most effective means of legislative program oversight and control. In general, legislatures ended the 1970s with a strengthened budget process." A recent movement to share budget information and participation among all legislators rather than just budget and appropriation committees has been furthered by development in some states of "computerized legislative fiscal information systems." Also popular in recent years is the requirement of economic impact statements on certain kinds of bills, use of "fiscal notes" on bills, and zero-base budgeting techniques. *Id.* at 83. Finally, as to federal funds: "Over three-fourths of the legislatures now have some provision for review of federal funds received by state agencies. Legislatures have identified the effect of federal monies on state planning and priorities as a major problem and become concerned with how such funds are received and spent by state agencies and integrated with state funds," as well as becoming concerned with legal issues like "separation of powers, federalism, the legislative power to appropriate monies, and the authority of a legislative committee to make decisions on behalf of the legislature during interim periods." *Id.* at 82-83.

232. See text below between nn. 241-243 & 313-315. Concerning the function of "service to constituents," the improvement described for the state level in n.229

Executive" and "Legislature and Administrative Agencies." One may note, meanwhile, that the deficiency in policy and program formulation is not the only factor undermining the stereotype of Congress as the effective source of national legislative power. Students of Congress have often noted that the organization of this large, unwieldy body involves such a dispersion of power among its committees and subcommittees as to sorely weaken its national leadership role in planning and promoting legislative policies.[233] Another point made is that, compared to members of the executive bureaucracy, Congressmen are more "oriented towards local needs and small-town ways of thought. The leaders of the administration and of the great private national institutions are more likely to think in national terms"[234] — a state of affairs perhaps less prevalent today than previously.

An alternative analysis of congressional function is in terms of (1) "declaring standards and rules of behavior,"[235] (2) "resource allocation,"[236] and (3) "investigation."[237] The two analyses can profitably be combined.

---

supra applies on the federal level as well. There is more openness about campaign funding under the Federal Election Campaign Act of 1971, as amended, which also limits honoraria for appearances, speeches, and articles (see 2 U.S.C. §§431-455); there was, as a result of the 1977 Ethics Resolutions of both Houses, disclosure not only of member finances but also of the receipt of gifts of $100 or more, and a limit on outside earnings. Under the Ethics in Government Act of 1978, amended in 1979 (92 Stat. 1824; 93 Stat. 37) members of Congress are included, along with other officials including the President, Supreme Court Justices, and presidential nominees and candidates for federal office, in the requirement of annual public financial disclosure reports (see 2 U.S.C. §§701-709; and analysis of the 1981 financial disclosures made by members of Congress, in 39 Cong. Q. 1677 (1981)). The occasions when votes in Congress must be recorded have been increased; most committee meetings have been opened to the public, with members' votes recorded and made public. Proposals for additional openness include televising Congress and closing loopholes in the Federal Regulation of Lobbying Act. See Bullock, Congress in the Sunshine, in Rieselbach, *supra* n.229 at 209-221. Bullock notes (at 216-220) that increased openness may have had some unintended consequences, such as making members less willing to compromise their positions; causing more delay in decisionmaking in committees and on the floor; introducing a conservative bias, both because delay supports the status quo, and because heeding constituent preferences more closely may mean more conservative voting on some issues like civil liberties or abortion funding; and turning lobbyists' interests towards influencing staff members instead of Congress members.

233. Dodd & Schott, Congress and the Administrative State 124-129, 326-328 (1979); Huntington, Congressional Responses to the Twentieth Century, in Truman, ed., The Congress and America's Future 18-22 (1965).

234. Huntington, *supra* at 15.

235. Hurst, Law and Social Order in the United States 97-105 (1977). For the states, see *id.* at 82-97.

236. *Id.* at 112-122. This includes taxing and spending for the debts, defense, and general welfare of the United States; borrowing money; and controlling the coin and currency. For the states, see *id.* at 105-112.

237. *Id.* at 122-132, 153-154. See also Note, 70 Harv. L. Rev. 671 (1957); Auerbach et al., *supra* n.5 at 606-623 (1961).

3. The Chief Executive

I confine myself here to the President and the sources and nature of his power. The primary definition of his position is Article II of the Constitution. Its listing of powers is less extensive than Article I's enumeration of Congress's powers: "The executive power" is vested in him, and he is to "take care that the laws be faithfully executed." A few more provisions add some specificity: He has military power as "Commander-in-chief"; he has veto power over congressional bills;[238] "he may require the opinion, in writing, of the principal officer in each of the executive departments, upon any subject relating to the duties of their respective offices"; he "shall have power to grant reprieves and pardons for offenses against the United States, except in cases of impeachment"; he has the power to make treaties with the concurrence of two-thirds of the Senators present; and he can, with the concurrence of a Senate majority, make certain appointments.[239] He also is obliged to "from time to time give to the Congress information of the state of the Union, and recommend to their consideration such measures as he shall judge necessary and expedient."[240]

The other source of presidential power is statutory. When Congress has authorized a President to do certain things, "his authority is at its maximum," Justice Jackson once said, because "it includes all that he possesses in his own right plus all that Congress can delegate." When he acts "in absence of either a congressional grant or denial of authority, he can only rely upon his own independent powers." By so relying he may undertake a course of action that, according to a

238. Under Article I, §VII, cl. 2, this veto can be overridden by two-thirds vote of each house; if a bill after passage by both houses is presented to the President and not returned by him "within ten days (Sundays excepted) . . . the same shall be a law in like manner as if he had signed it, unless [this being the "pocket veto" provision] the Congress by their adjournment prevent its return, in which case it shall not be a law." That is, where Congress adjourns within the ten-day period, the President may effectively sign the bill within that period, but if he does not it will not become law. See Edwards v. U.S., 286 U.S. 482 (1932).

239. These are "ambassadors, other public ministers and consuls, judges of the Supreme Court, and all other officers of the United States whose appointments are not herein otherwise provided for, and which shall be established by law; but the Congress may by law vest the appointment of such inferior officers, as they think proper, in the President alone, in the courts of law, or in the heads of departments." And he has "power to fill up all vacancies that may happen during the recess of the Senate, by granting commissions which shall expire at the end of the next session."

240. In addition, "he may on extraordinary occasions, convene both Houses, or either of them, and in case of disagreement between them with respect to the time of adjournment, he may adjourn them to such time as he shall think proper; he shall receive ambassadors and other public ministers"; and "shall commission all the officers of the United States." He is to be "removed from office on impeachment for and conviction of treason, bribery, or other high crimes and misdemeanors."

subsequent court decision, is not within the constitutional concept of "executive" power. Moreover, as Jackson further remarked, his decisions may fall within "a zone of twilight in which he and Congress may have concurrent authority, or in which its distribution is uncertain"; or they may be "incompatible with the expressed or implied will of Congress."[241] This conflict between executive and legislative power will be developed more fully in "Legislature and Executive" below.

Of interest here is how Congress itself has expanded the scope of executive power — a bolstering of the Executive Office begun in Franklin D. Roosevelt's day. The Executive Office has now become a "powerful organization [consisting] of a group of personal advisors, staff offices, and advisory councils (among them the Office of Management and Budget, the National Security Council, the Council of Economic Advisors) designed to supply Presidents not only with intelligence about what is happening in the depths of the administration, but also with public policy options and the organizational tools to coordinate both the formulation and execution of public policy."[242] The OMB is of particular importance. It "has emerged as the presidential staff agency par excellence. Its duties have grown beyond assisting in budgetary formulation to include budget administration, the clearance of legislative proposals emanating from executive branch agencies, coordination of broad, government-wide programs, assistance in the formulation of the president's legislative program, and advice to the president on whether to veto bills proffered by Congress. It also conducts executive oversight of program management and administration, reviews executive branch organization, and assists in the career development and assignment of top-level officials." It "has grown so powerful that Congress recently required that its director, heretofore appointed solely at the pleasure of the president, henceforth be confirmed in office by the Senate."[243]

Congress has enhanced presidential power in other ways, such as authorizing the President to reorganize executive agencies, subject to certain congressional checks. Though high-level appointments of officers have to be made with the advice and consent of the Senate, the Senate has traditionally afforded great discretion to Presidents in this regard.[244] And Congress has in a few instances lodged in the President the final decisionmaking authority to be exercised after the relevant agencies had completed their proceedings and recommendations (e.g., decision on tariff changes; decision on natural gas pipeline route from

241. Jackson, J., concurring in Youngstown Sheet & Tube Co. v. Sawyer, 343 U.S. 579, 635-637 (1952).

242. Dodd & Schott, *supra* n.233 at 3 (1979).

243. *Id.* at 43-44.

244. On this and the preceding paragraph, see *id.* at 3-4.

Alaska across Canada to terminals in the United States, but subject, in this instance to congressional review; and review of Nuclear Regulatory Commission decisions against licensing the export of nuclear material).[245]

Another important characteristic of the Chief Executive's power is that it extends beyond the strictly executive domain. His constitutional power to "recommend [to Congress] such measures as he shall judge necessary and expedient" is closer to legislation than to executive power (his office is responsible for most of the bills introduced and passed in Congress). So too is his power to approve or veto legislation, while the power to pardon or commute sentences has a judicial cast; its exercise resembles an adjudication that the facts in a particular case warrant leniency.[246]

Further aspects of presidential power are discussed later under "Chief Executive and Executive-Administrative Agencies" and "Legislature and Executive."

4. Executive and Administrative Agencies

While we have in the two previous sections encountered a legislative role of the executive in the formulation and promotion of legislation, we normally think of the executive part of the government as "carrying out" or "executing" the law made by the legislature. The jobs most of us associate with the executive branch, for instance, are posts that involve carrying out laws: tax officials, inspectors, licensing officers, policemen, prosecutors, motor vehicle commissioners, Presidents, governors, mayors, and their subordinates.

There are really two main forms of the executive. On one hand are the departments, bureaus, and divisions (agriculture, labor, public health, tax, etc.) that report to the Chief Executive. The second grouping contains the "administrative agencies" — such as the Securities and Exchange Commission, National Labor Relations Board, and Federal Trade Commission on the federal level; or the public service commission, workmen's compensation commission, and zoning commission on the state level — that are *semi-independent* of the Chief Executive, as we shall see, and are sometimes called "independent agencies" as distinguished from executive departments.

1. Either form of agency can exhibit a mixture of functions. In

245. See Gellhorn et al., *supra* n.211 at 141-142.

246. See also Ledewitz, The Uncertain Power of the President to Execute the Laws, 46 Tenn. L. Rev. 757 (1979); Nowak et al., *supra* n.222 at 172-176 & chap. 7; Swindler, The Executive Power in State and Federal Constitutions, 1 Hastings Const. L.Q. 21 (1974); Hurst, *supra* n.235 at 143-153.

the first place, in order to execute or administer the law laid down by the legislature, a department or agency may be authorized by the legislature to exercise a *lawmaking* function (i.e., issue rules and regulations, with the force of law, that implement the statute) — as, for instance, when the Treasury Department issues tax regulations, or the SEC issues rules regarding the sale of securities. The regulations are issued after notice of a so-called "notice and comment" hearing[247] on the proposed regulations. Unlike a court hearing, this hearing is more like that of a legislative committee, during which written and often oral comment is received, but there is no cross-examination, and no detailed findings of fact and conclusions of law are made by the issuing agency. Statutes for particular federal agencies, however, have sometimes imposed some or all of the characteristics of a trial-type hearing upon rulemaking.[248]

So too, both forms of agencies may exercise a kind of *judicial* function. In the first form of agency, consider the office of a district attorney: The prosecutor has to make some judgments that might be called "adjudicative," such as whether criminal proceedings should be brought, or whether the nature of the case, the condition of the office workload, and other factors justify substituting a lesser charge in return for a guilty plea to that charge. The police, too, are constantly making instant adjudications when they determine whether the facts justify making an arrest. A Veterans Administration or a Social Security office adjudicates claims for pensions, though usually informally.

But it is the second form of agency — the "administrative agency" — that we are prone to recognize as more clearly exercising a judicial function. This seems to be because of the hearings held prior to adjudication of, let us say, whether an FTC cease-and-desist order, or an NLRB unfair labor practice order, should issue. These hearings in many respects resemble the hearings in civil court proceedings. Often called *"quasi-judicial"* agencies, therefore, these administrative agencies are distinguished from ordinary executive departments. (But the dividing line is somewhat blurred: There are some executive departments, too, e.g., the federal Department of Agriculture, Commerce, or Interior, in which constituent bureaus hold rather formal adjudicative hearings as well as making more informal adjudications.)[249] The question of whether there is a *constitutional right* to a full, or an almost full, court-like hearing before the making of adjudications of particular individual rights (as distinct from the making of general

247. See §4 of the Administrative Procedure Act, 5 U.S.C. §553.

248. See 1 Davis Administrative Law Treatise, chap. 6, esp. §§6.1, 6.9 (2nd ed. 1978).

249. See Verkuil, A Study of Informal Adjudication Procedures, 43 U. Chi. L. Rev. 739, 757-796 (1976).

regulations) — e.g., administrative revocation of probation or parole, discharge of a public employee, termination of welfare benefits, debarment of contractors from further dealing with the government, or revocation of an automobile license — arose frequently in the 1970s. The result was "a greater expansion of procedural due process in the last five years [1970-1975] than in the entire period since ratification of the Constitution."[250]

2. The typical "administrative agency," then, has the power to issue rules and regulations and/or to issue individual adjudicative orders depending on its statutory authority. The rulemaking might be authorized for such purposes as protecting the quality or safety of products; informative labeling; labor or price standards; environmental quality; and honest, fair, or non-monopolistic business behavior. Individual orders might be authorized for such purposes as license issuance, setting rates, or fixing an injured worker's compensation. Individual enforcement activity might be authorized, like suspending or revoking licenses, suspending a government contractor, issuing cease-and-desist orders, making a negotiated settlement, giving publicity to orders, recalling products, seizing a product, requiring corrective advertising, withholding a subsidy, assessing a monetary penalty.[251] And enforcement actions in *court* might be authorized, such as criminal prosecutions, fixed monetary penalties of a civil nature, double or triple damages, "restitution," or injunctions that either restrain or command.

3. In terms of sheer volume of disputes handled, it is clear not only that executive agencies (including, e.g., Internal Revenue Service in the Treasury Department, the Veterans' Administration, Social Security Administration in the Department of Health and Human Services, Occupational Safety and Health Administration in the Labor Department, various agencies within the Departments of Agriculture, Interior, and Transportation) carry a far greater burden than the administrative agencies,[252] but that agencies of either type carry a

250. Friendly, Some Kind of Hearing, 123 U. Pa. L. Rev. 1267, 1273 (1975). See 2 Davis, Administrative Law Treatise, chaps. 10-13 (2d ed. 1979).

251. On administrative sanctions, see Hazen, Administrative Enforcement: An Evaluation of the SEC's Use of Injunctions and Other Enforcement Methods, 31 Hastings L.J. 427 (1979); Diver, The Assessment and Mitigation of Civil Money Penalties By Federal Administrative Agencies, 79 Colum. L. Rev. 1435 (1979); Note, 73 Nw. U.L. Rev. 957 (1978); Lawrence, Judicial Review of Variable Civil Money Penalties, 46 U. Cin. L. Rev. 373 (1977); Thomforde, Negotiating Administrative Settlements In SEC Broker–Dealer Disciplinary Proceedings, 52 N.Y.U.L. Rev. 237 (1977); Thomforde, Controlling Administrative Sanctions, 74 Mich. L. Rev. 709 (1976); Note, 11 Wake Forest L. Rev. 83 (1975); E. Gellhorn, Adverse Publicity By Administrative Agencies, 86 Harv. L. Rev. 1380 (1973); W. Gellhorn, Administrative Prescription and Imposition of Penalties, 1970 Wash. U.L.Q. 265; McKay, Sanctions In Motion: The Administrative Process, 49 Iowa L. Rev. 441 (1964).

252. See 1 Davis, *supra* n.250 at §1.3.

heavier burden than do the courts. In a given recent year, the federal district courts will have tried several thousand civil cases, but the federal agencies will have tried ten times as many, counting only those involving an oral hearing and verbatim transcript. If federal informal adjudications were counted, the annual number would run into the hundreds of millions and perhaps billions. And remember that the average state may have more than a hundred agencies with powers to adjudicate or issue rules (or both) with the force of law.[253]

4. It is not hard to see the advantages of lawmaking and enforcement by agencies. The legislature has neither the time nor the expertise to handle the detailed requirements of regulatory schemes for a myriad of ever-changing industrial and non-industrial problem areas, and to provide the continuous, day-to-day supervision that may be needed.

Could the legislature meet the lawmaking aspect of the problem by regulating in general rather than detailed terms? Of course, it sometimes does this. But it is an unsatisfactory technique: (a) it is unsatisfactory to the industry or other subject of the regulation because the vagueness gives unsatisfactory notice, and indeed would sometimes be unconstitutional on this account; (b) it, at any rate, tends to maximize the amount of litigation over the meaning of the standard.

As to the enforcement aspect of the problem, could the legislature leave it to the district attorney, or to aggrieved individuals, rather than administrative agencies, to bring court enforcement suits? Again, of course, it sometimes does this. But it foregoes certain advantages of administrative agency adjudications and agency enforcement suits in court. The advantages here would be: quantitatively greater enforcement as a result of continuous supervision; qualitatively better enforcement because of the development of a uniform enforcement policy and because of specialized knowledge on the part of the plaintiff enforcers.

But while this expertise of the agencies is important, you should beware of attempts to exaggerate its extent and its value. Top members of administrative commissions and boards are not always experts in the field involved; and though there are experts on the staff, they are not always expert in the precise area of the agency's field (e.g., a power commission concerned with water power problems may have to hire an engineer whose expertise in water problems is acquired after rather than before the hiring). Moreover, agency experts, like other personnel of bureaucratic organizations, tend to become congealed and conservative in their positions. Federal Judge Wyzanski once put it this way:

253. In support of this paragraph, see Davis, Administrative Law Text 4 (3d ed. 1972).

"One of the dangers of extraordinary experience is that those who have it may fall into the grooves created by their own expertness. They refuse to believe that hurdles which they have learned from experience are insurmountable can in fact be overcome by fresh, independent minds."[254] In addition, the extent of disagreement among the experts is still substantial in many fields. Finally, remember that agency expertise does not necessarily go hand in hand with wise policymaking; that "expertness is not wisdom and that the relative ordering of values in a society — the ultimate problem of choosing between alternative courses of action — is something we do *after* the expert has completed his task of collecting data, describing, and, to a limited extent, predicting."[255] (Emphasis added.)

Some of the interrelations of agencies with legislatures, the Chief Executive, and courts will be treated under other headings below.

5. The Public

Only two aspects of the influence of the public on law will be touched on here: (a) the role of public opinion, and (b) public participation in governmental processes.

a. *Public Opinion*

Consider first a well-known passage from Justice Cardozo about the role of public opinion or public values in the shaping of a judicial decision: "When the legislature has spoken, and declared one interest superior to another, the judge must subordinate his personal or subjective estimate of value to the estimate thus declared. . . . Even when the legislature has not spoken, he is to regulate his estimate of values by objective rather than subjective standards, by the thought and will of the community rather than by his own idiosyncrasies of conduct and belief."[256] What is not so often noted is the subsequent passage in which Cardozo observes that when the objective and subjective standards differ, there is no authoritative declaration or definition of the difference to help the judge. He will "have no standard of value available except his own"; "the objective will for him be merged

254. U.S. v. United Shoe Mach. Corp., 110 F. Supp. 295, 346 (D. Mass. 1953).

255. Schwartz, Legal Restriction of Competition in the Regulated Industries: An Abdication of Judicial Responsibility, 67 Harv. L. Rev. 436, 472 (1954). See generally Freedman, Expertise and the Administrative Process, 28 Ad. L. Rev. 363 (1976).

256. Cardozo, The Growth of the Law 95 (1924).

in the subjective." The judge thus "interprets the social conscience and gives effect to it in law, but in so doing he helps to form and modify the conscience he interprets. Discovery and creation react upon each other."[257]

This rather inevitable personal or creative contribution of the judge even when he purports to be effectuating "the thought and will of the community" is still stronger in a constitutional as distinguished from a common law case — though Chief Justice Stone coalesced the two kinds of cases when he said that the "sober second thought of the community . . . is the firm base on which all law must ultimately rest."[258] Constitutional cases receive my special emphasis since the very reason the clauses being construed ("due process," "equal protection," "unreasonable searches and seizures," etc.) were put into the Constitution was to *restrain* the community majority — acting through its legislatures or officials — from actions prohibited by those clauses. It is true, however, that in interpreting what those clauses prohibit, the court need not and should not ignore whatever light might be thrown on them by both historical and contemporary community values. So too in determining the "rationality" of the legislative judgment on a subject, a court can find some relevance in public opinion on the subject. Such opinion belongs in the category of "legislative facts" that are relevant to constitutional decision (i.e., facts bearing directly upon the policy judgments to be made, as distinct from the facts about what the parties did and the happenings that affected them, known as "adjudicative facts").[259]

Though not in definitive fashion, the Supreme Court has in fact referred to contemporary public opinion from time to time in considering constitutional issues. The 1972 death penalty case is an example. In this *Furman* decision, two of the five-man majority that found a violation of the "cruel and unusual punishment" clause[260] referred to public opinion. Their decisions had to take into account opinion polls *approving* the death penalty; and Justice Brennan did so by claiming the extremely infrequent application of the death penalty undermined the significance of the polls and showed that "contemporary society views this punishment with substantial doubt."[261] Justice Marshall thought that public opinion on this subject may well be based on ignorance or misinformation, and that it would change in the light of accurate knowledge.[262] The four dissenters joined in

257. *Id.* at 95-97.
258. Stone, The Common Law in the United States, 50 Harv. L. Rev. 4, 25 (1936).
259. See Karst, Legislative Facts in Constitutional Litigation, 1960 S. Ct. Rev. 75.
260. Furman v. Georgia, 408 U.S. 238 (1972). The death penalty cases are discussed earlier in this chapter, at nn. 25-29, and in App. 2 at nn. 214, 216-220.
261. *Furman* at 300.
262. *Id.* at 361-369.

the skeptical or equivocal feelings of Chief Justice Burger[263] and Justice Powell[264] about the significance of public opinion for this litigation or other constitutional litigation.

In the 1973 abortion decision invalidating the then typical state prohibition against abortion (on grounds of a privacy right embodied in the due process clause),[265] public opinion was not discussed except for the glancing treatment in the Rehnquist dissent: "Even today, when society's views on abortion are changing, the very existence of the debate is evidence that the 'right' to an abortion is not so universally accepted as the appellants would have us believe."[226] That the majority did not cite the opinion polls may be due to the fact that while society's views were indeed changing (i.e., as scholars have observed "the level of support [for abortion] was increasing in the late 1960s and early 1970s") still it was "not evident that a majority (or even a plurality) supported the pro-choice position by 1973. Even by early 1974, the margin of preference for that position was small enough to have resulted only from sampling error in the Gallup surveys."[267]

Thus both the death penalty and abortion decisions went to the verge of judicial power in invalidating the legislative judgment of a multitude of states on matters of great public moment, in spite of the absence of clear support in public opinion for the invalidation. I do not suggest, as some have done, that the decisions represent a usurpation of power. For I remind you of the fact that public opinion while relevant, is not a controlling consideration; and that constitutional restraints, which are of course to be interpreted by courts, were *in-*

263. *Id.* at 385-386: "Without assessing the reliability of such polls, or intimating that any judicial reliance could ever be placed on them, it need only be noted that the reported results have shown nothing approximating the universal condemnation of capital punishment that might lead us to suspect that the legislatures in general have lost touch with current social values."

264. After noting that public opinion had not been shown to be against capital punishment, he said, "[b]ut however one may assess the amorphous ebb and flow of public opinion generally on this volatile issue, this type of inquiry lies at the periphery — not the core — of the judicial process in constitutional cases. The assessment of popular opinion is essentially a legislative, not a judicial function" (at 443).

265. See *supra* n.42. See also *supra* nn. 58 & 59.

266. Roe v. Wade, 410 U.S. 113, 198 (1973).

267. Uslaner & Weber, Public Support for Pro-Choice Abortion Policies in the Nation and States: Changes and Stability After the Roe and Doe Decisions, 77 Mich. L. Rev. 1772, 1773 (1979). The authors say that support then rose slowly to 59% in 1976, dropped to 53% in 1977, and rose to 60% in 1979 (at 1775). Support was much higher when questions were focused on certain specific circumstances (defect in baby, mother's health threatened, pregnancy resulting from rape). On the general question of abortion for up to a three- or four-month pregnancy, and on the questions concerning special circumstances, there was a rise in support in 1973 over 1972 (the Supreme Court decision was in January 1973) ranging from 7 to 9% according to Harris and NORC polls (at 1775-1776), but a substantially smaller increase according to Gallup polls measuring the change from 1972 to 1974 (at 1777).

tended to restrain legislative majorities. And I suggest further that, as we shall later see,[268] when the rights involved are as deeply personal as those in these two cases, it has been customary for courts to shed the traditional presumption favoring legislative judgment in constitutional interpretation.

Nonetheless, the Court surely feels the need to tread carefully in its infrequent role as educator, rather than reflector, of opinion. It risks loss of prestige as well as retaliation. We are familiar with public hostility (sometimes geographically concentrated) to the Supreme Court over the Warren Court's personal liberty and equal protection decisions.[269] We know that the California public overruled by constitutional amendment (Art. I, §27) the California Supreme Court invalidation of the death penalty.[270] We know that the United States Supreme Court decisions on abortion, school prayers, and busing to implement school desegregation have recently provoked drastic congressional proposals aimed at circumventing those decisions. In general, the Court must reckon with what has been called the "profound antiliberalism latent throughout our society."[271] These pressures the Court deals with help to explain why the death penalty and abortion decisions represent what I describe earlier in this chapter (p. 14) as "the *unusual* instance of a strong legal change, in an area of controversial moral attitudes, being made by a court's invalidation of a legislative judgment even though popular sentiment for the change does *not* represent a strong majority."

b. Public Participation

The other legal aspect of the public that I want to say something about is the relatively recent phenomenon described as "public participation." Of course the phenomenon is not wholly new; but by reviewing developments over the last couple of decades or so, one sees a rather steady expansion of the public's right to participate in government processes. In the field of elections, statutes and decisions

268. See Chap. 5 herein under **C1**.

269. See Choper, Judicial Review and the National Political Process 165-166 (1980).

270. People v. Anderson, 6 Cal. 3d 628, 493 P.2d 880 (1972).

271. "Over the years a series of carefully structured studies, surveys and polls, as well as assorted grab-bag questionnaire arrangements ascertaining the views of groups of questionable representatives, all have probed and examined the attitudes of Americans toward civil liberties. Apparently without exception, these studies record profound antiliberalism latent throughout our society." Choper, *supra* n.269 at 163, quoting from Krislov, The Supreme Court and Political Freedom (1968) and citing discussion at 39-53 of the latter. Other sources are cited in Choper's discussion at 163-164.

have worked substantially to overcome barriers to voting and to participation by would-be candidates.[272] Direct participation in government administration was called for by the Economic Opportunity Act of 1964 with its "community action" boards and its requirement of "maximum feasible participation." Analogous provisions were in other antipoverty, housing, health, and education legislation of the 1960s.[273] In addition, the 1972 Federal Advisory Committee Act authorized and controlled the agency practice of using committees of unpaid representatives of particular interests in the community as sounding boards for policy development;[274] and a trend has developed in the states for inclusion of public representatives on state licensing boards.[275] As distinguished from participation in administration, opportunity to be heard administratively received a big boost in the 1960s and early 1970s, both when the individuals or groups involved were the specific object of adverse government action,[276] and when they simply wished to participate in an agency proceeding that might adversely affect their interest — a participation that Congress was in some instances willing to subsidize.[277] Three recent (though attenuated) forms of participation or opportunity to be heard administratively should also be mentioned: (1) making use of an "ombudsman" (official receiver of public complaints about the action or inaction of government officials) — a European technique that has been making very slow headway in American state and local governments;[278] (2) seizing the opportunity afforded by the "freedom of information" type of statute to obtain information from government files — a statute enacted by many states, and by Congress in 1966 (and strengthened in 1974);[279] (3) utilizing the "sunshine" or "open meeting" laws (throwing open to the public most of the meetings of most public bodies) enacted in all the states, and by Congress in 1977.[280]

272. Mermin, Participation in Governmental Processes, in Pennock & Chapman, eds., Participation in Politics 136-137 (1975).

273. *Id.* at 137-138.

274. See 86 Stat. 770 (1972), 5 U.S.C., App. I; Perritt & Wilkinson, Open Advisory Committees and the Political Process: The Federal Advisory Committee Act After Two Years, 63 Geo. L.J. 725 (1975); Markham, The Federal Advisory Committee Act, 35 U. Pitt. L. Rev. 557 (1974). Some agency statutes have provided specifically for representation from the general public as well as from industry. Also the Advisory Committee Act provided for *open* committee meetings with some exceptions that Congress in the Sunshine Act (5 U.S.C. §552b) amended, making them the same exceptions provided in the latter Act.

275. See N. Y. Times, Feb. 20, 1977, §E, at 6.

276. Mermin, *supra* n.272 at 138-140; Friendly, Some Kind of Hearing, 123 U. Pa. L. Rev. 1267 (1975); Mashaw, The Supreme Court's Due Process Calculus For Administrative Adjudication . . . ," 44 U. Chi. L. Rev. 28 (1976).

277. Mermin, *supra* n.272 at 140-143; Gellhorn et al., *supra* n.211 at 634-674.

278. Mermin, *id.*, references at 156, n.52.

279. Gellhorn et al., *supra* n.211 at 579-624.

280. *Id.* at 628-634.

Public participation in government processes might be viewed as also including the opportunity to be heard *in court*. The threshold requirement of "standing" to sue — which is discussed in Chapter 2 — has generally been loosened in recent years. The significance of this increasing freedom is heightened by the growth of two techniques for maximizing the public's access to courts: the "class action," which makes economically feasible the bringing of lawsuits by consumers, welfare recipients, etc. who could not afford to bring individual lawsuits; and the bringing of suits by "public interest" law centers and law firms. Specifically concerning the poor, an enlarged participation in both civil and criminal cases has been made possible by substantial provision of free legal services and invalidation of at least some fee barriers to suits and appeals. Also, the Supreme Court has been recognizing a right to be heard in court at an *earlier* stage of certain legal processes than has traditionally been permitted. Courts have been requiring greater court hearing rights than previously enjoyed for juveniles, defendants under certain sex deviate laws, defendants who are to be committed for institutional examination after a finding of insanity, and persons who are the subject of civil commitment proceedings.[281]

Miscellaneous additional trends of participation might be mentioned. One proposal now being urged is that a citizen who is a party in that governmental process known as a lawsuit should participate more fully by a more complete control of his lawyer. The proposal envisages a "participatory model" for lawyer-client relations (as distinct from the more "traditional model" in which the lawyer is almost in complete charge, in spite of the fact that theoretically the 1969 ABA Code of Professional Responsibility seems to favor the participatory model).[282] Public participation in the court process has also been enlarged by broadened participation in juries — i.e., through court decisions invalidating systematic exclusions of racial minorities, and more recently, of women, from jury service in criminal cases. Finally, some statutes on particular subjects have specifically authorized citizen enforcement suits against law violators.[283]

6. Some Interrelations Among the Law's Agencies

In the course of dealing with the major categories of the agencies of law, I have already hinted at some interrelations among them, as in the

281. On this paragraph, see Mermin, *supra* n.272 at 144-146; this chapter under D1b(4).

282. Mermin, *id.* at 147-148; Rosenthal, Lawyer and Client: Who's In Charge? (1974). See also Chap. 5 herein, text at nn. 68-71.

283. Mermin, *supra* n.272 at 148-149.

case of executive pressure on legislatures and legislative supervision over the agencies. What I want to do here is sketch a broader — though still not complete — picture of interrelationships. I hope to explain why it can be said that instead of the theoretical ideal of a "separation" of judicial, legislative, and executive power we have in fact a sharing or integration of power — not only a mixture of functions within each of the three major institutions, but also mutual interactions among them, of control and countercontrol.

a. Chief Executive and Executive-Administrative Agencies

Before considering examples of truly *inter*agency relations, let me first dispose of what looks, in part at least, like an *intra*agency relation. I refer to the relation between the Chief Executive and the executive and administrative agencies.

1. I referred earlier to the fact that an administrative agency has more independence from the President than does the executive department within the President's Cabinet. This has given rise to two major criticisms. One is that semi-independence makes more difficult the effective coordination of policies and programs by the Chief Executive (who, moreover, has been popularly elected, whereas the agency members have not). The second criticism is that relative lack of executive control makes more possible an often-noted phenomenon: an agency tendency to lose its initial regulatory zeal, and to identify the public interest with the interest of the regulated industry.

The second criticism is more vulnerable to rebuttal than the first, since the regular departments may have as much tendency toward industry orientation as the administrative agencies. Says a veteran administrative law scholar: "Anyone who follows the activities of the Department of Agriculture, for example, comes to feel (though this too is no doubt an exaggeration) that the Department is a glorified farmers' lobby." And it is doubtful "that an executive agency will be much different from an independent agency in periods when public opinion or statutory policy [or, he might have added, executive policy] is slack, indeterminate, or lacking in conviction."[284] Notice that the last sentence includes a reference to indeterminate statutory policy — a particular point of comment by students of the administrative agency. There is much room for improvement, it is argued, in the legislature's formulation of standards: it could, by clearer policy guidance than is afforded by statutory phrases like "the public interest,"

284. Jaffe, Book Review, 65 Yale L.J. 1068, 1071, 1074 (1956).

counteract the tendency to industry orientation, and help resolve uncertainties for the public and courts as well as for the agencies.[285]

Semi-independence has another interesting aspect worth noting: its impact on the executive power of removal of officers. The Supreme Court has held that the President could freely remove a subordinate executive employee (a postmaster) from office without the congressional consent that Congress had specified as necessary;[286] but that the President could not remove a quasi-judicial officer (Federal Trade Commissioner; War Claims Commissioner) on the ground of disapproval of his policies or wanting a man of his own selection, when Congress had specified not these but other grounds (inefficiency, neglect of duty or malfeasance) as a basis for removal,[287] or when Congress had been silent on removal.[288] These cases, however, do not seem to prevent a President from achieving removal of such a commissioner by a different path. If he were to file charges of inefficiency and neglect of duty and, after hearing, remove him, a court's deference to executive fact finding in such a situation would probably lead it to affirm, even if the proof were slight. Moreover, "[e]ven though members of most of the so-called independent boards and commissions are dismissable only for cause and sometimes only for very explicitly stated causes such as malfeasance or neglect of duty, an unelaborated request for a resignation has rarely been ignored, perhaps because the person involved preferred not to risk too explicit a statement of why he should give up his office."[289]

2. What comes before removal of course is appointment. The President's appointing power is a potent one, not only in relation to the high level personnel in the various departments of his Cabinet but also to the members of the independent agencies. The latter serve terms of five, six, or seven years, with one member's appointment expiring each year; and there is a tendency of members not to serve for a full term. Hence the President has a real chance to influence

285. *Id.* at 1072-1074; Friendly, The Federal Administrative Agencies: The Need for a Better Definition of Standards (1962).

286. Myers v. U.S., 272 U.S. 52 (1926).

287. Rathbun, Humphrey's Executor v. U.S., 295 U.S. 602 (1935).

288. Wiener v. U.S., 357 U.S. 349 (1958).

289. Gellhorn et al., *supra* n.211 at 130. In explanation of the reference to "most" independent agencies: "The members of the Federal Communications Commission, the Federal Energy Regulatory Commission, and the Securities and Exchange Commission, unlike their counterparts in other agencies are not statutorily protected against summary removal from office . . ."—apparently because those agencies were created after the postmaster case and before the FTC and War Claims Commission cases, "at a time when legislative draftsmen believed the President's power to be illimitable." *Id.* at 131 & n.7. Members of the three agencies mentioned doubtless have no less protection against summary removal, in view of the fact that the statute in the War Claims Commissioner case (*Weiner, supra* n.288) had also been silent on removal.

administrative agency policy through appointments — a majority of which, some studies also suggest, have been made for "partisan political reasons."[290] Congress cannot take this appointing power to itself. In 1976 the Supreme Court invalidated the statutory requirement that some members of the Federal Election Commission be congressional rather than presidential appointees.[291]

3. Equally important as an executive control over administrative agencies is a presidential bureau (the Office of Management and Budget, previously described under the "Chief Executive" heading), which exercises a coordinating and "oversight" function over executive and administrative agency activity as well as handling their requests for substantive legislation and for funds.[292] The OMB played the central role in the Executive Order efforts of Presidents Ford, Carter, and Reagan to coordinate and control more closely than hitherto the regulations issued by executive and administrative agencies. Under the Ford Order,[293] major rules, regulations, or legislative proposals emanating from "executive branch agencies" had to be accompanied by an "inflation impact" statement; and OMB developed the criteria for identifying these "major" rules and proposals and prescribed procedures for their evaluation by the agencies. The Carter Order covered broader ground. It required that the heads of executive agencies (the "independent regulatory agencies" were again exempted) make specific determinations regarding understandability and burdensomeness of "significant" regulations, and that a "regulatory analysis" be prepared for those significant regulations that "may have major economic consequences for the general economy, for individual industries, geographical regions or levels of government," among other requirements.[294] And the OMB was to "assure the effective implementation of this Order." After publication in the Federal Register of their preliminary plans and criteria for compliance with the Order, the agencies had to submit their revised drafts to the OMB for approval before final publication.

290. *Id.* at 126-127.

291. Buckley v. Valeo, 424 U.S. 1 (1976).

292. See Berman, The Office of Management and Budget and the Presidency, 1921-1979 (1981).

293. Exec. Order No. 11,821 (1974), 3 C.F.R. 926-927 (1971-1975 Compilation).

294. Exec. Order No. 12,044 (1978), 43 Fed. Reg. 12,661, *reprinted in* 7 U.S. Code Cong. & Ad. News 9680 (1978). The agencies had to publish at least semiannually an agenda of "significant" regulations under development or review. The agency head had to exercise "oversight" before development of any significant new regulation. An early and meaningful opportunity had to be given to the public to participate in the development of regulations. Before a proposed significant regulation was published for comment, the agency head must first have found that certain specified criteria had been met (e.g., the regulation had to be the least burdensome of acceptable alternatives, written in plain English, and understandable to those subject to it; an estimate of the new reporting or recordkeeping burdens involved had to be

The Reagan Executive Order is broader still, and the power of the OMB stronger and more explicit. The Order, it has been said, gives "OMB tremendous power over the substance and timing of regulations," and "new opportunities for interested persons to influence the regulatory process," i.e., by attempting to influence the OMB.[295] Under the Order, executive agencies (again the "independent federal regulatory agencies" are exempted) must find, before undertaking regulatory action, that "the potential benefits to society outweigh the potential costs to society"; they must aim at "maximizing the net benefits to society" and select "the alternative involving the least net cost to society"; and they must establish regulatory priorities that maximize the "aggregate net benefits to society, taking into account the condition of the particular industries affected by the regulations, the condition of the national economy, and other regulatory actions contemplated for the future." "Major" rules, affecting the economy in a substantial way, must meet special requirements, including issuance of a "Regulatory Impact Analysis," for existing as well as proposed major rules.[296] This RIA would analyze costs and benefits and explain why less costly alternatives could not legally be adopted.

---

included; and a plan had to be developed for evaluating the regulation after issuance).

Agencies were ordered to establish criteria, including effect on competition, burdensomeness, and relation to other programs and agencies, for identifying which regulations were "significant." The criteria for determining which of the significant regulations required a "regulatory analysis" had to ensure that such analyses were performed for all regulations resulting in "an annual effect on the economy of $100 million or more," or "a major increase in costs or price for individual industries, levels of government or geographic regions"; and had to permit such analyses to be performed at the agency head's discretion, for any proposed regulation. Agencies had to periodically review existing regulations to determine whether their standards were achieving the policy goals of the Executive Order. Among the exemptions were regulations issued on a formal trial-type hearing record (the usual regulation is not).

President Carter also established a Regulatory Analysis Review Group (RARG) to review the analyses accompanying proposed regulations, and a Regulatory Council, composed both of executive departments and independent regulatory agencies. The Council coordinated and dealt with problems of overlapping, duplicating, and conflicting regulations. It also published a Calendar of Federal Regulations to give an overview of the most important federal regulatory activities under development. The Administrative Conference of the United States issued a guide to assist the agencies. 43 Fed. Reg. 36,412 (1978).

295. Rosenthal, Executive Order on Regulation Boosts OMB's Power, Legal Times of Washington, March 16, 1981, at 14. It is Exec. Order No. 12,291, Feb. 17, 1981, 46 Fed. Reg. 13,193 (1981).

296. When I say "substantial way" I am referring to the definition of "major rule," which repeats the Carter Order's conditions for mandatory regulatory analysis (see the reference *supra* n.294 to annual effect on the economy and major increase in cost or prices) and adds the following concern: significant adverse effects on competition, employment, investment, productivity, innovation, or on the ability of United States-based enterprises to compete with foreign-based enterprises in domestic or export markets.

The OMB exercises close supervision in this respect, subject to direction of the Presidential Task Force on Regulatory Relief. And before approval of a major rule, the agency, in a memorandum of law published in the Federal Register, must determine that the rule is authorized by the statute and the factual conclusions have "substantial support in the agency record, viewed as a whole."

Though obviously influential, the OMB cannot legally force its position on the agency; but it can require an agency to make an RIA and demand that its critical comments along with the RIA be part of the public record. It also has discretion, subject to Task Force direction, to exempt any class of regulations from any or all requirements of the Order. The Order applies only "to the extent permitted by law," and would therefore bow to contrary provisions of any statute.[297]

Among other problems,[298] doubtless the greatest difficulty presented by the Order is how to weigh economic costs against non-economic benefits (health, life, safety, fair and equal treatment, conservation of resources and environment, esthetic satisfaction, and the like). Along with other issues in the methodology and proper role of cost-benefit analysis, this crucial consideration has produced, and will continue to produce, a lively literature.[299]

4. Whatever the difficulties in administering the specific economic concerns of this Order, there is no doubt that its function of *coordination* under the President of heterogeneous agencies' rulemaking activity

297. One such statute was the Occupational Safety and Health Act, which the Supreme Court in 1981 interpreted as not having intended a cost-benefit standard to be applied to OSHA's "cotton dust standard." American Textile Mfrs. Instit. v. Donovan, 69 L. Ed. 2d 185 (1981).

298. Criticisms have been made, for instance, that the judgments of the OMB and the presidential Task Force will be more political than expert; that the additional burdens put on agencies by the Order will substantially aggravate the problem of delay and cost in agency operations; that the Order is excessively concerned with economic considerations; and that there are ambiguities to be resolved, such as: What statutory language of the agency's governing statute will allow a court to say that the different criteria of the Order are "permitted by law"? What standard of judicial review is to be applied by the courts in reviewing the record of adoption of a regulation pursuant to the Order? Bliss, Regulatory Reform: Toward More Balanced and Flexible Federal Agency Regulation, 8 Pepperdine L. Rev. 619, 633-637 (1981).

299. See Note, Benefit Analysis: An Inadequate Basis for Health, Safety and Environmental Regulatory Decisionmaking, 8 Ecology L.Q. 473 (1980); Use of Cost-Benefit Analysis By Regulatory Agencies: Joint Hearings Before Subcomm. on Oversight and Investigations and Subcomm. on Consumer Protection and Finance of the House Interstate and Foreign Commerce Comm., 96th Cong., 1st Sess. (1979); Symposium, Cost-Risk-Benefit Assessment and the Law, 45 Geo. Wash. L. Rev. 901 (1977); Subcomm. on Oversight and Investigations, House Comm. on Interstate and Foreign Commerce, Federal Regulation and Regulatory Reform, 94th Cong., 2nd Sess. 505-515, 555 (1976) [Subcommittee Print]; Symposium, Valuing Lives, 40 L. & Contemp. Probs., No. 4, esp. 5-72 (1976); Green, The Risk-Benefit Calculus in Safety Determinations, 43 Geo. Wash. L. Rev. 791 (1975); Handler, A Rebuttal: The Need For A Sufficient Scientific Base For Government Regulation, *id.* at 808.

(in addition to development of more uniform criteria in the approach to economic regulation) represents a defensible and increasingly popular idea. Thus a 1975 proposal by two practitioners, under which Congress would authorize the President to have even *more* control over regulations than under the 1981 Order (i.e., *"to modify or direct"* both executive and independent agency rulemaking when necessary to achieve "an important national objective," as well as "to set priorities among competing statutory goals) — subject to a one-House congressional veto and to expedited judicial review"[300] — has been well received even in academic circles.[301] Inclusion of the one-House veto, a technique discussed later under "Legislature and Administrative Agencies," is important. Without it, Congress would not be likely to accede to the proposed heightening of presidential power. The power would apply, remember, to even the independent agencies (agencies that Congress tends to think of as closer to itself than the executive bureaus). Rather than answering only to the executive branch, agencies, through the inclusion of the veto, would come under the close supervision of both Congress and the President. This bringing of agencies into line with the "politically accountable branches of government" is presumably a worthy goal in a democracy.

However, is the proposal constitutionally valid? As will appear in a later discussion, it is not yet clear whether the one-House veto as applied to regulations is constitutional; nor is its validity clear as applied to presidential directives. Validity of just the congressional permission for substantive control by the President over rules of executive and independent agencies is somewhat more clear.[302] What

300. Cutler & Johnson, Regulation and the Political Process, 84 Yale L.J. 1395, 1414 (1975).

301. Byse, Comments on a Structural Reform Proposal: Presidential Directives to Independent Agencies, 29 Ad. L. Rev. 157 (1977); Gellhorn et al., *supra* n.211 at 134, n.10. But see Robinson, On Reorganizing Independent Regulatory Agencies, 57 Va. L. Rev. 947, 984 (1971); Friendly, The Federal Administrative Agencies 153 et seq. (1962). An ABA Commission has supported similar statutory rulemaking powers for the President with respect to "critical regulatory issues" (those that are of major significance to the national economic interest and "to the achievement of statutory goals other than the goal primarily entrusted to the regulatory agency in question"). ABA Commission on Law and the Economy, Federal Regulation: Roads to Reform 101 (1978).

302. It is true that previously discussed decisions distinguished between executive agencies and the "independent" or quasi-judicial, quasi-legislative agencies (so as to permit presidential removal of a postmaster without the congressional consent that a statute had specified as necessary, but to *preclude* removal of a Federal Trade Commissioner or War Claims Commissioner on grounds other than those expressly or impliedly contemplated by Congress for removal). But these decisions do not seem to stand in the way. In the latter two Commissioner cases the will of Congress stood in the way of the particular presidential control of independent agency personnel. Under the proposal, the will of Congress does not stand in the way of presidential direction of independent agency rulemaking; it *authorizes* presidential direction. As for the objection that the Chief Executive would be exercising legislative rather

may be legally more questionable are presidential exercises of such powers (and some have already occurred)[303] *without* the proposed statutory authorization. I.e., a statute that has entrusted the rulemaking authority to a particular official or agency (rather than, as sometimes happens, to the President who then delegates authority) *might* be read as a grant of exclusive authority, precluding presidential rule modification or direction, or perhaps even presidential "jaw-boning."

5. There are still other modes of Chief Executive influence over the agencies. One is a power to organize a new agency to carry out some of the President's executive powers — as, for instance, was done in World War II with creation of labor, price, and transportation agencies by Executive Order (with Congress sometimes displacing the authority

---

than executive power, the executive and independent agencies have been doing so all along, by delegation from Congress of the rulemaking power; Congress would now be delegating to the Chief Executive. Further, under the proposal any agency rule resulting from the President's directive would be subject to judicial review for conformity with the statutory powers of the agency and other applicable statutes as well as with constitutional requirements. Conceivably, though, a court might object that the grant of power to the President is *standardless* and hence an invalid delegation of legislative power, Note, 89 Yale L.J. 561, 573-578 (1980).

As for an objection that constitutional due process considerations bar the White House from making "ex parte" contacts (i.e., unrecorded contacts with government personnel by an interested party, in what purports to be an "open" agency proceeding): The judicial ban on such "ex parte" contacts has indeed been applied to contacts by private persons, and by Congressmen, in *formal* proceedings; and there has been some lower court extension of the ban to *some kinds* of agency informal proceedings including rulemaking, and some thinking that courts might take the more controversial step of extending the ban further to White House contacts. See Bruff, Presidential Power and Administrative Rulemaking, 88 Yale L.J. 451, 500-508 (1979). But (1) it is doubtful that the Supreme Court would thus extend the ban to White House contacts in connection with informal (i.e., "notice and comment") rulemaking. See Verkuil, Jawboning Administrative Agencies: Ex Parte Contacts By the White House, 80 Colum. L. Rev. 943, 970-982 (1980). (2) In any event, the proposed presidential powers differ from the influence exerted in the "ex parte" cases not only in being congressionally authorized but also in not fitting the "ex parte" description. The President's Executive Order could not be issued until 30 days after publication in the Federal Register of his proposed action, together with supporting findings, and an opportunity in that period for written comment; and a public record of such comments and ex parte contacts would have to be kept. See Cutler & Johnson, *supra* n.300 at 1415; Verkuil, *supra* at 983-985. Similarly inapplicable would be the *statutory* ban under the Administrative Procedure Act (5 U.S.C. §557(d)) against ex parte communications "relative to the merits of the proceeding," from any interested person outside the agency to anyone who is, or may be expected to be, involved in the decisional process of a *formal* proceeding. Any such written communications, memoranda stating the substance of oral communications, written responses and memoranda stating the substance of oral responses, must be made part of the public record. "Ex parte communication" is defined in 5 U.S.C. §551(14) as "an oral or written communication not on the public record with respect to which reasonable prior notice to all parties is not given, but it shall not include requests for status reports. . . ."

303. See Verkuil, *supra* n.302 at 944-947 (concerning the Secretary of Labor's cotton dust standard, the Environmental Protection Agency's ozone level standard, and the Secretary of Interior's stripmining rules).

of the Order by a statute on the subject), and as was done by Nixon in creation of the Cost of Living Council in 1971 to administer wage and price restraints. On this matter of delegation by the President — either of his existing executive power or powers delegated to him by statute — it is of course true that an occasional statute may require particular decisions to be made only by the Chief Executive, or only by the head of an agency. But in the absence of such provision, it is usually assumed that the authority to delegate to subordinates does exist; and in 1950 Congress officially recognized the President's authority, within certain broad limits, by the Presidential Subdelegation Act. Not only can the President organize, he can reorganize agencies, and has done so — by virtue of a series of short-term statutes commencing in 1932, under which a Reorganization Plan sent to the Congress is subject to disapproval by either House.[304]

In addition, the President can influence the attitudes and actions of executive and administrative personnel through policies communicated in Cabinet meetings, speeches, press conference statements, and informal contacts.[305]

6. In spite of the foregoing catalogue of presidential influences, some strong practical limits must be recognized. Scholars point to the fact that agencies become allied to or influenced by legislative committees and subcommittees, the industries being regulated, and other interest groups. This alignment, along with the "transitory nature of political leadership, the entrenched position of an increasingly professionalized public service [serves] to undermine the already limited capacity of the president to function as 'administrator-in-chief' of the modern administrative state."[306] The Hoover Commission is described as reporting a generation ago that "administrative organizations have become so fragmented by Congressional interest in their management that 'many departments and agencies are but loose federations of bureaus and subdivisions, each jealously defending its own jurisdiction.' "[307] President Truman claimed that presidential power amounted to the power "to bring people in and try to persuade them to do what they ought to do without persuasion"; and the Russian Tsar Nicholas is quoted as saying that Russia was ruled not by himself but by 10,000 clerks.[308]

304. On this paragraph, see Gellhorn et al., *supra* n.211 at 142-144. For details on reorganizations see Dodd & Schott, *supra* n.233 at 331-348; Mansfield, Federal Executive Reorganization: Thirty Years of Experience, 29 Public Ad. Rev. 341 (1969).

305. See Verkuil, *supra* n.302; Robinson, The Federal Communications Commission: An Essay on Regulatory Watchdogs, 64 Va. L. Rev. 169, 206-212 (1978).

306. Dodd & Schott, *supra* n.233 at 322.

307. Gellhorn et al., *supra* n.211 at 143.

308. *Id.* at 144-145. The disease affects agency heads as well as Presidents. Warner Gardner, an experienced Washington practitioner, once said, "I have discovered to my cost that the directions of an Assistant Secretary of Interior to the

While the OMB has had some coordinating effect, the tendency of the independent agencies is to follow the clearance procedure less fully than the executive bureaus have. Congress, in the creation of particular agencies, has sometimes called for direct submission of budgetary and substantive requests and comments to Congress *no later* than the submission to OMB; and bills have been introduced to free all independent agencies from the OMB's prior coordination process.[309] This refusal of Congress to give up control introduces the subject of the next section.

b. Legislature and Executive

The indicated clash between the President and Congress in the control of the agencies is not the only area of conflict.

1. First established in the Constitution's outlining of those powers of the two branches that curb each other, and later developed in the practical operation of government, the thrusts and counter-thrusts of the legislature and executive have become a prominent feature of our government. The President's veto power[310] over congressionally approved bills is just one of these checks. He also of course exerts influence over Congress through his power over patronage, the allocation of funds and projects, and the doing of favors asked by legislators or their constituents. More indirect presidential pressure is wielded through, for instance, the kind of direct appeals to the voter that were mentioned above in discussing presidential pressure on the agencies.

You know, too, that Congress exerts counter-controls. By a two-thirds vote of both Houses, a veto can be overridden. Congress also exercises a veto of its own — the "legislative veto" by which Congress or one House or committee thereof may, pursuant to a statute, disapprove the exercise of authority that it has delegated to the President

---

Bureau of Reclamation, with its wide congressional and popular support, can hardly be more than hortatory. I have been consoled by the discovery that the same may be said of the directions of the Secretaries of War as to the civil work of the Corps of Engineers." Gardner, The Administrative Process, in Paulsen, ed., Legal Institutions Today and Tomorrow 123 n.47 (1959).

309. Gellhorn et al., *supra* n.211 at 140-141.

310. A counterpart, of course, exists on the state level: In the case of appropriation bills, twentieth-century state constitutional amendments gave governors authority to veto in whole or in part (the latter being an "item veto"). The item veto power "materially increased not only the governor's formal power but also his bargaining power with the legislature, compared with the all-or-nothing options to which the general veto restricted him. By late twentieth century the item veto has become a firmly entrenched part of state fiscal policy, in controversy only insofar as a governor might in practice try to stretch it to allow him to strike substantive policy items from a bill because the bill appropriated money." Hurst, Law and Social Order in the United States 111-112 (1977).

or to the agencies (a device that we have referred to in the preceding section on relations between the President and the agencies and that will be discussed more fully below).[311] Presidential appointments are subject to Senate approval, by majority vote, under the constitutional clause that such appointments of federal "officers" be "by and with the advice and consent of the Senate" (though the appointment of "inferior officers" may be vested by Congress "in the President alone, in the courts of law or in the heads of departments"). Congress can remove the President by impeachment, with the House investigating and bringing charges, and the Senate sitting in judgment; you will recall that the impeachment articles voted by the House Judiciary Committee at the end of July, 1974 pressured President Nixon's resignation on August 9, 1974.[312]

2. In general, even though Executive Orders (issued pursuant to the constitutional vesting of executive power in the President) can be significant exercises of power of both an executive and legislative nature, they cannot go beyond certain bounds expressly or impliedly set by the legislature. The legislature may of course expressly confer considerable power on the executive — as, for instance, when it passes a statute authorizing certain authority over a particular subject and authorizes promulgation of legislative-type regulations. And there may be times when the Executive can act without such authorization from Congress if he is acting in an area where executive and legislative authority is deemed to be "concurrent." But if a court concludes that the executive action is inconsistent with the express or implied will of the legislature, the executive action cannot stand. President Truman discovered this truth when the Supreme Court invalidated his 1952 attempt to avert a steel strike by seizing the steel mills during the Korean War.[313]

3. Presidential power over the budget (through the OMB) was substantially modified by Congress's reassertion of budgetary power in the Budget and Impoundment Control Act of 1974. The Act "created new House and Senate budget committees, the Congressional Budget Office (a full-time professional staff for analytical studies), a complex set of budgetary procedures, a time-table for budgetary actions, a change in the fiscal year [to begin October 1], requirements for standardized budget terminology and information for the President's

311. A fuller discussion is to be found under "Legislature and Administrative Agencies."

312. See House Judiciary Comm., Impeachment of Richard M. Nixon, President of the United States, Report No. 93-1305, 93 Cong., 2d Sess. (1974); Black, Impeachment: A Handbook (1974); Berger, Impeachment: The Constitutional Problems (1973).

313. Youngstown Sheet & Tube Co. v. Sawyer, 343 U.S. 579 (1952); Marcus, Truman and the Steel Seizure Case: The Limits of Presidential Power (1977).

budget, and provisions for controlling presidential impoundments."[314] Recent observation suggests that the congressional budget committees "have not been able to take complete control of the budget, but each year they have managed to be more assertive, and their decisions have been reinforced by the House and Senate. Budget-making is still incremental, but the mechanism is in place to allow the Congress to address broad problems generated by the uneven process of accumulation that the previous decisionmaking pattern had difficulty confronting. The 'larger' perspective is encouraged by the Congressional Budget Office."[315]

The provision on "presidential impoundments" in the 1974 law deals with the presidential practice — which had provoked much controversy during the Nixon administration — of refusal to allow spending of actual appropriations for particular purposes. The practice was nothing new, but its limits had never been clearly fixed. The 1974 law introduced an accommodating solution: The Act allows an executive "rescission" or permanent impoundment if the President has sent a special detailed message to both Houses proposing such a move and both Houses respond by approving it within 45 continuous days of congressional session. A "deferral" or temporary impoundment for 12 months or less is allowed if the President sends a special message as above, and neither House passes a resolution disapproving the deferral (no time limits on disapprovals are mentioned).[316] "The new impoundment control process has worked smoothly and has had a significant impact on the pre-1974 trend toward centralization of budget power in the president."[317]

4. Another important aspect of legislative-executive relations is the question of limits on legislative power to obtain information from the executive. Congress has a potent power of investigation,[318] but the executive branch sometimes counters with a power of nondisclosure stemming from the doctrine of "executive privilege." President Eisen-

314. Ellwood & Thurber, The Politics of the Congressional Budget Process Reeexamined, in Dodd & Oppenheimer, Congress Reconsidered 251 (2d ed. 1981).

315. Brenner, An Approach to the Limits and Possibilities of Congress, in Dodd & Oppenheimer, *id.* at 380. The previous pattern referred to was thus described by Ellwood & Thurber, *id.* at 248: "Each year Congress would take the President's total budget, chop it up into small pieces, and parcel them out among committees and subcommittees that would work on them with little regard for the impact their particular changes might have on the whole."

316. See Ellwood & Thurber, *id.* at 246, 264-267; Munselle, Presidential Impoundment and Congressional Reform, in Rieselbach, Legislative Reform 173-181 (1978).

317. Ellwood & Thurber, *supra* at 267. Presidential "deferrals" during 1976-1980 have had a success rate per year ranging from 63 to 99% with a median in the upper 90s; but "rescissions" have been less successful, ranging from 0 to 80% per year: 0 for one year; and 4%, 37%, 46%, and 80% for the other four. *Id.* at 265.

318. See references *supra* n.237.

hower sketched the doctrine broadly when he wrote to a congressional committee that "throughout our history the President has withheld information whenever he found that what was sought was confidential or its disclosure would be incompatible with the public interest or jeopardize the safety of the nation";[319] and the Department of Justice has claimed that a similar privilege exists in the heads of departments.[320] The privilege is seldom invoked, however, against Congress. The Department of Defense reported in 1958 that in a three-year period it had complied with 300,000 inquiries from Congress and had refused to comply in only 13 instances.[321]

There has been more occasion for refusal under the 1966 Freedom of Information Act, pursuant to which the executive and administrative agencies have received multitudinous inquiries from the public as well as from congressional sources. The Act requires disclosure of government records to "any person," with stated exemptions (in 5 U.S.C. §552(b)). While executive privilege is not mentioned as such, something similar is included in the *first exemption,* preserving "national defense or foreign policy matters" that are "(A) specifically authorized under criteria established by an Executive order to be kept secret . . . and (B) are in fact properly classified pursuant to such Executive order"; and in the *fifth exemption,* for "inter-agency or intra-agency memorandums or letters which would not be available by law to a party other than an agency in litigation with the agency"; and in the *seventh exemption,* for "investigatory records compiled for law enforcement purposes," to the extent that disclosures would interfere with enforcement proceedings, disclose investigative techniques and procedures, endanger law enforcement personnel, deprive a person of procedural or privacy rights, disclose identity of a confidential source, or disclose certain confidential information in specified types of cases. "Any reasonably segregable portion of a record shall be provided to any person requesting such record after deletion of" the exempt portions.[322]

319. Hearings on S. 921 (Freedom of Information and Secrecy in Government) Before the Subcomm. on Constitutional Rights, Senate Comm. on the Judiciary, 85th Cong., 2d Sess. 271 (1958).

320. See *id.* at 63-146.

321. *Id.* at 383-387.

322. The wording of the first exemption stems from a 1974 Amendment. The latter attempted to liberalize a holding of E.P.A. v. Mink, 410 U.S. 73 (1973). In that case some members of Congress sought under the Freedom of Information Act to obtain several government documents containing recommendations to the President with respect to underground nuclear testing. The Court held that the executive classification as "Top Secret" or "Secret" was *enough* to trigger the exemption, and that the Act did not authorize or permit the judges' in camera inspection of the classified documents in order to authorize disclosure of nonsecret components. Further, the *fifth* exemption was held not to exempt purely factual material appearing in a form which is severable without compromising the private remainder of the memoranda; but instead of authorizing automatic in camera

Some dramatic executive privilege cases, not under the Freedom of Information Act, were decided in the Nixon era. I am referring not to the "Pentagon Papers" case, whose central problem was not a legislative-executive conflict,[323] but to litigation involving the embattled President in his scandal-wracked second term. After a White House aide had disclosed to Senate investigators that the President had tape recordings of all conversation in the President's office, two subpoenas were issued against the President. One, obtained by Special Prosecutor Archibald Cox from the District of Columbia District Court, required the production, before the grand jury investigating the Watergate alleged criminal conspiracy to obstruct justice (a conspiracy by the President, his Attorney General, and key White House aides),[324] of the tapes and written memoranda recording nine specified conversations. The other, seeking various tapes, was obtained by Senator Sam Ervin's Select Committee investigating the Watergate affair.

a) The suit of the Senate Committee to enforce its subpoena was dismissed by the district court on the ground that the court lacked "jurisdiction," i.e., authority to hear such a case.[325] A later suit under a new jurisdictional statute was dismissed for other reasons. The district

---

inspection by the district court for factual material, the Court said the government should have the burden of showing by affidavits or oral testimony that documents or portions contained no purely factual material. Only if this burden is not met may the district court order an in camera inspection.

The few courts that have had to interpret the new language "have in fact tended to accord substantial weight to executive branch views on classification, and to avoid in camera inspection where circumstances permitted judgment on the basis of a sufficiently detailed affidavit. See, e.g. Weissman v. CIA, 565 F.2d 692 (D.C. Cir. 1977); Note, 26 U. Kan. L. Rev. 617 (1978)." Gellhorn et al., *supra* n.211 at 594.

In 1975 the Supreme Court ruled that the fifth exemption calls for "disclosures of all 'opinions and interpretations'—which embody the agency's effective law and policy, and the withholding of all papers which reflect the agency's group thinking in the process of working out its policy and determining what its law shall be." The Court further ruled that the fifth exemption was intended to include the "attorney work product privilege" which exempts the attorney's work product from civil "discovery" procedures (see, on discovery, Chap. 2 herein under **B9**); and "whatever the outer boundaries of the attorney work product rule are, the rule clearly applies to memoranda prepared by an attorney in contemplation of litigation which set forth the attorney's theory of the case and his litigation strategy." NLRB v. Sears Roebuck & Co., 421 U.S. 132 (1975). Generally on the Act see Gellhorn et al., *supra* n.211 at 579-624; O'Reilly, Federal Information Disclosure (1977).

323. This 1971 decision held that the government had not met its burden of proof to show justification for an injunction (a "prior restraint") against newspaper publication of a confidential Pentagon history of Vietnam War policy; and it left open the question of criminal liability of those doing the publishing and those who unauthorizedly take such documents and supply them for publication. New York Times Co. v. U.S., 403 U.S. 713 (1971). See Henkin, The Right to Know and the Duty to Withhold: The Case of the Pentagon Papers, 120 U. Pa. L. Rev. 271 (1972); Developments in the Law: The National Security Interest and Civil Liberties, 84 Harv. L. Rev. 1130, 1189-1244 (1972).

324. The President was named as a conspirator but was not charged with a criminal offense as were the others.

325. Senate Select Comm. v. Nixon, 366 F. Supp. 51 (D.D.C. 1973). Federal court

court's reason was that the publicity might prejudice the expected criminal trials. Its judgment was affirmed on a different ground: True, "presidential conversations are presumptively privileged," to ensure "that the President and those upon whom he directly relies in the performance of his duties could continue to work under a general assurance that their deliberations would remain confidential." The presumption "can be defeated only by a strong showing of need by another institution of government." But here the subpoenaed evidence was not "demonstrably critical to the responsible fulfillment of the Committee's functions." Since creation of the Senate Committee, the House Judiciary Committee had begun its impeachment inquiry and already possessed copies of each of the five subpoenaed tapes; and the President had publicly released transcripts, with partial deletions, of each of the tapes in question, and had transmitted the originals of four of the tapes to the district court in response to a grand jury subpoena.[326]

b) The litigation involving the grand jury subpoena and a later subpoena after the grand jury indictment does not squarely reflect a Congress-President conflict, but is relevant to such conflicts because the litigation ended in the Supreme Court and revealed that Court's attitude on executive privilege. In spite of Nixon's claim of executive privilege, District Judge Sirica ordered the President to produce the tapes and papers for the grand jury and was affirmed by the court of appeals.[327] At this point, Nixon changed his tactics. Claiming he would no longer submit the issue to the courts, he agreed to let the court have only those of the nine tapes which Senator Stennis of Georgia (a conservative, friendly to the idea of executive privilege) thought should be delivered, and he would not turn over any subpoenaed papers. He instructed the Special Prosecutor not to seek court aid for production of evidence withheld under claim of executive privilege. On Cox's refusal, Nixon dismissed him. This "evoked a public reaction which [Nixon's] chief aide later described as a 'fire storm.' Within seventy-two hours the President changed his mind and promised to comply with the decree. A bit later, a new Special Prosecutor [Leon Jaworski] was appointed. . . ."[328]

After the grand jury had returned an indictment, Jaworski obtained a further subpoena to Nixon from the district court,[329] whose judgment was appealed to the court of appeals. By a special by-passing

jurisdiction depends upon the existence of a statute giving jurisdiction for the type of case involved. No such statute for this type of case was found to exist.

326. Senate Select Comm. v. Nixon, 498 F.2d 725, 730, 731, 732 (D.C. Cir. 1973), affirming 370 F. Supp. 521 (D.D.C. 1974). See Cox, The Role of the Supreme Court in American Government 26-27 n.4 (1976).

327. Nixon v. Sirica, 487 F.2d 700 (D.C. Cir. 1973), affirming 360 F. Supp. 1 (D.D.C. 1973).

328. Cox, *supra* n.326 at 8.

329. U.S. v. Mitchell et al., 377 F. Supp. 1326 (D.D.C. 1974).

procedure ("certiorari before judgment" of the court of appeals, used for cases of public importance requiring prompt resolution), the Supreme Court quickly granted certiorari, and affirmed the district court unanimously, Justice Rehnquist not participating. Chief Justice Burger's opinion acknowledged that the "President's need for complete candor and objectivity from advisers calls for great deference from the courts." But a generalized claim of executive privilege (as distinct from a specific claim of "need to protect military, diplomatic, or national security interests") could not outweigh in this case the "demands of due process of law in the fair administration of criminal justice"; it was "difficult," in this case, "to accept the argument that even the very important interest in confidentiality of Presidential communications is significantly diminished by production of such material for in camera inspection with all the protection that a district court will be obliged to provide."[330]

Thus the courts have made clear, just as the Freedom of Information Act exemptions had made clear, that there is a legitimate role for executive privilege — though the precise character of that role in differing circumstances is still uncertain.[331]

5. Congress as part of the post-Vietnam and post-Watergate reaction to the "imperial Presidency" has also taken anti-executive action in the area of military and emergency matters. The War Powers Resolution of 1973,[332] enacted over Nixon's veto, declared its purpose to be insuring "that the collective judgment of both the Congress and the President will apply to the introduction of United States Armed Forces

330. U.S. v. Nixon, 418 U.S. 683, 706, 713 (1974). The Court outlined guidelines for the district court's in camera inspection of the subpoenaed materials. The Court made other rulings, including the point that the Attorney General's statutory powers to conduct government criminal litigation and to appoint subordinate officers authorized his issuance of a regulation with the force of law that did the following: It appointed the Special Prosecutor, giving him a special independence with explicit power to contest the claim of executive privilege, and assuring him, pursuant to assurances from the President, that the latter would not remove him from his duties — except for "extraordinary improprieties" and after the President's consulting and finding an approving consensus in the Majority and Minority Leaders and Chairmen and ranking Minority Members of the House and Senate Judiciary Committees. The Court further found, inter alia, that the controversy was "justiciable" (see Chap. 2 herein under **B6**) despite the fact that it was between a subordinate and superior officer of the executive branch. In 1978 Congress itself enacted, as part of the Ethics in Government Act, a special prosecutor statute to be in effect for five years. 5 U.S.C. §§591-598. See Civiletti, Post-Watergate Legislation in Retrospect, 34 Sw. L.J. 1043, 1052-1056 (1981).

331. See generally on executive privilege, Berger, Executive Privilege (1974); Cox, Executive Privilege, 122 U. Pa. L. Rev. 1383 (1974); Symposium, United States v. Nixon, 22 U.C.L.A. L. Rev. 4 (1974); Note, 76 Colum. L. Rev. 142 (1976); U.S. v. Reynolds, 345 U.S. 1 (1952).

332. 87 Stat. 555 (1973). For committee reports see 2 U.S. Code Cong. & Ad. News 2346 et seq. (1973).

into hostilities, or into situations where imminent involvement in hostilities is clearly indicated by the circumstances, and to the continued use of such forces in hostilities or in such situations."[333] The purpose of the National Emergencies Act of 1976,[334] according to the Senate Committee Report, was "to terminate, as of 2 years from the date of enactment, powers and authorities possessed by the Executive as a result of existing states of national emergency, and to establish authority for the declaration of future emergencies in a manner which will clearly define the powers of the President and provide for regular Congressional review."[335]

My exploration of the interrelations between Congress and the President is now completed.[336] Certainly not all such interrelations have been identified or developed in detail,[337] but at least some major ones have been broached.

333. In rough summary: When the President unilaterally decides to send United States military forces "into hostilities or into situations where involvement in hostilities is clearly indicated by the circumstances," he must within 48 hours report to Congress concerning the circumstances, justification, and estimated duration of the involvement, and must periodically report thereafter during its continuance. He must *terminate* the use of armed forces within 60 days from the date required for the report or date of the actual report, whichever is earlier (with possible extension of another 30 days) *unless* Congress declares war or otherwise votes approval or is unable to meet because of armed attack on the United States. Any time that United States armed forces are engaged in external hostilities without a declaration of war, Congress can direct their removal by concurrent resolution. The Resolution states that it gives the President no powers he did not have before; nor is it "intended to alter the constitutional authority of the Congress or of the President or the provisions of existing treaties." For Professor Charles Black's views of the Resolution as "a series of puzzling repugnancies and contradictions," see Black, The Working Balance of the American Political Departments, 1 Hastings Const. L.Q. 13, 18 n.21 (1974).

334. 90 Stat. 1255, 50 U.S.C. §§1601, 1621, 1622, 1631, 1641, 1651. For committee reports see, 3 U.S. Code Cong. & Ad. News 2288 et seq. (1976). See also the International Emergency Economic Powers Act, 91 Stat. 1626 (1977), 50 U.S.C. §§1701-1706 and committee reports in 3 U.S. Code Cong. & Ad. News 4540 et seq. (1977).

335. S. Rep. No. 94-1168, 94th Cong., 2d Sess. 1 (1976). Provisions of law conferring emergency powers were to be effective (1) only when the President specifically declared a national emergency, and (2) only in accordance with the Act. In declaring an emergency he must specify the legal provisions under which he or other officers will act. There are provisions for termination of emergencies; for presidential and executive agency maintenance of a file and index of emergency Orders and regulations and transmittal of such Orders and regulations to Congress; for presidential reports to Congress of expenditures attributable to the emergency; and for repeal or continuation of various emergency and other statutory provisions.

336. For a good general treatment of the subject see Fisher, The Constitution Between Friends — Congress, The President and the Law (1978).

337. Thus, for instance, the ability of Congress to intrude on the executive is enhanced by court interpretation of the Constitution's "speech and debate clause" (Art. I, §6, declaring with respect to members of Congress that "for any speech or debate in either House, they shall not be questioned in any other place"). In 1971 Senator Gravel of Alaska at a public meeting of his Senate Subcommittee on Buildings and Grounds read extensively from the government's confidential "Pentagon Papers" on the Vietnam War and made all 47 volumes part of the public

c. *Legislature and Administrative Agencies*

This topic encompasses two major areas I wish to explore: (1) One is the pronounced trend in recent years towards legislative cutting down of the administrative bureaucracy, through "deregulation" or through the process of "oversight" of administrative agencies and their rules and regulations, including the use of a "legislative veto." (2) The other is the further cluster of "separation of powers" issues that arise over the legislative creation of an agency that not only "administers" or "executes" but also has powers partly judicial and partly legislative.

(1) Deregulation; "Oversight" (Including the Legislative Veto)

1. The movement supporting drastic legislative curtailment of government regulation in favor of the relatively free operation of the market has strongly accelerated in the last several years because of the belief that regulation has "failed." The deregulation approach already taken, in varying degrees, in such areas as airlines, trucking, and securities brokers' commissions is urged for much broader application. Others are more cautious, arguing that deregulation is much less defensible in some regulatory areas than in others.[338] At the start of the Reagan administration, it appeared that deregulation would be given high priority.

2. Perhaps an equally high priority was being given to legislative "oversight" of administrative agencies. As in the case of deregulation, the initial big push had come in the latter Carter years. In 1980 the Paperwork Reduction Act set up an agency within OMB to reduce the amount of information collection by government agencies and make

---

record. Also, his aide negotiated with Beacon Press for publication of the documents in book form. In Gravel v. U.S., 409 U.S. 606 (1972) the Court ruled that the speech and debate clause extended only to "legislative acts," and hence would protect the Senator and his aide from grand jury questioning about events at the subcommittee meeting, but would not protect them from questioning concerning arrangements for private publication of the papers. Nor was there in the latter type of inquiry any general "legislative immunity" stemming from a nonconstitutional source. The Court cautioned that the speech or debate clause "does not privilege either Senator or aide to violate an otherwise valid criminal law in preparing for or implementing legislative acts." On the latter point, see U.S. v. Brewster, 408 U.S. 501 (1972).

338. For a sampling of the growing literature on deregulation, see Symposium, Managing the Transition to Deregulation, 44 Law & Contemp. Prob. 1 (1981); Gellhorn, Deregulation: Delight or Delusion? 24 St. Louis U.L.J. 469 (1980); ABA Commission on Law and the Economy, Federal Regulation: Roads to Reform (1979); Breyer & Stewart, Administrative Law and Regulatory Policy 135-138 (1979); Breyer, Analyzing Regulatory Failure: Mismatches, Less Restrictive Alternatives, and Reform, 92 Harv. L. Rev. 549 (1979); Colloquium, The Deregulation of Industry, 51 Ind. L.J. 682 (1976); Stewart, The Reformation of Administrative Law, 88 Harv. L. Rev. 1667, 1689-1693 (1975).

the process more efficient.[339] In the same year the Regulatory Flexibility Act, primarily pushed by small business, stated as its purpose that agencies should "fit regulatory and informational requirements to the scale of the businesses, organizations and governmental jurisdictions subject to regulation." Agencies when giving notice of a proposed rule were to submit an "initial regulatory flexibility analysis," giving the rule's objectives; its *impact on small entities;* identification of all federal rules which may duplicate, overlap, or conflict; and description of "significant alternatives" to the rule that minimize any significant impact of the rule on small entities. The final rule was to be accompanied by a "final regulatory flexibility analysis" showing agency reactions to comments on the initial analysis and why any significant alternatives were rejected.[340] Moreover, by approximately July 1, 1981, each agency was to publish in the Federal Register a plan for periodic review of agency rules having significant impact on a substantial number of small entities — in order to determine whether rules should be changed or rescinded in order to minimize the impact on small entities.[341]

"Sunset" legislation which, we have seen, has been popular in the states, has been promoted on the federal level, but thus far not successfully since the financial and administrative problem for Congress is far greater than for the states. The major federal sunset bill, introduced in 1977, had mandated congressional committee review of most government programs every ten years as a condition to possible renewal. But the substitute agreed on by the Rules Committee in September, 1980 would *not require* the review of any programs; the committees would choose which, if any, programs would be reviewed, subject to approval by the appropriate House. This easing of review requirements was a result of the awareness of the members of Congress of the potentially enormous workload for committees, as well as the disruption, delay, or paralysis of agency programs that would result unless sunset reviews were undertaken at a measured pace.[342]

339. 94 Stat. 2812 (1980), 44 U.S.C. §§3501-3520. See committee reports in 5 U.S. Code Cong. & Ad. News 6241 et seq.

340. 94 Stat. 1164 (1980). It adds chap. 6 (§§601-612) to Title 5, U.S. Code. For committee reports see, 4 U.S. Code Cong. & Ad. News 2788 et seq. (1980). The requirements as to flexibility analysis are inapplicable if the agency head certifies in the Federal Register that the rule will not have a significant economic impact on small entities, succinctly explains the reasons, and also provides such certification and explanation to the Chief Counsel for Advocacy, Small Business Administration.

341. There are further provisions concerning the agency's review of its rules; concerning restriction of judicial review; and concerning the power of the Chief Counsel for Advocacy, Small Business Administration, to monitor compliance with this law by the agency and to appear in court to present views on the effect of a rule on small entities, in any federal suit to review a rule. The said Chief Counsel discusses the Act in Stewart, The New Regulatory Flexibility Act, 67 A.B.A.J. 66 (1981).

342. See Cong. Q., Sept. 6, 1980, at 2645. The ABA Commission on Law and the Economy had recommended that Congress delegate to the President the authority to

3. Carter, who had backed a broad sunset bill, had also backed the core of a measure or measures that (a) would have required agencies to execute a *"regulatory analysis" for any proposed major rule* — i.e., a preliminary analysis discussing the need, the alternatives, and the potential consequences, and a final analysis (after allowing time for public comment and debate); (b) would have required *periodic review* of rules and programs, and a biannual "regulatory agenda" from the agencies, outlining the major rules contemplated for the coming year; and (c) would have provided more public funds to encourage *public participation* in agency proceedings. Three other provisions proved so controversial that passage of the whole program was prevented;[343] a similar program described earlier, however, which Carter had established by Executive Order, continued until revoked by the Reagan Executive Order previously discussed.[344]

4. Often overlooked in discussion of legislative oversight of the agencies is the authority of Congress's watchdog, the General Accounting Office, headed by the Comptroller General. Concerned not only with seeing that public funds are not spent for unauthorized purposes, he is also specifically authorized by Section 204(a) of the Legislative Reorganization Act as amended in 1974 to "review and evaluate the

---

designate which agencies or regulatory functions were to be reviewed. A good example of negative sentiment on federal sunset is the following from a 1976 Brookings Institution study called "Are Government Organizations Immortal": "Imagine the paralysis, the sense of suspended animation that would overtake agencies, their clients, and their beneficiaries as expiration dates approached. Think of trying to do business and plan for the future under such conditions. Visualize the dilatory tactics of interests that, having lost an immediate battle over federal intervention, strove to delay implementation until the automatic reopening of the struggle rolled around. And finally consider the crush and confusion of legislatures as they tried in each session both to dispose of current business and to renegotiate the accumulating body of prior settlements. Time limits would soon be abandoned or ignored. Organizations would be routinely and uncritically renewed. Things would soon revert to their present state."

For some discussion of sunset legislation see Price, Sunset Legislation in the United States, 30 Baylor L. Rev. 401 (1978); Note, 11 U. Mich. J.L. Ref. 269 (1978); Vidas, The Sun Also Sets: A Model For Sunset Implementation, 26 Am. U.L. Rev. 1169 (1977).

343. First was the "Bumpers amendment" that would have given greater scope to court review of regulations by removing the presumption of validity that has attached to regulations; see O'Reilly, Deference Makes A Difference: A Study of Impacts of the Bumpers Judicial Review Amendment, 49 U. Cin. L. Rev. 739 (1980); second was a provision for a "legislative veto" of regulations by vote of one House (later weakened by requiring a vote of both Houses, with power in the President to veto the congressional veto); and third was a provision that the rulemaking process be of a "hybrid" form, so that instead of the legislative-type hearing in which comments (written, and not always oral) on proposed rules are received, interested parties would have not only the right of oral presentation but also, in certain circumstances, the right of cross-examination of other participants. See Cong. Q., Dec. 13, 1980, at 3576.

344. See discussion of both Orders under **D6a** above.

results of government programs and activities" when "ordered" by either House or "requested" by any congressional committee or "upon his own initiative." "This kind of reviewing and evaluating had in fact long been done by the Comptroller's staff, which since 1970 has included an Office of Program Review and Evaluation as a formally recognized entity."[345]

5. I come next to the "legislative veto" as applied to administrative regulations. An example would be Congress's insertion into a statute of a provision to the effect that an administrative regulation adopted under the statute can be vetoed by one House within 60 days of promulgation. (Less often, the veto is to be by both Houses, or by a legislative committee of one House).

The device seems to have been born in 1932 when Congress authorized President Hoover to consolidate existing administrative agencies and activities — any of his reorganization plans to be subject to a veto by a single House of Congress. That scheme for presidential reorganization plans has been continued ever since, having been used in hundreds of laws to allow legislative negation of action taken by administrative agencies (or executive departments).[346] Congress has even seriously considered bills to amend the Administrative Procedure Act so as to extend the system to all administrative rules.[347] Every President has opposed the veto, whether taken against his own action or against that of an executive or administrative agency. President Reagan, however, will presumably follow the 1980 Republican platform, which endorsed the veto.

Constitutional validity of the scheme is sharply debated. There are able critics[348] as well as supporters[349] of the validity of one form

345. Gellhorn et al., *supra* n.211 at 103 n.1. See Brown, The GAO, Untapped Source of Congressional Power (1970).

346. For examples of recent use of the device in prominent statutes on subjects like education, energy, and airline deregulation, see Cohen, Legislative Veto Battle Escalates — Should Congress Have the Last Word? Natl. L.J., Sept. 6, 1980, at 1476-1477. Recently a cognate weapon has been used: Congress, under Carter, had been attaching riders to appropriation bills to prohibit agencies from spending money to effectuate a particular regulation — e.g., an IRS regulation eliminating the tax-exempt status of private and religious schools that fail to meet affirmative action requirements. *Id.* at 1474.

347. Bruff & Gellhorn, Congressional Control of Administrative Regulation: A Study of Legislative Vetoes, 90 Harv. L. Rev. 1369, 1370 n.4 (1977).

348. See e.g., Dixon, The Congressional Veto and Separation of Powers, 56 N.C.L. Rev. 423 (1978); Bruff & Gellhorn, *supra* n.347; Administrative Conference of U.S. Recommendations 77-1, 1 C.F.R. §305.77-1 (1977); Address of Assistant Attorney General Scalia, Symposium on "Oversight and Review of Agency Decision-making," 28 Ad. L. Rev. 577, 684-698, 700-701 (1976); Note, 1976 Duke L.J. 285; Barber, The Constitution and the Delegation of Congressional Power 112-117 (1975); Watson, Congress Steps Out: A Look At Congressional Control of the Executive, 63 Calif. L. Rev. 926 (1975).

349. See, e.g., Nathanson, Separation of Powers and Administrative Law: Delegation, The Legislative Veto, and the Independent Agencies, 75 Nw. L. Rev. 1064,

or another of the scheme. Without attempting to probe deeply into the arguments, perhaps I can summarize the major criticisms by saying that the critics perceive (a) a legislative usurpation of executive power to carry out the laws through regulations; (b) an invalid delegation of legislative power from Congress to one House or to a legislative committee, there being no explicit standards to guide the discretion of the delegate; (c) a legislative by-pass of the constitutional veto power of the Chief Executive (one House or a committee is said to be legislating, in preventing a regulation from having the force of law; legislation to be effective must meet the approval of the President or be passed over his veto; where the legislative veto provision requires concurrence of both Houses, a specific constitutional provision seems to require, for at least some resolutions, a presentation to the President, and perhaps *a fortiori* should apply to an important resolution in which only one House has concurred);[350] and (d) an exercise of "judicial" power by a House or committee, to the extent that it is engaging in statutory interpretation to hold that the regulation is not within the intent of the agency's statute.

The response is: (a) Congress is not exercising executive or judicial power, nor is it even legislating, by the veto: In the statute authorizing the agency to make rules, Congress could have delegated this power to the agency with no strings attached; it chose instead to make a *lesser* or conditional delegation to the agency by reserving the power to act within a fixed period to invalidate the rules in a particular way. When it so acts, it is merely effectuating the specified condition.[351] (b) The delegation from Congress to a part of itself (one House

---

1078-1092 (1981); Schwartz, The Legislative Veto and the Constitution — A Reexamination, 46 Geo. Wash. L. Rev. 351 (1978); Javits & Klein, Congressional Oversight and the Legislative Veto: A Constitutional Analysis, 52 N.Y.U.L. Rev. 455 (1977); Miller & Knapp, The Congressional Veto: Preserving the Constitutional Framework, 52 Ind. L.J. 367 (1977); Stewart, Constitutionality of the Legislative Veto, 13 Harv. J. Legis. 593 (1976). Among other general discussions, see Ivanhoe, Congressional Oversight of Administrative Discretion: Defining the Proper Role of the Legislative Veto, 26 Am. L. Rev. 1018 (1977); McGowan, Congress, Court, and Control of Delegated Power, 77 Colum. L. Rev. 1119 (1977).

350. Article I, §7 provides for presentation to the President not only of "bills" approved by both Houses, but also of every "order, resolution or vote to which the concurrence of the Senate and the House may be necessary." This has been construed by the Department of Justice as applicable to "all final Congressional action of public effect," including "*all* Congressional attempts to evade the President's veto power" — as distinguished from the many other concurrent and simple resolutions that by long accepted congressional practice have not been presented to the President. See Letter of Attorney General Civiletti, quoted in Nathanson, *supra* n.349 at 1079.

351. The Supreme Court has already ruled that it is not an invalid delegation of legislative power for Congress to make the effectiveness of certain Secretary of Agriculture marketing regulations depend on prior referendum approval of two-thirds of the farmers affected — i.e., by private groups rather than Congress or a

or a committee) is said to be as permissible as the delegation of legislative power to the executive or administrative agency in the basic regulatory provisions of the statute; the courts are liberal today in the matter of "standards." (See p. 119 below.) (c) The President's veto power on legislation is not by-passed. As explained above, this is not a case of legislation. Moreover, the President did approve the original law specifying the condition.

No Supreme Court decision has thus far resolved the constitutional issue.

Aside from the constitutional objections, critics have pointed to a number of practical difficulties. One is the delay of administrative action — which can stretch out far beyond the specified 60 or 90 days when a House disapproves the proposed rule and the agency then revises and negotiates and revises again. Congressional disapproval might be of only part of a rule or program: How would that affect other related rules; and when would the agency's subsequent, modified rule be so similar to the disapproved rule as to come within its ban? The veto enormously expands the workload for Congress (perhaps mainly for its staff). Unlike an administrative rule, which is issued with the Administrative Procedure Act safeguards assuring opportunity for full input into the decision through hearings, the decision by one House or a committee has no such safeguards; it would be a "low visibility" decision in which intensive lobbying or log-rolling may be more determinative than merit. There may be other, unintended impacts on administrative agencies and administrative law.[352]

6. Still other important techniques of congressional oversight should be catalogued here briefly. Congress, as we know, has a role in appointments to agencies. Substantive policy may be affected through the control of Congress over the size of appropriations — for the agen-

---

part of Congress. Currin v. Wallace, 306 U.S. 1 (1939); U.S. v. Rock Royal Co-op, 307 U.S. 533 (1939). The Court said in *Currin* that there was no delegation. "Here it is Congress that exercises its legislative authority in making the regulation [through the Secretary] and in prescribing the conditions of its application. The required favorable vote upon the referendum is one of these conditions." (at 16).

352. The prestige of an agency as a responsible, autonomous body may be diminished, and recruiting capable people may be more difficult. Agencies may be induced to rely less on rulemaking than on adjudication to announce rather new policies — which contrasts with what is generally thought to be a salutary opposite trend in agency practice. Judicial review of regulations may become narrower: A court may conclude that failure of a house or committee to disapprove within the specified period signifies that the regulation had been ratified as being statutorily authorized (see Fredericks v. Kreps, 578 F.2d 555, 563 (5th Cir. 1978)). For examples of some of the practical difficulties mentioned in the text above, see Bruff & Gellhorn, *supra* n.347.

Critics have suggested alternatives to the veto: Bliss, *supra* n.298 at 644-651; Kaiser, Congressional Action to Overturn Agency Rules: Alternatives to the "Legislative Veto," 32 Ad. L. Rev. 667 (1980).

cy's work generally, or for particular programs. Quite apart from its enactment of sunset provisions, Congress may put a short expiration date on a statute, e.g., a year, so that hearings can be held annually on whether agency policies are to be approved through reenactment. Still other channels by which Congress keeps informed about what is happening in the agencies include: committee investigations; a statutory requirement of regular agency reports; committee hearings on appropriations and other matters within the committee's jurisdiction; the required publication in the Federal Register of agency rules and regulations; and a watchdog committee that might be established over all the operations of a particular agency (a state may have a committee for watching *all* agency rules and regulations). Moreover, the existence in both Houses of the standing ("subject matter") committees, appropriations committees, and committees on government operations means that each agency has at least six committees — plus subcommittees — which, while perhaps not watchdog committees, are capable of keeping in close contact with, and influencing, the agency's operations.[353] Whether or not they are on such committees, members of Congress (acting usually in behalf of constituents) are known to intercede with and put pressure on the agencies.[354] All this accountability, however, does not necessarily result in efficient "oversight." Senator Ribicoff in 1976 lamented the "fragmentation" of responsibility and the "chronic absence of coordination and cooperation between committees." The "standing committees do not coordinate their oversight with either the Government Operations Committees or the Appropriations Committees on a systematic basis."[355]

7. Finally, you should realize that there is more than just "oversight" in the interaction between legislature and agency. Agencies may develop a close relation of mutual assistance with particular legislative committees or members. This includes — in spite of the funneling of agency legislative requests through the Office of Management and Budget — direct legislative-agency contacts over content and drafting of proposed legislation. Scholars have observed that "the norms of legislative committees often differ from those of appropriations [committees]; the former often attempt to expand an agency's jurisdiction and view an agency as a partner rather than an adversary, whereas in

353. See Gellhorn et al., *supra* n.211 at 108.

354. *Id.* at 112-114. Recall the "due process" and Administrative Procedure Act barriers to "ex parte" contacts in formal proceedings. See *supra* n.302. And see Gelfond, Judicial Limitation of Congressional Influence on Administrative Agencies, 73 Nw. U.L. Rev. 931 (1978); Parnell, Congressional Interference in Agency Enforcement: The IRS Experience, 89 Yale L.J. 1360 (1980).

355. Ribicoff, Congressional Oversight and Regulatory Reform, 28 Ad. L. Rev. 415, 420 (1976). Generally on this paragraph, see Gellhorn et al., *supra* n.211, at 103-116.

the appropriations committees, norms of restraint and scarcity usually dominate. Through the dual subsystems, the tension (often hostility) within Congress between legislative and appropriations committees is transmitted to the agencies, whose stance vis-a-vis their legislative master is thereby made more complex and difficult."[356]

(2) Agency Functions and "Separation of Powers" Issues

Nor should we forget that the legislature plays a vital role before there is any administrative agency to "oversee." That is, it is the legislature that brings the administrative agency into being, by a statute describing (among other things) its composition, functions, and powers. It is the legislature that determines whether the agency is to hold hearings and exercise the judicial power to adjudicate disputes, whether it is to have the power to issue rules and regulations with the force of law, make investigations and inspections, issue subpoenas, and bring enforcement suits in court.

Among the questions thus raised, I wish briefly to discuss four separation of powers issues.

(a) When an agency is vested with judicial power, can it be objected that the legislature has transgressed the constitutional separation of powers by giving an agency what the constitution contemplates for courts? Generally, the answer nowadays is no. To sustain this objection, said the Supreme Court in 1940, "would be to turn back the clock on at least a half century of administrative law."[357] The reasons that administrative law has developed in this direction are probably (1) the courts are aware of the impossible burden that would be placed on the courts themselves if the agencies could not help in shouldering the adjudicative burden (recall the statistics in my earlier discussion of the functioning of administrative agencies); (2) the courts are aware that the typical agency adjudication is not the final word — it is subject to court review. Still, there are a few maverick decisions in state courts finding, some decades ago, that agency adjudication violates the separation of powers principle under the state constitution.[358]

(b) Even if exercise of a judicial function by a noncourt is permissible, does it not become impermissible when the legislature allows

356. Dodd & Schott, *supra* n.233 at 225.

357. Sunshine Anthracite Coal Co. v. Adkins, 310 U.S. 381 (1940). See also NLRB v. Jones & Laughlin Steel Corp., 301 U.S. 1 (1937); Union Bridge Co. v. U.S., 204 U.S. 364 (1907); Brown, Administrative Commissions and the Judicial Power, 19 Minn. L. Rev. 261 (1935).

358. A New Mexico court so held in 1957 with respect to the Workmen's Compensation Commission (State v. Mechem, 63 N.M. 250, 316 P.2d 1069 (1957)), and a New Hampshire court so held with respect to a proposed administrative agency system for adjudicating auto accident cases (In re Opinion of the Justices, 87 N.H. 492, 179 A. 344 (1933)).

this function to be *joined* in the same body with prosecutorial and other executive as well as legislative functions? Has not the integrity of the adjudicative process been impaired? A 1972 empirical study suggests, on the basis of a limited sample, a negative answer.[359] Nor, as we shall see, have courts ruled against the joinder as such. The Administrative Procedure Act aims at internal separation of functions within an agency, including independence of the hearing officers (now called administrative law judges or ALJs).[360] The Merit Systems Protection Board rather than the agency has the power over the ALJs' appointment and removal, and determines their salaries "independently of agency recommendations or ratings."[361] Performing no tasks "inconsistent with their duties and responsibilities as hearing examiners," no ALJ may "be responsible to or subject to the supervision and direction of" any officer "engaged in the performance of investigative or prosecuting functions for any agency"; and generally those participating in investigation or prosecution of an administratively adjudicated case are not to "participate or advise on the decision" of that case or a factually related case.[362]

True, the Act makes these latter provisions specifically inapplicable to the *heads* of agencies — who make the final adjudication. But a leading textbook points out that agency heads are rarely concerned with the details of cases at preliminary stages in a way that could accurately be characterized as investigative or prosecutive. In general, "federal courts have been scantily impressed by lawyers' outcries against the combination of responsibilities to be found in large administrative bodies."[363] At any rate, even in the case of a small agency — a medical board — the Supreme Court in 1975 held that the due process clause

359. See Posner, The Behavior of Administrative Agencies, 1 J. Legal Stud. 305, 323-344 (1972).

360. A 1978 statute enhanced the prestige of hearing officers or examiners by classifying them (as had a previous regulation) as administrative law judges; it also designated approximately one-third of the 1,000 or so positions as entitled to pay comparable to certain senior government executives' salaries. Gellhorn et al., *supra* n.211 at 754 n.9.

361. The agency presently selects ALJs from among the three highest rated candidates in the lists provided by the Office of Personnel Management. Experience in the agency's field (e.g., by being a former employee of the agency) is an element of qualification and not deemed to introduce an impermissible element of bias. *Id.* at 760-762. Some concern has been expressed over "whether sufficient controls over the quality and productivity of the ALJ performance has been retained." *Id.* at 755.

362. For the most pertinent provisions of the Act, see 5 U.S.C. §§554(d), 556, 559, 3105. Particular statutes may effect a still more drastic internal separation of adjudication from policymaking. Thus the 1947 Taft-Hartley Act saw to it that the adjudicative and prosecutorial staffs handling labor-relations cases were not reviewed by the same administrative entity. The General Counsel of the National Labor Relations Board has final authority over investigatory and prosecutorial policies. He is not controlled by the Board, which has final authority over adjudication.

363. Gellhorn et al., *supra* n.211 at 859.

would not prevent the joinder of *investigation* with adjudication. The board could adjudicate charges aimed at suspension of a physician even though the same board, after investigation, had brought the charges. The Court did differentiate those cases in which there might be a basis for suspecting that the board had been prejudiced by its investigation and could not adjudicate fairly on the basis of the evidence at the hearing; but no foundation for such a view had been presented in this case.[364]

(c) Even though constitutionality of joinder of functions be conceded, many have urged the desirability of safeguarding the integrity of adjudication and strengthening the process of policymaking by separating these two functions — i.e., removing the adjudicative functions from quasi-judicial agencies and transferring them to the regular *courts,* or to new specialized courts like a trade regulation court, a tax court, or a labor court.

Why have such proposals so far been unsuccessful? To begin with, a significant amount of separation of functions *within* the agency exists, as described above, though the agency *heads* generally have the last word on adjudications as well as the supervision of the non-

364. Withrow v. Larkin, 421 U.S. 35 (1975). The Court observed that a criminal court judge is not disqualified from presiding at trial by the fact that he earlier issued an arrest warrant on probable cause for the defendant, or decided at a preliminary hearing that there was probable cause to hold him for trial; that a civil judge is not "disqualified from presiding over injunction proceedings because he has initially assessed the facts in issuing or denying a temporary restraining order or a preliminary injunction"; and that the Court had recently sustained against due process objection a non-adversary procedure in which "a Social Security examiner has responsibility for developing the facts and making a decision as to disability claims."

The *Larkin* case was relied on in the following year when the Court held that a school board's decision to fire teachers striking in violation of state law (and who had objected to the board's proposed disciplinary hearings, questioning the board's objectivity) did not violate due process merely because the board had previously negotiated with the strikers. The prior involvement was "not enough to overcome the presumption of honesty and integrity in policymakers with decisionmaking power." A decisionmaker is not disqualified by "mere [prior] familiarity with the facts of a case," or by the fact that "he has taken a position, even in public, on a policy issue related to the dispute in the absence of a showing that he is not capable of judging a particular controversy fairly on the basis of its own circumstances." Hortonville Joint School Dist. v. Hortonville Educ. Assn., 426 U.S. 482 (1976).

Note that neither of these two constitutional cases involved the federal Administrative Procedure Act and its provision against the investigator's participation in the decision. (For criticism of the provision and general discussion of separation of functions, see Davis, Administrative Law Treatise chap. 18 (2d ed., 1980); see also Gellhorn et al., *supra* n.211 at 899-907). The *Larkin* opinion contains this dictum about the APA: "It is also very typical for the members of administrative agencies to receive the results of investigations, to approve the filing of charges or formal complaints instituting enforcement proceedings, and then to participate in the ensuing hearings. This mode of procedure does not violate the Administrative Procedure Act, and it does not violate due process of law." The reference to non-violation of the APA seems to be to the exemption for agency *heads* ("members").

adjudicatory staff. Further, as opponents of complete separation point out, it is often difficult to distinguish adjudication from policymaking — e.g., the process of licensing or granting of subsidies involves elements of both. More positively, they assert that there are *advantages* in amalgamation of the two functions in one body; that experience in one function helps in discharging the other. When Louis Hector, a proponent of separation, had argued that planning an air route is an executive function, but that selecting which carrier should operate it is a judicial function for a court, Professor Carl Auerbach replied: "The CAB . . . planned its international air routes pretty much as Mr. Hector would have wished. But in the subsequent [adjudicative] proceedings involving the selection of carriers, evidence was introduced to cause it to modify its plans in important respects. The selection of the carrier affects the route to be chosen, and vice versa."[365]

The argument is roughly this: (i) an agency stripped of its adjudicative functions would be lacking in an important source of information for its executive and legislative functions as above illustrated, would lack a significant means for the development of policy in areas that do not lend themselves to control by general rules,[366] and would not be as able to develop a *coordinated* policy; and (ii) the proposed administrative court would lack the knowledge that comes from exercise of executive and legislative functions (including the concomitant day-to-day contact with the specialized staff and the problems of the industry). It would therefore be making less-informed policy, for it is a mistake to assume that adjudication does not involve policy judgments. This is a point you will see more clearly from the discussion in Chapter 4. While I have summarized the arguments that have thus far been persuasive, I should add that from time to time a responsible official announces his views the other way — one of the most recent being Commissioner Philip Elman, who ended an active two-term career on the Federal Trade Commission in 1970. Newton Minow so spoke in 1963 on leaving the Federal Communications Commission,

365. Auerbach, Some Thoughts on the Hector Memorandum, 1960 Wis. L. Rev. 183, 186. See also Auerbach, Should Administrative Agencies Perform Adjudicatory Functions? 1959 Wis. L. Rev. 95; Cary, Why I Oppose the Divorce of the Judicial Function From Federal Regulatory Agencies, 51 A.B.A.J. 33 (1965).

366. The Supreme Court has recognized the wisdom of allowing federal agencies to assess the relative merits of announcing an innovative principle in an adjudicatory proceeding as against a rulemaking proceeding, and to make a reasonable choice between the two procedures. See Gellhorn et al., *supra* n.211 at 211-248; Shapiro, The Choice of Rulemaking or Adjudication in the Development of Administrative Policy, 78 Harv. L. Rev. 92 (1965); SEC v. Chenery Corp., 332 U.S. 194 (1947); NLRB v. Bell Aerospace Co., 416 U.S. 267 (1974).

and Louis Hector on leaving the Civil Aeronautics Board in 1959.[367]

(d) Insofar as the legislature confers *legislative* power on the agency, i.e., power to make rules and regulations with the force of law, can this be attacked as another violation of the separation of powers principle; has not the legislature abdicated its own constitutional responsibility for exercising the legislative power? Again, speaking generally, the answer is no. True, there have been plenty of cases in which the courts have asserted that the legislature cannot make a "delegation" (or an "undue delegation") of its legislative power. But in the entire history of the Supreme Court to the present, there have been only two cases in which that Court thought Congress had made such an invalid delegation to another branch of government — both of them involving aspects of the National Industrial Recovery Act of 1933.[368] Whatever may be the special factors that explain those decisions that found the statute lacking in sufficient "standards" to guide the delegate's discretion, the Supreme Court has since upheld numerous statutes no less lacking in standards. The trend in the federal cases is to look less at statutory standards than at the fairness of the agency procedures and results.[369] Explanation of the trend probably lies in the increased judicial awareness that for complex and changing regulatory problems, a legislature simply cannot lay down precise, detailed standards in advance.

Still, the "nondelegation doctrine," as it is sometimes called, is not dead. From time to time, two or three dissenting members of the Court will be found invoking the doctrine, which still enjoys some scholarly support.[370] Moreover, the doctrine is taken more seriously in state courts interpreting their state constitutions.[371]

367. The Hector memorandum was published as Problems of the CAB and the Independent Regulatory Commissions, in 69 Yale L.J. 931 (1960). Minow's position, originally in the form of a May 31, 1963 letter to President Kennedy, appears in Suggestions for Improvements of the Administrative Process, 15 Ad. L. Rev. 146 (1963). Elman's position appears in his A Modest Proposal for Radical Reform, 56 A.B.A.J. 1045 (1970). William L. Cary, former SEC chairman, after leaving the SEC took specific issue with both Minow and Hector in his article cited in n.365 *supra* and in his later book, Politics and the Regulatory Agencies (1967).

368. Panama Refining Co. v. Ryan, 293 U.S. 388 (1935); Schecter Poultry Corp. v. U.S., 295 U.S. 495 (1935).

369. See Davis, *supra* n.248, chap. 2.

370. See dissents in American Textile Mfrs. Inst. v. Donovan, 69 L. Ed. 2d. 185 (1981), and in Arizona v. California, 373 U.S. 546 (1963); Barber, The Constitution and the Delegation of Legislative Power (1975); Wright (Judge Skelly Wright), Beyond Discretionary Justice, 81 Yale L.J. 575 (1972); Lowi, The End of Liberalism 297-299 (1969); Merrill, Standards — A Safeguard For the Exercise of Delegated Power, 47 Neb. L. Rev. 469 (1968).

371. See 1 Cooper, State Administrative Law, chap. 3, esp. 79-80, 84-85, 87-90 (1965); Gellhorn et al., *supra* n.211 at 81-83.

d. Court and Executive-Administrative Agencies

Under this heading it might have been appropriate to include some of the issues discussed above. For in talking about the legislature in relation to the agencies, I also talked about court reactions — i.e., court reactions to legislative vesting of judicial power in the agency, and legislative joinder of it with executive powers in the same agency; and court reactions to legislative delegation of legislative power to the agency.

But my chief concerns under the present topic are three other questions: First, what are the kinds of questions that courts may properly consider in reviewing the action of administrative agencies? Second, what is the scope of the court's review? Third, what are some ways in which courts pay deference to the agency?

Judicial Review of Agencies

(i) The Kinds of Questions That May Be Reviewed

There are some limits on the kinds of questions a reviewing court can consider. Not all questions qualify as "judicial." There is a "political question" doctrine, for instance, under which a court may conclude that a particular issue is not "judicial" but "political," to be resolved by the other branches of government.[372] This doctrine was applied to the issue of legality of presidential action in the Vietnam War.[373] The Supreme Court made clear, a long time ago, that the question whether a state has a "republican form of government" as required by the Constitution is a political question.[374] The scope of the doctrine has been diminishing in recent years. But where the President's action involving other countries is concerned, the hands-off attitude expressed by the "political question" doctrine is reinforced by a traditional def-

372. The doctrine is also discussed in Chap. 2 herein under **B6,g&h.**

373. In Atlee v. Laird, 347 F. Supp. 689 (E.D. Pa. 1972) a three-judge federal court dismissed as raising a political question a case attacking constitutionality of the Vietnam War. This was *summarily affirmed* by the Supreme Court in Atlee v. Richardson, 411 U.S. 911 (1973), with dissents by Justices Douglas, Brennan, and Stewart. Earlier, some other lower courts had applied the doctrine (see, e.g., Velvel v. Nixon, 415 F.2d 236 (10th Cir. 1969), *cert. denied,* 396 U.S. 1042 (1970); Luftig v. McNamara, 373 F.2d 664 (D.C. Cir. 1967), *cert. denied,* 387 U.S. 945 (1967); Holtzman v. Schlesinger, 484 F.2d 1307 (2d Cir. 1973). But a contrary view was taken in Massachusetts v. Laird, 451 F.2d 26 (1st Cir. 1971); Berk v. Laird, 429 F.2d 302 (2d Cir. 1970); Orlando v. Laird, 443 F.2d 1039 (2d Cir. 1971), *cert. denied,* 404 U.S. 869 (1971). Also, in a number of cases in which the Supreme Court denied certiorari (discretionary) review, there were individual dissents from the denial. See, e.g., the dissents in Da Costa v. Laird, 405 U.S. 979 (1972); Moria v. McNamara, 389 U.S. 934 (1967); Mitchell v. U.S., 386 U.S. 972 (1967).

374. Luther v. Borden, 48 U.S. (7 How.) 1 (1849).

erence to his broad constitutional power in foreign affairs.[375] Even here, though, change may be in the wind. In the 1979 summary dismissal of the suit by several members of Congress challenging President Carter's termination of the defense treaty with Taiwan without Senate participation, the Court's attitude on justiciability was far from unified. Supporting dismissal of the suit on the ground that the question was a nonjusticiable political question was only a plurality of four Justices. Another concurred in the dismissal, without opinion. Two others found the issue justiciable. Two more urged that the justiciability issue should have full briefing and argument rather than be disposed of summarily.[376]

Another reason for saying a particular question is not a "judicial" one appropriate for a court's resolution is that it looks like the kind of executive or administrative question that has in the past been handled only by executive or administrative agencies. Thus, if a statute authorizes licensing by an agency, and authorizes a *de novo* judicial review — i.e., not limited to questions of law and to determining whether the agency fact findings were supported by substantial evidence, but rather covering the entire exercise of *administrative discretion* on issuance or revocation of the license, including an independent determination of fact and law — you *may* find a court saying the statute invalidly lodges a "nonjudicial" question in the court. Or you may find the court saving the constitutionality of the statute by *interpreting* it narrowly — in spite of its broad language — to allow only the normal, limited judicial review.[377] De novo judicial review of agency action is rarely authorized — even when a strong element of discretionary administrative policy is *not* involved. But there are special situations in which a court might hold de novo review (in the sense of an independent determination of fact and law, though not necessarily on the basis of a new evidentiary trial in court) to be constitutionally required.[378]

375. See, e.g., Chicago & Southern Airlines v. Waterman S.S. Corp., 333 U.S. 103 (1948).

Another aspect of judicial deference to the executive in the foreign affairs area is the so-called "act of state" doctrine. This doctrine bars inquiry by courts into the legality of acts of foreign governments done within their own territories, partly because (and some justices think solely because) such adjudication may embarrass the executive conduct of foreign policy. But a Supreme Court majority in 1972 seemed to believe that the doctrine can apply even in a case in which the executive has expressly advised the Court that American foreign policy interests would not be advanced by applying the doctrine. See First Natl. City Bank v. Banco Nacional de Cuba, 406 U.S. 759 (1972).

376. Goldwater v. Carter, 444 U.S. 996 (1979).

377. See Davis, *supra* n.253 at §29.09.

378. See Davis, *supra* n.253 at §29.08; Jaffe, Judicial Control of Administrative Action, chap. 16 (1965); Strong, The Persistent Doctrine of Constitutional Fact, 46 N.C.L. Rev. 223 (1968).

(ii) The Scope of Review

What then are the judicial questions that a court can properly handle in its review of executive and administrative action, and what is the nature of that review? One such question is whether the evidence at a hearing by an executive or administrative agency adequately supports the fact findings of the agency. In answering this question, a court does not weigh the evidence in the way it would if it were the initial fact finder, to see whether a preponderance of the evidence supports the fact findings in question. It asks, rather, whether there is "substantial evidence" to support the findings.[379] This question means: Could a reasonable mind believe such evidence to be enough to support the findings even though the court (presumably another reasonable mind) might not, if it were the original fact finder, have believed it to be enough? The court is thus paying some deference to the agency; it is not substituting its own independent judgment.

When you shift from a strictly fact question to a question of "law" or a "mixed question of fact or law," the cases on the scope of court review of agency determinations are in great confusion. The problem is easy enough if the agency procedure or decision is alleged to violate a constitutional standard or some clear statutory mandate whose application by the court requires no deference to the agency, because its expertise, or its face-to-face confrontation with witnesses, is not involved in the matter. On these questions of law, the court substitutes its own independent judgment.

But suppose the case involves interpretation of the statutory language to determine whether or not the language applies to the facts of the case. For example, is a newsstand operator who has, according to agency findings, certain economic relationships with the newspaper publisher, an "employee" within the meaning of that term as used in the National Labor Relations Act? This kind of question has sometimes been called a question of law, sometimes a "mixed question of fact and law." In this type of case you will find *some* Supreme Court cases deferring to the administrative judgment in the way the Court does toward fact findings (i.e., saying the agency determination will be upheld if it has a "rational basis," or "warrant in the record and a reasonable basis in law"); in other cases the Court has substituted its own independent judgment on the question.

When it does the former, (a) the Court may nonetheless use its independent judgment on *some* aspects of the problem (e.g., on what was the overall purpose of the statute, what was the common law

379. The leading case is Universal Camera Corp. v. NLRB, 340 U.S. 474 (1951). See generally, Davis, Administrative Law Treatise, chap. 29 (1958) and forthcoming corresponding chapter of second edition; Davis, *supra* n.253, chap. 29.

meaning of the disputed statutory word);[380] or (b) it is likely to be found asserting the oft-heard proposition that an administrative agency's interpretation of its own statute is entitled to receive great weight by the reviewing court — especially when the interpretation has been long-continued and had been, in effect, "ratified" by subsequent legislative appropriations for continued enforcement of the statute and/or legislative reenactments of it without any change in the interpreted language.[381]

When, on the other hand, the Court calls it a question of law it will usually substitute its independent judgment. But (a) this does not necessarily mean it will disagree with the agency interpretation; and (b) the Court sometimes seems to be saying that there are *some* questions of *law* on which the agency is so competent that it is entitled to deference.

In these cases of applying statutory language to the facts, predicting when the Supreme Court will take the deferential attitude and when the independent is extremely difficult. The Court has thus far done a poor job of rationalizing its decisions in this area.[382]

(iii) Forms of Judicial Deference to Agencies

It may be helpful to round up some other ways in which courts may or may not pay deference to agencies — i.e., other than in review of fact findings and other than in the kind of review they *sometimes* give to agency applications of statutory language to the facts.

1. Consider first the case of rulemaking. Here the agency is *not* conducting a formal (trial-type) hearing to adjudicate whether an unfair labor practice order or cease-and-desist order or monetary penalty order should be issued against a company. That is the kind of hearing in which the "substantial evidence" test for fact findings is obviously pertinent. Instead the agency, let us assume, is exercising its "legislative" rather than "judicial" function; it is conducting a hearing as a step toward issuance of a regulation with the force of law. Of the "informal" or "notice-and-comment" rulemaking type, the hearing is analogous to a congressional hearing on proposed legislation. Under the Administrative Procedure Act (5 U.S.C. §706) the major standard for testing validity of the rule in court is not "substantial evidence," but whether the rule is "arbitrary, capricious, an abuse of discretion or otherwise not in accordance with law." This is roughly related to

380. See NLRB v. Hearst Publications, Inc., 322 U.S. 111 (1944); Nathanson, Administrative Discretion in the Interpretation of Statutes, 3 Vand. L. Rev. 470 (1950).

381. See Davis, *supra* n.253 at 126-133; Annot., 39 L. Ed. 2d 942 (1975).

382. Davis, Administrative Law Treatise, chap. 30 (1958) and forthcoming corresponding chapter of second edition; Davis, *supra* n.253, chap. 30.

the 1935 Supreme Court determination[383] that there is generally a "presumption" of validity of an administrative regulation just as there is of a statute. The effect is a deference to the agency with the burden of persuasion put on the side of the party attacking the regulation.

But there are complications. One is the fact that as the APA (§553(c)) recognizes, a specific statute governing the agency may require that a rulemaking hearing should be "on the record"; and if so, the APA's provisions in Sections 556 and 557 for trial-type hearings (including the "substantial evidence" requirement on review, and evidence and cross-examination as in a court) will apply.

Another complication is this: Instead of saying that the rulemaking is to be "on the record," a statute may specify that to be upheld on judicial review a rule should be supported by "substantial evidence" on the record as a whole.[384] Is the effect equivalent to that of saying "on the record"? Or should the agency use the informal notice-and-comment procedure on the assumption that "substantial evidence" was being used loosely rather than in the sense of trial evidence; that the agency rule was to be sufficiently supported by the record's informal comment evidence *to avoid being arbitrary or capricious.* On this point, the "law is divided but the view that is tending to prevail" is the latter view.[385] Still further complications have arisen from the fact that some recent statutes for particular agencies have added to the normal notice and comment rulemaking procedure some attenuated elements of "on the record" rulemaking, e.g., right of cross-examination, but subject to certain qualifications.[386]

This statutory trend has been accompanied by an effort in Congress to enlarge the scope of *judicial review* of rules — mainly to re-

383. Pacific States Box & Basket Co. v. White, 296 U.S. 176 (1935).

384. For examples see the Occupational Safety and Health Act of 1970, 84 Stat. 1597, 29 U.S.C. §655(f); Consumer Product Safety Act of 1972, 86 Stat. 1218, 15 U.S.C. §2060(c); Federal Trade Commission Improvements Act of 1975, 88 Stat. 2195, 15 U.S.C. §57a(e)(3)(A); Toxic Substances Control Act of 1976, 90 Stat. 2040, 15 U.S.C. §2618(c)(1)(B)(i).

385. Davis, Administrative Law Treatise, §6.6 at 465 (2d ed. 1980). Judge Friendly's oft-quoted observation in Associated Indus. v. Department of Labor, 487 F.2d 342 (2d Cir. 1973) is that the substantial evidence test and the arbitrary and capricious test "tend to converge." Davis comments: "After all, the heart of both standards is the requirement of reasonableness or rationality, and that is what matters. The literal words, 'substantial evidence,' have always been a total misfit for rules that may properly rest only on interpretation or policy, and the nonliteral interpretation of "substantial evidence" has always been synonymous with "reasonable." Davis, *id.* at 468.

386. Davis, *id.* at §6.9. For example, the Federal Trade Commission Improvements Act of 1974 (15 U.S.C. §57a) allows oral as well as documentary evidence; and if the agency finds it necessary for resolution of disputed issues of material fact, an interested person is entitled to submit rebuttal evidence and conduct cross-examination (or have it conducted by the agency) subject to certain agency controls. The Toxic Substances Control Act of 1976 (15 U.S.C. §2605(c)(3)(A)) is rather similar.

quire the reviewing court to decide legal questions "independently"; to eliminate the long-standing presumption of validity of rules and the "arbitrary or capricious" standard for review of rules; and to require "substantial support" in the rulemaking file for the factual basis of the rule. An early variant of the chief measure to accomplish this (the "Bumpers amendment") passed the Senate in 1979, but neither it nor its other variants has yet been successful.[387]

Thus the anti-regulatory agency trend we have seen manifested in efforts at greater control through the *President,* and through legislative veto as well as other techniques of *congressional* oversight, manifests itself in the drive for greater controls by the third branch of government, the *judiciary*. The political conservatives who support this latter movement have also been opposed, however, to "judicial activism," arguing for judicial deference to the legislative branch on constitutional issues. The elected legislature is thus being distinguished, as an object of deference, from the unelected administrative agency.

Another point: If a change is to be made in the way that agencies conduct their rulemaking, could the courts accomplish this *without* statutory help? Could they themselves add to the rulemaking requirements set down by the Administrative Procedure Act, e.g., by requiring stricter rules of evidence or requiring the agency to allow cross-examination (assuming no provision in the agency's statute for such additional requirements)? The Supreme Court has said no.[388]

2. Suppose the National Labor Relations Board sent a company a notice that the Board would hold a hearing on a specified date to determine whether the company had engaged in an unfair labor practice under the Act. The company, claiming that the business of the plant involved intrastate rather than interstate commerce and there-

387. See generally, O'Reilly, Deference Makes A Difference: A Study of Impacts of the Bumpers Judicial Review Amendment, 49 U. Cin. L. Rev. 739 (1980); Bliss, *supra* n.298 at 640-643; Woodward & Levin, In Defense of Deference: Judicial Review of Agency Action, 31 Ad. L. Rev. 329 (1979). See also on rulemaking generally, Gellhorn & Robinson, Rulemaking Due Process: An Inconclusive Dialogue, 48 U. Chi. L. Rev. 201 (1981); Delong, Informal Rulemaking and the Integration of Law and Policy, 65 Va. L. Rev. 259 (1979); Pedersen, The Decline of Separation of Functions in Regulatory Agencies, 64 Va. L. Rev. 991, 1011-1020 (1978); Davis, *supra* n.385, chaps. 6 & 7.

388. Section 553 of the APA on rulemaking "established the maximum procedural requirements that Congress was willing to have the courts impose upon agencies in conducting rulemaking procedures. Agencies are free to grant additional procedural rights in the exercise of their discretion, but reviewing courts are generally not free to impose them if the agencies have not chosen to grant them. This is not to say necessarily that there are no circumstances which would ever justify a court in overturning agency action because of a failure to employ procedures beyond those required by statute. But such circumstances, if they exist, are extremely rare." Vermont Yankee Nuclear Power Corp. v. National Resources Defense Council, 435 U.S. 519 (1978). See "*Vermont Yankee* . . . Three Perspectives" (comments by Professors Stewart, Byse, & Breyer), 91 Harv. L. Rev. 1804 (1978).

fore did not come under the Act, went into federal court for an injunction to restrain the Board from holding the hearing. The Supreme Court has said that a "long-settled rule of judicial administration" should be applied to this situation, the rule of "exhaustion of administrative remedies." The Board having initiated an administrative proceeding, it was the company's duty to exhaust this remedy before going to the court.[389] The exhaustion rule has been riddled with exceptions by some courts — typically where wholly non-factual determinations are involved — but the basic rule does illustrate a court deference to the agency. The court wishes to gain the benefit of agency expertise before it concerns itself with the problem.

3. Analogous to the exhaustion rule is that of "primary jurisdiction." Here, unlike the situation in an exhaustion case, no administrative proceeding has been or is about to be commenced. The case has been brought in court and at least one of the issues is an issue that an administrative agency has special competence and adequate authority to handle (and no statute has given exclusive authority to either court or agency), so the court says the agency should have priority on the issue. The court either dismisses the suit or retains the case on its docket to await the agency action.[390]

4. One other illustration of court deference to the agency is the law applicable to "mandamus." Mandamus is a court remedy, one of whose uses is to command an official to perform a public duty. The remedy is qualified, to minimize interference with the functioning of officials. Thus, courts may say that the remedy is available to command the exercise of only "ministerial" (nondiscretionary) duties, or to compel an officer to perform a discretionary duty, but not to compel him to exercise his discretion in a particular way. True, exceptions are sometimes recognized where an official's exercise of discretion has been "arbitrary," and indeed alternative remedies like injunction may avoid the limits on the mandamus remedy, but mandamus doctrine does reflect a concern by courts for the prerogatives of a sister agency of government.[391]

e. Court and Legislature (Relations Additional to Those Shown in Chapters 3 and 5)

The sharpest confrontation between court and legislature occurs when a court strikes down a statute as unconstitutional. This phenom-

389. Myers v. Bethlehem Shipbuilding Corp., 303 U.S. 41 (1938). See Davis, Administrative Law Treatise, chap. 20 (1958) and forthcoming corresponding chapter of 2d edition; Davis, *supra* n.253, chap. 20.

390. Davis, *id* (treatise), chap. 19; Davis, *supra* n.253, chap. 19.

391. On mandamus generally, see Davis, *id.* (treatise) §23.09; Davis, *supra* n.253, §23.06.

enon will not be treated at this point, because it is considered at some length in Chapter 5. So too, I am postponing until Chapter 3 two other aspects of court-legislature relations: the process of court interpretation of statutes, and the phenomenon of a court resolving a common law problem (i.e., a nonstatutory problem) in the light of a statutory policy in a related field. At this point, I want to deal with a number of miscellaneous other aspects of the coexistence of courts and legislatures.

(1) Differences of Kind and Degree in the Functioning of Courts and Legislatures

Consider, first, some salient differences in the functioning of these two institutions.

What a court can do is rather strictly limited by what the parties bring to it. In general, the issues considered by the court are only those raised by the parties, and the facts considered are only those in the "record" of oral and documentary evidence presented by the parties. The court's judgment represents *not* its view of the optimum solution for all people who find themselves facing the same kind of social problem presented by the case, but primarily whether the particular record justifies the granting or denial of the particular relief requested by the particular plaintiff. There are some qualifications to this generalization, including occasions when courts considered issues not raised by the parties and granted a form of relief not requested. And persons other than the parties are being listened to when an appellate court grants permission to, say, the American Civil Liberties Union or the Association of American Railroads to file a written argument as "amicus curiae" (friend of the court).[392] From that source, moreover (or, indeed, from the parties' written arguments or from the court's own investigation or general knowledge), certain facts not in the record may properly be "judicially noticed" by the court. The doctrine of judicial notice traditionally has allowed a court to give weight to facts that are outside the record but so reliable that no proof is needed. The doctrine has been rather loosely applied in recent years, modifications are being suggested, and its boundaries are presently unclear.[393]

One other feature of a court's functioning should be added: At the same time that it is attempting to do justice in the particular case, it is attempting to integrate the case into the body of preexisting principle. This continuing, reasoned elaboration of principle was stressed

392. See Comment, The Amicus Curiae, 55 Nw. L. Rev. 469 (1961); Auerbach et al., *supra* n.5 at 228-231 (1961).

393. See McCormick, Evidence, chap. 35 (2d ed. 1972); Davis, *supra* n.385, chap. 15.

by Henry M. Hart as a distinctive virtue of the judicial process in legal development.[394]

In the respects discussed above, a legislature is more freewheeling than a court. Though it pays some attention to how its new laws fit in with existing statutes, it is not focusing on the weaving of a consistent body of principle. Further, the facts and issues and solutions that the legislature considers do not depend on what the parties to a particular dispute put before it. A legislative committee may receive input from anyone interested in its investigation or in the bill the committee is considering. Nor is the committee limited by that input; it may supplement it by its own staff studies or other material bearing on the relevant facts, as well as on arguments and possible solutions to the problems being considered. Compared to the court's limited options, the legislature's range of solutions is broad: It may choose from a variety of different forms of statutes, with different kinds of sanctions, perhaps with provision for an administrative agency to provide continuous attention to the problems giving rise to the statute. (One thing the legislature can *not* do consistently with the Constitution is to enact a "bill of attainder" — one that singles out persons or groups for punishment without trial.)[395]

In general, the legislature is concerned with rules for people generally or for large groups of people, rather than with a dispute between two antagonists; and it is formulating rules for the future rather than being concerned with the rights of two parties with respect to some past happenings. There is a maxim of statutory interpretation to the effect that a statute is "presumed" to have been intended to operate prospectively only, unless it deals with a matter of procedure rather than substance. However, this is only a rebuttable presumption, and some substantive statutes have been construed as operating retroactively. As so construed, the statute may be upheld where the court is convinced that the legislature had good reason to make it retroactive and the backward impact is not unreasonably harsh.[396]

To this qualification on the distinction between legislatures and courts there should be added another: A court decision need not always address itself to past facts. A comparatively recent development in judicial practice is this: Where there is announced a new rule, that either overrules an earlier decision or applies to a situation never before adjudicated, the court may avoid a possibly harsh retroactive

394. Hart's comments are in Paulsen, ed., Legal Institutions Today and Tomorrow 46-48 (1959).

395. See U.S. v. Brown, 381 U.S. 437 (1965); Annot., 4 L. Ed. 2d 2155 (1959).

396. See, e.g., Nowak et al., Constitutional Law 428-436 (1978); Hochman, The Supreme Court and the Constitutionality of Retroactive Legislation, 73 Harv. L. Rev. 692 (1960); Auerbach et al., *supra* n.5 at 173. For analysis of the concept of retroactivity, see Munzer, Retroactive Law, 6 J. Legal Stud. 373 (1977).

impact by making the new rule apply only to future cases, or to future cases and the case being decided but to no others.[397]

Under the orthodox approach, the new rule would apply not only to similar future cases and the case being decided but also to anyone whose situation arising before the decision was similar to the situation in the decided case. That individual would, generally speaking, have the benefit or burden of the decision when his situation was brought to court — assuming that the "statute of limitations," which puts a limit on the time within which a suit can be brought, had not yet expired. If his case had already been decided the other way prior to the case announcing the new rule, traditionally he would not be affected by the new rule, because of the principle of "res judicata" (the matter has been adjudicated). However, in spite of this salutary policy against the constant relitigation of cases, some exceptions have developed in this "new law" situation, especially in criminal cases.[398]

Finally, there is a sense in which statutory law has more of a *planned* quality about it — even discounting the fact that pressures from those who stand to gain or lose from the proposed legislation make the planning process something less than balanced and disinterested. That is, statutory law is not so dependent on a *chance* element which afflicts the system of nonstatutory law — the fact that a court will not deal with a problem until a genuine controversy between two parties has happened to occur and been placed by them before the court.

This chance element in the case law system requires some elaboration. One wonders how a legal system can develop in a socially desirable way when its rules are made *ad hoc* for particular parties who happen to have come into the kind of conflict that brought them to court. Karl Llewellyn once explained the social efficacy of the case law system by saying that litigation arises out of conflict, and conflict arises in fields of social activity where growth is taking place — where the relative strength of interest groups is changing. To which Lon Fuller responded: Where social change is rapid, case law with its crowded calendars cannot keep up; the pecuniary interest of an individual may be so slight as to make litigation or appeal impracticable (citing the abuses that grew up without judicial curb in the field of weekly premium "industrial life insurance"); and the chance element may have an unhealthy effect on the direction of legal growth.[399]

In explanation of the last point: Llewellyn himself had recognized

397. Schaefer, The Control of "Sunbursts": Techniques of Prospective Overruling, 41 N.Y.U.L. Rev. 631 (1967); Levy, Realist Jurisprudence and Prospective Overruling, 109 U. Pa. L. Rev. 1 (1960); Auerbach et al., *supra* n.5, at 175-178. The problem is discussed more fully in chapter 4 at nn. 50-61.

398. See Auerbach et al., *supra* n.5 at 174-175.

399. Fuller, American Legal Realism, 82 U. Pa. L. Rev. 429, 438-442 (1934).

that often a whole field of law may be (as paraphrased by Fuller) "influenced permanently by the particular turn taken by the first case arising in the field. This case may have carried a certain factual and ethical complexion which was actually the determinative element in its decision. The court in deciding it, however, may lay down a categorical rule which subsequently becomes divorced from the particular circumstances of its first utterance, and controls perhaps hundreds of cases which from an ethical or factual viewpoint are quite different from the first and 'critical' case." And "organized interest-groups . . . may see to it that these cases 'come up in the right way.' "[400]

To this importance of the "first case," Fuller added the importance of the *order* in which the later cases come up. There might be an "accidental absence of a decision which might serve as a doctrinal bridge between existing rules and needed new law." He cited as an example the case of Shuey v. United States,[401] in which the Supreme Court decided that a published offer of a reward could be effectively revoked by an announcement given equal publicity, even though the revocation was not then known by the plaintiff, who thereafter expended his efforts to do the things for which the reward was offered. Prior to this decision, the general rule was that a revocation of an offer was not effective until communicated. Hence, while Pollock, a leading British writer on contracts, found the decision reasonable, he thought it a "strong piece of judicial legislation." Fuller commented: Suppose that between the earlier cases and the Shuey case, a case had come up "in which a letter of revocation had been promptly delivered at the place of business of the offeree and had been allowed to remain unopened on his desk. Without much question a court would have held that such a revocation was 'communicated' so soon as the offeree had had a fair opportunity to become familiar with it. And had such a case existed before the Shuey case is it likely that anyone would have regarded that decision as a 'strong piece of judicial legislation'? Pollock's attitude was influenced by the purely fortuitous circumstances that there did not exist a case which could operate to carry his mind, without shock, from the older cases to the decision in the Shuey case."[402]

(2) Legal Change: By Court or By Legislature? And Who Has the Last Word?

The differences already mentioned in the functioning of courts and legislatures have some bearing on the recurrent question of

400. *Id.* at 440.
401. 92 U.S. 73 (1875).
402. Fuller, *supra* n.399 at 441.

whether a reform in the law should be by way of common law or by statute.

In recent years the issue has been posed sharply by cases in a number of states dealing with the issue of whether a particular immunity from tort liability should be abolished. Largely because of the widespread availability of insurance to potential defendants, we live in an era of expanding pressures for the proposition that injured people should be compensated for their injuries. So, long-standing tort immunities have been under attack, in state after state: immunity of the municipal and state governments, of hospitals and other charitable corporations, of parent to child and spouse to spouse.[403] One of the problems raised was whether the court should overrule its precedents establishing the immunity or whether it should leave it up to the legislature to make the reform. Most of the courts facing the issue have decided to take the plunge themselves — even, in some instances, when a legislative bill to make the change had died in committee or had been voted down by the legislature. A legislature that failed to act, or that acted negatively, was viewed by these courts as wanting to leave it up to the courts to retain or modify their own judge-made doctrines, rather than as wanting the courts to retain those doctrines.[404]

The choice that a court makes between judicial reform and possible legislative reform requires an assessment of the competing virtues of courts and legislatures for the job. As I have already suggested, the legislature typically has an advantage in broader access to relevant facts, broader representation of interests, and broader range of solutions. This was why Justice Brandeis dissented in a well-known case that recognized for the first time a kind of property right in the news. The International News Service had been copying, and distributing as its own, news items that had appeared in early editions of newspapers affiliated with the Associated Press or in publicly posted AP news bulletins. The Supreme Court majority supported AP's claims and enjoined the INS practices. Justice Brandeis's dissent recognized that the common law has a "capacity for growth," but thought that in this case, court "recognition of a new private right may work serious injury to the general public unless the boundaries of the right are

403. See Prosser, Law of Torts 984-987 (governments), 992-996 (charities), 859-867 (parent-child and husband-wife) (4th ed. 1971).

404. See, e.g., Holytz v. City of Milwaukee, 17 Wis. 2d 26, 36-39, 42-43, 115 N.W.2d 618, 623-625, 626-627 (1962), and cases cited therein. See also Battala v. State, 20 N.Y.2d 237, 176 N.E.2d 729 (1961); Collopy v. Newark Eye & Ear Infirmary, 27 N.J. 29, 141 A.2d 276 (1958). An instance of the same point of view being taken by a court to defend its abolition rather than recognition of a common law right of action is the Washington Supreme Court's abolition in 1980 of the action for alienation of affections — an abolition that had been accomplished legislatively in more than a score of states. Wyman v. Wallace, 94 Wash. 2d 99, 615 P.2d 452 (1980).

definitely established and wisely guarded." The legislature might wish to bar injunctions while allowing damages, perhaps in fixed amount; it might allow remedies only if the AP had assumed the obligation of supplying news at reasonable rates and without discrimination to all newspapers applying; it might wish to establish an administrative agency. "Courts are ill-equipped to make the investigations which should precede a determination of the limitation which should be set upon any property right in news, or of the circumstances under which news gathered by a private agency should be deemed affected with the public interest. Courts would be powerless to prescribe the detailed regulations essential to full enjoyment of the rights conferred, or to introduce the machinery required for enforcement of such regulations. . . . ."[405]

But note some limitations on the preference for legislative action. The situation is one in which the legislature, after all, *has not* acted. And this may not be the result of a deliberative choice, mindful of the public interest. Just as the blatant inaction of malaportioned state legislatures finally led the Supreme Court to change its mind and treat a constitutional attack on malaportionment as a justiciable controversy, some kinds of legislative inaction may induce courts to make common law reforms that might not otherwise have been made. Legislative action, for instance, may be stymied by the fact that the interest to be benefited by the reform — as in the case of the injured victim of a tort — is underrepresented before the legislature. It may be an unorganized interest, opposed by an organized interest that stands to lose from the reform. Or the relevant facts may be well enough known to (or available to) courts, so that legislative superiority in fact gathering is immaterial. Or no complex, regulatory solution may be needed — merely a right of action in court.

Such factors are pertinent to the court's intelligent choice — along with other facts about the characteristics and operations of state legislators, which are sometimes cited in order to question whether legislators are better representatives of the public interest than members of the typical state supreme court.[406]

405. International News Serv. v. Associated Press, 248 U.S. 215, 262-267 (1918). More recently, an important study, after pointing to some limits on the legislative and administrative process paralleling those on the courts, nonetheless finds a substantial difference in degree. It concludes that on certain issues of social policy, "the judicial process is a poor format for the weighing of alternatives and the calculation of costs," the anticipation of primary and secondary "consequences," the necessary "oversight" that is associated with a legislatively creative administrative agency, the exercise of a broad-based, informed insight unconfined by the walls of a particular piece of litigation. See Horowitz, The Courts and Social Policy, chap. 7 (1977).

406. See Peck, The Role of Courts and Legislatures in the Reform of Tort Law, 48 Minn. L. Rev. 265, 270-285 (1963). See also Bodenheimer, Power, Law and

Thus, a reasonable approach to the issue of court versus legislature in law reform seems to be not to favor one or the other for all law reforms, but to choose one or the other depending on its appropriateness for the particular reform being considered.[407]

Assuming the court has chosen judicial reform, this does not mean the legislature is barred from acting on the subject thereafter. In the tort cases I have mentioned, for instance, there were times when a legislature struck back by modifying the judicial reform. Thus when the Supreme Court of Wisconsin overruled its precedents supporting municipal immunity from tort liability, the legislature passed a statute making municipalities liable in tort but establishing certain exceptions and fixing a $25,000 maximum liability.[408]

So the legislature can have the last word when it comes to modifying a common law doctrine. It also has the last word when it modifies a judicial interpretation of the meaning of a statute. This was true, for instance, when the Supreme Court's ruling that the Sherman antitrust law applied to insurance transactions across state lines was followed by the McCarran Act renouncing federal antitrust controls and consenting to state regulation of the insurance industry.[409] Where the Court has the last word is in a ruling that a statute is unconstitutional. To change that ruling, if the Court cannot be persuaded to change its mind, the Constitution itself would have to be amended. This happened, for example, when the Supreme Court's invalidation of the federal income tax law[410] was followed by the Sixteenth Amendment, and invalidation of the federal provision for eighteen-year-olds' voting in state elections[411] was followed by the Twenty-sixth Amendment.

However, even on constitutional issues there may be some indirect and preventive weapons available to the legislature. One is control over court jurisdiction. Thus, you will recall that Article III of the Constitution, after specifying the Supreme Court's original jurisdiction, says that in other cases the Supreme Court shall have appellate jurisdiction "with such exceptions and under such regulations as the Congress shall make." This congressional control over Supreme Court

---

Society 107-114 (1973), which lists some criteria for determining when a court should be innovative and when it should leave the change to the legislature.

407. Peck, *supra* n.406 at 296-312.

408. See Holytz v. City of Milwaukee, 17 Wis. 2d 26, 115 N.W.2d 618 (1962), and 1963 Wis. Laws, chap. 198 (Wis. Stat. §895.43(1969)). See also the legislative responses in Minnesota, Illinois, New Jersey, and California, described in Peck, *supra* n.406 at 287-289.

409. See U.S. v. South-Eastern Underwriters Assn., 322 U.S. 533 (1944), and 59 Stat. 33 (1945), 15 U.S.C. §§1011-1015 (1958). See also Prudential Ins. Co. v. Benjamin, 328 U.S. 408 (1946).

410. Pollock v. Farmers' Loan & Trust Co., 157 U.S. 429 (1895); rehearing, 158 U.S. 601 (1895).

411. Oregon v. Mitchell, 400 U.S. 112 (1970).

appellate jurisdiction was invoked by Senator Jenner in a bill he introduced after some Supreme Court decisions in 1956 and 1957. The decisions, which he considered too liberal, dealt with the power of congressional investigating committees, federal and state programs aimed at subversive activities, and state requirements for admission to the bar. His bill would have deprived the Supreme Court thereafter of appellate jurisdiction in these classes of cases.

The precedent that he thought supported the bill was the post–Civil War case of Ex parte McCardle.[412] Here Congress, in order to prevent Supreme Court determination of the constitutionality of certain Reconstruction legislation, had passed a law withdrawing from the Court's jurisdiction over "appeals" certain kinds of habeas corpus cases (of which McCardle's case was one). The case had already been argued before the Supreme Court and was awaiting decision at the time the law was adopted. Still, the Supreme Court unanimously decided that the law had validly deprived it of the authority to decide the case.

In 1980 and 1981 Senator Helms and others, because of this decision and Congress's control over jurisdiction of the lower federal courts, was sponsoring a congressional withdrawal of all federal court jurisdiction over cases relating to validity of prayers in the public schools, abortion, and busing for school desegregation, thus leaving the issue up to the 50 state supreme courts.

But at least as far as the Supreme Court is concerned, it is a mistake to suppose that this congressional power over court jurisdiction is unlimited. In the first place, the Court in the *McCardle* case had not sanctioned a major impairment of its power to deal with the issue in the case. This is because other statutes permitted the Supreme Court to consider habeas corpus petitions in the exercise of its "*certiorari*" jurisdiction, and in the following year it held that it had jurisdiction to grant habeas corpus in such a suit, raising the same issue of constitutionality of the Reconstruction legislation.[413] Secondly, remember that Article III vests in the Supreme Court, and in such inferior federal courts as Congress may establish, the federal judicial power — a power that extends to "all cases in law and equity, arising under" the Constitution, laws, and treaties; and remember further that the very concept of an effective Supreme Court under our constitutional plan seems to imply a court power to keep the Congress as well as the executive and the states within their prescribed powers. These considerations plausibly lead to a narrow reading of the power given to Congress over the Court's appellate jurisdiction. As Professor Henry

412. 74 U.S. (7 Wall.) 506 (1868).

413. Ex parte Yerger, 75 U.S. (8 Wall.) 85 (1869). There was no decision rendered on the constitutional issue, because Yerger was thereafter released from the challenged military custody, thus making the case "moot," i.e., presenting a dead issue.

M. Hart has put it, the exceptions that Congress may make to the Court's appellate jurisdiction must not be such as would "destroy the essential role of the Supreme Court in the constitutional plan."[414] Nor should they be such as would violate due process or other constitutional limits. Thirdly, there is some authority for invalidating statutes on the ground that their purpose or motive is to undo or obstruct, judicial protection of constitutional rights.[415]

Fortifying these arguments are certain practical considerations: If the lower federal courts or the state courts were left with final authority on the issues being withdrawn from the Supreme Court's appellate jurisdiction, a well-nigh intolerable situation arises: inconsistency among these courts in interpreting the Constitution (with perhaps some unanimity created by some courts' treating as precedent the very Supreme Court decision that had led to the congressional withdrawal of jurisdiction). "The federal system," as Professor Herbert Wechsler has said, "needs federal courts and the judicial institution needs an organ of supreme authority."[416]

Besides congressional regulation of federal court jurisdiction, there is another weapon that Congress might try to use — but again, I think, not a potent one. I refer to congressional control over the size of the Supreme Court (the Constitution being silent on the number of Justices). The Court originally had six Justices, and at various times had seven and ten, but has had nine since 1869. President Roosevelt's famous "court-packing" plan of 1937 (call it "court enlargement" if you would have favored the plan) differed from the earlier legislation changing the size of the Court because it was more clearly aimed at overcoming existing attitudes of the Court on constitutional issues. The reasons initially given were largely in terms of the volume of work, but these reasons were soon demolished by a letter from Chief Justice Hughes and Justices Van de Vanter and Brandeis to the chairman of the Senate Judiciary Committee. The real reasons seemed to most lawyers — even some New Dealers — to make the proposed legislation violative of the spirit if not the letter of the Constitution. This apparent breaking with the spirit of constitutional provisions safe-

414. Hart, The Power of Congress to Limit the Jurisdiction of Federal Courts, 66 Harv. L. Rev. 1362, 1365 (1953). See also Berger, Congress v. The Supreme Court 285-296 (1969); Bator, Mishkin, Shapiro & Wechsler, Federal Courts and Federal System 360-365 (2d ed. 1973).

415. For recent discussion of the problem, including limits on *McCardle,* see Sager, Foreword: Constitutional Limitations on Congress' Authority to Regulate the Jurisdiction of the Federal Courts, 94 Harv. L. Rev. 17 (1981). See Taylor, Limiting Federal Jurisdiction: The Unconstitutionality of Current Legislative Proposals, 65 Jud. 198 (1981); Nowak et al., *supra* n.222 at 41-48. For some pro and con discussions of the recent bills see Symposium, 65 Jud. 177 (1981).

416. Wechsler, The Courts and the Constitution, 65 Colum. L. Rev. 1001, 1006-1007 (1965).

guarding judicial independence (life tenure; no diminution of pay while in office) undoubtedly contributed to the defeat of the bill.[417]

7. Techniques: A Summary Outline

In the preceding sections on the functions and functioning of the various agencies of the law, I have already referred, in an incomplete way, to the distinctive techniques by which their respective functions are carried out. Here is a summary roundup of these techniques.[418]

(a) *Techniques associated with the legislature are:*

(1) Setting standards of conduct by statute, which may be accompanied by the fixing of one or more sanctions for violation — though sometimes the standards are announced without penalty, and sometimes they are requirements in a government contract, or standards of eligibility for subsidy or other government benefit.

(2) Providing machinery and rules pursuant to which such standards and sanctions can be set.

(3) Investigating to determine the need for new or amending legislation.

(4) Taxing and spending, and otherwise providing for distribution of benefits — which may be widely distributed like public health, education, and highways, or more narrowly as in the case of welfare payments and subsidies to particular industries.

(5) Using a civil or criminal "contempt" sanction — using it itself or referring the case to a prosecutor — where a legislative function is being wilfully obstructed, as in the case of a witness unlawfully refusing to answer legislative committee questions. (The civil contempt sanction is designed to induce cooperation from the witness; his decision to cooperate will terminate the sanction.)

(6) Providing machinery and rules pursuant to which people may make — subject to certain controls — their own private arrangements for association, self-regulation, and

417. Basic materials in the debate on the plan will be found in Hearings on S. 1392 Before the Senate Comm. on the Judiciary, 75th Cong., 1st Sess. (1937); S. Rep. No. 711, 75th Cong., 1st Sess. (1937); Baker, Back to Back: The Duel Between FDR and the Supreme Court (1967); Burns, Roosevelt: The Lion and the Fox 291-315 (1956). See also, on presidential, congressional, and public controls over the Supreme Court, Chap. 5 herein at nn. 52-62.

418. See generally Summers, The Technique Element in Law, 59 Calif. L. Rev. 733 (1971); Cranston, Reform Through Legislation: The Dimension of Legislative Technique, 73 Nw. U.L. Rev. 873 (1979).

dispute-settling (such as rules with respect to making wills, forming corporations and unions, and entering into contractual arrangements on commercial and non-commercial matters, including agreements to arbitrate disputes).

(b) *Techniques associated with executive and administrative agencies are:*

(1) Planning and policy making; setting standards of conduct and eligibility as in (a)(1) above — though sanctions or penalties are not normally prescribed by the agencies. (The normal pattern is for the legislature to prescribe the sanctions, with the agency going to court to have them imposed. But there are some instances, when the sanction is non-criminal, of legislative authorization for agency prescription and even for agency imposition.)

(2) Carrying on investigations, inspections, and negotiations, and making informal decisions — all aimed principally at administering statutory or agency standards, obtaining compliance with standards, and obtaining information relevant to establishment and modification of standards. Statutes rarely authorize agencies themselves to administer monetary "contempt" sanctions for noncompliance with an agency subpoena. The agency typically tries to get a court order of enforcement, which when violated, results in a court contempt proceeding.

(3) Using more formal efforts to enforce compliance with standards of conduct and eligibility, through (in some of these situations, after administrative hearing) administrative cease-and-desist orders, granting and revocation of licenses, granting and revocation of subsidies and other financial benefits, publicizing derelictions, seizing offending articles like adulterated or misbranded food and drugs, and engaging in various criminal enforcement activities — including surveillance, arrest, search and seizure, administering prison regulations, and probation and parole supervision.

(4) Providing procedural rules, interpretations, statements of agency organization and the like, that will assist people in dealing with the agency and meeting its requirements.

(c) *Techniques associated with courts are:*

(1) The ordering of punishment (i.e., imprisonment and/or fine) and semi-punishment (such as the award of "punitive damages" in addition to compensatory damages in a noncriminal suit, or civil monetary penalties, or forfei-

tures of goods). Other sanctions are civil and criminal contempt, to punish or to induce conduct (see (a)(5) above).

(2) Ordering actual performance of a named obligation (e.g., the obligation to convey a piece of real estate you had agreed to convey and now refuse to convey) or restraining the performance of a named activity (e.g., your continued selling of certain unregistered securities in violation of a statute, or an official's continued enforcement of a statute).

(3) Ordering compensation for a legal injury. This is typically the well-known remedy of "damages" to one suffering some legal injury to his personal or property rights — though sometimes compensation can take the form of a compelled return of an item of property. Damage compensation can take various forms, such as the value of plaintiff's expenditures in labor, goods, or services that he made in reliance on defendant's promise, or an amount that would put plaintiff in as good a position as he would have been in if defendant had not committed the wrong against him.

(4) In arriving at its decision, the trial court uses an adversary hearing procedure — which is not used by the legislature nor, for some of their activities, by the agencies. However, there are also some atypical activities of courts that may involve no adversary hearings, such as naturalizing aliens, establishing court rules of procedure, establishing and supervising administration of requirements concerning membership in the bar of the court, handling uncontested proceedings such as often occur, e.g., in the field of probate and divorce, and enforcing a decree by supervising an enterprise or public institution (see under **D1b(5)** in this chapter).

Chapter 2

The Illustrative Case (Initial Aspects)

Having tried to give you, however sketchily, an overview of the legal system as a whole, I propose now to treat some aspects of it in greater detail. I shall do this by presenting a specific court case, and supplementing some features of it with background notes, in this and succeeding chapters.

The case was brought in a federal district court of South Carolina in 1962. The two women plaintiffs each filed the same "complaint." Reproduced below is the text of one of the complaints and the defendant's "motion to dismiss." The district court's order and opinion granting the motion to dismiss are also reproduced, together with the Fourth Circuit Court of Appeals opinion supporting reversal of the district court, and a small portion of the lawyers' briefs on appeal.

A. How It All Happened

1. The Complaint

Patricia A. Nappier, Plaintiff	)	
vs.	)	
	)	
Jefferson Standard Life Insurance Company	)	COMPLAINT
and Jefferson Standard Broadcasting Co.,	)	
a subsidiary of Jefferson Standard Life	)	
Insurance Co., Defendants	)	

The plaintiff complaining of the defendants herein alleges:

1. That the plaintiff is a resident of the County of Spartanburg, State of South Carolina.

2. That the defendant, Jefferson Standard Life Insurance Company is a foreign corporation organized and existing under and by virtue of the laws of one of the States of the United States other than the State of South Carolina, is licensed to do and was at the times hereinafter alleged doing business in the State of South Carolina; that the defendant Jefferson Standard Broadcasting Company is a corporation duly chartered under the laws of the State of North Carolina, is a subsidiary of Jefferson Standard Life Insurance Company, and, the defendants operate television station WBTW at Florence, South Carolina. That, on information and belief, the defendant, Jefferson Standard Life Insurance Company owns 1326 shares of stock of Jefferson Standard Broadcasting Company, there being only 4 other outstanding shares, and that the defendant, Jefferson Standard Broadcasting Company is under the direct control and supervision of the Jefferson Standard Life Insurance Company, that both corporations have common officers and directors and Jefferson Standard Life Insurance Company formulates and establishes the policies for the operation of Jefferson Standard Broadcasting Company and television station WBTW. This action is within the jurisdiction of this Court as there is a diversity of citizenship between the plaintiff and the defendants and the amount in controversy exceeds Ten Thousand ($10,000) Dollars, exclusive of costs and interest.

3. That the plaintiff at the times hereinafter alleged and for several years prior thereto was employed by the Dental Division of the South Carolina Department of Health and she, together with another young lady with whom she constantly travelled throughout the state and particularly throughout the area served by WBTW, put on dental health demonstrations in the public schools of this state. That the plaintiff and her co-worker were the only individuals in the state engaged in this type of work, which consisted primarily of putting on puppet demonstrations using a puppet which was commonly referred to as "Little Jack," and that because of their work this plaintiff and her co-worker were known throughout the state as "The Little Jack Girls." To be used in their work, the South Carolina Department of Health furnished plaintiff and her co-worker a station wagon on which was conspicuously inscribed on both sides "Little Jack, Dental Division, South Carolina State Department of Health."

4. That on November 27, 1961, this plaintiff together with her co-worker was in Kingstree, South Carolina, for the purpose of putting on their Little Jack Show in the public schools of Williamsburg County.

5. That this plaintiff who is a young, unmarried lady, together with her co-worker, had retired for the night on November 27, 1961, in a quiet, secluded motel at Kingstree, when during the early morning hours on November 28, 1961, a man broke into the quarters which plaintiff and her co-worker were occupying and raped each of them; that her attacker stole the said station wagon which was parked near the quarters she was occupying and fled.

6. That some time during the daylight hours on November 28, 1961, the subject station wagon was found abandoned in or near the City of Florence, and the defendants through their agents or servants, while acting within the scope and course of their employment, took pictures of the abandoned station wagon and televised the same on the news broadcast on Station WBTW at 6:30 P.M., and later that same day on the 11 P.M. telecast. That at both telecasts the words "Little Jack, Dental Division State Board of Health" were clearly visible on each side of the vehicle, both sides having been shown on the telecast pictures; the news announcer for the defendants identified the station wagon as that being used by the two young women who had been ravished at Kingstree, and further, the license number of the station wagon was shown in at least one of these pictures; all of which was done notwithstanding the fact that the defendants knew or reasonably should have known that the publication of these pictures of the station wagon would identify the rape victims.

7. That Sec. 16-81, Code of Laws of South Carolina, 1962, prohibits the publishing of the name of any female upon whom the crime of rape or assault with intent to ravish has been committed or alleged to have been committed in any type or form of publication.

8. That notwithstanding the above statute and without the permission or consent of the court or this plaintiff, the defendants willfully and deliberately published the pictures of the station wagon which plaintiff used in her work which clearly and positively identified this plaintiff as one of the young ladies upon whom this horrible crime was perpetrated.

9. That many and various individuals saw either or both of these telecasts as the television station operated by these defendants has a vast and broad coverage throughout a large portion of South Carolina; that by reason of the exhibition and showing of plaintiff's vehicle it became common talk of people in South Carolina that plaintiff was one of the young ladies who was subjected to the rapist and that because of the showing of said pictures many of her friends and people generally know about the horrible episode that she experienced and by which she will be identified during her entire lifetime.

10. That the publication by the defendants was done willfully, wantonly and in utter disregard of the statute laws of this state and without regard or concern of the right of privacy of this plaintiff.

11. That as a result and in consequence of the foregoing publications, this plaintiff has been demoralized, embarrassed, has suffered great mental pain, humiliation, mortification, has become highly nervous and has been unable to perform her regular employment, all to her damage in the sum of One Hundred Seventy Five Thousand ($175,000) Dollars, actual and punitive damages.

WHEREFORE, plaintiff demands judgment against the defendants in the sum of One Hundred Seventy Five Thousand ($175,000) Dollars, actual and punitive damages, together with the costs of this action and further demands a jury trial in the cause above set forth.

2. The Motion to Dismiss

Patricia A. Nappier, Plaintiff vs. Jefferson Standard Life Insurance Company and Jefferson Standard Broadcasting Co., a subsidiary of Jefferson Standard Life Insurance Co., Defendants	)))))))	MOTION TO DISMISS

The defendant, Jefferson Standard Broadcasting Company, moves the Court as follows:

1. For a dismissal of the within action upon the ground that the complaint fails to state a claim against this defendant upon which relief can be granted.

McEachin, Townsend & Zeigler,
Attorneys for Defendant,
Jefferson Standard Broadcasting Company.

Florence, S.C.
June 4, 1962

[*Note:* Each defendant upon due notice made the above motion in both cases.]

3. District Court Opinion

The text of the federal district court's opinion (reproduced below) is taken from the series of case reports known as *Federal Supplement,* which is confined to cases in the federal district courts. If you turn now to look at the reproduced opinion, what I am about to say will be clearer to you. The private publisher of these reports (West Publishing Co.) has added, after the identifying caption of the case and before the opinion itself, a short summary of the decision, plus six numbered sentences digesting six aspects of the opinion and fitted under four topics (Torts, Names, Statutes, and Telecommunications). The six numbers also appear in brackets before the paragraphs of the opinion from which the six numbered sentences are derived.

The four topics are listed together with a "key number" for each; for instance, the "Statutes" topic is listed with the number 190. The explanation of the numbering is as follows: If you look under the "Statutes" topic of West's *American Digest System,* you will find a breakdown of subtopics, of which one is "general rules of construction." Under that, a further subtopic is "meaning of language"; and of the 16 subtopics under that (covering key numbers 188 to 203), number 190 is listed as "existence of ambiguity." So West's editors decided that one sentiment in the opinion (which they summarized as "Court must apply the plain wording of an unambiguous statute regardless of how severe the consequences may be") should be fitted under their *Digest* topic "Statutes," keynote number 190. A future researcher interested in examining all court opinions that talk about the existence or nonexistence of ambiguity will find this sentiment from the *Nappier* case plus its citation listed among hundreds of others under "Statutes," keynote number 190 in the *American Digest System.*

Because the case was decided in 1963 in the United States District Court for the Eastern District of South Carolina, and the opinion text begins on page 174 of volume 213 of the *Federal Supplement,* the citation is: Nappier v. Jefferson Standard Life Insurance Co., 213 F. Supp. 174 (E.D.S.C. 1963). (While the decision deals with complaints by two separate plaintiffs, and each complaint lists two different defendants, it is common to use only the first plaintiff and defendant in the name of the case.)

Patricia A. NAPPIER, Plaintiff,
v.
JEFFERSON STANDARD LIFE INSURANCE COMPANY
and Jefferson Standard Broadcasting Company,
a subsidiary of Jefferson Standard Life
Insurance Company, Defendants.

S. Maxine GUNTER, Plaintiff,
v.
JEFFERSON STANDARD LIFE INSURANCE COMPANY
and Jefferson Standard Broadcasting Company,
a subsidiary of Jefferson Standard Life
Insurance Company, Defendants.

Civ. A. No. AC/911, AC/910
United States District Court
E.D. South Carolina,
Florence Division.
Jan. 23, 1963.

Actions against owners of television station for violation of state statute prohibiting publication of name of any woman who has been victim of an assault with intent to ravish or victim of rape, and for violation of right of privacy. The District Court, Wyche, J., held that defendants who were owners of television station which showed on newscasts the picture of state motor vehicle which had inscribed on the side thereof in part the name under which plaintiffs produced a show for school children and identified the station wagon as the one being used by two young women who had been ravished, did not violate South Carolina statute.

Actions dismissed.

1. Torts → 8

Statute prohibiting the publication of the name of any woman or child upon whom crime of rape or assault with intent to ravish has been committed is penal and must be strictly construed in a civil as well as a criminal case, and one seeking relief thereunder must bring his case squarely within the statute affording the penalty or relief. Code S.C. 1962, §16-81.

2. Names → 2

A person's "name" consists of one or more Christian or given names and one surname.

See publication Words and Phrases for other judicial constructions and definitions.

3. Statutes → 190

Court must apply the plain wording of an unambiguous statute regardless of how severe the consequences may be.

4. Torts → 8

South Carolina statute prohibiting publication of name of any woman or child upon whom crime of rape or an assault with intent to ravish has been committed does not prohibit publication of "stage names" or "assumed names" of the victims of an incident of rape or assault. Code S.C. 1962, §16-81.

5. Telecommunications → 439

Defendants, who were owners of television station which showed on newscasts the picture of state motor vehicle which had inscribed on side thereof in part the name under which plaintiffs produced a show for children and identified station wagon as one being used by two young women who had been ravished, did not violate South Carolina statute, prohibiting publication of name of any woman who has been victim of rape or an assault with intent to ravish. Code S.C. 1962, §16-81.

6. Telecommunications → 439

Owners of television station, which showed on newscasts a picture of state vehicle which was used by plaintiffs in traveling about the state and which had inscribed on the side thereof in part the name under which plaintiffs produced a show for school children and stated that station wagon was being used by two young women who had been ravished, did not sufficiently identify plaintiffs to give rise to cause of action for violation of their right of privacy.

Yancey A. McLeod, McLeod & Singletary, Harry M. Lightsey, Jr., Columbia, S.C., for plaintiffs.

P. H. McEachin, McEachin, Townsend & Zeigler, Florence, S.C., for defendants Jefferson Standard Life Insurance Co. and Jefferson Standard Broadcasting Co.

WYCHE, District Judge.

The above cases are before me upon motion of the defendants to dismiss upon the ground that the complaints do not allege a claim upon which relief can be granted.

The plaintiffs were in 1961, employed by the State of South Carolina as puppeteers, producing a show known as "Little Jack" which demonstrated health facts to the school children of the State. The plaintiffs were known throughout the State as "The Little Jack Girls" and traveled about the State in a station-wagon on the side of which was conspicuously inscribed "Little Jack, Dental Division, South Carolina State Department of Health." The defendants were and are owners and operators of Television Station WBTW in Florence, South Carolina. In November, 1961, the plaintiffs were the victims of an assault while on a trip to Kingstree, South Carolina, their attacker stealing the station-wagon described above to make his escape. On the following day the station-wagon was found abandoned in Florence, South Carolina. That night on both its 6:30 P.M. and 11:00 P.M. newscasts, the defendants broadcast pictures of the station-wagon on which the words "Little Jack, Dental Division, State Board of Health" together with the license number of the vehicle, were visible to the viewers of the television program. The announcer on these newscasts identified the station-wagon as the one being used by the two girls who had been raped in Kingstree.

Plaintiffs thereafter commenced these actions seeking damages for their mental anguish and suffering which had resulted from their alleged identification as the rape victims. These actions seek the recovery of damages because of the humiliation, mental pain, embarrassment and the subsequent inability of the plaintiffs to continue their work as the result of this television broadcast.

These actions are based upon the theory that the defendants have committed a tort through the violation of a South Carolina Statute (§16-81, Code of Laws of South Carolina, 1962), and violated the right of privacy of the plaintiffs. The defendants contend that the allegations of the complaints are not sufficient to state a cause of action under Section 16-81 and the common law of privacy in South Carolina, or under either of them, and that the complaints should be dismissed.

Section 16-81, Code of Laws of South Carolina, 1962, provides: "Misdemeanor to publish name of person raped, etc. Whoever publishes or causes to be published the name of any woman, maid or woman child upon whom the crime of rape or assault with intent to ravish has been committed or alleged to have been committed in this State in any newspaper, magazine or other publication shall be deemed guilty of a misdemeanor and, upon conviction thereof, shall be punished by a fine of not more than one thousand dollars or imprisonment of not more than three years. But the provisions of this section shall not apply to publications made by order of court."

[1] This statute is penal and must therefore be strictly construed in a civil as well as a criminal case. One who seeks relief thereunder must bring his case squarely within the provisions of the statute affording the penalty or relief. State v. Lewis, et al., 141 S.C. 207, 139 S.E. 386; Darlington Theatres, Inc. v. Coker, Sheriff, 190 S.C. 282, 2 S.E.2d 782; State ex rel. Moody v. Stem, et al., 213 S.C. 465, 50 S.E.2d 175; Independence Ins. Co. v. Independent Life and Acc. Ins. Co., 218 S.C. 22, 61 S.E.2d 399; State ex rel. v. Nat. Linen Service Corp., 225 S.C. 232, 81 S.E.2d 342.

Publication of *the name* "of any woman, maid or woman child upon whom the crime of rape or an assault with intent to ravish has been committed" constitutes a violation of this statute.

[2] The word "name" as set forth in the statute is not ambiguous, does not bear two or more constructions, and is not of such doubtful or obscure meaning that reasonable minds may disagree as to its meaning. A person's "name" consists of one or more Christian or given names and one surname or family name. Therefore, when the word "name" as set forth in the statute is taken in its plain, ordinary and usual sense, it means that which is the given and family name of a woman.

[3] The statute is effective for the purpose which is plainly expressed therein, namely, to prevent publication of *the name* of a victim of rape or assault as referred to therein. The scope of the statute, without construction of the word "name" to mean identification also, is more limited than it would be if the word "name" as set forth therein were construed and enlarged to mean identification. However, it is not my function to define the scope of an ambiguous word or statute, but to apply the plain wording of a statute as it is written, since the statute speaks for itself. I must adopt the plain meaning of a statute, however severe the consequences. Jay v. Boyd, 351 U.S. 345, 76 S. Ct. 919, 100 L. Ed. 1242.

[4] The plaintiffs allege in their complaints that they were known as "The Little Jack Girls," and contend that they have been named by the alleged publications of the defendants. Section 16-81 does not prohibit the publication of "stage names" or "assumed names" of the victims of an incident of rape or assault, it only prohibits publication of *the name,* which in plain, ordinary and usual terms means, as to these plaintiffs the name of "Maxine Gunter and Patricia Nappier."

[5] There is no allegation in the complaints that the "stage" or "assumed" names "The Little Jack Girls" were published. The plaintiffs simply allege that a station-wagon on which the words "Little Jack, Dental Division, State Board of Health" was shown, with the statement that the station-wagon was identified as being used by the two young women who had been ravished. The plaintiffs do not allege in their complaints that they have the "assumed" name of "Little Jack," which words they allege appeared on the side of the station-wagon.

It is my opinion that the defendants have not violated the South Carolina Statute, Section 16-81, Code of Laws of South Carolina, 1962.

[6] It is also my opinion that the defendants have not identified the plaintiffs sufficiently in the allegations of the complaint to allege a cause of action for damages for the violation of their right of privacy.

It is, therefore, ordered, that the motion to dismiss in each of the above entitled cases be and the same is hereby granted.

4. Court of Appeals Opinion

The court of appeals majority and dissenting opinions are reproduced below exactly as they appear in the *Federal Reporter* system beginning at 322 F.2d 502 (4th Cir. 1963). The Fourth Circuit embraces, in addition to South Carolina, the states of Maryland, West Virginia, Virginia, and North Carolina. The summary and key-number paragraphs added by the publisher in the *Federal Reporter* are here omitted, as is the court's statement of facts.

ALBERT V. BRYAN, Circuit Judge.

. . . The motion argued that the actual name of neither girl — as is true — was mentioned in the pictures or narrative, that the report was a matter of public interest and record, and so no cause of action for breach of privacy could be rested either upon the statute or on the common law. We disagree. "Name", we hold in the context of this case, is to be read in the statute as the equivalent of "identity". Since the broadcast, as pleaded, sufficiently identified the victims other than by name, it transgressed the statute and trespassed on the plaintiffs' privilege of privacy.

The meaning of the term "name" cannot be given the narrow import ascribed it by Standard without impairing the purpose of the statute. Aside from the personal protection of the woman involved, the object of this law, concededly, is to encourage a free report of the crime by the victim. Cf. State v. Evjue, 253 Wis. 146, 33 N.W.2d 305, 13 A.L.R.2d 1201 (1948). Fear of publicity might deter her from notifying the police. Thus the public interest is advanced by the statute: the crime is investigated promptly and the injured person is shielded.

These aims could not be fully achieved if only disclosure of one's proper name was forbidden. Publication of a description of the woman by identifying her through circumstances would in effect name her. After all, a name is but a designation, and a description is frequently a more positive identification than a name. State ex rel Lane v. Corneli, 347 Mo. 932, 149 S.W.2d 815 (1941). We recognize faces, or know persons by reputation, when we do not know them by name. Cf. Peck v. Tribune Co. 214 U.S. 185, 29 S. Ct. 554, 53 L. Ed. 960 (1909). An episode can be more revealing than a family name, a sobriquet than a surname.

In South Carolina the penal aspect of the statute does not require an interpretation so rigid as to strip its wording of its plain connotation. Carolina Amusement Co. v. Martin, 236 S.C. 558, 115 S.E.2d 273 (1960), cert. denied, 367 U.S. 904, 81 S. Ct. 1914, 6 L. Ed. 2d 1248 (1961); State v. Firemen's Ins. Co., 164 S.C. 313, 162 S.E. 334 (1931). This is certainly sound construction when, as here, the statute is only employed to provide civil redress. McKenzie v. Peoples Baking Co., 205 S.C. 149, 31 S.E.2d 154 (1944).

The Legislature could, of course, have used "identity" instead of "name", or put both in the statute, as do the laws of other states. E.g. Wisconsin Statutes of 1945, §348.412, as quoted in the Evjue case, supra, 253 Wis. 146, 33 N.W.2d 305; Florida Statutes, §794.03; Georgia Code, §26-2105. But "name" alone in the environment of the policy evidenced by the South Carolina statute is sufficient to comprehend "identity". That a description serves the purpose of a name is amply demonstrated in defamation cases. A libelee is nonetheless libeled though his name be not mentioned. Peck v. Tribune Co., supra, 214 U.S. 185, 29 S. Ct. 554, 53 L. Ed. 960 (1909); Nash v. Sharper, 229 S.C. 451, 93 S.E.2d 457, 459 (1956); Prosser, Torts 583 (1955).

No support for Standard's position is found in decisions upon a statute prohibiting the unauthorized use of a personal name, portrait or picture in advertising. E.g.: Gardella v. Log Cabin Products Co., 89 F.2d 891 (2 Cir., 1937); Levey v. Warner Bros. Pictures, Inc., 57 F. Supp. 40 (S.D.N.Y. 1944). For advertising, only the name, pseudonym or picture of the person — usually because of his prominence — is significant. Any other description is of no value. Consequently, the object of the law is not impinged unless the publication embodies the name, portrait or picture. That is not so in the statute now in review.

To repeat, we think the allegations of the complaints adequately demonstrate that the television in effect divulged the names of the two women. Thus each states a cause of action for intrusion upon privacy. South Carolina recognizes the right of privacy and affords a cause of action for an infringement. In Meetze v. Associated Press, 230 S.C. 330, 95 S.E.2d 606, 608, 609 (1956), the Court said:

". . . The following has been suggested as a fairly comprehensive definition of what constitutes an actionable invasion of the right of privacy: 'The unwarranted appropriation or exploitation of one's personality, the publicizing of one's private affairs with which the public has no legitimate concern, or the wrongful intrusion into one's private activities, in such manner as to outrage or cause mental suffering, shame, or humiliation to a person of ordinary sensibilities.' . . .

" 'The right of privacy is one which was not definitely recognized by the law until comparatively recent times. But we find ourselves in agreement with a number of authorities to the effect that the violation of such a right is under certain circumstances a tort which would entitle the injured person to recover damages.' "

While the plaintiffs have premised their suits, first, upon the breach of the statute and, second, upon the common law, there is no necessity to determine whether an action may be pitched solely on the statute, for it is clear the plaintiffs may sue under the common law as fortified by the statute.

Standard counters that the incident was a matter of public concern and record and so is exempted from the rule of privacy. Jenkins v. Dell Publishing Co., 251 F.2d 447 (3 Cir.), cert. denied, 357 U.S. 921, 78 S. Ct. 1362, 2 L. Ed. 2d 1365 (1958); Frith v. Associated Press, 176 F. Supp. 671, 674 (E.D.S.C. 1959); Meetze v. Associated Press, supra, 230 S.C. 330, 95 S.E.2d 606, 609 (1956); Prosser, Torts 643-44 (1955). The ready replication is that the statute states an exception to the exemption. No matter the news value, South Carolina has unequivocally declared the identity of the injured person shall not be made known in press or broadcast. Cf. State v. Evjue, supra, 253 Wis. 146, 33 N.W.2d 305. No constitutional infringement has been suggested. Indeed, Standard conceded in oral argument that if the broadcast did in fact and in law "name" the plaintiffs, then they had a right of action.

Dismissal of the complaints was error and the order must be set aside, the actions remanded for trial. Whether or not the defendants did in fact "name" the plaintiffs will then be an issue to be settled by the court or jury. On this point we intimate no view.

Reversed and remanded.

BARKSDALE, District Judge (dissenting).

With due deference to the views of the majority so ably expressed in Judge Bryan's opinion, I find myself unable to agree with the majority opinion, and therefore I dissent.

Although no information as to the legislative history of the South Carolina statute here involved (Section 16-81, Code of Laws of South Carolina 1962) appears in the record, I am willing to concede that the apparent objects of the Act were the "personal protection of the woman involved," and "to encourage a free report of the crime by the victim". But I cannot agree that in a statutory inhibition of publication of the "name of the victim", "name" is equivalent to "identity": "identity" is a much broader term than "name". If the South Carolina Legislature had intended by its statute to proscribe the publication of information from which "identity" could be determined, it could quite readily have said so, as does the Wisconsin statute.

The common law right of privacy exists in South Carolina, and an unwarranted invasion of this right is tortious and actionable, but it is not an absolute right, and where the alleged invasion of privacy is the publication of matter of public concern and record, it is not tortious nor actionable. Meetze v. Associated Press, 230 S.C. 330, 95 S.E.2d 606.

The majority take the view that "the plaintiffs may sue under the common law as fortified by the statute". It seems clear to me that plaintiffs have no cause of action at common law, because the published matter came within the well recognized exceptions to the right of privacy, and that even a liberal construction does not justify the court in equating "name" with "identity".

I would affirm the judgment of the District Court.

5. Arguing the Case

a. A Glimpse at the Lawyers' Briefs

I think you should have some idea of the form in which lawyers' written arguments are cast. While it would take too much space to reprint any substantial portion of the briefs, I am reproducing below the index pages of the appellees' brief, followed by some short excerpts from the argumentation on a particular point.

INDEX

TABLE OF CASES

[Omitted here are 38 additional cases listed alphabetically in the brief.]

STATUTES

TEXT AND TREATISES

Below is a portion of the argumentation from the appellees' brief, Point One, Part E:

E. NEW YORK RIGHT OF PRIVACY STATUTE AND RELATED CASES

The state of New York has a right of privacy statute, the pertinent provisions of which are as follows:

"New York Civil Rights Law (Consol. Laws c. 6) Article 5 — Right of Privacy.

"Section 50: A person, firm or corporation that uses for advertising purposes, or for the purposes of trade, the name, portrait or picture of any living person without having first obtained the written consent of such person, or if a minor, of his or her parent or guardian, is guilty of a misdemeanor.

"Section 51: Any person whose name, portrait or picture is used within this state for advertising purposes or for the purposes of trade without the written consent first obtained as above provided may maintain an equitable action in the Supreme Court of this state against the person, firm or corporation so using his name, portrait or picture, to prevent and restrain the use thereof; and may also sue and recover damages for any injuries sustained by reason of such use and if the defendant shall have knowingly used such person's name, portrait or picture in such a manner as is forbidden or declared to be unlawful by the last section, the jury, in its discretion, may award exemplary damages. . . ."

The New York state courts, including the New York Supreme Court and the Federal courts in New York and other states, have had occasion to interpret, construe and apply this statute in a number of cases in the past. Inasmuch as this statute prohibits publication of a *name,* among other matters, and the statute is a right of privacy statute for the purposes therein expressed, the defendants submit that many of the decisions dealing with the word "name" as used in the New York statute are squarely in point with one of the vital issues involved in the cases at bar.

One of the earlier cases dealing with the word "name" in the New York statute is Pfaudler vs. Pfaudler Co., 114 Misc. 477, 186 N.Y.S. 725, affirmed without opinion at 197 App. Div. 921, 188 N.Y.S. 725, which case is directly in point with the cases at bar insofar as determining whether the defendants have violated Section 16-81 by publishing "the name" of the plaintiffs. The New York court said in the Pfaudler case:

"The cause of action alleged in the complaint rests upon the question whether or not the use of the plaintiff's surname by the defendants constitutes a violation of Civil Rights Law, Sections 50, 51, which prohibit a corporation from using *the name* (emphasis supplied) for advertising purposes or for purposes of trade." . . .

"The sole question is whether or not the Civil Rights Law prohibits the defendant from using the plaintiff's surname. The word 'name' as used in the statute, must mean a person's full name. It was evidently the purpose of the Legislature to prevent the use of the full name of a person, by which alone he could be identified. This identification is possible in the case of a portrait or picture, the use of which the statute also prohibits. It is not possible where only the surname of a person is employed. The word 'Pfaudler' does not identify the plaintiff as the person whose surname has been used, except to those persons who may know the origin of the company, and even then it is impossible to say whether the word refers to the plaintiff or to his brother Caspar, both of whom were at one time connected with the defendant's predecessor."

. . . Based on the authority of the Pfaudler case, it is submitted that a violation of Section 16-81 would not occur until the full name of a victim of rape or assault incident as contemplated by the statute, is published, and therefore, by no means has any such publication of the names of the plaintiffs in these cases occurred.

In 1954 in a proceeding entitled People on complaint of Maggio vs. Charles Scribner's Sons, et al, 205 Misc. 818, 130 N.Y.S. 2d 514, an action was brought by the state against a publisher and motion picture corporation under the aforementioned Section 50 on complaint that the character portrayed was that of the complainant and that he had been identified by the surname used in the publication. The book involved in this case was that entitled "From Here To Eternity," which had a wide and successful circulation. One of the characters portrayed is called "Angelo Maggio." The complainant, Joseph Anthony Maggio, was in the United States Army infantry regiment stationed in Hawaii during the period just before Pearl Harbor. The book and motion picture made therefrom tell a story about persons who were in the Army stationed in Hawaii during the period referred to. The court said that:

"To violate the statute, the name must be used in such a context as to unequivocally point to and identify the complainant. The use of the word 'name' in the statute, in association with the words 'portrait' or 'picture' clearly indicates that this was intended. A portrait or picture leaves no doubt as to the identity of the subject. Where a name is used, it, like a portrait or picture, must upon meeting the eye or ear, be unequivocally identified as that of the complainant. . . ."

In the Maggio case the complaints were dismissed on the ground that the complainant did not make out a case against the defendants sufficient to constitute a violation of Section 50 of the Civil Rights Law. The court in that case strictly interpreted and applied the New York statute with regard to the word "name" as used therein. The court said that: "Section 50, being penal in nature, must be strictly construed, (citing other New York cases) . . . and 'purely statutory offenses cannot be established by implication, . . .' " See also Levy vs. Warner Bros. Pictures, 57 F. Supp. 40 (D.C.S.D.N.Y., 1944) which is a case very similar to the Maggio case, involving Section 51 of the New York Statute. . . .

[The brief then invoked a 1936 federal district court case in New York which had said the New York statute was inapplicable to assumed names or stage names. (The plaintiff Claire H. Davis had, under an assumed name of Cassandra, become known as a psychic, palmist, etc., and her suit had been against the makers of a movie containing a character called Countess Casandra, a psychic presented in a derogatory way.) The brief also argued that not even an assumed or stage name had been used in the *Nappier* situation, since only "Little Jack" rather than "Little Jack Girls" had appeared on the televised picture of the station wagon.]

Below is an excerpt from appellant's reply brief purporting to respond to the argument on the New York cases:

III. The Term "Name" Is Not Limited To the Christian And/Or Family Name of a Person But Extends To Any Common Designation By Which He Is Known.

In seeking a restrictive interpretation of the word "name", defendants rely upon several New York cases. Reflection will show that these cases are not apposite. The State of New York has never recognized the common-law right of privacy, Roberson v. Rochester Folding Box Company, 171 N.Y. 538, 64 N.E. 442, and the cases upon which plaintiffs rely are designed solely to prevent the exploitation of a person's "name, portrait or picture" for commercial purposes. New York Consolidated Laws, C. 6, Article 5. As such, it is obvious that they are more analogous in their implementation to the law of property than to the law of torts. The New York law is not intended to preclude undesired publicity, it is not designed to protect a person's right to be let alone. What is "naming" a person for the purpose of New York law and its intent to prohibit commercial rape of a person's property is a very different thing from what is "naming" a person under South Carolina law in such a manner as to deprive a person of privacy. . . .

b. *Appellate Advocacy — In This Case and In General*

1. Consider now, for a moment, the reply brief's answer to the New York cases. Would not a more effective answer to these cases have been possible? Could it not be said that the *Pfaudler* and *Maggio* cases decide merely this: The New York statutory "name" requirement is not satisfied by an advertiser's use of a surname only,[1] or by use of a name not identical in both Christian name and surname with the plaintiff's — because these uses would not produce the clear identification of the plaintiff that the statute was aimed at deterring. Hence these New York cases leave open the possibility that an advertiser's use of a description, other than an actual name, which *does clearly identify* the plaintiff (perhaps "The Little Tramp" in Charlie Chaplin's heyday, or "The Manassa Mauler" in Jack Dempsey's) *would be covered* by the New York statute.

In fact, there were some New York cases that seem to suggest precisely this. The federal court of appeals sitting in New York had said in 1937: "Having in mind the evident purpose of the statute, its application to a public or stage name, as well as a private one, seems inevitable." Hence the court thought that Tess Gardella, a stage and radio performer who had adopted the stage name "Aunt Jemima," would not (because it was a stage name) be prevented from suing under the New York statute.[2]

1. That *some* surnames can give a sufficient identification is shown by cases like that involving "Adrian," a famous dress designer. Adrian v. Unterman, 281 App. Div. 81, 118 N.Y.S.2d 121, aff'd, 306 N.Y. 770, 118 N.E.2d 477 (1952).

2. Gardella v. Log Cabin Products Co., 89 F.2d 891 (2d Cir. 1937). She had sued because of the use, without her consent, of "Aunt Jemima" as the name of a performer in the Quaker Oats massive radio advertising campaign for Aunt Jemima pancake flour. (What made the suit unsuccessful was the fact that Quaker Oats did not need the plaintiff's consent, since its rights to the use of the "Aunt Jemima" name, on the product and for a performer, had preceded plaintiff's use of the name.)

Another New York case that could have been cited, in support of the proposition that clear identification through a stage name or popular name is enough for a valid claim under the statute, is one whose pertinence would rest on an *analogy* to the stage name situation. The statute is equally operative where a "portrait or picture" rather than a "name" is involved. Hence if a case decides that the statute applies to a clear identification through some means *other than an actual portrait or picture* — such as impersonation of the plaintiff through an actor in a movie — then why cannot the case be used as authority for saying that the statute applies to a clear identification through some means *other than an actual name* — such as a stage or popular name? The case I am thinking of involved a wireless operator, John Binns, whose distress signal when his ship collided with another in 1909 resulted in a dramatic sea rescue, making him famous as the first man to use wireless in this way. The state court of appeals thought the movie actor's impersonation of Binns could qualify under the statute because the word "picture" was to be construed as including "any representation" of the plaintiff.[3]

The arguments I have suggested in behalf of the *Nappier* plaintiff-appellants might have been used not only by them but also by the court of appeals majority that ruled in their favor. The actual argument by the court of appeals, you will recall, was curiously weak in the paragraph devoted to the New York cases. What it said was:

> No support for Standard's position is found in decisions upon a statute prohibiting the unauthorized use of a personal name, portrait or picture in advertising. E.g.: Gardella v. Log Cabin Products Co., 89 F.2d 891 (2 Cir. 1937); Levey v. Warner Bros. Pictures, Inc., 57 F. Supp. 40 (S.D.N.Y. 1944). For advertising, only the name, pseudonym or picture of the person — usually because of his prominence — is significant. Any other description is of no value. Consequently, the object of the law is not impinged unless the publication embodies the name, portrait or picture. That is not so in the statute now in review.

The court said this shortly after it had stressed the apparent South Carolina statutory policy to induce rape victims to report the crime by giving them broad protection against identification.

This case was decided a year later than, and by a higher court than, the *Davis* case cited by the appellees' brief as precluding suits based on assumed or stage names.

3. Binns v. Vitagraph Co., 210 N.Y. 51, 103 N.E. 1108 (1913). There seem to be limits to this approach. Can "representation" include a purely verbal portrayal in a novel — so as to support a plaintiff who claimed he had been the model for one of the major figures in John Hersey's *A Bell for Adano,* though neither his name nor his picture had been used? A New York court, with one dissenter, said no. It distinguished the *Binns* case by stressing that it had involved both the use of plaintiff's name and his representation through an actor. Toscani v. Hersey, 271 App. Div. 445, 65 N.Y.S.2d 814 (1st Dept. 1946). For other decisions limiting the concept of "repre-

Thus the court's argument seems to amount to this: (1) The policy of the New York statute is different from South Carolina's "name of rape victim" statute: The New York legislature must have been confining itself to the kind of name which clearly identified the plaintiff. Any description in terms merely of "circumstances" or an "episode" would not be appropriate or valuable for an advertiser; hence that would be outside the policy of the New York statute, but within the policy of the South Carolina statute aimed at inducing a woman to report the crime by assuring her against circumstantial, etc., forms of identification as well as against actual naming. (2) The policy of the two statutes being different, the New York cases are irrelevant.

I find the argument unnecessarily weak because the court need not have rested on this position. It could have supplemented the point with an "even if" argument: "Even if we are wrong in this view of a more limited policy under the New York statute, and hence the New York cases *are* relevant, *those cases are not unfavorable* to the plaintiff." Here the court could cite, for instance, the *Gardella* (Aunt Jemima) and *Binns* cases discussed above, as showing that publishing a *popular* name rather than an actual name could qualify for coverage under the statute. It could then have argued that the circumstances of publication (televised picture of "Little Jack" on the station wagon, coupled with the fact that the plaintiffs were widely known as the "Little Jack Girls") were the equivalent of publishing the popular name, "Little Jack Girls." Alternatively, the court might have put the argument in "a fortiori" terms.[4]

The argumentative techniques I have pointed to — use of analogy, "even if," "a fortiori" — are quite common in lawyers' briefs. I think

---

sentation," see Molony v. Boy Comics Publ., Inc., 277 App. Div. 166, 98 N.Y.S.2d 119 (1st Dept 1950); Levey v. Warner Bros. Pictures, 57 F. Supp. 40 (S.D.N.Y. 1944).

4. Such an argument could have been couched like this: (1) the cases under the New York statute *(Gardella,* etc.) are favorable as to the coverage of a popular name, and (2) they *apply even more strongly* (with "a fortiori" force, as lawyers like to put it) since they were decided under a statute whose policy in behalf of the plaintiff suggests a narrower coverage of "name" than under the South Carolina statute (here would follow the court's actual argument above on this policy).

The court of appeals' failure to capitalize on the favorable New York cases may have stemmed from an overly hasty assessment that they were unfavorable — since the two cases it referred to (*Gardella* and *Levey, supra* nn. 2 & 3) had both ruled against the plaintiff. But, as note 3 above indicates, there was an extraneous reason in the *Gardella* case why plaintiff Aunt Jemima did not win. And in the *Levey* case, the reason why the ex-wife of George M. Cohan was unsuccessful in her attack on the portrayal of her in the movie biography of Cohan was that the movie actress did "not look nor act like plaintiff." The statutory words "portrait or picture" require, said the court, "a representation of a person at least approaching likeness." Levey v. Warner Bros. Pictures, 57 F. Supp. 40, 41-42 (S.D.N.Y. 1944).

the "even if" gambit is the one most often encountered. It has the obvious advantage of "covering the waterfront" of possibilities, and hence playing it safe. One cannot be sure which of some multiple assumptions or analyses may be accepted by the court, hence it is safer to argue the case on the basis of alternative assumptions or analyses. One limit to this approach is the possibility of weakening one's position in the eyes of the court by seeming to concede the possibility of error in one's first position. Still, unless the first position looks impregnable, lawyers have generally opted for presenting alternative positions.

2. It may interest you to know that the plaintiffs, who lost in the trial court and won as appellants in the court of appeals, had in the latter court filed a 17-page printed brief, and a 5-page reply brief to the appellee broadcasting company's 45-page brief. The ultimate loser had filed a more elaborate (and more highly organized) brief — which merely emphasizes the fact that the advocates' contribution does not necessarily determine the decision. Still, the advocates' contribution *can* be crucial. Federal Judge Medina observed early in his experience on the Second Circuit that he had to

> admit that the cogency of a lawyer's argument, the skill and ingenuity with which he built up his propositions in logical sequence and the research he brought to bear upon his presentation of the case really did much more than merely clarify the issues and then leave the case for me to decide. After all, as I view the administration of American justice, it is a cooperative effort in which the best results are obtained by the interaction of the minds of the court and counsel, and it is silly to suppose that the judge loses any of his dignity or authority when he admits that the art of persuasion still flourishes.[5]

At the same time, as an experienced practitioner and student of appellate advocacy has observed: " . . . after making due allowance for the frailties of mankind, it is really amazing how few good arguments are presented and heard, quite irrespective of the tribunal concerned. About a dozen years ago, I was told by a Justice of the Supreme Court of the United States that four out of every five arguments to which he is required to listen were 'not good'. . . . "[6] While this was said of oral argument, similar observations have been made about briefs. Why so? An at least partial explanation is that a lawyer's busy schedule or the smallness of the amount at stake in the litigation may render unfeasible the expenditure of time required for a first-rate job. Nor can one discount the fact that God has not bestowed forensic talents lavishly or evenly, and what talent is available law schools have not had the resources to train intensively.

5. Medina, Some Reflections on the Judicial Function, 38 A.B.A.J. 107-108 (1952).
6. Wiener, Briefing and Arguing Federal Appeals 6 (1967).

Here is an interesting critical comment on the nature of current written and oral appellate argument, voiced by Justice Schaefer of the Illinois Supreme Court:

> Judges are interested of course in what has been said, and what has been decided, and the traditions and formal ritual of courtroom advocacy encourages lawyers to pitch their arguments on that ground. In most cases that may be enough. But in any case, it is desirable that the thrust go deeper, and in cases on the frontiers of the law a deeper thrust is imperative. Those cases are not decided just upon the ground that "it was so held" in such and such a case. They are decided upon a consideration of why it was so held and upon an appraisal of the results of that holding in actual operation plus the anticipated consequences of an expansion or curtailing of that holding. This is the level upon which [judicial] conference room advocacy operates. It is also the level upon which the most effective courtroom advocacy operates.[7]

Similar sentiments have been expressed by Chief Justice Currie of the Wisconsin Supreme Court[8] and Justice Rutledge of the United States Supreme Court,[9] among others.

It may seem to you that the court of appeals opinion did not follow the quoted advice about reconsidering the validity of a precedent and assessing the consequences of expanding or not expanding it to cover the new situation. But remember: (1) the advice was directed at advocacy in the courtroom and the judicial conference room, not at the form in which judicial opinions should be written (judges are often reticent about discussing in their opinions all the policy reasons that may have influenced the decision); (2) the court was not being confronted with precedents of its own that it might want to reevaluate; it was a federal court applying state law — which included no precedents on the specific problem of statutory interpretation, and involved a statute whose soundness the court had no authority to reconsider. The court's emphasis on the *purpose* of the statute, in considering whether the New York precedents were pertinent, did conform to the spirit of the quoted advice.

Of course, in addition to Justice Schaefer's basic point, the effective appellate advocate must bear many other do's and don'ts in mind. Not only does the Argument section of the brief[10] present certain

7. Schaefer, The Advocate in the Reviewing Courts, 1956 U. Ill. L. Forum, 203, 210.

8. Currie, Some Aspects of Appellate Practice Before the Wisconsin Supreme Court, 1955 Wis. L. Rev. 554, 558.

9. Rutledge, The Appellate Brief, 28 A.B.A.J. 251, 253 (1942).

10. From the vantage point of one who has authored and supervised the preparation of briefs for federal agencies, as well as taught appellate advocacy, the main deficiency I see in both student and practitioner briefs is the one mentioned by Justice Schaefer, quoted in the text above. There are others: the tendency to focus

problems, but there are difficulties with other standard sections: the Statement of Facts,[11] the Questions Involved,[12] and the Summary of Argument.[13]

In oral argument questions of technique of presentation[14] as well

---

only on the favorable cases, rather than giving a perspective picture of favorable *and* unfavorable cases, and showing why the policies underlying the favorable cases are to be preferred (this to be in addition to the usual tactic of "distinguishing" some cases by identifying their situations as too different to be classed as unfavorable); the failure to canvass the secondary literature (books and articles); the dearth of imaginative arguments made by analogy; and the failure to observe the usual standards of readability for argumentative literature. Under the latter standards, one should aim for short, punchy sentences, and paragraphs in which (usually) the body of the paragraph supports a theme stated in the lead sentence; one should also vigilantly connect paragraphs by the use of transitional words and phrases: e.g., moreover, furthermore, however, still, finally, nevertheless, on the other hand, even if, similarly, etc. The reader should not be allowed to lose the thread.

Finally, a rather innovative point made by Karl Llewellyn that builds on Justice Schaefer's point: "If," said Llewellyn, "a brief has made the case for what is right, and has made clear the reason of the rightness, and has found and tailored and displayed the garment of law to clothe the right decision fittingly, then it is not only unwise but indecent not to furnish also in that brief a page or two of text which gathers this all together, which clears up its relation to the law to date, which puts into clear words the soundly guiding rule to serve the future and which shows that rule's happy application to the case in hand" (The Common Law Tradition at 241 (1960)). He refers to New Hampshire Chief Justice Kenison's having suggested a standard heading in the brief for this kind of passage: "A Rationale For This Case."

11. Too often this section of the brief is given a cursory or casual treatment. Yet a skillful shaping of the statement of facts (without being untruthful) can influence the decision. Too often, also, statements are made as fact without citation to the supporting pages of the Record.

12. The defect I have seen most often here is the failure to make the Questions factually informative enough. For example, the Questions "Whether the judgment below should be reversed," and "Whether the affidavit supporting the search warrant was legally insufficient" are defective. Contrast these with the following Question by an appellant in an affidavit case in the Supreme Court, as stated in a recent United States Law Week report on pending cases: "Was affidavit supporting search warrant insufficient to establish probable cause (under the 4th Amendment) where it established that defendant had minor conviction for marijuana possession and had purchased a chemical precursor to manufacture of illegal drugs under suspicious circumstances, but neither traced that precursor into defendant's residence nor established that suspicious activity was observed in or about defendant's residence?"

13. This should *not* be virtually a recitation of the topical assertions in your outline of the Argument. It should give the gist of what you have written under those assertions — a condensed version of the *reasons* for the assertions. It should be written *after* the Argument, though it usually appears before it in the brief.

14. (a) Some techniques are strictly verboten (often by the appellate court's rules): reading your argument, or reading very long quotations, or interrupting an opponent's argument. (b) A largely memorized argument conveys an artificial quality and impairs your flexibility. (c) At the outset it is best not to plunge into the facts immediately, but rather to orient the court to your statement of facts by first stating the *issues* (and those you have selected to discuss orally) and the procedural steps by which the case has come to the appellate court. (d) Every separate point in an argument and its relation to earlier and later points should be sharply delineated. It is easy for a court to forget your total position; it should not be allowed to lose

as the content of the argument[15] sometimes also present difficult questions of choice. These questions cluster not only around the main oral argument but also around rebuttal.[16] A pervasive difficulty is created by the limited time allotted for argument, sometimes as low as zero.[17]

---

sight of where you are, where you have been, and where you are going. (e) Sometimes it is important to point out a certain relation between various issues in the case — e.g., that if issue A is decided in your favor, it will be unnecessary to decide issue B. (f) Answers to court questions should not be put off by saying, "I'm coming to that later, your Honor." For many judges the offensiveness of such a statement is compounded by their knowledge that counsel may in fact never fulfill that promise. If you had planned to come to it later, at least give the gist of your answer immediately, together with a promise of fuller treatment later. (g) If you are unable to answer a question, you should frankly so state and (if the point is important) request the court's permission to submit to the court and opposing counsel a written response within, perhaps, three to five days. (h) As in other attempts at oral persuasion of an audience, variation in emphasis is important — gained mainly by a somewhat greater degree of loudness or stress on critical phrases, and by pauses; and equally important is conveying the impression that you earnestly and sincerely *believe* what you are saying.

15. Given the limited time available, as appellant or petitioner you must not try to cover every point made, and certainly not every case cited, in the brief. You must select one vital point, or a few, and only the key cases; and you must let the court know what points will be left to the brief, though indicating your willingness to discuss any of those points if the court is interested. As appellee or respondent, your argument is directed at refuting your opponent's position, as you know it from the briefs, and as he may have modified it in the oral argument preceding yours. The more you concentrate on the words he has used in oral argument the more effective will be your refutation. All your time can be devoted to refutation; it is not desirable to repeat the kind of statement of facts your opponent has already given. But if his statement contained a significant omission or distortion of fact, you of course can profitably pounce on that.

16. It is well to incorporate into your argument as appellant or petitioner some rebuttals of arguments in your opponent's brief, both because (1) it undermines in advance his oral argument to come and (2) your opportunity may not be realized to use some minutes of your allotted time on a separate rebuttal *after* your opponent's arguments (a privilege denied to the appellee or respondent since his whole argument comes after yours and itself is essentially a rebuttal). You may find that the court decides not to hear any separate rebuttal, e.g., because you have used more than the allotted time for the main argument, or because it is simply tired of listening and wants to go home, or is running behind schedule, or thinks it already has a clear enough grasp of the opposing arguments. When a separate rebuttal is made, confine it to: (1) basic issues rather than the scoring of "debaters' points" on relatively minor questions; and (2) only those matters raised during your opponent's oral argument — your purpose being to underscore the weaknesses in his answers to the court's questions and in his answers to your position, as well as to emphasize the parts of your position he has left unanswered. You also have the opportunity at the very end to re-summarize briefly your total position. Advocates differ in their relative readiness to present a separate rebuttal; but if all indications point to your winning the main argument, it is probably too hazardous to get up again, to expose yourself to possible questions that will uncover a hidden weakness. Also too hazardous is the beguiling tactic of the English barrister who, as respondent, rose after the appellant's argument to say: "My lords, I will follow the example of my friend who has just finished, and submit the case without argument."

17. The recently mounting caseloads have led appellate courts to require that some cases be submitted on briefs without oral argument. Probably the most com-

Nor is the preparation process of the oral argument usually given enough attention.[18] But no matter how careful the preparation, "it

mon time allotment for an appellate argument by one side is 30 minutes. The amount of court questioning that eats into this varies with the case and the court. This unpredictability undermines any would-be tactic of leaving your strongest argument until last — a dubious tactic anyway. Of course, it also means that you cannot afford prolixity in your language. The terseness of the trial judge who, when the defendant said, "As God is my judge, I did not take the money," responded: "He isn't. I am. You did," is not required, but more conciseness than is customary in conversation will help your case. By shaving your prepared remarks down you will not be caught off guard if questioning takes one-fourth or one-half or more of your time. Even so, there can be unpredictable upsets of your planned timing. I remember, for example, that during my argument for the government as appellant in Fleming v. Rhodes, 331 U.S. 100 (1947), Justice Frankfurter's questioning on a jurisdictional issue that I had not thought would bother the court, and in fact did not bother the other Justices, consumed ten minutes of the time I had planned for the constitutional problem (I requested, and was granted, an opportunity to file a supplemental brief on the issue); and Justice Jackson was responsible for at least five more minutes by requiring me to give the gist of the appellee's argument too, because the appellee had failed to file a brief or to appear for oral argument.

The most frustrating situation of course is one wherein the questioning is so profuse that you do not have the time to get your full position across. One possible solution is this: Rather than wait until time has expired, a couple of minutes previously you might tell the court that, having realized time is unavailable to explain your position fully, you would like to spend the remaining two minutes summarizing your whole position. (This should be an incisive summary of the *heart* of your argument and the *crux* of its superiority over your opponent's position — a summary that you have carefully rehearsed, though not necessarily memorized.) If this tactic is not possible, and time does expire, you should ask permission, in view of the extensive time taken up by questions, for an additional two minutes for such a summary. Still another method when you expect considerable questioning is to explain near the outset your intention of spending four or five minutes summarizing your full position (the kind of incisive summary I have mentioned) before holding yourself open to questions. If the questions do not materialize, one or more of the summarized points can be more fully developed — but at least your full position will have been displayed in a connected and probably uninterrupted way.

18. You should certainly refresh your recollection of the printed Record by re-reading it, as well as both briefs and key cases. You should have your digests of important cases with you at the lectern, as well as the briefs and Record. Index tabs on the Record and briefs should show the page numbers you expect to refer to or quote in your argument. So too, the notes you made to guide your argument should contain the page numbers relevant to your references to the Record or briefs. The nature of these notes was best described by Justice Jackson (who had been Solicitor General arguing the government's cases before the Supreme Court): "My practice was to prepare notes, consisting of headings and catchwords rather than of details, to guide the order of argument and prevent important items from being overlooked. Such notes help to get back on the track if one is thrown off by interruptions. They will tend to limit rambling and irrelevance, give you some measure of confidence, and at the same time let you frequently meet your judges eye to eye."

Jackson went on to make another suggestion: "Do not think it beneath you to rehearse for an argument. Not even Caruso, at the height of his artistic career, felt above rehearsing for a hundredth performance, although he and the whole cast were guided and confined by a libretto and a score. . . . [I]f you have an associate, try out different approaches and thrash out every point with him. Answer the questions that occur to another mind. See what sequence of facts is most effective.

is a common experience," said Justice Jackson, "that questions upset the plan of argument before the lawyer has fairly started. I used to say that, as Solicitor General, I made three arguments of every case. First came the one that I planned — as I thought logical, coherent, complete. Second, was the one actually presented — interrupted, incoherent, disjointed, disappointing. The third was the utterly devastating argument that I thought of after going to bed that night."[19]

B. *Background Note: Procedural Aspects*

1. Federal Rules of Civil Procedure

The procedural rules governing the preceding lawsuit were not the South Carolina rules applying to courts of that state, but the separate Federal Rules of Civil Procedure applying to federal court suits throughout the country. Before adoption of these rules in 1938, federal statutes required federal court procedure in suits "at law" — which included damage suits like this one — to conform to the procedures of the courts of the state in which the federal court sat. Separate federal rules, prior to 1938, did apply in actions *not* "at law" — e.g., in maritime cases ("admiralty") and in "equity" cases.

A further word should be included here about "equity." Under the old English system, "equity courts" were separate from the common law courts. The latter courts had by the end of the thirteenth century developed a rigid system with a limited number of "forms of action" for particular types of subject matter, and limited remedies (money damages or possession of land or a chattel). In spite of some later expansion in coverage of the forms of action, the common law court was still an inadequate forum for many plaintiffs. The subject matter might not fall within the existing forms of action — e.g., problems involving fraud or mistake, or the "trust" device in conveyance of

---

Accustom yourself to your material in different arrangements. Argue the case to yourself, your client, your secretary, your friend, and your wife if she is patient. Use every available anvil on which to hammer out your argument" (Jackson, Advocacy Before the Supreme Court: Suggestions for Effective Case Presentation, 37 A.B.A.J. 801, 861 (1951)). If for no other reason than timing, rehearsal is necessary.

19. Jackson, *id.* at 803.

Among helpful books on appellate advocacy, in addition to Wiener, *supra* n.6, are Stern, Appellate Practice in the United States (1981); Dizenfeld, Kuperberg & Whitson, eds., Handbook of Appellate Advocacy (rev. ed. 1980); Stern & Gressman, Supreme Court Practice, esp. chaps. 13 & 14 on briefs and oral argument (5th ed. 1978).

property, or unreasonableness of the penalties embodied in bonds or other instruments. Alternatively the fact that no common law procedure existed for compelling testimony of the parties or production of documents might be fatal to the case. Or the plaintiff might be seeking a *remedy* that the common law court could not give: so-called "specific" relief, like ordering the defendant to convey (instead of paying damages for not conveying) a piece of land which in violation of his contract he had refused to convey to plaintiff; or ordering defendant to stop infringing plaintiff's patent, or stop trespassing on his land. Thus the development of the separate "equity" courts to deal with these problems was in response to real needs.

A dual system, however, produced great difficulties. Suits "in equity" would be dismissed because the proper remedy was "at law." So too, plaintiffs "and defendants at law could not in the law action establish equitable claims or defenses pertaining to the same occurrence. In many situations two or more suits had to be brought to adjust properly the rights and remedies of the same parties growing out of a single transaction. Too often mistakes of form led to loss of a suit by the party entitled to win on the merits."[20]

By mid-nineteenth century in America, and somewhat later in England, reforms for the merger of law and equity were starting to take root; and the movement slowly spread. The climax came with Congress's authorization of the Supreme Court in 1934 to make separate procedural rules for the federal courts, as well as to *unite* law and equity for those courts. The 1938 Rules were the result and proved highly influential in the states as well. Under the Rules, there is no longer a "suit at common law" as distinguished from a "suit in equity." Only one form of action, called a civil action, is recognized, and the court can grant whatever type of relief is appropriate.[21]

One problem arising from this union was that of jury trial: The right for such a trial had been recognized in most actions in common law courts, whereas the equity court had made decisions by judges without juries. This divergence was resolved by granting the right of a jury trial in cases in which it would have historically been given. That generalization does not cover all possible complications; but in general an action for damages includes the right to a jury, while an action for injunction or other specific relief would not.[22] You will recall that plaintiff's complaint in the damage suit under consideration here did demand a jury trial.

20. James & Hazard, Civil Procedure §1.5 at 17 (2d ed. 1977). On the rise of equity and its relation to common law, see *id.*, §§1.3-1.6.

21. On the separation of law and equity in federal courts and subsequent supersession by the Federal Rules, see *id.*, §1.7, and Wright, Handbook of the Law of Federal Courts §§61-62 (3d ed. 1976).

22. On the jury trial right under the system of merged law and equity, see

Even though Congress authorized the Supreme Court to formulate the Federal Rules, I should also note that opinion is divided on whether the legislature has constitutional authority over court procedure at all. There is, however, little dissent from the proposition that courts have more competence to regulate in this field.[23] The Supreme Court, incidentally, did not create the Rules by itself. It appointed an advisory committee of distinguished lawyers and professors and adopted their recommendations, together with some changes of its own, at the end of 1937. These proposals were submitted to Congress, as the enabling act required, and in the absence of adverse legislation by Congress, became effective in September 1938. (The Federal Rules of Evidence became effective by a somewhat different procedure in 1975.)[24]

The Rules effected many important changes besides the union of law and equity in a single form of action. Probably the most significant of these were: (a) a theory of the parties' written pleadings that puts little stock in technicalities and recognizes the sufficiency of a complaint that simply gives "a short and plain statement of the claim showing that the pleader is entitled to relief"; and (b) "discovery" procedures prior to trial that serve to inform each party of important aspects of the other party's case, and that tend to simplify the issues. I will have something to say about both of these changes later in this chapter.

About half the states have adopted the Federal Rules virtually unchanged for use in state courts, and many other states have been substantially influenced. The Rules also permit local rules for the individual districts, but the extent to which the latter can introduce basic variations is rather unclear.[25]

2. Service of Summons and Complaint

Under the Federal Rules of Civil Procedure, the date that the complaint is filed in court counts as the date of commencement of the

---

James & Hazard, *supra* n.20, §8.1-8.11, and specifically as to federal courts, Wright, *supra* n.21, §92.

23. See authorities cited in Wright, *id.*, §62 at 291 nn. 2-3.

24. For 40 years from the time the Supreme Court was given rulemaking powers (i.e., up to the time of submission of the Federal Rules of Evidence in 1972) Congress had not changed any proposed Rule. But on submission of the latter Rules, in view of protests from some members of the public and from members of Congress, Congress enacted a 1973 law requiring specific legislation before the Rules could go into effect. Congress then substantially revised the Rules before allowing them to go into effect in 1975. See Wright, *supra* n.21, §62 at 294; Friedenthal, The Rulemaking Power of the Supreme Court: A Contemporary Crisis, 27 Stan. L. Rev. 673 (1975).

25. The Supreme Court has said that Federal Rule 83's permission for local rules does not allow "basic procedural innovations" (Miner v. Atlass, 363 U.S. 641 (1960)); yet it did allow a local rule reducing the size of a civil jury from 12 to 6 (Colegrove v. Battin, 413 U.S. 149 (1973)). See Wright, *supra* n.21, §62 at 294-295.

action — though in some state courts, the date that "process" (i.e., a summons) is served on the defendant is the commencement date.

After filing of the complaint, the court clerk issues a summons and delivers it to the marshal, or other person specially appointed by the court, for service on the defendant, together with a copy of the complaint. An individual can be served by delivering the summons and complaint to him personally. This is the best way, but alternatives are permitted: leaving copies at his "dwelling house or usual place of abode" with "a person of suitable age and discretion residing therein"; or delivering them to an "agent authorized by appointment or by law to receive service of process." Moreover, for serving individuals or corporations, service is permissible in the manner that may be authorized by a particular federal statute, or by the law of the state for service in state courts of general jurisdiction.

In the case of corporations there are some alternatives in addition to those in the preceding sentence. The present suit, remember, involves two corporations as defendants. Service can properly be made on a corporate officer, a managing or general agent, or any other corporate agent authorized by appointment or by law to receive service.

Sometimes there is a problem about whether a corporation is subject to suit in the state if it is a "foreign" corporation — i.e., organized in a different state or different country. (Here we know that the two defendant corporations were incorporated outside the state of South Carolina.) The problem arises from the Supreme Court view that to subject to a lawsuit in X State a foreign corporation which has insufficient "contacts" with X State would violate its constitutional "due process" right to fair treatment. In order to be subject to suit in the state, the corporation must have such minimum contacts with the state as would show it wished to avail itself of the privilege of conducting activities there. It would then incur corresponding obligations, so that maintenance of the suit against it would not offend "traditional notions of fair play and effective justice."[26]

There are many cases litigating the question of what constitutes the necessary minimal contacts, and the matter is still unclear, though the Supreme Court has sometimes found a very slight amount of business in the state as sufficient.[27] In the present case — referring back to the complaint — the alleged operation of a television station in South Carolina by one defendant corporation clearly constituted enough contact with the state. The defendant life insurance company's doing of business in the state was alleged in the complaint, and the motion to dismiss did not assert lack of jurisdiction over the defendant corpora-

26. See International Shoe Co. v. Washington, 326 U.S. 310, 319-320 (1945).

27. McGee v. International Life Ins. Co., 355 U.S. 220 (1957). See generally Wright, *supra* n.21, §64 at 302-304; Annot., 62 L. Ed. 2d 853 (1981).

tion on the ground that the business done in the state was insufficient to subject the defendant to suit in the state. The defendant's motion to dismiss asserted simply that the facts alleged were insufficient to make out a case for damage liability; i.e., the facts did not state "a claim against this defendant upon which relief can be granted."

3. Federal Court Organization

In Chapter 1, in discussing the courts as agencies of the law, I described the organization of state courts. This is an appropriate point at which to describe the organization of federal courts, before going on to analyze their jurisdiction.

1. Three layers form the federal court hierarchy: the trial courts of general jurisdiction known as the district courts, the 12 courts of appeal, and the Supreme Court. There are also a few specialized courts, e.g., Court of Claims, Court of International Trade (formerly Customs Court),[28] Court of Customs and Patent Appeals.[29] The Tax Court, once an executive agency in spite of its name, was made a "legislative court" in 1969.[30]

28. See the Custom Courts Act of 1980, 94 Stat. 1727 (1980).

29. Pending in Congress at this writing is the creation of a new federal appeals court for patent and trademark cases and claims under federal government contracts (a 12-judge Court of Appeals for the Federal Circuit, merging the United States Court of Customs and Patent Appeals with the appellate division of the existing Court of Claims) and a new trial court (U.S. Claims Court superseding the existing trial division of the U.S. Court of Claims) handling mainly contract claims against the United States. 39 Cong. Q. 2028, 2070 (1981). Other specialized courts, now defunct, were: the Commerce Court, for review of Interstate Commerce Commission decisions, lasting from 1910 to 1913; and the Emergency Court of Appeals, for review of validity of World War II emergency regulations and orders. The Temporary Emergency Court of Appeals established in 1971, with a now diminishing docket, has heard appeals from district courts in cases arising under the Economic Stabilization Act of 1971, Emergency Petroleum Allocation Act of 1973, Energy Policy and Conservation Act of 1975, and Emergency Natural Gas Act of 1977 (see 1980 Annual Report, Director, Administrative Office of U.S. Courts 52). On specialized courts, see Wright, *supra* n.21 at 11-14; for discussion of their advantages and disadvantages, see Currie & Goodman, Judicial Review of Federal Administrative Action: Quest for the Optimum Forum, 75 Colum. L. Rev. 1, 63-85 (1975).

30. See 26 U.S.C. §§7441, 7443, as amended by 83 Stat. 730 (1969). Legislative courts are created by Congress under its Article I legislative powers, for the effectuation of those powers. Judges of such courts do not enjoy the independence of judges on courts created under Article III. Article III judges hold tenure during good behavior (which generally means life tenure), and their compensation cannot be diminished while they are in office. The doctrine of legislative courts has had a long and confusing history. The Court of Claims, Court of Customs and Patent Appeals, and Customs Court were once legislative courts and have been changed into constitutional courts (the latter being now the Court of International Trade, see text *supra* at n.28). Other legislative courts are the district courts for Guam, the Virgin Islands, and the Canal Zone. A 1966 law (28 U.S.C. §134(a)) gave life tenure to judges subsequently appointed to the federal district court of Puerto Rico.

About half the states have one federal district court each. In the others the greater volume of business has necessitated creation of additional districts within the state. For example, New York State has eastern, western, northern, and southern districts; Illinois has southern, northern, and central; Wisconsin has only eastern and western; and California has northern, eastern, southern, and central. As volume of business has increased still further, but been localized within highly populous areas, Congress has simply increased the number of judges within districts rather than creating a larger number of districts. Thus the Southern District of New York, in which most of New York City is located, presently has 27 judges; the Northern District of Illinois has 16; Wisconsin's Eastern District has 4 while the Western District has 2; and California's four districts have a total of 42.[31]

A federal district court case is heard by a single judge (with jury, when one has been rightfully demanded). In cases of special significance, all the judges of a particular district may sit together on a case ("en banc").

Also, before 1976 there were statutes requiring a three-judge panel to sit when the plaintiff was seeking to enjoin enforcement of a federal statute, or state statute or rule, because of its alleged violation of the Federal Constitution, and also in the review of certain anti-trust and ICC cases. This system put personnel strains on the federal judiciary, developed various procedural complexities, and burdened the Supreme Court docket (since direct appeals to that Court were allowed from three-judge courts). After much campaigning for reform, a 1976 law reduced the occasions for three-judge courts to virtually negligible proportions. It repealed the above-mentioned provisions and required a three-judge court only "when otherwise required by Act of Congress" (which, as of then, largely meant, certain cases under the Civil Rights Act of 1964 and under the Voting Rights Act of 1965) "or when an action is filed challenging the constitutionality of the apportionment of congressional districts or the apportionment of any statewide legislative body."[32] It is still true that a direct appeal to the Supreme Court may

The Court of Military Appeals is regarded as not part of the judiciary, but a military tribunal created pursuant to Article I powers over the military. On constitutional versus legislative courts, see Wright, *supra* n.21, §11.

31. The number of judges in each district is given in 28 U.S.C. 133. On organization and some general characteristics of the district courts, see 28 U.S.C. §§81-144; Wright, *supra* n.21, §2; Judd, The Expanding Jurisdiction of the Federal Courts, 60 A.B.A.J. 938 (1974); Surrency, Federal District Court Judges and the History of Their Courts, 40 F.R.D. 139 (1966); Acheson, Professional Responsibility and the Workload of the Federal District Courts, 52 Geo. L.J. 542 (1964).

32. See 28 U.S.C. §2284; Wright, *supra* n.21, §50; Stern & Gressman, Supreme Court Practice §2.15, §2.16 at 130 (5th ed. 1978). (The reference to cases under the Civil Rights Act of 1964 is to Attorney General suits for preventive relief against discrimination in employment or public accommodations in violation of that Act).

be taken from a three-judge court's granting or denial of a temporary or permanent injunction.[33]

Finally, mention should be made of the "magistrate" system. Established under a 1968 law, since amended, magistrates are judicial officers who are appointed to full-time (eight-year term) or part-time (four-year term) positions by the district court judges and exercise not only the narrow powers to which their predecessors, the United States commissioners, had been confined[34] but also broader powers — including powers of trial when both parties so consent.[35] In the year ending June 1980 there were close to 500 magistrates, more than half of whom were part-time.[36]

2. The 12 *courts of appeal* are assigned to 11 numbered circuits into which the country is divided, plus the separate circuit for the District of Columbia. One of the busiest is the Second Circuit, which includes the state of New York (as well as Connecticut and Vermont) and therefore handles much important commercial litigation. The District of Columbia Circuit handles more litigation involving government agencies than do the others. That circuit also covers the smallest area while the Ninth Circuit handles the largest (Alaska, Arizona, California, Guam, Hawaii, Idaho, Montana, Nevada, Oregon, Washington). Another large area — the Canal Zone and the whole lower tier of southern states (Alabama, Florida, Georgia, Louisiana, Mississippi, Texas) — until recently was covered by the Fifth Circuit. These two massive circuits, the Fifth and Ninth, had a workload so heavy that 26 and 23 judges respectively were employed by the end of the 1970s.[37] Then a 1980 law[38] split the unwieldy Fifth into a new Eleventh Circuit covering Alabama, Florida, and Georgia, and a new Fifth Circuit, consisting only of Texas, Louisiana, Mississippi, and the Canal Zone. The number of judges in the remaining circuits range

---

There are a few statutory provisions, other than those mentioned, calling for three-judge courts. Thus such a court is to be convened when the Federal Election Commission requests it, for injunctive or declaratory relief under the Presidential Election Campaign Fund Act. And there is a three-judge "Special Court" provided under the Regional Rail Reorganization Act, with its own organizational and procedural provisions. Stern & Gressman, *id.* at 126-130.

33. 28 U.S.C. §1253. Direct appeals are again referred to below, under Supreme Court appellate jurisdiction.

34. E.g., the magistrate issues arrest and search warrants, sets bail, administers oaths and depositions, and holds preliminary hearings.

35. Among other things, the magistrate may, when both parties consent, try any jury or non-jury criminal misdeameanor or civil case; he also has some restricted authority in juvenile and youth offender cases. See 28 U.S.C. §§631-639; Margolis, U.S. Magistrates Get Broad Powers, 66 A.B.A.J. 322 (1980); Annual Report, Director, Administrative Office of United States Courts 10-12, 23-25 (1980).

36. Annual Report, *id.* at 12.

37. 28 U.S.C. §44.

38. 94 Stat. 1994 (1980), effective Oct. 1, 1981.

from 4 for the First Circuit (Maine, Massachusetts, New Hampshire, Puerto Rico, Rhode Island) to 11 for the Second, Sixth, and District of Columbia Circuits. Any of these courts of appeal normally sits in a panel of three judges — sometimes including (when the spot cannot be filled by a regular circuit judge) a district judge from within the circuit, as in the *Nappier* case, or a district or circuit judge from another circuit. In an occasional case of particular importance, if a court of appeals' total membership exceeds three, all the judges will sit together ("en banc"). The unsuccessful litigant in a district court can take an appeal, as a matter of right, to the court of appeals.[39]

3. The Supreme Court of the United States has nine members. Its annual term begins in October and usually ends in June. Each case is handled by the entire Court, with the quorum being six, rather than by a panel. Data on the nature and size of the caseload of both the Supreme Court and other federal courts are presented in the next section on federal jurisdiction.

4. Federal Court Jurisdiction

On the matter of jurisdiction, I will reverse the order and start from the Supreme Court.

a. Supreme Court Original Jurisdiction

The Supreme Court has, to begin with, an "original" jurisdiction — i.e., power to consider and decide certain cases that are *started* in the Supreme Court. These are, according to Article III of the Constitution, "[c]ases affecting Ambassadors, other public Ministers and Consuls, and those in which a State shall be Party. . . ." The first of these two classes of cases has almost never come to the Court, whereas the second class comes occasionally, i.e., usually a few per Term.

Implementing statutes have not assumed that all cases in the two categories listed are *exclusively* for Supreme Court original jurisdiction. They do consider that such exclusivity applies to suits by *one state against another*. On the other hand, a suit by the United States against a state is within the Court's *original but not exclusive* jurisdiction; and so too with a state's suit against the citizens of another state or

39. On organization and general characteristics of the courts of appeal, see 28 U.S.C. §§41-48; Wright, *supra* n.21, §3; Shafroth, Surveys of The United States Courts of Appeals, 42 F.R.D. 243 (1967); Carrington, Crowded Dockets and the Courts of Appeals: The Threat to the Function of Review and the National Law, 82 Harv. L. Rev. 542 (1968); Lumbard, Current Problems of the Federal Courts of Appeals, 54 Cornell L. Rev. 29 (1968).

against aliens. In such suits the Supreme Court *may* refuse to exercise its jurisdiction, leaving the plaintiff to pursue its remedy in the district court or a state court, as the case may be. When the Court exercises its original jurisdiction and the case requires fact finding, the Supreme Court does not itself hold a trial but rather appoints a Master to take evidence and make a report to the Court, on which briefs and arguments can then be presented to the Court.[40]

Finally, there are some limits on the coverage of the constitutional language reading "cases . . . in which a State shall be Party": (1) The case must fall within the federal "judicial power" as defined in Article III, section 2.[41] This means that requirements such as "standing," "political questions," etc. are applicable.[42] It also means that suits between a state and a citizen of *that* state would (with some possible exception) not be covered, and hence would be relegated to a state court. (2) The original jurisdiction has been construed to cover only non-penal cases. (3) In some situations — suits by a state against the United States or by a foreign government against a state[43] — consent by the defendant is necessary.

b. Supreme Court Appellate Jurisdiction

The Constitution does not spell out the Supreme Court's appellate jurisdiction, but instead leaves it to Congress, as we saw in the Chapter 1 discussion of the ways in which Congress could exert some control over the Court.

1. To relieve the Court from an intolerable burden of cases, Congress has seen to it, particularly by a 1925 statute, that the bulk of cases that come before the Court do not have to be considered by it. They are within the Court's discretionary "certiorari" jurisdiction. Recall my earlier reference to the bulk of the Court's cases being now disposed of by *denial* of certiorari. The Court's Rule 19 shows it is more likely to grant the writ of certiorari under circumstances when (in very rough summary) the lower court has ruled contrary to decisions of the Supreme Court or other courts, or has decided an important question of federal law that should be settled by the Supreme Court, or has departed too much "from the accepted and usual course of judicial proceedings." However, a denial of certiorari, the Court has often said, is not to be read as saying anything one

40. On this paragraph, see Wright, *supra* n.21, §109 at 556-558, 561-562.
41. See n.66 below and accompanying text.
42. See below under **B6.**
43. For a more elaborate discussion of original jurisdiction see Wright, *supra* n.21, chap. 13; Stern & Gressman, *supra* n.32, chap. 10.

way or the other on the merits of the issues presented. The denial means, Justice Frankfurter once commented,

> that fewer than four members of the Court deemed it desirable to review a decision of the lower court as a matter "of sound judicial discretion." A variety of considerations underlie denials of the writ, and as to the same petition different reasons may lead different Justices to the same result. This is especially true [with respect] to a State court. Narrowly technical reasons may lead to denials. Review may be sought too late; the judgment of the lower court may not be final; it may not be the judgment of a State court of last resort; the decision may be supportable as a matter of State law. . . . A decision may satisfy all these technical requirements and yet may commend itself for review to fewer than four members of the Court. Pertinent considerations of judicial policy here come into play. A case may raise an important question but the record may be cloudy. It may be desirable to have different aspects of an issue further illuminated by the lower courts. Wise adjudication has its own time for ripening.[44]

Still, there is plausible basis for thinking that the Justices' views on the merits of a case play a role in the decision on certiorari: E.g., substantial majorities of the decisions made *after granting* certiorari favor the *petitioner;* many dissents from the denial of certiorari have discussed the merits of the issues; the Court, like many lower courts, has occasionally treated a certiorari denial in a prior case as having a bearing on the merits in that case; strong correlations have been found between a Justice's vote on the merits after granting of certiorari and his recorded vote on the prior question whether to grant certiorari (the latter being shown in records left by Justice Burton of the Court's conference votes).[45]

2. What then of the small minority of cases that Congress has said the Supreme Court *must* review — the cases in which there is an "appeal" as a matter of right, rather than merely an opportunity to petition the Court to exercise its discretionary review by certiorari? Congress has set up various classes of cases for such appeal that, though typically concerned with the issue of constitutionality of federal and

44. Maryland v. Baltimore Radio Show, 338 U.S. 912, 917-918 (1950) (opinion of Frankfurter, J.).

45. See Linzer, The Meaning of Certiorari Denials, 79 Colum. L. Rev. 1227 (1979); Stern & Gressman, *supra* n.32, §5.7 & §§4.15, 4.18 (and generally on certiorari jurisdiction and procedure, see *id.* at §§4.1-4.27 & 5.1-5.15, chap. 6, and portions of chaps. 2 and 3). Concerning the point on high percentage of petitioner victories after the granting of certiorari: of the cases in which certiorari was granted in the October 1978 Term, lower court judgments in 57% of the cases with Supreme Court written opinions were reversed and 13% were vacated, a total of *70%;* and 92% of the judgments in cases with memorandum orders were vacated. Total reversal and vacations for both kinds of cases were *80%* of the cases decided after grant of certiorari. Corresponding figures for the preceding five Terms and for the subse-

state laws, are also inclusive of other concerns.[46] In some instances, a *direct* appeal from the district court is still allowed,[47] though Congress in recent years has drastically curtailed permission for such direct appeals, in order to reduce the burgeoning workload of the Supreme Court.[48]

Indeed the workload problem is such that there is strong support for further curtailment of appellate jurisdiction, perhaps by abolishing all appeals to the Supreme Court and making all review discretionary, i.e., on certiorari. The 1972 Report of the Federal Judicial Center Study Group on the Caseload of the Supreme Court (Freund Committee) developed this proposal, as well as suggesting the establishment of a National Court of Appeals whose primary function "would be to sift out and deny perhaps 80 percent of the petitions for certiorari which were clearly not worthy of Supreme Court review, sending the rest on to the Supreme Court to make the final selection";[49] and which would hear and decide the less important cases involving points on which there was conflict among the circuits.

---

quent Term were of a similarly high magnitude. For the source of the data, see below, n.59.

46. Congress has set up the following classes of cases for such appeal: (1) where a *federal law* has been held *unconstitutional* by any *federal* court in a civil suit to which the United States or federal officer is a party (28 U.S.C. §1252. Note: Even in private litigation in federal court, if the constitutionality of a federal statute is questioned, 28 U.S.C., Section 2403 would require certification of that fact to the Attorney General, allowing the United States to intervene as of right; in which case, if the statute is invalidated, the direct appeal provision applies); (2) where a *federal* law or treaty has been held unconstitutional by the *highest court of a state* (28 U.S.C. §1257 (1)); (3) where a *state law* has been held by a *federal court of appeals* to be unconstitutional or contrary to federal laws or treaties (28 U.S.C. §1254); (4) where a *state law* has been *upheld* by the *highest court of a state* against the claim of violation of federal Constitution, laws, or treaties (28 U.S.C. §1257(2)); (5) where a *three-judge district court* grants or denies an injunction in a civil action required to be heard by three judges (28 U.S.C. §1253) (on the presently limited availability of three-judge courts, see *supra* n.32 and accompanying text); and (6) where, in a federal civil *anti-trust* suit for equitable relief, the district judge finds that "immediate consideration of the appeal by the Supreme Court is of general public importance in the administration of justice," *and* the Supreme Court in its discretion allows the direct appeal. (15 U.S.C. §29(b)).

47. I.e., in Nos. 1, 5, and 6 in n.46 *supra.* If in a direct appeal situation, a quorum of six in the Supreme Court cannot be obtained, 28 U.S.C. §2109 allows the case to be remitted to the Court of Appeals, whose decision will be final.

48. Thus, government appeals in criminal cases that used to go directly to the Supreme Court now go to the Court of Appeals. So too with appeals from three-judge court decisions in suits to enjoin ICC orders and rules, or in suits to enforce the Interstate Commerce Act or Title II of the Federal Communications Act; suits to enjoin on constitutional grounds a federal statute or state statute or rule; or appeals from district court decisions in the government's civil anti-trust suits (subject to a rare exception, n.46 *supra*). See Stern & Gressman, *supra* n.32, §2.9 at 71; 12 Moore's Federal Practice §429.01[3] (1980).

49. Stern & Gressman, *supra* n.32, §1.16 at 44. §1.16 surveys the literature.

Neither this report nor the 1975 Report of the Commission on Revision of the Appellate Court System (Hruska Commission) and its differently oriented proposal for a National Court of Appeals[50] has escaped strong criticism. However, both reports as well as the commentators favor elimination or virtual elimination of the Court's nondiscretionary jurisdiction. What has recently been pending in Congress is a bill that would, among other things, abolish all appeals to the Supreme Court from state courts and confine appeals from federal courts to those few that now are authorized to come from three-judge courts.[51] The Court's appellate jurisdiction would thus become almost wholly discretionary.

3. When a litigant takes an "appeal" to the Supreme Court, he files a "jurisdictional statement" that has to show why he thinks the Court has jurisdiction of the appeal. But it is important to note that under Supreme Court Rule 15 he must also show "why the questions presented are so substantial as to require plenary consideration, with briefs on the merits and oral argument, for their resolution." And under Rule 16 the appellee's motion to dismiss the appeal or affirm the lower court judgment may be based "on any other grounds which the appellee wishes to present as reasons why the court should not set the case for argument." That is, the Court long ago decided that even when an appellant shows he comes within one of the jurisdictional statutes governing appeals so that he can appeal as a matter of right, the Court need not give *full* consideration to all appeals. It need not give such consideration to an appeal which, from the jurisdictional papers (the jurisdictional statement, appellee's motion to dismiss the appeal or affirm the judgment, and appellant's reply), it determines to be *clearly* without legal merit. In such case, instead of taking the normal course of issuing an "order noting probable jurisdiction" after which briefs with fuller treatment of the merits could be filed and oral argument would be heard, it disposes of the case summarily. It may simply affirm the judgment or dismiss the appeal "for want of a sub-

50. The report focused not on relieving the Supreme Court's workload but on the idea that the Court was not hearing enough cases of national importance, especially in the area of statutory interpretation, and on the fact that many certiorari denials had been in cases involving points on which circuits had been in conflict. The Commission proposed a National Court of Appeals that would hear cases of "intermediate national importance." "Selected cases would be referred to the new court by the Supreme Court, or transferred to that court by the courts of appeals, and would still be ultimately subject to discretionary review by the Supreme Court after decision by the national court of appeals." *Id.* at 45.

51. See S. 450, 96th Cong., 1st Sess. (1979); H.R. 2700, *id.;* S. Rep. 35, *id.* The latter report, in its first appendix contains a letter from all nine justices supporting an earlier, similar bill.

stantial federal question" — and write no opinion or very scant opinion, or present a bare citation of authority.[52]

These summary dispositions of appeals, unlike the denial of certiorari, are officially judgments on the merits of the case. However, students of the Court have suggested that considerations similar to those affecting the granting or denial of certiorari (importance of the question; whether there are conflicts in the lower courts; pressure of the Court's workload) help account for the growing increase in such summary dispositions. In recent years a majority of appeals have been handled in summary fashion.[53] A consequence is that appellant's counsel desiring to avoid summary affirmance or dismissal should advert in the jurisdictional papers not only to the lack of merit in the decision of the lower court but also to the importance of the issue, and to conflicts, if any, in the lower courts. So too the appellee's counsel should stress the opposite on these matters. He cannot assume that he will have a later opportunity to brief and argue the merits of the judgment received from the lower court; the Supreme Court has been known to *summarily reverse*. The unfairness of this tactic to the appellee (whose judgment is being taken away from him without his having briefed and argued the case) seems even greater than unfairness of summary dispositions to appellants or to the parties in certiorari proceedings.[54]

4. The approximately 150 *dispositions with written opinions* in October Term 1979 were distributed among the following types of suits: The largest group (86) were civil actions from inferior federal courts (more than half of these involved the federal government). Then came federal criminal cases (21), civil actions from state courts (18), state criminal cases (15), and federal habeas corpus (4).[55]

A striking feature of the Burger Court operations compared to those of the preceding Warren, Vinson, and Stone Courts has been the expansion in its caseload, in the number of separate opinions (dissents and concurrences), and in the volume of "in forma pauperis" petitions (which are typically from indigent criminal defendants and prisoners, and go on the "Miscellaneous" docket of the Court).[56]

52. Stern & Gressman, *supra* n.32, §§4.28, 5.17-5.18. Generally, because of different appellee motions called for by the Court's rules in appeals from state and federal courts respectively, the Court's "dismissals" of appeals for want of a substantial federal question are in appeals from state courts, and its summary "affirmances" are in appeals from federal courts. *Id.* at §5.18.

53. *Id.* at §§4.28-4.30, 5.17.

54. *Id.* at §5.19. For similar and more frequent practice in the case of certiorari review, see *id.* at §5.12.

Generally on jurisdiction and procedures in appeals to the Supreme Court, see *id.* at §§4.28-4.32, 5.16-5.23; chap. 7; and portions of chaps. 2 & 3.

55. For the source of the data, see below, n.59.

56. See, e.g., Frank, The Burger Court — The First Ten Years, 43 Law & Contemp. Prob. 101 (1980).

A look at statistics for the Court's work in the last seven years (October Term 1973–October Term 1979) reveals that the total cases disposed of annually has generally been under but close to 4,000 — a range of 3,806 for the 1975 Term to 4,006 in the 1976 Term. But the cases disposed of with opinions containing sufficient legal reasoning to be classed as written opinions necessarily were very much fewer: The range was from 155 cases in the 1979 Term to 188 in the 1973 Term. (The number of written *opinions* was somewhat less, since sometimes a single opinion disposes of more than one case. The range was from 135 dispositive opinions in the 1977 Term to 157 in the 1973 Term.) Thus the great bulk of dispositions did *not* include written opinions. Some were by "per curiam" or "memorandum" decisions, ranging from 112 in the 1978 Term to 339 in the 1973 Term. And the huge number of remaining dispositions were by *refusals* to review, i.e., were largely denials or dismissals of appeals or of petitions for review, ranging from 3,347 cases in the 1973 Term to 3,713 in the 1975 Term.[57] "In forma pauperis" petitions and appeals hovered around the 2,000 mark, with a drop to 1,828 in the 1979 Term; the percentage of these that were denied or dismissed was uniformly in the upper 90s.[58] In the cases with written opinions, unanimity of the Justices was low, existing in only 20 to 25 percent of the cases, with a dip to 18 percent in the 1977 Term. In the cases with memorandum orders, the range of unanimity was 74 to 83 percent of the cases, except for the 1973 Term, which hit a low of 55 percent. Finally, in a recent almost 20-year period the rate of Supreme Court *reversal,* in the cases decided on the merits, averaged approximately two-thirds.[59]

c. *Court of Appeals Jurisdiction*

What of the jurisdiction of federal courts below the Supreme Court? The courts of appeals of course have jurisdiction over appeals from the district courts. As noted before, these are appeals as of right. Appeals are from "final" decisions, though some decisions on orders

57. Primarily, these figures reflect denials of petitions for certiorari, i.e., petitions invoking the Court's discretionary jurisdiction. But also included are dismissals or withdrawals of "appeals," and denials of petitions for writs of habeas corpus or writs of mandamus.

58. On "in forma pauperis" cases, see Stern & Gressman, *supra* n.32, chap. 8. These filings have consistently outnumbered the paid filings since October Term 1958. *Id.* at 43.

59. Casper and Posner, The Workload of the Supreme Court 69 (1976). The other observations in the text paragraph are based on the statistics appearing in the November issues of the Harvard Law Review for the years 1974-1980. The November issue annually presents a statistical analysis of the Court's business for the preceding Term.

not finally disposing of the whole case ("interlocutory" or "collateral" orders) have been made appealable by statute or court decision — notably in the case of preliminary injunctions. In addition, a 1958 law gave the courts of appeals *discretion* to review *any* interlocutory order in a civil case if the trial judge certifies that the question of law is debatable and an immediate appeal would materially advance the ultimate termination of the litigation.[60]

A second important class of appeals consists of those from administrative agencies. Here the most common statutory basis for review is a specific provision in the statute creating the agency directing that exclusive jurisdiction over appeals will be in the appropriate court of appeals, any review thereafter being by petition for certiorari in the Supreme Court.[61] (A less common pattern is review, under express or implied authority, by a district court action for injunction and/or declaratory judgment).[62] Review of administrative agencies is generally on the basis of the record before the agency. Agency findings of *fact* will be accepted if based on substantial evidence in the light of the whole record. The latter review is regarded as *more* accepting of the findings than court of appeals review of district court fact findings, which are accepted if not "clearly erroneous." Where there had been no formal record, e.g., in the case of ordinary rulemaking, or where a determination is regarded as a mixture of fact and law, the standard of review has varied confusingly.[63]

The workload in the courts of appeals has been steadily increasing since 1945. In the year ending June 30, 1980, over 23,000 appeals were commenced, almost 21,000 were terminated, and over 20,000 were still

60. Wright, *supra* n.21, §§101, 102. Also, in spite of the "policy against piecemeal appeals," there are times when an appellate court is willing to issue to a lower court the so-called "extraordinary" writ of mandamus, or of prohibition — for instance, in some cases in which the latter court has erroneously assumed jurisdiction of a case or has refused to exercise its lawful jurisdiction. *Id.*, §1.02 at 515-517.

61. This pattern has come to embrace review of some ICC orders as well. Actions to enjoin or suspend an ICC order were formerly heard by a three-judge district court, and direct appeal allowed to the Supreme Court. Presently in the case of certain kinds of ICC orders, such an action is heard by a single district court judge, with appeal to the court of appeals; other ICC orders are reviewed directly in the court of appeals. Wright, *id.*, §1.03 at 520.

62. For review of agencies by the district court, see Gellhorn, Byse & Strauss, below n.63 at 918-923.

63. Davis, Administrative Law of the Seventies, chaps. 29-30 (1976). An "arbitrary or capricious" standard may be applied in the absence of a formal record, and has been viewed as giving a narrower scope of review of facts than the substantial evidence standard; but there is confusion in the opinions. *Id.*, §29.00. We have more fully treated the scope of review in Chapter 1 at nn. 379-388.

Generally on jurisdiction and procedures in appeals to the courts of appeals, see Wright, *supra* n.21, chap. 11; Gellhorn, Byse & Strauss, Administrative Law, Cases and Comments 917-918 (7th ed. 1979).

pending on June 30.[64] Of the appeals from district courts in that year, about 4,500 were criminal appeals, about 15,000 civil appeals (two-thirds of these were in private litigation; one-third in suits with United States as plaintiff or defendant), about 3,000 appeals from administrative agencies, and about 1,000 other cases (bankruptcy appeals and certain original proceedings).[65]

d. District Court Jurisdiction

Remember that Article III of the Constitution vests the "judicial power of the United States" in the Supreme Court "and in such inferior courts as the Congress may from time to time ordain and establish." Congress in establishing the inferior federal courts was limited in its grant of jurisdiction by the scope of the judicial power as defined in Article III. The most significant part of this definition covered (1) what has come to be known as "federal question" cases (cases arising under the Constitution or federal laws or treaties); (2) what is known as "diversity of citizenship" cases (cases between citizens of different states); and (3) cases to which the United States is a party.[66]

64. The following table, somewhat abbreviated, is from the Annual Report of the Director, Administrative Office of U.S. Courts 1 (1980):

Table 1
Appeals Commenced, Terminated, and Pending on June 30, 1940 through 1980

		Appeals Commenced			
Year Ended June 30	*Authorized Judgeships*	*Number*	*Cases Per Panel*	*Appeals Terminated*	*Appeals Pending June 30*
1940	57	3,446	184	3,434	1,678
1950	65	2,830	131	3,064	1,675
1960	68	3,899	172	3,713	2,220
1970	97	11,662	361	10,699	8,812
1975	97	16,658	515	16,000	12,128
1979	132	20,219	460	18,928	17,939
1980	132	23,200	527	20,887	20,252
Percent Change 1980 over					
1960	94.1	495.0	206.4	462.5	812.3
1970	36.1	98.9	46.0	95.2	129.8
1975	36.1	39.3	2.3	30.5	67.0
1979	—	14.7	14.7	10.3	12.9

65. *Id.* at 2.

66. The other categories of the "judicial power of the United States" are: cases affecting ambassadors, other public ministers, and consuls; admiralty and maritime

These three categories account for the bulk of cases in the federal courts. The largest category by far is of the cases in which the United States is a party, if you count the *criminal* cases; otherwise the three categories are somewhat more evenly divided. Thus, statistics for the year ending June 1980 show that total *civil* cases commenced in the district courts were 168,789 (about triple the rate in the 1950s), of which almost 64,000 were cases in which the United States was a party (almost 40,000 as plaintiff and almost 24,000 as defendant), about 65,000 were private cases involving a federal question,[67] and about 40,000 were private cases involving diversity of citizenship (almost wholly contract and tort cases).[68] *Criminal* cases commenced numbered

---

cases; cases between two or more states; between a state and citizens of another state; between citizens of the same state claiming lands under grants of different states; and between a state or its citizens and foreign countries, citizens, or subjects.

67. This is a rather misleading figure since it is swollen by inclusion of almost 20,000 prisoner petitions — which one might not expect to be classed as private civil suits. Some 3,700 other prisoner petitions are classed as having been brought against the United States.

68. See 1980 Annual Report, *supra* n.64, Table 17, p. 59. The following is an abbreviated version of Table 3 (at 3) showing the growth of civil litigation:

Table 3
Civil Cases Filed, Terminated, and Pending on June 30, 1940-1980

		Civil Cases Commenced			
Year Ended June 30	*Authorized Judgeships*	*Number*	*Cases Per Judgeship*	*Civil Cases Terminated*	*Civil Cases Pending June 30*
1950	215	54,662	254	53,259	55,603
1960	245	59,284	242	61,829	61,251
1970	401	87,321	218	80,435	93,207
1975	400	117,320	293	104,783	119,767
1980	516	168,789	327	160,481	186,113
Percent Change 1980 over					
1960	110.6	184.7	35.1	159.6	203.9
1970	28.7	93.3	50.0	99.5	99.7
1975	29.0	43.9	11.6	53.2	55.4
1979	—	9.1	9.1	12.0	4.7

There were, among other categories, over 11,000 real property cases, mainly with United States as plaintiff; almost 13,000 cases classed as "civil rights"; almost 9,000 social security cases; about 8,400 under labor laws; about 3,000 brought by the United States for civil penalties or forfeitures; about 1,500 antitrust cases the great bulk of which were private suits, only 26 being filed by the United States. The almost 50,000 contract actions were fairly evenly divided between private cases and those with the United States as plaintiff. The approximately 32,500 tort cases were mainly private cases. *Id.*, Table C2, at A-16.

about 28,000 — which is somewhat lower than in the 1950s, though the rate has been somewhat higher in the intervening year.[69]

Federal jurisdiction is a complicated legal specialty, and I can here only indulge in a few basic generalizations about each of the three major categories of civil jurisdiction.

(1) Cases to Which the United States Is a Party (Herein Also of Sovereign Immunity and Consent of the United States to Be Sued)

Consider first the cases to which the United States is a party. A federal statute follows up the constitutional grant of federal judicial power in this type of case by, in general, granting federal jurisdiction in suits *commenced* by the United States or by an agency or officer expressly authorized to sue (though if the particular type of suit has not been expressly authorized by statute, the courts ask whether the United States has sufficient pecuniary or governmental "interest" to give it *"standing"* to sue, a problem to be discussed below). No statute, however, attempts to confer jurisdiction for suits *against* the United States. Indeed, there is some shaky Supreme Court authority that the latter type of suit is not covered by the constitutional clause on the federal judicial power. But this seems to have stemmed from the fact that at the time of the Constitution, suits against the sovereign were unknown. The ancient "sovereign immunity" doctrine maintains the sovereign cannot be sued without its consent.

Several statutes, however, now give the consent of the United States to be sued in various situations, notably for certain contract and tort claims and, more broadly, in cases for non-monetary relief, as discussed in the next paragraph. If authority is given under such a statute *to sue* the United States (in a court of competent jurisdiction), this does not mean that the necessary *jurisdictional statute* exists — conferring jurisdiction on the district court over that type of suit — but usually "courts have not hesitated to accept jurisdiction of suits against the United States if consent has been given." Notice that the consent statutes referred to are a basis for arguing not only the United States-as-a-party category of jurisdiction but also the "federal question" category discussed below (suits "arising under" a federal statute).[70]

69. *Id.,* Table 40, at 90. The recent decline of filings in many offense categories (e.g., crimes against property) has been attributed to the recent enforcement policy of the Justice Department that puts a priority on prosecution of "white collar crimes, public corruption, organized crime, and trafficking in narcotics and dangerous drugs." *Id.* at 91.

70. On these paragraphs, see Wright, *supra* n.21, §22. The quotation is from p.83.

The sovereign immunity defense had been successfully invoked by the Government even when the suit was for injunctive or declaratory relief against an *officer* rather than the United States (particularly when Government property rights were involved) — though exceptions were usually recognized if the officer was alleged to be exceeding statutory or constitutional constraints on his powers, or operating under an unconstitutional statute. The widely recognized confusion in the case law on this subject[71] was finally clarified by a 1976 law that *waived* the sovereign immunity defense in suits seeking *relief other than money damages, against the United States or agency or officer thereof,* based on the latter's action), or failure to act, in an official capacity or under color of legal authority.[72] Suits that do seek money damages against the United States will have to come within the permissions given by other statutes for such claims, primarily the Federal Tort Claims Act (which makes the United States liable for negligence and some other torts of its employees under certain conditions)[73] and under statutes governing the Court of Claims (which has jurisdiction of money claims against the United States based on the Constitution, federal statutes, or executive department regulations; or on express or implied contracts with the government)[74] and statutes governing the district courts insofar as they have been given concurrent jurisdiction with the Court of Claims.[75]

For an example of the distinction between statutory authority to sue and statutory conferral of jurisdiction, see Califano v. Sanders, 430 U.S. 99, 107 (1977).

71. See Gellhorn et al., *supra* n.63 at 1055-1069.

72. The described suit "shall not be dismissed nor relief therein be denied on the ground that it is against the United States or that the United States is an indispensable party. The United States may be named as a defendant in any such action, and a judgment or decree may be entered against the United States." Where no statute specifies the form of the review proceeding, any applicable form of action (e.g., for declaratory judgment, prohibitory or mandatory injunction or habeas corpus) may be brought in a court of competent jurisdiction "against the United States, the agency by its official title, or the appropriate officer." However, "[n]othing herein (1) affects other limitations on judicial review or the power or duty of the court to dismiss any action or deny relief on any other appropriate legal or equitable ground; or (2) confers authority to grant relief if any other statute that grants consent to suit expressly or impliedly forbids the relief which is sought" (Pub. L. No. 94-574, 90 Stat. 2721, amending 5 U.S.C. §§702, 703). Another statute revealing congressional willingness to recede from a strong sovereign immunity position was the 1972 law declaring the United States may be named as a party defendant in a civil action to adjudicate disputed title to real property in which the United States claims an interest, other than a security interest or water rights. See 28 U.S.C. §2409a. (On security interest, see §2410.)

73. Wright, Miller & Cooper, Federal Practice and Procedure §3658 (1976).

74. *Id.,* §3657.

75. The district courts have concurrent jurisdiction in actions for recovery of taxes wrongly assessed or collected, and in actions for other monetary claims not exceeding $10,000. *Id.,* §§3656, 3657.

(2) Federal Question Cases

The 1875 federal statute granting "federal question" jurisdiction is in much the same language as the constitutional clause which recognizes this kind of case as falling within the federal judicial power. That is, the statute refers to a civil case that "arises under" the Federal Constitution, laws, or treaties. This quoted phrase has provoked much litigation. Attempts have been made to have it cover disputes that only remotely and indirectly involve federal law. The courts have struggled with tests that are formulated in terms of federal law being an "ingredient" of the claim; federal law creating the right of action; the case involving the validity, meaning, or effect of the federal law; or the claim being basic, essential to, or founded directly upon the federal law. No one formula has carried the day. Professor Charles Wright concludes that existing cases are neither consistent nor entirely analytical in their approach; they imply, he thinks, that certain "pragmatic considerations" are important. Another element worth noting is that the word "laws" in the jurisdictional statute is construed to include federal administrative regulations issued under a federal law.[76]

Until recently an important prerequisite to federal question jurisdiction was the statutory requirement (absent from the constitutional language) that the amount in controversy be *over $10,000,* exclusive of costs and interest (28 U.S.C. §1331).[77] At the same time, there were many special jurisdictional statutes (on *particular* federal questions) that eliminated the requirement.[78] Perhaps the most significant gap in these special statutes was the failure to cover some of the suits against the federal government or its agencies or officers, claiming invalidity of governmental action — and causing a substantial problem for plaintiffs who could not clearly meet the over $10,000 requirement.[79]

---

76. For broader and more intensive treatment of the statute see Wright, *supra* n.21, §§17-20.

77. Congress had increased the amount a number of times. The $10,000 figure was fixed in 1958; the previous amount, in existence since 1911, was $3,000.

78. Some prominent examples of these statutes covered cases arising under any federal law regulating commerce; cases in which the United States is plaintiff, and *some* cases in which it is defendant; certain civil actions for damages or injunctive or other relief against *state* officials for conduct alleged to deprive the plaintiff of rights under the Constitution or federal statutes; and actions to recover fines, penalties or forfeitures incurred under federal law. See Wright, *supra* n.21, §32.

79. Attempts to use the Administrative Procedure Act to fill the gap failed when the Supreme Court ruled that the APA did not itself make a grant of jurisdiction, but rather authorized judicial review by eligible plaintiffs "in a court of competent jurisdiction." Califano v. Sanders, 430 U.S. 99 (1977). Sometimes the plaintiff could bring himself under one of the special statutes specifying no jurisdictional amount, e.g., one for cases arising under a federal law regulating commerce (28 U.S.C. §1337),

This problem, as well as the similar predicament of plaintiffs who, though invoking federal question jurisdiction, were *not* suing the government or its agencies or officers, was finally laid to rest by laws of 1976 and 1980. The 1976 law abolished the over $10,000 requirement of Section 1331 as applied to actions against the United States or its agencies or officers in an official capacity; and the 1980 law took the next step by extending the abolition to *all* civil actions arising under the Federal Constitution, statutes, or treaties.[80]

One of the special jurisdictional statutes — giving jurisdiction to civil actions for damages or injunctive or other relief against persons who have, "under color of" *state or local* law, deprived others of *federal* constitutional or statutory rights — deserves special mention.[81] It is a post-Civil War enactment which has had a striking rebirth beginning with the 1960s. The civil rights movement and Supreme Court decisions expanding the scope of Fourteenth Amendment protections against the conduct of state and municipal officials contributed to the rebirth. So have recent decisions liberally interpreting the scope of

---

or a 1962 law granting district courts jurisdiction of "any action in the nature of mandamus to compel an officer or employee of the United States or any agency thereof to perform a duty owed to the plaintiff" (28 U.S.C. §1361). Where such possibilities were not applicable, the plaintiff might be barred because of the "extreme difficulty or impossibility of placing a monetary value on the interest which plaintiff sought to protect, as, for example, to be free from continuous police surveillance . . . or to distribute political leaflets. . . . In other cases, a plaintiff's claim to, say, welfare or government employment could be valued but the amount might be $10,000 or less." Gellhorn et al., *supra* n.63 at 922.

80. 90 Stat. 2721 (1976), amending 5 U.S.C. §702-703; 94 Stat. 2369 (1980), amending 28 U.S.C. §1331. Other statutes on particular subject matter can of course depart from the new 28 U.S. Code Section 1331 model by requiring a jurisdictional amount. Thus, Section 3 of the cited 1980 law amended 15 U.S.C. §2072(a) of the Consumer Product Safety Act to make clear that the $10,000 requirement in that Act was being retained for injured plaintiff suits against private parties. The Magnuson-Moss Warranty Act (15 U.S.C. §2301 et seq.) requires that any suit brought under it in a federal court involve at least $50,000 in total claims.

81. What was originally Section 1 of the Civil Rights Act of 1871, giving both jurisdiction and a remedy for violations of constitutional rights, was divided by the 1874 statutory revision into widely separated jurisdictional and remedial sections with somewhat different coverage. So it is that the present jurisdictional provision (28 U.S.C. §1343(3)) applies to suits to "redress the deprivation, under color of any state law, statute, ordinance, regulation, custom or usage, of any right, privilege or immunity secured by the Constitution . . . *or by any Act of Congress providing for equal rights* of citizens or of all persons within" United States jurisdiction; and the remedial section (42 U.S.C. §1983) provides: "Every person who under color of any statute, ordinance, regulation, custom, or usage of any State or Territory, subjects, or causes to be subjected, any [U.S.] citizen . . . or other person within the jurisdiction thereof to the deprivation of any rights, privileges or immunities secured by the Constitution *and laws,* shall be liable to the party injured in an action at law, suit in equity, or other proper proceeding for redress." (Emphasis added.) See Maine v. Thibotout, 448 U.S. 1, 4-8 (1980).

the remedial provisions (42 U.S.C. §1983) to which the jurisdictional provision applies.[82]

The importance of being able in a suit under 42 U.S. Code Section 1983 to use its special jurisdictional statute containing no jurisdictional amount requirement, rather than the general federal question jurisdictional statute (28 U.S.C. §1331), is of course deflated by the 1980 elimination of the $10,000 requirement from the latter statute.[83]

There is no statute comparable to Section 1983 giving a similar right of action against *federal* officers, but the Supreme Court has recognized an implied right under the Constitution itself to bring such actions (for violations of *constitutional* rights), and the jurisdictional statute is the federal question statute, 28 U.S. Code Section 1331.[84]

(3) Diversity of Citizenship Cases (Herein Also of the *Nappier* Case Jurisdiction and of Corporate Citizenship and Other Fictions)

The "diversity of citizenship" jurisdiction (28 U.S.C. §1332) is what was invoked in our South Carolina *Nappier* case, set out at the

82. Thus, the defendant's conduct is not made any less "under color of" state or local law by the fact that it was unauthorized or forbidden by such law. Monroe v. Pape, 265 U.S. 167 (1961). While the "person" who is liable under Section 1983 is held to exclude the state, Quern v. Jordan, 440 U.S. 337 (1979), it does comprise other important categories. Included first of all, are state and local executive officers, Scheuer v. Rhodes, 416 U.S. 232 (1974); Monroe v. Pape, *supra.* I use the word "executive" because traditional immunities from liability have been held to apply under Section 1983 to *judges* for conduct in the course of their judicial duties (Stump v. Sparkman, 435 U.S. 349 (1978)), to *prosecutors,* in the initiation of prosecution and presenting of the case (Imbler v. Pachtman, 424 U.S. 409 (1976)), and to *legislators* acting within the sphere of legitimate legislative activity (Tenney v. Brandhove, 341 U.S. 367 (1951)). Also included in coverage are municipalities — i.e., when the municipal officer's conduct was pursuant to a governmental custom or a promulgated municipal policy (Monell v. Department of Social Servs., 436 U.S. 658 (1978)) — and even a private person who wilfully participates in a joint activity with a covered "person" (Adickes v. S. H. Kress & Co., 398 U.S. 144, 152, 174 n.44 (1970)). While good faith is generally an affirmative defense for a defendant officer, municipalities *cannot* assert as a defense the good faith conduct of municipal officers, Owen v. City of Independence, 445 U.S. 622 (1980). Since Section 1983 refers to deprivation of rights under the Constitution "and laws," rights under federal statutory law are covered, Maine v. Thiboutot, 448 U.S. 1 (1980) (Social Security Act). Even a state court is not precluded from giving a remedy under Section 1983, *id.;* Martinez v. California, 444 U.S. 277 (1980). In spite of some uncertainty, there is good reason for saying that the plaintiff's exhaustion of state judicial and administrative remedies is not a prerequisite to a Section 1983 action. See Annot., 47 ALR Fed. 15, 21-22 (1980).

83. See *supra* at n.80.

84. See Bivens v. Six Unknown Named Agents, 403 U.S. 388 (1971); Butz v. Economou, 438 U.S. 478 (1978); Carlson v. Green, 446 U.S. 14 (1980); Annot., 64 L. Ed. 2d. 871 (1981). On the subject generally, see Cass, Damage Suits Against Public Officers, 129 U. Pa. L. Rev. 1110 (1981).

beginning of this chapter. Unlike the case of "federal question" jurisdiction just discussed, the over $10,000 jurisdictional requirement still applies (and you will note in the *Nappier* case complaint that the plaintiff alleges in paragraph 11 that she has suffered damage in the sum of $175,000). Proposals have been pending in Congress to raise the amount to $25,000, to eliminate diversity jurisdiction altogether, or to make it unavailable to a plaintiff who is a citizen of the state in which the court sits.[85] This category of jurisdiction has been persistently criticized.

The critics ask: Why should there be this kind of federal jurisdiction at all, when there is no federal question, the federal government is not a party, the federal court will be struggling with questions of *state* law (creating problems discussed in section 5 below on relations between state and federal courts), and federal court congestion is substantially aggravated — diversity cases being almost one-fourth of the civil cases now being filed? The major justification offered is the fear that the state court would be prejudiced against the out-of-state litigant, a reaction of particular significance in the case of those considering investment of capital outside the state. In our increasingly mobile and nation-oriented society, however, the justification of such a fear is doubtful; and in any event, no such reasoning should hold in the case of the in-state plaintiff. One of the other considerations motivating the defenders of diversity jurisdiction today is the allegedly higher quality of justice obtainable in the federal courts.

Those who offer proposals to substantially reduce the diversity jurisdiction try mainly to exclude from it those claims against which the risk of prejudice is deemed minimal. These might be claims arising out of substantial local involvement of the out-of-state party, as by the operation of a "local establishment"; or claims by an in-state plaintiff against an out-of-state defendant. A 1958 federal law went part of the way toward this objective by saying a corporation shall be deemed a citizen of any state in which it has been incorporated (which hitherto had, roughly speaking, been recognized), *and* of the state in which it has its *principal place of business.* Thus if a corporation organized in Delaware with principal place of business in New York is a party, diversity of citizenship is lacking if any party on the other side is a citizen of either Delaware or New York. The American Law Institute's 1969 proposals that would reach beyond the corporate "principal place of business" situation and probably cut the volume of diversity cases in half are still a matter of some debate. However, the weight of respectable modern authority seems to favor elimination or sharp curtailment of diversity,[86] and action on the part of Congress in the not

85. Wright, Miller & Cooper, *supra* n.73, §3701 (1976) (1980 Pocket Part, n.9.1).
86. Among strong critics from the bench have been Justices Frankfurter and

too distant future seems likely. According to Justice Jackson, that would be "the greatest contribution that Congress could make to the orderly administration of justice in the United States."[87]

An important matter of interpretation of the meaning of diversity arises in cases with multiple plaintiffs and/or multiple defendants. The statute granting diversity jurisdiction has been construed by the Supreme Court in such cases to mean that "complete diversity" is required. Each plaintiff must be a citizen of a different state from the state of which each defendant is a citizen. (The constitutional clause on diversity jurisdiction does not require this, so Congress could for a particular kind of situation change the rule, as it has done.)[88]

Look back now at the *Nappier* case complaint in the first part of this chapter. Notice that while the plaintiff alleges she is a South Carolina resident, one defendant is alleged to be incorporated in a state "other than the State of South Carolina," and the other in North Carolina. And while both defendants are alleged to be doing business in South Carolina, there is no indication that South Carolina is the principal place of business of either defendant — which, if it were true as to any party, would, under the 1958 law, destroy diversity as to that party and require dropping that party. This might result in dismissal of the suit if the dropped party is deemed indispensable to the suit.

From what I have said, it might appear that the complaint has properly alleged the elements of diversity jurisdiction. In fact it has not, though the defendants' motion to dismiss did not make an issue of this. The complaint was defective, in varying degrees of importance, in at least these respects: (1) Plaintiff describes herself as a South Carolina "resident." This was insufficient because citizenship, in diversity jurisdiction, involves not mere residence but rather the legal concept of "domicil." This refers to residing in a state, plus the intention of making that state one's home (or the lack of fixed intention to go elsewhere). The pleading defect here might be disregarded by the court when it is clear that residence in the domicil sense was intended, as indeed could be inferred from all the facts of this complaint. (2) The specific state under whose laws the defendant life insurance company was organized should have been named, rather than merely

---

Jackson, and Judge Friendly of the Second Circuit. Academic critics have included Herbert Wechsler, Charles Wright, Richard Field, and David Currie. Though judicial and other supporters of diversity jurisdiction seem to be in a minority in recent years, they include some well-known names, such as Judge Skelly Wright, James Wm. Moore, Donald Weckstein, and Attorney John Frank. Extensive citations of writings pro and con appear in nn. 16-20 & 23 of Wright, *supra* n.21, §23.

87. Jackson, The Supreme Court in the American System of Government 38 (1955).

88. For this and for other issues arising in the field of diversity jurisdiction, see Wright, *supra* n.21, §§23-31.

alleging that the state was other than South Carolina. (3) It was not enough to allege that both defendants did business in South Carolina and then to remain silent on the principal place of business. Ever since the 1958 law, the complaint in a diversity case would have to specifically allege that a corporate defendant's principal place of business was in a state other than the plaintiff's state. Finally, you should be aware that there is considerable freedom to *amend* the jurisdictional allegations of the complaint.[89]

A final word about corporations as citizens. How did they ever get to be considered as "citizens" of a state in the first place? Originally, it was held that the artificial entity known as a corporation was *not* a citizen for purposes of the diversity jurisdiction. But by mid-nineteenth century the Supreme Court was saying in Marshall v. B. & O. Railroad[90] that though a corporation was not itself a citizen, and hence the citizenship of its stockholders was what counted, fairness required that *all stockholders* of a corporation be *conclusively presumed* to be citizens of the state where the corporation was incorporated. (This has since been accepted law, until modified by the above-mentioned 1958 law declaring that a corporation "shall be deemed a citizen of any State by which it has been incorporated and of the State where it has its principal place of business."[91]) What the Court was doing was indulging in a "legal fiction" — since it would rarely be true that all stockholders of a publicly held corporation were citizens of the state of incorporation. It was doing the same thing that courts did when they held that a buyer in good faith of real estate as to which a previous deed or mortgage has, unknown to him, been recorded, has notice ("constructive notice") of the recording. They could have spoken more realistically and said: For various practical reasons a recorded mortgage as to which the buyer has no actual notice must be treated by the law as effective in the same way as one that he did know about; i.e., where the mortgage was recorded, notice is *no longer a requirement*.

And the Supreme Court might have reasoned more realistically, too, in dealing with the corporate citizenship problem. True, it was not free to discard the "citizen" category in the way the courts could have discarded their own "notice" category; the "citizen" category was specified by statute, pursuant to the Constitution. But they might have dealt more candidly with their changed interpretation of it instead of clinging to the old interpretation[92] as supplemented by the assumption

89. On this paragraph, see *id.*, §§26 & 69; Appendix of Forms (Form 2) at 666-667.

90. 57 U.S. (16 How.) 314 (1853).

91. 28 U.S.C. §1332(c).

92. By the "old interpretation" I refer to the opinion by Chief Justice Marshall in Bank of United States v. Devaux, 9 U.S. (5 Cranch) 61 (1809), declaring that the corporate artificial entity was "certainly not a citizen"; citizenship of the *members*

of palpably untrue facts. In the above-mentioned *Marshall* case, instead of using a more realistic rationale[93] — either for *changing* the doctrine that a corporation was not a citizen for any purpose, or changing the doctrine that all stockholders had to have a state citizenship different from that of the plaintiff (who was, in the *Marshall* case, a Virginia plaintiff) — the court found that all of the far-flung stockholders of the B. & O. Railroad, incorporated in Maryland, indeed "are citizens of that State" (i.e., are conclusively "presumed" to be so).[94] The language of such a statement, like the language of the courts that said the ignorant buyer of the real estate did have notice of the recorded mortgage, made the statement seem contrary to fact.

Why do courts indulge in this fictional way of talking? M. R. Cohen's explanation is that "in moments of innovation, we cling all the more to old linguistic forms. The latter minister to the general feeling of security, especially where the prevailing myth or make-believe is that the judge merely declares the law and cannot change or extend it. . . . From the point of view of social policy, fictions are, like eloquence, important in giving emotional drive to propositions that we wish to see accepted. They can be used . . . to soften the shock of innovation."[95]

Seeing the way in which fictions function outside the law helps illuminate their legal role. One of the most apt analogies to legal fictions is furnished by this passage from Roscoe Pound's article, "Law in Books and Law in Action":[96]

> When Tom Sawyer and Huck Finn had determined to rescue Jim by digging under the cabin where he was confined, it seemed to the uninformed lay mind of Huck Finn that some old picks the boys had found were the proper implements to use. But Tom knew better. From reading

---

would be controlling. Actually, just nine years prior to the mid-nineteenth-century view announced in *Marshall* (*supra* n.90) as described in the text, a short-lived decision had held that a corporation was "entitled, for the purpose of suing and being sued, to be deemed a citizen" of the chartering state. Louisville C. & C. R. Co. v. Letson, 43 U.S. (2 How.) 497 (1844).

93. The court might have said something like this: The developing role of corporations in the country make it a practical and equitable necessity to *change* our interpretation of "citizen." We will give a different and looser construction to "citizen" so as to bring a corporation within it for limited, diversity litigation purposes, as distinct from such other purposes as voting. Alternatively, and for the same reasons, the Court might have continued to assume, as it did, that a corporation was *not* a citizen, so that stockholder citizenship was controlling, and then gone on to say (1) the state of incorporation can be viewed as making *all* stockholders limited "citizens" of the state for limited group enterprise purposes including litigation, *or* (2) that it was time to *change* the requirement that *all* stockholders of the corporation being sued had to have a state citizenship different from that of each plaintiff.

94. Marshall v. B. & O. R.R., 57 U.S. (16 How.) 314, 329 (1853).

95. 6 Ency. Soc. Sci. 228 (1931). See generally Fuller, Legal Fictions (1967).

96. 44 Am. L. Rev. 12 (1910).

he knew what was the right course in such cases, and he called for case-knives. "It don't make no difference," said Tom, "how foolish it is, it's the *right way* — and it's the regular way. And there ain't no other way that I ever heard of, and I've read all the books that gives any information about these things. They always dig out with a case-knife." So, in deference to the books and the proprieties, the boys set to work with case-knives. But after they had dug till nearly midnight and they were tired and their hands were blistered, and they had made little progress, a light came to Tom's legal mind. He dropped his knife and, turning to Huck, said firmly, "Gimme a case-knife." Let Huck tell the rest:

"He had his own by him, but I handed him mine. He flung it down and says, 'Gimme a *case-knife*.'

"I didn't know just what to do — but then I thought. I scratched around amongst the old tools and got a pickaxe and give it to him, and he took it and went to work and never said a word.

"He was always just that particular. *Full of principle*."

Tom had made over again one of the earliest discoveries of the law. When tradition prescribed case-knives for those tasks for which pickaxes were better adapted, it seemed better to our forefathers, after a little vain struggle with case-knives, to adhere to principle — but use the pickaxe. They granted that law ought not to change. Changes in law were full of danger. But, on the other hand, it was highly inconvenient to use case-knives. And so the law has always managed to get a pickaxe in its hands, though it steadfastly demanded a case-knife, and to wield it in the virtuous belief that it was using the approved instrument.

5. Relations Between State and Federal Courts

1. Could the *Nappier* case have been brought in a state court of South Carolina? The answer is yes. A damage action for invasion of privacy would typically be brought in the state court of general jurisdiction. It is not one of those classes of action over which federal courts are by statute given *exclusive* jurisdiction (e.g., cases involving federal crimes, federal penalties, forfeitures or seizures, federal anti-trust actions, bankruptcy proceedings, patent and copyright actions, certain maritime actions, and a few others). Thus, there was in this case a state court jurisdiction as well as a "concurrent" federal court jurisdiction based on diversity of citizenship. If there had been no such diversity, there would have been no federal jurisdiction, since the complaint had raised no issue that would qualify the case under the "federal question" jurisdictional statute or any of the special jurisdictional statutes. Incidentally, if the *Nappier* plaintiff had sued in the state court, the case could still have wound up in the federal court — because the defendants had the right under "removal" statutes to re-

move the case to a federal court because the case qualified for federal court jurisdiction.[97]

2. Suppose, now, that the Federal Communications Act, regulating commerce in broadcasting, had prohibited broadcasts violating a person's right of privacy, and had declared that the person aggrieved by such broadcast could sue for damages in a court of competent jurisdiction. It is clear that a federal district court would qualify, even in the absence of diversity, since the action would arise under a federal act regulating commerce. Would a state court of general jurisdiction also qualify? Would the mere fact that the right of action had been specified by a federal statute mean that only a federal court could have jurisdiction? The answer is that when Congress has created a right of action and has *not intended to make federal jurisdiction exclusive* (as it has in the case of federal crimes and other actions mentioned in the preceding paragraph), then the appropriate state court is authorized to take jurisdiction.

Indeed, it cannot *refuse* to take jurisdiction — at least if it would be the appropriate court for suits involving analogous rights created by state rather than federal law — i.e., it cannot "discriminate" against the federally created right. These principles have been applied many times to state court suits under the Federal Employers' Liability Act of 1908 and the Emergency Price Control Act of 1942 — in the first type of case, for damages to injured workers on interstate railroads, and in the second for treble-damages (even if considered "penal") by an overcharged tenant or consumer.[98] Congress had in both statutes specifically authorized a concurrent jurisdiction by state and federal courts. Where Congress has been silent, when can intent to authorize be presumed? And to what extent is the procedure in the action to be governed by federal rather than state rules? Should the recent revival of the Tenth Amendment (see Chap. 5 under **C3**) mean that a constitutional limit exists on federal power to impose such procedural rules, and indeed on power to burden (or overburden) the state courts with such litigation? These and other questions are not fully resolved.[99]

Of course this is not the only type of situation in which a state court may properly be dealing with questions of federal law. In *any* action in a state court that has authority to hear the case (including those in which the authority comes from state law), the court does not refrain from considering a particular issue merely because it is one of federal law — such as whether a state statute violates the Federal

97. See Wright, *supra* n.21, chap. 6.

98. See Testa v. Katt, 330 U.S. 386 (1947); Mondou v. New York, N.H. & H. R.R. Co., 223 U.S. 1 (1912).

99. See Redish, Federal Jurisdiction 124-138 (1980); Wright, *supra* n.21, §45.

Constitution. It decides the federal law issues along with any state law issues. And the decision on federal issues by the highest state court empowered to make the decision may be reviewable by certiorari or appeal, as previously described, in the Supreme Court.

3. One of the most important aspects of relations between state and federal courts is this: When a plaintiff like the *Nappier* plaintiff has a damage claim under the law of the state and could sue in a state court, but chooses to invoke the diversity jurisdiction of the federal court, might this choice change the legal principles applicable to his claim? Might that individual choose the federal court simply because federal judge-made principles of privacy law present more favorable prospects than the judge-made privacy law that would be applied by the state court? This line of strategy was once available to a plaintiff (or to a defendant who considered removal to a federal court), but, in general, is no longer a possibility. A brief account of the change is as follows: Section 34 of the Judiciary Act of 1789 — the so-called Rules of Decision Act, which in substantially similar language still exists[100] — declared that the "laws of the several states" shall apply in the federal courts unless the Federal Constitution, statutes, or treaties provided otherwise. In 1842 in the celebrated case of Swift v. Tyson[101] on an issue of commercial law, the Supreme Court held that "laws of the states" referred to statutes and not to the body of judicial decisions making up the common law. This came to mean that the federal courts were free to develop their own federal common law, in the fields of torts, contracts, and commercial relations not covered by state statutes.

But there was persistent objection that on a matter not governed by the Constitution or federal statutes (typically in a diversity of citizenship case), the applicable law for a given state should not depend on whether the case was in a federal or state court. Finally, almost a century later, the 1842 decision was overruled. The Supreme Court declared in the 1938 case of Erie R.R. v. Tompkins that the 1842 decision had misconstrued not only the Rules of Decision Act but the Constitution itself. Henceforth the rule was to be: "Except in matters governed by the Federal Constitution or by Acts of Congress, the law to be applied in any case is the law of the state. And whether the law of the state shall be declared by its Legislature in a statute or by its highest court in a decision is not a matter of federal concern. There is no federal general common law."[102] A qualification of the principle that, in the cases described, the outcome should not depend on whether the case was in state or federal court, is this: Generally speaking, if the issue is regarded as one of "procedure" rather than substantive law, the

100. See 28 U.S.C. §1652.
101. 41 U.S. (16 Pet.) 1 (1842).
102. 304 U.S. 64, 78 (1938).

federal court will apply its own rather than the state's procedural rules. There are vexing problems, however, in applying the *Erie* doctrine.[103] And the Supreme Court has indeed recognized a federal "common law" in some special situations.[104]

The result of all this, as far as the *Nappier* case is concerned, is that the federal court sitting in a "diversity of citizenship" case in South Carolina, faced with a question of the substantive law of privacy, had to apply the judge-made privacy law of the state of South Carolina (as well as give the South Carolina criminal statute whatever relevance the court thought it had for this damage suit).

4. An important federal statute on the subject of relations between federal and state courts is the one which prohibits certain kinds of federal court interference with state court proceedings. The present statute, which has in some form been on the books from almost the beginning, was revised in 1948 to read as follows: "A court of the United States *may not grant an injunction to stay proceedings in a State court except* as expressly authorized by Act of Congress, or where necessary in aid of its jurisdiction, or to protect or effectuate its judgments."[105] (Emphasis added.) Some other special anti-injunction statutes — directed at restraint against certain state officers[106] — are in effect, but this is the important general statute.

The "except" clauses have produced many judicial interpretations, to be treated here only in terms of one problem of interpretation — the relation of the "except as expressly authorized by Act of Congress" clause to a type of case that I discussed earlier in connection with federal question jurisdiction. I refer to the cases under U.S. Code Title 42, Section 1983, which allows injunctive and other redress against persons who act under color of state or local law to deprive another of federal rights. Suppose that a man is indicted by a state grand jury under a "criminal syndicalism" statute (prohibiting certain activities directed at overthrow of the government), and he then sues in a federal district court under Section 1983, requesting an injunction to stay or restrain the state criminal proceeding on the ground that the prosecution and the statute violate his federal constitutional rights of free speech and press. Would such a federal court injunction against a state court proceeding be treated as "expressly authorized by Act of Congress" (i.e., by Section 1983) so as to be outside the ban of the statute mentioned in the preceding paragraph?

103. See Wright, *supra* n.21, chap. 9.

104. *Id.*, §60.

105. 28 U.S.C. §2283.

106. For example, there is the Johnson Act withdrawing federal court jurisdiction from suits to enjoin certain state public utility orders. Another statute prohibits federal court injunctions against the assessment, levy, or collection of certain state taxes. See Wright, *supra* n.21, §51.

The Supreme Court ducked answering this question in a 1971 case like the one just described. The Court said there was no need in that case to answer it, because even if the ban on injunctions were inapplicable (on the debatable ground that Section 1983 had "expressly" authorized injunctions against state court proceedings), there were *other* reasons for saying that the injunction should be denied. The Court referred to "the basic doctrine of equity jurisprudence that courts of equity should not act, and particularly should not act to restrain a criminal prosecution, when the moving party has an adequate remedy at law and will not suffer irreparable injury if denied equitable relief." This "is reinforced by an even more vital consideration, the notion of 'comity,' that is a proper respect for state functions . . . and a continuance of the belief that the National Government will fare best if the States and their institutions are left free to perform their separate functions in their separate ways."[107]

Exceptions could be recognized, the Court thought, for cases in which the state prosecution is conducted in bad faith, for harassment purposes rather than good faith enforcement purposes; or the highly unusual case in which a statute is "flagrantly and patently" unconstitutional "in every clause" and no matter how, or against whom, it is applied. The Court disapproved of language in earlier opinions that had seemed to treat less extreme situations as sufficient.

These principles were left undisturbed in a 1972 Supreme Court decision[108] squarely facing the question that had been ducked earlier. The Court held that the anti-injunction statute did not stand in the way of a Section 1983 injunction against a state court proceeding (i.e., such an injunction was "expressly authorized by Act of Congress") — though of course the other factors mentioned in the 1971 case would, in the typical case, stand in the way.

5. The considerations of "comity," mentioned by the Court in the above-mentioned 1971 case as a traditional brake upon federal court interference with state courts, are often referred to in connection with an "abstention" doctrine. The purport of this doctrine is that even when the necessary conditions for federal court jurisdiction exist, the court does not necessarily have to exercise its jurisdiction; it may under certain circumstances "abstain" from such exercise. Application of the doctrine is not limited to situations of federal court interference with an already pending state court proceeding.

Let us say no state court enforcement proceeding has yet been brought under a state law but one is about to be, on account of alleged violation by Mr. X of a regulation issued by a commission under a

107. Younger v. Harris, 401 U.S. 37, 43-44 (1971).
108. Mitchum v. Foster, 407 U.S. 225 (1972).

state law. Mr. X sues in federal court to restrain enforcement on the ground of federal unconstitutionality of the law, and the further ground that the law had not authorized the regulation in question. The federal court may be unwilling to decide the constitutional issue, because courts traditionally avoid decisions of such issues if possible, and here there might be no need to decide it because (1) under one of two reasonably possible interpretations of the ambiguous statute, let us say, no constitutional issue would arise, and the state court has not yet resolved the ambiguity; and (2) if the statute were construed not to authorize the regulation (an issue not yet resolved by the state court), then that too would dispose of the case without the necessity of deciding the statute's constitutionality. Both these questions deal with the *meaning* of the state statute — an issue of state law on which the state courts are the final authority. So the federal court may choose to abstain from decision, and either dismiss the case or retain it on the docket, while the plaintiff seeks state court adjudications of the unresolved questions of state law. There are complexities in the abstention doctrine, and it has been applied in somewhat different situations, too, but the foregoing example manifests the general method of its application.[109]

6. The Necessary "Standing" and "Justiciability"

The *Nappier* case presented no problem of standing or justiciability, but since I am trying to familiarize you with some fundamental procedural aspects of a lawsuit, I want to include these important questions with the others that may or may not be specifically involved in the case.

a. General (Herein Also of "Advisory Opinions" and Declaratory Judgments)

Under the Anglo-American adversary system, not everyone qualifies as an adversary entitled to set the court machinery in motion. Not every kind of alleged injury to an alleged interest will suffice. The court must be satisfied that the plaintiff has suffered the necessary kind of injury to the necessary kind of interest. The courts have required

109. For general discussion, see Wright, *supra* n.21, §52; Joiner, In Search of a Federal Forum: Overcoming the Abstention Rules, Natl. L.J., April 14, 1980, at 26. Wright mentions four overlapping objectives of the abstention doctrine: "(1) to avoid decision of a federal constitutional question where the case may be disposed of on questions of state law; (2) to avoid needless conflict with the administration by a state of its own affairs; (3) to leave to the states the resolution of unsettled questions of state law; and (4) to ease the congestion of the federal docket" (at 218).

that the dispute be a live one, rather than one laid to rest by subsequent events (i.e., made "moot"); involve plaintiff's own injury, not someone else's; be concrete and immediate, rather than a "hypothetical" dispute or one presenting a "premature" question for a mere "advisory opinion"; be not feigned or collusive; and not involve a question that is "nonjusticiable" — for instance, the kind of "political" question discussed in Chapter 1. In some circumstances, some kinds of interests and injuries, such as a federal taxpayer's or a competitor's, have been held insufficient to give standing.

In discussing these requirements, the Supreme Court has often invoked a constitutional source for some or all of them, in Article III, section 2, which extends the judicial power of the United States to specified categories of "cases" and "controversies."[110] Thus a dispute that lacks the adversary character described by the above requirements may be characterized as not a case or controversy within the meaning of the Constitution. The states, by state constitutional provision or otherwise, have adopted a similar view of the judicial function. As we shall see, the Supreme Court does not base its standing decisions solely on the Article III requirement. Even a plaintiff who meets the requirement may be barred by what the Court calls "prudential considerations."

Before presenting some of the situations to which the above-mentioned concepts refer, I want first to deal with certain conditions to which they do *not* refer.

As I have said, *advisory opinions*, in the sense of judicial answers to hypothetical or premature questions, are frowned on — and I will develop this further later. However, there is a special kind of advisory opinion that is viewed as legitimate in several states. Such an opinion is authorized by the constitutions of those states only when it is sought by specified public bodies rather than by private litigants. It is "not available to private or corporate or group parties generally. It is restricted, usually to the two houses of the legislature and the executive," and "designed for use during the process of legislation, or in the process of executive action."[111]

Second, the legitimacy of the *declaratory judgment* proceeding is not undermined by the above-mentioned requirements, though the proceeding lacks some aspects of the typical court controversy. Under an applicable declaratory judgment statute (and one exists for federal

110. "The two terms can be used interchangeably, for, we are authoritatively told, a 'controversy,' if distinguishable at all from a 'case,' is distinguishable only in that it is a less comprehensive term, and includes only suits of a civil nature." Wright, *supra* n.21 at 38, citing Aetna Life Ins. Co. v. Haworth, 300 U.S. 227, 239 (1937).

111. Field, The Advisory Opinion — An Analysis, 24 Ind. L.J. 203, 222 (1949). See also Comment, 44 Fordham L. Rev. 81 (1975); Wright, *supra* n.21, §12 at 40-42.

courts in addition to the statutes of practically all the states for state courts), the plaintiff has standing in court even though he does not claim the defendant has committed or is immediately about to commit a wrong, and even though the plaintiff does not seek relief in the form of damages or injunctive restraint against the defendant. What he seeks is "declaratory" relief — a court declaration of respective rights of plaintiff and defendant. It is particularly useful as a means of obtaining an authoritative interpretation of a statute, contract, or will, to avoid the adverse effect of conduct that would be taken in reliance on a mistaken interpretation. The court declaration is of course an official judgment, which may be supplemented by further relief (e.g., damages or injunction) in case the losing party refuses to abide by it. There is still a requirement, for declaratory relief, that the case involve a present live controversy, with the threat of real though not necessarily immediate injury. And even when this requirement is met, circumstances can justify a court's denial of relief in the exercise of a sound "discretion" in the public interest.[112]

We turn now to some cases illustrating the basic concepts discussed above.

b. Whether a "Legal" Right or Interest Is Necessary; Types of Interests Covered

Not so many years ago, leading Supreme Court cases on standing were announcing a prerequisite in terms of a "legal right" having been invaded; there had to be "injury" to a "legally protected right."[113] This did not mean that the Court had to decide the merits of the case before dealing with the standing issue, nor that the recognition by the Court of "legal right" or "legal interest" meant the litigant would ultimately win on the merits. Rather, by this phrase the Court may be said to have been posing the question whether the litigant was alleging the kind of substantial interest to which a court has been in the habit of listening.[114] But the phrase did lend itself to the above interpretations, and in 1970 the Supreme Court repudiated its use.[115] Data-processing service organizations had sued to challenge the Comptroller of the Currency's permission to national banks to render

112. See generally James & Hazard, Civil Procedure §1.10; Wright, Miller & Cooper, *supra* n.73, §§2751-2771.

113. See Tennessee Elec. Power Co. v. TVA, 306 U.S. 118 (1937); Joint Anti-Fascist Refugee Comm. v. McGrath, 341 U.S. 123 (1951).

114. See Justice Frankfurter's concurring opinion in the *Joint Anti-Fascist* case cited in preceding footnote.

115. Association of Data Processing Serv. Org. v. Camp, 397 U.S. 150 (1970).

data-processing services to bank customers and other banks. The court of appeals held that plaintiffs lacked standing because they had no legal right or interest in being free from this competition. But the Supreme Court said: "The 'legal interest' test goes to the merits. The question of standing is different." It then announced a newly formulated test (applicable at least to cases involving statutory or constitutional provisions, and, as later cases showed more clearly, only as an interpretation of the *Administrative Procedure Act's* application to administrative agency action): plaintiff's allegations must show (1) that the challenged conduct has caused him "injury in fact," and (2) that "the interest sought to be protected by the complainant is arguably within the zone of interests to be protected or regulated by the statute or constitutional guarantee in question."

Moreover, the relevant interests, said the Court, are not merely economic; they may be aesthetic, conservational, recreational, or spiritual. Here the Court cited recent cases recognizing the standing of environmentalists to contest construction projects damaging to the environment, and the standing of consumers and consumer organizations, including TV listeners wishing to persuade the FCC that a TV station's license should not be renewed.

While I cannot here make any detailed examination of all the types of interest that have been recognized, the taxpayer interest deserves a special word. It had long been the rule that a federal taxpayer alleging, e.g., unconstitutionality of a federal statute, lacked standing to enjoin expenditure of general funds from the Treasury for administration of the statute. Largely, this was because the taxpayer's interest in such moneys " — partly realized from taxation and partly from other sources — is shared with millions of others, is comparatively minute and undeterminable, and the effect upon future taxation of any payment out of the funds, so remote, fluctuating and uncertain. . . ."[116] However, in the 1968 case of Flast v. Cohen,[117] the Supreme Court recognized a federal taxpayer's standing to attack the expenditure of federal funds under the Elementary and Secondary Education Act of 1965 as allegedly violating the church-state separation clause of the First Amendment. The taxpayer's standing as taxpayer will exist, said the Court, (1) when he is attacking constitutionality of exercises of congressional power under the taxing and spending clause of the Constitution (as distinguished from attacking constitutionality of an essentially regulatory statute that involves incidental expenditure of tax funds to administer it); and (2) when the constitutional clause the individual claims to be violated is one that specifically restricts expendi-

116. Frothingham v. Mellon, 262 U.S. 447 (1923).
117. 392 U.S. 83 (1968).

tures of federal funds. The First Amendment was viewed as such a "specific" restriction, but it is still unclear whether any other constitutional restriction will qualify. The Court has already applied the *Flast* limitations to bar some taxpayer suits.[118]

The standing of a state or municipal taxpayer in a state court is, in general, treated by the state courts with greater liberality; and sometimes the taxpayer's standing to sue is recognized even when the challenged governmental action does not involve an expenditure of public funds.[119]

c. *Confusion As To the Nature and Application of the Basic Standard; Can One Invoke the Rights of Others?; Why All the Confusion?*

The law of standing has long been plagued by shifts in the basic test for standing and by uncertainties in applying the test.

1. Thus, while the 1970 *Data Processing* case, previously described, did have some clarifying influence on the law of standing, its reformulation of the test created a new set of ambiguities in the "zone of interest," and "interests to be protected or regulated by the statute or constitutional guarantee in question."[120] In addition, the scope of the new test's application was not altogether clear. It could reasonably be

118. One well-known instance was U.S. v. Richardson, 418 U.S. 166 (1974). A taxpayer who claimed that the executive branch's failure to reveal CIA expenditures violated the statement and account clause of the Constitution (Art. I, §9, cl. 7: ". . . and a regular statement and account of the receipts and expenditures of all public money shall be published from time to time") was held not to have standing as a taxpayer to enforce the clause. The Court declared that the double test announced in Flast v. Cohen had not been met: The challenge was not to an exercise of the taxing and spending power; and the constitutional provision allegedly violated was not a specific restriction on taxing and spending. The Court took the same attitude in Schlesinger v. Reservists Comm. to Stop the War, 418 U.S. 208 (1974), insofar as plaintiff anti-war activists were suing as taxpayers. They were claiming that the Constitution's compatibility clause (Art. I, §6, cl. 2: ". . . no person holding any office under the United States shall be a member of either House during continuance in office") was violated by the Pentagon policy allowing members of Congress to retain their status in the Armed Forces Reserves.

119. See generally on taxpayer standing, Comment, 81 Dick. L. Rev. 495 (1977); Notes, 61 Geo. L.J. 747 (1973); 69 Yale L.J. 895 (1960).

120. For vigorous criticism of the test and its language, see Davis, Administrative Law of the Seventies (1976) (1980 Supp., §22-02.11). One ground of criticism is its *restrictive* effect on standing: Cases that previously had been heard by a court without any question as to standing because of plaintiff's obvious "injury" might now be dismissed because of "zone of interest" considerations. In some respects though, the case had a liberalizing effect on standing: its dispensing with the confusing "legal right" barrier; its willingness to recognize a competitor's interest as sufficient, contrary to some previous cases; and its dictum affirming that noneconomic interests could qualify.

asserted, however, on the basis of the opinion and later Supreme Court opinions referring to the case, that the test was to be confined to Administrative Procedure Act cases involving statutory or constitutional claims. Even with this limitation the difficulties in defining the zone of interest and the strong criticism of the test probably account for the Court's failure to mention the zone of interest aspect of the test "in any of the later twenty-seven major opinions on standing, except in 1977 and 1979 footnotes."[121]

Thus, when the Court referred in a 1978 case to the two-pronged test applied in its recent cases, it was referring not to the *Data Processing* test (of (1) injury and (2) the zone of interest concept) but rather to (1) injury and (2) the "substantial likelihood that the judicial relief requested will prevent or redress the claimed injury."[122] Thus stood the test as far as Article III considerations were concerned, with "prudential considerations" described as adding another hurdle.

The 1979 *Gladstone* case took the same approach and elaborated as follows: (1) The minimum requirement, embodied in Article III, is that: "[a] plaintiff must always have suffered 'a distinct and palpable injury to himself' . . . that is likely to be redressed if the requested relief is granted" (elsewhere in the opinion the necessary injury is described as "an actual or threatened injury"). (2) Even while meeting Article III requirements, a plaintiff "may still lack standing under the prudential principles by which the judiciary seeks to avoid deciding questions of broad social import where no individual rights would be vindicated, and to limit access to the federal courts to those litigants best suited to assert a particular claim. For example, a litigant normally must assert an injury that is peculiar to himself or to a distinct group of which he is a part, rather than one 'shared in substantially equal measure by all or a large class of citizens'. . . . He also must assert his own legal interests rather than those of third parties." Relegated to a footnote, as though the Court were reluctant to let go entirely of a now tarnished concept, was the zone of interest test that "in appropriate circumstances" the plaintiff might have to meet, as another of the "nonconstitutional limitations on standing." The Court also recognized that Congress may expand standing by abrogating any of the prudential considerations, if the Article III constitutional minimum is met.[123]

121. Davis, *id.*, §22.20 at 188.

122. Duke Power Co. v. Carolina Environ. Study Group, Inc., 438 U.S. 59, 79 (1978).

123. Gladstone Realtors v. Bellwood, 441 U.S. 91, 100 (1979). The point last mentioned is not new. Some prior recognitions of this permissible role of Congress are in U.S. v. Richardson, 418 U.S. 166, 178 n.11 (1974); Schlesinger v. Reservists Comm., 418 U.S. 208, 224 n.14 (1974); Trafficante v. Metropolitan Life Ins. Co., 409 U.S. 205 (1972). Can Congress confer standing on a plaintiff who has *not* met the

What makes the cases confusing and unpredictable is not only the shifts in the test but the fact that all the test factors listed in the preceding paragraph seem to have been inconsistently applied. (1) Thus, in determining whether the injury was "distinct and palpable" (sometimes referred to as concrete, direct, non-abstract, non-speculative, or non-remote) the Court's attitude has sometimes been very loose and sometimes very strict[124] — as is illustrated by the *SCRAP*[125] and *Linda*

"injury" requirement of Article III? Congress can do so indirectly, by creating a *right or interest* in him or in the class to which he belongs, the invasion of which can then qualify as the necessary injury. Linda R.S. v. Richard D., 410 U.S. 614, 617 n.3 (1973); Warth v. Seldin, 422 U.S. 490, 514 (1975).

Congress can also, as in a "qui tam" statute (e.g., Federal False Claims Act, 31 U.S.C. §§231-235) authorize a citizen to sue on behalf of the Government for a civil penalty and to share recovery with the Government. See U.S. ex rel Marcus v. Hess, 317 U.S. 537 (1943). Here — and in other instances, like the Federal Election Campaign Act authorization to any voter to sue to test the Act's constitutionality (2 U.S.C. §437h) — the rationale would be the *"private Attorney General"* doctrine. In one version (that of Judge Jerome Frank in Associated Indus. v. Ickes, 134 F.2d 694 (2d Cir. 1943) the doctrine means this: Just as the Attorney General is designated by Congress to sue and represent the public interest in government litigation, and he need not show injury to himself, private parties may also be designated by Congress to sue in the public interest without having to show personal injury; they are surrogates for the Attorney General.

It has also been argued that the Court should *change its mind* about the personal injury view of "case or controversy"; that a wider access to the federal courts is desirable, especially because of "standing" difficulties encountered in "public interest litigation"; and that congressional redefinition of "cases" and "controversies" may help persuade the Court to adopt a looser interpretation of Article III. See generally, Tushnet, The New Law of Standing — A Plea for Abandonment, 62 Cornell L. Rev. 663 (1977); Braveman, The Standing Doctrine: A Dialogue Between the Court and Congress, 2 Cardozo L. Rev. 31 (1980); Note, 2 W. New England L. Rev. 71 (1979). A defense of a more traditional Article III requirement by Brilmayer in The Jurisprudence of Article III: Perspectives on the Case or Controversy Requirement, 93 Harv. L. Rev. 297 (1979) was replied to by Tushnet, The Sociology of Article III: A Response to Professor Brilmayer, *id.* at 1698 (1980), followed by Brilmayer, A Reply, *id.* at 1727 (1980).

124. See Davis, *supra* n.120, §§22.02-2 – 22.02-10; and 1980 Supp., §§22.00-1 – 22.00-4.

125. U.S. v. Students Challenging Regulatory Agency Procedures (SCRAP), 412 U.S. 669 (1973). Here a group of five law students in the Washington, D.C. area formed an association that sued to restrain enforcement of an ICC order allowing a two and one-half % emergency surcharge on railroad freight rates to go into effect. The chief injury claimed was that the freight rate increases caused "increased use of nonrecyclable commodities as compared to recyclable goods, thus resulting in the need to use more natural resources to produce such goods, some of which resources might be taken from the Washington area, and resulting in more refuse that might be discarded in national parks in the Washington area." In spite of the seemingly indirect and speculative nature of this injury, the Court characterized the injury as "direct" and "perceptible": Plaintiffs had alleged actual use of the Washington metropolitan area resources in question (for camping, hiking, fishing, and sightseeing) rather than a mere "interest" in environmentalism. And while the chain of causation assumed in the allegation may have been dubious, the case, the Court emphasized, was at the pleading stage. Hence, since it was conceivable that the plaintiffs could prove their assumptions, the allegations were sufficient to withstand

R.S.[126] cases, both decided the same year — while a 1980 case showed a perhaps unequalled degree of looseness.[127] (2) As to the likelihood-of-redress factor, the Court has sometimes, as in the *Gladstone* case above, linked this with the injury factor as constituting together the Article III requirement;[128] and it has sometimes invoked the related idea of a *causal relation* between the claimed illegality and the injury as an alternative to the likelihood-of-redress factor,[129] though in the same

---

a pretrial motion to dismiss. The Court also made clear that standing was not to be denied because the plaintiffs would be suffering the injury together with large numbers of others who were not suing, or because the alleged injury was small.

126. Linda R.S. v. Richard D., 410 U.S. 614 (1973). Here the mother of an illegitimate child sought an injunction to require a Texas prosecutor to bring a criminal prosecution against the father for non-support. The prosecutor had interpreted the relevant statute to apply only to legitimate children, and the plaintiff claimed the statute as thus construed violated the equal protection clause. In denying her standing the Court stressed that the injury must be "direct"; that the lack of support payments was not shown to be caused by the prosecutor's failure to try to put the father in jail; and the requested relief (putting him in jail) would not alleviate the injury. "The prospect that prosecution will, at least in the future, result in payment of support can, at best, be termed only speculative." The case lacked the necessary " 'direct' relationship between the alleged injury and the claim sought to be adjudicated. . . ." Query: Is the causal relation more speculative here than in the *SCRAP* case?

127. In U.S. Parole Commn. v. Geraghty, 445 U.S. 388 (1980), a prisoner who had been denied parole brought a "class action" on behalf of all parole-eligible prisoners, attacking validity of the Parole Commission guidelines, but the district judge denied his request for "class certification," as well as his claim on the merits. In a 5 to 4 decision, the Supreme Court held he had standing to pursue his appeal from the denial of class certification, even though, shortly after filing the appeal, his prison term expired and he was released. In addition to certain technical arguments belittling the extent to which the decision was departing from traditional Article III interpretations, the majority responded to the minority's concern over the lack of the traditional "injury" or "personal stake in the outcome" element by saying (n.11): "The erosion of the strict, formalistic perception of Article III was begun well before today's decision. . . . [T]he strict formalistic view . . ., while perhaps the starting point of all inquiry, is riddled with exceptions. And in creating each exception the Court has looked to practicalities and prudential considerations. . . . We do not attempt to predict how far down the road the Court will eventually go toward premising jurisdiction 'upon the bare existence of a sharply presented issue in a concrete and vigorously argued case' [quoting the dissent]. . . . Each case must be decided on its own facts."

128. See Warth v. Sedlin, 422 U.S. 490, 508 (1975); Simon v. Eastern Ky. Welfare Rights Org., 426 U.S. 26, 38 (1976); *Duke Power, supra* n.122 at 75 n.20.

129. See *Warth, supra* n.128 at 505; *Simon, supra* n.128 at 44-45; *Duke Power, supra* n.122 at 72, 74. That the two factors are alternatives that do not always point in the same direction, see Justice Powell's opinion in Regents Univ. Cal. v. Bakke, 438 U.S. 265, 280-281 n.14, in which a rejected white applicant to medical school had claimed that the school's affirmative action program was unconstitutional: ". . . Even if Bakke had been unable to prove that he would have been admitted in the absence of the special program, it would not follow that he lacked standing. The constitutional element of standing is plaintiff's demonstration of any injury to himself that is likely to be redressed by favorable decision of his claim."

opinion specifying both factors as necessary.[130] Again, in the propensity to recognize the existence of these factors the Court has sometimes been surprisingly quick, and sometimes surprisingly slow.[131] (3) The point that the injury must not be one that is "shared in substantially equal measure by all or a large class of citizens" is contradicted by the language in *SCRAP* (past cases "have already made it clear that standing is not to be denied simply because many people suffer the same injury." Otherwise "the most injurious and widespread government actions could be questioned by nobody")[132] and in *Sierra Club.*[133] (4) Finally the point about not invoking the rights of third parties has often been departed from. It is sufficiently complex and recurring to justify some extended analysis below.

2. The principle against such invocation of rights has been fortified by a parallel point developed in constitutional law cases, that the *constitutional* rights you invoke must be your own. Still, the principle has been departed from in constitutional cases. A well-known illustration of the principle is the 1943 case of Tileston v. Ullman[134] — the first in a trilogy of cases on the validity of the Connecticut birth control law prohibiting the use, and the counseling or assisting in the use, of contraceptive drugs and instruments. The plaintiff was a physician, Dr. Tileston, whose constitutional attack upon the statute was rejected by the Supreme Court because he was asserting the rights not of himself but of his patients, whose lives would allegedly be endangered by childbearing. "His patients are not parties to this proceeding and there is no basis on which we can say that he has standing to secure an adjudication of his patients' constitutional right to life, which they do not assert in their own behalf. . . ."

The second Connecticut birth control case was Poe v. Ullman.[135] Here the procedural deficiencies in *Tileston* seemed to have been

130. *Warth, supra* n.128 at 504.

131. E.g., compare the *Linda R.S.* and *Warth* opinions cited *supra* nn. 123 & 128 with *SCRAP* and *Duke Power* cited *supra* nn. 125 & 122. See Davis, *supra* n.120, §§22.00-3, 22.19-1.

132. 412 U.S. 669 at 687-688.

133. Sierra Club v. Morton, 405 U.S. 727, 734 (1972): ". . . The fact that particular environmental interests are shared by the many rather than by the few does not make them less deserving of legal protection through the judicial process." An illustration of the Court's point in the *Gladstone* opinion is the *Reservists Committee* case cited *supra,* n.118. The plaintiff anti-war activists had sued as citizens as well as taxpayers. As to citizen standing, the Court said that "[s]tanding to sue may not be predicated upon an interest of the kind alleged here which is held in common by all members of the public because of the necessarily abstract nature of the injury all citizens share." 418 U.S. at 220. For criticism of this statement see Davis, *supra* n.120, §22.02-7 at 502.

134. 318 U.S. 44 (1943).

135. 367 U.S. 497 (1961).

rectified: The declaratory judgment complaint by a physician alleged that the statute violated *his* own liberty and property rights under the Fourteenth Amendment; and also included were declaratory judgment complaints by a married couple and by a wife, who alleged certain dangers to the women's lives or health unless the physician were legally free to prescribe birth control information. Nonetheless, a Supreme Court majority of five dismissed the appeal from the state court decision dismissing the complaints. This time the Court found another kind of deficiency in standing: the long record of nonenforcement of the Connecticut statute showed it had become a dead letter. There was no genuine and immediate threat of prosecution.

In 1965, in Griswold v. Connecticut, the Supreme Court finally recognized sufficient standing in the litigants to attack the Connecticut law.[136] Officials of a birth control clinic had been prosecuted as accessories to the crime of use, for the advice they had given to married persons in the use of contraceptives. In holding that the statute unconstitutionally invaded the right of privacy of married persons, the majority said: "We think that appellants have standing to raise the constitutional rights of the married people with whom they had a professional relationship." The strict attitude against invocation of the constitutional rights of others that was taken in the *Tileston* case was inapplicable here, said the Court. Here, instead of a declaratory judgment suit by a doctor invoking his patients' rights, we have an actual "criminal conviction for serving married couples in violation of an aiding-and-abetting statute. Certainly the accessory should have standing to assert that the offense which he is charged with assisting is not, or cannot constitutionally be, a crime."

The Court also cited a number of cases in which parties had indeed been permitted to invoke the constitutional rights of others. One example is the 1953 case of Barrows v. Jackson.[137] In that case, residential property owners had entered into an agreement — a "covenant running with the land" — prohibiting sale or rental to non-whites. One owner, Jackson, violated the covenant by selling to a black, and was sued for damages by the other owners. Thus the situation was somewhat different from two 1948 cases generally treated together as Shelley v. Kraemer,[138] in which the defendant was not the violating owner but the black buyer, against whom other owners sought an injunction. In one case the injunction was to oust him from possession, and in the other to restrain him from taking possession. There the Supreme Court had held that the state court judgment ousting the black from possession, or restraining his taking possession, would vio-

136. 381 U.S. 479 (1965).
137. 346 U.S. 249 (1953).
138. 334 U.S. 1 (1948).

late his right to equal protection of the laws under the Fourteenth Amendment. But in the present case, the white defendant, Mrs. Jackson, who had sold the property to a black purchaser, could not claim that a damage judgment against her by the other property owners would violate *her* constitutional rights. (Nor would it violate the constitutional rights of the black buyer in possession of the property.) The Court did allow her to invoke the constitutional rights of others. It said a damage judgment against her would unconstitutionally discriminate against *future black buyers,* since owners, under threat of damage suits, would either refuse to sell to blacks or charge them higher prices.

And these future black buyers, the Court thought, could not easily get their grievances before a court (apparently because the future sellers' refusals to sell, or their higher prices, would not be illegal, according to the statutory and constitutional law of the period). "Under the peculiar circumstances of this case," said the Court, "we believe the reasons which underlie our rule denying standing to raise another's rights, which is only a rule of practice, are outweighed by the need to protect the fundamental rights which would be denied by permitting the damages action to be maintained."

The phrase "only a rule of practice" in the above quotation embodies the point that we have seen referred to, in the more recent cases like *Gladstone,* about "prudential considerations." I.e., the rule against allowing a party to invoke the rights of others is not a rigid rule stemming from Article III requirements but can be departed from when prudence permits. The Supreme Court's stance is not clear however, on when prudence should be allowed to permit. No overall rationale has been provided, nor has the Court always mentioned its reasons when permitting the invocation. Indeed, there are some well-known older cases in which the Court seemed to think that the clear injury to plaintiff's own property or other interests was *enough* to justify consideration of the constitutional rights of others.[139] Still, the most recent opinions, like *Gladstone* mentioned above, espouse the less liberal view that *even if* the party has standing because of actual

139. In Buchanan v. Warley, 245 U.S. 60 (1917), a white seller of real estate to a black buyer was seeking specific performance of the contract and arguing that an ordinance purporting to invalidate the sale was unconstitutional because discriminatory against non-whites. The Court considered the arguments and invalidated the ordinance, stressing that "the property rights of the plaintiff . . . are directly and necessarily involved" (at 73). In Pierce v. Society of Sisters, 268 U.S. 510 (1925), a parochial school attacked a state law generally requiring children to attend only public schools, and argued the constitutional rights of parents and children. The Court considered the arguments and invalidated the law, stressing that the parochial school's property was "threatened with destruction through the unwarranted compulsion which appellants are exercising over present and prospective patrons of their schools" (at 535).

or threatened injury to his own interests, he will *usually not* be heard to assert the rights of others. Assuming this attitude persists, the question is, in what unusual situation will prudence permit *such* a party to assert the rights of others?

In spite of the lack of a clear and consistent rationale, the cases suggest or imply that some factors will tend to favor the permission. Among these are the non-feasibility of third-party assertion of rights on their own (illustrated by the *Barrows* case above among others);[140] the fact that a party's advocacy on behalf of third-party rights has been vigorous and cogent (thus rebutting the fear that a party who is allowed to assert others' rights will not present them adequately), at least when coupled with certain other special facts;[141] the fact that the party making the assertion is not a plaintiff whose attempt to set the court machinery in motion is based partly on other people's rights, but a *defendant,* as in *Barrows,* calling the court's attention to the illegal impact of plaintiff's position on other people's rights — an argument that the court (pursuant to its obligation to avoid illegality) could consider on its own without the urging of any party;[142] the fact that because of the Court's special concern over First Amendment rights, an allegedly vague and overbroad statute might be said to be unconstitutional on its face because of an invalid "chilling effect" on the legitimate exercise of free speech rights by others — even though the litigant's own conduct was clearly and validly covered by the statute.[143]

3. Why so much confusion in the law of standing? Why is it that "generalizations about standing are largely worthless as such";[144] that

140. Another illustration is NAACP v. Alabama ex rel Patterson, 357 U.S. 449 (1958), in which Alabama sought to compel the NAACP to disclose its membership lists, and the Court allowed the NAACP to assert the members' First Amendment associational right to be free from such disclosure. One reason was that to "require that [the right] be claimed by the members themselves would result in nullification of the right at the very moment of its assertion" (at 459).

141. In Craig v. Boren, 429 U.S. 190 (1976), a female licensed vendor of beer was allowed to assert the violation of equal protection rights of her male customers by a state law prohibiting beer sales to males under 21 and to females under 18. In addition to the point about vigorous and cogent argument, the Court pointed out that the other party too had sought, or had not objected to, resolution of the constitutional issue; and that "vendors and those in like positions have been uniformly permitted to resist efforts at restricting their operations by acting as advocates for the rights of third parties who seek access to their market or function" (at 195). On the latter point, authorities cited included the *Barrows* racial covenant case I discussed earlier, and Eisenstadt v. Baird, 405 U.S. 438 (1972), which had allowed a distributor of contraceptive foam to assert the constitutional privacy right of unmarried women against a state law prohibiting such distribution to them.

142. The Court has not made much of this point as such — but it is strongly urged by Davis in Administrative Law, §22.07 (1st ed. 1958) (the relevant volume of the second edition has not yet been published).

143. See Wright, *supra* n.21 at 51-52; Nowak, Rotunda & Young, Constitutional Law 79-80, 722-727 (1978).

144. Douglas, J., in *Data Processing, supra* n.115 at 151.

the problem of standing is "among the most amorphous in the entire domain of public law"?[145] Commentators have often explained the phenomenon (partly because of hints in the Supreme Court opinions themselves) on the following grounds: The Court has been allowing its decisions on the preliminary question of standing to be influenced by its attitude on whether the merits of the issue ought, at that time, be decided,[146] and on whether expansion of the judicial role as against legislative and administrative roles in decisionmaking should be avoided.[147] The blunt criticism from Kenneth Davis is: "The law of standing has to do with who may be a plaintiff" and "is not designed to control what questions may be decided or how far courts should substitute judgment for that of legislators or administrators. . . . The way to avoid undue government by judges is not by denying standing to those who are injured in fact but is by declining to decide issues that are not appropriate for judicial determination and by limiting the scope of review."[148]

d. *Mootness*

Mootness has been defined as "the doctrine of standing set in a time frame: The requisite personal interest that must exist at the commencement of the litigation (standing) must continue throughout its existence (mootness)."[149]

Illustrating a once "live" case that was made "moot" by the passage of time is a well-known case on a New Jersey Bible-reading law. Some New Jersey taxpayers appealed to the Supreme Court from a

145. Paul Freund, quoted in Nowak et al., *supra* n.143 at 68.

146. See Nowak et al., *supra* n.143 at 78-79; Tribe, American Constitutional Law, §3-21 at 93 (1978); Davis, *supra* n.120, §22.06 at 518-519; Tushnet, The New Law of Standing — A Plea for Abandonment, 62 Cornell L. Rev. 663, 663-664 (1977). While unwillingness to decide the merits seems to influence a restrictive decision on standing, sometimes the converse is true: The public importance of deciding the merits may push the Court to a permissive extreme on standing. See concurring opinions by Justices Stewart and Stevens in *Duke Power, supra* n.122 at 94-95 & 102-103 respectively.

147. See, e.g., Justice Powell's concurring opinion in U.S. v. Richardson, 418 U.S. 166 (1974) and his discussion of the Court's "antipathy to efforts to convert the judiciary into an open forum for the resolution of political or ideological disputes about the performance of government."

148. Davis, *supra* n.120, §22.21 at 521. Davis's stripped down test is: "A person whose legitimate interest is injured in fact or imminently threatened with injury by governmental action should have standing to challenge that action in the absence of legislative intent that the interest is not to be protected." Davis, Administrative Law Text, §22.08 at 438 (3rd ed. 1972).

149. Monaghan, Constitutional Adjudication: The Who and When, 82 Yale L.J. 1363, 1384 (1973), quoted with apparent approval in U.S. Parole Comm. v. Geraghty, 445 U.S. 388, 397 (1980).

state court decision upholding validity of a New Jersey law requiring Old Testament verses to be read at the opening of each public school day. In addition to a ruling that, under the circumstances of the case, the necessary "standing" to sue as taxpayer or as parent did not exist, the Court ruled that the claim of a parent had been made moot by the fact that the child in question had graduated before the case reached the Supreme Court.[150]

Illustrating the *rejection* of a mootness claim is the case involving the late Congressman Adam Clayton Powell. When he was reelected to the House as a member of the 90th Congress in 1966, the House by resolution excluded him from membership because of certain alleged misconduct reported by a House committee. While his suit for injunctive and declaratory relief (including a back salary claim) was awaiting review by the Supreme Court, the 90th Congress terminated, Powell was elected to the 91st Congress, and a House resolution permitted him to sit in that Congress, though fining him $25,000 and annulling the seniority he had gained prior to the 91st Congress. Part of the Supreme Court's decision held that Powell's exclusion from the 90th Congress was unlawful, because the House could not impose for admission qualifications additional to the age, citizenship, and residence qualifications specified in the Constitution. But the Court also had to consider, at the outset, the mootness issue. The Court concluded that whatever other claims had been mooted, "Powell's claim for back salary remains viable even though he has been seated in the 91st Congress"; hence the question of his right to sit in the already terminated 90th Congress was not moot.[151]

On whether a criminal case is moot after the defendant has served his sentence and been released, the Supreme Court has vacillated, but it now admits "the obvious fact of life that most criminal convictions do in fact entail adverse collateral legal consequences. The mere 'possibility' that this will be the case is enough to preserve a criminal case from ending 'ignominiously in the limbo of mootness.' "[152]

On the whole, decisions in the mootness area of standing are as unpredictable and "riddled with exceptions"[153] as in other areas of standing. One of the recognized exceptions to the mootness principle is the situation in which an issue is "capable of repetition, yet evading review." For instance, the fact that a pregnant woman who sued to invalidate an abortion statute was no longer pregnant at the time of

150. Doremus v. Board of Educ., 342 U.S. 429 (1952).

151. Powell v. McCormack, 395 U.S. 486 (1969). *Cf.* Geraghty, *supra* n.127.

152. Sibron v. New York, 392 U.S. 40, 55 (1968). And see Pennsylvania v. Mimms, 434 U.S. 106, 108 n.3 (1977).

153. See quotation from *Geraghty, supra* n.127.

the Court's decision did not moot the case; such a plaintiff might never get her case decided if her status at the time of appellate decision was controlling.[154] However, it has been remarked that in "applying this principle . . . the Court has drawn distinctions too subtle for many observers, as it has in other aspects of the law of mootness."[155]

e. *Collusiveness*

Consider now an illustration of the requirement that a dispute be not "feigned" or "collusive." A landlord who wanted a chance to invalidate in court the rent controls established under the Emergency Price Control Act of 1942 got his tenant to sue him under the act for treble the amount of the rent overcharge. The tenant had been assured that the landlord would finance the suit, and his attorney was selected by the landlord's attorney and filed no brief. The Supreme Court held the case had to be dismissed, since there had been no " 'honest and actual antagonistic assertion of rights' to be adjudicated — a safeguard essential to the integrity of the judicial process, and one that we have held to be indispensable to the adjudication of constitutional questions by this Court."[156]

A collusive suit such as this is not the same as a "test case." The latter need not lack the necessary element of adverseness. Though both parties may welcome the "test," and may maneuver for the "creation of real facts specifically for the purpose of supporting the suit,"[157] a genuine, unfeigned controversy can still lie between them over their respective rights. The line, however, is not easily drawn; and there are even cases illustrating a "proposition that the requirement of adversariness may be disregarded if a sufficiently profound public interest is perceived."[158] The scope of the proposition extend beyond such familiar examples as a court's adjudicating an alien's petition for naturalization in spite of the absence of an adversary party, or a court's rendering a "default" judgment, or judgment on a criminal defendant's guilty plea.[159]

154. Roe v. Wade, 410 U.S. 113, 124-125 (1973).

155. Wright, *supra* n.21, §12 at 39-40. In general on mootness, see Annot., 44 L. Ed. 2d 745 (1976); Wright, Miller & Cooper, *supra* n.73, §3533; Kates & Barber, Mootness in Judicial Proceedings: Towards A Coherent Theory, 62 Calif. L. Rev. 1385 (1974); Note, 88 Harv. L. Rev. 373 (1974).

156. U.S. v. Johnson, 319 U.S. 302, 305 (1943).

157. Wright, Miller & Cooper, *supra* n.73, §3530 at 171.

158. *Id.* at 170.

159. See generally, *id.*, §3530.

f. Hypothetical or Premature Issues

That the issues presented must not be "hypothetical" or "premature" so as to call for a merely "advisory" opinion is one of the most frequently stated aspects of the standing requirement. We encountered this aspect in Poe v. Ullman, the second Connecticut birth control case, in which the Supreme Court saw no immediate threat to plaintiff's rights because the state's policy had been not to enforce the statute. While the policy against advisory opinions is often applied in cases raising the issue of constitutionality of statutes (which also is typically the issue in the cases as to which several states, noted earlier, specifically allow a legislature or governor to seek an advisory opinion from the state supreme court on a constitutional issue), the "advisory opinion" language has been used in nonconstitutional cases, too.[160] The advisory opinion concept is also reflected in the language often used in cases involving court review of administrative agency action — language to the effect that the case must be "ripe" for adjudication.

However, just *when* a case is so premature or hypothetical or unripe that adjudication would amount to an "advisory opinion" is a question that the courts have not found any easier to answer than other questions in the area of standing.[161] One well-known example from the more modern cases is the 5 to 4 decision in 1972 involving the Army Intelligence data gathering system for surveillance of such political activities as might be related to future domestic disorder. The sources for the data were mainly news media, publications of general circulation, and public meetings. Most if not all of the plaintiff individuals or their organizations had been the subject of army surveillance reports. Plaintiffs complained of the "chilling effect" of the system on their First Amendment rights of free expression and association. But they were held to have no standing to complain, in the absence of more specific present harm or threat of specific future harm. The premature claim was treated like a request for an "advisory opinion."[162]

g. Political Questions

The "political question" doctrine was briefly described in Chapter 1.[163] Its vitality still extends to a number of areas, including cases in-

160. See, e.g., U.S. v. Fruehauf, 365 U.S. 146 (1961).

161. See Wright, Miller & Cooper, *supra* n.73, §3529 generally and at 150, bottom; and the cases' confusion and inconsistency delineated in Davis, Administrative Law Text, chap. 21 (3rd ed. 1972) and Davis, *supra* n.120, chap. 21.

162. Laird v. Tatum, 408 U.S. 1, 14 (1972).

163. See at nn. 372-376.

volving foreign affairs and war making; validity of the process by which a statute or constitutional amendment was adopted; or the Article IV, section 4 guaranty of a republican form of government to every state. But the doctrine has been slipping. It did so noticeably in the 1962 case of Baker v. Carr[164] when the Supreme Court decided that a claimed violation of the equal protection clause by a state legislative apportionment was not properly viewed as a political question. A series of cases were then decided on the merits, involving apportionment of congressional seats as well as those in state and local government bodies.

Thereafter, among other decided cases that might previously have been thought to present political questions, was the 1969 case of Congressman Adam Clayton Powell discussed earlier under the heading of mootness. You will recall that the Court dealt with the issue of whether the House had validly denied Powell his seat in the 90th Congress. Even *Baker* had included in a listing of possible types of political questions, a question presented in the context of a "textually demonstrable constitutional commitment of the issue to a coordinate political department";[165] and it would have been easy to hold in the *Powell* case that such a commitment existed in the Article I, section 5 provision that "[e]ach House shall be the Judge of the . . . Qualifications of its own Members." The Court interpreted this clause to be a commitment to Congress of the duty to judge the qualifications *expressly* set forth in the Constitution (age, citizenship, and residence). Since the denial of Powell's seat had been based on other grounds — certain alleged misconduct — the validity of the denial was deemed justiciable rather than political.

In general we seem to be witnessing some loosening of the political question doctrine, though the uncertainties in spotting those questions on which the courts will pin the "political" label have still not been eliminated. The *Baker* opinion made progress in fashioning several abstract categories of political questions, but they are not self-applying. Thus, President Nixon unsuccessfully argued, among other points, that the language of the *Baker* analysis made a political question out of the Watergate Special Prosecutor's demand (through a court subpoena)

164. 369 U.S. 186 (1962).

165. *Id.* at 217. The other types listed were those presented in the context of: "a lack of judicially discoverable and manageable standards for resolving [the issue]; or the impossibility of deciding without an initial policy determination of a kind clearly for non-judicial discretion; or the impossibility of a court's undertaking independent resolution without expressing lack of the respect due coordinate branches of government; or an unusual need for unquestioning adherence to a political decision already made; or the potentiality of embarrassment from multifarious pronouncements by various departments on one question. Unless one of these formulations is inextricable from the case . . ., there should be no dismissal for non-justiciability on the ground of a political question's presence." *Id.*

for the President's production of certain tapes and documents to be used at the criminal trial of Haldeman, Ehrlichmann, Mitchell, and other Nixon aides.[166] As yet, there "is no workable definition of characteristics that might be found to distinguish political questions from judicial questions. It remains accurate to observe that the category of political questions is 'more amenable to description by infinite itemization than by generalization.' "[167]

h. Standing vs. Justiciability

In the discussion up to now, both the terms "standing" and "justiciability" have been used. In the past some confusion has been created by courts' using the terms interchangeably. Thus if the court felt a nonjusticiable question were involved, it might say that a litigant therefore had no "standing" to raise it. In the more recent cases, the Supreme Court has sometimes been careful to distinguish the terms. For instance, separate discussions were given in the *Baker* case discussed above under the respective headings of "standing" and "justiciability." As the Court explained in Flast v. Cohen, *standing* was *one aspect* of the broad concept of *justiciability*. "[N]o justiciable controversy is presented when the parties seek adjudication of only a political question, when the parties are asking for an advisory opinion, when the question sought to be adjudicated has been mooted by subsequent developments, and when there is no standing to maintain the action." The quoted passage separates the "standing" problem even from the "advisory opinion" and mootness problems, though they have often been treated as the same problem, and I have up to now so treated them. As the Court observed in the same opinion, "Standing has been called one of the 'most amorphous [concepts] in the entire domain of public law.' Some of the complexities peculiar to standing problems result because standing 'serves, on occasion, as a shorthand expression for all the various elements of justiciability.' "

But, in general, the Court continued, the

> fundamental aspect of standing is that it focuses on the party seeking to get his complaint before a federal court and not on the issues he wishes to have adjudicated. The "gist of the question of standing" is whether the party seeking relief has "alleged such a personal stake in the outcome of the controversy as to assure that concrete adverseness which sharpens the presentation of issues upon which the court so largely depends for

166. U.S. v. Nixon, 418 U.S. 683, 693, 697 (1974).

167. Wright, Miller & Cooper, *supra* n.73, §3534 at 296-297. On political questions generally, see *id.*, §3534; Nowak et al., *supra* n.143 at 100-111; Jackson, The Political Question Doctrine, 44 U. Colo. L. Rev. 477 (1973); Bean, The Supreme Court and the Political Question, 71 W. Va. L. Rev. 97 (1969).

illumination of difficult constitutional questions." . . . [I]n other words, when standing is placed in issue in a case, the question is whether the person whose standing is challenged is a proper party to request an adjudication of a particular issue and not whether the issue itself is justiciable. Thus a party may have standing in a particular case, but the federal court may nevertheless decline to pass on the merits of the case because, for example, it presents a political question.[168]

7. The "Motion to Dismiss" and Other Pleadings

Recall that the defendants in our *Nappier* case filed a motion to dismiss. How does this pleading relate to other pleadings in a civil lawsuit in federal court?

Under the Federal Rules of Civil Procedure, the plaintiff's complaint is required to set forth (1) a short and plain statement of the grounds upon which the court's jurisdiction depends, (2) a short and plain statement of his claim showing that he is entitled to relief, and (3) a demand for judgment for the relief to which he deems himself entitled. The basic pleading of the defendant is an "answer." In the answer (1) he must admit or deny each allegation ("averment") of the complaint, or state he is without knowledge or information sufficient to form a belief as to the truth of the averment (which has the effect of a denial). Averments not denied are deemed to be admitted. (2) He must state whatever constitutes an "avoidance or affirmative defense" to the complaint — for instance, a legal defense to the effect that the plaintiff's claim based on defendant's alleged negligence was barred because of the plaintiff's own ("contributory") negligence, or that it was barred because the statute of limitations had already run.

But some defenses, according to Rule 12(b), may "at the option of the pleader" be made by *motion*. Lack of jurisdiction is one of these defenses. Another — and this is the one invoked by the defendant's motion in the *Nappier* case — is *"the failure to state a claim upon which relief can be granted."* Such a motion to dismiss is analogous to what in many state courts is called a "demurrer" (which, according to one wag, is not to be confused with the comparative form of an obsolete adjective formerly applied to young ladies). Instead of denying any facts in the complaint, the motion is in effect saying: Even assuming, for purposes of this motion, that the facts alleged are true, your claim is legally insufficient; the law does not, on such facts, permit the granting of the requested relief against me. Thus you will note that in granting the motion to dismiss in the *Nappier* case

168. Flast v. Cohen, 392 U.S. 83, 95, 99-100 (1968).

the district judge did not question the truth of any of the facts stated in the complaint.

If the motion to dismiss had been denied, then the defendants would have had the right to file an answer denying any of the factual averments, or stating they were without knowledge or information sufficient to form a belief as to the truth of an averment. They might say the latter, for instance, about the averment in paragraph 3 of the complaint that the two girls were "known throughout the state" as The Little Jack Girls; or the averment in paragraph 9 that as a result of the broadcast "it became common talk of people in South Carolina" that plaintiff was one of the young ladies who had been raped, and that "people generally know about" the episode "by which she will be identified during her entire lifetime"; or the averment in paragraph 11 that plaintiff "has been demoralized, embarrassed, has suffered great mental pain, humiliation, mortification, has become highly nervous and has been unable to perform her regular employment." Plaintiff then would have the burden of establishing by his proof the averments that have been thus denied. While the averments that are not denied are deemed admitted, this is not true of averments as to amount of damage.

Some additional pleadings and additional motions are permitted in special situations.[169]

8. The Trial That Might Have Been: Jury and Judge

Assuming for the moment that defendants had filed an answer and the case went to trial, would the plaintiffs have had a right to the jury trial they demanded in the final clause of their complaint? The answer is yes. The Seventh Amendment of the Constitution, applicable to the federal courts, requires a jury trial in "suits at common law, where the value in controversy shall exceed twenty dollars." (Practically all state constitutions have a similar guarantee for state courts.) Under Federal Rule of Civil Procedure 38, a party is deemed to have "waived" or given up his right to a jury trial by failure to make timely demand for it under the rules — though under Rule 39 the judge has discretion, in spite of such failure, to grant a motion for jury trial of any or all issues.

What qualifies as a suit "at common law" is determined, in general, by reference to the type of suit that could be heard in the law courts rather than the equity courts at the time the Seventh

169. On pleadings and motions generally, see Wright, *supra* n.21, §§66-69; James & Hazard, *supra* n.20, chaps. 2-5.

Amendment was adopted in 1791. An action for damages, such as the *Nappier* case was, would so qualify — even though the kind of injury claimed (invasion of privacy) may not have been redressable at that time.

This does not mean that the jury would have to be composed of 12 persons, the traditional number, or that they would have to be unanimous in their verdict. Federal Rule 48 allows the parties to "stipulate that the jury shall consist of any number less than twelve or that a verdict or a finding of a stated majority of the jurors shall be taken as the verdict or finding of the jury"; and a 1973 Supreme Court case held that neither the Seventh Amendment, statute, nor Federal Rules barred local district court rules requiring use of a six-person federal civil jury.[170] Even in criminal cases the Supreme Court has allowed states to make certain departures from the 12-person and unanimity requirements.[171]

You are also reminded at this point of the discussion in Chapter 1 of the moderating role that the jury can play, and of the University of Chicago studies on the comparative attitudes of judge and jury in civil suits for personal injuries.

Finally, a word about the respective roles of judge and jury at the trial.[172] The rule of thumb is that the judge decides questions of law and the jury decides questions of fact — a rule that is not always easy to apply, and the complexities of which we cannot go into here. In the *Nappier* case, prior to any impaneling of a jury, the judge disposed of a legal question, i.e., the legal sufficiency of the complaint. If there had been a jury trial, there would have been a number of legal matters handled by the judge. First of all (disregarding the judge's role as to various pretrial matters, such as a motion for "judgment on the pleadings" or the "discovery" procedures I shall be discussing in the next subsection), the judge at the federal trial of a jury case could be called on to rule on various motions designed to have *him* rather than the jury decide the case. There could be a "motion for directed verdict," under Rule 50, by either party at the close of the evidence offered by his opponent. Such a motion would be based on the idea that reasonable men could not differ as to the conclusions to be drawn from the evidence; hence there was no role for the jury to play. After the jury verdict, a Rule 50 motion could be made for a "judgment notwithstanding the verdict" — based on the idea that a reasonable jury could not have arrived at that verdict. Under Rule 59, there could also be a

170. Colegrove v. Battin, 413 U.S. 149 (1973). Also on juries: Postscript, n.19.

171. See App. 2 herein at nn. 175-179. Generally on the jury trial right in criminal cases, see *id.* at nn. 171-188.

172. For general analysis, see James & Hazard, *supra* n.20, chap. 7, esp. §§7.3, 7.4, 7.10, 7.14.

"motion for new trial," or the judge could order a new trial on his own initiative, for such reasons as that the verdict is against the evidence; damages awarded are excessive or inadequate; newly discovered evidence; misconduct of jury, judge, or counsel; error in rulings on admissibility of evidence, or in the instructions to the jury.

The two last-mentioned errors point to the second and third major types of questions within the judge's province at the trial: rulings on admissibility of evidence and the final instructions to the jurors prior to their retirement to deliberate on the verdict. In the *Nappier* case, the judge's instructions would have explained the circumstances in which damages for invasion of privacy could be recovered under the law of South Carolina, and would have asked the jury to apply the legal principles thus expounded to the facts it found from the evidence.

That the jury does not understand the instructions has long been one of the criticisms of the jury system, strongly put by Federal Judge Jerome Frank[173] among others, and perhaps buttressed by more recent studies.[174] On the other hand, Professor Harry Kalven argued that the University of Chicago jury studies showed judges' agreement with jury verdicts in about 80 percent of the cases, civil or criminal; and that analysis of the criminal cases showed this same percentage of agreement in those cases rated by the judge as difficult.[175]

9. Adversary Nature of the Procedure; Limits on Adversariness

Our system of trial court procedure is often described as an "adversary system," meaning that the opposing parties to a dispute have the burden of bringing the dispute to court, of investigating it, and of present-

173. Frank, Courts on Trial 116-118 (1950); Skidmore v. Baltimore & O.R.R. Co., 167 F.2d 54, 64-65 (2d Cir. 1948); Sunderland, Verdicts, General and Special, 29 Yale L.J. 253, 259 (1920). Another aspect of jury misunderstanding is this: In recent years the issue has been coming up whether a particular case was so complex that it made jury trial unsuitable and the Seventh Amendment jury trial right inapplicable. See Annot., 54 A.L.R. Fed. 733 (1981); Devlin, Jury Trial of Complex Cases: English Practice at the Time of the Seventh Amendment, 80 Colum. L. Rev. 43 (1980); Notes, 8 Pepperdine L. Rev. 189 (1980); 32 Stan. L. Rev. 99 (1979); 92 Harv. L. Review 898 (1979). See also Lunberg & Nordenberg, Specially Qualified Juries and Expert Non-Jury Tribunals: Alternatives for Coping with the Complexities of Modern Civil Litigation, 67 Va. L. Rev. 887 (1981).

174. See, e.g., Charrow & Charrow, Making Legal Language Understandable: A Psycholinguistic Study of Jury Instructions, 79 Colum. L. Rev. 1306 (1979).

175. Kalven, The Dignity of the Civil Jury, 50 Va. L. Rev. 1055, 1064-1066 (1964). He observed further that "although the trial judges polled gave a wide variety of explanations for the cases in which there was disagreement, they virtually never offered the jury's inability to understand the case as a reason" (at 1066-1067). As to the point made about the *difficult* criminal cases, Kalven's belief that "there

ing the facts in court through witnesses called by each side — with the judge acting as a relatively passive umpire and adjudicator. By contrast, in the systems of some other countries, the judge is in more active command. Lawyers inform the judge of their intended documentary proofs and the names of potential witnesses, and he makes his own investigation (directly or through another) and his own study before trial. He actively manages the trial. It is he who calls the witnesses (they are viewed as the *court's* witnesses; they will not have been previously interviewed by the lawyers) and questions them, though the lawyers can also do so. If necessary he calls impartial experts, drawn from a standing panel nominated by responsible agencies in each specialized field such as medicine or engineering.

What is the basis of the criticism leveled at the adversary system? One of the most distinguished critics, Judge Frank, viewed the system as based on the "fight theory" rather than the "truth theory." Combat between two adversaries, he argued, was a poor way of getting at the truth. He pointed to inequalities between the combatant lawyers, and economic inequalities between opposing clients (leading to differing abilities to expend funds for investigation and for a lawyer). In addition he thought the emphasis on adversariness led to undesirable tactics: the lawyer's use of surprise, his unwillingness to concede harmful facts and willingness to discredit even truthful adverse witnesses, and his conscious or unconscious distortion of facts in the process of interviewing and coaching his witnesses.[176]

The indictment is strong but, I think, not fatal. In fact Judge Frank conceded that the existing system has qualities that we cannot afford to dispense with, and that a policy of reform within the adversary system was the best course.

1. One favorable aspect of the system is that a *fuller presentation* of relevant facts and arguments on both sides of a point is more likely to occur when opposing lawyers, spurred by partisan interest, have been beating the bushes to dig up the relevant facts and arguments. Moreover, there is reason to think that the adjudication itself will be of a less partisan, *more objective* character when the combatants rather than the adjudicator have done this digging before trial, and when the proceedings at trial consist of opposing presentations managed by them, as distinct from a presentation managed primarily by the adjudicator himself.

The argument for such objectivity was well stated by a Report of

---

is no reason to believe the point will not hold for civil trials as well" (at 1066 n.23) may be questioned. I suspect the degree of difficulty in the instructions in the more difficult civil cases is substantially greater than in the more difficult criminal cases; and that difficult instructions occur more frequently in civil than in criminal cases.

176. Frank, Courts on Trial 80-102 (1950).

the Joint Conference on Professional Responsibility of the Association of American Law Schools and the American Bar Association. Speaking first of the trial presentation managed by the adjudicator, the Report observed:

> [A]t some early point, a familiar pattern will seem to emerge from the evidence; an accustomed label is waiting for the case and, without awaiting further proofs, this label is promptly assigned to it. It is a mistake to suppose that this premature cataloguing must necessarily result from impatience, prejudice or mental sloth. Often it proceeds from a very understandable desire to bring the hearing into some order and coherence, for without some tentative theory of the case there is no standard of relevance by which testimony may be measured. But what starts as a preliminary diagnosis designed to direct the inquiry tends quickly and imperceptibly, to become a fixed conclusion, as all that confirms the diagnosis makes a strong imprint on the mind, while all that runs counter to it is received with diverted attention.
>
> An adversary presentation seems the only effective means for combatting this natural human tendency to judge too swiftly in terms of the familiar that which is not yet fully known. The arguments of counsel hold the case, as it were, in suspension, between two opposing interpretations of it. While the proper classification of the case is thus kept unresolved, there is time to explore all of its peculiarities and nuances.

This contrast was viewed as accentuated by the trial-managing adjudicator's pretrial investigation and study. The tribunal then

> cannot truly be said to come to the hearing uncommitted, for it has itself appointed the channels along which the public inquiry is to run. If an unexpected turn in the testimony reveals a miscalculation in the design of these channels, there is no advocate to absorb the blame. The deciding tribunal is under a strong temptation to keep the hearing moving within the boundaries originally set for it. The result may be that the hearing loses its character as an open trial of the facts and issues, and becomes instead a ritual designed to provide public confirmation for what the tribunal considers it has already established in private. When this occurs, adjudication acquires the taint affecting all institutions that become subject to manipulation, presenting one aspect to the public, another to knowing participants.

Finally, the Report thought it significant that "the experienced judge or arbitrator desires and actively seeks to obtain an adversary presentation of the issues. Only when he has had the benefit of intelligent and vigorous advocacy on both sides can he feel fully confident of his decision."[177]

177. Report of the Joint Conference on Professional Responsibility (Lon L.

2. True, there are disquieting aspects of the adversary system, but I think they do not outweigh the stated advantages, nor are they immune to reform. Inequalities do exist among advocates, but judges can to some extent correct the imbalance and are particularly apt to take a more active role when confronted with the inexperience of the fledgling lawyer. Indeed, a leading text on civil procedure points out that in spite of some judges' reluctance to exercise their powers, the common law tradition and especially its modern development does give them authority to do more than an umpire's job: to go beyond a litigant's legal theory of his case or the specific relief requested, to put the court's own questions to witnesses examined by the parties, and even to call additional witnesses.[178] Statutes also commonly provide for the use of the court's neutral expert on particular issues such as insanity. Some states have successfully experimented with the use of a panel of such neutral experts for medical testimony in auto accident cases.

True, also, economic inequalities between the opposing parties can create serious imbalance in legal representation.[179] Thus, one party may be at a disadvantage because funds needed for thorough pretrial investigation of the case are not available. The time may come when, as Judge Frank once speculated,[180] there will be public financing of investigative as well as other functions of a public prosecutor of civil actions, who would function as an alternative to a private lawyer. That step — as well, of course, as the more radical step of complete socialization of the legal profession — is not exactly imminent in this country. The Supreme Court has recently decided that no criminal defendant who has not waived his right to counsel can be sentenced to any jail term without having been represented by counsel of his own or by

---

Fuller and John D. Randall, Co-chairmen), 44 A.B.A.J. 1159 (1958). For an experimental study supporting this report's assumption that an adversary procedure is more likely to counteract bias in the decisionmaker, see Thibaut, Walker & Lind, Adversary Presentation and Bias in Legal Decisionmaking, 86 Harv. L. Rev. 386 (1972), and discussion of the study in 45 U. Colo. L. Rev. 1 (1973). See also Thibaut & Walker, Procedural Justice (1975); Lind, Thibaut & Walker, A Cross-cultural Comparison of the Effect of Adversary and Inquisitorial Processes on Bias in Legal Decisionmaking, 62 Va. L. Rev. 271 (1976); Lind, Thibaut & Walker, Discovery and Presentation of Evidence in Adversary and Non-adversary Proceedings, 71 Mich. L. Rev. 1129 (1973); Thibaut & Walker, A Theory of Procedure, 66 Calif. L. Rev. 541 (1978). Concerning the participants' *perception* of procedural fairness and outcome fairness ("distributive justice"), the conclusion was "that an adversary decisionmaking model enhances the perceptions of both procedural and distributive justice," Walker, Lind & Thibaut, The Relation Between Procedural and Substantive Justice, 65 Va. L. Rev. 1401, 1416 (1979).

178. James & Hazard, *supra* n.20 at 5-8 (1977).

179. See Note, Right to Aid in Addition to Counsel for Indigent Criminal Defendants, 47 Minn. L. Rev. 1054 (1963).

180. Frank, *supra* n.176 at 94-99.

free counsel if he cannot afford his own; but presumably only a minimal investigative expense would thereby be covered. This right of the indigent to counsel in a criminal case is a matter of constitutional right.[181] The Supreme Court has not yet recognized such a right in civil cases generally, but "legal aid" services for civil cases are in fact available in larger cities — not enough to fill the need, though on a broader scale than existed prior to the federal antipoverty program of recent years. The major source of funding, the federal Legal Services Corporation, is currently threatened by the budget-cutting efforts of the Reagan administration.[182]

To the argument that the adversary system lends itself to tactics like the use of surprise and the concealment or distortion of the adverse aspects of one's case, there are two answers.

(a) The first is that the canons in the ABA Code of Professional Responsibility set some ethical limits on adversariness — limits which doubtless need more vigorous bar association enforcement, though violations are hard to ferret out. Thus, one disciplinary rule in the Code prohibits a lawyer from engaging in "conduct involving dishonesty, fraud, deceit, or misrepresentation." Another declares he shall not "knowingly use perjured testimony or false evidence when he knows or it is obvious that the evidence is false," or "counsel or assist his client in conduct that the lawyer knows to be illegal or fraudulent." Another requires him to disclose to the court "legal authority in the controlling jurisdiction known to him to be directly adverse to the position of his client and which is not disclosed by opposing counsel."[183]

In other words, a lawyer has duties not only to his client but also to the public and the legal system, including the court; he is an "officer of the court." Even the "attorney-client privilege," which requires the lawyer not to disclose his client's confidences, can give way when the disclosure would be of "the intention of his client to commit a crime and the information necessary to prevent the crime."[184]

It is true that private practitioners have been hostile to interference with confidentiality of client communications, and have often honored the above listed duties in the breach. But more elevated views of their ethical responsibilities, usually urged by their academic brothers,[185] made enough headway to be at least partially embodied in an

181. On the right to counsel, see App. 2 herein at nn. 200-224.

182. See Postscript herein at nn. 11-32 for current modes of broadening the access to legal services.

183. ABA Code of Professional Responsibility, Disciplinary Rules 1-102, 7-102, and 7-106 (1970).

184. *Id.*, DR 4-101(C).

185. See Thurman, Limits to the Adversary System: Interests That Outweigh Confidentiality, 5 J. Legal Profession 5 (1980); Rotunda, Book Review, 89 Harv. L. Rev. 622 (1976); and articles cited in Postscript, n.78.

ABA Commission draft report. These views may not survive ABA consideration due in 1981 or 1982, but they have had more support than in prior years.[186]

(b) More important than the canons in dealing with surprise and concealment are the "discovery" procedures established by the Federal Rules of Civil Procedure for the federal courts and substantially adopted in most states. These procedures enable a party to discover, in advance of trial, facts that are known to, or evidence in possession of, the adverse party. Under the federal rules, either party may before trial do any of the following: (1) Take a sworn statement ("deposition") of any person upon *oral examination* or *written interrogatories* "for the purposes of discovery or for use as evidence in the action or for both purposes." (In the absence of a different agreement by the parties, the deposition is inadmissible as evidence at the trial unless the witness making it cannot be produced in court or unless it is used to contradict or "impeach" the witness.) (2) Request from the other party an *admission* of the genuineness of "relevant documents" or "the truth of any relevant matters of fact set forth in the request." (3) Seek a court order allowing *inspection* of documents, persons, or things. In addition, "pretrial conferences" among the judge and the opposing lawyers may eliminate some issues and possibly result in a settlement of the case without trial.

This is not to say that all is well on the discovery front. A current concern of the profession is over the *abuse* of discovery procedures, e.g., using them excessively in order to wear down an adversary, and thus adding to litigation costs and delays.[187]

10. Aspects of Criminal Proceedings under the Statute

Let us remind ourselves at this point that the statute involved in the *Nappier* case was a criminal statute. The suit actually brought was a civil suit — a tort suit for damages — but the suit specifically contemplated by the statutes was a criminal prosecution. If, then, the state prosecutor had decided to invoke the statute so as to prosecute the broadcasting corporations and/or the relevant corporate employees, what would those proceedings have been like? In other words, what are: (a) the Bill of Rights protections that would be given to the individual and corporate defendants against government procedures in

186. A broader discussion of ethical responsibilities is in the Postscript herein at nn. 72-80.

187. See Postscript herein at n.18; Brazil, Civil Discovery: Lawyers' Views of Its Effectiveness, Its Principal Problems and Abuses, 1980 Am. B. Foundation Research J. 787.

such a criminal case; (b) the nature of the criminal liability of a corporation, such as the broadcasting corporation; and (c) the procedural steps in a criminal case?

a. Bill of Rights Protections

This is extensively treated in Appendix 2 herein.

b. Nature of Corporate Criminal Liability

It may seem strange that a corporation, an *artificial entity* whose officers and employees are the real actors, should ever itself be "punished" (the punishment being confined of course to fines since imprisonment is not physically possible). And it may further seem strange that criminal liability, whether of an individual or a corporation, should ever be "vicarious," i.e., a liability inflicted on X because of *another's* criminal conduct occurring *without* X's intent or reckless neglect.

1. Taking the latter strangeness first, it is indeed true that vicarious liability is unusual in the criminal law. But it does occur. An example is a statute that states something like this: "Whoever by himself or his agent sells liquor to a minor is guilty of a misdemeanor." The American Law Institute's Model Penal Code has recommended that such a crime, lacking the usual requirement of an individual's own fault, should be re-classified by the legislature — i.e., it should be characterized not as a crime, with all the attendant stigma and other adverse consequences, but rather as falling into a newly created category ("offense") that would be subject only to *civil* penalties.[188]

You will recall that in the case of "strict liability" crimes (discussed in Chap. 1) the Institute has proposed a similar approach. In strict as in vicarious liability, personal fault is dispensed with; the difference is that in the former the conduct at issue was performed by the defendant himself. The two kinds of liability might occur together: A strict liability statute may also impose vicarious liability so that a defendant employer can be held criminally liable for his employee's act when neither one was at fault. But an interpretation that the legislature intended such a harsh combination is not often reasonable. The United States Supreme Court has been criticized for too readily assuming, in a 1930 food and drug case, that *because* the statutory liability was strict, it was also vicarious.[189]

Often the statute in question will not impose vicarious liability

188. LaFave & Scott, Criminal Law 227-228 (1972).
189. *Id.* at 226.

as clearly as does the statutory language quoted above ("by himself or his agent"). If, for instance, the language "whoever intentionally sells liquor to a minor" or "whoever sells liquor to a minor" is used, courts will generally be loath to impute the agent's intent, or the agent's sale to a minor, to an employer who was unmindful of it. Some courts have been willing to do so, however, when the penalty is light.[190]

2. Since, then, the law sometimes (though seldom) recognizes vicarious liability even when no corporation is involved, the fact that courts will view some statutes as imputing to a corporation the criminal mental element of officers or employees should not be too surprising. Still, as earlier decisions have pointed out, is it not absurd to suppose that a corporate artificial entity possesses the necessary mental element for commission of crime?

Nowadays courts — and legislatures — are not bothered by such a question. They are willing to assume (for reasons of policy that I shall treat more fully in a moment) that a corporation *can be* criminally responsible when the combined act and mental state of its officer — at least if he is a high officer — violates a criminal statute. The reason I say "can be" is because not every criminal statute will be aimed at covering corporations, or be so interpreted. Thus it is harder, though not impossible, to conclude that corporate criminal liability was intended if "person" or "whoever" (against whom the criminal prohibition is directed) is not specifically *defined* so as to include corporations, partnerships, and associations — a specificity written into many business crime statutes. On this basis it might well be argued that the absence of such a definition in the *Nappier* case statute rendered unauthorized a criminal case against the corporation, as distinct from the individuals involved in its operation.[191]

Also, statutes on *some types* of crime, e.g., homicide, might strike

190. *Id.* at 225.

191. For the statutory language, see the district court opinion under A3 in this chapter. In contrast to this statute, the prohibitions of the similar Georgia statute involved in Cox Broadcasting Corp. v. Cohn, 420 U.S. 469 (1975) (Chap. 5 herein at n.5), ran against "any news media or any other person," and ended by making the punishment applicable to "any person or corporation violating" the statute. Even so, no criminal case was apparently brought against the corporation; the *Cox* case was a civil suit for damages by the father of the rape victim. The Wisconsin statute made its punishment applicable to "any person who shall publish or cause to be published" the identity of a victim of rape or similar sexual assault. The only reported criminal case under this law was not against the corporate newspaper but against its individual editor or publisher. State v. Evjue, 253 Wis. 146, 33 N.W.2d 305 (1948).

Another relevant consideration is this: Does the jurisdiction in question have a general provision on statutory interpretation similar to this federal provision (1 U.S.C. §1): "[i]n determining the meaning of any Act of Congress, unless the context indicates otherwise, . . . [t]he words 'person' and 'whoever' include corporations, companies, associations, firms, partnerships, societies, and joint stock companies, as well as individuals."

us as inapplicable to corporations. Here, however, we must beware of our intuition. What about a "Murder, Inc." situation? And what about the applicability of a reckless homicide statute to a corporate auto manufacturer whose managers maintained the rear-end location of the gas tank in spite of the known danger of death in a substantial percentage of rear-end collisions?[192] In other words, if behind the human actors in a crime there is a corporation one or more of whose managers had brought about the prohibited harm intentionally (i.e., with desire for, or virtually certain belief in, its occurrence), or through reckless disregard, then corporate criminal liability is possible — unless inferences from the nature of the statute and its particular wording point to a contrary legislative policy.[193]

On what grounds can we defend the Supreme Court's 1908 declaration in a criminal case that there was "no valid objection in law and every reason in public policy" for "imputing" to a railroad corporation the knowledge and purposes of its agents acting within the subject matter of their employment (fixing rates)?[194] The Court argued that the corporation profited from the illegal activities of the agents to whom it had entrusted the authority to act in the subject matter; that precedents for imputing the corporate agents' intent to the corporation existed in civil cases; and that extensive business abuses in interstate commerce could not be effectively controlled without the criminal remedy. The Court's argument requires a more extended analysis.

To begin with, as the Court apparently assumed, imputing to a corporation its officer's mental element of intent or reckless disregard in a criminal case is really not *more* fictional (though indeed more serious) than imputing the officer's physical behavior or negligent attitude — an imputation that commonly occurs in civil cases in which corporate employers are held liable for damage from the negligent acts of employees. But perhaps it is not even necessary to speak in terms of the fiction of "imputing" mental elements. The legislature can be

192. See, on corporate homicide, Notes, 8 Pepperdine L. Rev. 367 (1981); 17 Calif. W.L. Rev. 465 (1981).

193. A more careful statement in the American Law Institute's Model Penal Code (§2.07) can be roughly summarized thus: (1) If the statute clearly intends corporations to be covered by the criminal prohibition, then it is enough that the conduct was by *an agent* acting in behalf of the corporation within the scope of his office or employment; but the corporation usually has a defense if it can prove that the high managerial agent having supervisory responsibility over the subject matter had employed *due diligence* to prevent commission of the crime, unless recognition of such defense is "plainly inconsistent" with legislative purpose; and (2) if the statutory intent to cover corporations is *not* clear, then criminal liability is to be imposed only if the conduct was *"authorized, requested, commanded, performed or recklessly tolerated by the board of directors or by a high managerial agent* acting in behalf of the corporation within the scope of his office or employment" (emphasis added).

194. New York Cen. & H.R.R. Co. v. U.S., 212 U.S. 481, 495 (1908).

viewed as having offered a qualified privilege to those wishing to use the legally created artificial entity known as a corporation: "We will give certain protections to your corporate form of doing business, e.g., guaranteeing that for the corporation's debts and liabilities, shareholders will be liable only to the extent of their investment in that corporation, rather than having all their other assets reachable too, as would be true if the enterprise were unincorporated. But this does not mean that shareholders are also privileged to avoid completely certain burdens that would apply to investors in non-corporate enterprise. I.e., included in the corporate debts and liabilities for which shareholders are liable to the extent of their investment are those imposed (a) by agency principles of the civil law and (b) by certain criminal statutes under which particular acts and mental states of enterprise agents will, in some circumstances, result in fines depleting the enterprise assets. The impact on shareholders from such corporate fines is still not as great as the impact of fines on unincorporated enterprise — the shareholder's liability is still limited to the extent of his investment."

Nevertheless, shareholders might seem to have some basis for complaint. The business crime statute that extends its prohibitions to both incorporated and unincorporated businesses is generally applied *only* to corporations; we seem more willing to visit the harshness of vicarious criminal liability on corporations because of an unreal assumption that the impact is upon an impersonal artificial entity whereas in fact it is upon shareholders, who are human and relatively innocent of the transaction in question; punishing the corporate officers and employees at fault, it may be urged, would be enough.

The opposing policy argument is of course in terms of the requirements of effective law enforcement in the area of business crimes. Confining punishment to the wrongdoing officer or employee himself is said to be much less effective enforcement[195] than pressuring the corporate owners (the shareholders) into exerting greater vigilance in corporate affairs; pressure on profits through the fine and the stigma

195. Deterrence of corporate agents through punishment applicable to them is thought to be weak because imprisonment is rarely imposed in "white collar" crimes; conviction for such crimes does not seem to bear the same stigma as convictions for non-business crimes; business crimes are often difficult to prove; and the jury may be less willing to punish conduct whose immorality is not as clear as the conduct in non-business crimes, especially if the jury thinks the particular agent had little to do with the formulation of the corporate policy involved. There have been striking instances of such jury sympathy with individual corporate agents and expressions of astonishment by appellate courts at their acquittal. See U.S. v. General Motors Corp., 212 F.2d 376, 411 (7th Cir. 1941); U.S. v. Austin-Bagley Corp., 31 F.2d 229, 233 (2d Cir. 1929), *cert. denied,* 279 U.S. 863 (1929). See also AMA v. U.S., 130 F.2d 233, 252 (D.C. Cir. 1942). On the other hand, such acquittals would probably be less frequent if the corporation were not itself being fined.

on the corporate name may be persuasive. Moreover, it is often difficult, as well as unfair, to single out among many corporate agents connected with the transaction, the particular ones who ought to be prosecuted; hence, prosecuting the corporation should be an available alternative. Also supporting this position is the response to the previous argument on unfair impact upon shareholders: (1) The impact does not include a stigma attaching to the shareholder personally; (2) his economic loss, as earlier discussed, cannot exceed the amount of his investment in the corporation, and will in fact be far less; and (3) since the illegal transaction usually redounds to the economic benefit of the shareholder, it seems fair that he should bear the economic burden of disgorging his share of the "ill-gotten gains."

This latter argument has some vulnerable aspects. Not all existing stockholders may have benefited from the past transaction; the amount of loss from the fine may be unrelated to the amount of benefit received; and the giving up of illegal gains seems more like a goal of a civil law injunction rather than of the criminal law.

Responses are also possible to the alleged effectiveness of the corporate fine as a deterrent to wrongdoing. May not the corporation be able to "pass on" the fine to its customers? Are stockholders in a large, widely owned corporation really in a position to exert concerted pressure on management? Does a corporate fine substantially harm the finances and the image of the corporation? (Is the report of the fine usually widely disseminated to the public? Is there much impact on a corporation marketing a product under a name not related to the corporate name? Is there much impact when the fine is less than the probable amount of illegal profits?) And does not the availability of the corporation as defendant sometimes mean that the prosecution foregoes prosecuting, or the jury foregoes convicting, the individual agents?[196]

The above arguments in aggregate suggest that the effectiveness and fairness of the corporate fine are not as great as surface appearances may indicate. Yet such fines are doubtless here to stay — if only because *some* additional deterrence is created; *some* aspects are fair; and a "deeper pocket" is tapped than in the case of fines against individuals, thus more effectively helping finance government enforcement.

c. *Procedural Steps in the Criminal Case*

In Appendix 2 herein we shall encounter the procedural steps in a criminal case, but a more focused analysis here may be helpful.

196. See Developments in the Law: Corporate Crime, 92 Harv. L. Rev. 1227, 1367 & n.14 (1979).

Generally on corporate criminal liability, see *id.* (argues for a "system of cor-

1. First there is the *arrest*[197] stage (usually preceded by an investigation). Of course in the case of a crime involving a corporation, the only possible arrestees would be corporate agents, assuming the prosecution has chosen to make them defendants. But arrest in these "white collar crime" cases is rare. Instead, a "summons" procedure is generally used, for both corporate and non-corporate defendants. The summons describes the offense charged and summons the defendant to make a judicial appearance at a stated time and place. Service upon, and appearance by, the corporation is through its authorized agents.[198]

2. The arrest and transport of a suspect to the *police station* is not necessarily followed by further prosecution. The "desk sergeant" may

---

porate civil fines based upon the probable profit from illegal activities, supplemented by criminal sanctions against individuals in cases of moral culpability"); Symposium, 1 N. Ill. L. Rev. 3 (1980); articles in Symposium on White Collar Crime, Part 2, 17 Am. Crim. L. Rev. 409 et seq. (1980); Commentary to Section 2.07, Model Penal Code; LaFave & Scott, Criminal Law 228-234 (1972); Elkins, Corporations and the Criminal Law, 65 Ky. L. Rev. 73 (1977); Note, Decisionmaking Models and the Control of Corporate Crime, 85 Yale L.J. 1091 (1976) (concludes that "only under limited circumstances can effective deterrence be achieved by penalizing the corporate entity rather than corporate employees"). Coming to my attention too late to be examined was Coffee, No Soul to Damn: No Body to Kick: An Unscandalized Inquiry Into the Problem of Corporate Punishment, 79 Mich. L. Rev. 386 (1981).

197. See App. 2 herein at nn. 7-9. According to Professor Wayne LaFave: Of all police encounters, only 10 to 15% result in arrests. The ratio of arrests to population is larger in the larger cities; it is affected by, among other things, whether police handle drunkenness by arrest. Only a fifth to a third of all arrests are on felony charges. A similar percentage range within all felony arrests involves juveniles. Of adults arrested for a felony, most are under thirty, and less than 8% are over fifty. Though some arrests are made with a warrant, issued by a magistrate, most are without a warrant, particularly on the state level. And an officer's decision to make an arrest involves considerable exercise of discretion. See LaFave, Modern Criminal Law 75-76 (1978).

198. Thus, for federal courts, under Rules 9(a) and 9(b)(2) of the Federal Rules of Criminal Procedure, on request of the government attorney, or upon the court's direction if the government attorney has not requested an arrest warrant, a summons rather than arrest warrant may be issued, for each defendant named in an indictment or information. The summons describes the offense charged and orders the defendant to appear before the court (or in case of a minor offense before a magistrate) at a stated time and place. A corporation's "appearance" is by proxy: Under Rule 43(c)(1), "A corporation may appear by counsel for all purposes." Under Rule 9(c)(1), a summons to a corporation is to be "served by delivering a copy to an officer or to a managing or general agent or to any other agent authorized by appointment or by law to receive service of process and, if the agent is one authorized by statute to receive service and the statute so requires, by also mailing a copy to the corporation's last known address within the district or at its principal place of business elsewhere in the United States." Rule 9, above described, deals with issuance of warrants and summonses after the grand jury indictment or prosecutor's "information" has been filed. Rule 4 deals with such issuance at an earlier stage, upon a complaint sworn before a magistrate. Federal prosecutors are increasingly seeking an indictment before getting an arrest warrant. This may be because of the time constraints imposed by the Speedy Trial Act (see App. 2 herein at nn. 167-168), and because an indictment filed before the date set for a "preliminary hearing" eliminates the latter and its advantages for the defendant (see nn. 206 & 208 below and accompanying text).

think the officer has insufficient evidence, or that the minor offense involved need not be prosecuted. A negative conclusion may also come after in-station interrogation (preceded by the Miranda warnings[199] and the suspect's waiver of his protection against talking). A suspect who is thus released may not even have been "booked" — i.e., had his name, time of arrest, and alleged offense recorded — since in some jurisdictions that occurs only after a decision to detain. In the more serious offenses, booking is supplemented by fingerprinting and photographing.

3. Arrests are often made before the *prosecutor* has learned, or made a decision, about the case. Some suspects who have not been released at the station may be freed at this stage, namely, when the prosecutor decides not to file with a magistrate a "complaint" against the suspect, signed by the police officer or the complaining witness, and supplemented in some jurisdictions by an arrest warrant. The prosecutor considers the nature of the evidence, the crime, the suspect, the alternative remedies, and, in some jurisdictions, whether the case qualifies for a "pre-trial diversion" program,[200] which would result in release when the suspect and the crime met certain conditions.

Considering the informal dismissals *both* at the police station level and at the prosecutor level, it is believed that the percentage of adult arrestees released without filing of charges may rise to as high as 40 percent — the percentage of felony releases being lower than that for misdemeanors. Releases at the police level deal generally with minor offenses, like public drunkenness, whereas releases of arrested felony suspects are usually the responsibility of the prosecutor, who gives great weight to police recommendations.[201]

4. The next step for the suspect who has been booked is the *"initial appearance"* before a magistrate. (This is not to be confused with the "preliminary hearing," the later appearance during which the determination as to probable cause in felony cases is made; nor should it be confused with the "arraignment," the stage when the felony defendant makes his plea — usually guilty, not guilty, or nolo contendere.)

In the case of a felony defendant, at the initial appearance the magistrate informs him of the charges and of his rights, including the right to a preliminary hearing and to have counsel at that hearing. (The hearing, if not waived, will be scheduled usually within two or three weeks after the arrest.) "If the defendant is indigent most states will appoint counsel at this stage — at least if the defendant requests

199. See App. 2 herein at nn. 108-112.

200. See App. 2 herein at n.231.

201. LaFave, *supra* n.197 at 77. Statistics vary with different areas and with different kinds of offenses. But "typically, 20-30% [of adult felony arrestees] will be released in larger urban areas. In addition, the prosecutor will decide to proceed on a misdemeanor rather than a felony charge in 10-20% of the arrests." *Id.* at 78.

a preliminary hearing."[202] The magistrate also sets bail at this point, for the felony defendant and for those misdemeanor defendants whose case is not finally disposed of at the initial appearance itself.

The reason that the misdemeanor defendant's case may be finally disposed of at the initial appearance is that after he has been informed of his rights, he (unlike the felony defendant) is asked to enter his plea — which will be a guilty plea for 75 to 85 percent of misdemeanor defendants, a percentage even higher where public drunkenness cases are substantial. Sentence may be imposed immediately. Delay, however, can occur, pending receipt of a pre-sentence report from the probation staff available in larger cities. If the plea is not guilty, the case will be set for trial; but in some jurisdictions he will be tried immediately unless a delay or jury trial is requested. In such immediate trials, without jury, defendants often represent themselves, and the "judicial atmosphere" is often lacking.[203]

Applicable to both the felony and misdemeanor defendant is a common statutory requirement that he be brought *without unreasonable delay* before a magistrate for his initial appearance. "In most urban communities, a person arrested on a felony charge in the afternoon or evening will not be presented before the magistrate until the next day, and, when arrested on a weekend, will not be presented until the following Monday."[204] Sometimes, particularly in misdemeanor cases, "station-house bail" may be afforded by the police prior to the initial appearance.[205]

5. The next stage, called *preliminary hearing* or preliminary examination, applies to felonies, not misdemeanors. The prosecution must prove to the magistrate's satisfaction that there is "probable cause" to believe the defendant committed a felony. The defendant's counsel need not, and generally does not, put on his own witnesses, but usually does cross-examine the prosecution witnesses; it is an occasion to discover the nature of the prosecution's case, without revealing much about the case for the defense. There are some other benefits, too, for the defense, and even for the prosecution.[206]

202. *Id.* at 78.

203. *Id.* at 79. In about half the states, on most misdemeanor convictions, defendant in a magistrate's court has a right to a completely new trial in a court of general criminal jurisdiction. *Id.* at 73 note e.

204. *Id.* at 78.

205. *Id.* at 78 note n.

206. Cross-examination may reveal weaknesses in the prosecution's case that convince the magistrate probable cause is lacking. Also, the prosecution witnesses' testimony on examination and cross-examination may be used at trial as a basis for "impeaching" the same witnesses if their trial testimony is inconsistent with their prior testimony; the defense may wish to put on a witness in order that the testimony be available at trial in case the witness is then unavailable; or the defense may wish to argue for reconsideration of the bail decision. Even the prose-

The magistrate may find probable cause as to the crime charged (or as to a lesser, misdemeanor charge that he will substitute for the felony charge), or no probable cause as to any charge. In the latter case, the defendant is released. If probable cause is found on the felony charge, the defendant is "bound over" for trial before a court of general criminal jurisdiction; and the formal accusation against him is then presented. In about half the states the prosecutor's formal statement is the filing of an *"information"* with the trial court. In the other states, which use a *grand jury,* he must present evidence to that body, which, when a majority is convinced of probable cause, issues its accusation (an *indictment*). The grand jury, consisting usually of 16 to 23 citizens, hears only the prosecutor's evidence, sits in private, and usually follows the prosecutor's recommendations.[207]

It is not true that a preliminary hearing is given in every felony case. In fact, they are held in less than half the felony cases, either because (1) the defendant has waived the hearing, or (2) a grand jury already found probable cause and indicted the defendant prior to the date set for the preliminary hearing.[208]

Another element to note is this: *prior* to actual filing of an information or indictment (and after the complaint filed at the initial appearance) the *prosecutor commonly reexamines the charges,* sometimes in connection with new evidence. This move may occur during preparation for the case before the magistrate or grand jury or in discussion with defendant's counsel. It can result in the dropping of felony charges because plea negotiations that were started at the initial appearance stage reduced the charge to a misdemeanor; or because of defendant's prosecution or conviction on another felony charge; or (in as many as 10 percent of the felony complaints) because the prosecutor has decided that no criminal prosecution is warranted after all.[209]

---

cution gets some benefit — e.g., an early test of the strengths and weaknesses of its case, early riddance of cases that probably would have been lost at trial, and early commitment of witnesses who might be subject to intimidation by the defendant. See generally, Coleman v. Alabama, 399 U.S. 1, 9 (1970); Note, 51 Iowa L. Rev. 164 (1965).

207. In the federal courts, Federal Criminal Rule 7(a) provides: An offense that may be punished by death shall be prosecuted by indictment. An offense that may be punished by imprisonment for a term exceeding one year or at hard labor shall be prosecuted by indictment or, if indictment is waived, by information. Any other offense may be prosecuted by indictment or by information. An information may be filed without leave of court.

208. LaFave, *supra* n.197 at 80. In such cases the defendant does not get the benefits described in n.206 *supra.* See also last two sentences in n.198 *supra.*

209. *Id.* at 81. As a result of complaint dismissals and pre-complaint screening, those who are ultimately charged by information or indictment with a felony often constitute less than half of those who were arrested for a felony. *Id.*

6. After the indictment or information comes the *arraignment* — the stage at which defendant enters his plea to the trial court. Usually between 70 to 85 percent of felony defendants plead guilty at this point or later — though often as a plea of guilty to misdemeanor charges, with the felony charges dismissed.[210]

Even in the minority of felony cases where there is no guilty plea to either felony or misdemeanor, a portion, perhaps 10%, is likely to be dismissed — the result of "prosecution determinations that the evidence is now insufficient, conviction of defendants on other charges, and successful defense pretrial motions."[211]

7. The *pre-trial motion* that may have the most favorable impact for the defense is the motion to suppress illegally obtained evidence.[212] Other possibilities include motions for a change in venue (place of trial), perhaps because of excessive publicity; for severance of trial from that of a co-defendant; and for "discovery" of certain information in the prosecution's possession that defendant wishes disclosed. Some motions may have to be made before entry of a plea, such as those claiming legal insufficiencies in the grand jury, indictment, or preliminary examination; double jeopardy; or the expiration of the statute of limitations period.[213]

8. Characteristics of *the trial* itself vary a good deal among jurisdictions. Thus, in New Jersey about 85 percent of all felony trials are before juries, whereas in Maryland the figure is 10 percent, and in the nation as a whole it is 60 percent — with considerable variation among different offenses. The median time interval between the filing of the indictment or information and the trial has been reduced to seven months or less in many jurisdictions. Most trials before juries last two days or less; most of those before courts last one day or less. "The acquittal rate for most major felonies is below 33 1/3%, and the overall rate for all felonies can easily fall below 20%. Totalling both guilty pleas and trial convictions, ordinarily 75-85% of all persons charged with felonies by information or indictment are convicted of some offense" — with the rate of conviction and level of conviction varying a good deal with the offense charged.[214]

210. *Id.*

211. *Id.* at 82. The result of such dismissals plus the guilty pleas is that only about 10 to 20% of the felony indictments or informations will be disposed of by trial; and in most states less than 10% of adults arrested on felony charges will have a trial on those charges. *Id.*

212. A six-day survey in Cook County, Illinois showed that motions to suppress were made in 41% of all narcotics cases, and had a 75% success rate. *Id.*

213. *Id.*

214. *Id.* at 82-83. The figures assume "a fair degree of pre-charge screening. In a state where there is less screening, a considerably higher percentage of dismissals at trial might reduce the conviction rate of those charged to 55 or 60%." *Id.* at 83 note s.

9. The *sentencing* stage is one in which the defendant may still have no substantial hearing rights.[215] The modern statutory pattern of sentencing has been the "indeterminate sentence" — though very recently, a movement has developed toward "mandatory" or "determinate" sentencing.[216] In the indeterminate system, the judge sets a range of imprisonment within the legislative limits, the legislature having set a maximum for the offense, but no minimum (or having set as the highest minimum the judge can fix, a percentage of the maximum). Within the judge's range, the sentence actually served would be determined by a parole board. As alternatives to imprisonment the judge also has discretion, for most crimes, to grant probation and/or to levy a fine. (Sometimes probation is combined with a limited jail sentence.)

"Starting at the point of arrest and continuing through conviction and sentence, the number of persons facing a possible prison sentence is constantly diminishing. In California, for example, less than 5% of the adult felony *arrestees* will be sentenced to prison. Approximately 50% of the arrestees will eventually be released (combining initial decisions not to prosecute, dismissals of complaints, dismissals of felony informations, and acquittals), 35% will be convicted on misdemeanor charges, and 15% will be convicted on a felony charge, with less than a third of that group sentenced to prison."[217]

10. *Appeals* from those found guilty at trial are at a highly variable rate: from 30 percent in some jurisdictions to over 80 percent in others. In felony cases an appeal is allowed as of right in most jurisdictions; in the others it is discretionary. In about one third of the states, the appeal goes not to the highest state court but to an intermediate

215. See App. 2 herein at n.161.

216. The movement has many roots, such as growing dissatisfaction with sentencing disparities among different judges traceable to differences in their respective evaluations of the gravity of various crimes and their respective approaches to sentencing objectives; or the feeling that parole boards have been exercising their broad discretion improperly, e.g., by too much emphasis on how well the prisoner has behaved in prison; or pessimism about the possibility of rehabilitation in a prison environment, and about the present state of our knowledge on techniques of rehabilitation; or the view that the uncertainties of an indeterminate sentence are psychologically bad for the prisoner. Reforms suggested include: (1) moderating judicial disparities by means of sentencing guidelines based on analysis of existing judicial practice; (2) use of sentencing commissions (penologists, sociologists, and perhaps clergymen, psychiatrists, and ex-convicts) to formulate ideal guidelines for judges; and (3) rigid controls by legislatures. See generally, Zalman, The Rise and Fall of the Indeterminate Sentence, 24 Wayne L. Rev. 857 (1978); Coffee, The Future of Sentencing Reform, 73 Mich. L. Rev. 1361 (1975); Symposium on Sentencing, 7 Hofstra L. Rev. 1 (Part I), 243 (Part II) (1978). See also Chap. 1 *supra* at n.72.

217. LaFave, *supra* n.197 at 84. "Many major industrial states would appear more likely to have 20-40% dismissals, 50% misdemeanor convictions, 20-30% felony convictions, and 10-15% imprisonment." *Id.* at n.u.

court of appeals, and usually will not reach the highest state court. A common reversal rate is 10 to 20 percent, though often the reversal means that the defendant will be re-tried and perhaps re-convicted.[218]

In the federal courts, there is a right of appeal from the district court to the court of appeals of the particular circuit, and discretionary review (certiorari) of the latter court by the Supreme Court. When review of a state court case is sought in the United States Supreme Court by appeal or certiorari (see above under **B4(b)**) the federal (usually constitutional) claim will not be considered by the Court if the state court decision was based on an "adequate state ground," separate from the constitutional claim.[219]

11. Finally, there are post-conviction remedies described as "collateral" remedies, as distinguished from the "direct" review afforded by appeal. Long after the time for appeal has expired, for example, a prisoner may be interested in such collateral review. The typical remedy is *habeas corpus.*

Article I, section 9 of the Constitution declares that the writ of habeas corpus "shall not be suspended, unless when in cases of rebellion or invasion the public safety may require it." Federal statutes have implemented this provision, making it, among other things, applicable to anyone "restrained of his . . . liberty in violation of the Constitution," including since 1867 state prisoners as well. The writ directs a government officer (e.g., warden) who has custody of a person to bring the detained person before the court to have the ground of detention inquired into, so that he may be released if the custody is invalid. Originally confined to jurisdictional issues, habeas corpus now extends to all constitutional issues[220] — with at least one exception. As noted in the Appendix 2 discussion of the exclusionary rule,[221] the Supreme Court's growing dissatisfaction with that rule led it in 1976 to decide as follows: *Federal* habeas corpus relief is not available to a *state* prisoner on the ground that unconstitutionally seized evidence was introduced at his trial, if the state had provided an opportunity for full and fair litigation of the Fourth Amendment claim.

Federal habeas corpus relief for a *state* prisoner (provided under 28 U.S.C. §2254) is conditioned on prior exhaustion of currently available *state* court remedies. But the exhaustion requirement is inter-

218. *Id.* at 84-85.

219. Thus, if the state court refusal to consider a federal constitutional claim rested on defendant's failure to comply with a state procedural requirement, and the Supreme Court thinks this forfeiture and the procedural requirement itself serves a legitimate state interest, the Court will not review the federal claim. See Israel & LaFave, Criminal Procedure 374-375 (3d ed. 1980).

220. Fay v. Noia, 372 U.S. 391 (1963); Waley v. Johnston, 316 U.S. 101 (1942).

221. See App. 2 herein at n.77.

preted liberally.[222] So is the requirement of "custody."[223] And the "adequate state ground" doctrine, previously mentioned, does not apply in federal habeas corpus.[224] The federal court is not bound by the legal determination made by the state court, but the federal statute establishes a presumptive correctness of state court fact findings, unless one of eight specified circumstances exists.[225]

In the case of *federal* prisoners, because habeas corpus petitions were being filed in the courts of those relatively few districts in which federal prisons were located, thus overburdening those courts, Congress provided in a 1948 law (28 U.S.C., §2255) for a substitute post-conviction petition, to be filed in the court where sentence had been imposed. This petition is treated by the Supreme Court as providing "a remedy exactly commensurate with that which had been available by habeas corpus."[226]

State prisoners' post-conviction remedies in *state* courts vary a good deal from state to state. Many have adopted statutes or court rules allowing habeas corpus relief for all constitutional claims; some are confined to selected claims; some recognize other writs (e.g., "coram nobis") as appropriate for raising certain constitutional claims after conviction. Unlike the case of federal court consideration of a state prisoner's claim, "state courts generally will not reconsider on collateral attack cognizable claims that were raised and decided on the merits at trial and on appeal."[227]

The volume of post-conviction petitions has been considerable.

222. Thus when state remedies are alternative to each other, one need not exhaust them all. (If defendant's claim was reviewed on direct appeal, he is not also required to seek state collateral relief before seeking federal collateral relief.) Brown v. Allen, 344 U.S. 443 (1953). The exhaustion requirement does not include the seeking of the Supreme Court's certiorari review of the state highest court's denial of relief; the requirement applies only to state remedies that are still open to him at the time he seeks federal habeas corpus, and not those he might have pursued in the past (like an appeal to a higher state court from his conviction) that are not still open to him. But "a deliberate by-passing of state procedures," especially when the decision to do so is participated in by defendant as well as counsel, would permit a federal court to deny habeas corpus. *Fay, supra* n. 220. Justification for the denial would be lost, however, if despite a deliberate bypass, there was a subsequent state court consideration of the merits of the constitutional claim. Warden v. Hayden, 387 U.S. 294 (1967).

223. Thus, a parolee who is subject to restrictions on movement, employment, and association, and to the constant fear that a single deviation may return him to prison, could qualify. Jones v. Cunningham, 371 U.S. 236 (1963). See also related cases in Israel & LaFave, *supra* n.219 at 411-412.

224. *Fay, supra* n.220.

225. The circumstances so specified include lack of support in the state court record for the factual determination; lack of a full, fair, and adequate hearing; or other denial of due process of law.

226. Hill v. U.S., 368 U.S. 424 (1962). See generally Israel & LaFave, *supra* n.219 at 412-415.

227. *Id.* at 416. See generally, 415-416.

Over 10 percent of adult felony prisoners in federal prisons have filed such petitions in a single year. About one-sixth of a federal court's civil docket is devoted to such petitions from federal and state prisoners (about 13,000). While in many state courts the rate of application for collateral remedies is much less frequent than in the federal courts, there are a few states in which the rate is higher, i.e., in which the annual applications can equal 15 to 20 percent of the state's prison population.[228]

C. Background Note: The Tort Law of Privacy

I wish here to set the *Nappier* case ruling on privacy law against a broader background, so that various facets of the law of privacy can be distinguished, and the *Nappier* ruling can be better understood.

The idea of a tort action for invasion of privacy is a relative infant in the law, born in the fertile brains of Louis D. Brandeis and Samuel D. Warren. It was an idea whose time had come when these Boston lawyers wrote their article "The Right to Privacy" in 1890[229] — though it may startle you to find them saying so long ago:

> The intensity and complexity of life, attendant upon advancing civilization, have rendered necessary some retreat from the world, and man, under the refining influence of culture, has become more sensitive to publicity, so that solitude and privacy have become more essential to the individual; but modern enterprise and invention have, through invasions upon his privacy, subjected him to mental pain and distress, far greater than could be inflicted by mere bodily injury.[230]

Their argument for creation of a new category of tort liability was rejected in 1902 by a 4 to 3 vote of the highest New York court in a suit by an attractive young lady against a company that advertised its flour with a picture of the plaintiff, without her consent. But the New York legislature thereupon passed a statute authorizing both a criminal prosecution and a tort suit against use of the name, portrait, or picture of any person "for advertising purposes or for the purpose of trade" without the person's written consent. The Georgia Supreme Court accepted the Brandeis-Warren thesis in 1905 in a situation analogous to that in the New York case. By the 1930s the American

228. LaFave, *supra* n.197 at 85.
229. 4 Harv. L. Rev. 193 (1890).
230. *Id.* at 196.

Law Institute's *Restatement of Torts* had accepted it. Today only a few states reject it.[231]

Probably the most influential analysis of the privacy cases was made by Prosser in his widely used *Torts* treatise, an analysis that has been incorporated into the *Restatement of the Law of Torts*.[232] One argument against the analysis is that it treats privacy as "a composite of the interests in reputation, emotional tranquillity and intangible property" rather than as an "independent value" protective of "human dignity."[233] Without entering into that debate, I shall set forth the Prosser classification, in which the *Nappier* case easily finds a niche.

Prosser analyzed the privacy cases as representing four kinds of invasions of four different interests:[234]

(1) The first group of cases is like the New York case: They involve the defendant's appropriating the plaintiff's identity, through his name or likeness, for defendant's benefit. The emphasis seems to be upon the appropriation of a property interest of the plaintiff, and this kind of privacy is sometimes called a "right of publicity." Of the four categories it is the least similar to what we normally think of as privacy and perhaps would not even have been so labeled if the New York law had not provided a "right of privacy" caption for it.

(2) The second group of cases involves the defendant's engaging in publicity that puts the plaintiff in a "false light" — conduct that is objectionable though not necessarily defamatory. As with the cases in the first category, the unauthorized use of a name or photograph is frequent. Examples are cases of falsely and publicly attributing to the plaintiff the authorship of an opinion, book, or article, or unauthorizedly using his name on a petition or as a candidate for office.[235]

231. Prosser, Handbook of the Law of Torts 804 (4th ed. 1971).

232. Restatement (Second) of Torts, §§652A-D (1977).

233. Bloustein, Privacy as an Aspect of Human Dignity: An Answer to Dean Prosser, 39 N.Y.U.L. Rev. 962 (1964).

234. Prosser, *supra* n.231 at 802-818.

235. The Supreme Court in Zacchini v. Scripps-Howard Broadcasting Co., 433 U.S. 562 (1977) emphasized the difference between the kinds of interests involved in the first and second privacy categories. That case, illustrating the first category, upheld a claim by an entertainer at a country fair that a news program's televising of his "human cannonball" act had invaded his privacy. The Court contrasted this situation with that in Time, Inc. v. Hill, 385 U.S. 374 (1967), (see Chap. 5 herein at n.7), in which a magazine review of a Broadway play based on plaintiff's actual life experiences had allegedly put those experiences in a false light. In the latter case, the Court thought: there was a kind of reputational rather than "proprietary" interest; the Court had been asked to discourage such publicizing rather than determine whether it was plaintiff or defendant that had the right to publicize; and the defendant had reported an event, rather than broadcast a performer's entire act for which the performer would normally get paid. (In *Time,* the court concluded that First Amendment freedom would allow the magazine to escape liability unless the story was knowingly or recklessly false; in the performer case, the Court thought the First Amendment was no defense to the "appropriation" of his rights. Constitutional aspects of privacy are further discussed in Chap. 5 herein under A and B.

(3) The third group of cases involves intrusion upon plaintiff's solitude or seclusion, examples being illegal entry or search, or eavesdropping.

(4) The fourth group of cases includes our *Nappier* case. One characteristic of this category is the *public disclosure of certain "private" facts* — facts that may be true and hence would not support an action for defamation. Here we find cases such as the one in which the defendant put up a truthful notice in the street window of his garage proclaiming that the plaintiff owed him money and would not pay it; and the one in which a movie told the true story, and revealed the present identity, of a reformed prostitute who seven years before had been the defendant in a sensational murder trial.[236]

Note that in (2) and (4) above I have referred to defamation. Also known as libel (or slander when oral), *false* statements that tend to injure *reputation* fall under this term. A reputational interest is not necessary to, but may be present in, claims under (2) and (4); and sometimes the situations in (2) and (4) would *also* qualify for a defamation action. The *Torts Restatement* observes that the same acts may invade more than one of the four kinds of privacy, and may qualify as defamation as well. In such cases, the plaintiff can proceed on all of the applicable theories, although he can have but one recovery for a single instance of publicity.[237]

Relevant to the *Nappier* case is the fact that as the common law of privacy developed, certain "privileges" developed, i.e., certain valid legal defenses to the alleged privacy violation. Among them were two privileges that tended to coalesce: that of giving further publicity to a public figure or celebrity (including actors and entertainers), and that of publicizing news and other matters of public interest. Thus the latter privilege had prior to the *Nappier* case been recognized in a South Carolina case involving publicity to a twelve-year-old wife who had given birth to a child,[238] and a New Mexico case involving publicity to a girl who had been sexually assaulted by her older brother, aged sixteen, these facts being also part of a public court record.[239] At common law, therefore, the defendants in *Nappier* may well have had a good defense, as the dissenting court of appeals judge indeed concluded. As we have already seen, however, the appellate court majority thought the South Carolina criminal statute had the effect of removing the common law defense. We shall be discussing this reasoning in the next chapter.

236. Brents v. Morgan, 221 Ky. 765, 299 S.W. 867 (1927); Melvin v. Reid, 112 Cal. App. 285, 297 Pac. 91 (1931).
237. Restatement of Torts (Second) 377-378, 395 (1977).
238. Meetze v. Associated Press, 230 S.C. 330, 95 S.E.2d 606 (1956).
239. Hubbard v. Journal Publ. Co., 69 N.M. 473, 368 P.2d 147 (1962).

I should also like to alert you to the fact that there is a *constitutional* aspect of the problem, which neither the district court nor the court of appeals discussed, and which we will consider in Chapter 5. For even if the statute makes a difference, statutes are subject to the Constitution. In other words, in addition to the defendant's common law privileges, the court must also consider whether he has a constitutional privilege, such as freedom of the press. We shall see in Chapter 5 that the more recent cases have weighed First Amendment values more heavily than privacy values in situations comparable to the *Nappier* situation — a tendency that would probably result in the plaintiff losing if the same claim were litigated today.[240]

240. "Although some individuals have recovered for unwarranted and highly offensive press intrusions, the courts to date have been far more sensitive to the guaranties of a free press, and more solicitous of the 'newsworthy exception' than were Warren and Brandeis." Barron, Warren and Brandeis, *The Right to Privacy . . .* Demystifying A Landmark Citation, 13 Suffolk L. Rev. 875, 880-881 (1979). The author observes that the public disclosure of private facts (i.e., the *Nappier* pattern) was what Brandeis and Warren had most in mind by privacy; and that of the four privacy categories, this one has been least litigated and least successful in generating relief. In explaining its lack of success, he refers not only to First Amendment considerations but also to the fact that "the truly privacy-oriented person may be reluctant to expose himself to further invasions of his privacy by taking legal action"; that the Warren-Brandeis argument depended on reasoning by analogy (from the law of libel and of intellectual property); and that their description of journalistic excesses in their day was exaggerated. *Id.* at 880-883. Doubts about desirability of the creation of the new tort are raised in Kalven, Privacy in Tort Law — Were Warren and Brandeis Wrong? 31 Law & Contemp. Prob. 326 (1966).

Chapter 3

Further Aspects of the Case: The Statute

A. Court Treatment of the State Statute; Interpretation Problems Raised Thereby

From Chapter 2 you will recall that the South Carolina statute made it a criminal misdemeanor to publish "in any newspaper, magazine or other publication," the "name" of the victim of a rape or attempted rape.

Remember also that the district court's reasoning was: (1) The statute had no application to the broadcast in this case because (a) there was no reason not to give the statute its plain or literal meaning, and when so construed it covered only publication of the actual names, not stage names, of the victims; and (b) being a penal statute, it must be narrowly construed. (2) In any event, the complaint did not show that the defendants had identified the plaintiffs sufficiently to violate their common law right of privacy.

The court of appeals opinion took a different view: The statute applied to the broadcast because there was good reason to give a non-literal reading to the statute, so as to cover any identifications, whether or not by actual names; though penal, the statute did not have to be narrowly construed; though not framed in terms of defenses to common law liability for privacy violation, the statute did show a legislative policy that was inconsistent with recognition of the common law defense of publicizing newsworthy people and events, in this "name of rape victim" situation.

The Background Notes that follow shortly will deal with this latter problem of the statutory impact on a common law area to which the statute is not directly addressed, and also to the general theory of statutory interpretation. At this point, however, I wish to address myself mainly to the specific points of (1) literal vs. nonliteral reading of statutes, and (2) the narrow reading of penal statutes. I will do this by introducing you to a famous set of four cases, which went off in different directions on these points. They will serve as a good introduction, I think, to the going ways of treating these very common problems of statutory interpretation.

1. Ejusdem Generis

Before beginning, I want to point out that two of the four cases are concerned with a maxim of interpretation that might also have been argued in the *Nappier* opinions but was not — the "ejusdem generis" maxim.[1] According to this maxim (literally, "of the same genus or class"), when you have a series of specific enumerations followed by a catchall clause (e.g., "any other . . ."), the coverage of the catchall is to be construed in the light of the common characteristics of the specific enumerations. That is, it should represent the same class or "genus" that they represent. Thus, when the South Carolina statute prohibited publishing the name of the rape victim "in any newspaper, magazine *or other publication*," the catchall I have italicized might be construed to cover only printed publications, i.e., to exclude a televised broadcast, since printing is the common characteristic of the specifically enumerated categories. This argument might be buttressed by the fact that the statute was enacted in 1902, when the legislature could not possibly have been thinking of television.

The answering argument would be that courts do not always apply the "ejusdem generis" approach to catchall clauses, any more than they always read a statute literally or always read a penal statute narrowly. The court would have to ask itself whether in the light of the statute's history and policy, its relation to other statutes, the reasonable expectations of those subject to it, etc., the scope of the catchall clause should be read restrictively. As to whether a word should be construed to cover an activity or process that was completely unknown to the enacting legislature that used the word, again the multiplicity of relevant factors may or may not lead a court to an affirmative answer.[2] A "dangerous weapon" statute enacted in mid-nineteenth century, for instance, can be and has been interpreted to cover weapons thereafter invented. If the *Nappier* defendants had raised the argument that "publication" should exclude television broadcasts, this approach

1. Sutherland, Statutes and Statutory Construction, §§47.17-47.22 (4th ed., Sands, 1973); Annot., 94 L. Ed. 464 (1950).

2. Sutherland, *id.*, §49.02.

would probably have been rejected — though I am given pause by the fact that the district judge and one of the three appellate judges took an almost equally wooden approach to the word "name."

2. Cases Rejecting "Plain Meaning" (Herein Also of "Express Mention, Implied Exclusion" and the Rule on Penal Statutes)

I turn first, then, to two well-known Supreme Court cases that *rejected a proposed literal meaning* and instead adopted, as did the *Nappier* court of appeals, a meaning derived from the statutory "purpose" or "policy" or "spirit."

1. The first case is the 1892 case of Holy Trinity Church v. United States.[3] An 1885 federal statute had prohibited prepaying the transportation, or in any way encouraging the importation, of aliens under contract "to perform labor or service of any kind in the United States. . . ." For violation the civil penalty was $1,000. The United States attorney sued the Holy Trinity Church in New York for the penalty because it had contracted with an English clergyman to come over to New York to be the church minister. The Supreme Court unanimously held that the statute did not apply to this transaction. True, the plain and literal meaning of "labor or service of any kind" would cover the minister's services. But there were reasons for not applying a literal meaning here, said the Court. The title of the act plus the petitions and testimony before congressional committees, plus the reports of the House and Senate committees, showed that "the evil [the law] was designed to remedy" was the importation under contract of cheap manual labor. These indications together with the country's hospitable attitude toward religion led the Court to conclude, "We cannot think Congress intended to denounce with penalties a transaction like" this, involving services of a church minister.

Nor did the Court regard its departure from literal meaning as a novelty of the law. The Court said:

> It is a familiar rule that a thing may be within the letter of the statute and yet not within the statute because not within its spirit, nor within the intention of its makers. . . . [F]requently words . . . are . . . broad enough to include an act in question, and yet a consideration of the whole legislation, or of the circumstances surrounding its enactment, or of the absurd results which follow from giving such broad meaning to the words, makes it unreasonable to believe that the legislator intended to include the particular act.

3. 143 U.S. 457 (1892).

One other aspect of the opinion ought to be mentioned. The Court conceded the fact that "as noticed by the Circuit Judge in his opinion, the fifth section which makes specific exceptions, among them professional actors, artists, lecturers, singers and domestic servants, strengthens the idea that every other kind of labor and service was intended to be reached by the first section." The Supreme Court was unmoved by this, but the circuit judge had stressed the "well-settled rule of statutory interpretation" that an exemption proviso carves out the coverage provision "what would otherwise have been within it." Hence the exemption clause was "equivalent to a declaration that contracts to perform professional services except those of actors, artists, lecturers or singers are within the prohibition of the preceding sections."[4]

The circuit judge might also have cited a related "well-settled rule" sometimes described as "express mention, implied exclusion." More elegantly known as "expressio unius, exclusio alterius," it embodies the thought that when the only matters expressly specified by the legislature are A and B, then the intention is to exclude the disputed C. If you think about this a moment, I think you will conclude that such an inference is not always justified. Sometimes if you specify A and B, you do not mean *only* A and B; you may be using A and B as illustrative examples. Still, it is true that a legislative specification, especially one within an exemption clause, is more likely to be intended to be exclusive (even if the legislature does not say "only"). But remember that even when a court concludes that the specification was intended to be exclusive, it might still believe that the legislature had *inadvertently omitted* an additional category, that applying the statute without it would lead to an absurd result, or that someone should not be punished who acted on a reasonable belief to that effect. This was apparently the attitude of the Supreme Court toward the exemption categories in the Holy Trinity Church case.

The second of my two cases rejecting a literal construction is the 1931 case of McBoyle v. United States.[5] The National Motor Vehicle Theft Act of 1919 had prohibited interstate transportation of stolen motor vehicles known to be stolen, and had provided that "the term 'motor vehicle' shall include an automobile, automobile truck, automobile wagon, motorcycle, or any other self-propelled vehicle not designed for running on rails." The defendant McBoyle was convicted of having caused the stealing and interstate transportation of an airplane. The Tenth Circuit Court of Appeals affirmed by a 2 to 1 vote. But a unanimous Supreme Court, speaking through Justice

4. U.S. v. Church of the Holy Trinity, 36 F. 303, 305 (S.D.N.Y. 1888).
5. 283 U.S. 25 (1931).

Holmes, held that the conviction should be reversed because the statute did not cover airplanes.

Holmes *rejected* a *literal* approach to "vehicle." He conceded that "no doubt etymologically it is possible to use the word to signify a conveyance working on land, water, or air, and sometimes legislation [specifically does so, and sometimes specifically does otherwise]. . . . But in everyday speech 'vehicle' calls up the picture of a thing moving on land." The "not designed for running on rails" language strengthens this "popular picture" of a vehicle running on land. "It is a vehicle that runs, not something not commonly called a vehicle, that flies." This interpretation was fortified by contextual considerations (similar to those underlying the "ejusdem generis" maxim that had been invoked by the dissenting circuit court of appeals judge, though Holmes did not refer to the maxim as such): "It is impossible to read words that so carefully enumerate the different forms of motor vehicles and have no reference of any kind to aircraft, as including airplanes under a term that usage more and more precisely confines to a different class."

Moreover, "[a]irplanes were well known in 1919, when this statute was passed; but it is admitted that they were not mentioned in the reports or in the debates in Congress." The dissenting circuit court of appeals judge had treated the matter of legislative history more fully. He conceded that not all congressional proceedings can be given much weight in interpreting a statute; congressional debates have little weight compared to committee reports. But the debates can be used, the Supreme Court had previously held, to show the history of the period. And here, he said, "The discussions of the proposed measures are enlightening . . . from a historic standpoint in showing that the theft of automobiles was so prevalent over the land as to call for punitive restraint, but airplanes were never even mentioned." He also tied in this prevailing concern over automobile thefts and the rarity of airplane thefts — both of which he characterized as "familiar knowledge" — with the broad principle that had also been invoked in the *Holy Trinity Church* case: "The prevailing mischief sought to be corrected is an aid in the construction of a statute."

Finally, the idea that penal statutes are to be strictly construed (i.e., narrowly construed to favor the defendant) — which was invoked by the *Nappier* district court and by the dissenting circuit court of appeals judge in *McBoyle* — also figured in Justice Holmes's opinion though the maxim was not cited as such: "Although it is not likely that a criminal will carefully consider the text of the law before he murders or steals, it is reasonable that a fair warning should be given to the world in language that the common world will understand, of what the law intends to do if a certain line is passed. To make the warning fair, so far as possible the line should be clear."

2. Before turning to my second pair of Supreme Court cases on the plain-meaning rule, let me say that there are cases in which the Court's refusal to apply a plain-meaning approach yields even more striking results than in *McBoyle* and *Holy Trinity*. How do you react to a Court holding that the United States itself qualifies as a "resident of the United States"?[6] Or that a statute allowing a railroad shipper's rate complaint to be pursued "either" in the district court or before the ICC means that the initial complaint can be brought only before the ICC?[7] Or that "shall" means "may," or "may" means "shall"; or that "and" means "or," or "or" means "and"?[8] Do you wonder whether the Court is going too far?

Remember that in these cases, too, the Court was convinced that *in the particular circumstances* it was more reasonable to conclude that the legislature could not have intended the result to which a literal meaning would lead. For instance, an important Supreme Court case, Hecht Co. v. Bowles,[9] involved the interpretation of "shall" in the injunction section of the Emergency Price Control Act of 1942. The section said that upon the government's proof of the defendant's violation of the act or any regulations thereunder, the court "shall" issue an injunction. The case involved a defendant department store with a proven and unusually "good-faith" intensive effort to avoid violations. The Court held that since the exercise of judicial discretion was a hallmark of a court of equity's exercise of the injunction power, and since there was nothing in the legislative history to show that Congress was deliberately making a drastic departure from this centuries-old tradition, the Court could not give "shall" its literal, mandatory meaning.

6. Helvering v. Stockholms Enskilda Bank, 293 U.S. 84, 91-94 (1934). The issue was whether interest received from the United States by a foreign corporation on a tax refund was covered by a clause applicable to foreign corporations and aliens, imposing a tax on "interest on bonds, notes, or other interest-bearing obligations of residents, corporate or otherwise." Making the refund was held to be an interest-bearing obligation of a "resident," namely the United States. The unanimous Court realized that the statutory language was inept and that its holding ran contrary to a number of maxims and presumptions; but it invoked considerations showing that "a contrary holding would defeat the evident purpose of [the] statute" to cover interest received by foreign corporations and aliens on all government as well as private obligations.

7. Texas & Pac. Ry. Co. v. Abilene Cotton Oil Co., 204 U.S. 426 (1907). What persuaded the Court was that a basic statutory purpose of promoting uniformity of rates would not be achieved unless the initial complaints were brought to the Commission. In this instance, purpose overrode a specific intent that was treated as a legislative lapse. This is not the usual treatment of specific intent.

8. On "shall" vs. "may," see Crawford, Statutory Construction, §262 (1940); Cairo & Fulton R.R. Co. v. Hecht, 95 U.S. 168, 170 (1877); 73 Am. Jur. 2d, §§23-25 (1974). On "and" vs. "or," see 73 Am. Jur. 2d, §241 (1974); DeSylva v. Ballentine, 351 U.S. 570, 573-574 (1956); U.S. v. Fisk, 68 U.S. (3 Wall.) 445, 447 (1865).

9. 321 U.S. 321 (1944).

Cases like these do not mean that the courts have gone berserk; rather, the opinions point to justifying evidence of intent or purpose. The cases have not gone so far as one imagined opinion of the Canadian Supreme Court, holding that an Indian's pony saddled with a feather pillow was a "small bird" within the meaning of the Ontario Small Birds Act — so that when its owner shot the pony after it broke its leg, he could be convicted of killing a small bird in violation of the Act.[10] The opinion (by "Blue, J.") is too long to reproduce, but reads in part:

> . . . Counsel relied on the decision in *Re Chicadee,* where he contends that in similar circumstances the accused was acquitted. However, this is a horse of a different colour. A close reading of that case indicates that the animal in question there was not a small bird, but, in fact, a midget of a much larger species. Therefore, that case is inapplicable to our facts.
>
> Counsel finally submits that the word "small" in the title Small Birds Act refers not to "Birds" but to "Act", making it The Small Act relating to Birds. With respect, counsel did not do his homework very well, for the Large Birds Act, R.S.O. 1960, c. 725, is just as small. If pressed, I need only refer to the Small Loans Act R.S.O. 1960, c. 727 which is twice as large as the Large Birds Act.
>
> It remains then to state my reason for judgment which, simply, is as follows: Different things may take on the same meaning for different purposes. For the purpose of the Small Birds Act, all two-legged, feather-covered animals are birds. This, of course, does not imply that only two-legged animals qualify, for the legislative intent is to make two legs merely the minimum requirement. The statute therefore contemplated multi-legged animals with feathers as well. Counsel submits that having regard to the purpose of the statute only small animals "naturally covered" with feathers could have been contemplated. However, had this been the intention of the legislature, I am certain that the phrase "naturally covered" would have been expressly inserted just as "Long" was inserted in the Longshoreman's Act.
>
> Therefore, a horse with feathers on its back must be deemed for the purposes of this Act to be a bird, and *a fortiori,* a pony with feathers on its back is a small bird.
>
> Counsel posed the following rhetorical question: If the pillow had been removed prior to the shooting, would the animal still be a bird? To this let me answer rhetorically: Is a bird any less of a bird without its feathers? . . .

10. Regina v. Ojibway. The opinion is not officially reported, but appears in 8 Crim. L.Q. 137 (Toronto, 1965). Professor W. Barton Leach of the Harvard law faculty, who had a special penchant for legal humor, publicized the opinion in 1970 at Harvard. He later reported that he had discovered the opinion had been invented by some Quarterly staff members and that the editor had decided to print it without indicating it was a joke.

3. Cases Adopting "Plain Meaning" (Herein Also of Inferences from Legislative Action and Inaction)

Coming to two well-known Supreme Court cases in which a literal or plain-meaning approach was *adopted:* The first is Caminetti v. United States,[11] involving the Mann Act. This act made it a criminal offense knowingly to transport, or cause or aid the transportation of in interstate commerce, "any woman or girl for the purpose of prostitution or debauchery, or for any other immoral purpose. . . ." Caminetti's conviction under this law was for transporting a woman from Sacramento, California to Reno, Nevada, where she was to become, in the Court's words, his "concubine and mistress." A majority of the Supreme Court upheld his conviction.

Let me first summarize the view of the three dissenting justices. They opposed the view that "any other immoral purpose" must be given a plain, literal meaning so as to cover the admittedly immoral purpose of making a woman one's mistress. As you might have expected, they relied heavily on the principle of the *Holy Trinity Church* case, which they cited and quoted from. They said the "principle [of that case] is the simple one that the words of a statute will be extended or restricted to execute its purpose." And the sole purpose here, they said, was to punish those engaging in *commercialized* vice involving the crossing of state lines. This was clear from the House Committee Report and the statement of the bill's sponsor. The dissenters stressed that a congressional committee report was weighty evidence of legislative intent, much more so than the floor debates. They also cited an opinion of the attorney general, and the fact that Section 8 of the act declared that the "Act shall be known and referred to as the 'White-slave Traffic Act.'" The latter point was supplemented by the argument that "[i]t is a peremptory rule of construction that all parts of a statute must be taken into account in ascertaining its meaning, and it cannot be said that Sec. 8 has no object." Finally, the dissenters cited the principle that "a construction which leads to mischievous consequences" should be rejected if the statute is reasonably susceptible of another construction. And here, "[b]lackmailers of both sexes have arisen, using the terrors of the construction now sanctioned by this court as a help — indeed, the means — for their brigandage."

The *Caminetti* majority, on the other hand, relied heavily on the "plain-meaning rule," in the way the district judge in our *Nappier* case did. They saw the principle as making unnecessary any reference to committee reports, maxims of construction, or any other aids that were extrinsic to the substance of the statute:

11. 242 U.S. 470 (1917).

> [I]t has been so often affirmed as to become a recognized rule, when words are free from doubt they must be taken as the final expression of the legislative intent, and are not to be added to or subtracted from by considerations drawn from titles or designating names, or reports accompanying their introduction, or from any extraneous source. In other words, the language being plain, and not leading to absurd or wholly impracticable consequences, it is the sole evidence of the ultimate legislative intent.

"Plain" meaning tends not only to be the same as literal meaning but also the same as ordinary meaning (though remember that the literal or "etymological" meaning of "vehicle" in *McBoyle* was viewed differently from its meaning in "everyday speech"). The majority supplemented its general observations on the plain-meaning principle by declaring on ordinary meaning: "Statutory words are uniformly presumed, unless the contrary appears, to be used in their ordinary and usual sense, and with the meaning commonly attributed to them." To say that interstate transportation for the purpose of making someone a "concubine or mistress" is not for an "immoral" purpose "would shock the common understanding of what constitutes an immoral purpose when those terms are applied, as here, to sexual relations."

The majority recognized that the "ejusdem generis" principle would require that the conduct covered by "any other immoral purpose" be of the same general class as prostitution and debauchery. And they concluded that being a concubine or mistress *was* in that same class even though lacking the commercial element. The Supreme Court had already so held in construing a statute dealing with importation of alien women, and this construction, said the *Caminetti* majority, was presumably known to Congress when it enacted the similar language of the Mann Act. The reliance on construction of the other statute illustrates a principle that has been embodied in the "pari materia" maxim — to the effect that statutes involving the same subject matter be construed together. The maxim, not surprisingly, does not always result in a court's adopting the natural conclusion that results from such a construing together — simply because other considerations, including perhaps other maxims, are deemed more persuasive in the particular case.[12]

My second "plain-meaning" decision is the 1950 case of Alpers v. United States.[13] "The question in this case," said the Court, "is whether the shipment of obscene phonograph records in interstate commerce is prohibited by Sec. 245 of the Criminal Code, which makes illegal the interstate shipment of any 'obscene . . . book, pamphlet, picture,

12. See Sutherland, Statutory Construction, §§51.01-51.06 (4th ed., Sands, 1973).
13. 338 U.S. 680 (1950).

motion-picture film, paper, letter, writing, print, or other matter of indecent character.' " The majority answered in the affirmative and upheld the conviction.

The three dissenting judges of course invoked the maxim about penal statutes, and the particular importance thereof in the field of freedom of expression.

> Our system of justice is based on the principle that criminal statutes shall be couched in language sufficiently clear to apprise people of the precise conduct that is prohibited. Judicial interpretation deviates from this salutary principle when statutory language is expanded to include conduct that Congress might have barred, but did not, by the language it used. . . . The reluctance of courts to expand the coverage of criminal statutes is particularly important where, as here, the statute results in censorship.

The dissenters further invoked the "ejusdem generis" maxim, though not referring to it as such, when they complained that while the statute's specific list of indecent articles "applied only to articles that people could read or see," the majority "now adds to it articles capable of use to produce sounds that people can hear."

The majority's response to these positions was couched in these words: "We are aware that this is a criminal statute and must be strictly construed. This means that no offense may be created except by the words of Congress used in their usual and ordinary sense." Quoting from an earlier Supreme Court opinion, they said, "while penal statutes are narrowly construed, this does not require rejection of that sense of the words which best harmonizes with the context and the end in view."

The "ejusdem generis" maxim also received short shrift: "We think that to apply the rule of *ejusdem generis* to the present case would be 'to defeat the obvious purpose of legislation.' The obvious purpose . . . was to prevent the channels of interstate commerce from being used to disseminate any matter that, in its essential nature, communicates obscene, lewd, lascivious or filthy ideas." The statute was intended to be a broad one, for it included other prohibitions, such as those against interstate shipment of contraceptives. "Statutes are construed in their entire context. This is a comprehensive statute, which should not be constricted by a mechanical rule of construction."

Nor was there anything in the legislative history to indicate a congressional intent to limit the catchall clause

> to such indecent matter as is comprehended through the sense of sight. True, this statute was amended in 1920 to include "motion picture film." We are not persuaded that Congress, by adding motion-picture film to the specific provisions of the statute, evidenced an intent that obscene matter not specifically added was without the prohibition of

> the statute; nor do we think that Congress intended that only visual obscene matter was within the prohibition of the statute. The First World War gave considerable impetus to the making and distribution of motion-picture films. And in 1920 the public was considerably alarmed at the indecency of many of the films. It thus appears that with respect to this amendment, Congress was preoccupied with making doubly sure that motion-picture film was within the Act, and was concerned with nothing more or less.

The majority therefore applied the plain meaning of the catchall clause — though it was not applying a "plain meaning rule" in the sense of ignoring any evidences of legislative intent located outside the statutory words.

A further word on the majority's attitude toward the motion picture film amendment: Its attitude was analogous to a rejection of an "express mention, implied exclusion" argument. That is, in cases in which that maxim is rejected, you are likely to find the Court assuming that the legislature was merely giving examples, or — as the majority says in this *Alpers* case — was making "doubly sure" about the matters expressly mentioned.

The "doubly sure" line may also be taken in cases in which a court wants to apply a law to conduct occurring prior to an amendment that explicitly covers that type of conduct. The inference from the amendment, that the conduct was not covered prior to the amendment, may be rejected by this reasoning: The legislature by its amendment wanted to "emphasize" or "clarify" or make "unmistakable" or "doubly sure of" the coverage. Consider for instance, Coplon v. United States, in which the District of Columbia Court of Appeals was dealing with the FBI's power to make an arrest without a warrant of a Department of Justice employee suspected of espionage. Another circuit court had already ruled that the statute governing FBI arrests did not authorize arrests without a warrant for felonies in the presence of the officer. Congress had then amended the statute so as to expressly grant such an authority. The situation presented to the District of Columbia court had arisen prior to the amendment, but the court refused to conclude that the fact of the amendment itself showed a lack of arresting authority prior to its passage. The amendment had simply "made unmistakable what we think was true before revision. . . ."[14]

But if you suspect that a court must have often, indeed usually, concluded that a legislative amendment — in the course of a bill's passage, or after its adoption — did reflect an intent to *change* the previously existing bill or statute, you are of course right.[15]

While on the subject of permissible interpretive inferences from

14. Coplon v. U.S., 191 F.2d 749, 755 (D.C. Cir. 1951). See also U.S. v. Lowden, 308 U.S. 225, 239 (1939); State v. Boliski, 156 Wis. 78, 145 N.W. 368 (1914).

15. See, e.g., U.S. v. Plesha, 352 U.S. 202, 208 (1957).

what goes on in the legislature, I think you should know about this additional facet of the subject though I cannot stop to elaborate on it: There are numerous cases on the issue of whether the court can infer legislative approval of an administrative[16] or judicial interpretation of a statute from the fact that (a) the legislature did nothing to change it; or (b) during the process of passage of the statute, or after its enactment, the effort to adopt a view contrary to the interpretation in question died in a legislative committee or was rejected by vote of one or both houses of the legislature. Naturally, the vote of both houses against the opposing view is much more likely to be taken as approval of the interpretation in question than are the other kinds of legislative action or inaction mentioned. But you will find that cases go both ways in each of these categories — simply because an inference of legislative approval is sometimes outweighed by opposing considerations present in the particular case.[17]

Now to develop a little further some aspects of the interpretation problems common to the four cases I have summarized as well as *Nappier*.

4. Problems in the "Plain Meaning" Rule

1. First, a reminder of some ambiguities in the plain-meaning rule. I have already referred to the point that a plain or unambiguous meaning generally seems to coincide with a "literal" and with an "ordinary" meaning, but that given a divergence between the latter two, the Supreme Court in the stolen airplane case chose what it conceived to be the ordinary meaning.

Another issue that may cause confusion is the relation of a plain-meaning interpretation to a choice between *narrow or broad* interpretation. I think we may tend to associate a literal or ordinary meaning with the *broader* interpretation. This association did indeed occur in the *Holy Trinity Church* case (the rejected plain meaning of "labor or service of any kind" would have *included* the minister's services), in *Caminetti* (the plain meaning of "any other immoral purpose" was

16. Apart from any question of legislative approval of an administrative interpretation through legislative inaction or legislative reenactment or continued appropriations, an administrative interpretation of a statute is often given considerable deference by a court, depending on the circumstances. See Chap. 1, *supra* at n.381.

17. See Kernochan, Statutory Interpretation: An Outline of Method, 3 Dalhousie L.J. 333, 359-360 (1976); Paulsen, ed., Legal Institutions, Today and Tomorrow 11-15 (Breitel), 45-48 (Hart) (1959); Reynolds, Judicial Process, §§5.21, 5.22 (1980); Sutherland, *supra* n.1, §§48.18, 49.10.

adopted and held to *include* noncommercialized immorality), and in *Alpers* (the plain meaning of "other matter of indecent character" was adopted and held to *include* obscene phonograph records). Yet this association was not true in *McBoyle* — where the ordinary meaning of "vehicle" in the phrase "any other self-propelled vehicle not designed for running on rails" was adopted and held to *exclude* airplanes. Nor was it true in our *Nappier* case in which the plain meaning of "name" as adopted by the district court and rejected by the court of appeals gave the *narrower* coverage.

Another erroneous association would be between the plain-meaning rule and the concept of "strict" construction. There is, no doubt, a sense in which a literal construction is a strict one. But in the field of statutory interpretation the term "strict" is generally used in the sense of *narrow*. Thus when we say a penal statute is to be construed strictly, we mean construed to give the narrower coverage that would favor the defendant, if such a construction is reasonably possible. So "strict" should not be used to characterize a literal construction via the plain-meaning rule, since (as we have already seen) such a construction sometimes yields the narrower, sometimes the broader interpretation.

Causing still another confusion is the fact that the rule is formulated in different ways by different courts, and sometimes even by the same court. Thus, a court might say: When the statutory language is plain, the court does not look beyond the statute[18] to legislative history or other extrinsic material for evidence of intent or purpose;[19] or the "does not" may be replaced by "cannot" (making it stronger) or by "need not" (making it weaker). The court may or may not include in the statement of the rule the exception that it in fact would recognize if the appropriate situation existed — namely, one in which a plain meaning leads to an absurd or unreasonable (or "wholly unreasonable," or "grossly impractical") result. A rule recognizing the existence of such an exception has been called "the golden rule."[20]

The question of what constitutes "extrinsic" material does not usually receive as strict an answer as the statement of the rule may suggest. That is, even when the exception is *not* being applied, a court often allows itself to look at *some* matters extrinsic to the words being construed, in order to assure itself that the meaning *is* plain. Included can be the relation of such words not only to other parts of the statute but also to other statutes, to prior decisions, and to a statutory purpose

18. Or it might say that when the meaning is plain, there is "no need for construction or interpretation."

19. Or it might say that when the meaning is plain, the court need not concern itself with intent at all. See below at n.48.

20. See Dickerson, The Interpretation and Application of Statutes 230, 231 n.43 (1975).

that is obvious, as distinct from one that would have to be hunted in the legislative history.

2. What can be said *in favor* of the plain-meaning rule? As good a statement as any was made by Justice Jackson, concurring in the 1951 case of Schwegmann Bros. v. Calvert Distillers Corp.[21] and protesting against the majority's unwillingness to rest the decision on the clear words of the statute, i.e., without reference to congressional debates and other items of legislative history:

> Resort to legislative history is only justified where the face of the Act is inescapably ambiguous, and then I think we should not go beyond Committee reports, which presumably are well considered and carefully prepared. . . . The Rules of the House and Senate, with the sanction of the Constitution, require three readings of an Act in each House before final enactment. That is intended, I take it, to make sure that each House knows what it is passing and passes what it wants, and that what is enacted was formally reduced to writing. . . . Moreover, it is only the words of the bill that have presidential approval, where that approval is given. It is not to be supposed that, in signing a bill, the President endorses the whole Congressional Record. . . .
>
> Moreover, there are practical reasons why we should accept whenever possible the meaning which an enactment reveals on its face. Laws are intended for all of our people to live by; and the people go to law offices to learn what their rights under those laws are. Here is a controversy which affects every little merchant in many states. Aside from a few offices in the larger cities, the materials of a legislative history are not available to the lawyer who can afford neither the cost of acquisition, the cost of housing, nor the cost of repeatedly examining the whole congressional history. Moreover, if he could, he would not know any way of anticipating what would impress enough members of the Court to be controlling. . . .

Another point can be added to the defense of the plain-meaning rule. As we have seen, it contains explicitly or implicitly within itself a reasonable qualification. When the *Caminetti* majority stated the rule, they included the limitation that the plain meaning must not be one "leading to absurd or wholly impracticable consequences."

3. What can be said *against* the plain-meaning rule?

(a) To begin with, it deliberately cuts off from judicial consideration even the clearest evidence from extrinsic sources, such as legislative history, of what was the so-called legislative intent on the question in dispute. Cogent reasons may exist for doing so, as is argued in the above-quoted opinion of Justice Jackson. But the evidentiary sacrifice involved is considerable.

(b) A more important difficulty stems from ambiguities within the

21. 341 U.S. 384, 395 (1951).

rule. We may not be as confused about the rule as was Lord Mildew (in A. P. Herbert's "The Uncommon Law") who paraphrased it as: "If Parliament doesn't mean what it says, it must say so." Plenty of cause remains, though, for befuddlement, ranging from some preliminary confusions already dealt with to the deeper ambiguity now under consideration. A real uncertainty surrounds the question as to when the conditions exist for application of the rule: When are the statutory words *so clear* as to bar the court from looking beyond the words to the statute's underlying policy and legislative history? This dearth of surety has led one writer to refer to the "ambiguity of unambiguous statutes." That is, there are plenty of instances in which, in spite of a rather obvious ambiguity on the face of the statute, attested to in the opinions of a divided court, one group of judges within the divided court is unwilling to view the *degree* of ambiguity as sufficient to make the plain-meaning rule inapplicable; hence they proclaim that the statute is unambiguous.

For example, in Packard Motor Co. v. NLRB[22] in 1947, the Supreme Court had to decide whether a plant foreman was an "employee" within the meaning of the National Labor Relations Act, so that a union of foremen would be entitled to rights of organization, collective bargaining, etc. under that Act. The Act declared that "[t]he term 'employee' shall include any employee. . . . " This definition looked in the direction of coverage. But "employer" was also defined: "The term 'employer' includes any person acting in the interest of an employer, directly or indirectly. . . . " Read together, the definitions at least created an ambiguity. The three dissenting Justices resolved the ambiguity by saying foremen were not covered as employees, and drew support from the absence — in the entire statute and its legislative history — of any reference to the problem of unionized supervisory personnel. They drew further support from the fact that certain other statutes in defining "employee" had specifically included subordinate officials. Yet the majority, speaking through Justice Jackson, read the statutory words as covering foremen, and solemnly intoned, "There is . . . no ambiguity in the Act to be clarified by resort to legislative history. . . . "

(c) Still another uncertainty remains as to when the conditions exist for application of the rule: When does the *exception* (quoted earlier from the *Caminetti* opinion) come into play so as to make the rule inapplicable when "absurd or wholly impracticable consequences" result? Practically the same question can be posed thus: When does the rule of the *Holy Trinity Church* case come into play? For that case counseled rejection of a plain or literal meaning "when a consideration

22. 330 U.S. 485 (1947).

of the whole legislation or of the circumstances surrounding its enactment, or of the absurd results which follow from" that meaning "makes it unreasonable to believe that the legislator intended to include the particular act." This of course was also the approach of the court of appeals in the *Nappier* case when it looked at the purposes of the statute and thought that such purposes would be frustrated by giving a literal reading to the word "name." In other words, in any case on the plain-meaning rule that is at all debatable, we are faced with a choice between that rule and its exception (or the *Holy Trinity Church* rule), and are given no precise way of choosing between opposite rules.

As a matter of fact, this point as to uncertainty over whether the rule or its opposite applies is even stronger than I have so far made it. There is in fact an opposite rule *additional* to the opposite rule just mentioned. What I have in mind is a rule that is an even more direct negation of the plain-meaning rule — an actual *denial* that a plain meaning on the face of the statute *ever* bars the interpreting court from looking beyond the face of the statute. Seven years before Justice Jackson refused in the *Packard Motor* case to look beyond the words of the National Labor Relations Act because the meaning of "employee" was plain, the Supreme Court had said in construing "employee" under the Motor Carrier Act:

> Frequently, . . . even when the plain meaning did not produce absurd results but merely an unreasonable one "plainly at variance with the policy of the legislation as a whole," this Court has followed that purpose, rather than the literal words. When aid to construction of the meaning of words, as used in the statute, is available, there certainly can be no "rule of law" which forbids its use, however clear the words may appear on "superficial examination."[23]

And in the same year, 1940, the Court said:

> It would be anomalous to close our minds to persuasive evidence of intention on the ground that reasonable men could not differ as to the meaning of the words. Legislative materials may be without probative value, or contradictory, or ambiguous, it is true, and in such cases will not be permitted to control the customary meaning of words or overcome rules of syntax or construction found by experience to be workable; they can scarcely be deemed to be incompetent or irrelevant. . . . The meaning to be ascribed to an Act of Congress can only be derived from a considered weighing of every relevant aid to construction.[24]

These 1940 cases were buttressed by a strong 1976 Supreme Court case that described as "error" the Court of Appeals refusal, on the

23. U.S. v. American Trucking Assn., 310 U.S. 534, 543-544 (1940).
24. U.S. v. Dickerson, 310 U.S. 554, 562 (1940). See also Harrison v. Northern Trust Co., 317 U.S. 476, 479 (1942).

ground of plain meaning, to look at legislative history.[25] Yet this case was ignored in some subsequent cases invoking the rule again.[26]

Thus, there are Supreme Court cases (1) applying the rule — sometimes the main rule, sometimes its exception;[27] and (2) rejecting the rule by declaring the Court can always look at legislative history or other relevant extrinsic aids.[28] In addition, in many instances the Court has neither applied nor rejected the rule but simply ignored it — i.e., it has, without first noting the existence of any ambiguity, considered extrinsic aids, and on that basis has adopted a non-literal meaning.[29] Such extraordinary inconsistency no doubt produces more flexibility both for the Court and the advocates. At the same time, though, we surely have here an example of the judicial process at its worst.

The sum of all the above arguments creates a persuasive argument against the plain-meaning rule. A number of scholars, indeed, have urged its abandonment.[30] Not that they believe courts should not pay primary attention to the statutory words; or that courts should not recognize the merit in a party's showing that he had reasonably relied on the words and hence should not be penalized for so doing. Rather, I think these scholars believe there should not be a cut-off — occurring regardless of reliance, and regardless of whether some Court members *do not* find the meaning "plain" — of extrinsic evidence of intent or purpose.

5. Problems in the Rule on Penal Statutes

What now of the rule on strict construction of penal statutes? Again there is something to be said *for* the policy underlying the rule: When something as drastic as a penal sanction is involved, it makes sense to say that of two reasonable alternative interpretations, the one favoring the defendant should be preferred in the absence of strong countervailing factors.

25. Train v. Colorado Pub. Interest Research Group, 426 U.S. 1, 9-10 (1976).

26. United Airlines v. McMann, 434 U.S. 192, 199 (1977); TVA v. Hill, 437 U.S. 153, 184 n.29 (1978).

27. In addition to the examples already discussed, see, e.g., Lake County v. Rollins, 130 U.S. 662, 670 (1889); U.S. v. Missouri Pac. Ry., 278 U.S. 269, 278 (1929); Commissioner v. Brown, 380 U.S. 563, 571 (1965).

28. See the *American Trucking, Dickerson, Harrison,* and *Colorado P.I.R.G.* cases *supra* in nn. 23, 24 & 25.

29. See the cases discussed in Jones, The Plain Meaning Rule and Extrinsic Aids in the Interpretation of Federal Statutes, 25 Wash. U.L.Q. 2, 12-20 (1939).

30. Jones, *id.* at 21-26; Murphy, Old Maxims Never Die: The "Plain Meaning Rule" and Statutory Interpretation in the "Modern" Federal Courts, 75 Colum. L. Rev. 1299, 1313-1317 (1975); Kernochan, Statutory Interpretation: An Outline of Method, 3 Dalhousie L.J. 333, 341-345 (1976).

But again we are left in doubt about when the rule will be applied. One source of the doubt is the existence and scope of these countervailing factors and the lack of any precise formula for weighing all the competing factors. Another source of doubt is the ambiguity of "penal." Criminal statutes, the prosecution under which entails criminal procedure and can result in a penalty of imprisonment and/or fine, would clearly qualify. But there are civil sanctions, such as treble damages or property forfeitures or license revocations, that a particular court may or may not view as qualifying. Moreover, if one rule is that a penal statute is to be strictly construed, and another is that a remedial statute is to be broadly construed, how helpful can these rules be when a court concludes that a statute is partly remedial and partly penal?[31]

There is still another ambivalence: The fact that a court has determined a statute to be penal for one purpose (such as whether the time period under a separate statute of limitations applying to "penal" actions should apply to this case) does not mean that the same court will necessarily view the same statute in another case as penal for another purpose (such as strict statutory construction).[32] Indeed, this kind of variability in the determination of whether a statute is penal is illustrated by the court of appeals opinion in the *Nappier* case. Here again are the court's words:

> In South Carolina the penal aspect of the statute does not require an interpretation so rigid as to strip its wording of its plain connotation. Carolina Amusement Co. v. Martin, 236 S.C. 558, 115 S.E.2d 273 (1960), cert. denied, 367 U.S. 904 . . . (1961); State v. Firemen's Ins. Co., 164 S.C. 313, 162 S.E. 334 (1931). This is certainly sound construction *when, as here, the statute is only employed to provide civil redress.* McKenzie v. Peoples Baking Co., 205 S.C. 149, 31 S.E.2d 154 (1944).[33] (Emphasis added.)

Thus, the court was suggesting that however rigid the interpretation might have to be in a criminal prosecution under the statute, it need not be that rigid in a civil suit for damages at common law, when the statute was involved in only an auxiliary way.

Notice also that the first sentence of the quotation, as well as the cases cited in support, illustrate anew that the rule contains qualifications and does not necessarily result in giving a penal statute the narrower of alternative interpretations. One of the cited cases puts it this way, quoting from a legal encyclopedia: " 'The rule that a penal statute must be strictly construed does not prevent the courts from calling to

31. The courts are not agreed on how to handle this problem. See, e.g., Sutherland, Statutory Construction, §60.04 (4th ed., Sands, 1974).

32. Compare Schiffman Bros. v. Texas Co., 196 F.2d 695 (7th Cir. 1952), with Roseland v. Phister Mfg. Co., 125 F.2d 417 (7th Cir. 1942).

33. 322 F.2d 502, 504 (4th Cir. 1963).

their aid all the other rules of construction and giving each its appropriate scope, and is not violated by giving the words of the statute a reasonable meaning according to the sense in which they were intended, and disregarding captious objections and even the demands of exact grammatical propriety.' "[34] Remember, in this connection, that *Caminetti* and *Alpers* were criminal prosecutions under the Mann Act and the federal obscenity statute, yet in both cases the broader interpretations of statutory coverage were adopted.

I should mention, finally, the fact that in more recent decades, the Supreme Court seems to have preferred to talk about the present problem in terms of the "rule of lenity" in construing criminal statutes. The difference in the meaning of this terminology and the terminology of the earlier cases on "strict construction of penal statutes" is unclear, though perhaps the more recent cases put greater emphasis on the idea that ambiguity must exist before the rule can be applied.[35]

Our discussion until now shows, if it shows anything, that the two rules figuring in the *Nappier* case (the plain-meaning rule and the rule as to penal statutes) as well as other rules encountered along the way, such as ejusdem generis, are not by themselves conclusive. They have qualifications; they may have opposites; they must be considered along with all other relevant factors before the Court's final decision is reached. I shall return to this theme again in the ensuing background note.

B. Background Note: A Further Word on Statutory Interpretation; The Search for Legislative Intent or Purpose

Having explored the nature of the interpretation issues that were central in the *Nappier* case, I should like to now look at the problem of interpretation against a somewhat broader background.

1. You will have noted that the interpreting court generally assumes a subordinate power relationship to the legislature. That is, it plays the subservient role of discovering and effectuating the "legislative intent." After all, the lawmaking or legislative power is lodged by federal and state constitutions in the legislature.

34. State v. Firemen's Ins. Co., 164 S.C. 313, 162 S.E. 334, 338 (1931), quoting 25 Ruling Case Law 1085 (1919).

35. See Annot., Supreme Court's Views As To The "Rule of Lenity" In The Construction of Criminal Statutes, 62 L. Ed. 2d 827 (1981).

An exception is those cases in which the legislature itself has made rather clear that the *court* is to exercise the dominant role. This happens, for instance, when a legislature deliberately enacts a vague provision — perhaps because it feels it does not know enough about the subject to be precise, or because conditions are expected to change too rapidly for a rigid standard, or because legislative compromise phrased in indeterminate language was the only way to get the statute passed. A statute prohibiting "unreasonable speed" rather than setting a specific maximum is one example. The Sherman Act prohibitions against monopolization and restraint of trade, with the courts left to develop the precise meaning of these standards, are other examples. In these instances, the court's freedom operates within elastic boundaries, although those boundaries have of course been laid down by the legislature. Still, these limits must not be *so* vague that any attempt to penalize conduct on the basis of them would violate "due process of law";[36] or *so* loose in the control of an agency's or court's discretion that the constitutional restriction against undue delegation of legislative power would be violated.[37]

2. In view of the basic premise of legislative supremacy, it is not surprising that the overwhelming number of court opinions will be found talking in terms of the overriding goal of effectuating "legislative intent" — though sometimes "purpose" is used instead of, or interchangeably with, "intent." Justice Frankfurter once said he always used "purpose" instead of "intent." Why the distinction?

In the typical appellate case of statutory interpretation, the court is dealing with a specific situation that the legislature never thought of. When Congress passed the Alien Contract Labor Act, it had not thought specifically about whether a New York church bringing over a minister from England would be covered; when it passed the Motor Vehicle Theft Act, it had not thought specifically about whether a stolen airplane would be covered; when the South Carolina legislature passed its 1902 law on publication of rape victims' names, it had not thought specifically about whether television broadcasts would be covered that allegedly identified without expressly naming the victim. To speak of a legislative intent in the sense of a conscious desire to have a specific situation treated in a particular way would therefore be to speak of a fiction. To avoid that fictional aspect of the search for legislative intent,[38] a court may regard itself as operating more realistically

36. See Library of Congress, The Constitution of the United States of America — Analysis and Interpretation 1154-1158, 1440-1443 (S. Doc. No. 92-82, 92d Cong., 2d Sess. (1973)) and 1978 Supp.; Annot., 96 L. Ed. 374 (1952); 40 L. Ed. 2d 823 (1974).

37. This is the issue discussed in Chap. 1, *supra* at nn. 368-371.

38. There is another fictional aspect to be dealt with, centering about *whose* intent: How can we talk about the intent of the *legislature* or even of the majority

by asking itself not "Did the legislature intend to cover this situation?" but rather this question: "Considering the *general* policy objective or *purpose* of the statute as shown by its provisions, its history, and other extrinsic aids, what *would* the legislature *probably* have said of the specific situation if it had thought of it?" Such a distinction between "intent" and "purpose" makes some sense, though, as I have said, you will find some judges using the terms interchangeably.

And the indicated conditional, subjunctive, or hypothetical way of talking about intent (which might be called "hypothetical specific intent") can be found in the writing of a number of scholars and jurists — including Aristotle,[39] Plowden,[40] J.C. Gray,[41] Justice Cardozo,[42] Justice Reed,[43] Judge Learned Hand,[44] and Judge Leventhal.[45] Some judges have disapproved of that mode of expression, but seem to have done so in cases in which they thought the language was too *clear* to justify speculation about hypothetical intent.[46]

3. But in spite of the prevailing judicial emphasis on intent, and the frequent assertion that *the* task of statutory interpretation is to discover the legislative intent, we know that judicial practice *sometimes belies the assertion.*

(a) Thus, judicial principles like the plain-meaning rule or strict

who voted for the bill, when the constituent members do not necessarily have the same situation in mind, and in fact the courts seem to pay attention to the intent of legislative sponsors, draftsmen, and reporting committees? One response has been that the legislature has in effect delegated the initial intent formation to sponsors, draftsmen, and committees, and has adopted that intent by its vote approving the bill. See Breitel, The Courts in Lawmaking, in Paulsen, ed., Legal Institutions Today and Tomorrow 27 (1959); Dickerson, *supra* n.20 at 71-72; SEC v. Robert Collier & Co., 76 F.2d 939, 941 (2d Cir. 1935). This theory, however, is not fully satisfactory since the intent of the sponsors, committees, and draftsmen is not necessarily uniform and easy to ascertain; nor can we assume that even *they* had thought of every specific situation before the court; nor that their intent was *in fact* always concurred in by the majority of voting legislators.

39. Aristotle, Ethics, Book V, chap. 10, fol. 1137, lines 12-28, quoted in Hand, The Bill of Rights 18 (1964).

40. Plowden, vol. 2, at 459, 467, quoted in Hand, *id.* at 20.

41. Gray, The Nature and Sources of Law 165 (1909).

42. Burnet v. Guggenheim, 288 U.S. 280, 285 (1933).

43. Vermilya-Brown Co. v. Connell, 335 U.S. 377, 387-388 (1948).

44. Hand, *supra* n.39 at 18-22; Hand, J., in U.S. v. Klinger, 199 F.2d 645, 648 (2d Cir. 1952), *aff'd per curiam,* 345 U.S. 979 (1953). See also Hand, How Far Is A Judge Free in Rendering A Decision, in Dilliard, ed., The Spirit of Liberty 106 (2d ed. 1953); Hand, Thomas Walter Swan, *id.* at 217, reprinted from 57 Yale L.J. 167, 171 (1947).

45. International Harvester Co. v. Ruckelshaus, 478 F.2d 615, 648 (D.C. Cir. 1973).

46. Jackson, J. in Western Union Tel. Co. v. Lenroot, 323 U.S. 490, 501 (1945); Burger, C.J. in TVA v. Hill, 437 U.S. 153, 185 (1978); Frankfurter, Some Reflections On the Reading of Statutes, 47 Colum. L. Rev. 527, 539 (1947). Frankfurter thought that purpose was to be preferred to intent as the focus, and especially preferred to a hypothetical intent, which he thought made the inquiry more subjective and speculative.

construction of penal statutes can operate to defeat clear evidence of intent. If the statutory words seem as a matter of general common sense, or ordinary meaning, to support an inference in one direction but the legislative history addressing the *specific* situation points specifically in the opposite direction, the latter may be prevented by the above principles from prevailing. We have seen this result in *Caminetti;* it was also strikingly evident in the *Acker* tax liability case.[47]

(b) In these instances the judicial principles had the effect of *outweighing* the stronger evidence (stronger because it dealt with specific intent). Sometimes the principles can result in *ignoring* the evidence of intent. This can happen when an occasional court formulates the plain-meaning rule in terms of not looking for legislative intent at all unless the words are ambiguous (instead of in terms of *confining the search for legislative intent* to the statute unless the words are ambiguous.)[48]

(c) Evidence of intent can also be outweighed by a court's concern for statutory *purpose*. "Intent" answers the question "What did the legislature want to do with certain situations or classes of situations?" whereas "purpose" answers the question "*Why* did the legislature want to do it (what policies, goals, anticipated consequences motivated the legislature)?" True, purpose is usually invoked as a guide to discovering intent, so that in case of conflict, intent would prevail; but there are unusual cases in which purpose triumphs over an intent that was mistaken, i.e., the legislature had in a particular provision apparently forgotten the basic statutory purpose.[49] The unusual triumph of purpose over intent is to be distinguished from the less unusual triumph of purpose over a plain meaning that leads to an absurd or wholly unreasonable result (as in the *Holy Trinity Church* case). The latter triumph is generally regarded as *effectuating* an intent that was obscured by the plain meaning.

(d) We have already seen 'that the legislature itself may deny a primary role to its own intent by a delegation of discretion to an agency

47. Commissioner v. Acker, 361 U.S. 87 (1959). In this case, a Senate Committee Report, a Conference Committee Report, and a Treasury Regulation had embodied the Internal Revenue Commissioner's interpretation of the tax law, yet the Court majority ruled against the interpretation. This rejection of traditionally strong evidence of specific intent was based on a natural inference that could be made from the general statutory words plus the familiar maxim that when a penalty is involved, the statute should be construed strictly in the direction of penalty avoidance.

48. See, e.g., In re Hiliker, 9 F. Supp. 948, 950 (S.D. Calif. 1935); Miller v. Wadkins, 31 Wis. 2d 281, 284-285, 142 N.W.2d 855 (1966); Wisconsin Envir. Decade v. Public Serv. Commn., 81 Wis. 2d 344, 350, 260 N.W.2d 712 (1978). (There are other Wisconsin cases using the more usual formulation. See, e.g., Ahlgrimm v. State Elections Bd., 82 Wis. 2d 585, 590, 263 N.W.2d 152 (1978)). I have not noticed illustrations of the unusual type of formulation in modern United States Supreme Court opinions.

49. This is illustrated by the *Abilene Cotton Oil* case, *supra* n.7.

or to the courts — though a court may find certain constitutional or statutory limits to the delegation.

(e) Finally, intent may play *no* role if the court concludes that the evidence of intent permits no clear inference one way or the other. In this situation, the court is forced to engage in a "creative" or "lawmaking" role, though somewhat limited by inferences of probable intent drawn from other sources in the legal order beyond the particular statute.[50]

4. I have talked about "purpose" rather tangentially up to now; and the subject should now be more directly faced. An emphasis on purpose was a distinctive mark of sixteenth-century jurisprudence, as exemplified in "the mischief rule" announced by Lord Coke's celebrated *Heydon's Case,* and also in Plowden and others.[51] While that emphasis waned, it has never been eclipsed, and certainly scholars in modern times have almost uniformly accepted it. One writer, terming purpose "the primary and most usual guide," refers to a "swelling chorus of scholars and judges in favor of purpose interpretation."[52] The number of scholars who can be cited in support is indeed impressive[53] — and the Law Commissions of England and Scotland joined their ranks in 1969 by endorsing a new emphasis on the "general legislative purpose underlying" the provision being interpreted.[54] Of course

50. See Landis, A Note On "Statutory Interpretation," 43 Harv. L. Rev. 886, 893 (1930); Dickerson, *supra* n.20 at 18-21, 22-28 & chap. 13.

51. Heydon's Case, 3 Co. Rep. 7a at 7b, 76 E.R. 637 at 638 (Ex. 1585); 2 Plowden 459, 467, quoted in Hand, The Bill of Rights 20 (1964); Radin, Early Statutory Interpretation in England, 38 Ill. L. Rev. 16, 39-40 (1943). According to *Heydon's case,* the court is to interpret the statute in the light of the "mischief" at which it was aimed, the judge's duty being to make the interpretation that will "suppress the mischief and advance the remedy . . . according to the true intent of the makers of the Act, *pro bono publico.*"

52. Kernochan, Statutory Interpretation: An Outline of Method, 3 Dalhousie L.J. 333, 336 (1976).

53. McDonnell, Purposive Interpretation of the Uniform Commercial Code: Some Implications for Jurisprudence, 126 U. Pa. L. Rev. 795, 853-855 (1978); Kernochan, *supra* n.52 at 333; Bishin, The Law-Finders: An Essay in Statutory Interpretation, 38 S. Calif. L. Rev. 1, 29 (1965); Witherspoon, The Essential Focus of Statutory Interpretation, 36 Ind. L.J. 423, 428-429, 433-436, 441 (1961); *Id.,* Administrative Discretion to Determine Statutory Meaning: "The Middle Road": I, 40 Tex. L. Rev. 751, 765, 785, 790-791 (1962); Hart & Sacks, The Legal Process 1411, 1413-1417 (1958, mimeo); Fuller, Positivism and Fidelity to Law — A Reply to Professor Hart, 71 Harv. L. Rev. 630, 661-669 (1958); Ekelöf, Teleological Construction of Statutes, 2 Scandinavian Stud. in Law 77 (1958); Frankfurter, Some Reflections On the Reading of Statutes, 47 Colum. L. Rev. 527, 533, 543 (1947); Corry, Administrative Law and the Interpretation of Statutes, 1 U. Toronto L.J. 286, 290, 293 (1947); Jones, Statutory Doubts and Legislative Intention, 40 Colum. L. Rev. 957, 972-974 (1940); *Id.,* Extrinsic Aids In the Federal Courts, 25 Iowa L. Rev. 737, 757-764 (1940); DeSloveere, Extrinsic Aids In the Interpretation of Statutes, 88 U. Pa. L. Rev. 527, 538 (1940); Davies, The Interpretation of Statutes in the Light of Their Policy By the English Courts, 35 Colum. L. Rev. 519 (1935); Landis, *supra* n.50 at 891, 892 (1930).

54. The Law Commission and the Scottish Law Commission, Statutory Interpretation 48-49, par. 80(c), par. 81(b); 51, §2(a) (1969).

eminent American judges, among them Holmes,[55] Hand,[56] and Jackson,[57] can be quoted in a similar vein.

But there are difficulties: The evidence of purpose may be ambiguous, so much so that both parties may be found invoking it.[58] Purposes may sometimes at least be no easier to discover than intent,[59] and often appear multiple and conflicting.[60] An alleged purpose may be given less weight when the statute was drawn as a compromise between strongly supported countervailing policies.[61] And because of different purposes of statutory provisions, the same words in different provisions (of the same or different statutes) may have strikingly different meanings; or the same statute may be given two opposite characterizations (e.g., substantive and procedural; penal and remedial) depending on the purpose context. Courts, including the Supreme Court, have recognized this phenomenon.[62]

Hart and Sacks have stressed two limits on the use of the purpose standard: A purpose interpretation must not result in meanings that the words "will not bear," and must not "violate an established policy of clear statement" (referring to situations in which the law's policy is to require a particularly high level of clarity, as in the case of penal statutes).[63] Still, as we have seen, there are times when a court is willing to deviate, and even accept meanings opposite to ordinary usage (e.g., "shall" meaning "may," "services of any kind" meaning "services of some kinds") when the evidence of purpose is strong enough, and hardship or unfairness to the litigant is weak enough.

5. Both "intent" and "purpose" focus on the "sending" end of the legislative communication. A third concept, "meaning," focuses on the "receiving" end. We have already encountered one form of the meaning standard in discussing the plain-meaning rule. A broader form than the plain-meaning rule — one that is not focused on plainness of mean-

55. Holmes, J. in U.S. v. Whitridge, 197 U.S. 135, 143 (1905), and as Circuit Judge in Johnson v. U.S., 163 F.2d 30, 32 (1st Cir. 1908).

56. Hand, J. in Cabell v. Markham, 148 F.2d 737, 739 (2d Cir. 1945); Cawley v. U.S. 272 F.2d 443, 445 (2d Cir. 1959); and as lecturer in The Bill of Rights 19 (1964).

57. Jackson, J. in SEC v. Joiner Leasing Corp., 320 U.S. 344, 350-351 (1943).

58. See, e.g., City of Milwaukee v. Department of I.L.H.R., 80 Wis. 2d 445, 453-455, 259 N.W.2d 118 (1977).

59. See MacCallum, Legislative Intent, 75 Yale L.J. 754, 780 (1966); Dickerson, *supra* n.20 at 91-92; but *cf.* McDonnell, *supra* n.53 at 841.

60. See McDonnell, *supra* n.53 at 847-851.

61. U.S. v. Sisson, 399 U.S. 267, 297-298 (1970).

62. Atlantic Cleaners & Dyers v. U.S., 286 U.S. 427, 433-434 (1943); Civil Aeronautics Bd. v. Delta Airlines, 367 U.S. 316, 328 (1961); Grant v. McAuliffe, 41 Cal. 2d 859, 264 P.2d 944, 948 (1953); Matczak v. Mathews, 250 Wis. 1, 5, 60 N.W.2d 352 (1953). For analysis of the phenomenon, see Mermin, Functionalism, Definition and the Problem of Contextual Ambiguity, in Hubien, ed., Legal Reasoning 319-327 (Brussels, 1971).

63. Hart & Sacks, The Legal Process 1412-1413 (mimeo, 1958).

ing as the crucial element, though the same result is usually achieved — is in terms of meaning-to-the-typical (or reasonable)-reader. This approach has been highlighted in Sands's fourth edition of Sutherland on Statutory Construction (the standard American reference) as an *alternative* to the approach in terms of intent and purpose.[64] He thinks the cases are tending in that direction, and that the approach is impliedly endorsed by the many cases expressing preference for ordinary or dictionary meanings. He refers to Holmes, Jackson, and Frankfurter as supporting the approach.

However, Holmes's brief essay along this line[65] is contradicted by his expressed attitude in judicial opinions;[66] the views of Jackson[67] and Frankfurter[68] are similarly contradicted by some of their judicial opinions;[69] and many cases seem to be using a "meaning" criterion as a way of arriving at, rather than as a substitute for, legislative intent. Courts continue to state overwhelmingly that the job of statutory interpretation is to discover the legislative intent. The Constitution, when the principle of legislative supremacy is considered, seems to require continuance of that attitude — but difficulty is created by constitutional arguments on the other side.[70]

64. Sutherland, Statutes and Statutory Construction, §§45.07, 45.08 (4th ed., Sands, 1973).

65. Holmes, Theory of Legal Interpretation, 12 Harv. L. Rev. 417, 419 (1899), reprinted in Holmes, Collected Legal Papers 203 (1920).

66. Olmstead v. U.S., 277 U.S. 438, 469 (1928) (dissenting opinion); Boston Sand & Gravel v. U.S., 278 U.S. 41, 48 (1928); as Circuit Judge in Johnson v. U.S. 163 F.2d 30, 32 (1st Cir. 1908).

67. Jackson, The Meaning of Statutes: What Congress Says Or What the Court Says, 34 A.B.A.J. 535 (1948); Schwegmann Bros. v. Calvert Distillers Corp., 341 U.S. 384, 395-397 (1951) (concurring opinion).

68. Frankfurter, Some Reflections On the Reading of Statutes, 47 Colum. L. Rev. 527, 538 (1947).

69. Jackson, J. dissenting in the following: U.S. ex rel Marcus v. Hess, 317 U.S. 537, 556 (1943); Federal Crop Ins. Corp. v. Merrill, 332 U.S. 380, 386 (1947); Jewell Ridge Coal Corp. v. Local 6167, UMW, 325 U.S. 161, 177 (1945).

Frankfurter, J. dissenting in: Commissioner v. Acker, 361 U.S. 87, 95 (1958); U.S. v. Monia, 317 U.S. 424, 431 (1943). Further, while his 1947 essay *supra* n.68 did reject the intent standard, what he substituted for it (i.e., purpose) focuses, as does intent, on the sending rather than receiving end of the communication.

70. Thus, Sands finds some support for his view in the constitutional due process requirement that statutes be not unduly vague. It is true that a person is not to be subjected to punishment or liability when the statutory requirement had not been clearly enough communicated. But this can function as an outer limit to the application of an intent standard. It need not mean that *all* types of statutes in all circumstances must be interpreted as the typical reader would interpret them.

Dickerson makes the following constitutional argument. Underlying the grant of legislative supremacy is an implied condition: that the legislative will is to be expressed and interpreted in accordance with *accepted standards of language use;* so the court is to search for the meaning to the typical reader, reading the provisions in their proper context (this being the best working approximation to actual intent, which he says is unknowable). Dickerson, *supra* n.20 at 10-11, 36-38. One might object to thus freezing the meaning-to-the-typical-reader approach into the Constitu-

6. Our difficulties in interpretation are aggravated by the fact that principles or maxims such as the plain-meaning rule and the rule on penal statutes are in fact quite numerous, and as in the case of both those "rules," can lead in opposite directions. You have seen that each of these rules sometimes carried the day and sometimes gave place. When the latter occurred, opposing considerations (and usually an opposing maxim) were available. Professor Karl Llewellyn once illustrated the pairing of these maxims by presenting a table of 28 "thrusts" and "parries" among the "canons of construction" used by state courts.[71] Sample selections from these are reproduced below, omitting his footnoted authorities.

CANONS OF CONSTRUCTION

Thrust	But	Parry
2. Statutes in derogation of the common law will not be extended by construction.		2. Such acts will be liberally construed if their nature is remedial.
4. Where a foreign statute which has received construction has been adopted, previous construction is adopted too.		4. It may be rejected where there is conflict with the obvious meaning of the statute or where the foreign decisions are unsatisfactory in reasoning or where the foreign interpretation is not in harmony with the spirit or policy of the laws of the adopting state.
5. Where various states have already adopted the statute, the parent state is followed.		5. Where interpretations of other states are inharmonious, there is no such restraint.
6. Statutes *in pari materia* (i.e., on the same subject matter) must be construed together.		6. A statute is not *in pari materia* if its scope and aim are distinct or where a legislative design to depart from the general purpose

tion, so that it would have to apply even to a case where (a) there is strong extrinsic evidence of contrary intent or purpose, *and* (b) there is no evidence of detrimental reliance on the typical or reasonable meaning. Dickerson makes a further constitutional argument that extrinsic aids like legislative history should not be used unless they meet implied constitutional conditions: that the typical reader has reasonable access to them and can reasonably assume they were taken into account by the authors of the legislation. *Id.* at 9-12. This position is more hard-line on extrinsic aids than usual. The Supreme Court and other courts now making a more free use of legislative history than he would allow clearly do not believe they are thereby violating any implied constitutional prohibitions.

71. See Llewellyn, Remarks On the Theory of Appellate Decision and the Rules or Canons About How Statutes Are To Be Construed, 3 Vand. L. Rev. 395, 401-406 (1950). The full table also appears, together with another 19 thrusts and parries from federal court opinions, in Appendix C of Llewellyn, The Common Law Tradition 521-535 (1960).

	or policy of previous enactments may be apparent.
9. Definitions and rules of construction contained in an interpretation clause are part of the law and binding.	9. Definitions and rules of construction in a statute will not be extended beyond their necessary import nor allowed to defeat intention otherwise manifested.
12. If language is plain and unambiguous it must be given effect.	12. Not when literal interpretation would lead to absurd or mischievous consequences or thwart manifest purpose.
13. Words and phrases which have received judicial construction before enactment are to be understood according to that construction.	13. Not if the statute clearly requires them to have a different meaning.
15. Words are to be taken in their ordinary meaning unless they are technical terms or words of art.	15. Popular words may bear a technical meaning and technical words may have a popular signification and they should be so construed as to agree with evident intention or to make the statute operative.
16. Every word and clause must be given effect.	16. If inadvertently inserted or if repugnant to the rest of the statute, they may be rejected as surplusage.
19. Exceptions not made cannot be read in.	19. The letter is only the "bark." Whatever is within the reason of the law is within the law itself.
23. Qualifying or limiting words or clauses are to be referred to the next preceding antecedent.	23. Not when evident sense and meaning require a different construction.

Llewellyn's listing is by no means exhaustive. One thrust and parry he omits concerns penal statutes; while another neglected thrust defines the construction to be chosen as that which can reasonably avoid a constitutional doubt about the statute, and its parry could read that "the canon of avoidance of constitutional doubts must, like the 'plain-meaning' rule, give way where its application would produce a futile result, or an unreasonable result 'plainly at variance with the policy of the legislation as a whole.' "[72]

72. Shapiro v. U.S., 335 U.S. 1, 31 (1948). Another point he omits mentioning is that "Court reports abound in decisions reflecting and endorsing a presumption against repeal by implication," and that on the other hand, "the presumption against implied repeal runs directly counter to the real probability, sufficient to support an

The phenomenon illustrated by these thrusts and parries is not confined to the law. Back in 1939 Robert Lynd made an analogous list of contrasting assumptions or values in American culture.[73] Herbert Simon, writing on administrative organization, has made a similar point about contradiction among some "proverbs of administration."[74]

In my teaching of statutory interpretation I have found this "proverb" notion fruitful. I have likened the maxims or canons to folk-sayings. I have gone down a list of "thrusts" with students, and asked for their "parries." I have found that if I present "He who hesitates is lost" or "The early bird catches the worm," someone will come up with "Look before you leap" or "Haste makes waste." If I say, "A penny saved is a penny earned," I get back, "Penny wise, pound foolish." If I say "Out of sight, out of mind," I am told that "Absence make the heart grow fonder." While "Faint heart never won fair lady" and "Nothing ventured, nothing gained," still on the other hand, "Discretion is the better part of valor," and "The meek shall inherit the earth."

I also discovered that folk-sayings can change meanings as the times change. I had suggested that the saying "A rolling stone gathers no moss" could be counterpointed by "Variety is the spice of life." I had always supposed that the "moss" in the saying represented something good — stability or maturity — and hence the saying was frowning on the rolling stone. But I found that about half the class viewed the gathering of moss as undesirable, and the saying was therefore praising the rolling stone: If one would savor the spices of life, one did not stay in one place and be a mossback. To these people my thrust and parry were synonomous: It was good to be a rolling stone and gather no moss, it was good to seek variety as the spice of life. I confess that nothing that has happened in class in a quarter-century of teaching has had such an unsettling or aging effect upon me. While I found authorities to support my understanding of the saying in various quotational encyclopedias, I am afraid the sources could not be described as contemporary: Tusser's sixteenth-century work, *Five Hundred Points of Good Husbandry,* or Mrs. Jameson's nineteenth-century volume, *Detached Thoughts.*

Folk-sayings are a particularly illuminating analogy to the above construction maxims because we readily discount a folk-saying as being only sometimes true. We recognize that it is not a complete and balanced assessment of its subject. The construction maxims too are

---

assumption on which a *presumption* could justifiably be premised, that the purpose of new legislation is to change prior law and in so doing to displace or *repeal* some part of it." Sutherland, Statutory Construction, §23.10 at 230, 232 (italics in original) (1972).

73. Lynd, Knowledge For What? 60-62 (1939).

74. Simon, Administrative Behavior 20-36 (2d ed. 1957).

simply reminders of relevant, not conclusive, bits of experience. I well remember an oral argument in the Second Circuit, with Judge Learned Hand presiding, in which a lawyer was unsophisticated enough to say: "Your honor, this case is governed by the fundamental principle of American law that a penal statute is to be strictly construed." Judge Hand responded, "Young man [he used this appellation though the lawyer must have been about 60; but Hand, you see, was about 75], that is not a fundamental principle of American law, it is just one of the maxims of construction. We might end up construing this statute strictly, but if we do it won't be because we were compelled by that maxim to do so."

7. The difficulty presented by ambivalent maxims of construction leads me to another point: Courts ought to be more open and realistic about the interpretation process.

Courts still tend to leave the impression that a particular maxim has led unerringly and inevitably to the result in the case. This is often little more than pretense — though it is true that some maxims may be weightier than others.[75] The process is complex and the tendency of a maxim's policy to move decision in one direction may be overborne by opposite tendencies because of, e.g., the clarity of the words; the relation to other parts of the statute; the relation to other statutes and interpretations thereof; the legislative history; the prior interpretations of this statute; other jurisdictions' analogous statutes and interpretations thereof; the developments subsequent to the statute, such as administrative interpretations and attitudes of subsequent legislatures in their treatment of proposed amendments or in later statutes; the common law meaning of relevant words; and the avoidance of absurd or wholly unreasonable results if reasonably possible. Hence more open acknowledgment of the nature of the process would be welcome.

Another way in which courts could be more open is in acknowledging that in the typical appellate situation — i.e., a situation in which the legislature simply had not thought of the *specific* situation confronting the court — if the court is to talk in terms of intent, then the question "What did the legislature intend for this situation?" is simply not realistic. More realistic (though still not easy to answer) would be the kind of question I referred to earlier: "What would the legislature probably have said about this situation if it had thought of it?" ("hypothetical specific intent"). This form of the question has been put, as I have indicated, by a number of scholars and jurists. (Also more realistic would be Dickerson's alternative question: "What

75. Dickerson, *supra* n.20 at 227-236 has made a start at sorting them out in this respect.

is the meaning carried by this language when read in its proper context by a typical member of the audience to which it is addressed?")

8. Perhaps the question in terms of hypothetical specific intent should carry some further inquiries with it, as urged by Professor Julius Cohen, so that in difficult cases the court would ask what the legislature would have done if it had "the time and awareness of the problems that *hindsight* now permits," *and* if it were seeking to avoid absurdities, inequalities, and policy oversights, as well as to promote consistency and harmony in the rest of the law. Cohen thus envisages a search for the probable meaning of an idealized version of the enacting legislature. He distinguishes that from the kind of judicial lawmaking in which the court consciously substitutes its *own* policy for a *known* legislative policy.[76] Dickerson too would tolerate Cohen's kind of judicial lawmaking provided it is the kind of case in which the court, on the basis of traditional techniques, can see no clear balance favoring one meaning over another.[77]

Understandably, courts hesitate to exercise lawmaking power, and hence have been slow to conclude that the evidence of intent, purpose, or meaning is completely absent or completely stalemated. This hesitation has been seen even in Switzerland where Article I of the Swiss Code specifically empowers the judges to act as *legislators* when "no rule can be drawn from the statute" or from customary law. A student of the Swiss Code has observed that in spite of this provision, the Swiss high court is still influenced by the orthodox view of a court's proper role, and refuses to accept the lawmaking role.[78]

We are thus reminded, I think, that whatever rough formula we may devise for statutory interpretation is likely to be modified, in application, by *prevailing judicial attitudes and ideals.* And such qualification can occur even when the evidence of intent, purpose, or meaning is not absent or stalemated, but is *close* to being so, as so often happens today. Especially in a court whose decision to review the case was discretionary rather than mandatory (thus resulting in a higher percentage of close cases), the opposing indications of intent, purpose, and meaning will often be either evenly or almost evenly balanced. In such situations the most likely critical judicial goal is the arrival at the most just and reasonable result for the type of situation involved.

9. I just referred to the fragility of any rough "formula" we may devise for statutory interpretation. Is there nonetheless a possibility

76. Cohen, Judicial "Legisputation" and the Dimensions of Legislative Meaning, 36 Ind. L.J. 414-423 (1961).

77. Dickerson, *supra* n.16 at 27-28; 238 n.1; 247 n.23; 249 n.25.

78. Mayda, Francois Gény and Modern Jurisprudence 63 (1978). The text of the Swiss Code appears at 162.

for improvement in that direction? And may some root sources of statutory ambiguity be removed?

Perhaps in the future more enlightened judges, more appreciative of the multi-factored nature of the problem, the inevitability of a "lawmaking" role in some cases, and the need for more candor, can follow a more satisfactory course if not a precise formula. Proposals for the creation of usable legislative history materials on the state level comparable to those on the national level may eventually be adopted. But proposals for a specific legislative code of interpretive rules — even if held not to be an unconstitutional infringement of judicial power — will have no easy path to success.[79] At any rate, statute books have generally been less ambitious. Some go part of the way by presenting, as applicable to all statutes, definitions of recurring words and some interpretive rules with respect to gender, tenses, number, computation of time, etc. Some, like the Wisconsin statute book, make their clarifications with the caveat "unless [such] construction . . . would produce a result inconsistent with the manifest intent of the legislature."[80] A more general rule of construction often found in statute books is: "All general provisions . . . shall be liberally construed in order that the true intent and meaning of the legislature may be fully carried out." A rule of this kind is not specifically helpful; and its relation to other rules, like the classical rule on penal statutes, is not clear. Assuming that statutory rules of construction are not ignored by courts, as they often have been, they too may have to be interpreted. And if they are formulated very precisely in an attempt to avoid interpretation, their resulting rigidity can prove too inequitable for some situations.

One of the more imaginative special statutory rules, recently suggested, is based on the fact that applying the legislative "intent" or

79. The Illinois Supreme Court has made a surprising ruling of such unconstitutionality in People v. Crawford Distrib. Co., 53 Ill. 2d 332, 291 N.E.2d 648, 652 (1973). The state antitrust law had required that provisions similar to those of a federal antitrust law should be construed in the same way as the federal provisions. This was deemed to violate the state constitutional provisions separating the judicial from the legislative power.

Optimism over the efficacy of a code of interpretive rules is shown in Silving, A Plea for a Law of Interpretation, 98 U. Pa. L. Rev. 499 (1950), and by the Commissioners on Uniform State Laws' promulgation in 1965 of a proposed and still largely ignored Uniform Statutory Construction Act. (§15: "If a statute is ambiguous, the court in determining the intent of the legislature, may consider among other matters: (1) the object sought to be obtained; (2) the circumstances under which the statute was enacted; (3) the legislative history; (4) the common law or former statutory provisions, including laws upon the same or similar subjects; (5) the consequences of a particular construction; (6) the administrative construction of the statute; and (7) the preamble".) For criticisms of the Act, and suggestions for the proper limits of this type of statute, see Dickerson, *supra* n.16 at 262-281.

80. Wis. Stat., §990.001 (1977).

other standard grows more difficult as a statute grows older. A "Non-primacy of Statutes Act" would declare that after 20 years a statute would become "comparable to a principle of common law," i.e., subjected "to the judicial scrutiny accorded judicial precedents; that is, [it] can be limited, extended, qualified, and even overruled by courts."[81]

The sources of statutory ambiguity themselves are not likely to be much reduced. Avoidable ambiguities attributable to bad draftsmanship can perhaps be reduced but most sources of ambiguity will remain: the prevalence of ambiguity in language generally; the unintended but almost inevitable ambiguities that may be introduced by amendments in the course of passage — particularly in amendments from the floor, but sometimes in committee amendments — that are not carefully integrated with the rest of the bill and with other statutes; the introduction of deliberate ambiguities (because the legislature does not know enough about the subject and wants to delegate broad authority to the court and/or administrative agency, or because more abstract language was necessary in order to get the statute passed); and, perhaps most important, the impossibility of the legislature's foreseeing and making provisions for all the situations that might arise.

10. When we have the ingredients of a formula for a chemical product but no precise weight for each ingredient, perhaps the best we can do is rely upon a skilled chemist who is knowledgeable about each ingredient and the purposes of the product, to produce a mixture that he senses to be the best one for those known purposes. A similar last-ditch reliance upon the quality of the human beings assigned to a baffling task was expressed by Justice Frankfurter at the close of his 1947 lecture on interpreting statutes. He was of course dealing with a more confusing task than the chemist's because more value-laden; factors like integrity and statesmanship were relevant. After saying that "perfection of draftsmanship is as unattainable as demonstrable correctness of judicial reading of legislation," he concluded, "Fit legislation and fair adjudication are attainable. The ultimate reliance of society for the proper fulfillment of both these august functions is to entrust them only to those who are equal to their demands."[82]

This emphasis on the quality of judges also calls to mind an observation once made by Judge Learned Hand. Since a judge must pass upon fundamental issues of power and justice, he must have, said Hand, "at least a bowing acquaintance with Acton and Maitland, with Thucydides, Gibbon and Carlyle, with Homer, Dante, Shakespeare and

81. Davies, A Response to Statutory Obsolescence: The Nonprimacy of Statutes Act, 4 Vt. L. Rev. 203, 205 (1979). See also the two related articles, Gilmore, Putting Senator Davies in Context, *id.* at 233; Calabresi, The Nonprimacy of Statutes Act: A Comment, *id.* at 247.

82. Frankfurter, *supra* n.68 at 546.

Milton, with Machiavelli, Montaigne and Rabelais, with Plato, Bacon, Hume and Kant." A purplish tint may adhere to the above words, but the point is valid and recognizable. "The words he must construe," Hand continued, "are empty vessels into which he can pour nearly anything he will." His "outlook [must not be] limited by parish or class. [He] must be aware that there are before [him] more than verbal problems, . . . aware of the changing social tensions in every society. . . ." Hand was thinking at the moment of constitutional interpretation, but his remarks apply, though with somewhat less force, to statutory interpretation. He was of course aware of the inevitably creative role of a judge in construing a statute and of the statesmanship, wisdom, and integrity needed to keep that creativity within bounds. As he further observed:

> . . . On the one hand, he cannot go beyond what has been said, because he is bound to enforce existing [legislative] commands and only those; on the other hand, he cannot suppose that what has been said should clearly frustrate or leave unexecuted its own purpose. . . . When a judge tries to find out what government would have intended which it did not say, he puts into its mouth things which he thinks it ought to have said, and that is very close to substituting what he himself thinks right. Let him beware, however, or he will usurp the office of government, even though in a small way he must do so in order to execute its real commands at all.[83]

And as we have seen, some authorities (perhaps including Hand) would add: The "small way" is forced to expand into a larger way when the case is one of those "hard cases" in which the words as well as other traditional indicia of intent, purpose, and meaning offer no clear path out of the jungle.

If you now feel that perhaps my presentation has exaggerated the complexity and uncertainty of the subject of statutory interpretation, may I plead in defense Justice Frankfurter's words in his 1947 lecture: "Though my business throughout most of my professional life has been with statutes, I come to you empty-handed. I bring no answers." He continued by calling the process an "art" rather than a science.[84] Further in my support is the conclusion of two prominent Harvard scholars (Hart and Sacks) who once pointed out that the "hard truth of the matter is that American courts have no intelligible, generally accepted, and consistently applied theory of statutory interpretation."[85] And finally, a distinguished British scholar has observed: "Reviewing these many problems of interpretation, we are driven, in the end, to the

83. Dilliard, ed., *supra* n.44 at 81, 106-107, 108.
84. Frankfurter, *supra* n.68 at 530.
85. Hart & Sacks, *supra* n.63 at 1201.

unsatisfying conclusion that the whole matter ultimately turns on impalpable and indefinable elements of judicial spirit or attitude."[86]

Not a happy situation. There is solace, of course, for the advocate. The diversity of theories and applications of theories enlarges his arsenal of techniques, precedents, and arguments with which to persuade the court. But the process of persuasion is not likely to be effective if the advocate draws on the arsenal indiscriminately. He must bear in mind that interpretive maxims, rules, or principles, and their interpretations in turn, are so diverse that invoking them in the abstract, divorced from *concrete* context, will not count for much. Rather, their appropriateness in light of the *particular* statute's[87] language, structure, history, purpose, and relation to other law; the pull exerted on the court from the concrete facts of the parties' situations; and the fact that the court will try if reasonably possible to reach a just and reasonable *result* — these are likely to exert magnetic force in the court's choice among the varieties of principle.

C. *Background Note: Interrelations of Common Law and Statute*

As you know, the common law represents non-statutory, judge-made law. When a statute is passed, it typically changes the law — either the preexisting common law or the preexisting statutory law. When South Carolina passed its 1902 statute making criminal the publication of rape victims' names, it changed the preexisting legal situation. Until that statute, such a publication could be made without criminal penalty. Conduct generally is not punishable unless a statute has previously made it punishable.

1. Common Law Crimes

I say "generally" because while this is true on the federal level and in many states, the doctrine of "common-law crimes" still exists in probably a majority of states, though with some restrictions. Even under that doctrine, however, in order to permit prosecution for conduct that has

86. Allen, Law in the Making 515 (Oxford paperback ed. 1961).

87. Justice Holmes once remarked that "every question of [statutory] construction is unique, and an argument that would prevail in one case may be inadequate in another." U.S. v. Jin Fuey Moy, 241 U.S. 394, 402 (1916).

not been made punishable by statute, the conduct would generally have to strike the court as clearly falling within some residual broad category of conduct whose "criminality" seems unmistakable. Conduct like that of the *Nappier* defendants would not seem to fit.[88]

Remember that the only legal change expressly made by the statute was the imposition of a criminal penalty. The litigation we are concerned with was not a criminal prosecution by the state; it was a damage suit by private parties claiming invasion of privacy. The court of appeals concluded that "the plaintiff may sue under the common law as fortified by the statute." Why "fortified by the statute"? Because the common law recognized a defense to a privacy action where, as in this case, "the incident was a matter of public concern and record"; and the statutory policy had, in effect, eliminated this defense, though the statute had not explicitly addressed itself to the common law right of privacy. As the court of appeals put it, "the statute states an exception to the exemption. No matter the news value, South Carolina has unequivocally declared the identity of the injured person shall not be made known in press or broadcast."

The case thus illustrates one facet of an important phenomenon: the intermeshing of common law and statute, the doctrine of common law crimes being another facet. I want now to sketch some further features of that phenomenon for you — including but not confined to the problem of civil rights and remedies in relation to criminal statutes.

2. Problems When Statutes Creating Rights Omit All or Some Remedies; Relevance and Irrelevance of Common Law

1. In order to gain some perspective, consider first the situation when a statute contains *no* remedy, criminal or civil, to enforce the standard of conduct it lays down. The statute simply prohibits the doing of certain things or simply declares a right to do certain things. In this situation, courts have sometimes viewed the statute as merely "hortatory," i.e., urging people to act in a certain way, but not contemplating a sanction to back up the urging. However, in recent years, the Supreme Court has often taken a "where there's a right there's a remedy" approach.

For instance, the federal civil rights law of 1866, which has been held to be authorized by the enabling clause of the Thirteenth Amendment (antislavery), declared simply that "[a]ll citizens of the United

88. On common law crimes, see LaFave & Scott, Criminal Law 57-69 (1972).

States shall have the same right in every State and Territory, as is enjoyed by white citizens thereof to inherit, purchase, lease, sell, hold and convey real and personal property."[89] The Supreme Court decided in the 1969 case of Sullivan v. Little Hunting Park, Inc. that in spite of the lack of a specific provision for a remedy, a plaintiff claiming discrimination in private housing could sue for damages and injunctive relief. "The existence of a statutory right implies the existence of all necessary and appropriate remedies. . . . 'A disregard of the command of the statute is a wrongful act and where it results in damage to one of the class for whose especial benefit the statute was enacted, the right to recover the damages from the party in default is implied . . . .' "[90] (An analogous case is one in which, without any implementing statute, the constitutional prohibition in the Fourth Amendment against unreasonable searches and seizures was held by the Supreme Court in 1971 to imply a damage remedy against federal narcotics agents who allegedly violated the amendment.[91])

A case like the *Sullivan* case, then, is a case of implying from a statute that is *silent on remedies* that the *legislature intended that a right it has created* should be enforced by *preexisting remedies* available to courts, like damages and injunction.

2. The situation gets more complex where the statute is not silent on remedies, but rather specifies one or more, e.g., a government remedy (criminal and/or injunctive, and perhaps also administrative sanctions, or perhaps withdrawal of government funds from violators of the prohibition) but not a private remedy, and the plaintiff seeks a private remedy like damages, injunction, restitution; or the government seeks a public remedy other than the one specified. You can see how natural it would be to conclude that the legislature wanted to allow *only* those remedies that were specified. Such a conclusion would be in the spirit of the maxim of statutory construction previously discussed, "expressio unius exclusio alterius" — i.e., express mention impliedly excludes the unmentioned.

And this is what courts often do conclude. But courts have

89. 42 U.S.C. §1982.

90. 396 U.S. 229, 230 (1969). The injunctive and damage remedies held available to enforce the federal right were also held to be available in this state court suit.

91. Bivens v. Six Unknown Named Federal Narcotics Agents, 403 U.S. 388 (1971). Similarly, in 1979, the Court recognized that a woman discharged from employment by a United States Congressman had a right of action arising directly under the Fifth Amendment due process clause, to recover damages for the Congressman's alleged sex discrimination (subject to the defense, not reached by the Court, of congressional immunity under the "speech and debate" clause of the Constitution). Davis v. Passman, 442 U.S. 228 (1979). The Court pointed out that its usual analysis of whether to imply a private right of action from a statute (see further discussion below) is inapplicable to the issue of implication from the Constitution. See also Butz v. Economou, 438 U.S. 478 (1978).

continued to struggle uncertainly with the problem over the years,[92] finally coming up with a "formula" in the Supreme Court's 1975 Cort v. Ash[93] opinion listing four factors to be considered: (1) whether plaintiff is a member of "the class for whose especial benefit the statute was enacted"; (2) whether there is "any indication of legislative intent, explicit or implicit," to create or deny the additional remedy; (3) whether implying the remedy is "consistent with the underlying purposes of the legislative scheme"; and (4) whether "the cause of action is one traditionally relegated to state law, in an area basically the concern of the states," making an implied federal cause of action "inappropriate."

However, the formula was rendered dubious in 1979. The initial 1979 case did apply the formula, and found its tests were met by a suit that claimed sex discrimination in the University of Chicago Medical School's denial of admission, and that sought relief under Title IX of the Educational Amendments of 1972.[94] But the other two cases[95] —

92. The history is traced from 1916 to 1979 in Justice Powell's dissent in Cannon v. University of Chicago, 441 U.S. 677, 732-742 (1979). Two 1967 cases illustrated the contrasting results. In one, the Supreme Court held that under the Lanham Act, which specified particular compensatory remedies for trademark infringement, the further remedy of recovering reasonable attorney's fees should not be implied. Though strong opposing considerations were urged in dissent, the Court was persuaded by the principle. "[w]hen a cause of action has been created by a statute which expressly provides the remedies for vindication of the cause, other remedies should not readily be implied." Fleischmann Distilling Corp. v. Maier Brewing Co., 386 U.S. 714, 720 (1967).

Note that the Court said "not readily" rather than "never." In the same year it found there was good reason to imply a further remedy under the Rivers and Harbors Act of 1899. The Act declared that one who sank a vessel in a navigable waterway was subject to (1) criminal penalties for a negligent sinking; (2) a requirement of removal, and forfeiture of interest in the vessel and cargo in case of nonremoval; and (3) a risk that if the government removed the vessel, it could sell vessel and cargo and retain the sales proceeds. The Court held that in one of the two cases, the government could properly sue to hold the sinkers of the vessel responsible for *removal;* and in the other case, in which the government had already removed the vessel, it could sue for *reimbursement of removal expenses.* The Court found, in light of the Act's purposes, and its relations to prior decisions and statutes, that the specified statutory remedies "were not intended to be exclusive." Wyandotte Transp. v. U.S., 389 U.S. 191, 201 (1967).

93. 422 U.S. 66 (1975). The case involved the federal criminal prohibition against corporate expenditures and contributions in connection with federal elections. The Court refused to imply a statutory right to an action against the corporate directors by a Bethlehem Corporation shareholder on behalf of the corporation, to recover monies expended allegedly in violation of the statute.

94. *Cannon, supra* n.92. The only express statutory remedy was the public remedy of cutting off educational funds.

95. In Touche Ross & Co. v. Redington, 442 U.S. 560 (1979), the Court refused to imply the right to a private damage action for customers of a broker against the broker's accountant for improper certification of financial statements (which certification allegedly led to the broker's financial difficulties). The relevant statutory provision required brokers to keep records and file reports as required by the SEC in the public interest and for investors' protection. The only express statutory sanctions

both of them in the corporate financial field and both rejecting the implication of a private action — showed a decided shift in the Court's attitude. The Court made clear that the four factors in the formula were not of equal weight; that the key problem in an implied remedy case was the discovery of legislative intent rather than judicial remedying of an ineffective statute, or exercise of alleged federal *common law* judicial power to redress tortious conduct;[96] that the "exclusio" principle of construction (applicable when the statutory provision mentions only public remedies, or private remedies under other sections or under provisions of related statutes) created a kind of presumption *against* implying the remedy that could only be overcome by persuasive evidence of a contrary legislative intent. The Court acknowledged awareness of its application of a stricter standard than previously applied in some past cases of implied private remedies.[97] The basic policy seemed to be one of avoiding judicial encroachment on legislative power, and goading Congress into accepting responsibility for more explicit provisions on intended remedies.[98] Some 1981 cases continued this stricter line.[99]

---

were criminal, administrative, and SEC injunction suits. Other sections of the Act did provide for private actions in various other situations.

In Transamerica Mortgage Advisors v. Lewis, 444 U.S. 11 (1979), the Court refused to imply the right to a private damage action against an investment advisor company on account of its alleged frauds and breaches of trust (in violation of §206 of the Investment Advisors Act) against a company in which plaintiff was a shareholder. The only express statutory sanctions were criminal, administrative, and SEC injunction suits. The Court did recognize a right under Section 215 (which makes investment contracts "void" when their performance violates the Act) to rescind the contract and get restitution of fees paid under it — these being normal legal incidents of voidness.

96. See n.100 below.

97. The Court in *Touche Ross, supra* n.95, did not overrule the leading case on implied private remedies in the securities field, J.I. Case Co. v. Borak, 377 U.S. 426 (1964), which had allowed a shareholder's damage action for losses resulting from deceptive proxy solicitation that violated a section of the Securities and Exchange Act. Rather, it said, "to the extent our analysis in today's decision differs from that of the Court in Borak, it suffices to say that in a series of cases since Borak we have adhered to a stricter standard for the implication of private causes of action, and we follow that stricter standard today."

98. The literature on the problem of implied statutory remedies is voluminous. In addition to the many studies treating the issue under particular statutes, there are many treating the problem more generally, including the following sample: Hazen, Implied Private Remedies Under Federal Statutes: Neither A Death Knell Nor A Moratorium — Civil Rights, Securities Regulation, and Beyond, 33 Vand. L. Rev. 1333 (1980); Annot., 61 L. Ed. 2d 910 (1979); Notes, 51 U. Colo. L. Rev. 355 (1980); 30 Stan. L. Rev. 1243 (1978) (focus on state courts); 9 U. Mich. J.L. Ref. 294 (1976); 123 U. Pa. L. Rev. 1392 (1975); O'Neil, Public Regulation and Private Rights of Action, 52 Calif. L. Rev. 341 (1964) (focus on whether preexisting remedies are being preserved).

99. See the rejection of the implication of certain private rights of action under the Rivers and Harbors Appropriations Act (Calif. v. Sierra Club, 68 L. Ed. 2d 101 (1981)); under the Davis-Bacon Act (Universities Research Assoc. v. Coutu, 67 L. Ed.

3. Relevance, to Common Law Issues, of Statutory Policy on Related Issues: Using Statutes "By Analogy" (Herein Also of "Common Law Public Policy")

The category in which the *Nappier* case falls is different from both of the categories mentioned above. In this third category, a plaintiff is not asserting a right of action created by the statute or invoking an implied statutory remedy. He is asserting a preexisting *common law right of action and remedy,* and pointing to the defendant's statutory violation as *proof* that the plaintiff has a good case under the common law right of action. The most common and well-established example of this is in the negligence field. Suppose the plaintiff claims his injuries were caused by the defendant's driving his car at a negligently high rate of speed. Suppose further that defendant's rate of speed violated the penal statutes on speeding. That violation of a penal statute would furnish at least evidence (and in most states conclusive evidence) that defendant's conduct was negligent, i.e., violated the standard of care of a "reasonable man." Thus, the statutory violation *influenced the determination of whether the common law right* (of freedom from injury caused by negligence) *had been violated.*[100]

The *Nappier* case is analogous. In South Carolina the plaintiffs

---

2d 662 (1981); and under the Federal Water Pollution Control Act and the Marine Protection, Research and Sanctuaries Act (Middlesex County Sewerage Auth. v. National Sea Clammers Assoc., 69 L. Ed. 2d 435 (1981)).

100. This is of course different from arguing that when the legislature *created a right* and provided no remedy, there was no intent to preclude enforcement of the statutory right by a preexisting common law remedy (*supra* at 271-272). We are here dealing with a common law *right and remedy.* Further: when the legislature makes a prohibition and provides some public remedies rather than the private remedy sought by plaintiff (*supra* at 272-274) is it also possible to argue (as in the present §3) that a *common law right* has been violated and violation of the statutory prohibition reinforces that claim? The common law right in question might be fitted into some preexisting category of, say, the law of torts (e.g., injury from deceit or unfair competition) or might be a common law right newly recognized by the court. One difficulty here is that a statute creating a prohibition or right, and a remedy, may be viewed as intended to be the exclusive source for determination of rights and any remedies on the subject — so as to prevent assertion of any preexisting common law rights and remedies or judicial creation of new ones. See, e.g., discussion in O'Neil, *supra* n.98. Another difficulty as far as the *federal* courts are concerned is that, as we noted in Chapter 2 in the discussion of Erie R.R. v. Tompkins, the common law powers of federal courts, even in diversity of jurisdiction suits, are much more limited than those of state courts. It is interesting that the Court in *Touche Ross, supra* n.95 said (at 568): "The question of the existence of a statutory cause of action is of course one of statutory construction. . . . [The] argument in favor of implication of a private right of action based on tort principles, therefore, is entirely misplaced." For an elaborate argument in support of a common law rather than statutory construction approach to the problem, even in federal courts, see Note, 51 U. Colo. L. Rev. 355 (1980).

had a common law right not to have their privacy violated by someone not in an excepted category (e.g., the category of newsman making legitimate comment on a newsworthy event or figure), and had a common law damage remedy for the privacy invasion. The South Carolina criminal statute *influenced the determination of whether the common law right had been violated* because the statutory policy against news comment identifying a rape victim influenced the court in refusing to recognize that kind of news reporting as coming within the exception to the common law right. Notice that the statute had its impact on the common law right even though the statute said nothing specifically about common law rights.

This process — by which a judge handles a common law problem in the light of whatever policy clues he can derive from a statute that operates in a related area but does not address itself to the specific common law problem — has been called "applying a statute by analogy," or using statutes "as principles," "as premises," or "as precedents." Distinguished legal scholars and judges — including Roscoe Pound,[101] James Landis,[102] Chief Justice Stone of the Supreme Court,[103] Chief Justice Schaefer of the Illinois Supreme Court,[104] and Chief Justice Traynor of the California Supreme Court[105] — have all broken some lances in behalf of the practice, and deplored the reluctance of judges to engage in it.

Sometimes of course there is legitimate reason for the reluctance. A judge may regard the legislative policy in the related field as inappropriate for transplantation to the common law field. Or he may think that the legislature has in effect *forbidden* the transplantation. Suppose, for instance, a statute says that "bastards shall be regarded in the same way as legitimate children, for purposes of determining inheritance from a mother who dies intestate [i.e., without a will]." A case comes up in which a mother *had* left a will, making certain bequests to her "children." Does "children" include her illegitimate children? This is a common law problem, i.e., neither the quoted statute nor any other statute, let us assume, addresses the problem specifically. But you can see how the court might feel it desirable to apply, to the common law problem, the legislative policy on illegitimacy shown in the quoted statute. This some courts have done. But you can also see one barrier to such action: The court may feel that the statute showed a deliberate choice that in the law of the state, the approach

101. Pound, Common Law and Legislation, 21 Harv. L. Rev. 383 (1908).

102. Landis, Statutes and the Sources of Law, in Harvard Legal Essays 231 et seq. (Pound ed. 1934).

103. Stone, The Common Law in the United States, 50 Harv. L. Rev. 4 (1936).

104. Schaefer, Precedent and Policy, 34 U. Chi. L. Rev. 3, 18-22 (1966).

105. Traynor, Statutes Revolving in Common Law Orbits, 17 Catholic U.L. Rev. 401 (1968).

to illegitimacy taken in the statutory rule should apply *only* to cases of intestacy; so that interpreting "children" in a will to cover bastards would be impliedly *forbidden* by the legislature. (This would be a case of applying the maxim of "express mention, implied exclusion" that we have encountered before.)

In short, legislative silence about an area related to that which it is covering may mean it wants to leave that *open* for determination either way by courts as a common law problem — in which case the "statutes by analogy" approach would be permissible. But it *may* mean — on the basis of an "express mention, implied exclusion" approach — that the legislature has decided the related area should *not* be treated in the same way. In such event, the court would have to bow to the legislative will. Often, of course, it will seem that the legislature had *no* definite intent with respect to the related area, so that the court will probably ask itself: What would the legislature have said if its collective mind had been turned more definitely to the subject; would it have left the matter open to the court, or would it have forbidden the extension of the statutory policy to the related area?

As I have said, some courts did take their cue from the intestacy statute in handling the illegitimacy issue in a will case. And there are, in cases on other subjects, many instances of this approach.[106] Let me illustrate by two cases in divergent fields. One is a 1961 Wisconsin case in the field of real property. Four university students, who had entered into a nine-month lease for a furnished house and moved out after a month, were suing to get back their security deposits plus a sum for their labors in putting the house into a habitable condition. The students were arguing against application of a common law rule that the landlord makes no implied warranty of habitability of leased premises. In ruling for the plaintiffs, the court said:

> Legislation and administrative rules, such as the safe-place statute, building codes, and health regulations, all impose certain duties on a property owner with respect to the condition of his premises. Thus, the legislature has made a policy judgment — that it is socially (and politically) desirable to impose these duties on a property owner — which has rendered the old common-law obsolete. To follow the old rule of no implied warranty of habitability in leases would, in our opinion, be inconsistent with the current legislative policy concerning housing standards.[107]

106. See illustrations given in the articles in nn. 101-105 *supra;* also in Page, Statutes as Common Law Principles, 1944 Wis. L. Rev. 175; Gellhorn, Contracts and Public Policy, 35 Colum. L. Rev. 679 (1935); Notes, 65 Colum. L. Rev. 880 (1965), 43 Dick. L. Rev. 234 (1939); U.S. v. Lennox Metal Mfg. Co., 225 F.2d 302, 318-319 (2d Cir. 1955), and cases cited therein; Moragne v. States Marine Lines, 398 U.S. 375, 389-393 (1970).

107. Pines v. Perssion, 13 Wis. 2d 590, 595-596, 111 N.W.2d 409, 412-413 (1961). See also Javins v. First National Realty Corp., 428 F.2d 1071 (D.C. Cir. 1970), in

The other case is a 1906 New York case in the field of injuries to employees. The American Express Company had included in its employment contracts a clause absolving the company of any liability for injuries that might be suffered by employees while on the job, including injuries caused by negligence of the company or its officers or employees. The common law of course imposed liability for negligent infliction of injury, but also recognized a certain amount of freedom of contract. The highest court of New York decided that the "release from negligence liability" clause was void. One reason was its inconsistency with the statutory policy of the state as evidenced in laws safeguarding workers by imposing various health and safety requirements upon employers — "the course of legislation framed for the purpose of affording greater protection to the class of the employed." Such a release clause "defeats the spirit of existing laws of the state."[108]

Another reason given by the court illustrates another concept you should be familiar with. The court said the clause was also against "common-law public policy." The policy of the common law in imposing liability for negligent infliction of injury was based on "the conservation of the lives and of the healthful vigor of . . . citizens, and if employers could contract away their responsibility at common law, it would tend to encourage on their part laxity of conduct in, if not an indifference to the maintenance of proper and reasonable safeguards to human life and limb." You will find a variety of situations in which courts have found contracts to be in whole or part contrary to common law public policy.[109]

You should also know that among the cases dealing with the impact of a statute on a contract are many involving statutes that are more closely related to the contract than was the New York labor legislation to the negligence-release contract, and hence are even more likely to affect the contract adversely. Thus a contract might be entered

---

which the court ruled that housing code violations could be asserted as a defense to a landlord's suit to evict for nonpayment of rent; the effect of the housing code was "that a warranty of habitability be implied in the leases of all housing that it covers." Analogous to this case is Dickhut v. Norton, 45 Wis. 2d 389, 173 N.W.2d 297 (1970), in which the analysis was in terms of carrying over legislative policy in the urban renewal field to a problem under a different statute, i.e., the eviction statute. The case recognized the defense, in a landlord suit to evict the tenant, that the eviction was wholly "retaliatory" — i.e., was provoked by the tenant's having complained to health authorities of the landlord's housing code violation. This defense was implied into the eviction statute in the light of the public policy shown in urban renewal legislation and its implication that violations should be reported. For argument that direct legislative change is preferable if common law attitudes on warranty of habitability are to be changed, see Meyers, The Covenant of Habitability and the American Law Institute, 27 Stan. L. Rev. 879 (1975).

108. Johnston v. Fargo, 184 N.Y. 379, 386, 77 N.E. 388, 390-391 (1906).

109. See 6A Corbin on Contracts, part 8 (1963).

into requiring the performance of certain acts that a statute has subjected to a criminal penalty, though it has not prohibited the contract itself. Typically, in a suit at common law to enforce the contract, the contract will be held wholly or partly void, but there are exceptions.[110]

4. Relevance of Statute - Common Law Interrelations to Lawyer Operations

The fact that common law and statute interrelate with each other has an effect, of course, on your operations as a lawyer. Suppose a client comes in with a case that appears to be a common law case; i.e., you know of no legislation on the subject. You would be foolish to research immediately into the court cases. For contrary to your faulty memory, there may just be a statute that nullifies what earlier court cases had decided on a purely common law basis. Furthermore, statutes, even if not applicable to the specific legal problem in your case, may be grist for your mill. They may be pertinent to a subsidiary aspect of the case. Or they may prohibit some acts, the legality of which you have assumed in framing the legal problem in the case. They may be pertinent, moreover, as embodying in a related field a policy analogous to the policy that you want to have the court apply to your common law problem. Finally, if you find the common law clearly adverse to the position of your client and wish to urge the court to overrule itself, again statutes are relevant: You will have to think about how to convince the court that it, rather than the legislature, is the better vehicle for the change in common law, a matter discussed in Chapter 1 under "Court and Legislature." And you may point to statutory rules in other jurisdictions as a possible model for the changed common law rule.

Conversely, if it is a case arising under a statute, and you are therefore primarily concerned with that statute, with analogous statutes, and with court interpretations of the statutes, you are still interested in common law attitudes. For instance, light may be thrown on ambiguous statutory words by referring to their common law meanings. There is also a maxim to the effect that "statutes in derogation of the common law are to be strictly construed."[111] That is, statutes changing the common law — and few statutes do not — are to be construed as making the narrower of two alternative changes. The maxim was born in the period when statutes were viewed as intruders in the

110. See Annot., Validity of Contracts in Violation of Statute Imposing Criminal Sanction but not Specifically Declaring Contract Invalid, 55 A.L.R.2d 481 (1957) and Later Case Service Supplementing vols. 49-55, at 687-688 (1978).

111. See Fordham & Leach, Interpretation of Statutes in Derogation of the Common Law, 3 Vand. L. Rev. 438 (1950).

house of the common law. It is not as much cited as it used to be, but still can be found in occasional modern opinions, buttressing a conservative statutory interpretation. It remains a weapon in the advocate's armory, along with other maxims that advise strict construction of certain kinds of statutes, and thus a fuller preservation of the common law.[112] Knowledge of the preexisting common law is therefore pertinent.

112. A number of chapters in vol. 3 of Sutherland, Statutory Construction (4th ed., Sands, 1974) are concerned with this point.

Chapter 4

Further Aspects of the Case: The Precedents

A. Court Treatment of the Prior Relevant Court Decisions; Aspects of Judicial Process

You have seen, in the *Nappier* opinions, the disagreement between the trial judge and two court of appeals judges, and between these two judges and their dissenting colleague. You may wonder why a legal system that is supposed to operate on a "precedent" basis can give rise to such disagreement. You may feel that a legal decision ought to emerge with all the inevitability of the conclusion of a logical syllogism; for does not the proposition of law derived from the precedents constitute the major premise of a syllogism, and does not the proposition stating the crucial facts in the instant case constitute the minor premise?

It is true that the reasoning in a judicial opinion can be cast into such syllogistic form, and once the premises are formulated, the conclusion flows inevitably therefrom. The trouble — i.e., the uncertainty about the result of a case — lies in the court's degree of freedom in the choice of premises. Quite often a reasonable difference of opinion can arise about what this "proposition of law derived from the precedents" is, or should be; and about what should be viewed as the "crucial facts in the instant case."

1. The Alternative Syllogisms

To illustrate the judicial freedom in choice of premises in the *Nappier* case, let me first cast the reasoning of the court of appeals majority on the one hand, and the reasoning of the dissenting judge on the other, into two different syllogisms:

Syllogism of court of appeals majority

Major premise: On the basis of the precedents, a person's right of privacy is violated by news reportage of *intimate facts that are not of legitimate public interest.*

Minor premise: In this case, the facts from which the identity of the plaintiff rape victims could be learned, which were broadcast on defendants' television news program, constituted *intimate facts that were not of legitimate public interest* (since the statute should be construed as making punishable, and hence not of legitimate public interest, the publication by private parties of facts from which the identity of a rape victim can be learned, rather than merely the publication of her actual name).

Conclusion: Therefore, defendants' broadcast violated plaintiffs' right of privacy.

Syllogism of court of appeals minority

Major premise: On the basis of the precedents, a person's right of privacy is *not* violated by "publication of *matter of public concern and record.*"

Minor premise: In this case, the defendants' TV broadcast of facts from which the identity of the plaintiff rape victims could be learned constituted "publication of *matter of public concern and record*" — and the statute does not make it any less a matter of public concern, since it should be construed as applying to publication of the rape victim's actual "name" rather than to facts from which her identity can be learned.

Conclusion: Therefore, defendants' broadcast did not violate plaintiffs' right of privacy.

Let me now examine more closely the sources of freedom in formulating the alternative premises of the judicial syllogism.[1]

2. Formulation of the Major Premise

I want to distinguish two different kinds of freedom here. One is in determining what any particular precedent stands for. The other is in choosing between competing precedents.

1. I shall be treating these sources of freedom in a rather general way. There have been some elaborate analyses of particular intellectual techniques through

a. *Determining What a Precedent Stands For; "Ratio Decidendi," Holding, and Dictum*

Both the majority and the minority opinions in *Nappier* cited, as the primary precedent on the South Carolina law of privacy, the 1956 case of Meetze v. Associated Press.[2] This case involved a girl who married at age eleven and produced a child at age twelve. Newspaper publicity about the birth featuring the mother's age was held not to violate the parents' privacy — with the court acknowledging that, in general, the right of privacy existed in South Carolina common law.

How did the *Nappier* majority and minority opinions differ in their treatment of the *Meetze* precedent? The minority cited it after making the observation that the privacy right in South Carolina "is not an absolute right, and where the alleged invasion of privacy is the publication of matter of public concern and record," it does not give rise to tort liability. The *Meetze* opinion had indeed made observations that supported this treatment:

> There are times when one, whether willingly or not, becomes an actor in an occurrence of public or general interest. When this takes place, he emerges from his seclusion, and the publication of his connection with such occurrence is not an invasion of his right of privacy. . . . The law does not recognize a right of privacy in connection with that which is inherently a public matter. . . . The facts in this article do not show an unwarranted invasion of the right of privacy. It is rather unusual for a twelve year old girl to give birth to a child. It is a biological occurrence which would naturally excite public interest. Moreover, it was an event which the law required to be entered as a public record. . . .

The majority, on the other hand, quoted some other observations in the *Meetze* opinion including a definition of actionable invasion of privacy, part of which read: "the publicizing of one's private affairs with which the public has no legitimate concern." Another passage in the *Meetze* opinion that might usefully have been quoted was the observation that "newsworthiness is not necessarily the test. . . . 'Revelations may be so intimate and so unwarranted in view of the victim's position as to outrage the community's notions of decency.'" These two passages together facilitate the making of an argument, based on the South Carolina statute, as to how the common law should apply here. One could say (as I think the majority rather inexplicitly

---

which courts make use of this freedom, e.g., Llewellyn, The Common Law Tradition, part 1 (1960); Stone, Legal System and Lawyers' Reasonings, chaps. 7, 8 (1964). I have tried, in Jurisprudence and Statecraft 84-103 (1963), to show, in more compact fashion, that the same complexities of the process can be delineated even within a narrow field of law in a single state.

2. 230 S.C. 330, 95 S.E.2d 606 (1956).

said) as follows: The statute showed that news reportage that revealed a rape victim's identity was not on a matter of "legitimate" public concern, and constituted "revelations . . . so intimate and so unwarranted . . . as to outrage the community's notions of decency," hence the common law right of privacy had been violated.[3]

My point is that *the language of the* Meetze *precedent did not compel a subsequent court to go in one direction rather than another.* In the first place, the above-quoted language of the opinion was not altogether consistent. At some points the words seemed to suggest an unqualified right to make news comment on matters of public concern and record; at others qualifications seemed to be recognized in terms of "illegitimate" concern and "unwarranted" revelations. Secondly, there is plenty of room for interpretation by the subsequent court, in applying such terms as "illegitimate," "unwarranted," and "public concern"; and in determining whether the precedent value of the case should be restricted to a situation in which the facts revealed by the news comment are *both* a matter of public concern and a matter of public record. In other words, the court looking back at the *Meetze* precedent can view the "rule" of that case broadly or narrowly (and thus include or exclude the type of facts facing this subsequent court) because of the ambiguity of the categories in which the elements of the rule are framed.

Is it inevitable that ambiguities will be introduced into the formulation of the rule of the precedent? *Some* ambiguity seems inevitable because of the necessity of putting the facts of the precedent into *categories* if the rule is to function as a precedent at all. If the rule of the *Meetze* case were formulated very narrowly in terms of the proposition that a newspaper identifying a twelve-year-old wife who had become a mother does not thereby violate the mother's right of privacy, the rule would have no explicit force as a precedent for the *Nappier* case or almost any other case, because the facts of *Nappier* would not fit into such a narrow formulation. When the *Meetze* rule is formulated *broadly,* into categories — in terms of *any news agency* reporting a matter which is of *legitimate public concern as well as a matter of public record,* or (more broadly) a matter of *legitimate public concern,* or (still more broadly) a matter of *public concern* — there is at least a possibility that the *Nappier* facts would be governed by the *Meetze* precedent. They *will* be so governed if the subsequent court resolves

3. The majority did not emphasize the legitimacy element in the first quotation, and, as I say, did not call attention to the second quotation at all. However, it was implying, I think, the line of argument I have suggested, when it said in reply to the argument that news comment on "matter of public concern and record" was exempt from privacy violation: "the statute states an exception to the exemption. No matter the news value, South Carolina has unequivocally declared the identity of the injured person shall not be made known in press or broadcast."

the ambiguities in the categories in a way that brings the subsequent situation within the rule.

In the *Nappier* case it happened that the key ambiguity to be resolved was in the statutory word "name." If the majority and minority had agreed on that, they would apparently have agreed on whether the elements of the *Meetze* precedent had been satisfied. But in other cases there could be great uncertainty as to the meaning and application of the indicated possible categories of the *Meetze* rule. Thus, would the concept of legitimate public concern cover additional news comment revealing intimate facts that concerned the person involved in the current event but were not related to the current event? How intimate or embarrassing must the facts be? How far could a magazine story on a former infant mathematical prodigy reveal embarrassing facts on his present activities?[4] Is a movie company publicizing a matter of legitimate public concern when its movie depicts the history and present identity of a reformed prostitute who had some years before been a defendant in a notorious murder trial?[5] These and many other actual cases attest to the ambiguity of the categories in precedent rules on the kind of privacy violation we have been considering: the allegedly unwarranted public disclosure of private facts.

A graphic representation of the point I am making can be found in an analysis by Julius Stone. He was responding to a theory that the rule or "ratio decidendi" of a precedent was to be determined by looking at the facts deemed important by the court that decided it, and then formulating the rule in terms of those facts, e.g.: When such-and-such facts occur, the plaintiff is (or is not) entitled to recover for the loss inflicted by defendant. Stone pointed to a number of difficulties. He said that you often cannot tell from the precedent opinion which facts were deemed significant by the court and which were not, and there are often inconsistent indications of significance. More important still, the facts have to be categorized and the opinion may be unclear as to the *breadth* of the fact-category that is deemed significant. He illustrated this by showing the varying breadth that could be assigned by a later court to each of the factual elements in the 1932 House of Lords decision in Donoghue v. Stevenson.[6]

In this case liability was imposed upon the manufacturer of an opaque bottle of ginger beer found to contain a dead snail, for injury (shock and gastroenteritis) to the plaintiff. She was a Scottish widow who drank from the bottle given her by an individual who purchased it from a retailer who had purchased it from the manufacturer.

4. See Sidis v. F-R Publ. Corp., 113 F.2d 806 (2d Cir. 1940).
5. See Melvin v. Reid, 112 Cal. App. 285, 297 P. 91 (1931).
6. A.C. 562 (H.L. 1932).

Stone analyzed the possible future breadth of the constituent fact-categories as follows:

> (a) *Fact as to the Agent of Harm.* Dead snails, *or* any snails, *or* any noxious physical foreign body, *or* any noxious foreign element, physical or not, *or* any noxious element.
>
> (b) *Fact as to Vehicle of Harm.* An opaque bottle of ginger beer, *or* an opaque bottle of beverage, *or* any bottle of beverage, *or* any container of commodities for human consumption, *or* any containers of any chattels for human use, *or* any chattel whatsoever, *or* any thing (including land or buildings).
>
> (c) *Fact as to Defendant's Identity.* A manufacturer of goods nationally distributed through dispersed retailers, *or* any manufacturer, *or* any person working on the object for reward, *or* any person working on the object, *or* anyone dealing with the object.
>
> (d) *Fact as to Potential Danger from Vehicle of Harm.* Objects likely to become dangerous by negligence, *or* whether or not so.
>
> (e) *Fact as to Injury to Plaintiff.* Physical personal injury, *or* nervous or physical personal injury, *or* any injury.
>
> (f) *Fact as to Plaintiff's Identity.* A Scots widow, *or* a Scotswoman *or* a woman, *or* any adult, *or* any human being, *or* any legal person.
>
> (g) *Fact as to Plaintiff's Relation to Vehicle of Harm.* Donee of purchaser, from retailer who bought directly from the defendant, *or* the purchaser from such retailer, *or* the purchaser from anyone, *or* any person related to such purchaser or other person, *or* any person into whose hands the object rightfully comes, *or* any person into whose hands it comes at all.
>
> (h) *Fact as to Discoverability of Agent of Harm.* The noxious element being not discoverable by inspection of any intermediate party, *or* not so discoverable without destroying the saleability of the commodity, *or* not so discoverable by any such party who had a duty to inspect, *or* not so discoverable by any such party who could reasonably be expected *by the defendant* to inspect, *or* not discoverable by any such party who could reasonably be expected *by the court or a jury* to inspect.
>
> (i) *Fact as to Time of Litigation.* The facts complained of were litigated in 1932, *or* any time before 1932, or after 1932, *or* at any time.[7]

One more example. This one is from the presidential address of Herman Oliphant to the Association of American Law Schools in 1927:

> A's father induces her not to marry B as she promised to do. On a holding that the father is not liable to B for so doing, a gradation of widening propositions can be built, a very few of which are:

7. Stone, The Ratio of the Ratio Decidendi, 22 Mod. L. Rev. 597, 603 (1959). An outstanding legal scholar in jurisprudence and international law, Stone is presently on the faculty of University of New South Wales in Australia, and of Hastings College of Law in this country.

1. Fathers are privileged to induce daughters to break promises to marry.
2. Parents are so privileged.
3. Parents are so privileged as to both daughters and sons.
4. All persons are so privileged as to promises to marry.
5. Parents are so privileged as to all promises made by their children.
6. All persons are so privileged as to all promises made by anyone.[8]

Karl Llewellyn made a similar point when he referred to the "strict" view of precedent as against the "loose" view. A court taking a strict view would veer away from the broader propositions in the prior opinion, addressed to situations other than that which was actually before the precedent court. It would tend to favor one of the narrower formulations. Sometimes its choice would be so narrow as to "confine the precedent to its precise facts," which would be a polite way of saying the precedent had been overruled; it had been deprived of any precedent value. Usually, of course, a court need not make its formulation that narrow in order to say that a case is not a precedent for the present case.

Llewellyn described the narrower formulations as those made for an "unwelcome" precedent, and the broader formulations as made for the "welcome" precedent. Each approach, he emphasized, is legitimate and part of the going judicial practice. Addressing Columbia Law School freshmen a half century ago, he said:

> What I wish to sink deep into your minds about the doctrine of precedent, therefore, is that it is two-headed. It is Janus-faced. That it is not one doctrine, nor one line of doctrine, but two, and two which, *applied at the same time to the same precedent, are contradictory of each other*. That there is one doctrine for getting rid of precedents deemed troublesome and one doctrine for making use of precedents that seem helpful. That these two doctrines exist side by side. That the same lawyer in the same brief, the same judge in the same opinion, may be using the one doctrine, the technically strict one, to cut down half the older cases that he deals with, and using the other doctrine, the loose one, for building with the other half. Until you realize this you do not see how it is possible for law to change and to develop, and yet to stand on the past. You do not see how it is possible to avoid the past mistakes of courts, and yet to make use of every happy insight for which a judge in writing may have found expression. . . .
>
> Nor, until you see this double aspect of the doctrine-in-action, do you appreciate how little, in detail, you can predict *out of the rules alone;*

8. Oliphant, A Return to Stare Decisis, 14 A.B.A.J. 71, 72 (1928).

> how much you must turn, for purposes of prediction, to the reactions of the judges to the facts and to the life around them. . . .[9]

At this point you may be thinking: "Granted that when the precedent opinion leaves open the possibility of a choice of interpretation of its rule by the later court, the later court is free to choose. But suppose the prior court has written the unusual opinion in which it indicated *precisely* the fact-category *breadth* deemed desirable for the rule it was applying. Would the later court still be free to choose a different breadth?" There is some difference of opinion here, but many would still say yes.[10] In this view, if the *Meetze* case had clearly formulated a rule allowing news reportage of private facts "on any matter of public interest," a later court could say: "We are not overruling that decision but we think the rule was formulated too broadly in relation to its facts. The facts indicated a matter of *legitimate* public interest, and the rule should have been qualified in that way. We do not feel bound by any prior formulation of a rule whose breadth (1) went unnecessarily beyond the type of situation presented, and (2) would produce, when applied to the present case, an unreasonable result." A textbook phrased the situation this way in 1961:

> True, the rule of the prior court — announced or otherwise — must necessarily go beyond the precise facts before it [e.g., beyond covering cases of newspaper publicity to the birth of a baby to a twelve-year-old wife] and thus has relevance for later courts operating under a precedent system. But assuming even that the prior court has a definite breadth of rule in mind which is ascertainable by the later court, is not the *later* court best able to decide whether the rule should be conceived broadly enough so as to apply to the particular "beyond" area brought before *it* for decision? The later court must determine whether the principles or policies underlying the prior decision are also applicable to the later case — i.e., whether the facts of the two cases are "similar" enough (or the differences without sufficient significance) to justify giving the explicit or implicit "rule" of the earlier case sufficient breadth to "apply" to the later case. To allow that breadth to be *fixed* by what was said in a prior court's opinion without the present situation before it, would be to stultify the process of wise decision. The precedent supplies guidance lines, not a straitjacket.[11]

What I have been talking about up to now in terms of the "ratio decidendi" or rule of decision can also be talked about in terms of the "holding" of a case. First, a word of background explanation.

9. Llewellyn, The Bramble Bush 68 (Oceana ed. 1951).
10. See, e.g., n.14 below.
11. Auerbach, Garrison, Hurst & Mermin, The Legal Process 65 (1961).

In the early days of the English precedent system, the opinion in a relevant prior case used to be treated like a textbook; everything in it had precedent value. By the end of the seventeenth century, the courts had begun thinking of precedent value in terms of the court's observations that were relevant to the specific situation before the court. The distinction came to be made, in other words, between "holding" and mere "dictum." A case was a precedent for what it "held," not for its "dicta." The latter were observations in the opinion that were "not necessary" to the decision.

The "not necessary" mode of expression has its difficulties. One pitfall is in its application to a decision that decides more than one issue. Suppose the facts presented two issues, and both were ruled on for the appellant, and the judgment of the lower court was reversed. Is the ruling on the second issue mere dictum? Does it have little or no weight because it was not "necessary" — i.e., the reversal would have occurred because of the first ruling anyway? Courts have been known to fall into the trap of thinking in this way. But the mere fact that the second ruling was not necessary for reversal does not mean that it was unnecessary in the sense that a dictum is said to be unnecessary. What is that sense?

Apparently the reference is to observations in the opinion that are directed at types of *facts not present in the case.* In the case I have supposed, the two rulings were directed at issues presented by the facts in the case, so that each was a holding. Both rulings also met a supplementary test sometimes used for distinguishing holding from dictum: the *judgment* (of reversal) *logically followed from* the ruling. I said the rulings favored the appellant; hence the judgment logically following from such rulings would be reversal.

Getting back to a single-issue decision: The "facts not present" test is generally easy to apply. Thus, suppose the *Nappier* court of appeals had included, in its opinion holding there had been a privacy violation, the following additional observation: "If the girls' assailant had attempted unsuccessfully to rape them our decision would be different." Such an observation would have been dictum. It was not "necessary" to the decision; it was directed at a type of facts not present in the case facing the court. No force of precedent would be created for a subsequent court faced with a case that resembled the *Nappier* case except for involving only an attempted rape.[12]

Spotting a dictum is not always easy. My example of the *Nappier* court addressing itself to a hypothetical issue not presented by the

12. I am not saying the subsequent court would not decide the case the same way; it probably would, in view of the "assault with intent to ravish" clause of the statute. I am merely saying the observation in the prior opinion would not have the force of a holding.

facts is a clear case. But suppose the court had said: *"We hold* that whenever a woman has been subjected to *sexual assault,* and publicity is given to it in a manner that identifies her, so that she suffers embarrassment, mental anguish, and possible damage to her social relations, she may recover damages for violation of her right of privacy; hence these plaintiffs may recover." Here the court has done what is not usually done: It has itself formulated what it conceives to be the holding of the case. And included in that purported holding is a type of facts not present in the case, i.e., sexual assaults other than actual rape. In addition, the judgment for plaintiff logically follows from the court's generalization on who may recover (judgment for plaintiff would *not* have logically followed from the previously imagined dictum about non-recovery by victims of attempted rape).

In this situation, you will find some difference of opinion. Some will say that since the court determination with respect to a type of facts not before the court was included in what it labeled its holding, that determination has the force of precedent for the subsequent court (e.g., a court faced with a case involving attempted rape).[13] Others would disagree, saying that insofar as the court's statement of the holding covers a type of facts not before the court, the statement is mere dictum.[14]

This difference of view corresponds of course to the difference previously discussed, when I posed the situation of a court indicating precisely the fact-category breadth that it deemed desirable for the rule it was applying.[15]

But whether the point is put in terms of ratio decidendi or in terms of holding, I think it fair to say that scholars nowadays tend to hold the view that there is *no single, authoritatively correct "ratio" or holding* for a particular judicial decision considered in isolation from how a later court views it; that there are many logical possibilities

13. This would be true in the case of those who, like Rupert Cross, in Precedent in English Law 71, 76 (3rd ed. 1977) define the ratio decidendi or rule of decision as a rule "*expressly* or impliedly treated by the [precedent court] as a necessary step in reaching [its] conclusion," having regard to the facts it deemed "material" and its "line of reasoning" (emphasis added). Cross notes (at 86) that when the later court thinks the rule had been formulated too broadly, the excess breadth might be referred to as a form of dictum, but it is "more in accordance with judicial practice" to discredit the excess by "explanation" or "interpretation" of the earlier rule.

14. Levi, An Introduction to Legal Reasoning 2-3 (1948; Phoenix ed. 1961); Oliphant, A Return to Stare Decisis, 14 A.B.A.J. 71-75, 159 (1927); Lord Halsbury in Quinn v. Leathem [1901] A.C. 495, 506.

15. See *supra* at n.10. I asked whether the later court would still be free to choose a *different breadth,* and said that contrary answers are given to this question. The same conclusion applies here. To talk of determining the "ratio decidendi" or rule of a case is to speak, in other terms, of determining its "holding." And talking, as I am doing now, about whether a rule of law is addressed to the "type of facts before the court" and hence is a holding raises the question: *What breadth* of facts should the court choose?

open to the later court, depending on how broadly or narrowly it classifies the facts of the prior case, and how independent in this respect it wishes to be of the prior opinion's own classification. I intend to elaborate on this subject at a later point in order to clarify any misimpressions perhaps left by this brief discussion.

b. Choosing Between Competing Precedents

I have been discussing the court's leeway in formulating the major premise of the syllogism — and have expounded upon the first aspect of that leeway, the freedom to determine what a particular precedent stands for. The second aspect is the choice between competing precedents. Again, the *Nappier* opinions furnish illustrations.

Thus, the district court cited five South Carolina cases for the proposition that the statute, being penal, should be narrowly construed. But the court of appeals majority was able to cite two South Carolina cases for the proposition that "the penal aspect of the statute does not require an interpretation so rigid as to strip its wording of its plain connotation."

On the question whether a description can serve the same legal purpose as actual naming, the court of appeals opinion referred to two competing lines of precedent. It cited with approval some libel cases to the effect that "a libelee is nonetheless libeled though his name be not mentioned." And it cited, in order to distinguish them, some cases (arising under a statute prohibiting unauthorized use of a personal name, portrait, or picture in advertising) holding that certain descriptions or references would *not* qualify as naming. These the court of appeals distinguished by saying: "For advertising, only the name, pseudonym or picture of the person — usually because of his prominence — is significant. Any other description is of no value. Consequently the object of the law is not impinged unless the publication embodies the name, portrait or picture. That is not so in the statute now in review."

3. Formulating the Minor Premise

So far the discussion of the legal syllogism has been in terms of formulating the major premise. Formulating the minor premise affords the court another area of choice.

The court must determine the reasonableness of categorizing the facts of the case in such a way as to bring them within the categories of the major premise. By that statement I do not mean that in the actual chronology of a court's deliberations the major premise comes first. The opposite is probably true usually. But when a court formulates its final, formal opinion, the principle of law functioning as the major premise will generally be presented first, and the categorization of the case will fit into the categories in the major premise. This was true of the two syllogisms formulated earlier about the *Nappier* case.

You will note that in the *Nappier* syllogisms, the two different minor premises fitted into two *different* major premises, with different conclusions resulting. But there are many instances of a difference in conclusion resulting from using different minor premises and the *same* major premise. For instance, assume that both the majority and minority of the court of appeals subscribed to the same major premise, e.g., " a person's right of privacy is violated by news reportage of intimate facts that are not of legitimate public interest." A difference of opinion might still remain between judges on *whether* that part of a news report that identified the rape victims was on a matter of "legitimate public interest."

The question of what is a matter of "legitimate" public interest involves a value judgment. But sometimes, of course, a difference in minor premises results from a difference in the fact findings — i.e., as to what actually happened in the case.

B. Background Note: More on the Precedent System

1. How Free Is the Appellate Judge, and How Unpredictable His Decision?

When you add up all the areas of freedom I have been discussing — determining what a precedent stands for, choosing between competing precedents, and formulating the minor premise — you may conclude that the legal system is shot through with uncertainty and unpredictability. Here is the misimpression I earlier promised to discuss further, and shall do so below.

a. High Predictability of Result in Typical Appellate Court (Not United States Supreme Court)

First of all, let me make clear what are, and are not, the subjects of discussion. We are talking about the freedom of an appellate court. Whatever freedom we may find to exist on that level is considerably greater than that which exists on the level of the practitioner advising a client on the state of the law, or the citizen attempting to be law-abiding on his own. Much of the practitioner's advice or the citizen's conduct is in situations to which the existing rules, principles, and customary standards of behavior speak rather *clearly*. The client or citizen orders his affairs accordingly, and court cases will usually not develop on account of his doing so. In contrast, the appellate court naturally has more "borderline" (or "problem" or "unprovided for" or "hard") situations to deal with. This description is especially applicable to the United States Supreme Court, most of whose cases are selected by the Court in the exercise of its discretionary "certiorari" jurisdiction, precisely because they are not routine cases and often because other courts have rendered contrary decisions.

A further relevant observation is that in a typical appellate court (not the United States Supreme Court) the "hard cases" are in a minority. Cardozo, while a member of the New York Court of Appeals, said that a "majority" of the cases coming before his court could reasonably be decided in only one way;[16] and at another point put the figure at "nine-tenths."[17] Federal Judge Jerome Frank thought that the latter figure was "perhaps not too wide of the mark."[18] Federal Judge Charles E. Clark, who said he agreed with Professor Edwin Patterson's judgment that the "nine-tenths" figure was too high, thought the "majority" figure was a fair statement.[19] Llewellyn's estimate of predictability was 80 percent or more, based partly on a study of cases decided by the New York Court of Appeals.[20] Possibly the current reliability of these estimates, made a generation or so ago, has been rendered suspect (overly high) by the subsequent proliferation of competing precedents.

b. Typical Appellate Court's Freedom Within the Rules, or to Overrule, Is Not a Freedom to Be Arbitrary; Non-Rule Factors, Including Considerations of Policy, Move the Court in a Fairly Predictable Direction

Any conclusions you may reach about appellate court freedom and the accompanying uncertainty or unpredictability of the law concern-

16. Cardozo, Nature of the Judicial Process 35 (1921).

17. Cardozo, The Growth of the Law 60 (1924).

18. Frank, Cardozo and the Upper-Court Myth, 13 Law & Contemp. Prob. 369, 374 (1948). Frank also stressed that predictability of result was much lower on the *trial* level than on the appellate level. E.g., the facts related by the client in the lawyer's office, on which the lawyer's confidence in a court victory is partly based, may be undermined on the witness stand.

19. Clark, Book Review, 57 Yale L.J. 658, 661 (1948).

20. Llewellyn, The Common Law Tradition 25 n.16, 45 (1960); Llewellyn, 14 U. Cin. L. Rev. 208, 219 (1940).

ing "hard" cases do not translate into conclusions about the uncertainty or unpredictability of the law generally. I assert this not only on the basis of the preceding two paragraphs but also because of the following consideration. The appellate court freedom described earlier in terms of the "many logical possibilities open to the later court" is not a freedom to be *arbitrary* in the exercise of those logical possibilities.[21] For there are *factors, other than the rules themselves,*[22] *that restrain the court and make predictability high.* I shall repeat below a summarization I once made of some aspects of this point.

One barrier to undue judicial freedom comes from language. That is, *some* words of prior judicial rules, of statutes, and of the Constitution strike in most of us a common chord of meaning, so that judicial repudiation of that meaning without solid basis in context or current need would strike most of us as arbitrary, and no judge wants to be considered arbitrary.

We must remember also the check on arbitrariness that comes from the *group* process of decision. If a judge holds capricious or ill-considered views, these must run the gauntlet of colleagues' critical reactions; if a court majority is inclined to arbitrary judgment, the judges must brook the critical reactions of the profession as a whole. Even when the maverick judge is unpersuaded by his colleagues, the tradition is for him to go along with the majority, except where strong convictions compel that he register dissent.

Efficacy of the group process of deliberation in influencing the individual case determinations of United States Supreme Court justices has been questioned by some, including Thurman Arnold. But, however apt his skepticism may be as applied to some individuals and some issues of fundamental judicial philosophy, those who have participated in meetings of corporate boards of directors, of committees of unions, university faculties, churches, fraternal societies; of law partners, of government commissions, of parole boards, or other groups charged with decisions, can surely attest to occasions when group discussion moderated, modified, or reversed the views of participants. More than one Supreme Court Justice indeed, has acknowledged that such changes of mind have occurred even after draft majority and minority opinions have circulated within the court.

21. See discussion in Llewellyn, *supra* n.1 at 19-61 which covers more ground than the selected factors I discuss in the paragraphs that follow.

22. Recall the Llewellyn quotation (*supra* at n.9) to the effect that "little, in detail, [can be predicted] out of the rules alone." The rule is of course always involved in the decision. But the appellate judges reinterpret an existing rule in the *context* of a particular new set of facts and the attendant policy considerations that seem persuasive to those judges at that time. One of the factors influencing that persuasiveness is the relative skill of the opposing attorneys, though I believe this is not usually the most critical factor on the appellate level.

Moreover, a tradition, embodied in Canons 20 and 21 of the old Canons of Judicial Ethics, counsels suppressing the expression of personal value judgments that are opposed to community value judgments, and suppressing a personal approach to decision that is not "the usual and expected method of doing justice." "Justice," said Canon 21, "should not be molded by the individual idiosyncrasies of those who administer it." Cardozo's observation in this connection was that the judge "is to regulate his estimate of values by objective rather than subjective standards, by the thought and will of the community rather than by his own idiosyncrasies of conduct and belief."

True, judges do not always adhere to traditions. But these traditions of responsible decision are coupled with another — the judicial duty and desire to do justice — and with some tendency for relatively disinterested minds to agree on the just policy for the situation in hand. That courts do not usually depart from all these traditions and tendencies is perhaps suggested by the fact that predictability of the result of the case is high.[23]

On the last-mentioned subject of prediction, let me elaborate on an earlier point: Even those scholars who have done most to detail the complexities and uncertainties in decision see a high rate of accurate prediction of appellate decision. If their estimates seemed overly high, remember this: they are talking about a prediction of which side will win (rather than the particular rationale that will be used), and about a prediction by a disinterested, trained lawyer familiar with the particular court. Moreover, they are talking about prediction "not just on the basis of precedent rules and facts and past attitudes, but also on the basis of subsequent developments — including those contemporary 'felt necessities' and 'intuitions of public policy' that tend to pull the malleable rules, facts, and attitudes into a particular shape."[24] Finally,

23. The foregoing five paragraphs draw on Mermin, Jurisprudence and Statecraft 111-112 (1963), which documents some of the above assertions. *Cf.* the discussion, in Chap. 1 *supra* at n.257, of what Cardozo meant by the words quoted above.

24. Mermin, Computers, Law and Justice, 1967 Wis. L. Rev. 43, 85. The reference to malleable rules, facts, and attitudes stems from a prior disparagement, in the cited article, of the attempts of political scientists to predict Supreme Court decisions by mechanical (statistical and computer analysis) methods. My criticism had been that these scholars assume the *same Court* will have the *same attitude* it had before in *factually similar* cases — but that each of the underlined factors is indeterminate. Thus the Court's personnel does change, and even without such change, attitudes of judges shift — sometimes because of the presence of issues (substantive, procedural, prudential) additional to the particular issue on which the predictor is interested in comparing the cases. Nor is the determination of "similarity" a mechanical process. Asking whether two cases are factually similar for purposes of judicial decision is to ask whether the policy underlying the rule of the prior case can reasonably apply and ought to apply to the present case, i.e., whether the *fact categories of the prior rule* can *reasonably* be read and *ought* to be read to include the facts of the present case. See also n.31 below.

they are talking about the ordinary appellate courts in which review may be had as of right, rather than the United States Supreme Court, in which, for the most part, review is on a discretionary basis and generally confined to the closer cases.[25]

c. *A Minority View: Judicial Freedom Moves and Should Move Within Legal "Principle" and Not "Policy," In an Effort to Discover the "Single Right Answer"; Judges Are to "Find" Rather Than "Make" Law*

And now a word of caution. What I have tried to capture in the foregoing discussion of the precedent system are the mainstream tendencies in American thinking and attitudes on the subject — at least in the sense that most judges and scholars would regard the analysis as substantially correct, whether or not they have previously thought about the subject in quite the same terms.[26]

But "most" is not "all"; some judges and scholars, while agreeing on high predictability and the barriers to arbitrariness, would view a judge's powers more narrowly than I have pictured. This would particularly be true of the judge who took the more conservative view of the concept of ratio decidendi or holding, i.e., would be deferential to the prior court's expressed view (in the distinct minority of instances in which the view is expressly stated) as to the proper level of *breadth,* for the future, of the ratio or holding. But whether holding this view or not, some authorities would lodge a further objection. According to their position, the judicial freedom within the diverse "logical possibilities" I have pointed to in the operating precedent system is restrained not only by the barriers to arbitrariness that I have mentioned, but also by another type of barrier I have not mentioned.

25. I have been talking about prediction of the individual case rather than statistical predictions as to percentages of affirmances and reversals. For the trends in these percentages in the Supreme Court and other appellate courts, see Chap. 1 *supra* n.196. Where states adopted a system of intermediate appellate courts and made review by the state's highest court discretionary, the latter court's reversal rate generally increased, though this effect was not as large or as prevalent in all states studied as might have been expected. Closeness of a case, or the highest court's disagreement with the result in the court below, seemed not to have been the only basis for selecting the case for review. See Kagan, Cartwright, Friedman & Wheeler, The Evolution of State Supreme Courts, 76 Mich. L. Rev. 961, 995-997, 999; Note, 33 Stan. L. Rev. 951, 960-961 (1981).

26. As samples of these mainstream tendencies, see Cardozo, The Nature of the Judicial Process (1921); Levi, An Introduction to Legal Reasoning (1948; Phoenix ed., 1961); Llewellyn, The Common Law Tradition (1960); Stone, Legal System and Lawyers' Reasonings, chaps. 6-8 (1964); MacCormick, Legal Reasoning and Legal Theory (1978).

They would say that the *type of justification* that the judge can give for exercising his freedom by an expansive rather than restrictive interpretation of a precedent, or vice versa (or by overruling a precedent, or by deciding a case that has no apparent precedent) is subject to the following restraint: It must be in terms of legal "principle" and not in terms of "policy." Policies, it is argued, are the concern of the legislature. They set out "a goal to be reached, generally an improvement in some economic, political or social feature of the community. . . ."[27] Principles are "to be observed, not because [they] will advance or secure an economic, political, or social situation deemed desirable, but because [they are] a requirement of justice or fairness or some other dimension of morality. Thus, the standard that automobile accidents are to be decreased is a policy, and the standard that no man may profit by his own wrong a principle."[28]

Alternatively, principles have been said to justify a decision "by showing that the decision respects or secures some individual or group right"[29] that is recognized by the legal institutions of which the court is a part. And in "hard cases" the judge may have to search beyond the equivocal terms of judicial opinions, statutes, and constitutions, looking for underlying principles that are presupposed by those provisions and the legal system as a whole. The judge, it is said, remains a law *finder* rather than law *maker*. He searches to discover the *preexisting, single "correct" or "right" answer* to the problem. The legislature, on the other hand, is the law maker; and, relatively unhampered by requirements of principled consistency, it ideally concerns itself with the law's consequences for the ever changing needs of society.

d. Prevailing Doubts About the Minority View

But such a view of judicial decisionmaking as a virtually self-sufficient legal-logical process, isolated from the pressures and demands of the surrounding society and with the judge playing a minimally creative role, has in our times been viewed as old-fashioned nineteenth-century "formalism," "mechanical jurisprudence," or a "slot machine" judicial process. Justice Holmes at the turn of the century, and then Roscoe Pound and many scholars thereafter, stressed the folly of such a theory that would separate judicial principles and logic from judgments of social policy. Rather the prevailing view has been that policy judgments by judges are an inevitable and, within limits, desirable

27. Dworkin, Taking Rights Seriously 22 (1977).
28. *Id.*
29. *Id.* at 82. This is Dworkin's later explanation of "principles." The remainder of the paragraph draws generally on chap. 4 of the cited book.

element in judicial decisionmaking. The policy problem may receive little or no discussion in common law opinions — a fact that may give mechanical flavor to the opinion. Such a result led Holmes to the criticism that "the judges themselves have failed adequately to recognize their duty of weighing considerations of social advantage. The duty is inevitable and the result of the often proclaimed judicial aversion to deal with such considerations is simply to leave the very ground and foundation of judgments inarticulate, and often unconscious. . . ."[30]

Why is the duty "inevitable"? One reason is that the policy issue is involved in the very process of determining whether a precedent case is "similar" to the case before the court. Determining similarity is not a mechanical matter. Rules are illuminated by seeking the reasons underlying them. To determine similarity, the judge must ask *whether the policy behind the precedent* (and it is a rare precedent that is *not* based on some policy deemed desirable) *ought also to apply to* the facts of the current case.[31] The alternative offered, of relying solely on legal rules and principles, is an illusory alternative. Rules shorn of their policy base are a poor starting point for reasoning; and this is reflected in the fact that judges who are unwilling to be explicit about policy will consider it tacitly or unconsciously, as Holmes observed.

This (1) "inevitable duty" plus (2) the blurred line between "principle" and "policy," and (3) the ambiguity, multiplicity, and contrariety of rules and principles combine to block any inevitable line of deduction from legal rules and principles to the promised, single "correct" or "right" answer.[32]

30. Holmes, The Path of the Law, 10 Harv. L. Rev. 457, 467 (1897). See also Dworkin, *supra* n.27 at 466.

31. "It's not as though you were a sorter on a factory assembly line with the job of matching two colors or sizes or quantities and concluding when you made such a match that the two were similar and therefore were to be put in a can with the same label. As a judge you don't just match things for some kind of mechanical likeness and then decide they are similar. The process of determining similarity is one in which judgments of *oughtness* and *social reasonableness* are central — though the chronological order of the steps in the appellate judge's reactions to a case may differ for varying types of cases and judges." Mermin, *supra* n.24 at 77. (For extended analysis and discussion see Stone, Legal System and Lawyers' Reasonings 267-300 (1964)). This being so, the process of "applying" a rule is really "a clarification of the rule, through a value-judgment determining whether the rule should be regarded as covering the new facts; and it is an evaluation of the rule, through a value-judgment whether it should be retained" at all. Mermin, *supra* n.23 at 105-106.

32. See Hart, American Jurisprudence Through English Eyes: The Nightmare and the Noble Dream, 11 Ga. L. Rev. 969, 982-986 (1977); Hart, Perspective of Philosophy, in Schwartz, ed., American Law: The Third Century (The Law Bicentennial Volume) at 423-428 (1976); Greenawalt, Policy, Rights, and Judicial Decision, in Symposium, 11 Ga. L. Rev. 991 (1977), and other articles critical of Dworkin in the same Symposium — which oppose the proposed confinement of judges to rules and "principles" as against "policies," and oppose the "one right answer" thesis. Greenawalt's earlier article, Discretion and Judicial Decision: The Elusive Quest For

Rather, when combined with a consideration of underlying policies, the rules and principles yield results that depend on the court's *evaluative* judgments in answering (explicitly or otherwise) some such questions as these: "(a) Is this a *just and reasonable* result; and is it more so than the alternative result? (b) Is the result *reasonably* reconcilable with the policies of existing precedent; is it more so than the alternative result; and can I *reasonably* construe those policies at the breadth level that I have chosen (and if the result is not reasonably reconcilable with precedent policies, are there strong enough reasons for overruling precedent)? (c) If the answers to questions (a) and (b) lead in opposite directions, what factors in the particular case make one direction *more reasonable* than the other?"

Answering such questions obviously calls for judicial statesmanship in the inquiries into, among other things, probable social consequences and the demands of morality — inquiries to be conducted with "impartiality and neutrality in surveying the alternatives; consideration of the interest of all who will be affected; and a concern to employ some acceptable general principle as a reasoned basis for decision."[33]

What I have tried to present, I repeat, is an attitude in the mainstream of contemporary juristic thinking as opposed to what I have called a nineteenth-century attitude — though the latter attitude has been currently argued by Ronald Dworkin[34] with much greater subtlety and ingenuity than by any nineteenth-century writer.

e. Am I Defending "Result Orientation"? "Rationalization"?

I have already dealt with the objection that the modern attitude leaves the judge free to be arbitrary; I have indicated some barriers to arbitrariness, mainly in certain established judicial traditions. Another objection deserves mention. Does not the concern for consequences of

---

the Fetters that Bind Judges, 75 Colum. L. Rev. 243 (1975), contains much additional material illustrating judges' use of policy judgments in a variety of types of decision, as does Summers, Two Types of Substantive Reasons: The Core of A Theory of Common Law Justification, 63 Cornell L. Rev. 707 (1978), and see at 717 n.28.

33. Hart, The Concept of Law 200 (1961). Hart goes on to say: "No doubt because a plurality of such principles is always possible it cannot be *demonstrated* that a decision is uniquely correct: but it may be made acceptable as the reasoned product of informed impartial choice. In all this we have the 'weighing' and 'balancing' characteristic of the effort to do justice between competing interests." These are "characteristic judicial virtues, the special appropriateness of which to legal decision explains why some feel reluctant to call such judicial activity 'legislative.'" *Id.*

34. See the Dworkin book cited *supra* n.27, and his Seven Critics, 11 Ga. L. Rev. 1201 (1977), a reply to the critical articles in the Symposium cited in n.32.

decision mean that the judge becomes so "result-oriented" that he works *backward* from a socially desirable result to the kind of premises that will give him that result, then deceptively writes the opinion in forward fashion, showing how the premises lead to the conclusion? At least two answers can be made to this objection. First, there is nothing wrong with result-orientation as such.[35] After all, law was established as a means to social ends, not as an end in itself. But result-orientation *alone* is an insufficient basis for decision. Except in certain unusual situations, the judge has the simultaneous task of (1) announcing fair and reasonable principles that are (2) reasonably reconcilable with precedent — or not reconcilable when precedent is, for strong reasons, being overruled. When Holmes said, "It is the merit of the common law that it decides the case first and determines the principle afterwards,"[36] he did not mean that for *any* result preferred by the judge he could find *acceptable* supporting premises from the precedents. The judge may have to reject a tentatively preferred conclusion because the precedents cannot reasonably be read to yield the necessary major premise. The quotation does, however, reflect the familiar tendency in human thinking to approach problems non-deductively — i.e., by considering tentative solutions first (arrived at by "hunch" or by more deliberate consideration) and seeing if persuasive reasons can be found to serve as premises.[37]

Second, the process is not one of deception or of "rationalization" in a derogatory sense. The court is not asserting that the deductive logic that is explicit or implicit in its opinion (the "logic of justification") represents its *entire* decisional process, so as to include the preliminary groping for premises that might support a tentative conclusion (the "logic of discovery"[38]). Rather, the court's justification — the part that matters — stands and is offered independently (1) as an attempt to persuade others that the court's conclusion is rational and just, and is consistent with such prior principle as is reasonably applicable; and (2) as the procedure by which the court has persuaded itself that its conclusion is rationally justified as a principled conclusion. Many opinions are admittedly not as open as they should be about all the policy reasons that may have figured in the "logic of discovery" stage — a

35. See, for a careful analysis, Stone, "Result-Orientation" and Appellate Judgment, in Pound, Griswold, Sutherland, eds., Perspectives of Law; Essays for A.W. Scott 347 (1964).

36. Holmes, Codes, and the Arrangement of the Law, 5 Am. L. Rev. 1 (1870).

37. See Dewey, Logical Method and Law, 10 Cornell L.Q. 17 (1924); Radin, The Method of Law, 1950 Wash. U.L.Q. 471, 489. For some quotations from English judges acknowledging this sequence of thought, see Cross, Precedent in English Law 51-52 (3d ed. 1977). For a similar statement by Chancellor Kent of New York, see Kent, ed., The Memoirs and Letters of James Kent 158-159 (1898).

38. The phrases "logic of justification" and "logic of discovery" are borrowed from Wasserstrom. See his discussion in The Judicial Decision 24-30 (1961).

deficiency that Justice Holmes deplored, as is evident in the previously quoted statement urging judges to be more articulate about "considerations of social advantage." Such articulateness is on the increase and has long been characteristic of public law opinions, especially in the United States Supreme Court. But even its absence cannot prevent the rest of us, including a later court, from critically examining the policy soundness of the conclusion as well as the reasonableness of the derivation of the major premise from precedents and the minor premise from the facts of the current case.

2. The Binding Force of a Precedent; The Problems of When and How to Overrule

1. You may wonder whether a decision's binding force on later courts varies with the relationship between the later court and the court that rendered the decision. It does. As you might expect, a higher court decision, within either the state or federal hierarchy, will bind the lower court within the same hierarchy, but the reverse is not true.

A state court is not bound by the decisions of other states' courts. Suppose a state court has to decide a federal issue, e.g., arising under a federal statute or the Federal Constitution, and a federal court below the United States Supreme Court has already decided the issue. The decision may have persuasive force but is not binding, though it would be if it had been rendered by the Supreme Court.

Suppose now a federal district court is deciding a federal issue, and the same issue has been decided by: a state court; or another federal district court; or by the federal court of appeals of another circuit. None of these courts would set a binding precedent. But the decision of the court of appeals of the circuit in which the now deciding district court is located (assuming there is no contrary Supreme Court decision on the issue) would do so.

Suppose an issue of state common law or statute is presented to a federal court because of the parties' diversity of citizenship. The federal court is bound to follow the state's decisions on the issue. (Recall the discussion of the famous Erie R.R. v. Tompkins case in Chap. 2 at nn. 100-104).[39]

Finally, consider some points peculiar to United States Supreme Court decisions. As earlier mentioned, the denial of discretionary review (certiorari denial) does not have the force of precedent;[40] nor does

39. For documentation of the assertions in the preceding four paragraphs, see IB Moore, Federal Practice, ¶0.402[1], at 60-67 (2d ed., 1980); Traynor, Some Open Questions On the Work of State Appellate Courts, 24 U. Chi. L. Rev. 211, 215 (1957).

40. Stern & Gressman, Supreme Court Practice, §5.7 (5th ed. 1978).

an affirmance by an equally divided Supreme Court, though it is binding on the parties to that case.[41] Because a quorum has since 1869 been fixed at six, then if six or seven out of the nine justices are sitting, only four justices (a majority of the quorum) can authoritatively author a precedent. I.e., the decision as to whether plaintiff or defendant should win in a particular situation, when adhered to by a majority of the quorum, is binding on future parties in similar situations. Lawyers nonetheless may regard that precedent as more vulnerable to overruling because decided by less than a majority of the full court.

Sometimes, regardless of the size of the quorum, the majority vote is based on differing *rationales* in two or more opinions. Lower courts have struggled and differed in assessing the *rule* of such a precedent, and the Supreme Court itself has made only a partial and unsatisfying attempt at such an assessment.[42]

Another feature of Supreme Court opinions is the frequent appearance of a "summary" affirmance, reversal, or dismissal, e.g., for lack of a substantial federal question (summary in the sense that the case is disposed of without full briefing, oral argument, and full opinion). These are decisions on the merits (unlike certiorari denials) and lower courts are to give them as much weight as other precedents[43] — though the Supreme Court itself has been known to give them less weight.[44]

2. The kind of judicial freedom I discussed earlier occurs within the process of "following" favorable precedents and "distinguishing" unfavorable precedents. But there is also the possibility of breaking with precedent altogether — acknowledging that an unfavorable precedent cannot be reasonably distinguished and should be overruled. In the American precedent system, this drastic step is allowable but is not to be taken lightly, being justified only by the strongest kind of reasons.

41. U.S. v. Pink, 315 U.S. 203, 216 (1942).

42. "When a fragmented court decides a case and no single rationale explaining the result enjoys the assent of five Justices, 'the holding of the Court may be viewed as that position taken by those Members who concurred in the judgments on the narrowest grounds. . . .'" Marks v. U.S., 430 U.S. 188, 193 (1977). But this approach "is only useful in those cases where the plurality and concurring opinions stand in a 'broader-narrower' relation to each other. Many of the most troublesome plurality opinions, however, do not fit into this mold, and lower courts have been left to their own devices to determine the precedential value of most plurality opinions." Note, 80 Colum. L. Rev. 756, 767 (1980). Difficulties in the meaning and application of the broad-narrow test are analyzed, *id.* at 761-767; alternative approaches are analyzed, *id.* at 767-781. For other discussions see Davis & Reynolds, Juridical Cripples: Plurality Opinions in the Supreme Court, 1974 Duke L.J. 59; Notes, 94 Harv. L. Rev. 1127 (1981); 2 Fla. St. U.L. Rev. 312 (1974); 24 U. Chi. L. Rev. 99 (1956).

43. Hicks v. Miranda, 422 U.S. 332, 343-345 (1975). But a summary affirmance does not necessarily affirm the reasoning of the lower court. Fusari v. Steinberg, 419 U.S. 379, 391-392 (1975). See also on summary decisions, Chap. 2 at 173-174.

44. Edelman v. Jordan, 415 U.S. 651, 671 (1974); Tully v. Griffin, 429 U.S. 68, 74 (1976). On this subject, see Stern & Gressman, *supra* n.40, §§4.28-4.31; Notes, 64 Va. L. Rev. 117 (1978); 29 Me. L. Rev. 325 (1978); 76 Colum. L. Rev. 508 (1976).

The English system has been more rigid. Not until 1966 did the House of Lords decide that it had power to overrule its own decisions.[45]

There are a number of aspects of overruling that I should touch on, at least briefly:

(a) Militating in general *against* overruling are the overall reasons for having a precedent system at all: the greater stability and certainty and integrated quality of the law; the greater assurance that different people who find themselves in similar situations will be treated by law in the same way; the saving of human energy and time that comes from building on past analyses of possibly similar problems. It is true that some of these virtues are diminished by the flexibility or leeway with which, as I have tried to show, the precedent system operates. But I suppose the virtues would be still less in evidence if a court operated under a system that did not consult precedent at all.

(b) The court may feel that the legislature, if it has failed to adopt proposals to change the existing judicial doctrine, has in effect approved or ratified the doctrine, so as to preclude the change by court overruling. Courts are less apt to take this attitude than they used to be. You may recall an earlier discussion of the attitudes of various state courts on the overruling of certain tort immunities.[46] They were willing to say that an immunity doctrine that they had themselves created, they could themselves abolish. Legislative failure to make the proposed change was not determinative. It is true, however, that a specific rejection of the proposal by unfavorable vote of the legislature weighs more heavily with the court than legislative inaction or death of the bill in committee, or unfavorable committee vote.[47]

(c) Some courts have adopted another kind of legislative ratification argument. They have said that if the precedent in question consists of a decision *interpreting a statute,* then it cannot be judicially overruled because the interpretation becomes part of the statute; so only the legislature can change it. Even courts that have announced such a principle have sometimes, I have noticed, changed their statutory interpretations, without saying anything one way or the other about the principle. The United States Supreme Court, be it noted,

45. See Dias, Precedents in the House of Lords — A Much Needed Reform, 1966 Camb. L.J. 153; Leach, Revisionism in the House of Lords, 80 Harv. L. Rev. 797 (1967).

46. See Chap. 1 *supra* at nn. 403-404. For discussions of overruling in tort cases in recent years, see Henderson, Expanding the Negligence Concept: Retreat From the Rule of Law, 51 Ind. L.J. 467 (1976); Keeton, Judicial Law Reform — A Perspective on the Performance of Appellate Courts, 44 Tex. L. Rev. 1254, 1255-1259 (1965); Keeton, Venturing to Do Justice 169-170 (1969).

47. See generally, Breitel, The Courts and Lawmaking, in Paulsen, ed., Legal Institutions Today and Tomorrow 11-15, 25 (1959); and on the related matter of inferences concerning the status of statutory interpretation precedents from legislative action or inaction, see Chap. 3 *supra* at nn. 16-17; Auerbach et al., *supra* n.11 at 848-849 (1961); Reynolds, Judicial Process, §5.21 (1980).

has not adopted the principle, having many times changed its interpretations of federal statutes.[48]

(d) The Supreme Court has, however, recognized this principle: It will be more prone to overrule its decision on an issue of *constitutional* interpretation than it will be to overrule its decision on other issues. The reason is that if great dissatisfaction is caused by the Court's decision on a federal nonconstitutional issue, Congress can rather readily change it. But Congress cannot change the Court's interpretation of the Constitution; only the cumbersome process of constitutional amendment can do that. Hence, the Court feels it should be more ready to overrule. It observed in 1944 that while it was "not unmindful of the desirability of continuity of decision in constitutional questions," in such questions, "where correction depends upon amendment and not upon legislative action, this Court throughout its history has freely exercised its power to reexamine the basis of its constitutional decisions."[49]

(e) Courts are much less likely to overrule where to do so would work hardship on those who substantially and reasonably *relied* on the previous state of the law. In fact, in an extreme case, such an upsetting of reliance could be unfair enough to be unconstitutional, as a violation of "due process of law." An occasional case, for instance, has had this pattern: A man does something, e.g., sells intoxicating liquor in 1908, after a state supreme court decision declaring that the statutory prohibition against such conduct is unconstitutional. In 1909 the court changes its mind and holds the statute valid. Later in 1909 the state successfully prosecutes the seller for his 1908 sales. The state supreme court reverses the conviction; the defendant's reliance on the earlier decision gives him a good defense as a matter of statutory interpretation. Courts generally would probably also say the conviction violated his due process rights. If Congress or a state *legislature* makes criminal what was not criminal when it was done, this would run afoul of the "ex post facto" clauses of the Constitution. Those clauses do not apply to courts, but the due process clauses do. Unduly harsh retroactivity —

48. ". . . We have never applied *stare decisis* mechanically to prohibit overruling our earlier decisions determining the meaning of statutes." Monell v. Department of Social Services, 436 U.S. 658, 695 (1978). See in support of this position, Mishkin & Morris, On Law In Courts 481-513 (1965); Traynor, Comment, in Paulsen, ed., Legal Institutions Today and Tomorrow 66 (1959); Keeton, Venturing To Do Justice 79-80 (1969). The other side (for which, see Levi, An Introduction to Legal Reasoning 32-33, 54-57 (1948); Horack, Congressional Silence: A Tool of Judicial Supremacy, 25 Tex. L. Rev. 247, 250-253 (1947)) is argued mainly on the theory that the legislature will be more alive to its democratic responsibilities if it knows that it alone, and not the courts, can correct erroneous judicial interpretations of statutes. There is also a fear that judicial overruling involves possibly harsh retroactive impact on those who relied on the earlier decision — though the "prospective" overruling decision used in common law and constitutional overruling as discussed below at nn. 50-61 could be used here too.

49. Smith v. Allwright, 321 U.S. 649, 665 (1944).

on the part of courts or any other agency of government, and whether in a criminal or civil suit — may be held to violate due process of law.

In the tort immunities cases referred to in paragraph (b) above, some courts hesitated about overruling the tort immunity of, say, a charitable hospital, or of a city, precisely because of the reliance element. The defendant hospital or city, in reliance on the existing state of the law, had not taken out insurance for tort liability. *After* the decision it could of course do so, to cover contingencies arising in the future. But sudden imposition now of tort liability for past occurrences that were, on reasonable grounds, not covered by insurance would be harsh — even if not unconstitutional. It would also be harsh on all other defendants in similar cases that were either pending in court or might yet be filed because the claims (while arising out of events in the period prior to the overruling decision) were not yet barred by the statute of limitations. These were largely the reasons why some courts chose to leave the change to the legislature. Legislative decisions are typically *prospective;* judicial decisions are typically retroactive.

(f) A key word above is "typically." Just as legislation is occasionally retroactive, and validly so when judged not so harsh as to violate the ex post facto or due process clauses,[50] judicial decisions have sometimes been prospective. Indeed, the last two decades have witnessed the flowering of judicial decision prospectivity.[51]

These very cases on tort immunities have had much to do with this development. They have dealt with the problem of harsh retroactivity of judicial overruling decisions by introducing some kinds of prospectivity into them. A parallel development, occurring simultaneously, was the Supreme Court's introduction of prospectivity into its overruling decisions in the area of constitutional rights of criminal defendants.

The major techniques departing from complete retroactivity have been these:

(i) *Complete prospectivity of the decision*

This means the decision does not apply to past situations, not even to the past situation that is the subject of the decision. Only situations

50. See, e.g., Nowak, Rotunda & Young, Constitutional Law 428-436 (1978); Hochman, The Supreme Court and the Constitutionality of Retroactive Legislation, 73 Harv. L. Rev. 692 (1960).

51. See Traynor, Quo Vadis, Prospective Overruling: A Question of Judicial Responsibility, 28 Hastings L.J. 533 (1977); Schaefer, The Control of "Sunbursts": Techniques of Prospective Overruling, 42 N.Y.U.L. Rev. 631 (1967); Mishkin, Foreword, The Supreme Court, 1964 Term, 79 Harv. L. Rev. 56 (1965); Schwartz, Retroactivity, Reliability and Due Process: A Reply to Professor Mishkin, 33 U. Chi. L. Rev. 719 (1966); Levy, Realist Jurisprudence and Prospective Overruling, 109 U. Pa. L. Rev. (1960); Annot., 22 L. Ed. 2d 821 (1969); 10 A.L.R.3d 1371 (1967); Note, 55 Wash. L. Rev. 833 (1980).

arising after the decision are affected. This had been the approach taken in a famous *Sunburst Oil* case, in which the Montana Supreme Court overruled a rule of law, but applied the old rule to the case before the court, declaring that the new rule would apply only to transactions occurring after the decision. Justice Cardozo's opinion for the United States Supreme Court declared that the Constitution did not stand in the way of the Montana court's decisional method.[52]

But it is worth noting that the Supreme Court had not used this technique in overruling its *own* decisions. In the decade of the 1960s when the Warren Court was overruling so many constitutional decisions on criminal procedure, the Court for the first time gave frontal consideration to the problem. And it concluded in the 1967 case of Stovall v. Denno that complete prospectivity in a federal court decision would be contrary to "the command of Article III of the Constitution that we resolve issues solely in concrete cases or controversies." Merely to announce a rule, and not apply it to the parties in the concrete case before the court, would be to announce a "mere dictum." And such a practice would have a possibly adverse "effect upon the incentive of counsel to advance contentions requiring a change in the law" since the reward of application to the present case would be removed.[53] The Court ignored a decision three years earlier that had been completely prospective;[54] and two years after *Stovall,* a sentence in a Court opinion suggested merely that complete prospectivity would be "most unusual."[55]

(ii) *Partial retroactivity*

One technique of partial retroactivity was applied in a number of the state cases abolishing tort immunities[56] — i.e., the new rule was to apply not only to similar situations arising in the future but also *to the case before the court* (not, however, to other similar situations arising prior to the decision). Sometimes the additional device of postponing the effective date of the decision was used, in order to exclude injuries occurring after the date of actual decision but before potential defendants have had time to adjust by getting insurance.[57] Such a

52. Great Northern Ry. v. Sunburst Oil & Refining Co., 287 U.S. 358 (1932).

53. Stovall v. Denno, 388 U.S. 293, 301 (1967).

54. England v. Louisiana State Bd. of Medical Examiners, 375 U.S. 411 (1964).

55. "Formulation of a rule of law in an Article III case or controversy which is prospective as to the parties involved in the immediate litigation would be most unusual, especially where the rule announced was not innovative." Simpson v. Union Oil Co., 396 U.S. 13, 14 (1969).

56. See, e.g., Molitor v. Kaneland Community Dist. No. 302, 18 Ill. 2d 11, 163 N.E.2d 89 (1959), *cert. denied,* 362 U.S. 968 (1960); Kojis v. Doctors' Hosp., 12 Wis. 2d 367, 107 N.W.2d 131, supp. opinion 12 Wis. 2d 373, 107 N.W.2d 292 (1961); Holytz v. City of Milwaukee, 17 Wis. 2d 26, 115 N.W.2d 618 (1962).

57. See *Holytz* opinion, *supra* n.56; Widell v. Holy Trinity Catholic Church, 19

postponement can of course be added to a completely prospective decision, too.

The Supreme Court has also used this partial retroactivity technique, as is manifest in its dealing with the right to counsel at police lineups in *Stovall.* The Court had just ruled in some other cases that such a right to counsel existed. But in *Stovall* the Court said the decision applied only to the defendants in those cases, and to future litigants — not retroactively to Mr. Stovall. It defended this "inequity . . . to other litigants similarly situated in the trial or appellate process who have raised the same issue" by pointing to: first, the above-mentioned reasons against the alternative of complete prospectivity; second, other reasons against the alternative of complete retroactivity.

These latter reasons showed the Court's attitude to be substantially as follows: *Some* overrulings should be, and have been, made completely retroactive. E.g., the Gideon v. Wainwright decision[58] recognizing a free counsel right for certain indigent defendants was later applied to cases of prisoners who had been convicted years before, who were now bringing habeas corpus cases to get the benefit of the new rule. The relative impact of the right involved upon the "integrity of the truth-determining process" is one of the relevant factors. It is a matter of degree; the unfairness to defendant of not having counsel present at the lineup was not as great as not having counsel at trial. Thus the nature of the particular ruling can make a difference. Second, when "the extent of the reliance by law enforcement authorities on the old standards" is substantial, as here, it can make a difference. Third, when retroactive application will have a "disruptive" effect on the "administration of justice" by throwing a possibly intolerable burden of reopened cases on the courts, it can make a difference. So the nature of the ruling and its probable effect on the truth-determining process "must be weighed against the prior justified reliance upon the standard and the impact of retroactivity upon the administration of justice."[59]

Of further note are the instances of partial retroactivity in which the Court has taken a position somewhere between the *Stovall* position and complete retroactivity. That is, the new rule has sometimes been applied not only in the case in which it was announced but also in *some* similar cases whose facts occurred prior to the overruling decision. Sometimes, for instance, the standard was in terms of cases which, at the time of the overruling decision, had not yet been brought to trial;[60]

Wis. 2d 648, 121 N.W.2d 249 (1963); Spanel v. Mounds View School Dist. No. 621, 264 Minn. 279, 118 N.W.2d 795 (1962) (postponement to adjournment date of the then current legislative session).

58. 372 U.S. 335 (1963).

59. *Stovall, supra* n.53 at 298.

60. See, e.g., Johnson v. New Jersey, 384 U.S. 719 (1966), taking this approach to

sometimes, more broadly, it covered all cases not yet so "finalized" that further decision on direct review was precluded.[61]

3. The Lighter Side

The vagaries of the precedent system have their lighter aspects, too. What do you do if you are asked by the court for precedents to support your position and you have so far been unable to find any? Well, if you are the ingenious Rufus Choate, you might come up with this: "I will look, your Honor, and endeavor to find a precedent, if you require it; though it would seem to be a pity that the Court should lose the honor of being the first to establish so just a rule."[62]

The Honorable Sir Robert Megarry recounts an English case: "In one appeal, Fletcher Moulton L.J. objected that counsel's argument was supported by no precedent. Counsel's reply was that, 'the common law was the mother of precedents.' 'Yes, Mr. Blank,' came the reply, 'but she is a mother who is now past the age of child-bearing.' 'With your Lordship's assistance,' counsel promptly responded, 'I shall hope to prove the contrary.' "[63]

Gracefulness in confessing that one's prior views, enshrined in precedent, were erroneous was a special talent of Justice Jackson. "I see no reason," he once said, "why I should be consciously wrong today because I was unconsciously wrong yesterday."[64] And in a concurring opinion supporting a position contrary to one he had taken in an earlier case as Attorney General:

> I concur in the judgment and opinion of the Court. But since it is contrary to an opinion which, as Attorney General, I rendered in 1940, I owe some word of explanation. 39 Ops. Atty. Gen. 504. I am entitled to say of that opinion what any discriminating reader must think of it — that it was as foggy as the statute the Attorney General was asked to interpret. . . .
>
> Failure of the Attorney General's opinion to consider the matter in [the light of indicated history] is difficult to explain in view of the fact

---

the famous *Miranda* decision regarding the right of a person in custody to receive police warnings concerning right to counsel and privilege against self-incrimination.

61. See, e.g., Linkletter v. Walker, 381 U.S. 719 (1965), taking this approach to the Mapp v. Ohio (367 U.S. 643 (1961)) rule excluding unconstitutionally seized evidence from the trial; and Tehan v. Shott, 382 U.S. 406 (1965), taking this approach to the Griffin v. California (380 U.S. 609 (1965)) rule against a prosecutor or judge making adverse comment on the defendant's failure to testify.

62. 1 Brown, Works of Choate 292 (1862), quoted by Justice Gordon in Niedfelt v. Joint School District, 23 Wis. 2d 641, 648, 127 N.W.2d 800 (1964).

63. Megarry, A Second Miscellany-at-Law 294 (1973).

64. Dissenting in Massachusetts v. U.S., 333 U.S. 611, 640 (1948).

that he personally had urged this history upon this Court in arguing Perkins v. Elg, 307 U.S. 325, 83 L. Ed. 1320, 59 S. Ct. 884. Its details may be found in the briefs and their cited sources. It would be charitable to assume that neither the nominal addressee [of the Attorney General opinion, Secretary Stimson] nor the nominal author of the opinion read it. That, I do not doubt, explains Mr. Stimson's acceptance of an answer so inadequate to his questions. But no such confession and avoidance can excuse the then Attorney General.

Precedent, however, is not lacking for ways by which a judge may recede from a prior opinion that has proven untenable and perhaps misled others. See Chief Justice Taney, License Cases, (U.S.) 5 How. 504, 12 L. Ed. 256, recanting views he had pressed upon the Court as Attorney General of Maryland in Brown v. Maryland (U.S.) 12 Wheat. 419, 6 L. Ed. 678. Baron Bramwell extricated himself from a somewhat similar embarrassment by saying, "The matter does not appear to me now as it appears to have appeared to me then." Andrews v. Styrap, (Eng.) 26 [L.T. (n.s.)] 704, 706. And Mr. Justice Story, accounting for his contradiction of his own former opinion, quite properly put the matter: "My own error, however, can furnish no ground for its being adopted by this Court. . . ." United States v. Gooding, (U.S.) 12 Wheat. 460, 478, 6 L. Ed. 693, 699. Perhaps Dr. Johnson really went to the heart of the matter when he explained a blunder in his dictionary—"Ignorance, sir, ignorance." But an escape less self-depreciating was taken by Lord Westbury, who, it is said, rebuffed a barrister's reliance upon an earlier opinion of his Lordship: "I can only say that I am amazed that a man of my intelligence should have been guilty of giving such an opinion." If there are other ways of gracefully and good naturedly surrendering former views to a better considered position, I invoke them all.[65]

Justice Jackson would doubtless have included in his illustrations a Supreme Court of Minnesota gem had it come into being by then rather than two years later. It seems that that court had changed its position on a legal issue within a period of three months without referring to the prior case, because it had apparently forgotten about it! When the same issue came up in a third case, in which this sad situation was brought to light, the court straightened things out by overruling the second case, and observing: "Upon [this] issue, this court has displayed extraordinary impartiality by aligning itself on both sides of the question."[66]

65. McGrath v. Kristensen, 340 U.S. 162, 176-178 (1950).
66. Knuth v. Murphy, 237 Minn. 225, 54 N.W.2d 771, 774 (1954).

Chapter 5

Further Aspects of the Case: The Constitution

A. *The Constitutional Issue That Defendants Might Have Raised but Did Not (The First Amendment)*

You may recall from Chapter 2's discussion of the tort law of privacy the fact that the *Nappier* defendants might have raised a constitutional issue. They might have argued that they had a First Amendment right to make a news report on the identity of the plaintiff rape victims in spite of the privacy claim. This and other constitutional aspects of privacy will be canvassed in this chapter.

1. A First Amendment constitutional argument *was* made, and was rejected, in the 1948 Wisconsin case of State v. Evjue.[1] The case arose under a statute similar to the South Carolina one except that its prohibition was broader; it was against publishing the "identity of a female who may have been raped or subjected to any similar criminal assault." The Wisconsin Supreme Court first pointed to United States Supreme Court language in the 1942 case of Chaplinsky v. New Hampshire for the proposition that First Amendment rights of free speech and press are not absolute:

> Allowing the broadest scope to the language and purpose of the Fourteenth amendment, it is well understood that the right of free speech is not absolute at all times and under all circumstances. There are certain well-defined and narrowly limited classes of speech, the prevention and punishment of which has never been thought to raise any constitutional problem. These include the lewd and obscene, the profane, the libelous, and the insulting or "fighting" words — those which

1. 253 Wis. 146, 33 N.W.2d 305 (1948). On remand, and after a plea of not guilty and a nonjury trial, the defendant was found not guilty, and the Wisconsin Supreme Court held that a statute permitting state appeals in criminal cases did not apply in this situation. 254 Wis. 581, 37 N.W.2d 50 (1949).

> by their very utterance inflict injury or tend to incite an immediate breach of the peace. It has been well observed that such utterances are no essential part of any exposition of ideas, and are of such slight social value as a step to truth that any benefit that may be derived from them is clearly outweighed by the social interest in order and morality.[2]

The same point applied, said the Wisconsin Supreme Court, to the kind of publication prohibited by the statute. The statute

> is intended to protect the victim from embarrassment and offensive publicity which no doubt have a strong tendency to affect her future standing in society. In addition to that it is a well-known fact that many crimes of the character described go unpunished because the victim of the assault is unwilling to face the publicity which would follow prosecution. . . . It is considered that there is a minimum of social value in the publication of the identity of a female in connection with such an outrage. Certain it is that the legislature could so find. At most the publication of the identity of the female ministers to a morbid desire to connect the details of one of the most detestable crimes known to the law with the identity of the victim. When the situation of the victim of the assault and the handicap prosecuting officers labor under in such cases are weighed against the benefit of publishing the identity of the victim in connection with the details of the crime, there can be no doubt that the slight restriction of the freedom of the press prescribed by [the statute] is fully justified.[3]

Circumstances can be imagined in which the court might have come to a different conclusion. Thus, a commentator observed:

> When identity is essential to a complete understanding of the story, the arguments for privacy, gallantry and law enforcement, are as strong, but the public's interest in knowing the identity increases. No longer can it be dismissed as curiosity or morbid desire, since it is part of the body of relevant information about a news event. Suppose a newsman hears that a rape suspect has been badly beaten in the jail to which he was taken. Authorities contend that the suspect fell down a flight of stairs. The suspect claims he was beaten by the sheriff. It is only by reporting that the alleged victim of the rape was the sheriff's daughter that the story can be fully understood. If an absolute statutory bar were to be upheld in such a case, the newspaper would be confronted with an unenviable choice: either omit the story completely or report only the details permitted by the statute, thereby providing an incomplete and possibly misleading account. Neither alternative is consistent with traditional notions of a newspaper's freedom to print a meaningful account of what is acknowledged to be news.[4]

2. 253 Wis. 146, 160-161, 33 N.W.2d 305 (1948). The quotation appears in the Chaplinsky case at 315 U.S. 568, 571 (1942).

3. 253 Wis. 146, 161, 33 N.W.2d 305 (1948).

4. Franklin, A Constitutional Problem in Privacy Protection: Legal Inhibitions on Reporting of Fact, 16 Stan. L. Rev. 107, 134-135 (1963).

But *even in the absence of such special circumstances,* the United States Supreme Court today would probably strike down a statute of the type in the *Nappier* case and the Wisconsin case. The validity of that statement is clearly supported by the 1975 *Cox Broadcasting* case (12 years after the *Nappier* decision) in which the Supreme Court invalidated a Georgia statute of the same type as South Carolina's. There the television reporter had based his report "upon notes taken during the court proceedings and obtained the name of the victim from the indictments handed to him at his request during a recess in the hearing." Public records "by their very nature are of interest to those concerned with the administration of government, and a public benefit is performed by the reporting of the true contents of the records by the media." The First Amendment (as applied to the states through the Fourteenth — a technique to be discussed below) bars "sanctions for the publication of truthful information contained in official court records open to public inspection."[5]

This cautious emphasis on the "public records" aspect of the case makes it a rather narrow holding, but the principle was widened in a rather analogous case in 1979, when the Court invalidated a West Virginia law making it a crime for newspapers to publish, without written approval of the juvenile court, the name of a youth charged as a juvenile offender. The Court recognized that *Cox Broadcasting* as well as some analogous First Amendment cases had emphasized the "public records" factor, but said, "That factor is not controlling. . . . A free press cannot be made to rely solely upon the sufferance of government to supply it with information." The information here having been lawfully obtained through "routine newspaper reporting techniques," the state "may not punish its publication except when necessary to further an interest more substantial than is present here."[6]

Other cases in the last several years have similarly shown the primacy, in their particular circumstances, of the First Amendment —

5. Cox Broadcasting Corp. v. Cohn, 420 U.S. 469, 495-496 (1975). Relying on this decision was the case of Oklahoma Publishing Co. v. District Court, 430 U.S. 308 (1977). Here a news media representative had already attended a juvenile's detention hearing, at which the juvenile's name was ascertained and his picture taken while leaving the hearing. News stories thereafter appeared revealing his name and picture. An Oklahoma statute had required that juvenile hearings be closed, unless the judge orders otherwise. Without reaching the issue of constitutionality of this statute, the Court held that in the circumstances of this case, a pre-trial order could not enjoin the media from thereafter disseminating the name or picture in connection with the pending juvenile proceedings.

6. Smith v. Daily Mail Pub. Co., 443 U.S. 97, 103-104, 105 (1979). The issue had been posed in terms of the state interest in avoiding impairment of the juvenile's rehabilitation, rather than specifically in terms of the juvenile's privacy. Note also that in Davis v. Alaska, 415 U.S. 308 (1974), a state's policy of preserving anonymity of a juvenile offender was subordinated to a defendant's Sixth Amendment right of cross-examination, so as to allow the defense to "impeach," i.e., discredit, the prosecution witness on the basis of the latter's juvenile record.

one concerning the "false light" type of privacy,[7] another involving a statutorily conferred confidentiality.[8] Still other recent cases have given greater weight to the First Amendment than to certain other competing claims in the context of a criminal trial[9] and of fair elections,[10] and

7. A magazine article about a Broadway play, *The Desperate Hours,* dramatizing the experiences of a family held captive by ex-convicts, gave the family's name as well as treating the play as a documentation of the family's actual experiences, though some of the play's representations (indicating brutalities by the convicts) were false. The plaintiff family sued for damages under the New York statute described in Chap. 2 (between nn. 230 & 231) claiming they had publicly been put in a false light — thus coming within the second of the four privacy tort categories described in Chap. 2 (at n.235). The Supreme Court ruled that the First Amendment would prevent an award of damages for privacy invasion stemming from this reporting of matters of public interest *unless* the reporting was knowingly or recklessly false. Time, Inc. v. Hill, 385 U.S. 374 (1967). However, it is argued that this standard (developed in *defamation* cases brought by *public officials or public figures* rather than private individuals) has been undermined by a defamation decision giving less constitutional protection to the media (i.e., applying a wider basis for defamation liability) when the plaintiff is a private individual. The Court's reasoning in this 1974 defamation decision was that, being neither a public official nor a public figure, the plaintiff neither has access to the media for rebuttal nor has assumed the risks of publicity, and is entitled to greater protection — i.e., the media are entitled to less constitutional protection. Gertz v. Welch, 418 U.S. 323 (1974). So the Court thought a state could properly make the media liable in such a defamation case even for mere negligence or gross negligence, as distinct from the intentional or reckless conduct required for liability to public officials (N.Y. Times Co. v. Sullivan, 376 U.S. 254 (1964)) and public figures (Curtis Publ. Co. v. Butts, 388 U.S. 130 (1967)). For argument that this broader basis for defamation of a private individual should now apply to a false light privacy case like *Time, Inc., supra,* see Ashdown, Media Reporting and Privacy Claims — Decline in Constitutional Protection for the Press, 66 Ky. L.J. 759, 781 (1978).

8. Virginia's interest in insuring confidentiality of proceedings of its Commission investigating complaints of disability and misconduct of judges, as well as its interest in protecting judges' reputations and maintaining institutional integrity of its courts was "insufficient to justify" criminal sanctions against the media for publishing truthful information about the proceedings, including the name of the state judge being investigated. Landmark Communications, Inc. v. Virginia, 435 U.S. 829 (1978).

9. The right to a fair jury trial did not authorize judicial "gagging" of the media's pre-trial publication of facts adverse to a criminal defendant because (1) the record did not show that judicial alternatives to this "prior restraint" on the media (e.g., change of venue, trial postponement, searching questioning of prospective jurors, instructions to jurors, sequestration of jurors, restraints on what police, witnesses, and contending lawyers may say to anyone) would not have sufficiently mitigated the adverse effects of such publicity; nor could the Court conclude that the order would even serve its intended purpose; (2) insofar as the gag order prohibited reporting or commentary on happenings at a public preliminary hearing, it was clearly invalid. Nebraska Press Assn. v. Stuart, 427 U.S. 539 (1976). Nor could a state law be upheld that allowed judicial *closure* of a criminal trial to media and public, in the unfettered discretion of the judge and the parties, and in the absence of any findings of necessity for closure. Richmond Newspapers, Inc. v. Virginia, 448 U.S. 555 (1980).

10. Despite a state's interest in fair elections and a political candidate's interest in reputation and expression, a state law granting a political candidate equal newspaper space to reply to the newspaper's criticism violates freedom of the press. Miami Herald Pub. Co. v. Tornillo, 418 U.S. 241 (1974). Nor are broadcasters

have strengthened the application of the Amendment to commercial and professional communicative activity.[11]

B. Background Note: Scope of Constitutional Protection of Privacy

To round out your understanding of the constitutional protection of privacy, some other aspects of the problem should be mentioned here. You should realize that not only can a constitutional provision like the First Amendment clash with a privacy interest recognized in tort law, but the *Constitution may itself protect a privacy interest.*

1. The Uncertain Scope of Constitutional Privacy Protection

The Supreme Court's 1973 abortion decision, Roe v. Wade,[12] tried to describe the source and field of operation of the constitutional right of privacy that it had recognized in Griswold v. Connecticut (the 1965 case invalidating for married persons the Connecticut prohibition against use of contraceptives).[13] The *Roe* Court confined the right to

---

required to accept paid political advertisements. Columbia Broadcasting System v. Democratic Natl. Comm., 412 U.S. 94 (1973). See also Buckley v. Valeo, n.11 below.

11. I refer to cases invalidating prohibitions on: price advertising of routine legal services by lawyers (Bates v. State Bar, 433 U.S. 350 (1977)); price adverstising of prescription drugs by pharmacists (Virginia State Bd. of Pharmacy v. Virginia Citizens Consumer Council, Inc., 425 U.S. 748 (1976)); advertisements for low cost abortion placement (Bigelow v. Virginia, 421 U.S. 809 (1975)); advertisement of contraceptives (Carey v. Population Services Intl., 431 U.S. 678 (1977)); utilities' promotional advertising (Central Hudson Gas & Elec. Co. v. Public Service Commn., 447 U.S. 557 (1980)); utilities' using inserts in billing envelopes to discuss controversial public policy issues (Consolidated Edison v. Public Service Commn., 447 U.S. 530 (1980)); posting of "For Sale" or "Sold" signs on residential property (Linmark Assocs., Inc. v. Willingboro, 431 U.S. 85 (1977)); independent expenditures beyond a specified ceiling by persons (including corporations) relative to a particular candidate for federal office (Buckley v. Valeo, 424 U.S. 1 (1976)). I refer also to the Court's recognition that business corporations have a First Amendment right to spend money to influence public referendum proposals, including those not affecting the corporation business, property, or assets. First Natl. Bank of Boston v. Bellotti, 435 U.S. 765 (1978). See O'Kelley, The Constitutional Rights of Corporations Revisited, 67 Geo. L.J. 1347 (1979).

12. 409 U.S. 817 (1973).

13. See Chap. 2 *supra* at nn. 36-37. The Court then invalidated a law prohibiting distribution of contraceptives to the unmarried. See Eisenstadt v. Baird, 405 U.S. 438 (1972) and comment in Carey v. Population Services, 431 U.S. 678, 687 (1977).

those privacy interests that are "fundamental." And it said: "Whether it be founded in the Fourteenth Amendment's concept of personal liberty . . . as we feel it is, or . . . in the Ninth Amendment's reservation of rights to the people, [it] is broad enough to encompass a woman's decision whether or not to terminate her pregnancy" — though certain restraints after the first trimester of pregnancy would be permissible.[14]

This preference for the Fourteenth Amendment's due process clause as the source was an adoption of the view of two concurring justices in the *Griswold* case. The majority in that case had rested instead on both the Ninth Amendment and on "zones" of privacy or "penumbras" emanating from certain Bill of Rights provisions (there being no clause specifically creating a right of privacy as such). The *Roe* opinion gave particular emphasis to certain areas of intimacy as being important in the constitutional concept of privacy: marriage, abortion, procreation, contraception, family relationships, and rearing and education of children[15] — and cited past cases that fitted (sometimes with a good deal of straining) into these categories. In the same year in an obscenity case, the Court observed that the privacy right was limited to "personal intimacies of the home, the family, marriage, motherhood, procreation and child rearing."[16] The 1977 Whalen v. Roe opinion reiterated that the liberty interest under the due process clause

14. See Chap. 1 *supra* at n.42.

15. Not all cases in these and related areas upheld the privacy claim. Some scholars had thought that the Court's attitude in the abortion and contraception cases, as well as its decision in Stanley v. Georgia, 394 U.S. 557 (1969), allowing obscene materials to be possessed and viewed in the privacy of the home, would doom laws against homosexual practices. But Doe v. Commonwealth's Attorney, 425 U.S. 901 (1976), summarily affirmed without opinion a three-judge federal court decision rejecting homosexuals' claims that the Virginia sodomy statute unconstitutionally invaded their privacy. See Note, 43 Fordham L. Rev. 553 (1976). So too the Court ruled that parents' privacy right to select a private school for their children was subject to the impact of 42 U.S.C. §1981 (§1 of the 1866 Civil Rights Act), construed to require the school to contract with parents on a non-discriminatory basis. Runyon v. McCrary, 427 U.S. 160 (1976). In courts below the United States Supreme Court, there tended to be a more expansive reading, and use by analogy, of the Roe v. Wade listing. Thus that opinion's recognition of a proper sphere for a woman's control over her own body (though not unlimited) helped lead to the idea that a person (or if the person is mentally incompetent, then responsible persons such as relatives, guardians, physicians) should be allowed to determine whether the "plug should be pulled" or certain kinds of treatment be refused, in terminal illness cases. See e.g., In re Quinlan, 70 N.J. 10, 355 A. 2d 647, 663 (1976), *cert. denied, sub nom.* Garger v. New Jersey, 429 U.S. 922 (1976); Superintendent of Belchertown State School v. Saikewicz, 370 N.E.2d 417 (Mass. 1977), supporting this idea and resting on the right of privacy; Annot., Patient's Right to Refuse Treatment Allegedly Necessary to Sustain Life, 93 A.L.R. 3d 67, 74-77 (1979); Symposium, Mental Incompetents and the Right to Die, 11 Suffolk L. Rev. 919 (1977); Note, Legal Aspects of the Right to Die: Before and After the Quinlan Decision, 65 Ky. L.J. 823 (1977).

16. Paris Adult Theatre I v. Slaton, 413 U.S. 49, 65 (1973).

was the basis of the right of privacy, and made a rather different formulation of the right by saying: Privacy cases have "involved at least two . . . kinds of interests. One is the individual interest in avoiding disclosure of personal matters, and another is the interest in independence in making certain kinds of important decisions."[17]

This formulation is apparently intended to cover, by its second "interest," the above *Roe* listing of categories; but the statement of the first interest is both too narrow and too broad. The narrowness lies in its being too unrevealing of the breadth of situations that had already been treated as involving a privacy interest — some of them even before *Griswold.* Even if we exclude the cases in which the privacy interest was linked to a specific Bill of Rights provision, as are arrest, search, wiretapping, and eavesdropping under the Fourth Amendment,[18] the 1977 formulation still seems either incomplete or unrevealing. For instance, the 1969 decision of Stanley v. Georgia,[19] as reinterpreted in 1973,[20] recognized "privacy of the home" as a basis for the right to possess and view obscene materials in the home.

Further, a group of privacy cases has dealt with protection from receiving unwanted or repugnant information or visual stimuli: upholding a federal statute authorizing a householder to petition the Postmaster General to order a mailer of erotically arousing or sexually provocative advertisements to refrain from further mailings to the householder;[21] upholding, again because of householder privacy, an ordinance prohibiting uninvited house-to-house solicitation by sales-

17. Whalen v. Roe, 429 U.S. 589, 599 (1977). The Court referred to an article by Professor Kurland that had listed three facets of the privacy right (freedom in private affairs from government surveillance and intrusion; right not to have government make one's private affairs public; right to be free in action, thought, experience, and belief from government compulsion) and said that the first "is directly protected by the Fourth Amendment; the second and third correspond to the two kinds of interests referred to" by the Court in the text *supra. Id.* at n.24. But Kurland's first category seems broader than the Fourth Amendment protection against searches and seizures etc., as summarized in App. 2 herein under **B.**

18. See App. 2, *id.* We might similarly exclude cases on the "privacy of association" interest that has been held to be part of the First Amendment, NAACP v. Alabama, 357 U.S. 449 (1958); Buckley v. Valeo, 424 U.S. 1, 64-76 (1976); or the privacy interest that Griswold v. Connecticut (*supra* at nn. 13-15) pointed to in the "penumbra" of the Fifth Amendment privilege against self-incrimination.

19. 394 U.S. 557 (1969).

20. Paris Adult Theater I v. Slaton, 413 U.S. 49 (1973); U.S. v. 12 200-Foot Reels, 413 U.S. 123 (1973); Notes, 26 Stan. L. Rev. 1161, 1185-1189 (1974); 48 N.Y.U.L. Rev. 670, 687-693 (1973).

21. Rowan v. Post Office Dept., 397 U.S. 728 (1960). But where a group tried to stop a realty broker from "blockbusting" and "panic peddling" activities by distributing leaflets in front of his home and church and at neighbors' doors, he could not, by invoking privacy, enjoin such distribution. "*Rowan* is not in point [because] respondent is not attempting to stop the flow of information into his own household, but to the public." Organization for a Better Austin v. Keefe, 402 U.S. 415 (1971).

men and peddlers, as applied to magazine salesmen;[22] upholding an FCC declaratory order against a "dirty words" broadcast, the broadcaster's First Amendment right being outweighed by "privacy of the home";[23] upholding an ordinance prohibiting "loud and raucous noises" from sound trucks;[24] upholding a city bus system's ban on the use of bus card ads on "political" matter or "public issues" coupled with permission for use of such ads for commercial and public service purposes,[25] but affirming a regulatory commission's permission to a street transit company to invade its passengers' privacy by soft broadcasts of news, music, and ads (where no one-sided political propaganda was broadcast, and a poll had shown that a great majority of the public supported the system);[26] invalidating, because of "the limited privacy interest of persons on the public streets," who "can readily avert [their] eyes," an ordinance prohibiting drive-in movie theaters from showing certain kinds of nudity films when the screen was visible from a public street or place.[27]

22. Breard v. City of Alexandria, 341 U.S. 622 (1951). The Court distinguished Martin v. Struthers, 319 U.S. 141 (1943), on the ground that the ordinance there had been invalidated as applied to the distribution of religious tracts. For other infirmities that may afflict such ordinances (such as vagueness or lack of standards to control administrative discretion in issuance of any required permits), see the opinion in Hynes v. Mayor of Oradell, 425 U.S. 610 (1976), and Annot., 48 L. Ed. 2d 917 (1977). The privacy interest has not always been deemed as strong as in *Breard, supra.* Thus, in Schaumberg v. Citizens for a Better Environment, 444 U.S. 620 (1980), an ordinance barring solicitations door-to-door or on streets by charitable organizations not using 75% of their receipts for charitable purposes was invalidated: Many charitable groups combine fund solicitation with information, discussion, and advocacy; against the First Amendment interests here, the government interest in preventing fraud and crime was insufficient; privacy protection is involved "only in the most indirect of ways," and householders were free to post signs against solicitations. In Carey v. Brown, 447 U.S. 455 (1980), an Illinois statute barring picketing of residences *except* for peaceful picketing of a place of employment in a labor dispute was held to violate the "equal protection" clause. The state's interest in insuring privacy of the home and giving special protection to labor protests did not justify *discriminating* among pickets based on the subject matter of their expression.

23. FCC v. Pacifica Foundation, 438 U.S. 726, 748 (1978).

24. Kovacs v. Cooper, 336 U.S. 77 (1949).

25. Lehman v. Shaker Heights, 418 U.S. 298 (1974).

26. Public Util. Commn. v. Pollak, 343 U.S. 451 (1952).

27. Erzoznik v. City of Jacksonville, 422 U.S. 205 (1975). Note the similar attitude in Cohen v. California, 403 U.S. 15 (1971), reversing a breach of peace conviction against an individual wearing a jacket bearing the phrase "Fuck the Draft" in a courthouse corridor. The Court thought that people in the corridor, unlike people in the street subjected to overly loud sound trucks, could avoid the unpleasant message by "averting their eyes." The Court did not discuss the ineffectiveness of this technique in avoiding the *first* look at the unpleasant message. Again, in Consolidated Edison v. Public Service Commn., 447 U.S. 530 (1980), in striking down as violating the First Amendment a state public service commission order barring utilities from including inserts discussing controversial public policy issues in billing envelopes, the Court said, "The customer . . . may escape exposure to objectionable material simply by transferring the bill insert from envelope to wastebasket."

Thus, the "individual interest in avoiding disclosure of personal matters," as it was described in the 1977 formulation referred to above, is too narrow to take account of certain kinds of government intrusions other than disclosure of personal information.

On the other hand, the formulation is too broad in the sense that this anti-disclosure (or "informational privacy") interest has *so far* had a *negligible* role in the Supreme Court cases on constitutional privacy. In the first place, it is well to remember that the cases discussed earlier in this section, showing the First Amendment triumph over a privacy interest against media disclosure of the name of a rape victim or juvenile, or against media "false light" publicity, were not discussing a constitutional privacy right. Their concern instead seemed to be privacy interests under *tort* law pitted against the media's First Amendment interests. Secondly, when litigants did invoke, in a few recent cases, a constitutional privacy right against disclosures of private matters by government, they did not succeed in the Supreme Court.[28] Litigants have occasionally succeeded in lower courts;[29] and there is reason to think that the courts of states like California and Alaska,

28. The Supreme Court has (in a strongly criticized decision) refused to find a violation of constitutional privacy in official publicizing of the fact of an arrest — even when the arrestee, whose photograph had been included in the circular of "active shoplifters" sent to 800 merchants, had pleaded not guilty and the charges, after distribution of the circular, were dismissed. The Court also thought that the reputational interest involved did not qualify as the necessary liberty interest under the Fourteenth Amendment due process clause. Paul v. Davis, 424 U.S. 693 (1976). Nor did the Court find an unconstitutional impairment of privacy in a New York law requiring doctors to give names and addresses of patients receiving certain prescription narcotics, such identification to be recorded in a central computer file maintained by the state health department, the tapes being kept in a locked cabinet, and public disclosure of identity of patients being prohibited. Whalen v. Roe, 429 U.S. 589 (1977). The Court cautioned that it was not dealing with a case of actual and unwarranted disclosure. In Nixon v. Administrator of General Services, 433 U.S. 425 (1977), President Nixon's personal privacy right in some of his papers and tapes made during his tenure in office had to bow to a statutory requirement that all of them go to the Administrator of General Services for screening, to determine which should be promptly returned to Nixon and which retained for historical and judicial purposes.

29. E.g., in York v. Story, 324 F.2d 450 (9th Cir. 1963), *cert. denied,* 376 U.S. 939 (1964), two years before *Griswold,* the court held that a woman's privacy rights under the Constitution, including the due process liberty interest, had been violated in the following circumstances: Having come to a local police station to report an assault, she was taken to a room by a male officer, told to undress and photographed nude in various suggestive poses, over her protest, for the alleged purpose of "preserving evidence" of her injuries; and the developed photographs were passed around the stationhouse. The Supreme Court might well have agreed with this decision. For lower court cases on dissemination and on requested expungement of arrest records of persons not convicted, see the conflicting authorities in DeBoice, Due Process Privacy and the Path of Progress, 1979 U. Ill. L.F. 469, 523-524, n.261. For cases on other records (bank, credit, medical, welfare) see *id.* at 523-524, nn. 262-265; 525, nn. 266-270; 526-529. Further on medical records, see Committee on Federal Legislation (Association of Bar of City of New York), Privacy of Medical Records, 35 Record 488 (1980).

which have adopted a state constitutional privacy right, will give a broader than usual protection to privacy in general.[30]

In *Whalen supra* the Court pointed to a special facet of the disclosure problem, "the threat to privacy implicit in the accumulation of vast amounts of personal information in computerized data banks or other massive government files,"[31] though it did not find that that particular case had presented an actual injury to privacy. Congress, too, has been aware of that danger and has responded with a number of statutes in the 1970s and early 1980s, including the general Privacy Act of 1974[32] and the following on specific kinds of privacy: the Fair Credit Reporting Act of 1971;[33] the Family Educational Rights and Privacy Act of 1974;[34] the Right to Financial Privacy Act of 1978;[35] and the

30. The Alaska Supreme Court ruled that adult possession of small amounts of marijuana in the home was protected by the Alaskan right of privacy, Ravin v. State, 537 P.2d 494 (Alaska 1975). (For more on marijuana, see DeBoice, *supra* n.29 at 516 n.232). The California Supreme Court declared that police surveillance of university classroom activity, if proven, would violate both the First Amendment and the California right of privacy. White v. Davis, 13 Cal. 3d 357, 533 P.2d 222 (1975). On Alaska and California, see DeBoice, *supra* n.29 at 530-533.

31. Whalen v. Roe, *supra* n.28.

32. 88 Stat. 1897 (1974), 5 U.S.C. §552a. For committee reports, see 4 U.S. Code Cong. & Ad. News 6916 et seq. (1974). The Act requires agencies to, among other things, disclose the categories of individuals and records, the topics, location, etc. that would identify the nature of their record systems, thus alerting citizens to the possibility that their names may be listed. Thousands of records systems have thus been identified in thousands of fine-print pages of the Federal Register. An individual has a right to see, copy, and challenge information about himself, and to learn why and under what authority information about him is being collected. The agency records of individuals are to be confined to those that are relevant and necessary for the agency's legally required purposes. The Act has criminal sanctions for violations by federal employees, and allows individuals to bring damage suits and other court actions against the government. It established the Privacy Protection Study Commission, which filed in 1977 a full report with five lengthy appendices that survey "record keeping and informational policy in consumer credit transactions, depository institutions, insurance transactions, medical service operations, investigative reporting services, federal government agencies, public schools, public assistance departments, statistical survey operations, and the IRS. It also studied the use of mailing lists, social security numbers, and other assigned identifiers. The appendices concern privacy law in the States (I), tax return confidentiality (II), employment records (III), technology and privacy (IV), and an assessment of the Privacy Act of 1974 (V) . . . ." DeBoice, *supra* n.29 at 522 n.257.

33. 84 Stat. 1128, Title VII (1970). For amended form, see 15 U.S.C. §§1681-1681t. Among other things, this gives to a person who is the subject of credit information the right to be informed of the contents of the file, the right to challenge the information, and the right to place a corrective statement in the file.

34. 88 Stat. 571, 1858; 93 Stat. 342; 20 U.S.C. §1232g. For committee reports, see 3 U.S. Code Cong. & Ad. News 4093 et seq. (1974); 4 *id.* at 6794-6796 (1974). This law, implemented by Department of Education regulations, denies federal funds to institutions (1) refusing parental access to school records on their children or postsecondary school students' access to their own records, or (2) allowing access by third parties except under certain defined conditions.

35. 92 Stat. 3697 (1978), 12 U.S.C. §§3400-3422. For committee reports, see 7 U.S. Code Cong. & Ad. News 9273 et seq. (portions dealing with Title XI) (1978). The Act establishes procedures that federal agencies must comply with in seeking access

Privacy Protection Act of 1980.[36] In addition, miscellaneous recent congressional proposals would go even further.[37] Not the least of the interpretation problems created by such measures is the determination of "whether personal information is required to be disclosed under the Freedom of Information Act or prohibited under the Privacy Act. Major problems arise with reconciling the Privacy Act with the Freedom of Information Act's exemption for 'clearly unwarranted invasions of personal privacy.' "[38]

2. A Summary Perspective

In conclusion, I offer the following perspectives on privacy and the Constitution:

(1) The privacy interest under tort law has generally been subordinated to the defendant media's First Amendment protections, and corporate First Amendment rights have been recently strengthened — so that the *Nappier* plaintiffs today would doubtless lose.

(2) While the *Nappier* plaintiffs could claim a tort privacy interest, they could not also claim a constitutional right of privacy, as far as disclosure of intimate information is concerned. This claim would not succeed because the disclosure was not by *government*, and government action is generally required for a constitutional violation (a requirement discussed later in this chapter).

Moreover, if it *had* been a governmental disclosure, the plaintiff's constitutional rights would not necessarily have been violated. For example, while unnecessary governmental publicizing of plaintiff's name without serving any valid governmental purpose might be such

to the records of banks and other financial institutions. E.g., the agency must notify an individual customer of a financial institution that a subpeona for his records with the institution has been issued, prior to the institution's compliance. The customer is given the right to challenge the subpoena and stay compliance until a court determination. See Note, The Right to Financial Privacy Act: New Protection for Financial Records, 8 Fordham Urban L.J. 597 (1980).

36. This law erects certain barriers to police searches of documents possessed by persons reasonably believed to have a purpose to disseminate to the public a newspaper, book, broadcast, or other similar form of public communication; and affords some limited protection, through Attorney General guidelines, in the case of documentary searches directed against other persons. See explanation in App. 2 at nn. 45-49 and citations in n.45.

37. See Note, 8 Fordham Urban L.J. 773 (1980); recommendations in Report of Privacy Protection Study Commission (1977).

38. O'Brien, Privacy and the Right of Access: Purposes and Paradoxes of Information Control, 30 Ad. L. Rev. 45, 88 (1978). See also, Vache & Makibe, Privacy in Government Records: Philosophical Perspectives and Proposals for Legislation, 14 Gonzaga L. Rev. 515 (1979); Leigh, Informational Privacy: Constitutional Challenges to the Collection and Dissemination of Personal Information by Government Agencies, 3 Hastings Const. L.Q. 229 (1976).

a violation, including plaintiff's name in the indictment would doubtless not be. Besides, it is not yet clear in the Supreme Court how much weight will be given to the interest in *nondisclosure of intimate information* as part of the due process clause protection[39] — as distinguished from (a) the same interest under tort law and (b) certain other privacy interests under the due process clause. Whalen v. Roe (on New York's maintenance of centralized records of names of those for whom physicians had prescribed certain drugs — see n.28 above) referred to the possible existence of such a constitutional interest. It found that the safeguards in the New York system were adequate and plaintiff had not been harmed; and that otherwise there *might* be a constitutional violation.

(3) Not only has there been some uncertainty in the Court about defining the concept of privacy — an uncertainty shared with the scholars[40] — but the Court has not been consistent in the "level of scrutiny" that it brings to bear on an alleged violation of privacy.[41]

(4) The Supreme Court has shown a tendency to keep the constitutional privacy right within tight boundaries. It has sometimes, not always, talked as though the categories singled out for special attention in the abortion opinion (Roe v. Wade) were the only possible privacy categories for consideration as part of the due process right; and the tendency is to interpret even those categories narrowly. Thus, in spite of the Court's recognition of the large latitude for one's control of one's body in the areas of birth control and abortion, and in spite of the "privacy of the home" concept recognized in the *Stanley* case as reinterpreted in later cases (see above at nn. 19 & 20), the Court was unwilling to include certain other kinds of control over one's body within the area of constitutional protection.[42] The Court has also

39. See *supra* at n.28.

40. See, e.g., Gavison, Privacy and the Limits of Law, 89 Yale L.J. 421 (1980); Silver, The Future of Constitutional Privacy, 21 St. Louis L.J. 211, 266-273 (1977); Gerety, "Redefining Privacy, 12 Harv. Civ. Rights & Civ. Lib. Rev. 233 (1977); O'Brien, *supra* n.38 at 63-75; Parker, A Definition of Privacy, 27 Rutgers L. Rev. 275 (1974); Lusky, Invasion of Privacy: A Clarification of Concepts, 72 Colum. L. Rev. 693 (1972); articles in Pennock and Chapman, eds., Privacy (1971).

41. See discussion of levels of scrutiny in this chapter between nn. 67 & 68.
Though privacy was labeled a "fundamental" right in Roe v. Wade, invasions thereof are not always given the "strict scrutiny" normally attached to alleged violations of fundamental rights. See, e.g., *Whalen, supra* n.17. "[O]nly Justices Brennan, Marshall and perhaps Blackmun are fully satisfied with a strict scrutiny standard in cases which involve burdens on, but not total denial of fundamental privacy rights." DeBoice, *supra* n.29 at 531 n.301. See also below at 333-334.

42. Homosexual activities were a notable example. (See *Doe, supra* n.15.) In a 1973 case the legitimacy of the statute against exhibiting obscene films was defended by the Court in part by referring to "constitutionally unchallenged laws against prostitution, suicide, voluntary self-mutilation," and also by suggesting the continued validity of laws against fornication, adultery, and bigamy. *Paris Adult Theatre I, supra,* n.20. See also Chap. 1 herein at nn. 51-60. In 1976, the Court

resisted expansion in the category of family-related privacy.[43] "[C]onstitutional privacy has always been little more than a slogan to fit only a few matters which are deemed important to a fleeting majority of the Court. There has been little doctrinal development. . . . Privacy is a doctrine capable of almost infinite expansion, and litigants have, of course, sought to stretch it to and beyond the breaking point. A natural resistance to the excesses of theory combined with the Burger Court's own general stance to insure a cautious — and ultimately hostile — reception."[44]

C. Background Note: Some Basic Features of Our Constitutional Jurisprudence

1. Judicial Review of Constitutionality

We have seen that the Wisconsin court considered (and the South Carolina federal courts would have considered had the issue been raised) the question whether the court should strike down the statute as unconstitutional. Such a power, exercised by one branch of government against a coordinate branch, is an awesome power. (a) You may wonder whether the Constitution clearly authorizes it, and do governments really have to be run this way? Could not the legislature be allowed to be its own judge of whether its enactments will violate the

---

rejected a claim that a privacy interest as to personal appearance could invalidate a departmental regulation as to policemen's hair length. Kelley v. Johnson, 425 U.S. 238 (1976).

43. When the Court struck down, as violative of due process, an ordinance limiting the occupancy of dwelling units to members of a single family (defined in such a way as to preclude the defendant's grandson from living with her), only four Justices were willing to ground the decision on a family privacy interest rather than other reasons. Moore v. City of East Cleveland, 431 U.S. 494 (1977). (Three years before, a clear majority had upheld zoning regulations permitting no more than two individuals *unrelated* by blood, marriage, or adoption to occupy a single family dwelling. Village of Belle Terre v. Boraas, 416 U.S. 1 (1974)). The privacy right of parents to select a private school for their children did not include selecting a racially segregated school that would be violating a federal Civil Rights Act (construed to require the school to contract with parents on a nondiscrimination basis). *Runyon, supra* n.15.

44. Silver, *supra* n.40 at 215, 222-223. A sample of the voluminous and growing literature on privacy might include the works cited *supra* in nn. 9, 38 & 40; Rule, McAdams, Stearns & Uglow, The Politics of Privacy (1980); Posner, The Uncertain Protection of Privacy By the Supreme Court, 1979 Supreme Court Review 173; Miller, The Assault on Privacy (1971); Pember, Privacy and the Press: The Law, The Mass Media and the First Amendment (1970); Westin, Privacy and Freedom (1967).

Constitution? (b) Would not that be more democratic, since the legislature is popularly elected, whereas some state courts and all federal courts are not? (c) Finally you may wonder whether there are any recognized limits on, or standards for, the court's exercise of this power. I'll take these points up in order.

a. The Constitutional Authorization

In fact, some countries of the world do *not* recognize such a power in the courts. England, for instance, does not. What was distinctive about English constitutional history was the development of an independent Parliament and independent courts, formerly subservient to the king. But as between these two independent bodies — the Parliament and the courts — the courts were never clearly recognized as supreme, in the sense of being empowered to hold a statute unconstitutional. Parliament is the sole judge of whether a proposed statute is in conformity with the usages and traditions embodied in England's unwritten constitution.

There were of course some written documents in English constitutional history that asserted certain basic rights, and certain barriers to legislative and executive domination. Among these are, for example, the Magna Carta of 1215; Cromwell's "Instrument of Government" of 1653; and Parliament's "Bill of Rights" of 1689. But none of these documents suggested that the *courts* could strike down statutes for infringement of a specified right — and rarely did any court opinion assert such a power. One instance was a 1610 dictum of Lord Coke in Dr. Bonham's Case, as follows: "When an Act of Parliament is against common right and reason, or repugnant, or impossible to be performed, the common law will control it and adjudge such act to be void."[45] But the alleged precedents cited by Coke did not support such a broad proposition, and his dictum was never accepted in England.

It did, however, take root in America, with some early manifestations of the idea occurring even in the period prior to the 1787 Constitutional Convention. The colonial legislatures were well aware that their legislation was subject to review and invalidation by the British

45. 8 Eng. Rep. 118a (C.P. 1610). See Bailyn, The Ideological Origins of the American Revolution 176-177 and n.19 (1967); Thorne, Dr. Bonham's Case, 54 Law. Q. Rev. 545, 549, 551 (1938). As Bailyn summarizes (at 177): ". . . By saying that the courts might 'void' a legislative provision that violated the constitution, he had meant only that the courts were to construe statutes so as to bring them into conformity with recognized legal principles" if possible, and if not possible, the will of the legislature would prevail (as Chancellor Kent observed, according to Bailyn's n.19).

Privy Council. There were a few judicial dicta in the colonial courts that the Stamp Act was unconstitutional. In addition, a few state court decisions in the 1780s held a law invalid as violating a state constitution. The latter eighteenth century was, moreover, a period in which "natural law" was in the ascendancy — a "higher law" against which enacted law must be measured. And the courts must have seemed the most objective external agency to do the measuring. Particularly after the Declaration of Independence and its talk of natural and inalienable rights, many felt that certain rights were so fundamental and inherent that no law could take them away.

As for the 1787 Constitutional Convention itself, the topic of judicial review was not fully discussed. It came up as a side issue, and opinion on it was divided, though probably a majority assumed the power existed. In the course of arguments in the various states over ratification of the Constitution, the power was assumed. The power was also strongly defended by Alexander Hamilton in Number 78 of the *Federalist* papers. In the decade or so after ratification, the power was defended in congressional speeches and university lectures; it was exercised in dozens of lower courts; and even a few Supreme Court cases assumed the existence of the power without any full analysis or actual invalidation of a law.[46]

Finally, in 1803, the Supreme Court in the famous case of Marbury v. Madison[47] authoritatively established the power of judicial review.

Essentially, the point of view expressed in this case was that the power was *implied* in the Constitution: A judge has a duty to decide what the law is; in case of actual conflict between a statute and the Constitution, he must have the power and duty to resolve the conflict in favor of the higher authority, the Constitution, in accordance with his oath to support the Constitution.

b. Judicial Review and Democracy

Those who have continued, from time to time, to raise the issue of constitutional authorization of the judicial review power have generally coupled it with an attack on the allegedly *undemocratic* character of the power.

A major response to this second strand of the argument is that the American system is not one of "pure" democracy. Not only is it not a

46. On historical antecedents for judicial review, see Nowak, Rotunda & Young, Constitutional Law 11-14 and sources there cited. See also Bailyn, *supra* n.45 at 175-198.

47. 5 U.S. (1 Cranch) 137 (1803). For analysis of the case see Van Alstyne, A Critical Guide to Marbury v. Madison, 1969 Duke L.J. 1; Nowak et al., *supra* n.46 at 2-11.

system in which all decisions are made by majority vote of the people themselves; it is not even a system of second-degree democracy in which the majority vote is by the people's representatives, elected by popular vote on the basis of population. After all, the Constitution does allot two Senators to each state regardless of population,[48] a right the Founding Fathers felt so strongly about that Article V prohibits any constitutional amendment that would deprive a state "of its equal suffrage in the Senate" without the state's consent. The Constitution also allots at least one Representative to each state.[49] Resulting from such representation is a further deviation from equal voting power, since the population in several states is less than that of the nation's average congressional district. In presidential elections the "electoral college" feature detracts from the democratic nature of the process: Presidents can be, and have been, elected who polled only a minority of the popular vote. Furthermore, the Constitution abounds, in the Bill of Rights and elsewhere, with specific prohibitions, requirements for public office, etc. that thwart, to that extent, any contrary desires by a majority of the public's representatives. The actual functioning of the legislature itself has some antimajoritarian features.[50]

You cannot conclude from the above that an appointed court is *more* democratic than, or *as* democratic as, the other branches of government. What is clear is that appointment instead of election of judges does not mark a basic inconsistency with the pattern of the Constitution generally.

That pattern, as our high school civics books informed us, is one of "checks and balances," of "separation of powers," designed to safeguard against undue concentration of power in any one branch.[51] Judicial review of constitutionality is one check on the legislature, and on unconstitutional executive acts as well. It does not give the Supreme Court unrestrained, supreme power since the legislature and other departments have their own checks on the courts: (1) A (popularly elected) President nominates new members of the federal courts, and (popularly elected) representatives in the Senate are empowered to approve or disapprove — though it is true that the Senate is not as representative a body as the House. The Senate has disapproved four

48. Article I, §3, ¶1.

49. Article I, §2, ¶3.

50. For discussion of these, as well as of antimajoritarianism in the Constitution, see Choper, Judicial Review and the National Political Process 12-45 (1980); Bishin, Judicial Review in Democratic Theory, 50 S. Calif. L. Rev. 1099, 1103-1112 (1977).

51. See Giraudo, "Judicial Review and Comparative Politics: An Explanation For the Extensiveness of American Judicial Review Offered From the Perspective of Comparative Government, 5 Hastings Const. L.Q. 1137 (1979); Rostow, The Sovereign Prerogative 149 (1962): ". . . The Constitution . . . does not establish a parliamentary government, and attempts to interpret American government in a parliamentary perspective break down in confusion or absurdity."

times in this century, 26 times in the last two centuries.[52] (2) In cases of extreme misconduct, Congress may remove a federal judge by impeachment.[53] (3) Congress has, as we have seen (Chap. 1 between nn. 411 & 417), power over the size of the Supreme Court, as well as a certain limited power to control its appellate jurisdiction and hence to withdraw some classes of cases completely from the Court's power to decide — as well as power over jurisdiction of the lower federal courts. (4) Congress controls the Court's budget (though under Art. III, §1, it cannot reduce judicial compensation). (5) Congress's control over the times when the Court sits permits it, for instance, to abolish a scheduled term and thus delay the incidence of decision — a device used once, early in the Court's history.[54] (6) Court decisions that are resisted cannot be effective without executive enforcement.[55] When the public and/or public officials dislike a court decision heartily enough, they have been known to defy it, with little or no steps being taken for enforcement. This check has been manifested in a substantial fraction of American public schools' noncompliance with the Court's decisions on religious practices in the public schools, as well as a number of other areas.[56] (7) The public may protect itself still further if its representatives utilize the constitutional amendment procedures to overcome the Court decision, as has happened four times in the Court's history.[57] (8) Indeed the public's representatives can abolish altogether, by constitutional amendment, the power of judicial review of constitutionality.

True, some of these checks on the Court are less effective than others. But the fact that public feeling, when strong enough and widely enough shared, can usually transform an ineffective check into an effective one; the rarity of such public feeling and checks against particular Supreme Court decisions; and the fact that the public, over more than 175 years, has not abolished or seriously modified the in-

52. Abraham, Justices and Presidents 31 (1974).

53. Art. I, §3, ¶¶6-7. See also, for statutory authority for lesser sanctions against federal district and court of appeals judges, Chap. 1 between nn. 187 & 190.

54. 1 Warren, The Supreme Court in United States History 222-224 (1922).

55. A famous example is President Lincoln's defiance of Chief Justice Taney's issuance of a writ of habeas corpus in the face of Lincoln's temporary suspension of habeas corpus for a particular district (without congressional authorization) during the Civil War. Se Ex Parte Merryman, 17 F. Cas. 145 (1861); Swisher, The Taney Period 844-854 (1974) (5 Oliver Wendell Holmes Devise History of the Supreme Court of the United States).

56. See, e.g., Choper, *supra* n.50 at 140-150, 164-165.

57. The Eleventh Amendment (on citizen suits against a state), adopted 1795, overruled Chisholm v. Georgia, 2 U.S. (2 Dall.) 419 (1793). The Fourteenth Amendment (§1, being on citizenship, due process, equal protection), adopted 1868, overruled Dred Scott v. Sandford, 60 U.S. (19 How.) 393 (1857). The Sixteenth Amendment (income tax), adopted 1913, overruled Pollack v. Farmers' Loan & Trust Co., 157 U.S. 429 (1895). The Twenty-sixth Amendment (on eighteen-year-olds' voting rights), adopted 1971, overruled Oregon v. Mitchell, 400 U.S. 112 (1970).

stitution of judicial review itself, all speak against the idea that judicial review has functioned in an "undemocratic" way.

At any rate, it should be clear by now that to isolate an express or implied provision of the Constitution and ask whether it is "democratic" in the sense of facilitating the fulfillment of the majority's will is a dubious procedure. Such isolation ignores the fact that a part that is torn out of a pattern cannot be evaluated alone; it ignores the surrounding "checks" that an aroused majority can exercise on the Court. Furthermore, let us not forget that a prime *purpose of a Constitution* with its Bill of Rights and other prohibitions is to set *limits* on what the *majority itself* can do. Hence it makes no sense to brand as undemocratic an express or implied constitutional provision merely on the ground that it may thwart fulfillment of the majority's will. Do we say the First Amendment is undemocratic because of the possible blockage of a majority will directed at suppressing minority opinion?

If it be argued that judicial review is *less* democratic than having the legislature be its *own* interpreter of the constitutional limits placed upon it, a common response is that this alternative would not effectively implement those limits. I.e., is not self-interpretation more likely to be an interpretation biased by self-interest than if it were made by a carefully screened judicial elite, with greater security of tenure, much more freedom from interest group pressure, and much more focal concern with the doing of justice and the analysis, exposition, and integration of constitutional principles and policies? Do not the legislative majorities as well as the public become more fully informed, through judicial opinions, of vital matters: the alternative possibilities in, and arguments concerning, our constitutional ideals?[58] Is it not valuable, for instance, for these judicial opinions to symbolize and dramatize for the American people the fundamental moralities to which law must be subject?

The preceding discussion also suggests two further points. One, which may be implicit in what has already been argued, is that "democracy" is not necessarily to be *defined* as simply the fulfillment of majority will. A system that gives greater protection to the rights of the *minority* (by conditions of political freedom and special devices such as judicial review) against a tyrannical, selfish, insensitive, or unthinking majority might, to that extent, lay greater claim to the democratic label. Perhaps such a system is democracy in the popular sense of "It's a free country."[59] The second point is that (even if some

58. "The Supreme Court is, among other things, an educational body, and the Justices are inevitably teachers in a vital national seminar." Rostow, The Sovereign Prerogative 167-168 (1962).

59. See Bishin, Judicial Review in Democratic Theory, 50 S. Calif. L. Rev. 1099, 1128-1137 (1977).

variant of "majority will" be the sole approach to defining democracy) any undemocratic vices of our judicial review system have to be *put in the balance* against the system's virtues, rather than result in condemning the system as undemocratic. Cardozo was performing this kind of balancing procedure when he decided to opt in favor of judicial review:

> The great ideals of liberty and equality are preserved against the assaults of opportunism, the expediency of the passing hour, the erosion of small encroachments, the scorn and derision of those who have no patience with general principles, by enshrining them in constitutions, and consecrating to the task of their protection a body of defenders. By conscious or subconscious influence, the presence of this restraining power, aloof in the background, but none the less always in reserve, tends to stabilize and rationalize the legislative judgment, to infuse it with the glow of principle, to hold the standard aloft and visible to those who must run the race and keep the faith. I do not mean to deny that there have been times when the possibility of judicial review has worked the other way. Legislatures have sometimes disregarded their responsibility and passed it on to the courts. [And courts have sometimes made disastrous decisions in exercising this power. — Ed.] Such dangers must be balanced against those of independence from all restraint, independence on the part of public officers elected for brief terms, without the guiding force of a continuous tradition. On the whole, I believe the latter dangers to be the more formidable of the two.[60]

While I am myself persuaded that Cardozo's balancing arrives at the right result, i.e., that the American form of judicial review is a desirable and compatible feature of a constitutional democracy, I do not pretend to have fully canvassed here all that might be argued on the other side,[61] or even all that can be argued on the side of judicial

60. Cardozo, The Nature of the Judicial Process 92-93 (1921). For discussions in addition to those already cited of the legitimacy of judicial review — including its constitutional authorization and its democratic character — see Nowak et al., *supra* Chap. 1, n.43; Levy, ed., Judicial Review and the Supreme Court (1967); Berger, Congress v. The Supreme Court, chaps. 1-8 (1969); Gunther & Dowling, Cases and Materials on Constitutional Law 15-23 (8th ed. 1970); Bickel, The Least Dangerous Branch, chap. 1 (1962).

On judicial review in other countries, see Symposium, Conference on Comparative Constitutional Law, 53 S. Calif. L. Rev. 401 (1980); Cappeletti, Judicial Review in the Contemporary World (1971); McWhinney, Judicial Review (4th ed. 1969); Cappelletti & Adams, Judicial Review — European Antecedents and Adaptations, 79 Harv. L. Rev. 1207 (1966).

61. It is argued, for instance, that judicial review weakens the sense of political "responsibility" of the other branches and the people (but see Bishin, *supra* n.59 at 1135-1137; Cox, Role of the Supreme Court in American Government 116-117 (1976)); and that it risks destructive retaliation against the Court by the other branches (but see Kurland, Foreword: Equal in Origin and Equal in Title to the Legislative and Executive Branches of the Government, 78 Harv. L. Rev. 143, 175 (1964)). Some classical criticisms of judicial review in general are Thayer, The

review.[62] But enough has been said to make clear the major lines of debate on the question.

The controversy today is not really over whether the allegedly undemocratic character of review justifies its present *abolition*. Few if any people think that feasible. The point of the debate today is that if judicial review is an undemocratic feature of our Constitution, then the *scope or intensity* of judicial review should accordingly be attenuated. That is the battleground to which I next turn.

c. Limits On, or Standards For, Judicial Review

The controversy centers mainly of course on the "open-ended" clauses (like "due process" and "equal protection") that leave so much room for the exercise of discretion by judicial interpreters. In recent years a number of scholarly voices have complained that the Supreme Court is exercising this discretion in a manner unbecoming a court. The Court is said to be reaching out to decide various broad issues of policy in the manner of a legislature, and reflecting its own personal values.[63] The Court, it is argued, should focus more on the development of a consistent body of principled decisions that honor the words, spirit, and structure of the Constitution.[64] Some suggest[65] that the "due

---

Origin and Scope of the American Doctrine of Constitutional Law, 7 Harv. L. Rev. 129 (1893); Commager, Majority Rule and Minority Rights (1943); Hand, The Contribution of An Independent Judiciary to Civilization, in Dilliard, ed., The Spirit of Liberty 159-165 (1953); Hand, The Bill of Rights 1-30 (1958). Examples of more recent advocacy of very *limited* review under the due process clause are Linde, Due Process of Lawmaking, 55 Neb. L. Rev. 197 (1976); Ely, Democracy and Distrust 14-21 (1980).

62. One can, for instance, point to a special virtue of review, stemming from the fact that ours is a federal system. If each *state* legislature was to be the sole judge of its laws' federal constitutionality, a practical unified federal system could scarcely exist. Justice Holmes once said: "I do not think the United States would come to an end if we lost our power to declare an Act of Congress void. I do think that the Union would be imperiled if we could not make that declaration as to the laws of the several states." Holmes, Law and the Court, in Collected Legal Papers 291, 295-296 (1920). In somewhat analogous spirit, Professor Choper has proposed that the Supreme Court treat as "non-justiciable" questions of whether a given exercise of national power offends "states' rights." Choper, *supra* n.50, chap. 4. He has a similar proposal for conflicts in the respective constitutional powers of Congress and the President. *Id.*, chap. 5. For summaries and critiques of the Choper book, see reviews by McGowan in 79 Mich. L. Rev. 616 (1981), by Monaghan in 94 Harv. L. Rev. 296 (1980) and Sager in 81 Colum. L. Rev. 707 (1981).

63. Kurland, *supra* n.61; Bickel, The Supreme Court and the Idea of Progress 175 (1970); Horowitz, Courts and Social Policy, chap. 7, esp. 293-298 (1977); Ely, Democracy and Distrust, chap. 3, 181-183 (1980); Cox, *supra* n.61 at 102, 114, 117-118 (1976).

64. Bickel, *supra* n.63 at 86-87, 175; Wechsler, Principles, Politics and Fundamental Law 3-48 (1961); Lusky, By What Right? 20-21 (1975).

65. See Ely and Linde, both cited *supra* in n.61.

process" clause should no longer be given the "substantive"[66] meaning it has acquired. While I cannot here explore the nuances of these criticisms, what I can do is attempt briefly to summarize the background and nature of the current, confusing standards for application of the "due process" and "equal protection" clauses.

1. When due process is given a procedural meaning, a statute would violate due process if it, for example, provided for certain court adjudications being made without an opportunity for a fair adversary hearing before an impartial judge. Or a statute might violate another kind of procedural due process if the very process of statutory enactment was not in accordance with legal requirements applicable to enactment of formally valid laws.[67]

The Supreme Court recognizes of course the procedural meanings of due process, but in addition, sometimes applies a *substantive* (nonprocedural) meaning. Substantive due process seems to have different meanings for different types of cases. In the case of statutes dealing with matters of economic regulation or general social welfare, due process is held to require that the legislative judgment not be "arbitrary." The statute must use a "rational" or nonarbitrary means of effectuating a constitutionally permissible goal. Still, the Court is theoretically not playing the role of a superlegislature. Rather it recognizes there is a "presumption" favoring the constitutionality of the statute. This gives weight to the expressed judgment of a coordinate and popularly elected branch of the government. The burden of proof is placed on the person attacking constitutionality.

There were times (notably in the decades preceding 1937) when the Supreme Court seemed to be giving only lip service to this principle of presumptive validity. At these times it was invalidating social legislation such as statutes governing maximum hours of labor, minimum wages, and maximum prices. The Court seemed to be in fact acting as a superlegislature and substituting its own judgment as to reasonableness of the legislation instead of asking merely whether reasonable men could have arrived at the legislative judgment. In 1937, however, this trend was reversed, and the presumption of constitu-

66. This concept is explained below.

67. See Linde, *supra* n.61 at 239. Judge Linde's proposal is that the due process clause should permit *only* this narrow kind of procedural review — a position not taken by American courts, but popular in some foreign countries. Professor Ely, *supra* n.61, shares the view favoring only a procedural meaning for due process, but apparently leaves room for vigorous judicial policymaking through *other* clauses, including a hopefully revived "privileges and immunities" clause and clauses that keep open the channels of political change, prohibit discrimination, and help insure equal participation in the processes and bounty of government. For criticism, see Tribe, The Puzzling Persistence of Process-Based Constitutional Theories," 89 Yale L.J. 1063 (1980); Lynch, Book Review, 80 Colum. L. Rev. 857 (1980); Cox, Book Review, 94 Harv. L. Rev. 700 (1981).

tionality is now more uniformly observed in fact as well as announced in the opinions — i.e., in cases involving statutes in the economic and social welfare realm.

But when it comes to statutes restricting those civil liberties that the Court decides are "fundamental" (the list is not altogether clear but probably includes rights under the First, Fourth, Fifth, Sixth, and Eighth Amendments, as well as voting rights, right of interstate travel, certain rights of privacy), the Court applies not the above deferential, "rational basis" test, but one described as "strict scrutiny." Here the Court will not allow the invasion of a fundamental liberty unless it is *necessary* to promote a *"compelling"* or "overriding" governmental interest. In other words, the usual presumption of constitutionality is treated as simply absent or as replaced by a presumption of *un*constitutionality.[68]

At this point I think it would be instructive to ask how the case upholding the Wisconsin name-of-rape-victim statute (above between nn. 1 & 2) fits in with my discussion concerning presumptions. Let me repeat two sentences from the previously quoted language: "It is considered that there is a minimum of social value in the publication of the identity of a female in connection with such an outrage. *Certain it is that the legislature could so find.*" These sentences illustrate my point about a presumption of, or a "rational basis" approach to, constitutionality. The Wisconsin Supreme Court, while apparently in agreement with the legislative judgment, was reminding us that the question was not what the court would have found or said if it were the legislature, but rather whether a reasonable legislature could have found and said what it did.

But is the case inconsistent with what I have described as the

68. For discussion of procedural and substantive due process, see Nowak et al., *supra* n.46 at 380-383 with more detailed treatment at 476-514 and 385-450; and Tribe, American Constitutional Law (1978) at 474-477, 501-563, 421-455, and 886-990. Note that from the early 1970s, particularly in cases involving claims to a due process hearing right, the Court's rationale has had a new emphasis. It generally rejects an earlier distinction between a person whose liberty or property interest was weighty enough to be a "right" entitled to due process protection, and one who had a mere "privilege" and hence was not entitled to such protections. The Court now usually asks whether the interest is of such a "nature" as to rise to the status of an "entitlement" and thus to trigger due process protection — and the Court pays particular attention to any "justifiable expectations" derived from an "independent source such as state law" or from "mutually explicit understandings." This approach has had a sometimes widening, sometimes narrowing effect on the coverage of interests deemed to trigger due process protections. See Tribe, *id.*, esp. 514-539; Nowak et al., *supra* at 478-498. The question of what *kind* of process is "due" (analytically though perhaps not psychologically separate from whether the kind of interest involved has triggered the due process clause at all) has been given varying, pragmatic answers by the Court in varying situations. See Tribe, *supra* at 532-557; Nowak et al., *supra* at 498-512.

United States Supreme Court attitude in many civil liberties cases? Since the case involved the defendant's freedom of expression, would not the Supreme Court have recognized no presumption or a reverse presumption? In light of the First Amendment cases cited in the preceding section on privacy and the Constitution, this seems likely. There, as here, the First Amendment right was confronted with competing personal rights, sometimes privacy rights in tort situations, and the First Amendment right generally triumphed. Indeed, you will recall that the cited 1975 *Cox Broadcasting* case in the Supreme Court *invalidated* a Georgia statute very similar to that in the South Carolina and Wisconsin cases.[69]

2. Just as due process protections apply against both federal and state governments (under the Fifth and Fourteenth Amendments respectively), so does equal protection. The latter is true because the Fifth Amendment due process clause has been interpreted to include an equal protection guarantee as a counterpart for the Fourteenth Amendment's "equal protection of the laws" clause.[70] And, as in due process cases, there are differing standards of review in the post-1937 equal protection cases. There is the distinction we have seen between (a) the deferential review in economic and social welfare cases (does the legislature's classification bear a "rational" relationship to a legitimate governmental purpose?) and (b) a "strict scrutiny" review of classifications that involve "fundamental" rights *or* that classify people on a "suspect" basis, like race or national origin (is this classification *necessary* for the achievement of a *compelling* or overriding government purpose?). The Supreme Court seems to have used a third approach in recent years for *some* cases in the *first* category, e.g., recent cases on gender-based classifications (is the classification *"substantially"* related to the achievement of *"important"* government objectives?). It is a more independent review than under the "rational basis" test though the Court has not clearly and consistently articulated a rationale for this intermediate approach.[71]

3. The flexibility inherent in these three-tiered tests, as well as in the two-tiered tests used in the due process cases, produces divisions

69. The rather narrow *Cox* rationale in terms of "public records" as the source is to be read in the light of the broader approach taken in the later *Smith* opinion on disclosure of the name of a juvenile charged as an offender. See *supra* at nn. 5 & 6.

70. Bolling v. Sharpe, 347 U.S. 497 (1954); Karst, The Fifth Amendment's Guarantee of Equal Protection, 55 N.C.L. Rev. 540 (1977).

71. See Nowak et al., *supra* n.46 at 524-527. For suggestions by scholars for improved approaches to equal protection, see articles cited *id.* at 526 nn. 12-16. The more detailed treatment of the equal protection cases is in *id.*, chap. 16. See also, Perry, Modern Equal Protection, 79 Colum. L. Rev. 1023 (1979); Barrett, The Rational Basis Standard For Equal Protection Review of Ordinary Legislative Classifications, 68 Ky. L. Rev. 845 (1980).

among the Justices as to their proper application. That is, decisions that are controversial as to their substance are also frequently controversial as to which of the tests applies. Thus in the due process area, the majority opinion in the famous abortion case of Roe v. Wade (see Chap. 1, n.42) treated the woman's right to abortion in the first trimester of pregnancy as a "fundamental" right, requiring a "compelling" state interest (not found to exist) to support the prohibitory abortion statute; the Rehnquist dissent argued that only the "rational basis" test need be applied.[72] In the equal protection area, the celebrated *Bakke* case on "benign" or "reverse" racial discrimination in medical school admissions posed a similar conflict over the applicable test as well as over substance. Of the five Justices applying the equal protection clause (the four others decided the case solely on statutory grounds), Justice Powell used a "strict scrutiny" approach because racial classifications were being made, whereas the other four used the "intermediate" approach above described.[73]

4. The criticism of the pre-1937 Court — that it was acting as a superlegislature in the area of economic regulation and social welfare — has also been made of the Court's "strict scrutiny" approach in civil liberties cases. Those who defend the Court on this issue usually argue that when we are dealing with rights like freedom of speech, equal voting power, freedom from adverse racial discrimination, or the rights of those accused of crime, we are generally dealing with minority voices in our polity — people who lack the organized power in the legislature to protect their interest in fair treatment. The courts may be virtually their only hope.

This more "activist" attitude in the civil liberties area has been usually associated with the Warren Court (though its roots go back

72. For discussions of Roe v. Wade and related issues in abortion, see Symposium, The Law and Politics of Abortion, 77 Mich. L. Rev. 1569 (1979).

73. They (Brennan, Marshall, White, Blackmun) asserted that the state medical school's pursuit of its purposes (i.e., purposes to compensate for past societal discrimination against minorities, to correct the underrepresentation of minorities in medicine, to improve delivery of medical services to under-served communities, and to diversify the student body) by setting aside a reasonable percentage of class positions for only qualified minority applicants, and applying the same standards of grading to all students once they are admitted, did not create a "suspect" classification in the usual sense, and did not stigmatize whites or minorities or "put the weight of the government behind racial hatred and separatism."

Justice Powell, together with the four who decided on statutory grounds only, affirmed the California Supreme Court's judgment ordering the admission of Bakke, the white applicant. He voted to reverse, however, what he construed to be an order of the California court against the medical school's *taking race into account* in admissions. He thought race, among other factors, could be considered in *diversifying* the student body and thus furthering a proper aim of universities. In this latter vote of reversal he was joined by the "Brennan four," who believed not merely that race could count as a factor in student body diversity but that even a racial "quota," reasonable in amount, was valid. For discussion of issues posed by this case of Regents v. Bakke, 438 U.S. 265 (1978), see Symposium, 67 Calif. L. Rev. 1 (1979).

further). But in this area, and indeed in some other areas, it is a mistake to suppose that the attitude of the more "conservative" Burger Court has been consistently and sharply different. A conservative Court is supposed to show more "judicial restraint" in invalidating legislation, more adherence to precedent, less active concern for civil liberties. But an analysis of Burger Court decisions during 1970-1978 shows that the "Court 'has nullified more national laws on first amendment and equal protection grounds than any predecessor,' and indeed on several issues has moved well beyond the lines established in 1969."[74] It has invalidated three federal and three state statutes on constitutional grounds never used by the Warren Court. Its overruling of precedents has occurred at least ten times, not more than half of which can be viewed as undoing Warren Court precedents. On individual rights one finds some retreats, some vacillations, and some advances.[75]

How to explain the fact that the contrast between the Warren and Burger Courts has not been much sharper? In the first place, no sudden and complete change jolted the nature of the Court's membership. When the Burger Court convened in October, 1970, its two new justices (Burger and Blackmun) were joined by seven members of the Warren Court, four of them generally regarded as "liberals" (Black, Douglas, Brennan, and Marshall) and three others as either conservatives or moderates (Harlan, Stewart, and White). In 1972 President Nixon appointed Powell and Rehnquist (both regarded as conservative, strict constructionists) after the deaths of Harlan and Black; and in 1975, President Ford appointed Stevens (regarded as a moderate) to succeed Douglas.

Moreover, one characteristic that differentiates the Court from the political branches and is important for continuing public respect for the Court — as well as being a limit on a new Justice's inclination to support overturning politically distasteful precedents — is a certain tradition: that clear precedents should "outweigh the arguments for change unless one is pretty clear that the change is impelled by one of the deeper lasting currents of human thought that give direction to the law."[76]

In addition, discussion about judicial activism versus self-restraint,

74. Choper, *supra* n.50 at 107.

75. On the last three propositions, see Choper, The Burger Court: Misperceptions Regarding Judicial Restraint and Insensitivity to Individual Rights, 30 Syracuse L. Rev. 767, 771-787 (1979); Howard, The Burger Court: A Judicial Nonet Plays the Enigma Variations, 43 Law & Contemp. Prob. 7 (1980).

76. Cox, *supra* n.61 at 111 (1976). I am not dealing here with certain other areas where the Burger Court, apparently because of a greater concern for federalism values, has been definitely more conservative, e.g., in tending to reduce access to the federal courts, in limiting the scope of federal judicial remedies, and limiting congressional power to apply its regulations to state governments themselves. See Cox, Federalism and Individual Rights Under the Burger Court, 72 Nw. U.L. Rev. 1 (1978).

or strict versus loose constructionism, can be very misleading. It is not true that the politically conservative judge has always been the strict constructionist judge. The conservative Justices of the pre-1937 Court who blocked the liberal New Deal legislation were giving not a strict or narrow construction but a broad and loose construction to the due process clause.

Also misleading is the assumption that a Justice's attitude is static and predictable. Many a President has ruefully perceived inconsistencies (perhaps not always accurately) in the attitude of his appointee, as between the periods prior to and after the appointment. President Theodore Roosevelt, the trust-buster who had appointed Holmes, was bitter about a Holmes anti-trust dissent, saying he could "carve out of a banana a judge with more backbone than that."[77] President Eisenhower thought his appointment of Earl Warren was the "biggest damn fool mistake I ever made."[78] President Truman, reacting to Justice Tom Clark's concurring opinion in the case invalidating Truman's seizure of the strike-bound steel mills during the Korean War, called Clark "that damn fool from Texas," and "my biggest mistake."[79] And finally, "so far as adherence to the principle of stare decisis is concerned, [the Burger court] is not the kind of Court promised by President Nixon at the time of his judicial appointments, nor [was its action] the course of action to which President Nixon's nominees subscribed at the time of their confirmations."[80]

Inconsistency can also be manifested *during* the period of judicial service. Thus, the later opinions of Justices Black and Frankfurter are viewed as much more conservative than their earlier opinions; the later opinions of Justice Blackmun, and to some extent of Chief Justice Burger, are viewed as more liberal than their earlier ones. In 1969, reflecting on 16 years of service, Earl Warren said he did not "see how a man could be on the Court and not change his views substantially over a period of years."[81] Finally, a Justice may show an activist and a loose constructionist attitude on some issues that he feels strongly about, and an opposite attitude on others — even when, like Justice Frankfurter, he is a Justice who strongly criticizes other Justices for their activism or loose construction.[82]

77. Harbaugh, Power and Responsibility: The Life and Times of Theodore Roosevelt 162 (1961).

78. Weaver, Warren, The Man, The Court, The Era 342-343 (1967).

79. Abraham, *supra* n.52 at 230n. For illustrations as to other Presidents and Justices, see *id.* at 62-63.

80. Choper, *supra* n.75 at 774.

81. N.Y. Times, Oct. 19, 1969 (Magazine), at 128-129.

82. Lewis, The Same Justice Can Be Both a "Strict" and "Loose" Constructionist, N.Y. Times, May 24, 1970 (Magazine), at 30; Rodell, For Every Justice, Judicial Deference Is a Sometime Thing, 50 Geo. L.J. 700 (1962).

2. The Fourteenth Amendment and the Bill of Rights

The Constitution formulated at the 1787 convention was ratified by the necessary number of states in 1788, and the new Congress began functioning in March 1789. Because of considerable apprehension that the rights of states and individuals were not sufficiently protected against abuses by the new federal government, a Bill of Rights was adopted soon after the Constitution, and became effective in November 1791. These were the first ten amendments to the Constitution. The first eight established certain rights *against the federal government*[83] — including freedom of speech, press, and religion, freedom from unreasonable searches and seizures, the privilege against self-incrimination, right to jury trial, right to counsel, etc. Here is the text:

AMENDMENT I

Congress shall make no law respecting an establishment of religion, or prohibiting the free exercise thereof; or abridging the freedom of speech or of the press; or the right of the people peaceably to assemble, and to petition the government for a redress of grievances.

AMENDMENT II

A well-regulated militia being necessary to the security of a free State, the right of the people to keep and bear arms shall not be infringed.

AMENDMENT III

No soldier shall, in time of peace, be quartered in any house without the consent of the owner, nor in time of war, but in a manner to be prescribed by law.

AMENDMENT IV

The right of the people to be secure in their persons, houses, papers, and effects, against unreasonable searches and seizures, shall not be violated, and no warrants shall issue but upon probable cause, supported by oath or affirmation, and particularly describing the place to be searched, and the person or things to be seized.

AMENDMENT V

No person shall be held to answer for a capital, or otherwise infamous crime, unless on a presentment or indictment of a grand jury, except in cases arising in the land or naval forces, or in the militia, when in actual service in time of war or public danger; nor shall any person be subject for the same offense to be twice put in jeopardy of life or limb; nor shall be compelled in any criminal case to be a witness against himself, nor be deprived of life, liberty, or property, without due process of law; nor shall private property be taken for public use without just compensation.

83. Barron v. Baltimore, 7 Pet. 243, 8 L. Ed. 672 (1833).

AMENDMENT VI

In all criminal prosecutions, the accused shall enjoy the right to a speedy and public trial, by an impartial jury of the State and district wherein the crime shall have been committed, which district shall have been previously ascertained by law, and to be informed of the nature and cause of the accusation; to be confronted with the witnesses against him; to have compulsory process for obtaining witnesses in his favor, and to have the assistance of counsel for his defense.

AMENDMENT VII

In suits at common law, where the value in controversy shall exceed twenty dollars, the right of trial by jury shall be preserved, and no fact tried by a jury shall be otherwise re-examined in any court of the United States, than according to the rules of the common law.

AMENDMENT VIII

Excessive bail shall not be required, nor excessive fines imposed, nor cruel and unusual punishments inflicted.

AMENDMENT IX

The enumeration in the Constitution of certain rights shall not be construed to deny or disparage others retained by the people.

AMENDMENT X

The powers not delegated to the United States by the Constitution, nor prohibited by it to the States, are reserved to the States respectively, or to the people.

The Constitution makes no similar list of protections against the *state* governments. But the Fourteenth Amendment, adopted after the Civil War, does, among other things, prohibit a state from depriving any person of life, liberty, or property without "due process of law," or denying to any person the "equal protection of the laws." So the question then came up in a number of cases whether this very broad "due process" language should be interpreted to include the same protections against the state government that the specific provisions of the Bill of Rights gave against the national government.

The Court's answer was that the due process clause does not automatically incorporate all of the Bill of Rights; it incorporates only those provisions that must be regarded as fundamental or essential to a free democratic society, or, as later phrased, are "fundamental to the American scheme of justice."[84] However, the Court has gradually changed its mind about many of those rights previously regarded as nonessential, so that now almost all parts of the Bill of Rights are regarded as incorporated into the Fourteenth Amendment due process clause and hence applicable to the states.[85] A large number were thus

84. Duncan v. Louisiana, 391 U.S. 145, 149 (1968).

85. See Lewis & Trichter, The Nationalization of the Bill of Rights: History,

incorporated in just the last couple of decades. Not yet incorporated are the Fifth Amendment provision for grand jury indictments in the case of major crimes,[86] and the Seventh Amendment provision for jury trial in civil cases.[87]

A majority of the Court has also ruled: "Once it is decided that a Bill of Rights provision is fundamental . . . the same constitutional standards apply against both the State and Federal governments."[88] This does not mean that Fourteenth Amendment due process can give *only* those types of protections afforded by provisions of the Bill of Rights; it is not so limited. There are many examples of the Justices' belief — both in majority and minority opinions — that a state provision can be ruled in violation of Fourteenth Amendment due process without determining whether a Bill of Rights provision affords parallel protection against the federal government.[89]

Development and Current Status, 20 Washburn L. Rev. 195 (1981); Nowak et al., *supra* n.46 at 414-416; Israel & LaFave, Criminal Procedure 14-16 (3d ed. 1980); Annots., 18 L. Ed. 2d 1388 (1967), 23 L. Ed. 2d 985 (1969). As to a few Amendments, the incorporation issue requires some special comment: The Second Amendment, being seen as a protection against federal interference with the state militia, is viewed as not intended to apply to the states. See Presser v. Illinois, 116 U.S. 252, 265 (1886). Whether the Third Amendment applies to the states has never been litigated in the Supreme Court. In the case of the Eighth Amendment, the "cruel and unusual punishment" clause has been specifically incorporated by the Court into Fourteenth Amendment due process (Robinson v. Califórnia, 370 U.S. 660 (1962)); the "excessive bail" clause has been at least impliedly incorporated (Schlib v. Kuebel, 404 U.S. 357, 365 (1971)); the "excessive fines" clause has not been directly ruled on but is very likely to be treated the same way as the punishment clause. The Ninth Amendment's protection of potential, unenumerated rights was apparently assumed to be incorporated, by the majority's fleeting reference to it (and the much stronger reliance on it in Justice Goldberg's concurring opinion, in spite of some confusing language) in Griswold v. Connecticut, 381 U.S. 479 (1965). The Tenth Amendment, being concerned with division of powers between federal and state governments rather than specification of rights against the federal government, has no bearing on the incorporation issue.

86. The 1884 ruling that that particular clause of the Fifth Amendment is inapplicable to the states (Hurtado v. California, 110 U.S. 516 (1884)) has been adhered to, and its overruling is not regarded as likely.

87. It is generally thought that the 1916 ruling that the clause is inapplicable to the states (Minnesota & St. L.R.R. Co. v. Bombolis, 241 U.S. 211 (1916)) will continue to be adhered to.

88. Benton v. Maryland, 395 U.S. 784, 795 (1969).

89. See, e.g., Justice Brennan's opinion for the majority in Matter of Winship, 397 U.S. 350 (1970) ("proof beyond a reasonable doubt is among the essentials of due process" in a juvenile delinquency case charging an act that would be criminal if committed by an adult; Justice Black's dissent argued there was no basis in the Bill of Rights for the rule). See also Justice Frankfurter's opinion for the majority in Rochin v. California, 342 U.S. 165 (1952); Justice Clark's opinion in Estes v. Texas, 381 U.S. 532 (1965); Justice Frankfurter's concurrence in Adamson v. California, 332 U.S. 46 (1947), and the dissenting opinions of Justices Murphy and Rutledge in the same case; Justice Harlan's concurrence in Griswold v. Connecticut, 381 U.S. 479 (1965) (dealing with substantive due process); Justice Blackmun's opinion for the majority in Roe v. Wade, 410 U.S. 113 (1973), and Justice Stewart's concurrence and Justice Rehnquist's dissent in the same case (substantive due process).

In what way was the freedom of expression issue, which was raised in the Wisconsin and Georgia cases and which might have been raised in the South Carolina case, rooted in the Constitution? The key language is in the First Amendment: "Congress shall make no law . . . abridging the freedom of speech or of the press. . . ." This restriction has been liberally construed to apply to other agencies of the federal government besides Congress; and the Fourteenth Amendment due process clause has been held, at least since 1925,[90] to incorporate the restriction so as to apply to agencies of state government.

3. Role of the Ninth and Tenth Amendments

You will note from the constitutional text quoted above[91] that the first eight Amendments are in the form of specified restraints on government activity, whereas the last two take a different form. In fact, references to the Bill of Rights have often been references just to the first eight amendments. The Ninth Amendment, however, has a greater similarity to the first eight than does the Tenth. The Ninth specifies no restrictions on the federal government, but does call attention to the possibility of restrictions other than those that have been enumerated. And, in fact, the Supreme Court in the case of Griswold v. Connecticut[92] construed its broad language to encompass at least one specific restriction. It found that the Ninth Amendment, together with policy emanations from other amendments in the Bill of Rights, protected a right of privacy of married persons sufficient to invalidate the Connecticut prohibition against use of contraceptives. But as we have seen, the Court seems to have retreated from this rationale in the 1973 abortion case of Roe v. Wade when, speaking of the privacy right, it said, "Whether it be founded in the Fourteenth Amendment's concept of personal liberty . . . *as we feel it is,* or . . . in the Ninth Amendment's reservation of rights to the people, [it] is broad enough to. . . ."[93] Since then the Court has seldom, and cautiously, referred to the Ninth Amendment.[94]

90. See Gitlow v. New York, 268 U.S. 652, 666 (1925).

91. At 337-338.

92. 381 U.S. 479 (1965).

93. 410 U.S. 113, 153 (1973) (emphasis added).

94. See, e.g., Justice Stevens, writing for the majority in Whalen v. Roe, 429 U.S. 589, 598 n.23 (1977). See also Chief Justice Burger writing for three Justices in Richmond Newspapers v. Virginia, 448 U.S. 555, 579-580 & nn. 15, 16 (1980). The broadest acceptance was voiced by Justice Douglas's concurrence in Roe v. Wade, 410 U.S. 113 (1973) and Doe v. Bolton, 410 U.S. 179 (1973). For scholarly discussion see Ely, Democracy and Distrust 33-40 (1980); Bertelsman, The Ninth Amendment and Due Process of Law — Toward a Viable Theory of Unenumerated Rights, 37 U. Cin. L. Rev. 777 (1968); Note, 33 U. Chi. L. Rev. 814 (1966).

The Tenth Amendment, on the other hand, focuses not on unenumerated rights but rather on the distribution of power between state and federal governments. It seems to be saying that if a power has not been granted by the Constitution to the federal government, then it is a power that the states can exercise — unless the Constitution has prohibited the states from exercising it.

In spite of the relative clarity of this provision, considerable confusion about its meaning is shown in the following colloquy on the floor of the Senate by two southern senators critical of the Supreme Court's 1954 decision invalidating state school segregation laws:

Mr. Thurmond: I should like to ask the distinguished Senator a question or two. Is it not true, speaking of the segregation decision, that in the first 10 Amendments to the Constitution, known as the Bill of Rights, which were drafted by a great citizen of the Senator's state, George Mason, the 10th Amendment to the Constitution provides that all powers not specifically delegated to the Federal Government are reserved to the states?

Mr. Byrd: The Senator is correct.

Mr. Thurmond: Is it not further true that the word 'education' is not even to be found in the United States Constitution?

Mr. Byrd: That is correct.

Mr. Thurmond: Is it not further true that since the field of education was not delegated to the Federal Government, therefore it was reserved to the States and should remain reserved to the States and to the people thereof?

Mr. Byrd: The Senator is correct.[95]

One confusion here may arise from the Senators' possible assumption that when the Tenth Amendment refers to powers not delegated "to the United States," the quoted phrase includes the Supreme Court as well as the legislature and executive. As far as I know, the cases under the Tenth Amendment are concerned with the scope of nonjudicial powers of the federal government, typically the powers of Congress, in relation to state powers. But even if we were dealing, in this segregation situation, with an exercise of congressional power rather than of Supreme Court power to apply the Constitution to a state segregation law, the following fallacies would be present in the quoted colloquy:

(a) The mere fact that the word "education" is not mentioned in the Constitution would not mean that Congress had no power over it. Congress has specific power, for instance, to spend money for the general welfare (which surely includes education). Further, Congress

95. 103 Cong. Rec. 10,676 (July 16, 1957).

has specific power under Section 5 of the Fourteenth Amendment to enforce the Fourteenth Amendment prohibition against a state's depriving people of the equal protection of "the laws."[96] No exception is made, in this prohibition, for education laws.

In the context of judicial rather than congressional powers, the colloquy argument is even more inept. For to say that a federal court has no power to decide a case whose subject matter (such as education) has not been specifically mentioned in the Constitution as coming within federal judicial power is to virtually eliminate the federal judicial power. As we have seen in Chapter 2, virtually all of the judicial power is stated not in terms of specific subject matter, but rather in terms of the nature of the parties and whether the case arises under the Constitution, federal laws, or treaties.

(b) Under the language of the Tenth Amendment, in order to qualify as a reserved state power, the power must not only have been (1) not granted to the federal government, but also (2) "not prohibited to the States." And the Fourteenth Amendment *does prohibit* states from depriving people of equal protection of "the laws," including, of course, education laws.

(c) Still another aspect of the Tenth Amendment is worth noting. At various times in its history the Supreme Court has subscribed (and did so at the time of the colloquy) to a particular narrow theory of the Tenth Amendment's role — the theory that the Amendment does *not* operate as a *limit* upon the scope of the granted federal power. In this view, a court is not supposed to decide first whether the subject matter has been reserved to the states and, if so, declare that the exercise of federal power violates the Amendment. Rather, a court faced with a federal statute would — as indeed the Amendment's literal language seems to require — first determine (by looking at the Constitution, its

96. This power is potent. Under it Congress could validly supersede New York's English literacy requirement for voting, by providing that lack of English literacy could not be a basis for denying voting rights to anyone who completed the sixth grade in a Puerto Rican school in which the predominant classroom language was not English. Katzenbach v. Morgan, 384 U.S. 641 (1966). For analysis of the complex opinion and the scope of congressional power under §5, see Nowak at al., *supra* n.46 at 690-697. Congressional power to enforce the Thirteenth and Fifteenth Amendments is analyzed at 697-703 and 703-708 respectively. Recently the attempt has been made to circumvent the Supreme Court 1973 abortion decision (Roe v. Wade) by legislation proposed pursuant to §5 of the Fourteenth Amendment that would define the term "life" in that Amendment so as to make human life commence at the time of conception. (See S. 158, 97th Cong., 1st Sess., Jan. 19, 1981.) It seems doubtful that Congress's power under §5 to "enforce" the Amendment can extend to enforcing constitutional interpretations that are contrary to those that are already announced, or might later be announced, by the Supreme Court — which is the supreme authority on interpretation of constitutional language. For literature on the problem of Congress's power under §5, see in addition to Nowak et al., *id.;* Tribe, Constitutional Law 261-272 (1978); Cox, The Role of Congress in Constitutional Determinations, 40 U. Cin. L. Rev. 199 (1971); Cohen, Congressional Power to Interpret Due Process and Equal Protection, 27 Stan. L. Rev. 603 (1975).

history, etc.) whether power over the subject has been granted to the federal government by the Constitution. If so, then the power has not been reserved to the states; if not so granted, then the power has been reserved to the states. The reserved power thus becomes a *residual* power, *not a limitation* on the scope of granted federal power. As the Supreme Court said in 1941, the Tenth Amendment "states but a truism that all is retained which has not been surrendered."[97] It instructs us that no power which the Constitution fails to allocate to the federal government exists in a no-man's-land free from both federal and state power; rather it is a power reserved to the states (unless specifically denied to the states).

The Supreme Court's upholding of this view at various times began in the Court's earliest period. Then, in the century between the death of Chief Justice Marshall and 1937, it occasionally invoked the opposing view that the Amendment was a limit on federal power. From 1937 to 1976 it reverted to the early view, exemplified in the above quoted 1941 opinion. But a shift occurred again in the 1976 opinion of National League of Cities v. Usery.[98] Here a 5 to 4 decision held that while the federal Fair Labor Standards Act's regulation of minimum wages and overtime pay in enterprises affecting interstate commerce fell within the congressional power to regulate commerce, the power was limited by the Bill of Rights, including the Tenth Amendment. Under that Amendment, considerations of local sovereignty invalidated the application of the Act to state and local government employees. The Court did not sanction as broad a limiting role for the Amendment as had been recognized in some earlier periods: The Amendment would not be construed as narrowing present tests of what is commerce or affects commerce; it would not limit federal power to regulate *non*governmental employees or entities, or to regulate those *governmental* activities that were not *traditionally* governmental (i.e., were not "integral operations in areas of traditional governmental functions.")[99] Nor would this decision be controlling where the federal power involved was not the commerce power but the spending power under Article I, Section 8 (pursuant to which certain regulatory conditions have been attached to money grants), or the congressional power to regulate by way of enforcing the Fourteenth Amendment, under Section 5 thereof.[100]

97. U.S. v. Darby, 312 U.S. 100, 124 (1941).

98. 426 U.S. 833 (1976). The history is reviewed in Corwin (Chase & Ducat revision), The Constitution and What It Means Today 442-448 (14th ed. 1978).

99. 426 U.S. at 852. Thus, a case like U.S. v. California, 297 U.S. 175 (1936), upholding application of federal monetary penalties to violations of the Federal Safety Appliance Act by a state operated railroad, was distinguished. The activities were "not in an area that the States have regarded as integral parts of their governmental activities."

100. See *supra* n.96. The Court stated in n.17 of the opinion: "We express no

Nonetheless, as one scholar recently observed, "The majority's performance in *National League of Cities* has been the target of wide-ranging criticism. Justice Rehnquist's opinion makes light of precedent and offers little guidance for the resolution of subsequent cases. . . ." He goes on, however, to note that the Court's "renewed interest in protecting the state's independent status is not misguided."[101] For the advantages of a federal system[102] are being lost by forces undermining the state's capacity to realize those advantages.[103] He suggests that

---

view as to whether different results might obtain if Congress seeks to affect integral operations of state governments by exercising authority granted it under other sections of the Constitution, such as the Spending Power, Art. I, sec. 8, clause 1, or Sec. 5 of the Fourteenth Amendment." Importance of the latter section in this connection is pointed up by Fitzpatrick v. Bitzer, 427 U.S. 445 (1976). It upheld a federal court suit under the Federal Civil Rights Act of 1964 by state employees against their state employer for damages and attorneys' fees because of employment discrimination, in spite of the fact that the Eleventh Amendment bars citizens' federal court suits against a state. The rationale was that the Fourteenth Amendment had in §5 authorized the 1964 legislation to enforce the anti-discrimination provisions made applicable by the Amendment against states, and the Fourteenth was of course *after* the Eleventh. The same reasoning can apply to a Tenth Amendment case in which the clash is between that Amendment and federal legislation passed pursuant to §5 of the Fourteenth Amendment rather than the commerce clause. For the Court's 1981 reiteration of the limits on the *National League of Cities* decision, see its rejection of the Tenth Amendment claim in Hodel v. Virginia Surface Mining & Reclam. Assoc., 69 L. Ed. 2d 1, 21-27 (1981) involving federal regulation of surface coal mining.

101. Kaden, Politics, Money, and State Sovereignty: The Judicial Role, 79 Colum. L. Rev. 847, 848, 849 (1979).

102. Kaden sees these as (1) the fact that "decisionmaking in smaller units makes possible more direct public participation in both the process of representative selection and the process of policy determination by the delegates chosen. . . . Simply put, proximity increases accountability by increasing access" (*id.* at 853-854); (2) federalism "promotes variety in political choice and counters the impulse toward social and ideological homogeneity by allowing cultural differences to find expression in different places" (*id.* at 854); (3) "the aphorism that a federal system permits the states to serve as laboratories for experimentation has also been borne out in our experience. Traditionally, federal government initiatives have drawn on the experience in the states" (*id.*). Because state autonomy fosters participation and accountability as above noted, it serves political liberty, and so judicial protection of that autonomy is "an essential part of the traditional judicial assignment to protect the individual's right to liberty against majoritarian abuse" (*id.* at 857).

103. Among such forces are the declining influence of state party organizations on voters and members of Congress, changes in the structure of Congress and its internal rules, and the burgeoning systems of either direct federal regulatory commands to the states or (more often) requirements imposed as conditions to much needed financial grants (*id.* at 857-883). One result is that "a state's views are increasingly represented by public officials with a direct stake in ever-expanding national programs even if expansion entails greater regulation and the imposition of more onerous burdens on the states." In short, "it is now far less likely that the states' interest in their continuing autonomy will consistently receive expression within the political branches of the federal government, or that the political process will yield dependable lines of accountability between the governed and the government" (*id.* at 868).

certain tentative guidelines[104] are more satisfactory than those offered by *National League of Cities.* These and other guidelines will have to be thoroughly explored for the future resolution of this basic problem in American federalism.[105]

4. Whether Constitutional Restraints Can Apply to Private as Well as Government Action

I have referred more than once to the fact that the major constitutional protections are restraints against government: the federal government in the case of the Bill of Rights, and the state government (and its subdivisions) in the case of the Fourteenth Amendment. The conduct of private parties is, in general, not covered by these restraints.

You should know, however, that there are some exceptions to this general proposition. I will touch briefly on the following categories of exception: (a) situations in which the executive or legislative governmental element is so intertwined with the private conduct as to make the private party a kind of "government instrumentality" (e.g., where the government aids, commands, encourages, approves, or authorizes

104. E.g., in the area of direct commands to the states: Compelling the states to (as Attorney General Levi expressed it in a 1975 statement expressing constitutional doubts) "donate their funds and personnel, and to create agencies or facilities to administer a federal law" would be beyond the pale (*id.* at 892). The federal government would be barred from coopting the state's political processes by significantly interfering with legislative and executive direction, as measured by fiscal impact, organizational structure, and allocation of nonfiscal resources. But requiring states, along with private parties, to abide by minimum wage and maximum hour requirements (involved in *National League of Cities*) or safety standards, bargaining practices, or liability rules would be legitimate (*id.* at 890-891).

In the area of conditions attached to grants: "If the federal government could lawfully impose the requirement directly on the states by regulation, it should be no less acceptable when imposed as a condition to federal aid" (*id.* at 895). If the condition could *not* have been imposed directly, e.g., under the commerce clause, because of interference with state autonomy, then the Court may properly apply to the condition an "intermediate level of scutiny" (*cf. supra* at n.71), putting a heavier burden of justification on the federal government than is customary in the review of regulatory legislation (*id.* at 896). And "given the drastic increase in the amounts of federal funds and the formula-based entitlements in aid programs enacted since 1960, it is unrealistic for anything to depend on the state's nominal right not to participate" (*id.*).

105. For further discussion of the Tenth Amendment and *National League of Cities,* see Nowak et al., *supra* n.46 at 159-163; Schwartz, National League of Cities v. Usery — The Commerce Power and State Sovereignty Recidivus, 46 Fordham L. Rev. 1115 (1978); Michelman, States' Rights and States' Roles: Permutations of "Sovereignty" in National League of Cities v. Usery, 86 Yale L.J. 1165 (1977). For the view that state interests are adequately represented on the national political level, and that questions of whether federal government action invalidly infringes on state rights should be treated by the Supreme Court as nonjusticiable, i.e., to be resolved by the political branches alone, see chapter 4 of Choper, *supra* n.50.

the private activity); (b) situations in which the private party is performing a function that is typically governmental ("public function" theory); (c) situations in which a court decision backing up the conduct is viewed as providing the necessary governmental element (a "judicial enforcement theory" of government action); and (d) situations governed by the unusual kind of constitutional restraint that is itself directed at private parties as well as government, e.g., the Thirteenth Amendment (and which can therefore be the basis of federal statutes directed at private conduct not reachable by other congressional powers).

a. "Government Instrumentality" Theory

1. An illustration of government *aid* that was sufficient to result in a "state action" conclusion is the case of a state loaning textbooks to students including those at racially discriminatory private schools.[106] The conclusion of unconstitutionality as to aiding the latter students also applies to tuition grants to such students.[107] But a line is drawn between particularized subsidies like those to schools, on the one hand, and generalized government services offered to all, like police and fire protection, parks, museums, etc. on the other.[108] And a relevant inquiry is whether the private entity's legitimate functions, assisted by the subsidy, can be *separated* from the challenged practices[109] — something that could not be done in the textbook case, in which the Court said, "discriminatory treatment exerts a pervasive influence on the entire educational process."[110] An additional problem is well illustrated in the cases on government financial aid to private hospitals. The cases, which are in sharp conflict (there being as yet no conclusive Supreme Court decisions), reveal that "the standards used for determining 'state action' for purposes of a case involving alleged racial discrimination may be different from [i.e., apparently more inclusive than] the standards used where allegations not involving race are concerned."[111]

106. Norwood v. Harrison, 413 U.S. 455 (1973).

107. See *id.* at 463, n.6. The opposite result can follow when the school is not discriminating racially but rather is a religious school exercising religious freedom under the First Amendment and the subsidy is confined to the school's secular rather than sectarian functions. *Id.* at 468-470; Board of Educ. v. Allen, 392 U.S. 236 (1968).

108. *Norwood, supra* n. 106 at 465; Gilmore v. City of Montgomery, 417 U.S. 556, 574-575 (1974).

109. See, e.g., Powe v. Miles, 407 F.2d 73 (2d Cir. 1968); Browns v. Mitchell, 409 F.2d 593, 596 (10th Cir. 1969); Grossner v. Trustees of Columbia U., 287 F. Supp. 535 (S.D.N.Y. 1968).

110. *Norwood, supra* n.106 at 469; and see preceding footnote.

111. Annot., 42 ALR Fed. 463, 471 (1979).

The much-cited case of Burton v. Wilmington Parking Authority[112] represents perhaps the outer limit of the Court's willingness to recognize state action under a government instrumentality theory. A state agency running a parking facility had *leased space* to a privately operated restaurant, which engaged in racial discrimination. The Court was impressed by the fact that the restaurant was an integral part of the state's plan to operate the building as a self-sustaining unit; that both the state and restaurant derived certain economic benefits from the scheme; and (apparently) the fact that there was the appearance of government authorization for restaurant practices.

This case was differentiated by an important 1972 Supreme Court decision involving the refusal of a Moose Lodge, located on private property, to serve food and beverages to a black guest of a Caucasian lodge member. The Supreme Court ruled that the fact that this private club received a liquor license from a state board and was subject to certain record-keeping and other regulations of the board did *not* "sufficiently implicate the State in the discriminatory guest policies of Moose Lodge so as to make the latter 'State action' within the ambit of the Equal Protection Clause of the Fourteenth Amendment."[113] The Court found lacking here "the symbiotic relationship between lessor and lessee that was present in" the parking facility restaurant case. It also noted that the board was not encouraging discrimination; and that the club was not in a liquor monopoly situation. (The Court did authorize enjoining a board regulation commanding club licensees to abide by their constitutions and bylaws — since the result, however unintended, was to put the force of the state behind bylaws requiring racial discrimination against guests.)

2. Cases involving public utilities offer further illustration. The fact that Metropolitan Edison Company was heavily regulated and had monopoly status was not itself enough to give "state action" status to its allegedly unconstitutional procedures for terminating electric service upon nonpayment of bills. The Court thought it significant that the state had not specifically *authorized or approved* the challenged termination procedure,[114] though it had generally authorized the public utility enterprise. This situation contrasted, said the Court, with that of the *Pollak* case because there the Commission, after hearing, had

112. 365 U.S. 715 (1961).

113. Moose Lodge No. 107 v. Irvis, 407 U.S. 163 (1972).

114. Jackson v. Metropolitan Edison, 419 U.S. 345 (1974). The Commission had done nothing after the company filed its tariffs, which included a reservation of the right to terminate services on reasonable notice of nonpayment of bills (a reservation which, under state law, the company was not clearly required to file or the Commission clearly empowered to disapprove, said the Court).

specifically approved a street car company's challenged practice of piping music, news, and ads to its passengers.[115]

3. An illustration of state action through *"encouragement"* of private conduct that would be unconstitutional if engaged in directly by the state is afforded by the case involving a California initiative measure adopted by popular referendum as a constitutional amendment. The measure in effect repealed, and forbade future enactment of, "fair housing" laws prohibiting discrimination in housing. The amendment prohibited the state from denying a person's freedom to decline to sell or rent his residential property, in his absolute discretion. Private racial discrimination in housing was thus made a state constitutional right. But to invalidate the amendment on an assumption of encouragement-of-discrimination might have the startling consequence of invalidating *any* state attempt to *repeal* any protective legislation analogous to the housing legislation. The Supreme Court therefore tread a narrow path in its rationale: The California Supreme Court had *found* that in this particular case, the effect and intent of the amendment was to encourage discrimination; the United States Supreme Court could find no reason to overturn that determination.[116]

4. Consider now the idea of a government *grant of authority* to a private party. A license or other grant was involved in the *Moose Club* and public utility cases discussed above, but in the circumstances of those cases was deemed insufficient. *Some* grants of authority, however, can be more significant.

Thus, an employee of a private amusement park who tried to exclude people from the park on racial grounds and then arrested

115. Public Util. Commn. v. Pollak, 343 U.S. 451 (1952). We have encountered this case in the discussion of privacy *supra* at n.26. The conclusion as to privacy invasion was negative.

116. Reitman v. Mulkey, 387 U.S. 369 (1967). It might further have been held in this case that the amendment constituted direct racial discrimination under the Fourteenth Amendment, because *racial minorities were thus prevented from using legislative remedies* to alleviate their housing problem, requiring them to use the more difficult avenue of constitutional amendment. See Black, "State Action," Equal Protection and California's Proposition 14, 81 Harv. L. Rev. 69 (1967). An encouragement rationale is not necessarily confined to encouragement of the challenged activity itself. It may be "enough that government influence(s) or encourage(s) private persons to perform functions or implement policies *in the course of which* a challenged activity occurred" (emphasis added). Note, State Action: Theories for Applying Constitutional Restrictions to Private Activity, 74 Colum. L. Rev. 656, 683 (1974). An example is Coleman v. Wagner College, 429 F.2d 1120 (2d Cir. 1970). Here the Court thought that if a New York statute requiring private colleges to file with state officials certain regulations (to be formulated by the college for maintenance of order on campus, together with the applicable penalties that must include the possibility of suspension or expulsion) was intended as a command to the colleges to adopt a more severe policy toward campus disruption, it would be a "meaningful state intrusion into disciplinary policies of private colleges"; and the private college's particular disciplinary procedures *implementing* this state policy would be subject to constitutional restraints.

them was held to have engaged in state action because he had been deputized as a sheriff for duty at the park and purported to be acting in that capacity.[117] The Reitman v. Mulkey "encouragement" case above might also be viewed as involving the state's grant of constitutional authority to discriminate, enlarging a pre-statutory common law right to discriminate by putting the right in the constitution and repealing the fair housing statute.

Here is another example: A labor union that was certified under the Railway Labor Act as sole bargaining agent of certain workers, including blacks, discharged its bargaining function in a racially discriminatory manner. Because of the government certification of the union for discharge of statutory obligations vitally affecting the workers, it could be argued that the union had been given a grant of authority to act as virtually a government agent; hence its discriminatory conduct could be treated as a violation of the due process clause of the Fifth Amendment, just as direct federal government discrimination would be. This was the view taken by the Supreme Court of Kansas in 1947.[118] A couple of years earlier, the United States Supreme Court in a similar case had found the union violative of the *statute,* and strongly intimated that if the statute were interpreted otherwise, *it* would be unconstitutional.[119]

b. "Public Function" Theory

There are some cases that are related to the grant-of-authority cases but do not depend on such a grant. These cases illustrate the *"public function"* theory — cases in which the private party is carrying on a function of a governmental nature, i.e., one typically carried on by government. Here are the so-called "white primary" cases, which found racial discrimination by political parties or political clubs unconstitutional because — *even where operating without specific statutory authority* — they were part of the total election machinery and hence discharging a function governmental in nature.[120] Similarly, the

117. Griffin v. Maryland, 378 U.S. 130 (1964).

118. Betts v. Easeley, 161 Kan. 459, 169 P.2d 831 (1946).

119. Steele v. Louisville & N.R.R., 323 U.S. 192 (1944). One more example: A state could not avoid the unconstitutionality of racial discrimination in primary election voting by granting authority to political party committees or a state political convention to determine who could vote in primaries. Nixon v. Condon, 286 U.S. 73 (1932); Smith v. Allwright, 321 U.S. 649 (1944). The political parties, though private organizations, had become agents of the state for discharge of the state's function in running elections, the primary system being part of the elective process.

120. Terry v. Adams, 345 U.S. 461 (1953); Rice v. Elmore, 165 F.2d 387 (4th Cir. 1947), *cert. denied,* 333 U.S. 875 (1948). *Cf.* the white primary cases in n.119 *supra.*

refusal of a town manager in a "company town" to grant a permit for distribution of religious literature was treated as state action. His functions were analogous to those of an official of an ordinary town; he was discharging a function governmental in nature.[121] The Court also took a "public function" approach to the running of a segregated private park.[122]

c. *"Judicial Enforcement" Theory*

Turning now from the "government instrumentality" and "public function" theories to the "judicial enforcement" theory: The landmark case here is the Supreme Court's 1948 decision in Shelley v. Kraemer already mentioned.[123] In this case blacks were involved in purchasing houses subject to racial covenants. These covenants embodied *private* discrimination. Hence, viewed by themselves, they were not subject to the Fourteenth Amendment's prohibition against a state's depriving people of the equal protection of the laws. But when one of the covenantors tried to enforce the discriminatory covenant by going to court — in one case to oust the black purchaser, and in the other to restrain him from taking possession — would the court's granting the injunction constitute the state action violating the Fourteenth Amendment? The Supreme Court so held.[124]

But there was qualifying language:

> These are cases in which the purposes of the [racially restrictive] agreements were secured only by judicial enforcement . . . . It is clear that but for the active intervention of the state courts, [defendants] would have been free to occupy the properties without restraint. These are not

121. Marsh v. Alabama, 326 U.S. 501 (1946).

122. Transfer of title from the city (which had received the land under a will for a whites-only park) to private trustees was not itself enough to avoid application of the Fourteenth Amendment to segregation practices — not only because the record failed to show complete cessation of municipal maintenance but because running this park was a "public function." Evans v. Newton, 382 U.S. 296 (1966). Then, after the state court ruling that the testator had intended the property to revert to his heirs in the event that the segregated park intention could not be enforced, the Court permitted this reversion to the heirs and discontinuance of the land's use as a park. Evans v. Abney, 396 U.S. 435 (1970).

123. 334 U.S. 1 (1948). See Chap. 2 *supra* at n.138.

124. This was not the first instance of *judicial* action being treated as state action. Thus, e.g., a trial judge's improper denial of appointed counsel to an indigent defendant has been treated as state action violating the due process clause. Powell v. Alabama, 287 U.S. 45 (1932). But that had been a direct judicial deprivation of constitutional rights. In *Shelley,* the immediate deprivation, i.e., the discrimination, was a private one, and only when the discriminator got the aid of a court to enforce it did the unconstitutional state action arise. Hence the *Shelley* theory may be called a "judicial enforcement" theory.

cases . . . in which the states have merely abstained from action, leaving private individuals free to impose such discrimination as they see fit.[125]

1. This language might be taken to mean that a judicial enforcement theory will *not* be applied to *denial* of relief to a plaintiff attacking an allegedly unconstitutional practice.[126] However, such a distinction between affirmative and negative action in this field has not been firmly established; it seems to rest on a largely accidental factor and is not clearly intended by the quoted language in *Shelley*.

2. The more obvious purpose of the above language is to establish that judicial action (whether positive or negative) will be state action if it *creates* or makes effective a discrimination that previously was nonexistent or ineffective. The Court was stressing that prior to the injunction, these defendants had not been effectively discriminated against; in spite of the covenants, they had actually purchased the properties.

3. Narrowing this approach somewhat is a third approach — the theory proposed by Judge Louis Pollak, writing as an academic in 1959: The *Shelley* principle should invalidate a judgment only when the judgment assists private persons in inducing or compelling *other* persons to do what is forbidden to the states by the Fourteenth Amendment.[127]

This third approach of course covers the *Shelley* situation — as well as other enforcements of contracts by which one covenantor compels another to discriminate in the sale of property. But it is narrower than the second approach since it would exclude those instances of discrimination-creating affirmative relief that involved no pressure against others to discriminate. Application of either approach, however, usually results in the same conclusion in certain well-known situ-

125. 334 U.S. 1, 13, 19 (1948).

126. See, e.g., Rice v. Sioux City Memorial Park Cemetery, 245 Iowa 147 (1953). The plaintiff had signed a contract with a cemetery for burial of her Indian husband — a contract that contained a clause against burial of non-Caucasians. When the cemetery managers discovered he was an Indian, they refused burial and successfully defended the damage suit on the contract by pointing to the "non-Caucasian" clause. The Court thought that the state in denying relief had "maintained neutrality" and not affirmatively or directly aided in an unconstitutional discrimination. The United States Supreme Court without opinion affirmed by virtue of the fact that it was equally divided. 348 U.S. 880 (1954). But it later vacated its judgment on the ground that the writ of certiorari had been improvidently granted. The reason was that an Iowa statute (passed after this litigation had started and not previously brought squarely to the Court's attention) prohibited racially discriminatory burial practices by cemeteries. This gave the present litigation "an isolated significance" for the future, so that certiorari should not have been granted.

127. Pollak, Racial Discrimination and Judicial Integrity: A Reply to Professor Wechsler, 108 U. Pa. L. Rev. 1, 13 (1959).

ations — whether the common conclusion is against state action,[128] or for state action.[129]

4. Perhaps the narrowest interpretation of the *Shelley* "judicial enforcement" theory is its confinement to government-like private conduct, i.e., involving concerted action in a field in which governments commonly operate. Thus when the group of co-covenantors in *Shelley* were regulating the conditions for ownership of land in their territory, they resembled the government in that they exerted a concerted power and were engaged in an activity analogous to a government's zoning activity. The *Shelley* Court had not reasoned in such narrow terms. However, in its actual application thus far, the "judicial enforcement" theory has not extended much beyond these narrow terms — in fact not much beyond *racial covenant* situations.

The reason apparently is the Court's well-known fear of opening the doors too wide. Obviously, to say that whenever a court sanctions, in whatever manner, *any* kind of private discrimination, it transforms the private action into state action, would obliterate the fundamental constitutional distinction between private and state action. All that

128. Thus, in the cemetery case discussed in n.126 *supra,* (1) the discriminatory situation was not created by the court's denial of relief — it already existed, and (2) there was no pressure on third persons to discriminate in the same manner as the cemetery.

So too, under either theory there would be no state action in the case of a court's convicting blacks of trespass, at the complaint of a private land-owner who complains only against black trespassers on his land, or the complaint of a businessman who complains only of black customers persisting in demanding service at a whites-only restaurant or lunch counter. The court's conviction would not initiate the discrimination or assist the property owner in any purpose to pressure others to discriminate. The prosecutions therefore seemed constitutionally possible. The reason most such trespass prosecutions against blacks were *not* successful were: (1) in some instances a clearer mark of state action had been present in the discrimination: the state or city, through legislation or executive pronouncements, had made racial segregation *official* policy, e.g., Peterson v. City of Greenville, 373 U.S. 244 (1963), Lombard v. Louisiana, 373 U.S. 267 (1963); (2) the remaining large number of sit-in cases of the 1960s were dismissed not because of some theory of state action, but for another reason: Title II of the Civil Rights Act of 1964, forbidding racial, or other discrimination in public accommodations, was interpreted not only to preclude future prosecutions of persons exercising rights under Title II but also to require "abatement" of criminal trespass convictions for sit-ins *prior* to the Act. Hamm v. City of Rock Hill, 379 U.S. 306 (1964).

129. Consider this type of case: A father's will has a provision that the son's interest will terminate if he marries outside the Hebrew faith. After the testator's death, the son marries a Catholic, and the sister sues to terminate his interest under the will. Perhaps the court should be viewed as facing an existing discrimination; but it could be argued that the court's granting of relief would create an actual discriminatory situation hitherto existing only potentially. It would also have the effect of enforcing a provision designed to pressure *another* person (the son) to adopt the father's prejudice. See *Pollak, supra* n.127 at 12-13. (Although the two theories might thus lead to a state action conclusion, the actual case, Gordon v. Gordon, 332 Mass. 124 N.E.2d 228 (1955), *cert. denied,* 349 U.S. 947 (1955), enforced the provision of the will, without coming to substantial grips with the *Shelley* principle. See also U.S. Natl. Bank v. Snodgrass, 202 Ore. 530, 275 P.2d 860 (1954)).

would be needed to make the Constitution relevant to any situation involving private discrimination would be the filing of a lawsuit. But at what point short of that extreme should the line be drawn? The Supreme Court has not yet formulated a firm theoretical basis for answering that question.

A word of caution now about the various theories already canvassed. Their judicial application is far from mechanical or readily predictable. Troubling questions of degree and of value always arise, e.g., how much and how important is the government involvement, how should the weight of the impact on the victim's asserted right, and the value of that right, be measured against the importance of preserving certain kinds of freedom to the private actor?

For example, in racial discrimination situations, some *limits* would be recognized on any theory that seemed to absolutely bar a person's preference, in personal relations, for one race over another. Thus, suppose a social fraternity on the campus of a private college plans a party. A member invites a black student though the fraternity rules forbid having blacks in the house. Another member, unable to persuade his fraternity brother to withdraw the invitation, seeks a court order restraining the black student from coming to the party, claiming it would violate fraternity rules and impair the value of his expensive fraternity membership. If the court were to grant relief, its order would *create* a discrimination and hence on the second variant of "judicial enforcement" theory *might* be viewed as unconstitutional. And on the third variant, it *might* be said that the court enforcement of the plaintiff's prejudices and the fraternity's rule compelling *other* persons — like the member issuing the invitation — to do what a state could not do under the Fourteenth Amendment was unconstitutional. (And if this situation occurred in a building owned by a state university and *leased* to the fraternity, it might further be argued that, on a "government instrumentality" theory, the private discrimination was state action).

Yet I think such conclusions strike most of us as highly dubious. People must be free to give rein to *some* preferences in personal relations if only for reasons of "psychic health," as Edmund Cahn put it.[130] A "balancing of interests" approach seems to be a factor in whatever theory may be adopted.

Moreover, it has been urged that a "balancing approach" should be used not merely in the course of applying one of the theories previously discussed but as an overall substitute for those theories.[131]

130. Cahn, Jurisprudence, 30 N.Y.U.L. Rev. 150, 156 (1955).

131. The argument deplores as mythical the idea that state action is a "unitary" concept in whose application the court is always looking for the necessary minimum quantum of active government involvement. It is said that the court's attitude on the

d. *Direct Constitutional Restraint on Private Parties and Effectuating Statutes*

Up to now I have been talking about the possibilities of private conduct running afoul of constitutional restraints purporting to apply to government rather than private conduct: restraints on states under the Fourteenth Amendment and on the federal government under the Bill of Rights. But the government action requirement is not included in every constitutional provision granting rights or protections. Thus it has been held that no such requirement is in the Thirteenth Amendment prohibiting slavery or involuntary servitude. The Amendment had authorized Congress to enforce it, so any enforcing statute could reach private conduct rather than just state and local governments and their officers. In the 1968 case of Jones v. Mayer[132] the Supreme Court declared the Amendment was a valid source of authority for the 1866 civil rights law declaring: "All citizens of the United States shall have the same right in every State and Territory as is enjoyed by white citizens thereof to inherit, purchase, lease, sell, hold and convey real and personal property."

Thus, private discrimination in the sale or rental of housing runs afoul of this statute, which has implied injunctive and damage sanctions.[133] The statute was thought, at the time of the *Shelley* case in 1948, not to apply to private discrimination. If the present interpretation had then been in effect, there would have been no need to wrestle with the "state action" problem under the Fourteenth Amendment.

The civil rights law in question (42 U.S.C. §1982) is not the only one that has been held to be based on the Thirteenth Amendment. An even broader law of thc same period (42 U.S.C. §1981) provides that "all persons" have "the same right . . . to make and enforce contracts, to sue, be parties, give evidence, and to the full and equal benefit of all laws and proceedings for the security of persons and property as is enjoyed by white citizens, and shall be subject to like punishment, pain, penalties, taxes, licenses, and exactions of every kind, and to no other." The Court has held that the statute bars a private school from discriminating racially in its admissions — the school having so-

---

allegedly preliminary issue of state action is in fact influenced by its attitude on the ultimate constitutional issue (whether the state's action or inaction has, in the language of the Constitution, "deprived" one private party of constitutional protection against another private party's impairment of his interests). There should be an "honest and open balancing" instead of the decision being "hidden behind a unitary concept" of state action. See Nowak et al., *supra* n.46 at 473-475. See also *id.* at 475 n.5 for articles espousing "balancing" approaches of a somewhat more limited nature.

132. 392 U.S. 409 (1968).

133. Sullivan v. Little Hunting Park, 396 U.S. 229 (1969).

licited the general public to enter into a contractual relationship and having refused the plaintiffs solely on racial grounds.[134] So too, Section 1981 gives a remedy (an alternative to the remedy under Title VII of the Civil Rights Act of 1964) against racial discrimination in private employment contracts.[135]

Still another post-Civil War civil rights law authorizes damage recovery against injurious *conspiracies* directed at depriving anyone of equal rights under the law (42 U.S.C. §1985(3)). Overruling an earlier view that state action was impliedly a required element, the Supreme Court has construed this law too as authorized by the Thirteenth Amendment's enforcement clause, and as applying where there is a "racial, or perhaps otherwise class-based, invidiously discriminatory animus behind the conspirators' actions."[136]

134. Runyon v. McCrary, 427 U.S. 160 (1976). Doubtless not all private contract discrimination is covered by the statute. Thus it has been suggested that if §1981 had been relied on in the case of the Moose Lodge social club discussed *supra* at n.113 the plaintiff might still have lost: "*Runyon* involved educational facilities which were open to any white who could pay the set fees. The only applicants refused were those who were black. Moose Lodge, on the other hand, was not open to the general public. One could become a member only by invitation and thus some whites as well as all blacks were denied membership. Although plaintiff in *Moose Lodge* did not attempt to rely on Sec. 1981, the key between the cases lies in the public nature of these schools. . . . One would expect that section 1981 would not apply to truly private matters such as marriage contracts. . . . Such contracts are not solicited from the general public. . . ." Nowak et al., *supra* n.46 at 703. See also Developments in the Law — Sec. 1981, 15 Harv. Civ. Rights & Civ. Lib. L. Rev. 29, 114-120 (1980).

135. Johnson v. Railway Express Agency, Inc., 421 U.S. 454 (1975). According to McDonald v. Santa Fe Trail Transp. Co., 427 U.S. 273 (1976), discrimination against whites is also covered. However, an affirmative action plan by employer and union to overcome the effects of past discrimination, though adversely affecting whites, is permitted by Title VII. See United Steelworkers v. Weber, 443 U.S. 193 (1979). See generally on §1981, Developments in the Law, *supra* n.134.

136. Griffin v. Breckenridge, 403 U.S. 88, 102 (1971).

Mention should also be made of the possibility that even legislation passed pursuant to authority of §5 of the *Fourteenth* Amendment could sometimes reach the kind of private conduct that would violate that Amendment if it had been engaged in by state officials. But "there has not yet been a Supreme Court case precisely holding that Congress by statute [pursuant to §5] may reach purely private actions, though some lower courts have so held" (Nowak et al., *supra* n.46 at 696-697). Supreme Court *dicta* in support may be found in the opinions in U.S. v. Guest, 383 U.S. 745 (1966) (See *id.* at 690).

Postscript

As I look back on these pages, I realize that there is much about the legal system that I have ignored or only hinted at. I intend here to partially fill those gaps on three topics.

A. The Future of the Legal Profession

To begin with, I have neglected the legal profession — its composition, its meeting of the public's needs and expectations, and the provocative changes now being wrought in these areas as well as in the bar's structure and operations. It will only be possible to touch upon some highlights below.

1. Composition

The number of lawyers in the country "has more than doubled in the last twenty years until there are now about half a million lawyers. This is one lawyer for each 440 persons in the population, a much higher percentage than in any other country."[1] This number — made up of private practitioners;[2] government lawyers, including prosecutors and

1. Griswold, Introduction: The Legal Profession in the 1980's, in Symposium, 11 U. Toledo L. Rev. 193, 195 (1980).

2. A 1980 estimate for the number of private practitioners is 335,650. Cantor, Managing Legal Organizations in the 1980's, Symposium, *supra* n.1 at 311, 314. It has been predicted that greater increases will occur in the number of lawyers employed in "government agencies, corporate legal departments and public service legal programs." Janofsky, The Future of the Legal Profession and the Role of the American Bar Association, *id.* at 202. Following is a portion of the breakdown made

public defenders; judges; corporate in-house counsel; "public interest" lawyers; and miscellaneous others — "is expected to grow to more than 600,000 by 1985, and a distinguished legal educator has estimated that by the year 2000 there will be one million lawyers."[3]

This burgeoning profession will not have the same demographic characteristics as in the recent past. There will be, and already are, far more women, minorities, and young lawyers than ever before. "[T]he percentage of women law students has risen from 8.5% in 1970 to 30.3% of all law students in 1978. Minority enrollment . . . has tripled in the past seven years as the percentage of minority law students has increased from 3.6% in 1970 to 8.2% of all law students in 1978." Since the recent expansion in number of law school graduates affects the overall age distribution within the profession, it is not surprising to find that "over one-half of the ABA's current membership is under the age of thirty-six. . . ." Somewhat related to composition of the profession, are features that have been much studied in the last two decades: lawyers' differing backgrounds; the social status and leadership roles of lawyers serving different types of clients; the subject and time distribution of lawyers' work; and the relative dominance of client's interests and professional interests.[4]

---

by Cantor (at 313) of the private sector (lawyers in private practice or with industry) using ABA data plus estimates for 1975 and 1980 and showing the percents of *all* lawyers:

		Private Practice				
Year	*Directory Listings*	*Total in Private Practice (and %)*	*Partners (%)*	*Associates (%)*	*Solo Practitioners (%)*	*With Private Industry (%)*
1980	490,000	335,650 (68.5)	32.0	8.5	28	11.5
1975	414,000	290,000 (70.1)	30.0	8.0	32.1	10.6
1970	324,000	236,085 (72.7)	28.5	7.6	36.6	10.3
1960	252,385	192,353 (76.2)	24.1	5.8	46.3	8.9
1954	221,600	189,443 (85.5)	23.3	4.7	57.5	5.5

He estimates (at 312) that of the 20% of all lawyers who are neither in private practice nor with private industry, "about 15% are in government (including the judiciary) and about 5% are inactive or retired." He further states (*id.*) that "an estimated 30,000 to 40,000 may not be included in the Martindale-Hubbel listings from which these data are derived."

3. Janofsky, *supra* n.2 at 209.

4. The quoted matter is from *id.* at 208. Some of the studies referred to are Laumann and Heinz, The Organization of Lawyers' Work: Size, Intensity and Co-Practice of the Fields of Law, 1979 Am. B. Foundation Research J. 217; Heinz and Laumann, The Legal Profession: Client Interests, Professional Roles, and Social Hierarchies, 76 Mich. L. Rev. 1111 (1978); Heinz, Laumann, Cappell, Halliday & Schaalman, Diversity, Representation, and Leadership in an Urban Bar: A First Report on a Survey of the Chicago Bar, 1976 Am. B. Foundation Research J. 717; bibliographies in Heinz & Laumann, *supra*, nn. 1-3, and in Auerbach, Unequal Justice 377 (1976).

2. Meeting Public Needs for Reasonable Access to Legal Services

1. Before turning to future legal needs of the public, we should take note of the public's legal needs in the recent past, as shown in the American Bar Association's 1977 national survey. Based on 1971-1973 experience gleaned through interviews, the following numbers of individuals yearly experienced the following selected types of *non-business* legal problems (i.e., the same number, though not necessarily the same people, experienced *each* of the problems listed after the number): (a) Between nine and nine and one-half million: acquiring real estate; serious property loss caused by another; (b) Between five and one-half and seven million: serious disputes with a government agency; consumer problems (including landlords, retail sellers, or creditors); (c) Between four and one-half and five million: execution of a will; (d) Two million: divorce; (e) Between one and one-third million and two million: employment problems; violation of constitutional rights; serious personal injury caused by another; (f) Between one-half million and one million: death of spouse.

An individual experiencing such problems, however, did not necessarily turn to a lawyer in order to cope with them. The probability of using legal services varied widely with the type of problem, ranging from 79 percent for execution of a will, to 77 percent for a divorce, to about 40 percent for acquiring real property and for serious personal injury caused by another, to 35 percent for death of spouse, to 10 percent for consumer problems, to 10 and 12 percent respectively for a violation of constitutional rights and difficulties with government agencies, to 5 percent for serious property loss caused by another, and to 1 to 8 percent for different kinds of employment problems.[5]

2. It seems plausible that the use of lawyers, and public legal needs even in categories not covered by the ABA survey, will expand in the future. Thus there will be more need for lawyers representing criminal defendants and suspects, in view of the rising crime rate and certain Supreme Court rulings: that an indigent defendant in a felony case has a constitutional right to free counsel; that an indigent even in a misdemeanor case cannot constitutionally suffer the imprisonment penalty if he had not been offered free counsel; and that a suspect's right to counsel accrues as early as he is taken into custody. Extension of the free counsel right into certain types of civil disputes is also on the horizon.[6] More legal services will be needed as certain other new

5. Curran, Survey of the Public's Legal Needs, 64 A.B.A.J. 848, 848-850 (1978). This article is a brief summary of highlights of Curran, The Legal Needs of the Public: Final Report of National Survey (1977).

6. See Note, 66 Geo. L. Rev. 113 (1977); Mermin, The Constitutional Right to Counsel in America, 50 Philippine L.J. 430, 447 et seq. (1975).

rights and liabilities are generated or earlier ones expanded: rights growing out of genetic engineering; "rights growing out of ecology . . . ; consumer's rights; students' rights; welfare and other poverty rights; space rights; communications rights; the right to medical care and the right to receive replacement of human organs; the right to privacy, especially against bugging through the use of electronic devices; and the whole maze of rights growing out of the struggle of the individual against big government, big business, big charities, and big institutions of every kind."[7] This is a partial list, and does not even attempt to portray the extent to which the *business* world is subjected — in spite of the "deregulation" movement — to new and increasingly complex rules that invite the use of lawyers.

Contributing to the expansion is the deepening tendency of Americans to turn to law for the solution of almost any social problem, what Bayless Manning has called "hyperlexis" (described as "America's national disease —the pathological condition caused by an overactive law-making gland").[8]

Counteracting, however, to some uncertain extent, the forces pushing for greater use of lawyers' services are some growing developments in the direction of curtailing certain kinds of legal services. Thus it is predicted, on the basis of a private survey of bar opinion, that there will be less involvement of attorneys in personal injury claims, because of the expected spread of "no-fault insurance"; less practice before a jury, because of the expected elimination of jury trials in some classes of civil cases; less practice before a court, because more disputes will be resolved by arbitration and mediation, and through government administrative procedures; and some areas of practice will be totally surrendered to nonlawyers (i.e., government officials and lay experts) since "uncontested divorces and other aspects of domestic relations problems, such as support, may be handled by direct application to a government official . . . without the assistance or intervention by a private attorney and without the requirement (in many cases) of the proof of fault. Other traditional legal transactions that may be handled by non-attorneys include the routine settlement of small estates, a variety of real estate transactions, simple tax problems and phases of so-called pension planning and estate planning."[9]

7. Fuchs, Lawyers and Law Firms Look Ahead, 57 A.B.A.J. 971, 972 (1971). On genetic engineering, see, for example, Tell, Genetic Engineers Create New Breed of Legal Practice, 4 Natl. L.J. 1 (1981), and citations on legal aspects of DNA and other areas of biotechnology in n.127 below.

8. Manning, Hyperlexis: Our National Disease, 71 Nw. U.L. Rev. 767 (1977). This explanation of the recent increase in American litigation along with others is critically examined in Lieberman, The Litigious Society (1981); Marks, The Suing of America (1981); Andrews, Book Review, 1981 Am. B. Foundation Research J. 851.

9. Fuchs, *supra* n.7 at 972.

3. One reason why the extent of the public's use of lawyers has not in the past kept up with the extent of the public's experience of legal problems has been the perceived high *cost* of legal services. The 1977 ABA survey showed that a substantial majority of interviewees thought that most lawyers charge more than their services are worth. The high cost of legal services, both to business and the individual, has often been remarked and criticized.[10] Is there reason to hope for future improvement (i.e., leaving aside the effect of general inflation in the economy)? Several considerations support an affirmative answer.

(a) One is the effect of more price competition within the profession as a result of Supreme Court decisions. The 1975 *Goldfarb* decision held that a minimum fee schedule of a bar association not run by the state violated the federal antitrust laws.[11] In addition, pro-"group practice" decisions have been handed down such as that in the *United Mineworkers* case, which held that when a union employed an attorney on salary to represent union members who wished to use him for workmen's compensation claims, no unauthorized practice of law by the union had occurred but rather an exercise of the union's First Amendment rights.[12] Finally the 1977 *Bates* case declared that while the Arizona Supreme Court's disciplinary rule prohibiting commercial advertising by the bar did not violate federal antitrust law (since the rule came within an exemption for acts of state government), it did violate the attorneys' First Amendment rights to advertise their prices for certain routine legal services.[13]

Competition is also increasing from *outside* the profession, as mentioned earlier: "Lay businesses and professions are now serious contenders for much legal work, primarily of a standardized, repeat character, and include bank trust departments, accountants, title insurers, real estate brokers, collection agencies, and architects, among

10. See, e.g., Green, The Gross Legal Product: "How Much Justice Can You Afford?" in Nader & Green, eds., Verdicts on Lawyers 63-79 (1976); Burger, Annual Report on the State of the Judiciary — 1980, 66 A.B.A.J. 295, 296 (1980); Address by President Carter, 64 A.B.A.J. 840 (1978); Carter Lashes Out at Nation's Lawyers, Asks Them To Decelerate Increase in Fees, Wall St. J., May 5, 1978, at 20, col. 2; Rosenberg, Contemporary Litigation in the United States, in Jones, ed., Legal Institutions Today: English and American Approaches Compared 168-171 (1977). In addition to the ABA's client attitude survey described above, a 1978 National Center for State Courts survey shows that "44% of the American public think high legal fees are a serious problem." Janofsky, *supra* n.2 at 206 n.19. That soaring legal fees are stimulating more corporations into the establishment of their own "house counsel" to replace outside attorneys, see Natl. L.J., March 30, 1981, at 1.

11. Goldfarb v. Virginia State Bar, 421 U.S. 773 (1975).

12. United Mine Workers v. Illinois State Bar Assoc., 389 U.S. 217 (1967). For other cases see n.22 below.

13. 433 U.S. 350 (1977). The Court recognized that this advertising could validly be subjected to regulation against false, deceptive, or misleading advertising and to reasonable time, place, and manner restrictions.

others. This competition undoubtedly will persist and new lay competitors will emerge."[14] In addition there is the movement for do-it-yourself legal work: the familiar books and self-help packets available for handling more routine tasks, e.g., simple divorce and probate matters.[15] Moreover, the movement for laymen's mediation or conciliation[16] is growing, receiving a considerable boost by the 1980 federal Disputes Resolution Act authorizing the Department of Justice to award $10 million per year for 1981-1984, to state and local governments and nonprofit organizations for dispute resolution programs for minor disputes, "such as that between neighbors, a consumer and seller, and a landlord and tenant."[17] How much of this will survive the Reagan Administration's budget cutting is not yet clear.

14. Johnstone, The Future of Private Law Practice, Yale L. Rep. (alumni magazine), Winter 1977-1978 at 9.

15. See Time, Dec. 8, 1980 at 112.

16. A wider perspective is furnished by the following: "The movement toward greater use of mediation and conciliation in community 'dispute resolution centers' and 'neighborhood justice centers' and the expanded use of these processes to deal with expanded categories of disputes must be seen in the context of a much larger picture. This picture includes the extended use of arbitration and ombudsmen; the diversion of a variety of juvenile and nominally criminal cases to a variety of community agencies; the growth and expansion of small claims courts; the emergence of medical malpractice tribunals designed to divert certain suits from the formal court system; the development of specialized courts with full jurisdiction over all civil and criminal disputes related to a particular subject matter, such as housing; the emergence of consumer complaint and consumer protection agencies; and the assumption by newspapers and magazines of the task of printing and investigating complaints about government agencies, companies and other institutions.

"Certain of these changes have taken place not only in urban and rural society at large but also within so-called 'total institutions' such as schools, prisons, and housing units where bargaining, negotiation, democratic assembly, ombudsmen, mediation and arbitration have been introduced to divert some disputes from the formal civil and criminal courts and to deal with other conflicts that were previously ignored or dealt with by administrative fiat." Smith, A Warmer Way of Disputing: Mediation and Conciliation, 26 Am. J. Comp. L. (Supp.) 205, 206 (1978). See also Rice, Mediation and Arbitration As A Civil Alternative to the Criminal Justice System — An Overview and Legal Analysis, 29 Am. U.L. Rev. 17 (1980). In a broader perspective — one of analyzing the modes of enhancing access to the law's benefits — Galanter looks at three variables in addition to legal services (institutions, rules, and parties) and recognizes that one of the many possibilities of institutional change is to "provide institutions that are mediative and conciliatory." Other modes of enhancing access are: modification of rule systems (e.g., no-fault schemes; simplified transactions); enhancing capabilities of parties (e.g., through enhanced knowledge and organizational strength); and upgrading of legal services. See Galanter, Delivering Legality: Some Proposals For the Direction of Research, 11 Law & Society Rev. 225 (1976); The Duty *Not* to Deliver Legal Services, 30 U. Miami L. Rev. 929 (1976).

17. The Act, 94 Stat. 17(1980), specifically declared (§2) that the use of "neighborhood, local or community resources, including volunteers (and particularly senior citizens) and available building space such as space in public facilities, can provide for accessible, cost-effective resolution of minor disputes." One of the Department of Justice's major earlier efforts had been to fund, in the late 1970s, three pilot Neighborhood Justice Center projects — in Atlanta (sponsored by a private non-

(b) A downward pressure on costs, with consequent potential for lower fees, may emerge from the still struggling movement to shorten litigation time, notably through the simplification of "discovery" procedures,[18] reducing the use of the civil jury,[19] and other procedural

---

profit organization), Kansas City, Missouri (sponsored by the city), and Los Angeles (sponsored by the county bar association). Slayton, Neighborhood Justice Centers — An Alternative, 6 Litigation, no. 2, at 28-29 (1980). The Slayton article gives details of the Atlanta experience. Further on lay processing of disputes, see Ebel, Bar Programs — Other Ways to Resolve Disputes, *id.* at 25; Salas & Schneider, Evaluating the Dade County Citizen Dispute Settlement Program, 63 Jud. 174 (1979); Smith, *supra* n.16; Law Enforcement Assistance Administration, A Preliminary Analysis of Alternate Strategies For Processing Civil Disputes (1978); *Id.*, Citizen Dispute Settlement (1975); Danzig & Lowy, Everyday Disputes and Mediation in the United States: A Reply to Professor Felstiner, 9 Law & Socy. Rev. 675 (1975); Felstiner, Avoidance As Dispute Processing: An Elaboration, *id.* at 695; Sander, Varieties of Dispute Processing (in Pound Conference proceedings), 70 F.R.D. 79 (1975).

18. See Griswold, *supra* n.1 at 198-199; Meserve, Lynch & Daniel, The Devitt Report In Context: Public Responsibility of Lawyers In the 1980's, 11 U. Toledo L. Rev. 216, 232-234, 235-236 (1980). The Griswold article observes that while pre-trial discovery (see my description in Chap. 2 *supra* between nn. 186 & 187) was once hailed as a means of eliminating the element of "surprise" at trial, getting all the relevant facts out into the open, and facilitating settlement of cases, it is being used to excess, often "as a means of wearing down the opposition simply because of the legal costs of responding, and the delay in bringing the case to actual trial. . . . [S]ome way should be found to induce the trial courts to keep close control of the discovery process and to impose strict time limits in all cases. . . . [I]t would have a considerable impact on the cost of legal services in many types of cases" (at 199). The other article cited in this note shows that the ABA committee's recommendations (to limit discovery to the "issues" rather than the "subject matter" of the action; to limit to 30 the number of interrogatories that may be served on a party without leave of court; and to provide a discovery conference at the request of any party) resulted in a committee of the Judicial Conference of the United States supporting only the third recommendation (and for "unusual cases"), in submitting proposed amendments to the Federal Rules of Civil Procedure.

19. Meserve et al., *supra* n.18 at 230-232. The Constitution offers a partial barrier, since the Seventh Amendment guarantees a jury trial in civil "suits at common law" when over $20 is involved. It covers rights of action created by a law authorizing enforcement in a damage action in the ordinary courts of law. Curtis v. Loether, 415 U.S. 189 (1974). However, the Amendment does not apply to suits in "equity" (e.g., injunction suits; bankruptcy proceedings) or "admiralty" (maritime cases). Nor does it apply to administrative proceedings even when the agency is imposing (civil) monetary penalties. Atlas Roofing Co. v. OSHA, 430 U.S. 442 (1977). The Amendment is construed to allow — what many local district court rules have done — reducing the number of jurors from 12 to 6. Colegrove v. Battin, 413 U.S. 149 (1973). And there is currently being debated the question whether the Amendment was intended to apply to certain highly technical or complex cases. See authorities cited *supra* at 214 n.173. Partly because of such complexity, Chief Justice Burger has called for the exploration of alternatives to jury trial. 48 U.S.L.W. 2118 (1979).

The state courts are free of Seventh Amendment restrictions; the Amendment was not incorporated into the Fourteenth Amendment due process clause so as to apply to the states. Hardware Dealers Mutual Fire Ins. Co. v. Glidden Co., 284 U.S. 151 (1931); Melancon v. McKeithen, 345 F. Supp. 1025 (E.D. La. 1972), *aff'd sub nom.* Mayes v. Ellis, 409 U.S. 943 (1972). (On "incorporation," see *supra* at 338-339 nn. 84-90.) However, there is usually a state constitutional provision, too, for jury trial.

shortcuts.[20] So too, in the larger private law offices cost savings may well result from efficiency improvements that are brewing in office structure and management, to be described later.

(c) There are other ways in which reasonable access to legal services will be furthered. The bar has long sponsored "referral"[21] plans under which the bar association maintains a list of lawyers willing to be consulted for a specified low fee by a person searching for a lawyer. But a development with more significance for the future is the spread of some newer forms of delivery, and new financing for delivery, of service. First is the growth in "group legal services" plans, previously mentioned, which are offered, e.g., by a labor union or fraternal society, for at least some kinds of legal claims at no extra cost to members, or at reduced fees — and involving usually a limited choice of one's lawyer ("closed panel plan"), but sometimes an unlimited one ("open panel"). Those involving monthly or other periodic payments, like insurance premiums, are called "prepaid" plans. Offerings of prepaid plans to the general public (as in the case of Blue Cross or private health insurance policies) rather than a particular group are not common. "Prepaid legal service plans and group legal service plans may well be the wave of the future."[22]

A second innovative form of service is the neighborhood or "storefront" type of "legal clinic" that tends to advertise heavily and handles fairly standardized legal problems at high volume and low cost. Clinics spread rapidly after the *Bates* decision on lawyer advertising, and their number must now approach about 1,000.[23]

20. The ABA has recently established an Action Commission to Reduce Court Cost and Delay (composed of lawyers, judges, law professors, and consumer representatives) to act chiefly "as a catalyst for implementing and encouraging experiments which reduce litigation cost and delay." Janofsky, *supra* n.2 at 206. An example of the type of program that will be encouraged by the Commission is the California three-year project begun in 1978 for four courts, covering cases not involving more than $25,000. The experiment provided for "1. narrative pleading and limited motions; 2. elimination of most traditional discovery other than party depositions; 3. substitution of compelled disclosure of certain types of information for discovery; and 4. relaxed rules of evidence in non-jury trials." *Id.* at 207.

21. See Carlin, The Advancing State of the Art of Lawyer Referral Service, 30 Baylor L. Rev. 643 (1978).

22. Janofsky, *supra* n.2 at 209-210. The author was ABA president during 1979-1980. He observes that recent membership in prepaid plans was from 3 to 5 million families; and that the ABA has been promoting this form of legal services delivery. Earlier it had opposed the plans, particularly the closed-panel type. See generally, Schwartz & Murphy, Prepaid Group Legal Services Plans: What They Are and How They Work (1979); Pfennigstorf & Kimball, eds., Legal Services Plans: Approaches to Regulation (1977). For Supreme Court upholding of group legal service plans, see the *UMW* case, *supra* n.12, as well as United Transp. Union v. State Bar, 401 U.S. 576 (1971); Brotherhood, Ry. Trainmen v. Virginia, 377 U.S. 1 (1964); NAACP v. Button, 371 U.S. 415 (1963).

23. "Not only have the *number* of clinics increased but the 'franchising' of legal clinics has become a 'booming business.' Jacoby and Meyers, a California-based legal

Those who are too poor to pay legal fees at all — the clients of "legal aid" societies traditionally funded in a limited way by local charities, bar groups, or municipalities — have in the last several years been getting much more access to legal services in civil cases as a result of a massive infusion of federal funds. The War on Poverty program of the 1960s had established the Office of Economic Opportunity, which included a Neighborhood Legal Services Program. The latter was replaced in 1974 by the Legal Services Corporation, a federal government corporation whose bi-partisan board of directors, serving for three-year terms, are presidential appointees. By the end of the 1970s, Congress was approving "an annual appropriation of $300 million for the Corporation, over three times the annual level than when the Corporation was first established," and there were "over 5,000 lawyers and 1,300 paralegals providing services in 335 programs throughout the country."[24] The program has had ABA endorsement but is vulnerable to

---

'retailer' has twenty-four offices in California and twelve in the New York area," reportedly serving "30,000 clients in its seventeen California clinics in 1978 and 3,500 clients in the first quarter of operation of its New York offices." Janofsky, *supra* n.2, at 213-214. The article cites Bodine, Proliferation of Legal Clinics Continues: 550 More Were Born in Last 10 Months, Natl. L.J., Dec. 31, 1979, at 5, col. 1, and Storefront Lawyers Reaping Benefits of Advertising, Chicago Tribune, May 15, 1979, at 11. The ABA had itself sponsored in 1976, together with the Philadelphia Bar Association, a storefront clinic experiment that lasted 13 months and is analyzed in Menkel-Meadow, The 58th Street Legal Clinic: Evaluation of the Experiment (1979). See also Muris & McChesney, Advertising and the Price and Quality of Legal Services: The Case For Legal Clinics, 1979 Am. B. Foundation Research J. 179.

24. Bellow, Legal Aid in the United States, 14 Clearinghouse Rev. 337, 340 (1980). The recent goal of the Corporation has been "minimum access," defined as two lawyers per 10,000 poor people (compared to ten lawyers per 10,000 people above the poverty line). *Id.* at 340. Erwin Griswold, former Dean of the Harvard Law School and former Solicitor General, has called the Legal Services Corporation "the most important development on the sociological side of the law in our time." Griswold, *supra* n.1 at 197. The main statutory provisions are in 42 U.S.C.A. §2996, 2996a-k (1980 pocket part). For discussions of the Corporation, see Bellow, *supra* at 339-345; Handler, Hollingsworth & Erlanger, Lawyers and the Pursuit of Legal Rights (1978); George, Development of the Legal Services Corporation, 61 Cornell L. Rev. 681 (1976). For studies of the OEO legal services program, see the bibliographical note in Handler, Ginsberg & Snow, The Public Interest Law Industry, in Weisbrod, Handler & Komesar, Public Interest Law — An Economic and Institutional Analysis 45-46, n.11 (1978). Some of the programs funded are of the "Judicare" type, under which the services are furnished by a client-chosen private attorney rather than by office staff attorneys. Typical of opposition to this is: "The private bar is not equipped to furnish volume service, lacks the skills necessary to perform the broad range of poverty law services, and is insufficiently involved in the problems of the poor to perform zealously or to perceive the need for difficult law reform litigation. Administratively, it is almost impossible to relate cost to effectiveness or insure a general uniformity of quality." Klaus, Civil Legal Services For the Poor, in Schwartz, ed., Law and the American Future 136 (1976). There has been much controversy during both the OEO period and the LSC period over the relative economy and other merits of the two systems. For an example of the controversy, see Johnson, Further Variations and the Prospect of Some Future Themes (in Cappelletti, Gordley & Johnson, eds., Toward Equal Justice: A Comparative Study of Legal Aid in Modern

the budget-cutting propensities of the Republican administration that took office in January 1981.[25] As for legal services to indigent defendants in *criminal* cases, they will, as already noted, continue to be furnished by the governmental unit involved, as a matter of constitutional right, except for those misdemeanants who are not punished by imprisonment. Statutes and court rules may go still further than the Constitution.[26] Also, a recent ABA-endorsed proposal is for national involvement in financing of criminal defense services for indigents, analogous to involvement of the National Legal Services Corporation for civil legal services — but federal funds (through a Center for Defense Services) would augment rather than supplant the state and local defense programs.[27]

A form of free legal service of a more generalized nature is that furnished by non-government organizations sponsoring litigation, usually of the law-reform variety.[28] The NAACP began its test-case or law reform litigation early in this century. The American Civil Liberties Union began developing its litigation strategy about a generation later. Ralph Nader in the 1960s began creating a number of public interest organizations for law reform, some of them engaging in litigation. The full fledged "public interest law firms" (some concentrating on a single issue, like environmental protection, most of them not) began being significant in the late 1960s and early 1970s, when foundations, notably Ford, began funding them concurrent with ABA approval. And while many private law firms had always donated services for *pro bono publico* work (unpaid public service),[29] the 1970s saw, in the case of

---

Societies (1975), criticized in Brakel, Styles of Delivery of Legal Services to the Poor: A Review Article, 1977 Am. B. Foundation J. 219.

25. For discussions of the financing problem, for both civil and criminal legal service programs for the indigent, see 37 NLADA Briefcase, 13 et seq. (1980). The Reagan administration seems to prefer the "Judicare" approach (see *supra* n.24) and the phasing out of federal financing in favor of state, local, charitable, or bar financing.

26. They do, for instance, in the federal courts, under the Federal Criminal Justice Act of 1964 as amended, 18 U.S.C. §3006A, and Criminal Rule 44(a). The controversy referred to in n.24 concerning use of private attorneys versus use of staff attorneys is paralleled in the criminal law field by the controversy over use of "public defender" office attorneys versus use of court-appointed private attorneys.

27. See Lefstein & Portman, Implementing the Right to Counsel in State Criminal Cases, 66 A.B.A.J. 1084 (1980).

28. See generally, Weisbrod, Handler & Komesar, *supra* n.24; Council for Public Interest Law, Balancing the Scales of Justice: Financing Public Interest Law in America (1976). For early symposia on public interest law practice, see 79 Yale L.J. 1005 (1970); 13 Ariz. L. Rev. 797 (1971).

29. In 1980 *mandatory* "pro bono" was being proposed to the ABA and meeting substantial opposition. Under the proposal an attorney would be bound to perform "unpaid public interest legal service" and to make an annual report of it to "appropriate regulatory authority." Acceptable service would include "activities for improving the law, the legal system, or the legal profession, or by providing professional services to persons of limited means or to public service groups or or-

some firms, a leap in the extent of this admixture of public activity with the normal business of the private law firm; they became part of the "public interest law industry."[30]

It is not at all clear whether the level of public interest law financing can be maintained in the years to come, especially since foundations have been substantially reducing their support. But continued financial help can be expected from Congress's authorization, in a number of statutes under which public interest lawyers might sue, for judicial award of reasonable attorney's fees to the successful plaintiff.[31] A more general statute, not superseding the special statutory

---

ganizations." See 66 A.B.A.J. 279, 280 (1980). For further discussion, and more general treatment of the private bar's involvement in both civil and criminal services for the poor, see 37 NLADA Briefcase, Nos. 3 & 4 (1980); Tucker, *Pro Bono* ABA, in Nader & Green, Verdicts on Lawyers 20-32 (1976); and discussion below at nn. 75-76.

30. "The core of the PIL [Public Interest Law] industry consists of some 86 voluntary sector PIL firms. These are nonprofit organizations engaged chiefly in PIL activities. Also included in the industry are 66 mixed private and public interest law firms that are for-profit organizations in the private sector engaged to varying but significant degrees in activities of the PIL type." Handler, Ginsberg & Snow, *supra* n.24 at 76. The authors go on to note: "Fourteen of the 24 Legal Services Backup Centers [part of the Legal Services Corporation] funded by the federal government, are engaged substantially in PIL-like activities. . . . A much smaller contribution . . . is made by the traditional private sector law firms and attorneys in solo practice through *pro bono* work involving law reform or impact litigation." The PIL industry as a whole "offers positions for nearly 1,000 lawyers and over 500 non-lawyer professionals. The total income of the industry exceeds $45 million, and the estimated total income devoted to financing PIL and PIL-like activities exceeds $29 million." *Id.*

31. The successful litigant in American courts is (in the absence of certain special circumstances recognized at common law) not entitled to recover his attorney's fees from the losing party—unless a *statute* allows such recovery. See Alyeska Pipeline Serv. Co. v. Wilderness Socy., 421 U.S. 240 (1975). There are about 75 federal statutes making this allowance (Note, 80 Colum. L. Rev. 346, 348 & n.20 (1980)), including the Securities Act of 1933, 15 U.S.C. §77k(e); the Consumer Product Safety Act, 15 U.S.C. §§2059(e)(4), 2072-73; Truth in Lending Act, 15 U.S.C. §1640(a); Privacy Act of 1974, 5 U.S.C. §552a(g)(2)(B); Federal Water Pollution Control Act, 33 U.S.C. §1365(d); Clean Air Act, 42 U.S.C. §1857h-2(d); and the Civil Rights Attorney's Fees Awards Act of 1976, 42 U.S.C. §1988.

The latter Act (which is analyzed in Note, 80 Colum. L. Rev. 346 (1980)) explicitly covered, in addition to United States civil enforcement suits under the Internal Revenue Code, the following civil rights statutes: 42 U.S.C. §§1981, 1982 (recognizing equal rights for all persons); §1983 (liability for depriving a citizen of his federal constitutional or statutory rights under color of state law); §§1985, 1986 (liability of conspirators who prevent citizens from securing the privileges of citizenship, and liability of officers who do not enforce the liability); Title VI of the Civil Rights Act of 1964, 42 U.S.C. §200d et seq. (barring discrimination based on race, color, or national origin in programs receiving federal aid); and Title XI of 86 Stat. 235 (1972), 20 U.S.C. §1681-86 (barring discrimination based on sex or blindness in educational programs receiving federal aid). In enforcement suits under the named statutes, "the court in its discretion may allow the prevailing party, other than the United States, a reasonable attorney's fee as part of the costs." The Act does not purport to cover the civil rights statutes already containing an attorney's fee provision. Thus, Title II of the Civil Rights Act of 1964 (barring discrimination in places of public accommodation) has such a provision, 42 U.S.C. §2000a-3(b).

provisions, which was effective in October 1981 with some provisions terminating in 1984, generally authorizes (with certain detailed refinements) the recovery of costs including attorney fees and expenses (1) by the prevailing party in any federal civil action brought by or against the United States or any federal agency or official acting in an official capacity, and (2) by the prevailing party other than the United States in certain administrative proceedings.[32]

3. Changes in Private Law Firm Structure and Operation

Many who have looked into the crystal ball predict a continuing trend toward larger law firms, sometimes through mergers with other firms.

Title VII (barring discrimination in employment) also has its own provision, 42 U.S.C. §2000e-5(k). See also Note, 66 Iowa L. Rev. 1301 (1981).

The Supreme Court has thus described various other statutes providing for attorney fee awards: "Some of these statutes make fee awards mandatory for prevailing plaintiffs; others make awards permissive but limit them to certain parties, usually prevailing plaintiffs. But many of the statutes [authorize] the award . . . to [prevailing] plaintiffs or defendants, and entrusting the effectuation of the statutory policy to the discretion of the district courts." Christianburg Garment Co. v. EEOC, 434 U.S. 412, 415-416 (1978). The Court here approved the idea that a successful Title VII *defendant* should be permitted an award "not routinely, not simply because he succeeds, but only where the action brought is found to be unreasonable, frivolous, meritless or vexatious" (at 421).

32. This is the "Equal Access to Justice Act," which is Title II of Pub. L. No. 96-481, 96th Cong., 2d Sess., 94 Stat. 2325-2330 (1980); 5 U.S.C. §§504, 551, 554; 26 U.S.C. §501; 28 U.S.C. §§604, 1920, 2412, 2414, 2517; 26 U.S.C. §1. For Committee reports, see 5 U.S. Code Cong. & Ad. News 4984-5003, 5009-5017. The administrative agency awards apply to adversary administrative adjudications, other than rate fixing or license cases. Some provisions apply to both administrative awards and court awards: (1) One of these is an "unless" clause. It applies adversely to agency awards when "the adjudicative officer of the agency finds that the position of the agency as a party to the proceeding was substantially justified or that special circumstances make an award unjust." A similar clause applies adversely to one of the provisions as to court awards (the provision that in a non-tort action, with the prevailing party not the United States, fees and expenses "shall" be awarded in addition to the other costs that "may" be awarded). (2) "Fees and other expenses" includes reasonable fees of expert witnesses; reasonable costs of studies, analyses, engineering reports, etc. that are "necessary" to the party's case; and reasonable attorney's fees (or agent fees where non-attorneys are used in the administrative adjudication). (3) The award provisions do not apply to individuals with specified wealth or numbers of employees. (4) Account may be taken, in the award decision, of the conduct of the would-be recipient that "unduly and unreasonably protracted the final resolution of the matter in controversy." (5) Annual reports to Congress (in the agency award situation, by the Administrative Conference of the United States after consultation with the Chief Counsel for Advocacy of the Small Business Administration; and in the court situation, by the Director of the Administrative Office of United States Courts) are to be made on the number, nature, and amount of awards during the year. (6) A 1984 repeal date is scheduled for administrative agency awards, and also for the particular provision that court awards of attorney fees and expenses shall be made (subject to the "unless" clause) to prevailing parties other than the United States in non-tort actions.

Expansions will occur not only in the firms' main offices but also by establishment of branch offices in suburbs and other cities such as Washington and New York, as has happened with the large accounting firms. A 1980 survey showed that 45 out of the 50 largest American law firms have Washington offices.[33] Another kind of chain phenomenon expected to grow is the use by a large firm of a network of independent lawyers regionally or nationally who have contracted to work for it part-time.[34] Still another predicted configuration is the "clinic" of legal and business specialists performing "a full range of professional business services for the client, running the gamut from business and financial planning to real estate, accounting and legal advice" — an alternative being to "place the clinic business specialist under the law firm's roof."[35]

Accompanying predictions are of the continuing efforts toward scientific "management" of law offices — both because growth requires more management, and because increased competition from the expanding number of lawyers in relation to population requires more efforts at efficiency.[36] One existing technique whose use will doubtless expand is the training of secretaries, or lay specialists ("paraprofessionals" or "paralegals"), "to take over and master lower-level legal tasks, such as preparing corporate minutes, probate accounts, deposition notices, interrogatories, simple pleadings and a host of other tasks. . . ."[37] More significant is the trend toward increasing productivity through automation of office processes, including use of improved computers, automatic typewriters, and dictation equipment. "The trend toward the use of technology . . . will continue into the 1980's."[38]

Specialization is another trend expected to intensify, in spite of some bar opposition being voiced at the outset of the 1980s.[39] "The

33. Wall St. J., Aug. 14, 1980, at 1. The survey was by the National Law Journal. For data showing enormous growth in the size of firms from 1963 to 1977, see Cantor, Law Firms Are Getting Bigger . . . And More Complex, 64 A.B.A.J. 215 (1978). See also Schwartz, The Reorganization of the Legal Profession, 58 Tex. L. Rev. 1269, 1274-1276 (1980).

34. Among other predictions of growth along all the lines above suggested are Bower, Law Firm Economics in the 1980's: Bigger and Better, 11 U. Toledo L. Rev. 302-304 (1980); Johnstone, *supra* n.14 at 10; Fuchs, *supra* n.7 at 973-974.

35. Fuchs, *supra* n.7 at 975.

36. Cantor, Managing Legal Organizations In The 1980's, 11 U. Toledo L. Rev. 311 (1980).

37. Fuchs, *supra* n.7 at 973.

38. Bower, *supra* n.4 at 307. "Areas which law offices have automated include bookkeeping, accounting and financial management functions, copying and duplicating, word processing, litigation support/evidence management, closed file storage and retrieval, legal research, timekeeping/billing, docket control, indexing and conflict of interest controls." *Id.* For expected technological improvements in the 1980s, see *id.* at 308-309. See also, Wall St. J., Dec. 23, 1980, at 32.

39. See Slonim, Specialization Plans Get A Divided Response, 66 A.B.A.J. 270 (1980). For further works on specialization, see Selected Checklist of Materials on

breadth and scope of the law is simply too great to enable one attorney to produce cost-effective, comprehensive legal services on behalf of a wide range of clients. The day of the legal generalist is practically over, except possibly in small rural communities."[40] "Behind the move to specialization is not only efficiency in the face of the growing complexity of the law, but also the threat of malpractice. The standard of care the courts are applying to lawyers in large firms today is such that the attorneys must be specialists for their own protection."[41] The ABA in 1979 proposed a "Model Plan of Specialization" for possible future adoption by the states.[42] Because of the danger of entrenching a kind of monopolistic power through certification, the proposed supervisory Board of Legal Specialization, to be appointed by the state's highest court, is to be composed of lawyers in general practice as well as those who specialize; an Advisory Commission, also appointed by the court, is to be composed of non-lawyers; and the fact that one has not been recognized as a specialist in a particular field does not prevent one's practicing in that field (regardless of whether one is a specialist in another field or in no field at all). Standards for determining qualifications for recognition as a specialist are also provided.[43] The Model Plan is expected to influence the specialization plans of some states, including those already operating plans containing less regulative

---

Specialization, 34 Record 441 (1979); Fromson & Miller, Specialty Certification, Designation, or Identification for the Practising Lawyer, 50 St. Johns L. Rev. 550 (1976); Petrey, Professional Competence and Legal Specialization, *id.* at 561; Zehnle, Specialization In the Legal Profession (1975); Hochberg, The Drive to Specialization, in Nader & Green, *supra* n.29 at 118-126; Mindes, Lawyer Specialty Certification: The Monopoly Game, 61 A.B.A.J. 42 (1975).

40. Bower, supra n.34 at 309.

41. Hector, Tomorrow's Lawyer, Yale L. Rep. (alumni magazine), Spring 1979 at 12.

42. It is reprinted as an Appendix to Mindes, Proliferation, Specialization and Certification: The Splitting of the Bar, 11 U. Toledo L. Rev. 273, 296-301 (1980).

43. The applicant must show, for the preceding three years, (1) "substantial involvement" in the specialty—which, if measured on a time spent basis, means at least 25% of the total practice of a lawyer engaged in normal full-time practice; (2) compliance with the continuing legal education requirements for the specialty (a minimum of ten credit hours per year in the specialty). (3) He/she must have satisfactory references as to his/her competence in the specialty from five lawyers or judges. The recognition as a specialist is for five years (during which he/she continues to be subject to investigation of specialist competence) and the recognition period is renewable on the basis of standards like those applicable to initial recognition. Specialty committees appointed by the Board for each specialty help the Board carry on its work, and may recommend more stringent standards, including but not limited to oral or written examinations. Waiver of an examination requirement may be permitted if additional and substantially more stringent standards are applied. There is provision for revocation or suspension of specialist recognition, after hearing. The Board's denials, suspensions, or revocations of recognition are appealable to the state's highest court.

elements. However, while specialization *in fact* is expected to intensify, there is still much opposition to the spread of certification plans.[44]

Finally, one predictor of lawyer operations adds the following: "Most states permit the incorporation of professional associations, and incorporation makes available most of the tax benefits of qualified profit-sharing and pension plans for business corporations. With attractive retirement benefits now possible, with the development of the large law firm, with the pressure of the younger generation for change, there will be a growing tendency for older lawyers to retire from the law practice and not, as heretofore, to 'die with their boots on.' "[45]

4. Meeting Public Expectations of Competency, Openness, and Ethical Responsibility

1. How can we expect lawyers to fare in the public's overall evaluation of them in the 1980s? To what extent is the profession lifting itself from those depths assigned to them in classic obloquy by the New Testament[46] — as well as by such litterateurs as Shakespeare,[47] Wordsworth,[48] or Carl Sandburg?[49]

If we look first at ratings by non-business *clients,* based on various characteristics like honesty in dealing with the client, promptness, interest and concern about client's problems, and fees, then the previously described ABA survey published in the latter 1970s (dealing with the public's legal needs) showed rather satisfying results, on the whole.[50] As for responses from business clients, a recent Wall Street

44. About ten states have a certification system; only three or four require an examination; and no state has adopted a certification plan in the last three or four years.

45. Fuchs, *supra* n.7 at 975. See also Natl. L.J., Nov. 16, 1981 at 1; Nester, Retirement Planning For the Lawyer: The Pros and Cons of Lawyer Incorporation, 53 Ohio St. B. Assoc. Rep. 939 (1980). For some other predictions of things to come, see the listing at 1090 of Rossiter, Looking Ahead: The Association in 2078, 64 A.B.A.J. 1084 (1978), a half-humorous, highly imaginative piece.

46. "Woe unto you also, ye lawyers, for ye lade men with burdens grievous to be borne, and ye yourselves touch not the burdens with one of your fingers." Luke 11:46.

47. "The first thing we do, let's kill all the lawyers." II Henry VI, act IV, sc. 2, 1.84 (Dick Butcher).

48. "A lawyer art thou? — draw not nigh! Go carry to some fitter place, the keenness of that practiced eye, the hardness of that sallow face." A Poet's Epitaph, in Wordsworth, Complete Poetical Works, vol. 2, at 172-174 (1911).

49. "Why is there always a secret singing/When a lawyer cashes in?/Why does a hearse horse snicker,/Hauling a lawyer away?" The Lawyers Know Too Much, in The Complete Poems of Carl Sandburg 189 (rev. ed. 1970).

50. On a scale from 1 to 4 (with 4 meaning excellent and 1 meaning poor) the ratings averaged in the "good" category — i.e., ranging from 3.16 for "keeping client informed of progress" to 3.48 for "honesty in dealing with client." The *order* of the average ratings for the various characteristics was generally repeated for different

Journal–Gallup survey of chief executives of large, medium, and small companies showed the executives' general satisfaction with their lawyers' services.[51] If we turn from these client categories to the amorphous "public," the story is rather different. A 1978 Harris poll, rating public confidence in 16 institutions, found law firms near the bottom along with Congress, advertising agencies, and labor unions.[52]

2. The profession itself has shown substantial concern about the level of *competence* of its members, particularly in the area of courtroom skills,[53] but also in drafting, investigation, counselling, and negotiation. The ABA has embarked on a program to remedy these deficiencies through "continuing legal education" offerings to practicing lawyers.[54] The 1979 Final Report of a committee (the "Devitt Committee") of the Judicial Conference of the United States,[55] approved by the Conference, calls for a pilot program in "a number of cooperating" district courts that would, among other things, raise the requirements

---

kinds of legal problems; but "the over-all positive or negative orientation of those ratings differs substantially by problem type," e.g., the ratings in the estate planning field are higher than in the consumer problem field. The average rating for all seven lawyer characteristics varied from 3.61 for estate planning to 2.98 for personal and property injury torts. Curran, *supra* n.5 at 851-852. There was a relation between outcomes and attitudes toward lawyers. Thus, "the highest average ratings were given to lawyers who handled the three problems in which 90% or more of clients reported optimal results: estate planning, estate settlements, and real property matters. In contrast, the lowest average ratings were given for tort matters, in which only 25% of the clients reported optimal results." *Id.* at 852.

51. Wall St. J., Dec. 2, 1980, at 37, col. 4. The figures for the larger firms (not much different from those for the other firms) showed the following rating of legal and other professional services:

	Very Good	*Fairly Good*	*Poor*	*No Opinion*
Accountants	45%	47%	6%	2%
Lawyers	39	43	14	4
Investment bankers	28	48	15	9
Public relations specialists	15	45	27	13
Business journalists	13	46	29	12
Executive recruiters	11	42	27	20

52. Time, April 10, 1978, at 56.

53. See Burger, The Special Skills of Advocacy, 42 Fordham L. Rev. 227 (1973); Partridge & Bermant, The Quality of Advocacy in the Federal Courts, A Report to the Committee of the Judicial Conference of the United States to Consider Standards for Admission to Practice in the United States (1978). The latter study showed that of the approximately 2,000 lawyer courtroom performances evaluated, 8.6% were rated as either "very poor," "poor," or "not quite adequate," and 16.7% were "adequate but no better"—by the 284 federal judges responding to the survey. Another survey showed judges rating 13% of lawyer performances as 'incompetent," either partially or predominantly. The remaining 87% were either "competent," "highly competent," or "exceptionally competent." Maddi, Trial Advocacy Competence: The Judicial Perspective, 1978 Am. B. Foundation Research J. 119.

54. Janofsky, *supra* n.2 at 202-204.

55. Final Report of Committee to Consider Standards For Admission to Practice in the Federal Courts, To the Judicial Conference of the United States (1979).

for admission to practice in the federal courts (including an examination and four trial experiences in actual or simulated trials); establish a performance review committee for instances of inadequate trial performance; and have more trial advocacy education programs, both for law students and for attorneys.[56] Efforts are also being made within the profession to strengthen the competency standard of the ABA's 1969 Code of Professional Responsibility.[57]

3. When competence (or integrity) sinks low enough, the client may sue the attorney for malpractice. The volume of such suits, rising in recent years,[58] may well continue to increase. The courts in these cases have expressed the applicable standard of conduct in various ways: whether the attorney had the skill and knowledge ordinarily possessed by attorneys under similar circumstances; whether the attorney was negligent, i.e., failed to use reasonable care and diligence; whether the attorney failed to exercise in good faith his best judgment. But the client's path is strewn with obstacles: The standards have been rather leniently interpreted; the client has the difficult job of proving causation, i.e., that *but for* the lawyer's deviation from the standard the outcome would have been different; the client has difficulty in finding a lawyer willing to sue another lawyer; judges seem reluctant to stigmatize a practitioner member of the profession; a judgment for the client may be frustrated by the lawyer's having no malpractice insurance;[59] and the alternative remedy of invoking the bar's own grievance machinery[60] is not likely to succeed,[61] and in any event will not result in monetary compensation to the client. However, a few of the more recent cases have been less lenient in interpreting the standard of care, particularly in dealing with an attorney specialist; and they have held that the statute of limitations on the suit starts running from the time of the plaintiff's discovery of the lawyer's misconduct

56. See discussion in Meserve et al., *supra* n.18 at 223-225.

57. *Id.* at 226-229.

58. Editorial, Suits Against Lawyers On The Rise, 65 A.B.A.J. 535 (1979).

59. For discussion of these points, see Rosenthal, Lawyer and Client: Who's In Charge? 123-127 (1974).

60. The fact that disciplinary enforcement of legal ethics was extremely lax ("a scandalous situation") was found in 1970 by the Report of the ABA Special Committee on Evaluation of Disciplinary Enforcement (commonly called the Clark Committee Report after the chairman, former Supreme Court Justice Tom C. Clark). See also Marks & Cathcart, Discipline Within the Legal Profession, 1974 U. Ill. L.F. 193; Countryman, Finman & Schneyer, The Lawyer in Modern Society, chap. 9 (2d ed. 1976). There is a trend toward some non-lawyer representation on disciplinary boards. See More States Adding Public to Disciplinary Boards, Natl. L.J., June 25, 1979, at 7, col. 1 (totalling 23 states); Wolfram, Barriers to Effective Public Participation in Regulation of the Legal Profession, 62 Minn. L. Rev. 619, 641-643 (1978). More effective *self*-regulation of the profession has been a declared objective of the "integrated bar" movement, for which see below at nn. 81-82.

61. See Martyn, Informed Consent in the Practice of Law, 48 Geo. Wash. L. Rev. 307, 309 (1980).

rather than (as usually held) from the time of its occurrence.[62] The "growing judicial disposition to impose more stringent standards upon lawyers has produced the collateral phenomenon of increased legal malpractice insurance premiums" — posing the dilemma of a lawyer's either operating without insurance or raising his own fees.[63] Concerned by the problem, an ABA committee in 1979 was undertaking a study of several thousand closed malpractice claims,[64] and the problem can be counted on to be with us in the years ahead.[65]

A word, finally, about the criminal defendant client. Here a constitutional element is added. The criminal defendant's Sixth Amendment right to "assistance of counsel" is construed to give him the right to "effective" assistance — meeting a certain minimum standard of competency.[66] In the absence of Supreme Court clarification of the standard, lower courts have usually required a showing that counsel's inadequate performance caused actual prejudice to the defendant's interest in obtaining an acquittal. This requirement is sometimes criticized as more stringent than was contemplated by the Sixth Amendment but the trend in recent cases is not such as to justify a prediction of imminent change.[67] When claiming ineffective assistance of counsel, a criminal defendant generally seeks reversal of the conviction; the civil malpractice suit against counsel is rarely pursued.[68]

4. The malpractice problem is also related to the issue of the lawyer's "openness." By this I mean that many complaints from defeated clients might be obviated if the lawyer imparted, for each aspect and stage of the case, full information and explanation to the client, discussing the problems with the client and allowing the client the ultimate authority to make the major decisions. This "informed consent" approach resembles the one developed in medical practice. Furthermore, language in the ABA Code of Professional Responsibil-

62. Schnidman & Salzler, Legal Malpractice Dilemma: Will New Standards of Care Place Professional Liability Insurance Beyond the Reach of the Specialist, 45 U. Cin. L. Rev. 541, 544-550 (1976).

63. *Id.* at 560.

64. See 65 A.B.A.J. 1033 (1979).

65. Some of the many discussions, other than those above cited, of lawyer malpractice are: ABA, Section of Insurance, Negligence and Compensation Law, Professional Liability of Trial Lawyers: The Malpractice Question (1979); Symposium, Legal Malpractice, 30 S.C.L. Rev. 201 (1979); Houser, Legal Malpractice — An Overview, 55 N.D.L. Rev. 185 (1979); Selected Materials on Legal Malpractice, 33 Record 238 (1978); Note, Should Legal Malpractice Insurance Be Mandatory, 1978 B.Y.L. Rev. 102 (1978); Symposium, 14 Willamette L.J. 355 (1978); Mallen & Levit, Legal Malpractice (1977); Countryman et al., *supra* n.60 at 81-102; Huszagh & Molloy, Legal Malpractice: A Calculus for Reform, 37 Mont. L. Rev. 279 (1976); Haughey, Lawyers' Malpractice: A Comparative Appraisal, 48 Notre Dame Law. 888 (1973).

66. McMann v. Richardson, 397 U.S. 759, 770-771 (1970).

67. See Note, 80 Colum. L. Rev. 1053, 1057-1060 (1980).

68. See Countryman et al., *supra* n.60 at 88-89; Annot., 53 A.L.R.3d 731 (1973).

ity suggests that lawyers should indeed act in this manner,[69] even though lawyers have traditionally acted otherwise. As it stands now, "[n]either the case law nor the Code of Professional Responsibility establishes a clear line between the lawyer's decisionmaking authority and the client's; even when the client is clearly given the decision, there is confusion over what information he must be given."[70] Recent scholarly analysis[71] has strongly enough argued for the explicit adoption of an "informed consent" approach to make future movement in this direction likely, or at least a matter of important controversy in the profession.

5. A much debated aspect of the present topic is the issue of ethical responsibility. The ABA's 1969 Code of Professional Responsibility had been regarded as a considerable improvement over the preexisting Canons of Ethics, but the winds of change were blowing hard in the 1970s. ABA President Janofsky observed in 1980 that in the preceding decade there had been "sweeping changes in the legal profession," and "even more important, . . . changes in what our clients, our government and our society expect of lawyers."[72] An ABA Commission on Evaluation of Professional Standards, created in 1977 and chaired by attorney Robert Kutak, prepared a draft of "Model Rules of Professional Conduct,"[73] which he described as "black-letter statements of the practice of ethical lawyering as it is perceived by our profession in the closing decades of the 20th century."[74] The Rules deal with such staple topics in this field as: lawyer advertising and solicitation; eliminating abuses in competitive tactics; conflicts of interest; relation between corporate house counsel and corporate officers; movement by lawyers between private firms and government agencies; the obligation of "competence" as adviser, negotiator, and courtroom advocate; the duty of contributing a portion of one's time to "pro bono" legal

69. See ABA Code of Professional Responsibility, Ethical Considerations 7-7 and 7-8 (1969); Chap. 1 *supra* at 91.

70. Spiegel, Lawyering and Client Decisionmaking: Informed Consent and the Legal Profession, 128 U. Pa. L. Rev. 41, 49 (1979). Elaboration of the quoted proposition appears at 49-72, and defense of an affirmative theory of informed consent is at 72-140.

71. See generally, Spiegel, *id.*; Martyn, *supra* n.61; Rosenthal, *supra* n.59. On the possibility of a co-counsel role for defendant, see DeFoor & Mitchell, Hybrid Representation: An Analysis of a Criminal Defendant's Right to Participate as Co-Counsel at Trial, 10 Stetson L. Rev. 191 (1981).

72. Janofsky, A New Code for the New Decade, 66 A.B.A.J. 6 (1980).

73. The proposed Model Rules of Professional Conduct, discussed below, more explicitly favor client control over all aspects of representation, within certain limits — though further clarifications are believed needed. Spiegel, The New Model Rules of Professional Conduct: Lawyer-Client Decisionmaking and the Role of Rules in Structuring the Lawyer-Client Dialogue, 1980 Am. B. Foundation Research J. 1003.

73. Janofsky, A New Code for the New Decade, 66 A.B.A.J. 6 (1980).

74. Kutak, Coming: The New Model Rules of Professional Conduct, 66 A.B.A.J. 46, 48 (1980).

activity; how to handle a client's perjury; and whether to disclose evidence favorable to the other side.

The Rules were the subject of hearings in various regions of the nation during 1980, being often the object of intense bar opposition.[75] Particularly criticized were (1) the Rule on pro bono activity and the requirement of annual reporting of the extent of that activity to an appropriate regulatory authority; and (2) the interference with the adversary model and the confidentiality of client communications, through certain provisions on mandatory or discretionary disclosures inimical to a client's interests.[76] Symptomatic of this discontent was a rival Code of Ethics being circulated simultaneously by the 40,000-member Association of Trial Lawyers of America and defended largely in terms of being free from the alleged defects just mentioned.[77] On the other hand, measured by some scholarly criticisms of the earlier

75. See, e.g., the reports of widespread hostility to the discussion draft in Slonim, More Volleys Fired At Kutak Commission Draft, 66 A.B.A.J. 704 (1980); Los Angeles Daily J., Sept. 30, 1980, at 1, col.2; Aug. 5, 1980, at 1, col.6. The latter story notes that the Commission "has compiled a telephone book-thick volume of comments about the rules — most of them critical — from bar groups and lawyers all over the country."

76. To illustrate: Mandatory pro bono is attacked as unconstitutional "involuntary servitude." Also it is said that "forced legal service, especially in fields where the particular lawyer has no proved competence, is likely to produce fifth-class legal service." Kaufman, A Critical Look At the Model Rules of Professional Conduct, 66 A.B.A.J. 1074, 1077 (1980). Generally on *pro bono* see Christensen, The Lawyer's Pro Bono Publico Responsibility, 1981 Am. B. Foundation Research J. 1; Rosenfeld, Mandatory Pro Bono: Historical and Constitutional Perspectives, 2 Cardozo L. Rev. 255 (1981); Natl. L. J., June 15, 1981, at 1.

The matter of attorney disclosure of client confidences had been dealt with rather uncertainly under the prior Code of Professional Responsibility: One had a duty to protect a client's confidences and zealously protect a client's interests; but a lawyer was not knowingly to use perjured testimony, and he "may" disclose his client's intention to commit a crime. There was controversy over the interrelations of these provisions. See, e.g. Rotunda, Book Review of Freedman (Lawyer's Ethics in An Adversary System (1975)), 89 Harv. L. Rev. 622 (1976). The discussion draft of the Rules proposed a compromise that has left many unsatisfied. In the case of intended crime, the attorney *must* disclose the information if the intended crime is death or serious bodily harm to another; otherwise he has the discretion to disclose information as to a "deliberately wrongful act." (An earlier draft had included certain additional crimes in the mandatory disclosure category.) However, as to perjury, the discussion draft proposed that in civil cases, the client's intended or actual perjury *must* be disclosed; in criminal cases, the same is true, except as disclosure is precluded by law (e.g., constitutional right to counsel and due process principles — whose application to the present issue is currently unclear). And if the law requires counsel to follow the client's demand for presentation of certain evidence, counsel must offer it regardless of a belief it is false. As for evidence favorable to another party, counsel has discretion to disclose it, except when forbidden by constitutional principles. Another new discretion attracting criticism was that permitting a lawyer representing a corporation to engage in certain kinds of "whistle blowing" on a corporate employee. For brief summaries of leading provisions of the Rules, see 66 A.B.A.J. 279 (1980) and Kaufman, *supra*. The latter criticizes, among other things, the "vast discretion" allowed by the Rules.

77. See 66 A.B.A.J. 705 (1980); 16 Trial 45 (1980).

Code,[78] the new Rules do not go far enough in the direction of serving the *public* interest.[79] Considering the pressures manifested in 1980, any revised drafts of the Rules, when presented to the ABA in 1981 or 1982, will probably satisfy the practitioners more than the scholars.[80]

6. Finally, some mention should be made of the "integrated" or "unified" bar — since this mode of bar organization has been defended in good part on the ground that it enhances lawyer competence and ethical responsibility and otherwise improves the administration of

78. See, e.g., Morgan, "The Evolving Concept of Professional Responsibility, 90 Harv. L. Rev. 702 (1977); Jones, Lawyers and Justice: The Uneasy Ethics of Partisanship, 23 Villanova L. Rev. 957 (1978); Wolfram, Client Perjury, 50 S. Calif. L. Rev. 809 (1977). A former law professor turned federal judge had written several articles critical of adversary system ethics and urging a more truth-seeking, truth-disclosure role for the lawyer, e.g., Frankel, The Search For Truth — An Umpireal View, 123 U. Pa. L. Rev. 1031 (1975) — which was followed by critical responses from Freedman at 1060 and Uviller at 1067. See also Nessen, Rethinking the Lawyers' Duties to Disclose Information: A Critique of Some of Judge Frankel's Proposals, 24 N.Y.L. Sch. L. Rev. 677 (1979); Frankel, Partisan Justice (1980).

79. However, appraisals from academia in the first law review symposium on the Model Rules, though varying in enthusiasm, generally acknowledged that in terms of explicitness, consistency, and ethical level, the Rules were a substantial improvement over the Code. See Review Symposium: The Model Rules of Professional Conduct, 1980 Am. B. Foundation Research J. 921. See also Landesman, Confidentiality and the Lawyer-Client Relationship, 1980 Utah L. Rev. 765.

80. The report of an interview with the chairman in 1980 stated that he contemplated at least four more drafts before submission to the ABA House of Delegates; that "commission members have already decided to tone down some of the most hotly contested provisions," including substitution of a discretionary for the mandatory requirement of disclosing information about a client who threatens death or serious bodily harm to another; that some limits on confidentiality of client communications would be retained, but provisions would be redrafted "to stress the importance of confidences between lawyers and clients"; that although the mandatory pro bono requirement will remain, "the commission is expected to drop a provision requiring lawyers to report their pro bono work to local or state bar associations." Los Angeles Daily J., Aug. 5, at 1, col. 6. However, early in 1981, the Commission "dropped its recommendation that lawyers be required to render unpaid public interest legal service. Instead, the commission plans to suggest that attorneys 'should' render public interest legal service, also dropping the reference to 'unpaid.' " Slonim, 67 A.B.A.J. 33 (1981). The Commission's final draft of the Rules was slated for publication in the October 1981 issue of the ABA Journal.

Another aspect of the responsibility topic is this: Ethical responsibility toward the legal system as a whole, as well as openness with clients, have been seen as adversely affected by the organizational changes within the profession — a profession that is young, crowded, "likely to be fiercely competitive, both within and without, that shows weakened local roots [i.e. "the local general professional community" has become less of a "lawyer's reference group for norms of practice and professionalism"] that is infused with lay participation, and that is increasingly organized in large public and private law firms." The challenge is to develop mechanisms "to ensure that lawyers treat each client, at least to some extent, as an individual, and not merely as a legal problem passing through the bureaucratic process"; and "to ensure that professionals regard the overall conditions of our legal system and legal institutions in their entirety and not merely as specific issues bearing no relationship to each other or to our general legal well-being."

Schwartz, The Reorganization of the Legal Profession, 58 Tex. L. Rev. 1269, 1277-1278, 1290 (1980).

justice. Under this system — in effect in more than half the states — the state's statutes, or the rules of the state's highest court, or a combination of both, require membership in the state bar association as a condition for law practice. The compulsory dues "provide greater resources and control for admission and disciplinary processes, continuing education, combatting the unauthorized practice of law and other activities clearly related to the administration of justice."[81] But there has been objection to some activities, particularly such other operations as legislative lobbying or support of political causes or candidates, on the ground that dues by compelled members should not be used for activities conflicting with the duespayer's beliefs. In the only Supreme Court case on validity of the integrated bar, the Supreme Court ruled that where the practice of law was conditioned on membership in the state bar association, and membership required nothing more than the "compulsory payment of reasonable annual dues," and the record showed that "the bulk of State Bar activities" was aimed at "elevating the educational and ethical standards of the Bar," there was no violation of First Amendment freedom of association. But there was no majority on the issue of whether the plaintiff attorney's First Amendment *free speech* rights were violated by the use of his dues for legislative or political causes that he opposed. (Some thought the issue was not "ripe" for decision; some found it ripe and thought the violation had occurred, while others found no violation.) However, the Court's attitude in closed shop or union shop labor cases suggests that the latter uses of an attorney's dues would indeed be a violation — but redressable merely by restitution of, or an injunction against collection of, the fraction of the attorney's dues represented by the ratio of such unconstitutional bar expenditures to total bar expenditures.[82]

B. *The Future of Legal Education*

1. The demand for a law school education — strikingly on the rise in the 1970s, as already noted — is expected to decline in the 1980s.[83] The

81. Aronson & Weckstein, Professional Responsibility 22-23 (1980).

82. The Supreme Court integrated bar case is Lathrop v. Donohue, 367 U.S. 820 (1961). For analysis of the relation between this case and the labor cases, see Parker, First Amendment Proscriptions on the Integrated Bar: *Lathrop v. Donohue* Reexamined, 22 Ariz. L. Rev. 939 (1980).

83. See Association of American Law Schools, Report of the Joint Committee on Demand For Legal Education In the 1980's (1980). The Report notes that the number of twenty-two-year-olds will be declining from the early 1980s to the end of the decade; and the number of high school graduates is expected to decline at

present pattern of a college degree followed by three years of law school followed by a bar examination is comparatively recent[84] though likely to be maintained for some time. Proposals for a two-year law degree,[85] or for some less than seven-year combination of a three- or four-year college program with a two- or three-year law program, are not well supported.[86] In spite of pressure from the ever-mounting costs of higher education, lawyers' opposition to such proposals are based on: the consequent aggravation of the already impending oversupply of lawyers; the difficulty of imparting the necessary knowledge, skills, and professional responsibility in one-third less time, in an era of expanding problems for the legal system; the likelihood, rather, of a narrow concentration on doctrinal analysis; and the improbability of a resulting diversity among law schools, i.e., the probability that if any

least until the mid-1980s. The decreasing total demand will be unevenly distributed among different states, since (1) the populational changes will differ among the states, and (2) there are non-population factors that will affect the applicant pool for particular schools. The report makes many recommendations to law schools and to concerned national organizations for coping with declining enrollment.

84. "Fifty years ago, academic training for aspiring lawyers was an ideal rather than a requirement, and it is only within the past few years that the completion of three years of formal legal education has become virtually the universal method of entering the profession." Boyer & Cramton, American Legal Education: An Agenda For Research and Reform, 59 Cornell L. Rev. 221, 224 (1974). As for admission to law school, "in the 1920's, admission . . . generally followed one, two, or three years of college. Today . . . the bachelor's degree is generally required . . ." (*id.* at 229). Passing a state bar exam (which nowadays generally includes some "objective" questions from a nationally standardized "multi-state bar examination") was not required in some 16 states in 1890; by now this "diploma privilege" persists in only a few states. For this and other issues connected with bar examinations, see Countryman et al., *supra* n.60 at 755-766.

85. Such a proposal for a "generalist" degree (coupled with a suggestion for an optional advanced program thereafter, to serve the needs of those who are interested in teaching, research, or specialized public service, or who have already had professional experience and wish to acquire a specialty) was made to the Association of American Law Schools in the 1971 Carrington Report. It appears in an Appendix at 95-328 of Packer & Ehrlich, New Directions in Legal Education (1972). The report suggested still another curriculum, to last only one year, for college juniors, seniors, or graduates who seek no degree for legal practice but wish an understanding of the legal system as part of their general education, or are uncertain about their career goals, or wish to attain professional competence in fields allied to law practice (e.g., counseling in such areas as family welfare, labor, taxation). A report prepared for the Carnegie Commission on Higher Education, appearing at 1-91 of Packer & Ehrlich, *supra,* was sympathetic to experimentation with a two-year optional curriculum, though it saw dangers in the plan. Another proposal for a two-year law school curriculum would allocate a third year ("for those graduates who wish to become legal practitioners") to "practical training and specialty training in . . . lawyer schools administered by the bar." Manning, Law Schools and Lawyer Schools, 26 J. Legal Ed. 379, 382 (1974).

86. When the ABA Council on Legal Education considered a two-year plan in 1972, there was strong opposition from law schools and the bar. See Stolz, The Two-Year Law School: The Day The Music Died, 25 J. Legal Ed. 37 (1973). *Cf.,* Boyer & Cramton, *supra* n.84 at 229.

law schools were allowed to adopt the plan, all or most others would be economically forced to do so.

2. Law school curricula have been expanding and are expected to continue expanding in areas posing pressing contemporary issues, such as: energy problems; environmental protection; welfare; poverty; consumer protection; housing; urban problems; communications; space; medical jurisprudence; alcoholism and drugs; and rights of women, homosexuals, prisoners, and racial minorities. "The explosive growth of new areas of legal practice and government regulation, the lack of a consistent intellectual structure for the law curriculum, and the autonomy of faculty members reluctant to abandon or restructure their favorite courses, have all contributed to a familiar process of curriculum growth by accretion" in the elective curriculum that follows the usually required first-year courses.[87] Included in the electives have been, and doubtless will be, courses or seminars attempting to integrate some aspects of law with other disciplines, notably history, sociology, economics, anthropology, psychology, or medicine.

In the sphere of teaching methods, some recent developments that do not yet have widespread significance but will probably be influential in the future for at least some courses are audio-visual aids, programmed learning, and computer simulation.[88] In addition, studies in the application to legal education of learning theory and educational psychology, including "humanistic" educational psychology, have already influenced some law professors and may influence more.[89] Still, the "large-class, case method of instruction, usually in a 'Socratic' question-and-answer format, has dominated law teaching since it was pioneered by Langdell nearly a century ago."[90]

The latter statement, however, is in a sense misleading. The full

87. Boyer & Cramton, *supra* n.84 at 230.

88. *Id.* at 231-232.

89. See *id.* at 231 n.38; 232-233; Shaffer & Redmount, Lawyers, Law Students and People (1977); Strong, The Pedagogic Training of a Law Faculty, 26 J. Legal Ed. 226 (1973); Himmelstein, "Reassessing Law Schooling: An Inquiry Into the Application of Humanistic Educational Psychology To the Teaching of Law, 53 N.Y.U.L. Rev. 514 (1978); Himmelstein, Shaffer, Lesnick, Meltsner, Swords, G. Friedman & Pepe, Reassessing Law Schooling: The Sterling Forest Group, *id.* at 561; Bellow, The Limits of Humanistic Law Teaching, *id.* at 644.

90. Boyer & Cramton, *supra* n.84 at 224. The authors go on to say: "The reasons for the longevity and popularity of the case method are several: its general pedagogical effectiveness, particularly in comparison to lectures; its adaptability to large classes, and thus its low cost; and perhaps most important, its ability to accommodate differing intellectual currents and differing conceptions of law" (at 224-225). The authors illustrate the latter point by saying that in Langdell's day the case method was viewed as extracting "fundamental principles from the raw material of printed decisions in the logical manner of the physical sciences"; and when the skeptical "realist" school of the 1930s emerged, casting doubt on the "scientific" nature of law, "the principle focus of the case method shifted from principles to process" (at 225).

potential of the "case method" has been extremely difficult to realize, and a cheap imitation is in its place. As Llewellyn complained back in 1948, case instruction could be, but was not being, used to develop craft skills of intensive analysis and imaginative problem-solving. Rather it was being used primarily to impart information about legal decisions and to raise queries about their probable scope and wisdom.[91] A 1976 study of law teaching methods in three Indiana and one California law schools indeed concluded that casebook classes were largely lecture classes.[92] The authors suggested, as possible explanation, the enormous increase in volume of information in practically all areas of law, student resistance to Socratic techniques, and their "demand" for information in class. Llewellyn would have argued that these reasons did not justify such use of the case class since "man could hardly devise a more wasteful method of *imparting information about subject matter* than the case class." Treatises, syllabus, and lecture can efficiently impart information. But the case class "is a class in doing — though the doing be mental and verbal; it is a cooperative, supervised, systematic exercise in diagnosis of a problem; in organization of data; in the arts of reaching for, building, and testing solutions or arguments, of making reasoned judgments of policy and putting them to the test; an exercise in the craft skill — and the human skill — of accurate, orderly, persuasive formulation in language of thoughts that need such organization and expression in order to accomplish a given purpose."[93]

Accordingly, we can add another reason for the tendency to attenuate the "case method": It takes, for optimum results, an uncommonly talented teacher with wide-ranging skills and knowledge, completely at ease in both the technical and policy aspects of the subject; able to evoke student participation; and resilient and resourceful enough to get all vital points across without hindrance from a too rigidly ordered pre-class "game plan." And, again for optimum results,

91. Such questions, he said, approached the case "from the rear," treated it as "something done and complete," providing an "authoritative datum about the state of the law." But the "less frequent, and more vital approach, 'from the front' is an approach to the case as a problem *for* solution, not as a problem already solved. Its essence lies in such questions as: What materials were there to work with before the decision and in the decision? How could the case, or the materials at hand, have been analyzed, presented and argued to give cogent reason for deciding for the losing party? How did the winning party arrange his case to win? Or did the court decide for the winner in spite of his blobs in presentation and argument, and, if so, how and why? . . . In this aspect, every case worked over becomes a direct exercise in living law and in dealing with an essential problem which the prospective lawyer will face in his life work — the persuasion of a court to reach the desired answer in a new case as yet undecided." Llewellyn, The Current Crisis in Legal Education, 1 J. Legal Ed. 211, 213-214 (1948).

92. Shaffer & Redmount, Legal Education: The Classroom Experience, 52 Notre Dame Law. 190, 197-201 (1976).

93. Llewellyn, *supra* n.91 at 215. (Italics in original.)

the materials assigned for the class should include background facts and other non-legalistic materials relevant to the policy aspects of the problems to be discussed. To make room for these, as Llewellyn observed, the number of actual cases in the usual text would have to be drastically reduced.

It seems, then, that in an attempt to improve case-method instruction and make it effective for more teachers, the textbook of the future should include, in addition to cases and relevant statutes or administrative rules, a higher proportion of non-legalistic materials than now appears; a much smaller number of cases; a sharper focus on problems for class handling; and, especially in areas not covered by the cases, more summaries of the law in certain areas, written by the editor or extracted from treatises and articles (thus not relying on cases for "imparting information"). A pattern something like this has been emerging in some casebooks and seems likely to become more pronounced and widespread.

3. Probably the most prominent point of curricular ferment at the outset of the 1980s was the teaching of "craft skills" — an objective to which the pure case method as described above makes only a partial contribution. A 1979 Report of an ABA Task Force on law schools and lawyer competency (Cramton Report)[94] stressed, among other recommendations,[95] that a law student should receive instruction in developing his ability to write, communicate orally, gather facts, interview, counsel, and negotiate; and students desiring it should also get instruction in litigation skills.[96] This was not intended to create a

94. ABA, Report and Recommendations of Task Force on Lawyer Competency: The Role of the Law Schools (1979). The 12-member Task Force was drawn from distinguished members of the bench, bar, and law school faculties, and was chaired by Dean Roger Cramton of Cornell University Law School.

95. The Report recommended that new instructional materials and teaching methods that focus on fundamental lawyer skills should be developed, and should be valued no less highly than research on legal doctrine. As researchers, law faculty should give more attention to what courts, lawmakers, and lawyers do, how they do it, how the relevant skills are learned, how legal services can better be performed, and how the legal system in operation can be improved. Small classes should be used, and more extensive instructional use should be made of experienced and able lawyers and judges. Experience in working together with other students should be encouraged. Student performance should be measured by more comprehensive methods than the typical end-of-term exam; and students should get detailed critiques of their performance. The curriculum should have greater coherence and avoid presenting the same kinds of tasks year after year; it should build in a structured way, with problems of successively broader scope and challenge. Law schools, instead of relying in their admission policy on LSAT and college grade point average, should also give weight to such factors as writing ability, talent in oral communication, work habits, interpersonal skills, dependability, and conscientiousness; and should consider the possibility of interviewing that portion of the applicant pool having middle-range records.

96. Report, *supra* n.94 at 3-4. A 1978 Law School Admission Council Study had shown lawyers rating their law school education low in the development of these

uniform pattern among law schools. The Report recognized that law schools may properly strike differing balances between the emphasis on lawyer skills and that on doctrinal analysis, research, etc. "Diversity and experimentation rather than mandated uniformity offer the most likely path to more effective law school education."[97] The Report rejected the idea that lawyers should rely on their first years of practice, or upon apprenticeship, to develop these skills.[98] And law school skill training, the Report recognized, would not be by itself sufficient; the proliferating "continuing legal education" (CLE) courses for lawyers were also essential.[99]

Financing of the new programs also received some attention. As against "other graduate and professional education, law school education has historically been a low budget operation characterized by unfavorable student-faculty ratios."[100] While the schools might gradually re-allocate available funds as new faculty are appointed and curriculum decisions are made, an influx of fresh funds from foundations, the bar, and from government was thought to be required. A ten-year subsidy beginning in 1968 and totalling $10 million to selected law schools from the Ford Foundation–sponsored CLEPR (Council on Legal Education for Professional Responsibility) for "clinical" pro-

---

skills. See Baird, A Survey of the Relevance of Legal Training to Law School Graduates, 29 J. Legal Ed. 264 (1978). A secondary virtue of skills training is in the hoped-for avoidance of the familiar second and third year student boredom. See Boyer & Cramton, *supra* n.84 at 230, 276-282.

97. Report, *supra* n.94 at 3.

98. The idea "that young lawyers should gain an acceptable level of competence in the practice, in effect learning at the expense of their first clients, is today not an acceptable one"; and "many believe that reliance on a period of informal apprenticeship to experienced seniors in a firm to bridge the gap between law school instruction and the demands of practice is no longer practicable for a large number of law school graduates, if it ever was. In all likelihood, the majority of law graduates never received first-rate on the job training. Many have always begun professional work in settings lacking both the resources and expertise necessary for effective supervision." Report, *supra* n.94 at 14-15.

99. There is a National Institute on Trial Advocacy, established with bar encouragement in 1971, that holds training sessions in trial skills for practicing lawyers and to a lesser extent for law teachers. NITA materials and instructional methods have also been used in some law school courses. Report, *supra* n.94 at 12-13. Attempts are being made to streamline and reduce the high cost of NITA training sessions. See Janofsky, *supra* n.2 at 204. An American Trial Lawyers Association's National College of Advocacy also exists. See Specter, ATLA's National College of Advocacy: An Educational Innovation, 15 Trial, no. 2 at 32 (1979). The ABA is sponsoring the creation of core materials and training to teach non-trial skills: fact gathering, interviewing, counselling, negotiation, and drafting. Janofsky, *supra* n.2 at 203. Various other organizations, both profit and nonprofit, have plunged into the growing market — a market enlarged by the adoption in several states of a mandatory CLE requirement. See Douglass, Lawyers' Competence and C.L.E., 15 Trial, no. 2, at 27 (1979); Friday, Continuing Legal Education: Historical Background, Recent Developments and the Future, 50 St. Johns L. Rev. 502 (1976).

100. Report, *supra* n.94 at 22.

grams[101] had terminated. The federal government, though, was still in the picture, having supplied funds totalling several million for law school clinical programs during 1977-1980. Coming after the Report, the Education Amendments of 1980 raised the annual subsidy by appropriating $5 million for fiscal 1981, and higher amounts for subsequent years, reaching $10 million by fiscal 1985[102] — though the Reagan Administration may take a less generous attitude.

In 1980 the ABA Special Committee for a Study of Legal Education recommended, for submission to the ABA House of Delegates in 1981, that the Cramton Report's skills training proposals be supported and implemented[103] — in addition to two other recommendations to the House of Delegates,[104] and some more "general" recommendations. One was that the ABA should "take the lead in exploring additional and creative funding resources for legal education and in developing methods to obtain such resources."[105] Others concerned the law student

101. These were either (1) "in-house" law school clinics, staffed by clinical law faculty or (2) part-time placements of students with lawyers, judges, prosecutors, administrative officials, legal services agencies, public interest law centers, or certain other placements, with law faculty attempting to maintain a substantial educational involvement.

102. Pub. L. No. 96-374, Title IX, §905 (Part E, §§951-953), 96 Cong., 2d Sess., 94 Stat. 1487-1488 (1980). For committee reports, see 4 U.S. Code Cong. & Ad. News 3195-3196, 3272. No law school was to receive more than $100,000 in any fiscal year, and financing was not to go beyond 90% of the costs of the clinical experience programs established or expanded by accredited law schools. Financial assistance roughly comparable to that mentioned in the text above was authorized "for legal training for people with disadvantaged backgrounds." §904 (Part D, §§941-942). In calling for increased federal support for legal education, the Report had argued the support should not be restricted to clinical programs, saying that support of such programs "may be best done through the Legal Services Corporation, since most law school clinics are engaged in delivering high quality legal services to the poor — the central task of the Corporation." Report, *supra* n.94 at 32.

103. Report of ABA Special Committee for a Study of Legal Education, Law Schools and Professional Education (1980). This Committee had sponsored the Boyer and Cramton 1974 Study, and its report was based on further ABA Foundation research studies as well. There is a valuable summary of the latter studies at 25-94, covering questions about choosing legal education and a legal career (who goes to law school and why; how students select law schools); questions about effectiveness of law school training (how students and graduates evaluate their legal education, including curriculum; knowledge and skills viewed by attorneys as important for law practice; how much time and energy students invest in law study; relation of law school to professional responsibility, and to quality of advocacy in the courts; impact of law school on student career goals); questions about transition from school to practice (how young lawyers learn on the job; how legal careers develop, and effect thereon of legal credentials); extent and effect of stratification in the profession; and background characteristics of law teachers. For a subsequently published study on one of the foregoing topics, see Zemans & Rosenblum, Preparation for the Practice of Law — The Views of the Practicing Bar, 1980 Am. B. Foundation Research J. 1.

104. The two others were: that existing law school programs in skill training be surveyed and evaluated, and that the American Bar Foundation continue its legal education research.

105. See Report, *supra* n.103 at 95-101.

body[106] and matters of curriculum and teaching.[107] In the same year, a joint report of an ABA–Association of American Law Schools committee offered some voluntary "guidelines" for clinical legal education.[108]

You should not assume that the current stress on craft skills is something new, or that it is being unanimously endorsed. A perennial issue in the legal education literature,[109] many law school professors

106. (1) As pre-law students they should have more precise curricular guidelines, with emphasis on "advanced writing skills and effective oral communication," though also important are "accounting, economics, psychology, and . . . historical and contemporary social and political processes." (2) As recommended by the Cramton Report, the law school admissions process should consider factors other than LSAT and grade point average, and law schools should "consider establishing guidelines for admission that assure the achievement of adequate writing ability on the part of those admitted." (3) The schools should "reevaluate the adequacy of their respective student financial aid systems." (4) Law students should have adequate "academic and career counselling throughout law school" and "should be made aware of the value of various skills that may be relevant to the practice of law."

107. Teaching materials, "particularly in the areas of the administrative process and regulatory law and of legislative process and statutory law" should be reevaluated. (2) Sufficient resources should be provided to law schools "to improve dramatically student/faculty ratios. . . ." (3) The schools should generally "remain on a three-year equivalent program. . . ." (4) Law schools in their criteria for faculty promotion and tenure should take into account differing workloads ("such as those experienced by clinical teachers"), and give "appropriate weight . . . to the effective teaching of legal skills." (5) The "law school recruitment process for full-time faculty [should] increasingly look to the practicing segment of the profession for its potential faculty members and seek creative ways to attract practitioners to teach, such as 'practitioner in residence' programs and law firm sabbatical programs." (6) Law schools should "provide means for the improvement of pedagogical skills." (7) Law schools should have more "effective communications" with the bar in order that they may play a role in "continuing legal education" of the bar. (8) As "part of the self-study process required by the ABA, . . . law schools [should] include as members of self-study task forces or committees, alumni, other members of the practicing bar, and academicians from other disciplines." (9) "[E]valuative research [should] be supported so that new teaching methods and strategies can be developed and evaluated and the results disseminated within the legal education community."

108. Report of the Association of American Law Schools–American Bar Association Committee on Guidelines for Clinical Legal Education (1980). The guidelines "are intended to provide advice to law schools in the creation, operation, and evaluation of clinical programs. They are emphatically not intended as standards for purposes of accreditation or in any other way to force clinical legal education into a particular mold. Clinical training, like other aspects of legal education, is too vital to be denied the flexibility of diverse experimentation and adjustment to meet the needs of individual legal education programs. . . . [T]he Committee also believes that each law school has a responsibility to provide its students with the opportunity to gain an understanding of the basic competencies required by lawyers in order to function in the attorney-client relationship."

109. A short bibliography of the literature might include: Reed, Training for the Public Profession of the Law (1921); Currie, The Materials of Law Study, 3 J. Legal Ed. 331 (1951) (parts 1-2), 8 *id.* at 1 (1955) (part 3); Packer & Ehrlich, New Directions in Legal Education (1972); Stevens, Two Cheers For 1870: The American Law School, in Fleming & Bailyn, eds., Law in American History 405 (1971); Boyer & Cramton, American Legal Education: An Agenda For Research and Reform, 59 Cornell L. Rev. 221 (1974); Symposia, 29 Cleve. St. L. Rev. 345 (1980), 50 St. John's L. Rev. 441 (1976), 1977 B.Y.U.L. Rev. 689, 53 N.Y.U.L. Rev. 291 (1978).

and ex-professors have been vigorously opposed to such an emphasis[110] — usually on the ground that skills training is very costly, cannot be done well in law schools, will have to be done at the expense of the necessary core curriculum, and neophyte lawyers lacking in skills training do get some help from other lawyers and from judges.

Still, some notable law professors have in somewhat different ways been on the other side, including Karl Llewellyn[111] and Jerome Frank,[112] who could hardly be accused of the anti-intellectualism or "trade school" bias sometimes attributed to the skills training emphasis. Nor was the Cramton Report written primarily by practitioners; of the twelve unanimous authors three were federal appellate judges and five had academic affiliations. The argument has been not only that a young lawyer's early clients should not have to bear the burden of the uncertain quality of skill training he receives by handling their cases, but that law school "exercise in the application of legal theory to legal problems is a broadening experience that promotes effective learning of ideas."[113] One academic who approaches skills training with caution and deplores the "anti-intellectualism" of some of its proponents concedes that "both clinical training and traditional instruction can be trivial or profound, and serve broad social and humanistic goals or the narrowest of ends. Indeed, properly conceived and executed, clinical programs advance the higher educational aspirations and support the objectives of classroom instruction. The student is given, among other things, an opportunity under field conditions to test his command of

110. See McGowan, The University Law School and Practical Education, 65 A.B.A.J. 374 (1979); Carrington, The University Law School and Legal Services, 53 N.Y.U.L. Rev. 402, 420-432 (1978); McClain, Legal Education: Extent To Which Know-how in Practice Should Be Taught In Law Schools, 6 J. Legal Ed. 302 (1954); Clark, "Practical" Legal Training An Illusion, 3 J. Legal Ed. 423 (1951).

111. Llewellyn, The Current Crisis in Legal Education, 1 J. Legal Ed. 211, 216-218 (1948); Association of American Law Schools Curriculum Committee Report, The Place of Skills in Legal Education (of which Llewellyn was the apparent drafter), 45 Colum. L. Rev. 345, esp. 364-377 (1945). The five other committee members subscribed to the Report without dissent from its major points.

112. Frank, A Plea For Lawyer-Schools, 56 Yale L.J. 1303 (1947); *id.*, Courts On Trial 225-246 (1950). Among other law professors' works see Bradway, Clinical Preparation For Law Practice (1946); Rutter, A Jurisprudence of Lawyers' Operations, 13 J. Legal Ed. 301 (1961); Strong, The Pedagogic Training of A Law Faculty, 25 J. Legal Ed. 226 (1973); Shaffer, Legal Interviewing and Counselling (1976); Gullickson, Structuring A General Practice Course (1976); Kelso & Kelso, The Future of Legal Education For Practical Skills: Can the Innovations Survive? 1977 B.Y.U.L. Rev. 1007; Brown & Dauer, Planning By Lawyers: Materials On A Nonadversarial Legal Process (1978); Hegland, Trial and Practice Skills (1978). Note also that the 1971 Carrington Report to the Association of American Law Schools, cited *supra* n.85, had proposed that in many courses the emphasis be not on doctrinal subject matter but on development of certain skills, technique, and understandings about operation of the legal system; that there be more instruction, and more individualized instruction, in research, writing, problem solving, planning, counselling, and advocacy; that more team-teaching be utilized; and that more incorporation of pertinent knowledge from other disciplines be attempted.

113. Boyer & Cramton, *supra* n.84 at 272.

analytical skills and a broader experience with which to evaluate the legal norms and the values expressed in the administration of justice."[114]

It is true that substantial expansion of skills training in law schools cannot be successful without the far greater monetary investment required by small-group instruction. It is also true that law schools would have to make more instructional use of practitioners, carefully chosen not only for competence but also for other desirable pedagogical qualities. These conditions being satisfied, the controversy in the coming years will be over the striking of a proper balance: When will a shift of resources from the core curriculum be "too much"?[115]

C. *Law and Other Disciplines*

We have encountered above advice that legal education pay increased attention to law's relations with other disciplines. I here try to offer some guidance to existing literature on such relations.

1. First, as far as the discipline of historical study is concerned, its relation to law has been relatively neglected in this country, and it usually has treated law in an unduly narrow way. The predominant (not exclusive) approach in the writing of American legal history, until about mid-twentieth century, was one of insularity — i.e., treating the development of legal doctrines and institutions without substantial attention to their interrelations with the surrounding society. By that time an opposite trend had become dominant,[116] in which Willard Hurst's influence through his own studies[117] and through other

114. Allen, The New Anti-Intellectualism in American Legal Education, 28 Mercer L. Rev. 447, 456 (1977).

115. To me, the "not too much" standard often calls to mind what the witty Professor Thomas Reed Powell of Harvard used to say about how one might formulate a statement on the interstate commerce power for a "Restatement" of constitutional law (the American Law Institute has published several summary "Restatement" volumes for various fields of law): "In the usual form the black-letter text would read: 'Congress may regulate interstate commerce.' A Comment would add: 'The states may also regulate interstate commerce, but not too much.' And then there would follow a Caveat: 'How much is too much is beyond the scope of this Restatement.'" Professor Paul Freund, introduction, Powell, Vagaries and Varieties in Constitutional Interpretation (1956) at ix.

116. The story of the shift from one emphasis to the other is impressively traced and discussed in Gordon, Introduction: J. Willard Hurst and the Common Law Tradition in American Legal Historiography, 10 Law & Socy. Rev. 10 (1975).

117. The Growth of American Law (1950); Law and the Conditions of Freedom in Nineteenth Century United States (1956); Law and Social Process In United States History (1960); Justice Holmes on Legal History (1964); Law and Economic Growth: The Legal History of the Lumber Industry in Wisconsin, 1836-1915 (1964); Legitimacy of the Business Corporation In the Law of the United States, 1780-1970

Rockefeller Foundation–sponsored studies for which he was advisor[118] played a significant role. Hurst has long counselled that, among other things, more attention be paid to interaction of law and society;[119] even recent legal historical scholarship, in his opinion, evinces various shortcomings in scope[120] as well as in theoretical orientation.[121] Never-

(1970); Legal Elements in American History, in Fleming & Bailyn, eds., Law in American History (1971); A Legal History of Money In the United States, 1774-1970 (1973); Law and Social Order In the United States (1977); The Functions of Courts In the United States, 1950-1980 (1980).

118. Hunt, Law and Locomotives (1958); Kuehnl, The Wisconsin Business Corporation (1959); Laurent, The Business of A Trial Court, 100 Years of Cases (1959); Kimball, Insurance and Public Policy (1960); Murphy, Water Purity (1961); Lake, Law and Mineral Wealth (1962); Mermin, Jurisprudence and Statecraft (1963); Friedman, Contract Law in America (1965); Mermin, The Fox–Wisconsin Rivers Improvement (1968).

119. In Legal Elements in American History, *supra* n.117 at 6-10, he summarized many of his previous suggestions by advising legal historians: to cover not only judicial activity (the study of which, moreover, he said, had concentrated on the Supreme Court to the relative neglect of other federal and state courts, particularly trial courts), but also the federal and state and municipal legislative, executive, and administrative processes, and the "operating public policy created by the ways in which lawyers and their clients, and laymen working without benefit of counsel, shape affairs with more or less use, avoidance, or evasion of the law emanating from official agencies"; to avoid "the conventional historical preoccupation with formal constitutional law" by paying attention to the "constitutive roles in this society of the market, the business corporation, public utilities, the church, trade associations, trade unions, public and private educational organizations, and welfare and research foundations" and the "aspects of law related to the legitimation and distribution of practical power within and among such institutions"; to study the development of not only the functions and procedures of legal agencies but "the substantive content of public policy," and in doing so, to avoid the over-identification of public policy with regulatory standards of conduct, by including study of the law's direct and indirect "allocation of resources," "indirect compulsion," and "situation structuring"; and to avoid exaggeration of the areas of interest conflicts and "directed" use of law, since much of "men's social experience in which the law was involved entailed neither combat nor consent, but merely the mindless cumulation of unperceived, unplanned, unchosen events," i.e., "drift and inertia."

120. In his Old and New Dimensions of Research In United States Legal History, 23 Am. J. Legal Hist. 1, 2-9, 19-20 (1979), he argues that research is still disproportionately focused on courts as against legislatures, administrative and executive agencies; that not enough account has been taken of "the likenesses and differences with which legal doctrine and uses of law have shaped or responded to sectional differences, different from, or in tension with, interests perceived on a national scale"; that we have neglected how "public policy has affected or has been affected by changes in the scale of private organization for collective action"—particularly the growth of large private organizations from the latter nineteenth century into the 1920s; that this period as well as others, such as the post–World War II generation, has been relatively neglected in favor of pre–Civil War decades; that in our preoccupation with "law and the market" we have given too little attention to the interplay of law and: the family, sex roles, the church, education, scientific and technical knowledge, and "the tension between conventional morality and individual goals"; and that, difficult though it is, we must try to ascertain the impact of public policy on "ordinary individuals" as distinct from extraordinary individuals or groups.

121. He criticizes aspects of the theories of "consensus history," "pluralism," and economic class domination. *Id.* at 9-20. He adds that the new interest in historical

theless, a surge of historical studies, particularly in the last decade or so, manifests a greater similarity than dissimilarity to Hurst's broad law-in-society model.[122] Ongoing work in American legal history appears, or is reviewed occasionally, in general legal (or historical or social science) periodical literature, but is more fully handled in some specialized legal periodicals.[123]

2. A number of other disciplines devoted to the study of people in society have been found relevant to the law — a fact that should hardly be surprising, in view of the point made in Chapter 1 on the mutual interaction of law and society. There is a growing body of literature researching law and psychology,[124] law and psy-

---

theory must avoid the temptation for armchair theory — i.e., theory not solidly based on persistent, grubby investigation of the facts.

Hurst's own work has in turn been subjected by admiring critics to some questions. See Scheiber, At the Borderland of Law and Economic History: The Contributions of Willard Hurst, 75 Am. Hist. Rev. 744 (1969); Tushnet, Lumber and the Legal Process, 1972 Wis. L. Rev. 114; Gordon, *supra* n.116 at 44-55; Book Reviews by Stone, 78 Harv. L. Rev. 1687 (1965), and by Abrams, 24 Stan. L. Rev. 765 (1972).

122. See Gordon, *supra* n.116 at 12 & 55. Some examples are Atiyah, The Rise and Fall of Freedom of Contract (1979); Konig, Law and Society in Puritan Massachusetts (1979); Horwitz, The Transformation of American Law, 1780-1860 (1977); Nelson, Americanization of the Common Law: The Impact of Legal Change In Massachusetts Society, 1760-1830 (1975); Friedman, A History of American Law (1973); Hyman, A More Perfect Union: The Impact of the Civil War and Reconstruction on the Constitution (1973); Haskins, Law and Authority in Early Massachusetts (1960). An unusually broad-based analysis and defense of a socio-historicist attitude is Gordon, Historicism in Legal Scholarship, 90 Yale L.J. 1017 (1981).

123. An American Journal of Legal History first appeared in 1957 and is flourishing. The N.Y.U. Annual Survey of American Law, published since 1942, usually has a section canvassing the year's major literature in legal history. The Law and Society Review, which has occasional historical articles, devoted two issues of vol. 10 (1975-1976), written by legal historians, to Law and Society in American History: Essays in Honor of J. Willard Hurst.

124. Loh, Psychological Research: Past and Present, 79 Mich. L. Rev. 659 (1981); Marshall, Law and Psychology in Conflict (2d ed. 1980); Parker, Legal Psychology (1980); Robinson, Psychology and Law (1980); Schwitzgebel, Law and Psychological Practice (1980); Farrington, Hawkins & Lloyd-Bostock, Psychology, Law and Legal Processes (1979); Yarmey, The Psychology of Eyewitness Testimony (1979); Walker, Lind & Thibaut, The Relation Between Procedural and Distributive Justice, 65 Va. L. Rev. 1401 (1979); Abt & Stuart, eds., Social Psychology and Discretionary Law (1979); Saks & Hastie, Social Psychology in Court (1978); Massery, ed., Psychology and Persuasion in Advocacy (1978, National College of Advocacy); Conley, O'Barr & Lind, The Power of Language: Presentational Style In the Courtroom, 1978 Duke L.J. 1375; Sales, ed., Psychology in the Legal Process (1977); Tapp & Levine, Law, Justice and the Individual in Society: Psychological Issues (1977); Note, 29 Stan. L. Rev. 969 (1977); Okpaku, Psychology: Impediment or Aid in Child Custody Cases, 29 Rutgers L. Rev. 1117 (1976); Thibaut & Walker, Procedural Justice: A Psychological Analysis (1975); Symposium, Law and Psychology, 26 Stan. L. Rev. 1245 (1974); Walker, Thibaut & Andreoli, Order of Presentation At Trial, 82 Yale L.J. 216 (1972); Marshall, Marquis & Oskamp, Effects of Kinds of Questions and Atmosphere of Interrogation, on Accuracy and Completeness of Testimony, 84 Harv. L. Rev. 1620 (1971); Singer, Psychological Studies of Punishment, 58 Calif. L. Rev. 405 (1970); Boehm, Mr. Prejudice, Miss Sympathy, and the Authoritarian Personality:

chiatry,[125] law and anthropology,[126] law and biology and medicine,[127]

An Application of Psychological Measuring Technique to the Problem of Jury Bias, 1968 Wis. L. Rev. 734; Winick, A Primer of Psychological Theories Holding Implications For Legal Work, 7 Am. Behavioral Scientist 45 (1963).

In the 1970s, at least two journals with a legal psychology orientation began publication: Law and Psychology Review (1975) and Law and Human Behavior (1977).

125. Symposium on Law and Psychiatry, 66 Va. L. Rev. 427 (1980); Robitscher, The Powers of Psychiatry (1980); Weisstub, ed., Law and Psychiatry (1978) and (1979); Bromberg, The Uses of Psychiatry In the Law: A Clinical View of Forensic Psychiatry (1979); Morse, Crazy Behavior, Morals and Science: An Analysis of Mental Health Law, 51 S. Calif. L. Rev. 527 (1978); Dix, Death Penalty, "Dangerousness," Psychiatric Testimony and Professional Ethics, 5 Am. J. Crim. L. 151 (1977); Cocozza & Steadman, The Failure of Psychiatric Predictions of Dangerousness: Clear and Convincing Evidence, 29 Rutgers L. Rev. 1084 (1976); Brooks, Law, Psychiatry and the Mental Health System (1974); Ehrenzweig, Psychoanalytic Jurisprudence (1971); Goldstein, Psychoanalysis and Jurisprudence, 77 Yale L.J. 1053 (1968); Watson, Psychiatry for Lawyers (1968); Halleck, Psychiatry and the Dilemmas of Crime (1967); Bienenfeld, Prolegomena To A Psychoanalysis Of Law and Justice, 53 Calif. L. Rev. 957, 1245 (1965).

The Journal of Psychiatry and Law started publishing in 1973.

126. Roberts, Order and Dispute: An Introduction to Legal Anthropology (1979); Pospisil, The Ethnology of Law (2d ed. 1978); Moore, Law As Process: An Anthropological Approach (1978); Nader & Todd, eds., The Disputing Process — Law in Ten Societies (1978); Cappelletti & Garth, eds., Access to Justice, vol. IV, The Anthropological Perspective (1978); Abel, A Comparative Theory of Dispute Institutions in Society, 8 Law & Socy. Rev. 217 (1973); Pospisil, The Anthropology of Law: A Comparative Theory (1971); Koch, Law and Anthropology: Notes on Interdisciplinary Research, 4 Law & Socy. Rev. 11 (1969); Nader, Koch & Cox, The Ethnography of Law: A Bibliographic Survey, 7 Current Anthropology 267 (1966); Hoebel, Three Studies in African Law" (Review of books by Howell, Bohannan & Gluckman), 13 Stan. L. Rev. 418 (1961); Hoebel, The Law of Primitive Man (1954); Llewellyn & Hoebel, The Cheyenne Way (1941).

127. Beckstrom, Sociobiology and Intestate Wealth Transfers, 76 Nw. L. Rev. 216 (1981); Wadlington, Waltz & Dworkin, Law and Medicine (1980); Clarke, The Choice To Refuse or Withhold Medical Treatment: The Emerging Technology and Medical-Ethical Consensus, 13 Creighton L. Rev. 795 (1980); Ufford, Brain Death — Termination of Heroic Efforts To Save Life — Who Decides?, 19 Washburn L.J. 225 (1980); Ryder, Implementing A Qualified Right To Die, 10 Kingston L. Rev. 24 (1980); Note, 32 U. Fla. L. Rev. 275 (1980); Humber & Almeder, Biomedical Ethics and the Law (2d ed. 1979); Capron, Tort Liability in Genetic Counselling, 79 Colum. L. Rev. 618 (1979); Symposium, Mentally Retarded People and the Law, 31 Stan. L. Rev. 541 (1979); Flannery et al., Test Tube Babies: Legal Issues Raised by *In Vitro* Fertilization, 67 Geo. L.J. 1295 (1979); Meisel, The "Exceptions" To The Informed Consent Doctrine: Striking A Balance Between Competing Values in Medical Decisionmaking, 1979 Wis. L. Rev. 413; Brock, Fetal Research: What Price Progress? 1979 Detroit C. of L. Rev. 403; Notes, 28 Emory L.J. 1045 (1979), 11 Sw. U.L. Rev. 1421 (1979), 1979 Detroit C. of L. Rev. 429, 9 Capital L. Rev. 191 (1979); Ramsey, Ethics At the Edges of Life: Medical and Legal Intersections (1978); National Commission For the Protection of Human Subjects of Biomedical and Behavioral Research, The Belmont Report (including two-volume Appendix) (1978); Bandman & Bandman, Bioethics and Human Rights (1978); Symposium, Biotechnology and the Law: Recombinant DNA and the Control of Scientific Research, 51 S. Calif. L. Rev. 969 (1978); Berger, Government Regulation of the Pursuit of Knowledge: The Recombinant DNA Controversy, 3 Vt. L. Rev. 83 (1978); Grad, Medical Ethics and the Law, 437 Annals 19 (1978); Gray, Complexities of Informed Consent, *id.* at 37; Symposium on Health Law, 22 St. Louis U.L. Rev. 397 (1978); Reilly, Genetics, Law

as well as law's relationship to other natural sciences and to science generally.[128] The huge political science literature is relevant, since the governmental institutions treated are of course legal institutions.[129] In

---

and Social Policy (1977); Shuman, Psychosurgery and the Medical Control of Violence (1977); Symposium on Legal Medicine, 22 N.Y.L. Sch. L. Rev. 873 (1977); Notes, 3 Colum. J. Envir. L. 344 (1977), 65 Ky. L. Rev. 880 (1977); Steele & Hill, A Plea For A Legal Right To Die, 29 Okla. L. Rev. 328 (1976); Veatch, Death, Dying and the Biological Revolution (1976); Symposium, Medical Experimentation On Human Subjects, 25 Case Western U.L. Rev. 431 (1975); Shapiro, Legislating the Control of Behavior Control: Autonomy and the Coercive Use of Organic Therapies, 47 S. Calif. L. Rev. 237 (1974); Shapiro, Who Merits Merit? Problems in Distributive Justice and Utility Posed By the New Biology, 48 S. Calif. L. Rev. 318 (1974); Notes, 72 Mich. L. Rev. 1182 (1974), 7 U. Mich. L. Ref. 615 (1974), 26 Stan. L. Rev. 1191 (1974); 47 S. Calif. L. Rev. 476 (1974), 48 *id.*, 489; Waltz & Thigpen, Genetic Screening and Counselling: The Legal and Ethical Issues, 68 Nw. U.L. Rev. 696 (1973); Symposium on Genetics, 48 Ind. L.J. 527 (1973); Freund, ed., Experimentation With Human Subjects (1970); Curran & Shapiro, Law, Medicine and Forensic Science (2d ed. 1970); Symposia, 35 Law & Contemp. Prob. 667 (1970), 32 *id.*, 561 (1967), 36 Fordham L. Rev. 631 (1968), 15 U.C.L.A. L. Rev. 267 (1968).

The American Journal of Law and Medicine began publishing in 1975.

128. Cohen, Ronen & Stepan, Law and Science: A Selected Bibliography (1980); Goldberg, Controlling Basic Science: The Case of Nuclear Fusion, 68 Geo. L.J. 683 (1980); Gianelli, The Admissibility of Novel Scientific Evidence, 80 Colum. L. Rev. 1197 (1980); Martin, Procedures for Decisionmaking Under Conditions of Scientific Uncertainty: The Science Court Proposal, 16 Harv. J. Legis. 443 (1979); Goldberg, Constitutional Status of American Science, 1979 U. Ill. L.F. 1; Ferguson, Scientific Inquiry and the First Amendment, 64 Cornell L. Rev. 639 (1979); Talbott, "Science Court": A Possible Way to Obtain Scientific Certainty For Decisions Based on Scientific Fact, 8 Envt. 827 (1978); Bazelon, Coping With Technology Through the Legal Process, 62 Cornell L. Rev. 817 (1977); Gelpe & Tarlock, The Uses of Scientific Information in Environmental Decisionmaking, 48 S. Calif. L. Rev. 371 (1974); Curlin, Fostering Understanding Between Science and Law, 59 A.B.A.J. 157 (1973); Stone, Knowledge, Survival, and the Duties of Science, 23 Am. U.L. Rev. 231 (1973); Lederburg, Freedoms and the Control of Science, 45 S. Calif. L. Rev. 596 (1972); Symposium, Implications of Science-Technology For the Legal Process, 47 Denver L.J. 549 (1970); Caldwell, ed., Science, Technology and Public Policy: A Selected and Annotated Bibliography (1969); Jones, ed., Law and the Social Role of Science (1966) (with bibliog. at 135-201); Loevinger, Law and Science As Rival Systems, 8 Jurimetrics J. 63 (1966).

129. Legal scholars, having a traditionally greater interest in judicial institutions, have been particularly aware of two aspects of political scientists' researches into courts: (1) One is the inquiry into "impact" of Supreme Court decisions. See Wasby, The U.S. Supreme Court's Impact, 49 Notre Dame Law. 1023 (1974); Becker & Feeley, ed., The Impact of Supreme Court Decisions (1973); Wasby, The Impact of the U.S. Supreme Court (1970); Symposium, Impact of Supreme Court Decisions, 23 J. Legal Ed. 77 (1970); Everson, ed., The Supreme Court As Policy Maker: Three Studies On the Impact of Judicial Decisions (1968); *cf.* Rabin, Impact Analysis and Tort Law, 13 L. & Socy. Rev. 987 (1979). (2) The other is the mathematicized or computerized analyses and predictions of appellate (particularly Supreme Court) decisions. These studies, which are still pursued from time to time, had flourished mainly in the 1960s. See, e.g., the rounding up of studies in Goldman, Behavioral Approaches to Judicial Decisionmaking, 11 Jurimetrics J. 142 (1971); Grossman & Tannenhaus, eds., Frontiers of Judicial Research (1969); Symposium, Social Science Approaches to Judicial Decisionmaking, 79 Harv. L. Rev. 1551 (1966). See also Schubert, The Judicial Mind (1965); Schubert, Judicial Behavior (1964) and most of the articles in Symposium, Jurimetrics, 28 Law & Contemp. Prob. 1 (1963). As-

recent years, growing attention has been paid to statistical analysis and probability theory for establishing facts, making predictions, and shaping legal policy judgment.[130]

Probably the most active and fruitful interdisciplinary area in the last few decades has been that of law-sociology. "Sociological jurisprudence" had been one of the banners under which the eminent legal scholar, Roscoe Pound, marched in the first decade or so of this century; and though some bold legal spirits, including "legal realists" of the 1930s, marched to the same general tune, the sociolegal research output was sparse. The two decades after World War II produced much more — for instance, valuable large-scale research efforts into jury operations, judicial administration, police practices, and compensation in auto accident cases, some of which studies have been cited in Chapter 1. Interest in sociolegal empirical research mounted sufficiently to justify the founding in the mid-1960s of the leading journal in the field, the *Law and Society Review*. Surveys at that time showed an

---

sumptions made by these studies about judicial behavior have been attacked. See, e.g., Friendly, Of Voting Blocs, And Cabbages and Kings, 42 U. Cin. L. Rev. 673 (1973); Howard, On the Fluidity of Judicial Choice, 62 Am. Pol. Sci. Rev. 43 (1968); Mermin, Computers, Law and Justice, 1967 Wis. L. Rev. 43, 72-87; Fuller, An Afterword: Science and the Judicial Process, 79 Harv. L. Rev. 1604 (1966); Stone, Man and Machine in the Search For Justice, 16 Stan. L. Rev. 515 (1964); Becker, Political Behavioralism and Modern Jurisprudence (1964). Some who have themselves made mathematicized analyses have also acknowledged their deficiencies in predictive power. See Spaeth, Supreme Court Policy Making: Explanation and Prediction 140-173 (1979); Kort, Simultaneous Equations and Boolean Algebra, 28 Law & Contemp. Prob. 143, 161 (1963).

130. Fisher, Multiple Regression in Legal Proceedings, 80 Colum. L. Rev. 702 (1980); Finkelstein, The Judicial Reception of Multiple Regression Studies in Race and Sex Discrimination Cases, 80 Colum. L. Rev. 737 (1980); Symposium, 55 Ind. L. Rev. 493 (1980); Book Review, 89 Yale L.J. 601 (1980); Kaye, The Laws of Probability and the Law of the Land, 47 U. Chi. L. Rev. 34 (1979); Underwood, Law and the Crystal Ball: Predicting Behavior With Statistical Inference and Individualized Judgment, 88 Yale L.J. 1408 (1979); Lermack, No Right Number? Social Science Research and the Jury-Size Cases; 54 N.Y.U.L. Rev. 951 (1979); Finkelstein, Quantitative Methods In Law: Studies In the Application of Mathematical Probability and Statistics To Legal Problems (1978); Brilmayer & Kornhauser, Review: Quantitative Methods and Legal Decisions, 46 U. Chi. L. Rev. 116 (1978); Nagel & Neef, Legal Policy Analysis (1977); *id.*, The Legal Process: Modeling The System (1977); Lempert, Uncovering "Nondiscernible" Differences: Empirical Research and the Jury-Size Cases, 73 Mich. L. Rev. 643 (1975); Zeisel & Diamond, "Convincing Empirical Evidence" On the Six Member Jury, 41 U. Chi. L. Rev. 281 (1974); Johnson & Tersine, The Mathematical Evaluation of Trial versus Settlement, Case and Comment, Jan./Feb., 1973; Zeisel, . . . And Then There Were None: The Diminution of the Federal Jury, 38 U. Chi. L. Rev. 710 (1971): Finkelstein & Fairley, A Bayesian Approach to Identification Evidence, 83 Harv. L. Rev. 489 (1970), responded to by Tribe, Trial By Mathematics: Precision and Ritual in the Legal Process, 84 Harv. L. Rev. 1329 (1971), followed by further exchanges at 84 Harv. L. Rev. 1801 & 1810; Annot., Admissibility in Criminal Case of Statistical or Mathematical Evidence Offered For Purpose of Showing Probabilities, 36 A.L.R.3d 1194 (1970); Kaplan, Decision Theory and the Factfinding Process, 20 Stan. L. Rev. 1065 (1968).

impressive amount and variety of existing empirical studies.[131] They have been abundantly supplemented since then in the pages of the *Review* and, to a lesser extent, of other legal and sociological journals. Substantial treatises, theoretical studies, and collections of essays have also been published both before[132] and since[133] this journal's establishment.

The University of Chicago Law School began publishing in 1972 a journal devoted to "the application of scientific methods to the study of the legal system" (*Journal of Legal Studies*) and welcoming contributions from all social sciences.

Predominant in these contributions have been those from economists and others interested in economic analysis. Their studies

131. Skolnick, The Sociology of Law in America — Overview and Trends (in Law and Society Supplement to the Summer 1965 issue of Social Problems); Auerbach, Legal Tasks for the Sociologist, 1 Law & Socy. Rev. 91 (1966); Skolnick, Social Research and Legality — A Reply to Auerbach, 1 Law & Socy. Rev. 105 (1966). Some other journals devoting themselves to law and society are: International Journal for the Sociology of Law, British Journal of Law and Society, European Yearbook of Law and Sociology, Research in Law and Sociology (annual volume beginning 1978).

132. Jones, A View From the Bridge (in Law and Society Supplement to Summer 1965 issue of Social Problems); Davis, Foster, Jeffery & Davis, Society and the Law (1962); Evan, Law and Sociology (1962); Rheinstein, ed., Max Weber on Law in Economy and Society (trans. Shils & Rheinstein 1954); Ehrlich, Fundamental Principles of the Sociology of Law (trans. Moll 1936); Llewellyn, Some Realism About Realism, 44 Harv. L. Rev. 1222 (1931); Pound, Scope and Purpose of Sociological Jurisprudence, 24 Harv. L. Rev. 591 (1911) and 25 *id.* at 140; 189 (1912).

133. Symposium, Contemporary Issues in Law and Social Science, 14 Law & Socy. Rev. 429 (1980); Abel, Redirecting Social Studies of Law, 14 Law & Socy. Rev. 805 (1980); Evan, ed., The Sociology of Law (1980); Burman & Harrell-Bond, eds., The Imposition of Law (1979); Griffiths, Is Law Important, 54 N.Y.U.L. Rev. 339 (1979); Macaulay, Lawyers and Consumer Protection Laws, 14 Law & Socy. Rev. 115 (1979); Handler, Social Movements and the Legal System (1978); Johnson, ed., Social System and Legal Process (1978); Thorne, The Impartial Jury and the Social Sciences, 5 J. Contemp. L. 43 (1978); Abel, Comparative Law and Social Theory (1978); Friedman & Macaulay, eds., Law and the Behavioral Sciences (2d ed. 1977); Hammett, ed., Social Anthropology and Law (1977); Sarat, Studying American Legal Culture: An Assessment of Survey Evidence, 11 Law & Socy. Rev. 427 (1977); See 1977 publications of Nagel & Neef, *supra* n.130; Unger, Law in Modern Society: Toward A Criticism of Social Theory (1976); Black, The Behavior of Law (1976); Feeley, The Concept of Laws In Social Science, 10 Law & Socy. Rev. 497 (1976); Friedman, The Legal System: A Social Science Perspective (1975); Podgórecki, Law and Society (1974); Symposium, Law and Social Science Research, 52 N.C.L. Rev. 974 (1974); Zeisel, Reflections On Experimental Techniques in the Law, 2 J. Legal Stud. 107 (1973); Black & Mileski, ed., The Social Organization of Law (1973); Rehbinder, The Development and Present State of Fact Research in Law in the United States, 24 J. Legal Ed. 567 (1972); Schwartz & Skolnick, Society and the Legal Order (1970); Aubert, ed., Sociology of Law (1969); Simon, ed., The Sociology of Law (1968); Kalven, The Quest For the Middle Range: Empirical Inquiry and Legal Policy, in Hazard, ed., Law in a Changing America 56 (1968); Stone, Social Dimensions of Law and Justice (1966); Stone, Law and the Social Sciences (1966); Macaulay, Law and the Balance of Power: The Automobile Manufacturers and Their Dealers (1966); Sawer, Law in Society (1965).

augmented other works with an economic focus on law,[134] including a pioneering work by the *Journal*'s editor, applying the distinctive approach of an economist throughout most of the law's fields.[135] The approach has engendered a lively literature of controversy.[136]

Incomplete though this picture of the expanding scope of socio-legal research may be, it is enough to make my point — the same point Cardozo made in a 1930 speech to lawyers: "Nothing in the whole realm of knowledge but is grist for our mill."[137] Holmes more than once expressed a similar view. In an 1897 speech to Boston University law students, he said: "For the rational study of the law, the black-letter man may be the man of the present, but the man of the future is the man of statistics and the master of economics."[138] Again, an 1886

134. The Journal of Law and Economics, published by the University of Chicago since 1957, is the richest single source, and the International Review of Law and Economics began publication in England in 1981; but see the voluminous literature cited in Samuels, Law and Economics: A Bibliographical Survey, 1965-1972, 66 Law Libr. J. 96 (1973); id., "Legal-Economic Policy: A Bibliographical Survey," 58 Law Lib. J. 230 (1965). These bibliographies include books as well as articles in the law journals of the law schools (currently more than 200 journals) and the miscellaneous economic and other social science journals. In years past, the legal scholar's concern with economics was confined to such fields as antitrust, business regulation, taxation, and corporations, in which the economic theories and economic facts were palpably relevant. Nowadays, one finds a good deal of writing on economic theory and economic fact in fields like judicial administration, tort (including economic aspects of accidents involving automobiles and defective products, theories of negligence and strict liability), contract law and contract damages, property law (including personal and real property, zoning, property restrictions in the interest of environment improvement), criminal law (including procedure and disposition of offenders), and areas of constitutional law, like "equal protection."

135. Posner, The Economic Analysis of Law (1st ed. 1973; 2d ed. 1977). See also Hirsch, Law and Economics (1979).

136. Symposium, Change in the Common Law: Legal and Economic Perspectives, 9 J. Legal Ed. 189 (1980); Symposium, Efficiency As A Legal Concern, 8 Hofstra L. Rev. 485 (1980); Interchanges between Kelman and Spitzer and Hoffman, in 52 S. Calif. L. Rev. 669 (1979) and 53 *id.* at 1187, 1215 (1980); Carroll, Two Games That Illustrate Some Problems Concerning Economic Analysis of Legal Problems, 53 *id.* at 1371 (1980); Coleman, Efficiency, Exchange and Auction: Philosophic Aspects of the Economic Approach to Law, 68 Calif. L. Rev. 221 (1980); Posner, Utilitarianism, Economics and Legal Theory, 8 J. Legal Studies 103 (1979); Schwartz, Economics, Wealth Distribution, and Justice, 1979 Wis. L. Rev. 799; Michelman, Norms and Normativity in the Economic Theory of Law, 62 Minn. L. Rev. 1015 (1978); Minda, The Lawyer-Economist At Chicago: Richard A. Posner and the *Economic Analysis of Law*, 39 Ohio St. L.J. 415 (1978); Krier, Book Review, 122 U. Pa. L. Rev. 1664 (1974); Leff, Economic Analysis of Law: Some Realism About Nominalism, 60 Va. L. Rev. 451 (1974); Buchanan, Good Economics — Bad Law, *id.* at 483; Lovett, Economic Analysis and Its Role In Legal Education, 26 J. Legal Ed. 385 (1974); Polinsky, Economic Analysis As A Potentially Defective Product: A Buyer's Guide To Posner's *Economic Analysis of Law*, 87 Harv. L. Rev. 1655 (1974); Samuels, The Coase Theorem and the Study of Law and Economics, 14 Natl. Resources J. 1 (1974).

137. Cardozo, The Home of the Law, in Hall, ed., Selected Writings of Benjamin Cardozo 405, 408 (1947).

138. Holmes, Collected Legal Papers 187 (1920). The black-letter reference is to the darker type in which important legal rules may appear in some legal texts.

speech to Harvard undergraduates reminded them that "a man may live greatly in the law as well as elsewhere; that there as well as elsewhere his thought may find its unity in an infinite perspective. . . . If your subject is law, the roads are plain to anthropology, the science of man, to political economy, the theory of legislation, ethics, and thus by several paths to your final view of life. . . . To be master of any branch of knowledge, you must master those which lie next to it. . . ."[139]

3. In this perspective, law's interconnections with other disciplines cannot be limited to social science. Jurisprudence or legal philosophy has not only its law-in-society phase, but also its "analytical" (law's relation to language, logic, conceptual analysis, system, decisional process)[140] and "ethical" (law and values)[141] dimensions. In that same

139. *Id.* at 30.

140. See the continuing series of "Nomos" volumes issued by the American Society for Political and Legal Philosophy, analyzing key legal-political concepts, ranging from topics like Authority (1958) and Rational Decision (1964) and Equality (1967) to the most recent Property (1980) and Human Rights (1981); Raz, The Concept of a Legal System (2d ed. 1980); Golding, Legal Reasoning (1980); Harris, Law and Legal Science (1979); Raz, The Authority of Law (1979); MacCormick, Legal Reasoning and Legal Theory (1978); Hacker & Raz, Law, Morality and Society (1977); Dworkin, Taking Rights Seriously (1977); Simpson, ed., Oxford Essays in Jurisprudence (2d series, 1973); Summers, ed., More Essays in Legal Philosophy (1971); Hubien, Legal Reasoning (Brussels, 1971); Hughes, ed., Law, Reason, and Justice (1969); Summers, ed., Essays in Legal Philosophy (1968); Gottlieb, The Logic of Choice (1968); Kelsen, Pure Theory of Law (1967); Stone, Legal System and Lawyers' Reasonings (1964); Hart, The Concept of Law (1962); Wasserstrom, The Judicial Decision (1961); Guest, ed., Oxford Essays in Jurisprudence (1st series, 1961); Llewellyn, The Common Law Tradition (1960); Levi, An Introduction to Legal Reasoning (1948; Phoenix ed. 1961); Kantorowicz, The Definition of Law (1958); Allen, Law in the Making (6th ed. 1958); M. R. Cohen, Reason and Law (1950); *id.*, Law and the Social Order (1933); Frank, Law and the Modern Mind (1930; Anchor ed. 1963); Cardozo, Nature of Judicial Process (1921); Holmes, Collected Legal Papers (1920); Hohfeld, Fundamental Legal Conceptions As Applied in Judicial Reasoning (1919).

141. Kamenka & Tay, eds., Justice (1980); Finnis, Natural Law and Natural Rights (1980); Grey, The Legal Enforcement of Morality (1980); Bodenheimer, Philosophy of Responsibility (1980); Feinberg, Rights, Justice, and the Bounds of Liberty (1980); Ackerman, Social Justice and the Liberal State (1980); Symposium on Law and Morality, 1980 B.Y.U.L. Rev. 721; Hart, Utilitarianism and Natural Rights, 53 Tulane L. Rev. 663 (1979); Stoljar, Moral and Legal Reasoning (1979); Leiser, Liberty, Justice, and Morals (2d ed. 1979); Rostow, The Ideal in Law (1978); Richards, The Moral Criticism of Law (1977); Pennock & Chapman, eds., The Limits of Law (Nomos 15) (1975); Hughes, The Conscience of the Courts (1975); Nozick, Anarchy, State and Utopia (1974); Lasswell & McDougal, Criteria For A Theory About Law, 44 S. Calif. L. Rev. 362 (1971); Rawls, A Theory of Justice (1971); Pennock & Chapman, eds., Political and Legal Obligation (Nomos 12) (1970); Feinberg, Doing and Deserving (1970); Fuller, The Morality of Law (2d ed. 1969); Freund, On Law and Justice (1968); Devlin, The Enforcement of Morals (1965); Stone, Human Law and Human Justice (1965); Friedrich & Chapman, eds., Justice (Nomos 6) (1963); Shuman, Legal Positivism (1963); Hart, Law, Liberty and Morality (1963); Perelman, The Idea of Justice and the Problem of Argument (1963); Cohen, ed., The Legal Conscience (1960); Cahn, The Sense of Injustice (1949);

1897 speech, Holmes, after calling jurisprudence "a study which is sometimes undervalued by the practical-minded," went on to defend it in nonpractical terms as well:

> We cannot all be Descartes or Kant, but we all want happiness. And happiness, I am sure from having known many successful men, cannot be won simply by being counsel for great corporations and having an income of fifty thousand dollars. An intellect great enough to win the prize needs other food besides success. The remoter and more general aspects of the law are those which give it universal interest. It is through them that you not only become a great master in your calling, but connect your subject with the universe and catch an echo of the infinite, a glimpse of its unfathomable process, a hint of the universal law.[142]

Most of us who study law and the legal system, in or out of the legal profession, may not tread all the paths that beckon, or hear the "echo" that Holmes heard. But for many it will be true that the study of law and the legal system, if I may alter a Baconian aphorism, "maketh a full person."

Garlan, Legal Realism and Justice (1941); F. S. Cohen, Ethical Systems and Legal Ideals (1933).

Some of the works in either nn. 140 or 141 could readily be cited in both footnotes. Nor does either footnote purport to present a complete coverage or to include collections of annotated Readings, such as Cohen & Cohen, Readings in Jurisprudence and Legal Philosophy (Schuchman ed. 1979); Lloyd, Introduction to Jurisprudence (4th ed. 1979); Christie, Jurisprudence (1973). Nor does either footnote cover those texts or treatises that are surveys of sociological *and* analytical *and* ethical jurisprudence or parts of them, such as Golding, Philosophy of Law (1975); Bodenheimer, Jurisprudence (rev. ed. 1974); Hall, Foundations of Jurisprudence (1973); Friedmann, Legal Theory (5th ed. 1967); Hook, ed., Law and Philosophy (1964); Pound, Jurisprudence (5 vol., 1959); Patterson, Jurisprudence (1953); Stone, Province and Function of Law (1946) (later revised into three independent volumes, each of which is cited in the appropriate place in nn. 133, 140 & 141 above).

142. Holmes, Collected Legal Papers 202 (1920).

Appendix 1

Tips on Some Mechanics of Law Study

A. Summarizing Assigned Cases

Most law school textbooks reprint the full or partial text of a good many court opinions — typically, appellate court opinions. As a student, you have to make summaries or "briefs" of the assigned cases. (The term "brief" is also used to refer to the printed argument that a lawyer files with a court.) These summaries are useful for you in the class discussion of the cases and in studying for examinations. Moreover, your understanding of the case is enhanced by your putting the important features of it down on paper in your own words. The process reveals gaps and other aspects of the case of which you would otherwise remain unaware. And it is a bread-and-butter process that a practicing lawyer engages in constantly, for which his skills should be sharpened in law school.

What then should a brief of a case look like? I submit below a sample brief, based on the court of appeals opinions in the *Nappier* case. (You can look again at the opinions, reproduced in the first section of Chapter 2 above (under **A4**). The facts of the case are reproduced in the district court opinion, under **A3**.) The letter P is used below to designate plaintiff, and the letter D to designate defendant.

NAPPIER v. JEFFERSON STANDARD LIFE INSURANCE CO.
322 F.2d 502 (4th Cir. 1963)

Damage action for privacy violation through TV broadcast.

Facts:

S.C. Stat.: Misdemeanor to publish in newspaper, magazine, or other publication, "name" of female victim of actual or alleged rape, or assault with intent to ravish.

Complaint allegations: The two young women Ps taught dental hygiene in S.C. public schools, using a traveling puppet show involving puppet called "Little Jack," and a state-furnished station wagon bearing prominent inscription: "Little Jack, Dental Division, S.C. State Dept. of Health."

Someone raped Ps at their Kingstree motel and fled with their station wagon, which was found abandoned later that day. D broadcasting co. in two newscasts that day showed pictures of station wagon revealing above inscription and license number, with announcer identifying wagon as "that used by the two young women who had been attacked in Kingstree."

Throughout the state, Ps were spoken of as "The Little Jack Girls." As a result of the broadcasts they became generally known in the state as the victims of the crime, to their embarrassment and humiliation, and in violation of their right of privacy.

Motion to dismiss for failure to state claim on which relief can be granted.

Dist. Ct.: grants motion.

Issues:

On basis of fact allegations of complaint, did D's broadcasts violate Ps' privacy under S.C. law?

Held (2 to 1):

Yes — under S.C. common law "as fortified by the statute." Reversed and remanded for trial the truth of the allegations (Did D *in fact* "name," i.e., identify, Ps?)

Reasoning:

1. The statutory prohibition against publication of "name" prohibits published *identification* of rape victim rather than merely publication of *proper name.*

   a. Only this interpretation would serve statutory purpose of protecting rape victims from publicity and encouraging them to report the crime to police.
   b. The narrower interpretation: (1) isn't required by fact that statute is penal. That fact "does not require an interpretation so rigid as to strip its wording of its plain connotation" — especially since statute here is being used not in penal suit but to help provide civil redress; (2) isn't required by fact that similar statutes of some other states use "identity" instead of or in addition to "name." "Name" alone can also be enough.
   c. Cases on defamation show that an identifying description can be the equivalent of a name: "A libelee is nonetheless libeled though his name be not mentioned."
   d. Cases under statutes prohibiting unauthorized use of personal name, portrait, or picture in advertising are not analogous: in advertising, "only the name, pseudonym or picture of the person — usually because of his prominence — is significant. Any other description is of no value."

2. Ps *can recover* for privacy violation *"under the common law as fortified by the statute."*

   a. S.C. recognizes a common law right of privacy — including "the publicizing of one's private affairs with which the public has no legitimate concern, or the wrongful intrusion into one's private activities, in such manner as to outrage or cause mental suffering, shame or humiliation to a person of ordinary sensibilities."
   b. The exemption from such common law liability in cases of news reporting of "matters of public concern and record" does not apply here because of the statute. "The statute states an exception to the exemption. No matter the news value, S.C. has unequivocally declared the identity of the injured person shall not be made known in press or broadcast."

3. No constitutional issue has been raised.

Dissent:

1. Statute does not apply: word "name," even on liberal construction, is not equivalent of "identity."

If S.C. legislature had identity in mind, would have used that word, as Wis. legislature did.

2. Under S.C. common law of privacy, exception for "publication of matter of public concern and record" applies here.

A brief of a case does not always have the same form, though some features are pretty standard, such as the full name of the case and citation (first three lines of the above brief) and an introductory capsule phrase to orient you in the legal field and situation when you start reading the brief (fourth line). Under the *Facts* heading, it would not be typical to have a "complaint allegations" subheading, because the typical appellate opinion recites as facts not those alleged in the complaint but those that have been found by the lower court on the basis of the evidence, and are either uncontested on appeal or if accepted have been contested by the appellate court. Here there was no evidence at any trial, since the defendants had moved to dismiss, and for purposes of that motion the factual allegations of the complaint are assumed to be true.

Another point: There will be times when you want to write not a full brief but a shorter version, which might omit the reasoning and telescope the facts, issues, and holding into one or two sentences. Such a brief for the *Nappier* court of appeals decision might be something like this:

> *Held:* (1) S.C. crim. prohib. vs. publishing rape victim's "name" was meant to include prohib. vs. identification without use of her proper name — hence where D's TV broadcast showed picture of victims' auto with license no. and prominent inscription, "Little Jack, Dental Div. S.C. State Dept. of Health" (they being known as "Little Jack Girls" in their travels to pub. schools of state with show featuring "Little Jack" puppet), this violated stat. (2) In victims' c/law dam. suit for privacy viol., fact that this stat. prohibited D's conduct eliminated c/law defense

in terms of reporting matters of legitim. pub. concern and record. *Dismissal of complaint reversed.*

Even in this shorter version, you will note that I have included some very specific facts about the particular case. It would not have been sufficient, for instance, to stop before the dash and omit the "hence" clause. To do so would communicate the thought that identification of some kind would fulfill the statutory purpose, but would omit the specific contribution of this case to the determination of what constitutes sufficient identification. It is true that a subsequent court faced with a different form and different area of alleged identification may read the fact categories of this precedent "broadly," and treat it in terms of a precedent for all forms of alleged identification (however different from this type of TV picture) and for any area of alleged identification (no matter how much smaller than the statewide area here). But this is up to the subsequent court, not you. When you are briefing a case, you are not engaged in predicting how broadly a subsequent court will read it. You are treating the fact categories *narrowly*. It is your record of precisely what happened in this case.

A final admonition to remember about briefing is this: do not brief the case as you go along in your first reading. Read the opinion all the way through first. Some complex cases you will have to read more than once. And in your reading it will be profitable to stop a moment after you have grasped the facts and issues, and before the court starts giving its solution to the problem. You might ask yourself at that point what strikes you as a wise solution. Of course sometimes your reaction will not be worth much, especially if the whole subject matter is entirely new to you. But at other times it can be valuable, by making possible an original, imaginative response to the problem instead of letting you fall into the easy groove of the court's thinking.

Assume now that you have briefed a case. The next step is *not* to turn to the next case assigned for briefing. Instead you are expected to do some thinking about the case you have just briefed. Consider whether you agree with the court's reasoning; if not, why not? Does it commit any logical fallacies? Has the opinion distorted what a precedent said or held (assuming you are familiar with the precedent)? Does the result violate your feelings of justice or fairness? Do the probable social consequences of the decision seem desirable? Could the losing attorney have done (or argued) better?

Further, consider how the case stacks up with any prior assigned cases in the same section of the book. Is it consistent with them? Is it distinguishable? What aspect of the general problem in that section is *added* by this case? You see, the cases in a particular section of the book are related to each other in a special way. After all, on the subject of any particular section — let us say, "contributory negligence" — there are thousands of cases in existence, and the editor has selected perhaps only four. Why these four? Perhaps the first one lays out the whole problem in an effective way, together with the historical background. Perhaps the second one illustrates an exception to, or limitation upon, the contributory negligence principle, such as the "last clear chance" doctrine. Perhaps the third one presents a borderline situation to which the doctrine has never been applied before but to which it might reasonably be so applied if the court desired. Perhaps the fourth shows the changes that a statute has made in the common law on the subject. Some perspective will be gained on the assigned cases, making you more ready for class discussion, if you have asked: Why is this case here? What does it add?

Still more understanding of the problem of an assigned case or group of cases may be achieved by consulting a treatise on the problem. Thus, reading the discussion of contributory and comparative negligence by Prosser,[1] or by Harper and James,[2] is very likely to enhance your understanding of the subject and of the assigned cases on it. This reading of a treatise, or of relevant law-review articles cited in the casebook, is a much-neglected final step in properly doing the assignment and preparing for class. In case you do not have time to devote such effort to a particular assignment, make a note to do it at some later point when time is more free.

Another method you will find very helpful is a group discussion, with a few of your fellow students, of the problems in a section of the course that has just been completed. If every participant prepares an outline of that section (based on his case briefs, his reading of treatises and articles, and his class notes), you are likely to find the discussion highly rewarding.

I should not have to add, finally, that there is *no painless substitute* for the process I have outlined of briefing the cases, critically evaluating them, and reading and thinking about what the scholars have said about them. It is incredible but true that a certain percentage of students every year is deluded into thinking that an equivalent training in the study of cases can be obtained by simply buying and reading ready-made briefs that someone else has written, sometimes accompanied by comments thereon that some usually anonymous nonscholar (paid on a piecework basis) has ground out. For a future lawyer, this makes just about as much sense as it would for a football team member, expecting to play in an upcoming game, to avoid the practice sessions, allowing a proxy to participate in his place and getting a written report on the sessions from his proxy.

B. Classwork

What are you expected to do in class? First of all, there is a lot that goes on in class that you will want a record of. Your memory alone will not be good enough. But of course it has to be a critical kind of note-taking, a "sifting and winnowing." You will want to jot down not only the significant ideas (a good many will not be) from the other side of the lectern, including significant questions that may remain unanswered, but also the ideas and questions that a classmember may express, and those that occur to you during the discussion.

Secondly, it will benefit you to participate orally in the discussion — by volunteering answers to questions, by asking questions, and by taking issue

1. Prosser, Handbook of the Law of Torts 416-439 (4th ed. 1972).
2. Harper & James, The Law of Torts, chaps. 22 and 23 (1956) and 1968 Supp.

with expressed ideas with which you disagree. Let me tell you a story about the importance of class work.

More than thirty years ago, I was teaching at the University of Oklahoma Law School in Norman, when a black woman applied for admission and was rejected because of her race, pursuant to state law. In an injunction suit to compel her admission to the law school at Norman, the NAACP lawyers (who included, among others, the present Supreme Court Justice Thurgood Marshall) rounded up a parade of prominent legal educators as witnesses. There was Dean Griswold of Harvard, Dean Harrison of Pennsylvania, Professor Max Radin of California, Professor Charles Bunn of Wisconsin, Professor Walter Gellhorn of Columbia, and perhaps others I cannot remember. They all knew that the state, if required to offer the woman applicant a legal education, would offer it on a racially *separate* basis (with few if any fellow students) — as indeed the state formally offered to do after the first Supreme Court opinion in the litigation.[3] And so a striking emphasis in these witnesses' testimony was on the importance, in legal education, of having a large number of fellow students. The importance was that of experiencing the *different viewpoints* that can be held on the same set of facts by people of varying backgrounds and temperaments. It is an experience that develops an awareness of or sensitivity to the latent richness in any given set of facts — like the variations in sparkle created by turning a gem slightly so as to reflect the light differently.

The same point can be seen by comparing the majority and dissenting opinions in some cases: you read the majority opinion and you are convinced; you read the dissent with its divergent slant on the facts — e.g., a different emphasis, or a pointing up of some facts' significance or some reason or argument that was neglected by the majority — and you change your mind completely. Another illustration of the hidden complexities or ambiguities in a set of facts is this: A professor preparing for class may read the same case for the sixth year, and in that reading may see significances that he did not see in any of his prior readings.

By not hesitating to express yourself in class, you not only improve your skill in oral discourse but you contribute to the development in the whole class of a sensitivity to (1) the varying interpretations that may be put on facts, and (2) the varying types of arguments that are possible for the ultimate decision on such facts. The practicing lawyer has to have this sensitivity when he listens to the facts of a client's story, and has to interpret them, relate them to a number of possible conceptual categories, and possible legal arguments pro and con.

Not surprisingly, such a sensitivity or flexibility is primarily what is called for in answering questions on the typical law examinations. An example is given below.

3. The first opinion is Sipuel v. University of Oklahoma 332 U.S. 631 (1948). The second is Fisher v. Hurst, 333 U.S. 147 (1948). For a description of the litigation, see Kluger, Simple Justice 258-260 (1976). In the second decision, the Supreme Court for technical reasons refused to declare that a state plan of this sort was evading the mandate in the Court's first decision requiring a legal education for her in conformity with the equal protection clause. Eventually, however, she was admitted to and graduated from the University of Oklahoma Law School in Norman.

C. Law Examinations

Law examinations take various forms. Occasionally there will be an "objective" question (true-false or multiple-choice) in which primarily the scope of your information is being tested. Occasionally, also, some "short answer" questions may be included that may call for information or for something more. The typical question, however, is the "problem" question. This gives the facts of a concrete situation, and expects you to find the issues and deal intelligently with those issues in the light of what you have learned about legal treatment of apparently similar issues. You may be asked to decide the issues, as judge. Or you may be asked to argue one side of the case, for plaintiff or defendant. (The question I shall present below asks you to argue for the defendant-appellant.) The examination may or may not be "open book." And it is not usually a "take-home."

The person reading your examination will start "climbing the walls" if he or she finds you talking all around the issues, spouting all the law that you have memorized on a particular subject and hoping that some of it will seem relevant to the reader. You are expected to confine yourself to law drawn from reasonably similar concrete situations. Your task is first to spot the issues, in all the areas of the problem in which controversy is reasonably possible. Your next task is to indicate the legal principles that might be applied to those areas, by showing the respects in which the policies underlying existing rules or doctrines in apparently similar situations would or would not apply. If you are asked to play the advocate's role, you try consistently to handle those rules and doctrines in a way that puts the best face possible (without intellectual dishonesty) on your side. If you are asked to be a judge, you must not make the mistake of leaving the solution hanging. You must take the plunge and decide the case, indicating why you think the considerations favoring one side outweigh those favoring the other.

I am going to set forth a situation which I once used on an examination. It is relatively simple but calls for some of the skills I have been talking about as well as for skill in logical organization of one's total material. I will follow it with a suggested answer. You would need to have a certain amount of legal education under your belt before you could give an answer like the one suggested. Still, the Chapter 3 material on statutes, together with your common sense, will enable you to anticipate much of the answer. Please think about the problem before you read the suggested answer.

PROBLEM

The "Condemnation" chapter of a state statute book included this provision: "§100. If it be desired at any time to establish a cemetery . . . or to enlarge any such already established, and the title to land needed cannot otherwise be acquired, land sufficient for the purpose may be condemned . . . [etc.]."

Subsequently there was added to the "Zoning" chapter of the same book a provision, effective June 1, 1940, reading: "§5. No cemetery shall be established within 250 yards of any house, home, hotel, inn, or other structure without the consent of the owner. . . . Violations of this section may be prosecuted as misdemeanors, and shall be enjoined at the suit of said owner. . . ."

Fairlawn Cemetery Corp., needing to enlarge its cemetery, has acquired a large tract of wooded land, through condemnation proceedings. The boundary of this tract is 200 yards from Mr. Will Full's property — the Heavenly Foods Grocery Store, which is a one-story affair, with a back room in which he sleeps and sometimes prepares meals. On May 15, 1940, Fairlawn commenced to improve, cultivate, and stake out the tract in contemplation of cemetery operations within it; and the workers so engaged would habitually purchase groceries from Mr. Full for their noontime lunches, joshing him about how much shorter his funeral ride was now going to be, etc.

On July 15, 1940, Mr. Will Burry introduces himself to Mr. Full as being the president of Fairlawn, and says to Mr. Full: "We trust you don't object to these expansion operations of ours." Mr. Full brusquely replies, "You should put your trust in God. I've got you dead to rights." In short, he soon sues to enjoin the operations. He claims that the zoning statute was violated and that it is therefore the court's duty to issue an injunction against the use of the newly acquired tract for a cemetery.

You are the attorney for Fairlawn. Outline, in logically coherent fashion, all the arguments that should go into your brief, in opposition to Will Full's position.

SUGGESTED ANSWER

1. *There Was No Violation of the Zoning Law.*

a. *The zoning law should be presumed to be prospective.*

Hence, it should not apply at all to a case in which the property is already acquired and preliminary operations have already begun.

Supporting this conclusion are the following considerations:

(1) There is a well-known *presumption* that substantive, as distinguished from procedural, statutes operate *prospectively* only.[4] This is to avoid an unduly harsh impact of a retroactive requirement — which is precisely what would be involved here, since Fairlawn had already bought, improved, and cultivated the tract prior to the June 1 effective date of the zoning law.

(2) Another established principle is that if reasonably possible a court should choose, of two alternative statutory constructions, the construction that *avoids a constitutional doubt.*[5] To construe the zoning statute as retroactively affecting Fairlawn's pre-June enlargement activities would raise a constitutional doubt as to its validity under the due process clause.[6] Further, the facts show that Fairlawn was

4. See Chap. 1 *supra* at 128.
5. See Chap. 3 *supra* at 263.
6. See *supra,* n.4.

acting pursuant to a court judgment in condemnation proceedings permitting use of this new tract for a cemetery — so retroactivity of the zoning statute would be of more dubious validity than if Fairlawn were acting without a court judgment.

b. *Anyway, the zoning law does not apply to "enlargement" operations.*

Note the contrast in language of the two statutes: *"establish"* in the zoning law, and *"establish . . . or enlarge"* in the condemnation law. There is a "pari materia" principle of construction[7] to the effect that statutes on roughly the same subject — here, the subject of land use — should be construed together. Hence it is a reasonable inference that "establish" in the zoning law does not include an enlargement operation. The legislature had in mind, in the zoning law, new cemeteries established thereafter, not old cemeteries enlarged thereafter. (Alternatively, even if "enlargement" operations constitute "establishing," this establishing occurred when the new tract was improved, staked out, etc., so the zoning law would be inapplicable under the retroactivity point, in "a" above.)

c. *The zoning law is further inapplicable because Will Full's property was not a "structure" within the meaning of that law.*

The statutory pattern of specific enumerations followed by a catchall clause ("any house, home, hotel, inn, or other structure") makes relevant the "ejusdem generis" principle of construction.[8] Since all the specific enumerations are used primarily for residence or lodging, the principle would exclude a building that was primarily for selling groceries, with the lodging element a minor or incidental feature.

While such maxims of construction are not controlling, the maxim should be given weight here, where there is nothing strong to rebut it and a particular legislative concern, in this cemetery situation, over *residential* structures would make sense.

d. *The above-urged narrow constructions are particularly appropriate since this is a penal statute.*

The zoning law carries a criminal sanction, and nothing is better established than the principle that criminal statutes are to be strictly or narrowly construed.[9] It is true that this is not a criminal case, but the question whether the statute has been violated by these operations would probably have to be answered the same way in a criminal suit as in this injunction suit.

e. *Even if the zoning law were otherwise applicable in this situation, there was no violation in view of Will Full's "consent."*

The statute's prohibition applies when the owner has not given his "consent." But here it seems that the owner did consent, since he put up no protest for more than two months after gaining knowledge from the workers of what was going on.

2. *Even If the Zoning Law Was Violated, No Injunction Should Issue.*

Will Full argues that because of the violation the court is under a "duty" to issue an injunction. It is true that there is a contextual argument for mandatory issuance — since the statute uses "may" in speaking of the bringing

7. See Chap. 3 *supra* at 245.

8. See Chap. 3 *supra* at 238-239, and discussion of *McBoyle* at 241 and of *Caminetti* and *Alpers* at 245, 246.

9. See Chap. 3 *supra,* at 253, 255.

of criminal prosecutions and "shall" in speaking of the issuance of injunctions.

However, it takes a whole lot to show a legislative purpose to abolish the traditional power of a court of equity to exercise its discretion over whether to issue an injunction. [The Supreme Court so stressed in Hecht Co. v. Bowles, 321 U.S. 321 (1944).] There is no strong reason here, shown in any legislative history or otherwise, to overcome the view that the difference in language was inadvertent. There are many cases, including the *Hecht* case, in which courts have held "shall" to mean "may" in a particular context.[10]

Since, then, a court is still free under the statute to exercise its discretion about issuance of an injunction, it should exercise it here *against* issuance. This could be justified by Will Full's apparent bad faith (one must come into a court of equity with "clean hands") in getting the benefit of the added grocery business while not objecting for over two months.

3. *Even If an Injunction Should Issue, It Should Not Grant the Full Relief Requested.*

Will Full requests an injunction "against the use of the newly acquired tract for a cemetery." He thus seeks to enjoin the use of the whole new tract. Yet the most he is entitled to under the statutory "within 250 yards" requirement is that the *closest 50 yards* (the tract is now within 200 yards of his store) be enjoined from use as a cemetery.

There is another possible, but rather weak, argument under "1" (that there was no violation of the zoning law). It would be premised on the continued availability of the condemnation procedure in spite of the zoning law. It would run like this:

The zoning law did not repeal the authority in the condemnation law to acquire, by condemnation, tracts that "cannot otherwise be acquired." Implied repeals are not favored by the law;[11] the two statutes should be read together in a reconciling way if possible.

So: previously if you wanted to acquire an adjoining tract without condemnation proceedings, all you needed was the tract-owner's agreement; after the zoning law, you have to *also* get agreement of the owner of the "structure" within 250 yards. *If that consent is lacking, the situation would be one of the situations in which title "cannot otherwise be acquired" than by condemnation* within the meaning of the "Condemnation" chapter. So you would proceed to condemn. (Here Fairlawn had already instituted condemnation proceedings and acquired the property; it should be in at least as favorable a position as it would have been in if it had waited to condemn the property *after* Will Full claimed to be refusing his consent.)

Note: The foregoing argument has not been included because it seems weak. It is unlikely that the legislature wanted the zoning provision to be so ineffectual — i.e., allowing the new requirement of owner's consent to be so easily nullified, by condemnation.

10. See Chap. 3 *supra* at 242.
11. See Chap. 3 *supra* at 263 n.72.

Appendix 2

Bill of Rights Protections Against Government Procedures in a Criminal Case

A. *Bill of Rights Protections in General*

You will note from the discussion of the federal Bill of Rights in Chapter 5 (337-338) that practically all of the defendant's procedural protections against the federal government in a federal criminal case apply also to state defendants by way of the Fourteenth Amendment's due process clause. The federal defendant's protections are found in: the Fourth Amendment on unreasonable searches and seizures; in various Fifth Amendment provisions (grand jury indictments required for infamous crimes; no double jeopardy; no compulsory self-incrimination; no deprivation of life, liberty, or property without due process of law); in various Sixth Amendment provisions (the right to a speedy and public trial by jury, to be adequately informed about the accusation, to be confronted by the adverse witnesses, to have compulsory process for obtaining witnesses, and to assistance of counsel); and in the Eighth Amendment's protection against excessive bail, excessive fines, and cruel or unusual punishment.[1]

You should bear in mind not only that these federal constitutional protections are virtually all applicable to state court as well as federal court cases, but that in state cases, a state constitution or statute may offer still broader protection. For example: The Federal Constitution's search and seizure provision (applicable against federal officials, and to

1. The Amendments not covered here, notably the First Amendment (see Bill of Rights text in Chap. 5 at 337-338), are omitted because I am limiting myself to Bill of Rights protections against government procedures in criminal cases.

state officials through the Fourteenth Amendment) has been construed not to preclude an officer's search, with a legitimate search warrant, of the office of a newspaper not reasonably suspected of complicity in a crime, there being probable cause to believe that the fruits, instrumentalities, or evidence of crime were located there.[2] But a state constitution or statute may be interpreted to preclude such a search — as distinct from, say, a subpoena to produce certain documents or things within a specified period. The federal constitutional provision, as interpreted, simply tells us the scope of federal protection against federal and state official conduct; it does not prevent a state from giving greater protection. But if the state attempted to give *less* constitutional protection, e.g., by permitting issuance of warrants on more lenient conditions than those required by the Federal Constitution for warrants, this conflict with the Federal Constitution would invalidate the state constitutional or statutory rule, under the Federal Constitution's Supremacy Clause.[3]

What I propose to do now is impart a brief, general knowledge of the above-enumerated federal constitutional protections. Remember, the decisions that I shall report were not rigid deductions from specific commands in the constitutional language. The constitutional words are often not confining (e.g., "unreasonable" searches and seizures; "due process" of law). Even when the words are specific (e.g., "jury trial"), they have to be interpreted against a background of "original intent" of the framers of the language, an intent that was rarely focused on the specific situation before the court, or was left unclear by the language used.[4] Recourse to broad purposes instead of specific intent will often yield no certain answer as to how the original framers would have responded to the specific situation. Moreover, the traditions of constitutional interpretation include not only the inquiry into

2. Zurcher v. Stanford Daily 436 U.S. 547 (1978).

3. Art. VI, ¶2, U.S. Constitution: "This Constitution, and the laws of the United States which shall be made in pursuance thereof, and all treaties made, or which shall be made, under the authority of the United States, shall be the supreme law of the land; and the judges in every State shall be bound thereby, anything in the Constitution or laws of any State to the contrary notwithstanding."

For general discussion of the contemporary role of state constitutions, with particular reference to filling gaps in federal constitutional protections, see Brennan, State Constitutions and the Protection of Individual Rights, 90 Harv. L. Rev. 489 (1977); Note, 29 Stan. L. Rev. 297 (1977); Comment, 12 Harv. Civ. Rights — Civ. Lib. L. Rev. 63 (1977); Howard, State Courts and Constitutional Rights in the Day of the Burger Court, 62 Va. L. Rev. 873 (1976); Mosk, The State Courts, in Schwartz, ed., American Law: The Third Century 220-228 (1976).

4. Thus, the plurality opinion in Apodaca v. Oregon, 406 U.S. 404, 410 (1972) upholding a state law permitting guilty verdicts by 10 out of 12 jurors in noncapital criminal cases said that "our inability to divine the 'intent of the Framers' . . . requires that in determining what is meant by a jury we must turn to other than purely historical considerations. Our inquiry must focus upon the function served by the jury in contemporary society."

original intent but also other principles. Thus, there is the idea expressed by Holmes to the effect that the "case before us must be considered in the light of our whole experience and not merely in what was said a hundred years ago,"[5] and the similar attitude expressed by Chief Justice Hughes,[6] among others. There is also the judicial use of principles or rules to *implement* the purposes of a constitutional provision, such as the "exclusionary rule" in applying the Fourth Amendment search and seizure provision, or the "Miranda rules" in applying the Fifth Amendment self-incrimination provision — both of which will be treated herein.

In short, while the process of constitutional interpretation has some differences from the process of interpreting statutes or common law rules, a basic similarity is this: Those cases reaching appellate courts (especially the United States Supreme Court) often require a serious grappling with issues of social policy and justice. In the cases I shall report, perhaps the most pervasive policy conflict is that between the requirements of effective crime control and the requirements of fairness to the criminal defendant. Behind the decisions I shall be cryptically summarizing were some earnest judicial efforts to resolve that conflict in a reasonable way.

B. Unreasonable Searches and Seizures (Including Arrests)

1. Arrests

As appears from the language of the Fourth Amendment (see Chap. 5 herein at 337) on "the right of the people to be secure in their persons" against unreasonable searches and seizures, as well as in their "houses, papers and effects," the Amendment includes in its coverage arrests and other unreasonable seizures of the person. Some arrests permitted by statute might be viewed as constitutionally unreasonable

5. Missouri v. Holland, 252 U.S. 416, 433 (1920) and see *supra* n.4.

6. Home Building & Loan Assoc. v. Blaisdell, 290 U.S. 398, 442-443 (1934): "If by the statement that what the Constitution meant at the time of its adoption it means today, it is intended to say that the great clauses of the Constitution must be confined to the interpretation which the framers, with the conditions and outlook of their time would have placed upon them, the statement carries its own refutation. It was to guard against such a narrow conception that Chief Justice Marshall uttered a memorable warning — 'We must never forget that it is a *Constitution* we are expounding . . . a constitution intended to endure for ages to come, and consequently to be adapted to the various crises of human affairs."

seizures of the person. However, there is no such constitutional violation by the typical common law or statutory standard for arrest — namely, that an arrest warrant is, upon sworn application, issued by a magistrate to an officer, only on "probable cause" that the arrestee committed the specified crime; that an officer can make an arrest *without* a warrant when he has reasonable grounds to believe that the arrestee has committed a felony (or when the arrestee has committed a misdemeanor or felony in his presence).[7] But when an arrest is to be made in the arrestee's dwelling, then the Fourth Amendment, said the Court in 1980, in "terms that apply equally to seizures of property and to seizures of persons, . . . has drawn a firm line at the entrance to the house. Absent exigent circumstances, that threshold may not reasonably be crossed without a warrant," despite the existence of probable cause for the arrest.[8] Also, some kinds of temporary "stops" that are not arrests are in some circumstances permissible.[9]

What consequences flow from an officer's arrest that fails to meet the standards? *First,* the fact that defendant was illegally arrested (or even kidnapped and brought to court) does *not* give him a defense to the prosecution, or oust the court of jurisdiction, though perhaps this rule will be changed.[10] *Second,* the arrestee can (with no great hope

7. See U.S. v. Watson, 423 U.S. 411, 416-424 (1976). There are statutory variations. One, for instance, would not attach the "in the presence" requirement to all misdemeanors or in all circumstances. Also, a private person has traditionally been allowed to make a "citizen's arrest" without a warrant when he had reasonable grounds for thinking that in his presence a crime was committed by the arrestee. On arrest generally, see LaFave, Arrest (1966); LaFave, Search and Seizure, §5.1 (1978).

8. Payton v. New York, 445 U.S. 573 (1980). If exigent circumstances do exist (e.g., "hot pursuit," or officer's reasonable belief that evidence would be destroyed or that the offender was expecting the police) they would probably also justify noncompliance with local legal requirements for officers' pre-entry announcement of their office and purpose. See Ker v. California, 374 U.S. 23 (1963); Israel & LaFave, Criminal Procedure 142-144 (3d ed. 1980); LaFave, Search and Seizure, §6.2 (1978). And a warrant for the arrest of A does not authorize the police to enter and search the home of B without a *search* warrant — in the absence of exigent circumstances. Steagald v. U.S., 68 L.Ed.2d 38 (1981).

9. If an officer has reasonable grounds for suspecting that criminal activity is afoot and that the suspect is armed and dangerous, he can, generally speaking, "stop and frisk" without violating the Fourth Amendment. Though there is no warrant and no probable cause to justify a warrantless arrest, and though it is a search and seizure within the meaning of the Amendment, it is not the kind of "unreasonable" search and seizure referred to by the Amendment. Terry v. Ohio, 392 U.S. 1 (1968); Sibron v. New York, 392 U.S. 40 (1968). Some temporary stops or "seizures" for investigative purposes made on reasonable suspicion, though less than probable cause, might also be upheld. See Israel & LaFave, *supra* n.8 at 159-164; LaFave, Search and Seizure, chap. 9 (1978). *Cf.* Brown v. Texas, 443 U.S. 47 (1979). So might stops of autos under some circumstances. Penn. v. Mimms, 434 U.S. 106 (1977). *Cf.* Delaware v. Prouse, 440 U.S. 648 (1978).

10. Ker v. Illinois, 119 U.S. 436 (1886); Frisbie v. Collins, 342 U.S. 519 (1952);

for recovery) sue the arresting officer for damages,[11] and in many jurisdictions has recourse against the governmental unit employing the officer.[12] *Third,* if evidence had been seized without a search warrant, on the established ground that a warrant is unnecessary when a seizure is reasonably incidental to a lawful arrest, then if the arrest was *not* lawful, a warrant was necessary and the seized evidence will have to be excluded from the trial. This last is an aspect of the "exclusionary rule" to be discussed later. The exclusionary rule not only excludes evidence unconstitutionally seized, but also evidence constituting the "fruits" of the seizure as well as the fruits of other unconstitutional procedures, including certain arrests[13] or certain line-up procedures.[14] This "fruits of the poisonous tree" doctrine will also be discussed later.

Gerstein v. Pugh, 420 U.S. 103, 119 (1975). For judicial questioning of whether this rule would still be followed on full consideration by the Supreme Court today, see U.S. v. Toscanino, 500 F.2d 267, 271-276 (2d Cir. 1974). See also LaFave, Search and Seizure, §1.7 (1978).

11. Davis, Administrative Law Treatise, §26.03 (1st ed. 1958); Foote, Tort Remedies for Police Violations of Individual Rights, 39 Minn. L. Rev. 493 (1955). Recovery against the officer is doubtful because juries are more inclined to believe the officer than the victim charged with a crime, and even when they do believe the victim, they are inclined to assess low damages. Furthermore, the officer may well be unable to pay a substantial judgment while the victim is often too poor to undertake the cost of litigation, especially when the prospect of substantial recovery is doubtful. If state or municipal police officers are sued, it is usually under local law. But if the victim claims they violated his federal (typically constitutional) rights, he can sue them under a much-invoked federal statute (42 U.S.C. §1983). See Chap. 2 herein at 182-183; LaFave, Search and Seizure, §1.8 (1978). If the suit is against a *federal* officer, no general statute comparable to 42 U.S.C. §1983 applies, but he may be sued for a tort under local law or, if the injury is to a constitutional right (e.g., arrest or search violating the Fourth Amendment) the suit can be based directly on the Constitution. See Chap. 2 herein at 183; Butz v. Economou, 438 U.S. 478 (1978); Bivens v. Six Unknown Federal Narcotics Agents, 403 U.S. 388 (1971); Carlson v. Green, 446 U.S. 14 (1980) (prison inmate's Eighth Amendment rights were actionable even though the complaint could also support a suit against the United States government under the Federal Tort Claims Act); Annot., 64 L. Ed. 2d 871 (1981).

12. State and local laws allowing suits against the government unit may have exemptions, e.g., for "intentional" torts. Since the 1974 amendments to the Federal Tort Claims Act, the victim can sue the federal government (after first pursuing an administrative remedy) for the conduct of federal enforcement officers that constitutes, under the law of the state involved, false arrest or one of a number of other intentional torts. Under 42 U.S.C. §1983 mentioned in the preceding footnote, where federal rights have been violated, the *municipal government* can be sued if the officer's conduct was implementing a municipal ordinance, regulation, policy statement, decision, or custom. Monell v. Department, Soc. Serv., 436 U.S. 658 (1978). On tort liability of governmental units, see Davis, Administrative Law of the Seventies, chap. 25 & §26.03 (1976).

13. The fruits could be the arrestee's statements closely following, and influenced by, the illegal arrest. See Wong Sun v. U.S., 371 U.S. 471 (1963).

14. The fruits could be an in-court identification by the witness who had identified defendant at the illegal line-up procedure. See U.S. v. Wade, 388 U.S. 218 (1967).

2. Fourth Amendment Coverage; Miscellaneous

We cannot fully explore the interpretations given to the "right of the people to be secure in their persons, houses, papers and effects, against unreasonable searches and seizures." But it should at least be noted that "houses" covers more than residences. The term includes certain other buildings in proximity to a dwelling and such places and things as autos, hotel rooms, and offices, though not jails.[15] In fact, an approach solely in terms of places was rejected when the Supreme Court in the 1967 *Katz* case emphasized that "the Fourth Amendment protects people not places." Hence the Government's eavesdropping on defendant's conversations in a public telephone booth had "violated the privacy upon which he justifiably relied."[16]

There are doctrines to the effect that no unreasonable search and seizure takes place when the property in question is "in plain view," or is "abandoned"; and that seizable property is not confined to instrumentalities, fruits of crime, or contraband but can include "mere evidence" of crime. These doctrines are not easy to apply, and have been complicated by addition of the *Katz* principle of justifiable expectations of privacy.[17]

3. Probable Cause

"Probable cause" has been held to be a requirement for warrantless arrests or searches[18] as well as for the issuance by a magistrate of a warrant for arrest or search. Probable cause for a warrant exists when the known facts are sufficient to warrant a "prudent man" or a man of "reasonable caution" in believing that an offense has been or is being committed (arrest warrant),[19] or that the things specified in the warrant were connected with criminal activity and were to be found in the specified place (search warrant).[20]

The Supreme Court prefers the use of warrants and is even willing to apply the probable cause standard somewhat less stringently when a warrant has been used.[21] It regards as significant the fact that a disinterested magistrate rather than an interested policeman has made the

15. Israel & LaFave, *supra* n.8 at 101-106; LaFave, Search and Seizure, chap. 2 (1978).

16. Katz v. U.S., 389 U.S. 347 (1967).

17. Israel & LaFave, *supra* n.8 at 103, 107-109; LaFave, Search and Seizure, §§2.2, 2.6 (1978).

18. Draper v. U.S., 358 U.S. 307 (1959).

19. See Henry v. U.S., 361 U.S. 98, 102 (1959); Beck v. Ohio, 379 U.S. 89 (1964).

20. LaFave, Search and Seizure, §3.1 at 441-444 (1978).

21. See U.S. v. Ventresca, 380 U.S. 102 (1965) (search); *Beck, supra* n.19 (arrest).

initial determination. *Some* assurance is thus provided — even though warrants are often issued by magistrates without careful consideration. The evidence of probable cause need not be confined to the kind of evidence that is necessary for admission in a trial; thus, hearsay or a prior police record are relevant.[22] Many cases have been concerned with this problem, including those on the sufficiency of information obtained from informers and others and the sufficiency of any necessary corroborating facts.[23]

Our daily experience has made most of us aware of some situations wherein for overriding practical reasons, the probable cause requirement is interpreted as having much *weaker* force: Searches at national borders[24] and airports[25] are examples. Another is inspections made for violations of regulatory laws (e.g., fire, health, and safety laws), made not because of a belief that violations have occurred but because inspection of buildings on an "area" basis or pursuant to some other administratively feasible standard is the practicable as well as traditional method of enforcement.[26] Though a judicial warrant is required for these inspections, the probable cause requirement is obviously attenuated; and in some licensed, "pervasively regulated" businesses even the warrant is not required.[27] Another example is the "stop and frisk" and certain other brief detentions.[28] Still other examples could be cited.[29]

22. *Draper, supra* n.18; Brinegar v. U.S., 338 U.S. 160 (1949); LaFave, Search and Seizure, §3.2 (1978).

23. Israel & LaFave, *supra* n.8 at 114-120; LaFave, Search and Seizure, §§3.3-3.5 (1978).

24. U.S. v. Ramsey and Kelley, 431 U.S. 606, 626-628 (1977). Complicated distinctions arise when stops and searches are not actually at the border. See generally, Israel & LaFave, *supra* n.8 at 168-169; LaFave, Search and Seizure, §10.5 (1978).

25. See Notes, 72 Mich. L. Rev. 128 (1973); 48 N.Y.U.L. Rev. 1043 (1973). The cases are largely influenced by the cases on border searches and on "stop and frisk" (both mentioned above), but there are differences. See LaFave, Search and Seizure, §10.6 (1978).

26. Marshall v. Barlow's, Inc. 436 U.S. 307 (1978); Israel & LaFave, *supra* n.8 at 166-168; LaFave, Search and Seizure, §§10.1, 10.2, 10.4 (1978).

27. U.S. v. Biswell, 406 U.S. 311 (1972) (gun dealer); Colonnade Catering Corp. v. U.S., 397 U.S. 72 (1970) (liquor dealer); Donovan v. Dewey, 69 L. Ed. 2d 262 (1981) (quarry); LaFave, Search and Seizure, §10.2 (1978).

28. See *supra* n.9; Israel & LaFave, *supra* n.8 at 157-164; LaFave, Search and Seizure, chap. 9 (1978).

29. There is relaxation of the probable cause requirement in the case of federal agency subpoenas issued for production of business documents to ascertain coverage and possible law violation (Oklahoma Press Publishing Co. v. Walling, 327 U.S. 186, 209 (1946)); in searches by probation and parole officers of parolees and probationers even when made without arrest or warrant (lower court authority) (Israel & LaFave, *supra* n.8 at 170-171; LaFave, Search and Seizure, §10.10 (1978)); in inspections related to government benefits and services: e.g., no probable cause or warrant was required for periodic home visits by a welfare caseworker at reasonable hours, after notice, to see if the welfare recipient continued to be eligible and dependent children were not being deprived of their benefits (Wyman v. James, 400 U.S. 309 (1971); LaFave, Search and Seizure, §10.3 (1978)); in certain searches directed at students,

4. Warrants; Execution of Warrant

Cases on the requirement that the warrant "particularly describ[e] the place to be searched and the persons or things to be seized" have of course produced numerous distinctions based on types of places and things.[30] A warrant for searching premises (a house, an office, an auto) does not itself authorize searching an *occupant*, but certain other bases for searching or frisking may exist;[31] and detention of the occupants of the premises during the search is permissible.[32] As for seizure of items not named in the warrant, this has been frowned on but more recently has been supported by the Supreme Court — at least when the police came upon the unnamed items inadvertently, and it was immediately apparent that they had probable cause to believe the items constituted the fruits, instrumentalities, or evidence of crime.[33]

Statutes often provide that the officer executing a search warrant can *break into* premises only if, after notice of his authority and purpose, he is refused admittance. An exeception is made for exigent circumstances, e.g., when giving notice prior to entry could reasonably be expected to result in destruction of the evidence or increased danger to the officers or others, or when the officers' authority and purpose is already known to those within.[34]

5. Searches Without Warrants

What about a search *without* a warrant? The typical situation is the search "incident to a lawful arrest." Whether or not the lawful arrest was with a warrant, the officer is authorized to "search the person arrested in order to remove any weapons that the latter might seek to use in order to resist arrest or effect his escape [and to] seize any evi-

---

even when made without a warrant or arrest (lower court authority) (*id.*, §10.11); in allowing checks on driver license and registration by general roadblock-type (as distinct from random) stops of vehicles, or the particularized stopping of an individual motorist on reasonable suspicion rather than probable cause (Delaware v. Prouse, 440 U.S. 648 (1979); LaFave, Search and Seizure, §10.8 (1978)); and in allowing certain searches, mail examinations, and eavesdropping against prisoners without compliance with Fourth Amendment requirements (id., §10.9).

30. Israel & LaFave, *supra* n.8 at 124-127; LaFave, Search and Seizure, §§4.5, 4.6 (1978). The magistrate must also be satisfied that not too much time has elapsed since the observations were made supporting the belief that certain things were to be found in a particular place. Israel & LaFave, *supra* n.8 at 123-124.

31. Israel & LaFave, *supra* n.8 at 129-130; LaFave, Search and Seizure, §4.9 (1978).

32. Michigan v. Summers, 69 L. Ed. 2d 340 (1981).

33. Coolidge v. New Hampshire, 403 U.S. 443 (1971); Israel & LaFave, *supra* n.8 at 130-132; LaFave, Search and Seizure, §4.11 (1978).

34. Israel & LaFave, *supra* n.8 at 128-129; LaFave, Search and Seizure, §4.8 (1978).

dence on the arrestee's person in order to prevent its concealment or destruction."[35] Moreover, this authority extends to "a search of the . . . area 'within his immediate control' — construing that phrase to mean the area from within which he might gain possession of a weapon or destructible evidence";[36] searching a broader area will require a search warrant, but there are exceptions.[37] And, as in the case of searches with warrants, a "plain view" doctrine applies, so as to permit seizure of probable cause-linked evidence.[38]

Besides searches incident to a lawful arrest, some other kinds of searches are recognized as exceptions to the warrant requirement because of "exigent circumstances." Thus, police who have entered premises in "hot pursuit" of the offender could search the whole house for him and for weapons.[39] The warrant requirement is inapplicable in at least some of the situations in which the delay incident to obtaining a warrant would probably mean destruction or removal of evidence or risk of death or bodily harm; but, typically, probable cause must be present.[40]

A final illustration of an exception is afforded by the numerous cases on automobiles and other vehicles. Special considerations apply here both because of the hazards to enforcement stemming from the mobility of vehicles, and because there is supposed to be a lesser expectation of privacy in them as opposed to a house or office.[41] So the car search incident to a lawful arrest can be broader than under the usual rule; searches on probable cause but without warrants are more freely allowed (though search of closed containers like luggage may still require a warrant); absence of the particularity aspect of probable cause is often condoned (e.g., when the police, if applying for a warrant could not have sufficiently particularized the fruits, instrumentalities, or evidence of crime that they were after); and there are circumstances permitting seizure and impoundment of the entire vehicle.[42]

35. Chimel v. California, 395 U.S. 752, 762-763 (1969); U.S. v. Robinson, 414 U.S. 218 (1973); Israel & LaFave, *supra* n.8 at 134-139; LaFave, Search and Seizure, §5.2 (1978). See also *id.,* §5.3 (later search during post-arrest detention). While searches may sometimes be made of body cavities, an uncertain limit exists by virtue of the Supreme Court's holding that forcible administration of an emetic to retrieve swallowed narcotics was a brutal method which shocked the conscience and violated due process. Rochin v. California, 342 U.S. 165 (1952). See generally, LaFave, *supra,* §5.3.

36. *Chimel, supra* n.35; LaFave, *supra* n.35, §§5.5, 6.3 (1978).

37. See LaFave, *id.,* §§6.4, 6.5 (1978). See also §6.3 (searches "before and incident to arrest").

38. This is so at least as to items not known by the police to be there. See generally, Israel & LaFave, *supra* n.8 at 147-148; LaFave, *supra* n.35, §§5.2, 6.7 (1978).

39. Warden v. Hayden, 387 U.S. 294 (1967); LaFave, *supra* n.35, §6.1(c).

40. See generally, Israel & LaFave, *supra* n.8 at 148-151; LaFave, *supra* n.35, §§6.5 (b), (d).

41. See, e.g., South Dakota v. Opperman, 428 U.S. 367-368 (1976).

42. LaFave, Search and Seizure, §§7.1-7.3 (1978); New York v. Belton, 69 L. Ed. 2d 768 (1981); Robbins v. California, 69 L. Ed. 2d 744 (1981). Also some warrantless

But it would be misleading to suggest that the auto cases are clear and consistent. Thus, for instance, the Court has said it is not *always* true that a search of the auto itself may "even with probable cause . . . be made without the extra protection for privacy that a warrant affords."[43] Some cases, turning on niceties of difference in detail and shifting emphases by the Court, are difficult to reconcile with the others. As the Supreme Court has ruefully observed, its decisions on "warrantless searches, especially when those searches are of vehicles, suggest that this branch of the law is something less than a seamless web."[44]

6. Statutory Barriers to Some Searches Even With Warrants

Even a search with a warrant, legitimate under the Constitution, can be restrained by statute — the legislature can give more protection than does the Constitution. After the 1978 Supreme Court decision upholding a search with warrant, upon probable cause, of the office of a newspaper not itself reasonably suspected of complicity in crime, Congress was concerned enough about the chilling effect of such searches (as distinguished from issuance of subpoenas) on First Amendment freedoms to pass the Privacy Protection Act of 1980.[45] (1) This made it unlawful for any government employee to search for or seize any "work product materials" possessed by a person reasonably believed to have a purpose to disseminate to the public a newspaper, book, broadcast, or other similar form of public communication, in or affecting interstate or foreign commerce, *unless* (a) there is probable cause to believe that the person in possession has a particular involvement in the offense concerned,[46] or (b) there is reason to believe that immediate seizure is necessary to prevent the death of, or serious bodily injury to, a human being. (2) There are similar provisions for docu-

---

searches of vehicles are allowed that have no purpose of obtaining evidence of crime. E.g., once a vehicle has been properly impounded, the police are permitted to make an "inventory" of its contents, provided it is reasonable in scope and not a pretext concealing an investigatory motive. South Dakota v. Opperman, 428 U.S. 364 (1976); Israel & LaFave, supra n.8 at 155-156; LaFave, *supra*, §7.4 (1978).

43. Chambers v. Maroney, 399 U.S. 42, 50 (1970).

44. Cady v. Dombrowski, 413 U.S. 433, 440 (1973). For cases involving "stops" of autos in various circumstances, see *supra* nn. 9 & 24.

45. 94 Stat. 1879 (1980), 42 U.S.C. §§2000aa, 2000aa5-2000aa12. For committee reports, see 4 U.S. Code Cong. & Ad. News 3950 et seq.

46. I.e., this person has committed or is committing the offense to which the materials relate, and the offense does not consist of receipt, possession, communication, or withholding of such materials or the information therein — though even there the search and seizure may be conducted if the information relates to national defense, classified information, or restricted data under specified statutes.

mentary materials other than work product materials possessed by persons with the above-stated purposes, plus some "unless" clauses adding to the (a) and (b) clauses above.[47] (3) The Act provides damage remedies for searches and seizures violating the Act.[48] (4) Some limited protections for persons other than those specified in (1) and (2) above are afforded by the fact that the Attorney General is required to issue certain *guideline* procedures for federal employees searching for documentary materials in the possession of persons *not* reasonably believed to *be suspects or related to suspects,* the materials being (e.g., as in the case of lawyers' or doctors' records) not contraband or the fruits or instrumentalities of an offense.[49]

7. Consent

A government contention that the defendant had *consented* to an otherwise invalid search and seizure will succeed only if the prosecution can sustain its burden of proving: "that the consent was in fact voluntarily given and not the result of duress or coercion, express or implied." The prosecution's burden does not include proving that the subject knew he had a right to refuse consent. Nor must he be warned of his right to refuse. But consent given in response to a false claim of authority to search is not voluntary. In making these points the Supreme Court stressed that the voluntariness issue is decided on the basis of the "totality of circumstances," and that its decision was directed at the typical consent-issue situation: a defendant who is not yet in custody.[50]

47. I.e., (1) "there is reason to believe that the giving of notice pursuant to a subpoena duces tecum would result in the destruction, alteration or concealment of such materials"; *or* (2) such materials have not been produced after a "court order directing compliance with a subpoena duces tecum, and (A) all appellate remedies have been exhausted; or (B) there is reason to believe that the delay in an investigation or trial occasioned by further proceedings relating to the subpoena would threaten the interests of justice."

48. The remedies are against federal or local governments and state governments that have waived immunity; and against employees of a state that has not waived immunity if the employees did not have a reasonable good faith belief in the lawfulness of their conduct. A government being sued cannot assert the immunity of an employee as a defense except in the case of a judicial officer. The remedy against a government is "exclusive of any other civil action or proceeding for conduct constituting a violation of this Act" against the employee or his estate. Minimum damages are $1,000 plus reasonable attorney's fees and costs. The Attorney General may settle damage claims.

49. Some matters to be included in the guidelines are specified, including "a recognition of special concern for privacy interests" when a documentary search "would intrude upon a known confidential relationship" like that between "clergyman and parishioner; lawyer and client; or doctor and patient." Noncompliance with the guidelines is not to be a basis for suppression or exclusion of evidence.

50. Schneckloth v. Bustamonte, 412 U.S. 218 (1973). Cases have also dealt with

8. Wiretapping and Eavesdropping

Wiretapping and electronic eavesdropping have had an interesting history under the Fourth Amendment. A 1928 Supreme Court case ruled that wiretapping was not a search and seizure within the meaning of the Amendment.[51] A subsequent federal statute prohibited anyone not authorized by the sender from intercepting and divulging to anyone the content, substance, purport, meaning, or existence of any "communication," as defined. In federal prosecutions thereafter, wiretap evidence obtained in violation of the statute by federal or state officers tapping interstate or intrastate communications was ruled inadmissible[52] (unless one party to the conversation had consented).[53] Ultimately the same ruling of inadmissibility was made for state prosecutions as well.[54]

In 1967 the *Katz* case overruled the narrow view of the Fourth Amendment exhibited by the 1928 case and by subsequent cases insisting on a "trespass" or physical property element. It ruled that the government's obtaining of recordings of defendant's end of phone conversations in a public telephone booth, through an electronic device on the outside of the booth, was a search and seizure made without a judicial warrant, violating the Fourth Amendment.[55] The Amendment protects people, wherever they are, in any expectations of privacy that are "justifiable." A warrant could have been obtained here, the Court thought, since the surveillance was conducted only after investigation had established a strong possibility that the suspect was illegally transmitting gambling information through the booth at the same time each morning; and the listening was limited to the times he used the booth, and, insofar as possible, only to his illegal transmissions of information, resulting in six recordings averaging three minutes each.

The *Katz* approach makes clear that both wiretapping and electronic eavesdropping are subject to the Fourth Amendment — but there are some exceptions or qualifications. One is the situation in which a "pen register" has been installed by the phone company at police request to record phone numbers dialed from the suspect's home phone, rather than to record the content of conversations; this is not a "search" requiring a warrant.[56] Another though somewhat un-

---

the circumstances in which consent may validly be given not by the defendant but by others, such as members of his family, his landlord, tenant, co-inhabitant, employer, employee, or bailee. On consent generally, see Israel & LaFave, *supra* n.5 at 171-183; LaFave, Search and Seizure, chap. 8 (1978).

51. Olmstead v. U.S., 277 U.S. 438 (1928).

52. Benanti v. U.S., 355 U.S. 96 (1957); Weiss v. U.S., 308 U.S. 321 (1939); Nardone v. U.S., 302 U.S. 379 (1937).

53 Rathbun v. U.S., 355 U.S. 107 (1957).

54. Lee v. Florida, 392 U.S. 378 (1968).

55. Katz v. U.S., 389 U.S. 347 (1967).

56. Smith v. Maryland, 442 U.S. 735 (1979).

certain exception is the situation in which one party to the overheard conversation has consented to the surveillance. In 1971 a four-Justice plurality opinion found no "justifiable" or "legitimate" or "reasonable" expectation of privacy had been violated when the defendant's conversations with an informer in a restaurant, in defendant's home, and in the informer's car were overheard by government agents through a transmitter concealed on the informer.[57]

Since warrants are generally required for wiretapping and eavesdropping, Congress saw fit to establish in Title III of the Omnibus Crime Control and Safe Streets Act of 1968, as subsequently somewhat amended,[58] detailed provisions for issuance of such warrants[59] and for related matters as well.[60] However, there are still some unresolved

---

57. U.S. v. White, 401 U.S. 745 (1971). Earlier decisions in similar vein (On Lee v. U.S., 343 U.S. 747 (1952); Lopez v. U.S., 373 U.S. 427 (1963)) are not as significant because they were decided before the *Katz* case with its new rationale.

The use of secret agents is of course not confined to situations of wiretapping or electronic eavesdropping. It may be well to remind you parenthetically at this point — i.e., even though the cases I have in mind may involve no search and seizure — that the use of secret agents sometimes gives rise to an "entrapment" argument by the defendant. Generally this occurs in crimes involving willing victims, such as prostitution, bribery, abortion, gambling, and illegal sales of liquor, narcotics, or obscene materials. But entrapment does not take place unless the agent "originates the idea of the crime and then induces another person to engage in conduct constituting such a crime when the other person is not otherwise disposed to do so." LaFave & Scott, Criminal Law 369 (1972). The defense has not been put by the Supreme Court in constitutional terms but rather in terms of the idea that statutes defining and punishing the crime impliedly exempt the situations involving entrapment by government agents. See U.S. v. Russell, 411 U.S. 423 (1973); Sherman v. U.S., 356 U.S. 369 (1958); Sorrells v. U.S., 287 U.S. 435 (1932). Some of the Supreme Court Justices have chosen to rely solely on the Court's implied supervisory power over the administration of justice in the federal courts.

58. 82 Stat. 212 (1968), 92 Stat. 1796 (1978); 18 U.S.C. §§2510-2520.

59. In the case of certain specified federal or state crimes, applications can be made, upon specified higher level authorization, to federal and state judges, respectively, for orders authorizing wiretapping or eavesdropping. Evidence obtained by such court orders will be admissible. Wiretapping or eavesdropping not thus authorized and without prior consent of a party to the conversation is criminal; evidence so obtained is not admissible in federal or state proceedings and the victim has a damage remedy. An interception order can be issued only if the judge finds that certain probable cause requirements are met, and that normal investigative procedures have failed or are unlikely to succeed or are too dangerous. The order must be specific as to various elements involved in the interception: the person, the offense, the facilities or place, the type of communication, the agency and authorizing officer, and the time period (for which there is a 30-day maximum, with extensions possible by full re-applications). There is provision for certain emergency interceptions without judicial order, to be followed by applications within 48 hours. The Supreme Court has ruled that an officer's covert entry to install a court-ordered electronic surveillance device is authorized by the Act and does not violate the Fourth Amendment. Dalia v. U.S., 441 U.S. 238 (1979).

60. Certain requirements must be followed for judicial notification (after termination of an interception or after denial of an application) of the named person and other parties to an intercepted communication, concerning the dates of the order and interception period, or of the application denial, and whether communications were intercepted. Both judges and prosecutors are to make periodic reports

questions about the compatibility of this statute with the *Katz* decision — perhaps the main one being whether the Court's stress on the carefully restricted and short nature of the surveillance in *Katz,*[61] as I have previously described, is compatible with the statute's tolerance of: (1) continuing surveillance up to 30 days on a single showing of probable cause (with possible extensions on a new showing of probable cause), and (2) overhearing of all conversations on the wire being tapped or the room being bugged, including the suspect's conversations on matters other than the suspected offense, and remarks of persons other than the suspect.[62]

A defendant in a criminal case is entitled to try to prove that the government's electronic surveillance was unlawful. If he succeeds, he can see all the surveillance records as to which he has standing (e.g., conversations to which he was a party, and conversations on his premises) and try to show that other evidence in the case was traceable to the surveillance and hence inadmissible as the "fruit of the poisonous tree."[63]

9. The Exclusionary Rule

I come now to a short treatment of a long subject: the "exclusionary rule" under which evidence obtained by the government "in violation of the Fourth Amendment cannot be used in a criminal proceeding

---

on wiretapping and eavesdropping matters to the Administrative Office of the United States Courts, which in return reports to Congress, giving summary analyses of the data thus submitted. The Act does not limit presidential power to make interceptions of communications when certain aspects of national security are at stake, such interceptions being admissible as evidence when reasonable; but the Court has ruled that the presidential power does not permit warrantless surveillance of suspected *domestic* subversion. U.S. v. United States District Court, 407 U.S. 297 (1972). A similar statutory provision regarding *foreign* intelligence has been amended (18 U.S.C. §2511) to take account of the Foreign Intelligence Surveillance Act of 1978 (92 Stat. 1783); 50 U.S.C. §§1801-1811) that permits, under high level authorization, foreign intelligence surveillance without court order in some situations and not in others. See Note, 78 Mich. L. Rev. 1116 (1980).

61. A similar emphasis on restricted surveillance, rather than continuous surveillance on a single showing of probable cause, occurred in Berger v. New York, 388 U.S. 41 (1967), which held the New York eavesdropping law unconstitutional, and also emphasized the restricted nature of the judicially authorized surveillance upheld in Osborn v. U.S., 385 U.S. 323 (1966) (agent with concealed tape recorder). Both *Berger* and *Osborn* were prior to *Katz,* and all were prior to the 1968 statute.

62. Justice White, dissenting in *Berger* (cited in preceding footnote), discounted this feature by analogizing it to what happens in an ordinary police seizure of material objects: "In searching for seizable matters the police must necessarily see or hear, and comprehend, items which do not relate to the purpose of the search." See also U.S. v. Cafero, 473 F.2d 489 (3d Cir. 1973).

63. Alderman v. U.S., Ivanov v. U.S., and Butenko v. U.S., 394 U.S. 165 (1969); Giordano v. U.S., 394 U.S. 310 (1969). The judge, to protect innocent third parties

against the victim of the illegal search and seizure."[64] The rule was first applied by the Supreme Court against the federal government in 1914[65] and against the states in 1961.[66] The theory today is not that the rule embodies a "personal constitutional right of the party aggrieved," but that it is "a judicially created remedy designed to safeguard Fourth Amendment rights generally through its deterrent effect" on the police,[67] with the subsidiary purpose of keeping the court's integrity unsullied by acceptance of unconstitutionally obtained evidence.[68] The 1961 opinion was apparently influenced by the Court's belief that "other remedies" against the police for lawless conduct had proved "worthless and futile." Rejected was the Cardozo scorn (expressed in 1926 on behalf of the New York Court of Appeals)[69] of the proposition that "the criminal is to go free because the constable has blundered." In the Supreme Court's view, it was better that some criminals should go free, and the constable be deterred from future misconduct, than that his misconduct be tolerated or encouraged by the courts, through a lenient rule on admissibility of evidence.

The hopes for deterrence of police misconduct, however, have been far from realized. The Supreme Court in 1976, after an elaborate survey of the literature, concluded: "No empirical researcher, proponent or opponent of the rule, has yet been able to establish with any assurance whether the rule has a deterrent effect. . . ."[70] A number of factors might be expected to thwart a substantial deterrent effect.[71]

In addition to skepticism about deterrence, the public doubtless continues to be shocked when it hears of court decisions applying the rule so as apparently to free the defendant in cases of serious crimes.[72]

---

in the conversations, can order defendant and his counsel to make no unwarranted disclosures of the records to others. *Alderman, supra.*

64. U.S. v. Calandra, 414 U.S. 338, 347 (1974).

65. Weeks v. U.S., 232 U.S. 383 (1914).

66. Mapp v. Ohio, 367 U.S. 643 (1961).

67. *Calandra, supra* n.64 at 348. Clear language in *Mapp* however (*supra* n.66 at 655, 657) had treated the rule as required by the Fourth Amendment.

68. See *Mapp, supra* n.66 at 659, 660.

69. People v. Defore, 242 N.Y. 13, 21, 150 N.E. 585, 587 (1926).

70. U.S. v. Janis, 428 U.S. 433, 450 n.22 (1976). And see Kaplan, The Limits of the Exclusionary Rule, 26 Stan. L. Rev. 1027, 1033-1034 & n.46 (1974).

71. There could be: (1) a possible attitude by police that they can continue their illegalities and successfully give false testimony about the methods used; (2) the policeman's imperfect knowledge of what a Supreme Court majority will later declare to have been the correct application of the Fourth Amendment to the facts; (3) the fact that he is not usually informed about the eventual court exclusion of the evidence; (4) and his knowledge that defendants usually plead guilty; they may, even when there is a strong search and seizure issue, decide against the risks and costs of litigation. See Kaplan, *id.* at 1032-1033 & nn. 40, 44; 1038 & n.63.

72. "The disparity in particular cases between the error committed by the police officer and the windfall given by the rule to the criminal is an affront to popular ideas of justice" and "demonstrates why the . . . rule cannot be justified

This public perception, though, is seldom based on the whole story. Actually the rule "rarely allows dangerous defendants to go free. In serious cases, there are often other charges not weakened by the exclusionary rule, or sufficient evidence of the crime charged apart from that unconstitutionally seized. Moreover, the courts have shown a remarkable ability in the most serious cases to stretch legal doctrine to hold doubtful searches and seizures legal."[73]

The rule may thus not be as favorable to criminals as appearances suggest. The question remains, however, whether improvements are possible, to make the rule even less favorable to the worst criminals and at the same time more deterrent in its effect on the police. One proposal along these lines would make the rule inapplicable (a) to "the most serious cases — treason, espionage, murder, armed robbery, and kidnapping by organized groups," and (b) to "cases where the police department in question has taken seriously its responsibility to adhere to the Fourth Amendment" by having "a set of published regulations giving guidance to police officers calculated to make violations of fourth amendment rights isolated occurrences, and perhaps, most importantly, a history of taking disciplinary action where such violations are brought to its attention."[74] Other proposals would make the rule inapplicable to cases in which the officer had a "good faith" belief in his actions being constitutional, or cases in which the court in its discretion decided against applying the rule.[75] These and other proposals have their difficulties.[76]

Meanwhile the Supreme Court clings to the rule. In 1976 the Court maintained its adherence to the assumption of deterrence "despite the absence of supportive empirical evidence," and to the assumption that the rule's "demonstration that our society attaches serious consequences to violation of constitutional rights" will encourage enforcement officers to "incorporate Fourth Amendment ideals into their value system." These statements were made, however, in a case that ruled that the benefits of the exclusionary rule would be "small in relation to the costs," and hence should *not* be applied so as to give to a *state* prisoner *habeas corpus* relief in a *federal* court on his claim that unconstitutionally seized evidence had been used against him (assuming the state had provided an opportunity for full and fair litigation of this Fourth Amendment claim).[77]

---

as a moral imperative preventing the courts from soiling themselves with tainted evidence." *Id.* at 1036.

73. *Id.*

74. *Id.* at 1046, 1050.

75. See Natl. L.J., June 8, 1981, at 1.

76. See LaFave, Search and Seizure, §1.2 (1978).

77. Stone v. Powell, 428 U.S. 465 (1976).

In other words, the uncertainty about the rule's deterrent effect, and the Court's concern over the social cost of excluding relevant and reliable evidence from the fact finding process, are at least partly responsible for its weakening the rule or holding it inapplicable in a variety of situations.[78] Some of these are cases of searches and seizures of premises and property of persons other than defendant — with the Court tending to conclude the rule was inapplicable because defendant lacked "standing" to invoke it. I.e., his own Fourth Amendment rights, as distinct from third-party rights, were not substantially enough involved.[79]

78. (1) One category covers certain situations in which evidence is not being presented in a criminal trial as direct proof of guilt — for instance, it is used to undermine defendant's trial testimony, in the cross-examination process ("impeaching" the witness); it is used as a basis for questions to a *grand jury* witness; it is offered at a preliminary hearing; or it is used (though not yet sanctioned by the Supreme Court) in sentencing proceedings or in probation and parole revocation proceedings. See Israel & LaFave, *supra* n.8 at 301-310; LaFave, Search and Seizure, §§1.4, 11.6 (1978). (2) A second category consists of those cases in which the Court has refrained from applying the rule to some of the "derivative evidence" ("fruit of the poisonous tree") situations — i.e., by being readily disposed to find that the alleged derivative evidence had been derived from an "independent" source or had been arrived at not by "exploitation of the illegality" but "by means sufficiently distinguishable to be purged of the primary taint." (X's statement to police following his illegal arrest was tainted fruit, but not Y's statement to police several days after his illegal arrest and after he had been arraigned and temporarily released and warned of his rights. Wong Sun v. U.S., 371 U.S. 471 (1963).) See Israel & LaFave, *id.* at 284-300; LaFave, *supra,* §11.4 (1978). (3) The Court's lack of enthusiasm for the rule again manifested itself on the issue of the standard of proof by the government. Dealing with the issue of voluntariness of a confession, the Court was "unwilling to expand current exclusionary rules," and thought it "very doubtful that escalating the prosecution's burden of proof in Fourth and Fifth Amendment suppression hearings" (from "preponderance of evidence" to proof "beyond a reasonable doubt," the standard applicable to proof of guilt) would be sufficiently productive in deterring police misconduct to justify the escalation. Lego v. Twomey, 404 U.S. 477 (1972); U.S. v. Matlock, 415 U.S. 164 (1974). See LaFave, *supra* §11.2 at 512-517 (1978). For discussion of "burden" as distinct from "standard" of proof, see *id.* at 498-512. (4) The Court has been unwilling to rule that the admission of unconstitutionally seized evidence is in that uncertain class of errors that require *automatic* reversal; rather, it has applied the rule of Chapman v. California, 386 U.S. 18 (1967), that some constitutional errors are "harmless" if it appears beyond a reasonable doubt that the error did not contribute to the conviction. Chambers v. Maroney, 399 U.S. 42 (1970). See Israel & LaFave, *supra* at 332-338; LaFave, *supra,* §11.7 at 735-749 (1978). (5) The Court has refused to apply the exclusionary rule to electronically recorded evidence obtained in violation not of the Constitution or statute but of federal administrative regulations. U.S. v. Caceres, 440 U.S. 741 (1979). (6) See the quotation from *Rakas* in n.79 below.

79. See, e.g., U.S. v. Payner, 447 U.S. 727 (1980). A defendant's possessory interest in the premises or in the property seized would generally give him the necessary expectation of privacy (but see U.S. v. Salvucci, 448 U.S. 83 (1980)). Lacking such an interest, his mere legitimate presence at the time of search is, contrary to an earlier view, not enough. On this type of issue, "misgivings as to the benefit of enlarging the class of persons who may invoke [the exclusionary] rule are properly considered." Rakas & King v. Illinois, 439 U.S. 128, 138 (1978). See Israel & LaFave, *supra* at 310-328; LaFave, *supra,* §11.3 (1978).

C. *Indictment by Grand Jury*

The requirement of grand jury indictments for infamous crimes means that if a person is to be charged with a federal offense punishable by more than one year's imprisonment, the decision to *charge* (i.e., to issue an indictment) must have been made by an investigative body known as the grand jury, which, after a hearing, indicts only if it finds "probable cause" that the suspect committed the offense. If the defendant pleads not guilty to the indictment, the trial follows. The grand jury indictment provision is virtually the only criminal procedural provision of the Bill of Rights that the Supreme Court has not yet regarded as applicable to the states by way of the Fourteenth Amendment (see Chap. 5 above at 338-339). It is permissible, therefore, as some states do, to charge a person by an "information," i.e., a formal charge issued by the prosecutor; and the states are not required by the Federal Constitution to provide a substantial adversary hearing on the probable cause issue. However, "almost all states provide for the screening of felony cases by preliminary hearing or grand jury review, and many states use both procedures."[80]

D. *Double Jeopardy*

". . . Nor shall any person be subject for the same offense to be twice put in jeopardy of life or limb." This clause protects not merely against multiple *punishment* for the same offense but also against the jeopardy of a second *prosecution* for the same offense, whether the first prosecution ended in acquittal or conviction.[81]

Even though the "life or limb" phrase is not to be construed literally,[82] it does suggest that the double jeopardy clause protects against twice being put in jeopardy by *criminal* proceedings for the same offense. Hence it would *not* apply to the many instances in which the same conduct is subjected not only to enforcement proceedings that are "essentially criminal" but also to others that fall short of being criminal, though containing a coercive or punitive element.[83]

80. Israel & LaFave, *supra* n.79 at 31.

81. North Carolina v. Pearce, 395 U.S. 711, 717 (1969). But see text below at nn. 88 & 90.

82. Breed v. Jones, 421 U.S. 519, 528 (1975); Ex Parte Lange, 85 U.S. (18 Wall.) 163 (1873).

83. E.g., a civil suit to recover monetary penalties for fraud in the tax field,

At what point in a proceeding does jeopardy "attach"? For instance, if the judge discharges the jury before any verdict is rendered, declaring a mistrial, has jeopardy attached so as to bar a second prosecution? As commonly understood, jeopardy attaches when the jury has been impanelled and sworn (or in a non-jury trial when the judge has begun to hear evidence);[84] but re-prosecution is not barred if termination of the first proceeding was a matter of "manifest necessity." This ambiguous phrase covers such situations as a "hung jury" (one that cannot agree)[85] or an illegally constituted jury,[86] but its applicability to the diverse situations that keep arising is not often clear.[87]

The situation after verdict is clearer. It is established, as we know from the stream of reported reversals and remands of criminal convictions in the law reports, that after defendant's successful appeal for reversal of his conviction (on any ground other than insufficiency of evidence to support his conviction), a retrial is not double jeopardy.[88] Also an *acquittal* is generally held to be final; the *Government usually cannot* appeal from an acquittal by jury verdict or court order, in spite of the claim that legal error was committed.[89] Still, some kinds of

---

Helvering v. Mitchell, 303 U.S. 391 (1938), and some other fields, U.S. ex rel Marcus v. Hess, 317 U.S. 537 (1943); Rex Trailer v. U.S., 350 U.S. 148 (1956); or a civil suit for forfeiture of property, Various Items of Personal Property v. U.S., 282 U.S. 577 (1931); One Lot Cut Stones & One Ring v. U.S., 409 U.S. 232 (1972) (but *cf.* U.S. v. U.S. Coin & Currency, 401 U.S. 715 (1971)); or a civil contempt proceeding involving imprisonment (since civil contempt imprisonment is viewed as primarily remedial rather than punitive, i.e., designed to get the defendant to do something, which when done will release him), Yates v. U.S., 355 U.S. 66 (1957). A juvenile delinquency proceeding is viewed otherwise; and even if the state, after adjudication of delinquency, foregoes punishment and shifts to prosecution-as-an-adult instead, there is double jeopardy. Breed v. Jones, 421 U.S. 519 (1975).

84. Serfass v. U.S., 420 U.S. 377, 388 (1975); Downum v. U.S., 372 U.S. 734 (1963).

85. U.S. v. Perez, 9 Wheat. 579 (S. Ct. 1824); Logan v. U.S., 144 U.S. 263 (1892).

86. Thompson v. U.S., 155 U.S. 271 (1894).

87. See, e.g., U.S. v. Scott, 437 U.S. 82 (1978); Arizona v. Washington, 434 U.S. 497 (1978); Lee v. U.S., 432 U.S. 23 (1977); Illinois v. Somerville, 410 U.S. 458 (1973); Downum v. U.S., 372 U.S. 734 (1963).

88. U.S. v. Scott, 437 U.S. 82, 90-91 (1978); North Carolina v. Pearce, 395 U.S. 711, 720 (1969); U.S. v. Tateo, 377 U.S. 463, 465 (1964); U.S. v. Ball, 163 U.S. 662 (1896). But if the conviction had been on a lesser, included charge (e.g., second degree murder when he had been charged with first degree), the new trial would be limited to a second degree charge, the prior conviction being viewed as an acquittal of first degree murder. Green v. U.S., 355 U.S. 184 (1957). Jury imposition of a harsher *sentence* on the second conviction than on the first would be permissible; and such harsher sentencing would also be permissible if sentencing were by the judge, but only if the reasons for his doing so affirmatively appeared in the record and were based on "objective information concerning [defendant's] identifiable conduct occurring after the time of the original sentencing procedure." North Carolina v. Pearce, 395 U.S. 711, 726 (1969); Stroud v. U.S., 251 U.S. 15 (1919). But see Bullington v. Missouri, 68 L. Ed. 2d 270 (1981).

89. U.S. v. Martin Linen Supply Co., 430 U.S. 564, 571 (1977); Fong Foo v. U.S.,

government appeals (where no re-trial would result) are permissible, sometimes even after acquittal;[90] and also permissible is a statutorily authorized government appeal, after conviction, of the sentence alone.[91]

Ambiguities in the "same offense" phrase have been somewhat clarified. Successive prosecutions by federal and state governments for the same conduct violating each sovereignty's laws would not be double jeopardy; different "offenses" would be involved.[92] Not so when the prosecutions are by state and local governments,[93] or by federal and territorial governments,[94] since in both instances the other government is a subordinate arm of the sovereign government rather than a sovereign entity itself. When only one sovereign prosecutes conduct violating more than one of that sovereign's laws, the initial question is whether the different laws were *intended* to create separate offenses. A negative answer avoids the constitutional double jeopardy issue, as in a case in which the Supreme Court thought punishment for the general offense of using a firearm in connection with any federal felony was not intended to be an additional penalty for a defendant being punished for the specific offense of bank robbery with the use of a dangerous weapon or device.[95] Even if separate offenses are intended,

---

369 U.S. 141 (1962); Kepner v. U.S., 195 U.S. 100 (1904); U.S. v. Ball, 163 U.S. 662 (1896).

90. Thus the Government can appeal when "it presents no threat of successive prosecutions," as when there is a dismissal of an indictment after a guilty verdict; "restoration of the guilty verdict and not a new trial would necessarily result if the Government prevailed." *Martin Linen Supply, supra* n.89 at 577 (1977), citing U.S. v. Wilson, 420 U.S. 332 (1975). The same is true if *before* any verdict the defendant has deliberately chosen "to seek termination of the proceedings against him on a basis unrelated to factual guilt or innocence of the offense" (in this instance, dismissal of some counts of the indictment because of pre-indictment delay) and thus avoided submission of the guilt issue to the jury. U.S. v. Scott, 437 U.S. 82, 98-99 (1978). See also Serfass v. U.S., 420 U.S. 377 (1975) (Government appeal from pre-trial order dismissing an indictment).

91. U.S. v. DiFrancesco, 66 L. Ed. 2d 328 (1980).

92. Bartkus v. Illinois, 359 U.S. 121 (1959). Abbate v. U.S., 359 U.S. 187 (1959). The same is true as to successive prosecutions by the United States and an Indian tribe exercising inherent rather than delegated power. U.S. v. Wheeler, 435 U.S. 313 (1978). For discussion of the federal government's policy of restraint in bringing a federal prosecution after a state prosecution, see Rinaldi v. U.S., 434 U.S. 22 (1977).

93. Waller v. Florida, 397 U.S. 387 (1970).

94. Grafton v. U.S., 206 U.S. 333 (1907).

95. Simpson v. U.S., 435 U.S. 6 (1978). For an analogous conclusion as to multiple offenses under the same statute, see Bell v. U.S., 349 U.S. 81 (1955) (transportation of *two* women across state lines, in the same trip, for prostitution). For some cases in which the Court concluded different offenses were intended and could be prosecuted without double jeopardy, see Morgan v. Devine, 237 U.S. 632 (1915) (defendant committed two separate offenses by (1) breaking into a post office with intent to commit larceny, and (2) thereupon stealing postage stamps and postal funds); Albrecht v. U.S., 273 U.S. 1 (1927) (separate offenses of possessing and selling the same liquor); Gore v. U.S., 357 U.S. 386 (1958) (single sale of narcotics constituted three separate

the double jeopardy clause may prevent their being so treated if the proof needed for one is too similar to the proof needed for the other, i.e., if each offense does not require *proof of a fact that is not needed to establish the other;*[96] and certain procedural barriers may also prevent double prosecution.[97]

Finally, let us assume that the broadcasting corporation involved in the *Nappier* case had been prosecuted criminally, and it wished to raise certain double jeopardy issues. Could it be argued in opposition that the double jeopardy clause is inapplicable to corporations, because the clause refers to "persons"[98] and to jeopardy of "life or limb," both of which references — and particularly the latter — seem inapplicable to corporations? To date the Supreme Court has not specifically discussed the issue, and in 1977 denied certiorari to a Government petition squarely raising the issue.[99] But it has *assumed* applicability by in fact applying double jeopardy protections to corporate defendants.[100]

---

offenses because defendant had sold not in pursuance of a written order, not in the original stamped package, and had facilitated concealment and sale); Albernaz v. U.S., 67 L. Ed. 2d 275 (1981) (conspiracy to commit offense of importing marijuana and offense of distributing the marijuana).

96. Whalen v. U.S., 445 U.S. 684 (1980); Brown v. Ohio, 432 U.S. 161 (1977); Blockburger v. U.S., 284 U.S. 299 (1932).

97. For instance, the "collateral estoppel" doctrine was held to be part of the double jeopardy clause. For present purposes it is enough to explain that as a consequence of this doctrine, in a case of successive prosecutions for robbery of different victims in the same robbery, an acquittal apparently based on a *question of fact in the first case* (defendant's absence from the robbery) that is *also crucial to the second charge bars* a trial on the second charge. Ashe v. Swenson, 397 U.S. 436 (1970). This decision pressures the prosecution to join at one trial all the charges growing out of a single criminal act or transaction. The federal government has said that out of "fairness to defendants and . . . efficient and orderly government," it follows this policy: "that several offenses arising out of a single transaction should be alleged and tried together and should not be made the basis of multiple prosecutions" (quoted in Petite v. U.S., 361 U.S. 529, 530-531 (1960)).

98. As to "person": In the same sentence of the Fifth Amendment, "person" includes corporations in the *"due process"* clause (Sinking Fund Cases, 99 U.S. 700, 718-719 (1879)), but excludes them in the *self-incrimination* clause (Hale v. Henkel, 201 U.S. 43, 69-70 (1906); Oklahoma Press Publ. Co. v. Walling, 327 U.S. 186, 208-210 (1946)).

99. U.S. v. Security National Bank, 430 U.S. 950 (1977).

100. See, e.g., U.S. v. Martin Linen Supply Co., 430 U.S. 564 (1977); Fong Foo v. U.S., 369 U.S. 141 (1962). For discussion see Annot., 50 L. Ed. 2d 830, 845-846 (1978); Schreiber, Double Jeopardy and Corporations: "Lurking in the Record" and "Ripe for Decision," 28 Stan. L. Rev. 805 (1976).

Generally on double jeopardy, see Annot., 50 L. Ed. 2d 830 (1978); Mead, Double Jeopardy Protection — Illusion or Reality? 13 Ind. L. Rev. 863 (1980); Note, 14 Ga. L. Rev. 761 (1980); Sigler, Double Jeopardy (1969).

E. *Privilege Against Self-Incrimination*

1. The well-known privilege against "self-incrimination" is explicitly guaranteed in federal criminal[101] cases by the Fifth Amendment, and in state criminal cases not only by state constitutions but also by the Fourteenth Amendment due process clause as interpreted by the Supreme Court.[102] The language of the Fifth Amendment, that the defendant shall not "be compelled in any criminal case to be a witness against himself," has been broadly construed; i.e., even a witness in a civil court case or an administrative hearing who would become a *potential* defendant in a criminal case because of an incriminating answer may invoke the privilege against being compelled to give such an answer.[103]

Similarly, the privilege applies in the early stages of the criminal process, so that *confessions* obtained in violation of the privilege would be inadmissible — though this has not always been recognized by all courts. In the federal courts, inadmissibility of "involuntary" confessions obtained by police interrogation has been based either on Fifth Amendment self-incrimination or on common law rules of evidence.[104] In the state courts for almost three decades after 1936 (because of the pre-1964 view that the Fifth Amendment privilege was not incorporated into Fourteenth Amendment due process so as to apply to the states, and because of the view that the Supreme Court could not prescribe state court rules of evidence), the Court's "voluntariness" standard was based instead on the fairness demands of Fourteenth Amendment "due process."[105]

Difficulties in applying this voluntariness test in the states on a case-by-case basis to the "totality of circumstances" involved[106] were greatly alleviated by the development of alternative tests that were less vague: (1) There was held to be a Sixth Amendment right to *counsel* (applicable to the states by way of Fourteenth Amendment due process) at critical stages of the pre-trial process, ultimately held to include

101. For discussion of when a case is criminal for purposes of the self-incrimination clause, see U.S. v. Ward, 448 U.S. 242 (1980).

102. Malloy v. Hogan, 378 U.S. 1 (1964).

103. McCarthy v. Arndstein, 266 U.S. 34, 40 (1924).

104. Israel & LaFave, *supra* n.8 at 213-214; U.S. v. Carrignan, 342 U.S. 36 (1951). Between 1943 and 1968, confessions in federal cases were also excludable on the ground of "unnecessary delay" in bringing the arrestee before a magistrate. McNabb v. U.S., 318 U.S. 332 (1943); Mallory v. U.S., 354 U.S. 449 (1957). Title II of the Omnibus Crime Control and Safe Streets Act of 1968 abolished the McNabb-Mallory rule, which had been based not on constitutional requirements but on the Court's power to supervise the administration of justice in the federal courts.

105. Israel & LaFave, *supra* n.8 at 213.

106. For various circumstances deemed relevant in the cases, see *id.* at 215-220.

police interrogation, so that a confession obtained at such a stage in the absence of counsel and the absence of a waiver of counsel was inadmissible.[107] (2) Going beyond this Sixth Amendment holding that had been stated cautiously in terms of the particular facts of the case was the more sweeping *Miranda* case of 1966,[108] which invoked the Fifth Amendment *privilege* (by this time applicable to the states), declaring the privilege "is fully applicable during a period of custodial interrogation" and listing specific rules to be followed by the police if a statement to them was to be admissible — assuming the person is "in custody at the station or otherwise deprived of his freedom of action in any significant way."[109] These rules are now the key approach to admissibility of confessions or incriminating statements obtained by police interrogation, but the voluntariness and right to counsel cases are still relevant, especially when the *Miranda* requirements have been met or are inapplicable.[110]

The *Miranda* rules were intended to safeguard the privilege against self-incrimination, but the Court recognized that a legislature

107. *Id.* at 220-226; Escobedo v. Illinois, 378 U.S. 478 (1964). Escobedo had requested and been refused an opportunity to consult with his lawyer.

108. Miranda v. Ariz., 384 U.S. 436 (1966).

109. (1) He "must first be informed in clear and unequivocal terms that he has the right to remain silent," together with an "explanation that anything said can and will be used against the individual in Court"; (2) he "must be clearly informed that he has the right to consult with a lawyer and to have the lawyer with him during interrogation"; and "that if he is indigent a lawyer will be appointed to represent him"; (3) if he "indicates in any manner, at any time prior to or during questioning that he wishes to remain silent, the interrogation must cease," and if he "states that he wants an attorney, the interrogation must cease until an attorney is present." In addition to these rules for the police, the government was given a "heavy burden" in proving any claim that "the defendant knowingly and intelligently waived" his privilege and right to counsel; a waiver is not to be presumed from silence or the ultimate obtaining of a confession (*id.* at 467-468, 469, 471, 473-474, 475).

110. Israel & LaFave, *supra* n.8 at 215. The rules have produced a substantial number of decisions, mainly in the lower courts, on such issues as the meaning of "custody," "interrogation," and "waiver," the adequacy of warnings, etc. *Id.* at 233-255. Recent Supreme Court decisions declare that the Miranda warnings need not be in the precise language of the *Miranda* opinion, California v. Prysock, 69 L. Ed. 2d 696 (1981); that "interrogation" is not limited to express questioning but also includes "any words or actions on the part of the police (other than those normally attendant to arrest and custody) that the police should know are reasonably likely to elicit an incriminating response from the suspect." Rhode Island v. Innis, 446 U.S. 291, 301 (1980); that once an accused has "expressed his desire to deal with the police only through counsel, he is not subject to further interrogation by the authorities until counsel has been made available to him, unless the accused himself initiates further communication, exchanges or conversation with the police." Edwards v. Arizona, 68 L. Ed. 2d 378, 386 (1981); and that a defendant interviewed before trial by a court-appointed psychiatrist should have been given the *Miranda* warnings and his counsel should have been given notice of the examination and of its scope. In the absence thereof, the psychiatrist's evidence as to defendant's future dangerousness was inadmissible at the penalty phase of the trial (which eventuated in a death sentence). Estelle v. Smith, 68 L. Ed. 2d 359 (1981).

could substitute "other procedures which are at least as effective in apprising accused persons of their right of silence and in assuring a continuous opportunity to exercise it." Congress did attempt a substitute in 1968 for *federal* prosecutions, but its (questionable) constitutionality has not yet been determined.[111]

Studies of the *Miranda* rules in operation show that in general "the *Miranda* warnings have not appreciably reduced the amount of talking by a suspect, and the police are now obtaining about as many confessions as before *Miranda*."[112]

2. Suppose that in the *Nappier* situation a criminal case were brought against the broadcasting corporation and relevant officers and employees, and a corporate officer was subpoenaed to be a witness. If he were also a named defendant, he would be entitled not to comply with the subpoena, because the self-incrimination privilege entitles a defendant in a criminal case not to take the stand at all (as distinct from a mere witness, who would have to take the stand and be entitled to claim a privilege against answering particular questions on the ground the answers would be incriminating).[113]

Can an officer or employee on the stand claim the privilege on the ground that a truthful answer would incriminate the *corporation* rather than himself? The answer is no, because the privilege is

111. Title II of the Omnibus Crime Control and Safe Streets Act of 1968 states in 18 U.S.C. §3501 that a voluntary confession is admissible in federal court; and whether the defendant was without counsel at the time of confession, and whether he had been advised of his right to counsel or his right to remain silent, are merely circumstances to be considered as relevant to voluntariness. The Court would probably not view this as meeting its "procedures which are at least as effective" standard, especially since this procedure of looking at all the circumstances bearing on voluntariness is one that the *Miranda* court had already found to be an ineffective protector of a suspect's rights.

112. Israel & LaFave, *supra* n.8 at 231.

113. The defendant's constitutional right not to take the stand includes the right not to take it at the outset of the case for the defense and to decide later whether to testify. Hence a statute requiring that if he does testify he must be the first defense witness violates both the self-incrimination privilege and due process. Brooks v. Tennessee, 406 U.S. 605 (1972). The right is also infringed by "either comment by the prosecution on the accused's silence or instructions by the court that such silence is evidence of guilt." Griffin v. California, 380 U.S. 609, 615 (1965). The defendant has a constitutional right to have the jury instructed that his failure to take the stand cannot give rise to any adverse inferences. Carter v. Kentucky, 67 L. Ed. 2d 241 (1981). But his constitutional right is not violated if the instruction is given to the jury over his objection. Lakeside v. Oregon, 435 U.S. 333 (1978). Nor is there such infringement where the prosecutor tries to impeach a defendant's testimony by reference (on cross-examination and in his closing argument to the jury) to his *pre-arrest* failure to communicate to the police his present claim of self-defense. Jenkins v. Anderson, 447 U.S. 231 (1980). See also Raffel v. U.S., 271 U.S. 494 (1926). The situation is distinguished from one in which the silence was after the arrest, i.e., it was preceded by the implicit promise of the *Miranda* warnings that his silence would not be used against him. Doyle v. Ohio, 426 U.S. 610 (1976).

personal; it cannot be claimed by or on behalf of corporations,[114] or for other artificial entities like labor unions, associations, or partnerships.[115] For the same reason, if the officer were required not to testify but to produce corporate documents or broadcasting tapes at the hearing, he could not refuse on the ground that production would incriminate the corporation. Nor could he claim that production would incriminate himself; again, the privilege is (in another sense) personal; the documents are not *his* documents or tapes.[116] But his own *testimony* is another matter; he can claim a privilege against his giving incriminating testimony concerning the documents or tapes, or their whereabouts.[117]

3. What if the prosecutor needs the testimony and all the available officers or employees can validly claim the privilege? He can usually, under the authority of an "immunity statute," ask the court to compel the witness to answer, in exchange for immunity from prosecution. By thus foregoing any conviction of the particular witness, the prosecutor hopes to obtain testimony that will convict other officers and/or the corporation.

The scope of immunity statutes varies among the states. A rather similar variation occurs *within* states depending on the subject matter involved — apparently because immunity provisions of differing subject matter laws were enacted at different times and little effort has been made to go back and unify the approach to the immunity problem. Thus in South Carolina at the time of the *Nappier* case, statutes in different areas of law either (1) authorized a grant of immunity, without explaining its scope,[118] (2) explained that the compelled testimony could not be "used in evidence" against the witness,[119] or (3) explained that the witness could not be prosecuted "for or on account of any transaction, matter or thing concerning which" he gave compelled evidence.[120]

The third type of statute obviously embodies a very broad concept of immunity. Instead of a prohibition merely against the *use* of the compelled evidence against the witness ("use immunity"), we have here a prohibition against prosecution for the *transaction concerning which* he gave the compelled evidence ("transaction immunity"). Thus under

114. Wilson v. U.S., 221 U.S. 361 (1911).

115. U.S. v. White, 322 U.S. 694 (1944) (labor union); McPhaul v. U.S., 364 U.S. 372 (1960) (Civil Rights Congress); Bellis v. U.S., 417 U.S. 85 (1974) (law partnership).

116. U.S. v. White, 322 U.S. 694, 699 (1944); Bellis v. U.S., 417 U.S. 85, 90 (1974).

117. Curcio v. U.S., 344 U.S. 118 (1957).

118. 1962 Code of Law of South Carolina, §10-1805 (nuisances).

119. *Id.*, §16-85 (abortion).

120. *Id.*, §66-115 (corporate violations); §62-307 (proceedings before Securities Commissioner). The latter statute makes exceptions from immunity in the case of perjury or contempt by the witness.

a "use immunity" statute a prosecutor would be free to prosecute on the basis of *other* evidence he obtained by using the compelled evidence as leads; under a "transactional immunity" statute, he could not.

On the federal level an interesting vacillation has existed between those two kinds of immunities,[121] culminating in a 1970 law, applicable to proceedings before federal courts, grand juries, congressional committees, executive departments, and specified, major federal agencies.[122] A witness can be compelled, in accordance with statutory procedures, to testify in spite of his claim of the self-incrimination privilege, and "no testimony or other information compelled under the order (or any information *directly or indirectly derived from* such testimony or other information) may be used against the witness in any criminal case, except a prosecution for perjury, giving a false statement, or otherwise failing to comply with the order" (emphasis added). Thus the witness does not get transactional immunity, but a full use immunity that seems to protect against the compelled evidence being used as leads to other evidence. The Supreme Court, in upholding this statute,[123] said this is all the witness is constitutionally entitled to, namely, an immunity "coextensive with the scope of the privilege." (He is just as well off as he would be if he had invoked the privilege in the absence of an immunity statute, the Government being free thereafter to use evidence, as it is under this statute, from independent sources.) And the prosecution will have the burden, said the Court, of proving affirmatively that the evidence proposed to be used is derived from a legitimate and independent source. To give the

121. A "use immunity" for witnesses before congressional committees was amended in 1954 to embody "transactional immunity" (and to apply to grand juries and courts as well) when the evidence was on *national security* matters, the amended act being upheld in Ullman v. U.S., 350 U.S. 422 (1956). Transactional immunity had been thought by many to be constitutionally required after an 1892 decision had invalidated a "use immunity" statute, applicable to evidence obtained from witnesses in any judicial proceeding, on the ground the immunity was not coextensive with the privilege. Since the compelled evidence could be used as leads to other evidence, the witness was not as well off as he would have been under the constitutional privilege of silence. Counselman v. Hitchcock, 142 U.S. 547, 564-565 (1892). The statute was amended to a transactional immunity type, and upheld in Brown v. Walker, 161 U.S. 591 (1896). However, some backtracking from transactional immunity occurred when the Supreme Court in addressing the state-federal aspects of immunity, declared: No matter which sovereign is asking the questions, the witness's constitutional privilege is against incrimination under the laws of the other sovereign as well, by the *use of the compelled evidence or its fruits;* and an immunity statute is not valid unless, after the compelled testimony, both governments are barred *from using it or its fruits,* in state or federal prosecutions. Thus the government can still prosecute the witness, but it would have the burden of showing that its evidence had an independent, untainted source. Murphy v. Waterfront Commn., 378 U.S. 52 (1964). This kind of *full* "use immunity" was adopted in the 1970 statute now to be discussed in the text.

122. 84 Stat. 926 (1970); 18 U.S.C. §§6001-6005.

123. Kastigar v. U.S., 406 U.S. 44 (1972).

witness transactional immunity would be to give him a bonus; he would be free from prosecution even on the basis of legitimate, completely independent evidence not traceable to the compelled evidence.[124]

A dissenting view was that the witness would *not* be just as well off: The prosecutor (or someone among the people who work up the case for him) might use the compelled evidence as leads to other evidence and falsely claim it was independent evidence. And while the prosecutor has the burden of proof on the issue of independence, the defendant would as a practical matter be hard put to present evidence undermining the prosecutor's assertions about how he got the evidence.

4. Finally, some miscellaneous limits on the applicability of the constitutional privilege should be mentioned: (1) generally, the witness would have to specifically claim the privilege;[125] (2) the claim that a truthful answer would be incriminating is not automatically accepted as true by the tribunal — though it should be accepted unless it is "perfectly clear" that the witness is mistaken in thinking the answer would "furnish a link in the chain of evidence needed to prosecute;"[126] (3) the privilege is inapplicable to evidence that is not of a "*testimonial or communicative* nature" (i.e., inapplicable to mere *production* of business papers in response to subpoena;[127] and inapplicable to evidence such as a blood sample taken by a physician under police direction from an objecting defendant after his arrest for drunken driving,[128] or modeling articles of clothing,[129] or appearing in a police

124. We have been unwilling to allow this, said the Court, in coerced confession cases. "A coerced confession, as revealing of leads as testimony given in exchange for immunity, is inadmissible in a criminal trial but it does not bar prosecution" on independent evidence (citing Jackson v. Denno, 378 U.S. 368 (1964)).

The Court later stressed that for immunity to be coextensive with the protections of the privilege, it is unnecessary for *all* the consequences of compelled testimony to be no more adverse to the witness than the consequences of silence. Even a transactional immunity statute, concededly constitutional, would not provide "a full and complete substitute" for silence, since it would not prevent (1) the use in civil proceedings of the compelled statements, or their use "for any purpose that might cause detriment to the witness other than that resulting from subsequent criminal prosecution"; or (2) the use of compelled statements both truthful and false, in prosecutions for perjury or giving false statements (prosecutions that were specifically provided for in the immunity statute). United States v. Apfelbaum, 445 U.S. 115 (1980). See also, Note, 19 Vill. L. Rev. 470 (1974).

125. Rogers v. U.S., 340 U.S. 367, 370-371 (1951); U.S. v. Monia, 317 U.S. 424, 427 (1943) (statute may dispense with this necessity of prior claim).

126. Hoffman v. U.S., 341 U.S. 479, 486-487 (1951).

127. Fisher v. U.S., 425 U.S. 391, 408-414 (1976).

128. Schmerber v. California, 384 U.S. 757 (1966). The Court said that "both federal and state courts have usually held that [the privilege] offers no protection against compulsion to submit to fingerprinting, photographing, or measurements, to write or speak for identification, to appear in court, to stand, to assume a stance, to walk, or to make a particular gesture" (at 764).

129. Holt v. U.S., 218 U.S. 245 (1910).

lineup and speaking for identification,[130] or yielding examples of one's handwriting);[131] and (4) is also inapplicable to the use of certain required records or reports — a doctrine whose scope is still uncertain.[132]

F. *Due Process of Law*

The "due process clause," protecting any person from being deprived of "life, liberty or property without due process of law" occurs both in the Fifth Amendment (protecting against the federal government) and the Fourteenth (protecting against state governments). "Due process" has an obvious *procedural* significance, which we are concerned with here, though it has also developed a non-procedural or "substantive" meaning.[133]

130. U.S. v. Wade, 388 U.S. 218 (1967).

131. Gilbert v. California, 388 U.S. 263 (1967); U.S. v. Euge, 444 U.S. 707 (1980).

132. Compare Shapiro v. U.S., 335 U.S. 1 (1948) in which the doctrine was applied to a grocer's business records required by the Office of Price Administration to be kept, with Marchetti v. U.S., 390 U.S. 39 (1968), in which the doctrine was held inapplicable to information required to be supplied in connection with an occupational tax on wagering. A major emphasis in the latter opinion was on the fact that *Shapiro* involved "an essentially non-criminal and regulatory area of activity," while *Marchetti* related to a "selective group inherently suspect of criminal activities." Some other decisions similar to *Marchetti* are Grosso v. U.S., 390 U.S. 62 (1968) (a different gambling tax); Haynes v. U.S., 390 U.S. 85 (1968) (firearms registration); Leary v. U.S., 395 U.S. 6 (1969) (marijuana tax). The inherent risk in reporting information in these situations was thought to be absent, and self-reporting was thought to be indispensable to fulfilling an essentially non-criminal statutory purpose, in a case upholding a state "hit and run" statute requiring the driver in an accident to stop and give his name and address. California v. Byers, 402 U.S. 424 (1971). On the business records problem, see generally, Note, 38 Ohio St. L.J. 351 (1977).

133. A judgment that a statute or official conduct violates substantive due process is a judgment that it is arbitrary, i.e., grossly unreasonable or unjust. Thus, a criminal statute that "either forbids or requires the doing of an act in terms so vague that men of common intelligence must necessarily guess at its meaning and differ as to its application violates the first essential of due process of law." Connally v. General Constr. Co., 269 U.S. 385 (1926). See Notes, 109 U. Pa. L. Rev. 67 (1960); 7 Conn. L. Rev. 94 (1974); 9 Houston L. Rev. 82 (1971); Annot., 96 L. Ed. 374 (1952). Also, courts have sometimes struck down a criminal statute on the ground that it "prohibits conduct that bears no substantial relationship to injury to the public. Or, although this same factor is likely to be present, a court will sometimes strike down a statute on the more specific ground that it does not contain one of the traditional elements of a criminal offense. The objection may be that the statute contains no *mens rea* requirement, that is, that it punishes conduct innocently engaged in without any sort of a bad state of mind, or it may be that the statute punishes mere status or condition instead of requiring some specific act or omission to act." LaFave & Scott, Criminal Law 137 (1972). The quotation does not mention the fact (recognized elsewhere by the authors, *id.* at 218-228) that there are narrow

A sampling of the ways in which "due process" gives a defendant procedural protection in a criminal case might include these points: "No principle of procedural due process is more clearly established than that notice of the specific charge, and a chance to be heard in a trial of the issues raised by that charge, if desired, are among the constitutional rights of every accused. . . ."[134] The right to a hearing includes "a right to examine the witnesses against him, to offer testimony and to be represented by counsel,"[135] as well as a right to an impartial judge,[136] and a trial free from excessive pre-trial publicity,[137] mob domination,[138] or certain prejudicial practices during trial. The latter include a "carnival atmosphere"[139] or unconsented obtrusive televising of the trial[140] or being compelled over objection to stand trial before a jury while dressed in prison clothes,[141] or the prosecutor's knowing use of perjured testimony[142] or his "suppression . . . of evidence favorable to an accused upon [the accused's] request [for disclosure] . . . where the evidence is material either to guilt or to punishment . . . ,"[143] or other pre-judicial conduct of the prosecutor in the courtroom (e.g., bullying witnesses, misstating the facts in his cross-examination, making assertions calculated to mislead the jury, and generally forgetting that his duty is not to convict but to see that justice is done).[144] A conviction violates due process if based on a rule of law that has been applied retroactively — i.e., a rule not in existence at the time of the alleged

---

legal areas, such as food and drug laws, in which criminal liability without fault is upheld. For recent Supreme Court discussion of the *mens rea* requirement, see U.S. v. U.S. Gypsum Co., 438 U.S. 422, 436-443 (1978).

134. Cole v. Arkansas, 333 U.S. 196, 201 (1948).

135. In re Oliver, 333 U.S. 257, 273 (1948). For some interferences with the right to present testimony and cross-examine that were held violative of due process, see Chambers v. Mississippi, 410 U.S. 284 (1973).

136. Ward v. Village of Monroeville, 409 U.S. 57 (1972); In re Murchison, 349 U.S. 133 (1955); Tumey v. Ohio, 273 U.S. 510 (1927).

137. Rideau v. Louisiana, 373 U.S. 723 (1963); Irvin v. Dowd, 366 U.S. 717 (1961); Groppi v. Wisconsin, 400 U.S. 505 (1971). *Cf.* Murphy v. Florida, 421 U.S. 794 (1975).

138. Moore v. Dempsey, 261 U.S. 86 (1923).

139. Sheppard v. Maxwell, 384 U.S. 333 (1966).

140. Estes v. Texas, 381 U.S. 532 (1965). In Chandler v. Florida, 66 L. Ed. 2d 740 (1981), the Supreme Court held that Florida's rule of court allowing under specified safeguards the radio, television, and still photographic coverage of a criminal trial for public broadcasting, over defendant's objection, did not in itself violate due process. Defendant would have to show that the jury's ability to judge fairly had been compromised, or that there was adverse impact on trial participants.

141. Estelle v. Williams, 425 U.S. 501 (1976). In the particular case, a failure to object to the court negated the necessary compulsion.

142. Mooney v. Holohan, 294 U.S. 103 (1935).

143. Brady v. Maryland, 373 U.S. 83, 87 (1963); Giglio v. U.S., 405 U.S. 150 (1972). See also Wardius v. Oregon, 412 U.S. 470 (1973). *Cf.* Moore v. Illinois, 408 U.S. 786 (1972).

144. Berger v. U.S., 295 U.S. 78 (1935).

offense.[145] A conviction must be based on evidence in the record,[146] and the prosecution must prove "beyond a reasonable doubt" "every fact necessary to constitute" the crime charged.[147] The burden of proof standard has produced some complexities in recent cases exploring its meaning[148] and in cases dealing with "presumptions" of various kinds.[149]

145. See, e.g., Marks v. U.S., 430 U.S. 188 (1977), applying this principle to a *judicial* change in rule. Applying to a criminal defendant a *legislative* rule not in existence at the time of the alleged offense would be constitutionally prohibited to the states (Art. I, §10) and the federal government (Art. I, §9) since the rule would be an *ex post facto* law.

146. Thompson v. Louisville, 362 U.S. 199 (1960).

147. In re Winship, 397 U.S. 358 (1970).

148. The rule of *Winship, supra,* means that if the state is charging murder and the defendant claims the facts fit a manslaughter requirement of "heat of passion upon sudden provocation," the state must prove beyond a reasonable doubt the intent necessary for murder *and the absence of* heat of passion upon sudden provocation. Mullaney v. Wilbur, 421 U.S. 684 (1975). Yet the case of Patterson v. New York, 432 U.S. 197 (1977) upheld a New York statute requiring that in order to reduce the charge of second degree murder (intentional causing of another's death) to manslaughter, the *defendant* must prove by a preponderance of evidence the affirmative defense of extreme emotional disturbance. The Court said the affirmative defense did not negative any facts of the crime (the death, the intent, causation) that the state had the burden of proving beyond a reasonable doubt. It said that *Mullaney,* in spite of some of its language, had not been intended to require the prosecution to prove beyond a reasonable doubt *all* facts affecting the degree of culpability; the legislature still had some discretion in allocating burden of proof. The Court also treated as still good law a 1952 decision upholding the Oregon law that required *defendant* to establish an insanity defense beyond a reasonable doubt (Leland v. Oregon, 343 U.S. 790 (1952)). See also Rivera v. Delaware, 429 U.S. 877 (1976) (appeal raising question of continued validity of *Leland* was dismissed as not raising a substantial federal question). In the case of a state's civil, involuntary commitment of a person to a mental hospital: This cannot occur on the basis of a "preponderance" of the evidence; a "clear and convincing" evidence standard is valid; and a "beyond a reasonable doubt" standard is permissible, but not required. Addington v. Texas, 441 U.S. 418 (1979).

149. The prosecution's burden of proof cannot be freely alleviated by statutory "presumptions"; such a presumption concerning the facts necessary to establish guilt must show a "rational connection" between the facts proved and the facts presumed. Thus, a statutory presumption that possessors of marijuana and cocaine had received the drugs through illegal importation was unconstitutional, but was rational enough to be sustained in the case of heroin since almost all heroin used in the United States is illegally imported. Leary v. U.S., 395 U.S. 6 (1969); Turner v. U.S., 396 U.S. 399 (1970). See also County Court of Ulster County v. Allen, 442 U.S. 140 (1979); Tot v. U.S. 319 U.S. 463 (1943); Casey v. U.S., 276 U.S. 413 (1928). In a recent homicide case, a jury instruction embodying a presumption that a person intends the natural and probable consequences of his acts was held an unconstitutional violation of the *Winship* beyond-a-reasonable-doubt rule, insofar as the jury may have interpreted the presumption as *conclusive* or as shifting the burden of persuasion from the prosecution to the defendant. Sandstrom v. Montana, 442 U.S. 510 (1979). While other instructions and the totality of other circumstances may make a presumption-of-innocence instruction unnecessary (Kentucky v. Whorton, 441 U.S. 786 (1979)), the case of Taylor v. Kentucky, 436 U.S. 478 (1978), shows that an instruction may sometimes have to be added to a beyond-a-reasonable-doubt instruction. Here the prosecution had repeatedly suggested that the fact of being an indicted defendant

The rights of mentally ill defendants have been protected by a number of due process decisions. If the individual is mentally incompetent to stand trial he has a due process right not to be tried in such a condition,[150] and not to be indefinitely committed to a mental institution solely because of that incompetency, i.e., without any further determination, such as of dangerousness to himself or others.[151] If the defendant was insane at the time of the *offense,* some courts would say he has a due process right not to be convicted for that offense.[152] And if he has been acquitted on the ground of insanity at the time of the offense, he may well have a due process right not to be automatically committed to a mental institution without prior hearing on the issue of his now existing insanity.[153]

In other areas, outside of the trial itself, due process claims of the defendant have been recognized in some situations and not in others. We have seen earlier that police tactics like searches and seizures are subject to a due process limit in terms of the kind of brutality that "shocks the conscience."[154] When a state prosecutor proceeds by filing an "information" rather than going before a grand jury, due process requires "a judicial determination of probable cause as a prerequisite to extended restraint on liberty following arrest." But in this "preliminary hearing" there is no constitutional right to a full adversary hearing; the magistrate can proceed on the basis of hearsay and written testimony.[155] In the typical plea-bargaining situation, no due process violation is created merely through the prosecution's inducement of the defendant to plead guilty, by offering a reduction of charges or promising to recommend a lenient sentence; or through the prosecutor's carrying out the threat made during plea negotiations to reindict the

---

tended to establish guilt, thus making it necessary to emphasize, by the requested presumption instruction, that defendant was to be judged solely on the trial testimony.

150. Drope v. Missouri, 420 U.S. 162 (1975); Pate v. Robinson, 383 U.S. 375 (1966).

151. Jackson v. Indiana, 406 U.S. 715 (1972). The Court said that one who is thus committed indefinitely solely because of incapacity for trial cannot be held more than the reasonable period necessary to decide if there is a substantial probability he will attain that capacity in the foreseeable future. If he probably will not, the government must either release him or institute the civil commitment proceeding necessary to commit indefinitely any other citizen. Even if he probably will be so capable, "his continued commitment must be justified by progress towards that goal." As to a civil commitment, "a state cannot constitutionally confine without more a nondangerous individual who is capable of surviving safely in freedom by himself or with the help of willing and responsible family members and friends." O'Connor v. Donaldson, 422 U.S. 563, 576 (1975).

152. Sinclair v. State, 161 Miss. 142, 132 So. 581 (1931); State v. Strasburg, 60 Wash. 106, 110 P. 1020 (1910).

153. LaFave & Scott, Criminal Law 318-319 (1972).

154. See Rochin v. California, *supra* n.35.

155. Gerstein v. Pugh, 420 U.S. 103, 114, 120 (1975).

accused on more serious charges (for which he was clearly subject to prosecution) if he did not plead guilty to the original charge.[156]

Due process entitles parolees and probationers to an almost full administrative hearing before revocation of parole or probation.[157] Additionally prisoners are entitled to full hearing rights before they can be transferred to a mental hospital,[158] but can claim no such rights when the transferal is from one prison to another;[159] and they have lesser hearing rights before imposition of discipline for alleged misconduct within the prison.[160] Due process apparently still requires no substantial hearing before a judge's determination of sentence,[161] no right to an appellate review of the sentence, and indeed no right to any appeal in a criminal case[162] — though of course criminal appeals are generally allowed by statute (and a "collateral" or indirect review is allowed to a prisoner through the constitutional guarantee of habeas

156. Bordenkircher v. Hayes, 434 U.S. 357 (1978). Plea bargaining, said the Court, "flows from the 'mutuality of advantage' to defendants and prosecutors each with his own reasons for wanting to avoid trial." The accused, with assistance of counsel, is "free to accept or reject the prosecutor's offer." The "fear of the possibility of a greater penalty upon conviction after a trial" does not render a guilty plea "involuntary in a constitutional sense." But some circumstances are distinguishable on the ground of likely prosecutor "vindictiveness." See, e.g., Blackledge v. Perry, 417 U.S. 21 (1974). See generally, Alschuler, The Changing Plea Bargaining Debate, 69 Calif. L. Rev. 652 (1981); McCoy & Mirra, Plea Bargaining As Due Process In Determining Guilt, 32 Stan. L. Rev. 887 (1980); Symposium, 13 Law & Socy. Rev. 189 (1979); Alschuler, Plea Bargaining and Its History, 79 Colum. L. Rev. 1 (1979); Annot., 50 L. Ed. 2d 876 (1978).

157. Morrissey v. Brewer, 408 U.S. 471 (1972); Gagnon v. Scarpelli, 411 U.S. 778 (1973).

158. Vitek v. Jones, 445 U.S. 480 (1980).

159. Meachum v. Fano, 427 U.S. 215 (1976); Montanye v. Haymes, 427 U.S. 236 (1976).

160. Wolff v. McDonnell, 418 U.S. 539 (1974). In the cases cited in the preceding two sentences of the text, the Court applied its fairly recent theory that the existence of the necessary "liberty interest" that would trigger due process protection can be dependent on state law creation of such an interest, with attendant justifiable expectation on the part of the party invoking due process. See, for the theory, Chap. 5 herein at 332 n.68.

161. Williams v. New York, 337 U.S. 241 (1949); Williams v. Oklahoma, 358 U.S. 576 (1959). But *cf.* U.S. v. Tucker, 404 U.S. 443 (1972) (sentence cannot, consistently with due process, be based on misinformation of a constitutional magnitude); Gardner v. Florida, 430 U.S. 349 (1977) (plurality views); Specht v. Patterson, 386 U.S. 605 (1967); Schulhofer, Due Process of Sentencing, 128 U. Pa. L. Rev. 733, 760-764 (1980); Annot., 63 L. Ed. 2d 872 (1981). Federal Criminal Rule 32(c)(3), as amended in 1975, requires *disclosure* of pre-sentence reports, exclusive of any sentence recommendations, when requested by the defense, unless certain exceptions apply. These exceptions are "designed to prevent disruption of rehabilitative programs, violations of promises of confidentiality, and the possibility of harm to the defendant or others." Fennell & Hall, Due Process at Sentencing: An Empirical and Legal Analysis of the Disclosure of Pre-sentence Reports in Federal Courts, 93 Harv. L. Rev. 1615, 1619 (1980).

162. McKane v. Durston, 153 U.S. 684 (1894).

corpus review), and the statutes of perhaps half the states, contrary to typical federal practice, allow review of the sentence.[163]

Mention might also be made here of a due process–like right that is covered not by the due process clause but by clauses entirely outside of the Bill of Rights, namely the "bill of attainder" clauses.[164] They prohibit both Congress and the states from passing a bill of attainder — which has been construed to mean a law that inflicts punishment without the opportunity of trial or hearing.[165]

G. *Speedy and Public Trial*

In the Sixth Amendment guarantee of a "speedy and public trial," the requirement of speed has not been interpreted in terms of any absolute standard. The Supreme Court has rejected "inflexible approaches" and adopted instead a "balancing test, in which the conduct of both the prosecution and the defendant are weighed" on the basis of four factors: length of delay; government justification of the delay (e.g., overcrowded docket as against attempt to hurt the defense); whether and how defendant asserted his right (there being no presumption of his acquiescence in delay because of his lack of request for trial); and prejudice to the defendant (e.g., greater pre-trial incarceration, greater anxiety, impairment of the defense).[166] On the federal level, the Speedy Trial Act of 1974[167] has created some more specific limits: Usually a charge must be filed within 30 days from arrest, the arraignment must occur within 10 days, and the trial must commence within 60 days thereafter.[168]

163. See Comment, 17 St. Louis U.L.J. 221 (1972). On sentencing generally, in addition to citations in n.161 *supra,* see Schwartz, Options in Constructing A Sentencing System: Sentencing Guidelines Under Legislative or Judicial Hegemony, 67 Va. L. Rev. 637 (1981); Crump, Determinate Sentencing: The Promises and Perils of Sentence Guidelines, 68 Ky. L.J. 1 (1979-1980); Perlman & Potuto, The Uniform Law Commissioners' Model Sentencing and Corrections Act: An Overview, 58 Neb. L. Rev. 925 (1979); Symposium, Parts 1 and 2, 7 Hofstra L. Rev. 1; 243 (1978-79); Zalman, The Rise and Fall of the Indeterminate Sentence, 24 Wayne L. Rev. 857 (1978); Coffee, The Future of Sentencing Reform: Emerging Legal Issues in the Individualization of Justice, 73 Mich. L. Rev. 1361 (1975); Frankel, Criminal Sentences: Law Without Order (1973).

164. They apply against Congress (Art. I, §9) and the states (Art. I, §10).

165. See Schwartz, Constitutional Law, 307-309 (2d ed. 1979); U.S. v. Brown, 381 U.S. 437 (1965).

166. Barker v. Wingo, 407 U.S. 514, 530-533 (1972). See, generally, Joseph, Speedy Trial Rights in Application, 48 Fordham L. Rev. 611 (1980).

167. 88 Stat. 2076 (1974), 93 Stat. 327 (1979); 18 U.S.C. §§3161-3174.

168. 18 U.S.C. §3161.

The "public trial" requirement, according to a 1979 Supreme Court ruling, does not prevent a court from protecting defendant's fair trial rights by an order (agreed to by defendant and prosecution) excluding members of the press and public from a *pre-trial* hearing on suppression of evidence in a murder case — and denying access to a pre-trial transcript until the danger to defendant's fair trial right has dissipated. The intended beneficiary to the "public trial" right, said the Court, is the defendant rather than the public.[169] In 1980, however, focusing on the First Amendment, the Court ruled that that Amendment guarantees public and media access to *trials*.[170]

H. *Jury Trial*

An "impartial jury of the State and district wherein the crime shall have been committed" is guaranteed by the Sixth Amendment against the United States Government, and, since 1968,[171] by Fourteenth Amendment due process against the states.

The jury trial right extends to all non-petty offenses (i.e., carrying potential imprisonment of more than six months),[172] but not to juvenile delinquency proceedings.[173] The defendant's desire to waive a jury in favor of a trial before the judge alone can constitutionally be made to depend on the prosecutor's consent.[174]

However, the Sixth Amendment does not require a 12-person jury, as has been the practice in federal courts;[175] a state's use of a 6-person jury in a non-capital felony case was upheld.[176] Nor does it require a state to adopt the federal court practice[177] of unanimous verdicts; 9 to

169. Gannett Co. v. De Pasquale, 443 U.S. 368 (1979). This does not mean that only the defendant actually receives a benefit from the public nature of the trial. An earlier case, striking down a summary commitment for contempt by a judge sitting in secret under a one-man grand jury system, referred to such benefits as protection against possible judicial abuse, the alerting of witnesses unknown to the parties, and the teaching of spectators about their government so that they acquire confidence in judicial remedies. In re Oliver, 333 U.S. 257, 270 (1948).

170. Richmond Newspapers v. Virginia, 448 U.S. 555 (1980).

171. Duncan v. Louisiana, 391 U.S. 145 (1968).

172. Baldwin v. New York, 399 U.S. 66 (1970). Criminal contempt proceedings are included, where the sentence imposed exceeded six months. Bloom v. Illinois, 391 U.S. 194 (1968); Codispoti v. Pennsylvania, 418 U.S. 506 (1974).

173. McKeiver v. Pennsylvania, 403 U.S. 528 (1971).

174. Singer v. U.S. 380 U.S. 24 (1965).

175. Fed. R. Crim. 23(b). The parties may stipulate otherwise with the court's approval.

176. Williams v. Florida, 399 U.S. 78 (1970). Use of a six-person jury in a federal *civil* case was upheld in Colegrove v. Battin, 413 U.S. 149 (1973).

177. Fed. R. Crim. 31(a).

3, 11 to 1, and 10 to 2 verdicts in non-capital felony cases were upheld,[178] but not a state's conviction of a non-petty criminal offense by a non-unanimous 6-person jury.[179]

The jury trial right does imply a requirement that the jury be chosen from a fair cross section of the community. Hence, intentional exclusion of certain "economic, social, religious, racial, political and geographical groups" would be unconstitutional.[180] Examples are systematic, intentional exclusion of all those "who work for a daily wage,"[181] or of any women who have not filed a written statement of their desire to serve.[182] But as the opinion in the latter situation observed, the "fair cross-section principle must have much lee-way in application." Thus, as is well known, most statutes exempt groups like lawyers, doctors, and ministers; and such statutory or administrative exclusions are thought to serve the public interest,[183] as does the excusing of particular individuals on grounds of hardship. So too, "blue-ribbon" juries with better qualifications for certain important or complex cases have been upheld,[184] as has a statute restricting jury service to persons "esteemed in the community for their integrity, good character and sound judgment" (though a *prima facie* case of discrimination in *administering* such a statute can be shown, as in other instances, by a striking disparity between the percentage of blacks in the community and the small percentage of blacks called to jury duty).[185] In the examination of prospective jurors, a prosecutor's use of his

178. Johnson v. Louisiana, 406 U.S. 356 (1972); Apodaca v. Oregon, 406 U.S. 404 (1971). Justice Powell, one of the five majority Justices in *Apodaca,* argued in a concurring opinion that the Sixth Amendment did require unanimity, but that unanimity was not so essential an element of the jury trial right as to have been incorporated into Fourteenth Amendment due process. Thus, five Justices (Powell and the four dissenters) believed that verdict unanimity is constitutionally required for the federal courts, and a different five (Powell and the other four in the majority) believed it not required for the state courts.

179. Burch v. Louisiana, 441 U.S. 130 (1979).

180. Thiel v. Southern Pac. Co., 328 U.S. 217 (1946).

181. *Id.*

182. Taylor v. Louisiana, 419 U.S. 522 (1975). The defendant was allowed to make this challenge in spite of being a male. Similarly a white defendant was allowed to challenge a jury from which blacks had been systematically excluded. Peters v. Kiff, 407 U.S. 493 (1972). Even blacks who are non-defendants can sue to restrain officials from administering a jury selection system in a manner that systematically discriminates against blacks. Carter v. Jury Commn., 396 U.S. 320 (1970).

183. See Rawlins v. Georgia, 201 U.S. 638 (1906).

184. Fay v. New York, 332 U.S. 261 (1947); Moore v. New York, 333 U.S. 565 (1948).

185. Turner v. Fouche, 396 U.S. 346 (1970) (grand jury). Cases condemning racial discrimination in the selection of juries (e.g., Strauder v. West Virginia, 100 U.S. 303 (1880); Norris v. Alabama, 294 U.S. 587 (1935)) or grand juries (Pierre v. Louisiana, 306 U.S. 354 (1939)) go back a long way. "Equal protection of the laws" as well as "due process," under the Fourteenth Amendment, have been commonly invoked in such racial discrimination cases.

"peremptory challenges" (those for which no reason need be given) that resulted in the striking of all the prospective black jurors was found not to be unconstitutional, there being no showing that the prosecutor had systematically achieved this result over a period of time.[186] Other examples could be cited.[187]

The Sixth Amendment requirement that the jury be drawn from "the State and district wherein the crime shall have been committed" (known as the "vicinage") means that the jury can be drawn from the whole federal district — there are approximately 90 districts — or from a part of the district.[188] The states usually have analogous vicinage requirements in state constitutions or statutes.

I. Notice of Charge; Confrontation; Compulsory Process

The defendant's Sixth Amendment rights "to be informed of the nature and cause of the accusation; to be confronted with the witnesses against him; [and] to have compulsory process for obtaining witnesses in his favor . . ." deal with some basic aspects of a fair trial.

The right-to-be-informed portion is of course similar to the "due process" right of notice previously mentioned, including the freedom

186. Swain v. Alabama, 380 U.S. 202 (1965).

187. No unconstitutional deprivation of a representative jury for the "young" occurs by virtue of the fact that a jury list, compiled every four years, necessarily failed to include those who became eligible in the interim between lists. Hamling v. U.S., 418 U.S. 87 (1974) (because of the "practical problems of administration," said the Court, there has to be "play in the joints of the jury selection process"). Exclusion, in a capital case, of jurors with "conscientious or religious scruples against capital punishment" was not an unconstitutional deprivation of a representative jury on the guilt issue (there being no showing that such excluded jurors would differ from other jurors in their attitude on the guilt issue). But the exclusion did violate jury impartiality on the issue of sentence (being decided in this capital case by the jury). The state was not limiting the exclusion to those who would reject capital punishment in all cases; it was sweeping more broadly, and in effect selecting a "hanging jury." Witherspoon v. Illinois, 391 U.S. 510 (1968). The fact that some or all of the jurors are federal employees does not itself violate the impartiality requirement; individual jurors can be examined for bias. U.S. v. Wood, 299 U.S. 123 (1936); Frazier v. U.S. 335 U.S. 497 (1948). A judge who, in examining prospective jurors in a case against a black, bearded defendant, asked whether the jurors were conscious of any bias or prejudice against the defendant acted in violation of Fourteenth Amendment due process in not questioning them (or permitting counsel to question) specifically as to *racial* bias, as requested. But he was not so required to ask, as requested, whether they were biased against beards. Ham v. South Carolina, 409 U.S. 524 (1973).

188. Ruthenberg v. U.S., 245 U.S. 480, 482 (1918); Barrett v. U.S., 169 U.S. 218 (1898).

from undue vagueness.[189] But the older tendency toward technicality and over-meticulousness in criminal pleading has dissipated. "The rigor of old common law rules of criminal pleading has yielded, in modern practice, to the general principle that formal defects, not prejudicial, will be disregarded."[190] Federal Criminal Rule 7(c)(1) requires that the indictment "shall be a plain, concise and definite written statement of the essential facts constituting the offense charged." The accusation must give the elements of defendant's offense, sufficiently apprise him of what he must prepare a defense against, and, together with the rest of the record, sufficiently identify the offense so as to enable him to argue double jeopardy against a future prosecution for the same offense.[191] A conviction cannot be affirmed on the ground that the evidence showed a certain statutory violation if the indictment had charged the violation of a different statutory provision.[192]

The "confrontation" part of the Amendment has sometimes been invoked in "hearsay" situations — i.e., a witness's statements made prior to the trial have often been treated as "hearsay" and hence inadmissible to prove the *truth* of the matters asserted therein, though they may be admitted to *"impeach"* the credibility of the witness. Some jurisdictions, however, allow the first type of use as well, a method of procedure that will violate the confrontation clause *unless* (1) the maker of the prior statement becomes subject to cross-examination as a witness, or (2) though he is clearly unavailable[193] as a witness, the prior statement had itself been subject to cross-examination or its equivalent.[194] There are other interesting confrontation rulings. E.g., the clause is violated by the court bailiff slipping some free advice to the sequestered jury he was in charge of, which creates a situation analogous to testimony not subject to cross-examination.[195] The clause is also violated when cross-examination is unduly restricted in certain

189. See *supra* 434 n.133 & 435.

190. Hagner v. U.S., 285 U.S. 427, 431 (1932).

191. *Id.*, Russell v. U.S., 369 U.S. 749 (1962).

192. Cole v. Arkansas, 333 U.S. 196 (1948); Stirone v. U.S., 361 U.S. 212 (1960).

193. E.g., the witness has died or transferred to a foreign country, as distinct from, for instance, being in a federal prison from which the state authorities had not made a good faith effort to get him temporarily released. Compare Mancusi v. Stubbs, 408 U.S. 204 (1972) with Barber v. Page, 390 U.S. 719 (1968).

194. Ohio v. Roberts, 448 U.S. 56 (1980); California v. Green, 399 U.S. 149 (1970); Pointer v. Texas, 380 U.S. 400 (1965). (The *Pointer* case made the Sixth Amendment confrontation clause applicable to the states by way of Fourteenth Amendment due process.) An example of a situation in which the author of the prior statement is not now testifying and the prior statement had *not* been subject to cross-examination, is the introduction in evidence of the confession of a co-defendant who does not himself testify. This violates the confrontation right. Bruton v. U.S., 391 U.S. 123 (1968). *Cf.* Harrington v. California, 395 U.S. 250 (1968); Nelson v. O'Neil, 402 U.S. 622 (1971); Dutton v. Evans, 400 U.S. 74 (1970).

195. Parker v. Gladden, 385 U.S. 363 (1966). *Cf.* Turner v. Louisiana, 379 U.S. 466 (1965) (based on impartial jury requirement).

ways.[196] However, defendant can forfeit the right to confront witnesses when his own disruptive behavior justifies his exclusion from the courtroom,[197] or if he has voluntarily absented himself from the courtroom.[198]

The "compulsory process" portion of the Amendment empowers the defendant to use court subpoenas to summon witnesses in his behalf. The Amendment of course assumes a right to present witnesses. In a 1967 case holding this provision applicable to the states through Fourteenth Amendment due process, the Court struck down a state law prohibiting one party to an alleged crime from testifying in behalf of another participant therein.[199]

J. "Assistance of Counsel for his Defense"

The final portion of the Sixth Amendment guarantees the right of an individual "to have the assistance of counsel for his defense." Relevant litigation here has been mainly concerned with defendants who were too poor to pay for counsel.

The indigent defendant's right to free appointed counsel in the federal courts was made clear in 1938.[200] The same right in the state courts had a rocky course before gaining full recognition. The Court recognized the right in state *capital* cases in 1932;[201] and in 1942 it declared that in a *non*-capital state case, due process did not require appointment of counsel unless the trial would be rendered obviously unjust by absence of counsel (e.g., when the defendant was illiterate, very young, or below average in intelligence).[202] When this rule proved unsatisfactory, the Court finally established, in the famous 1963 Gideon

196. Smith v. Illinois, 390 U.S. 129 (1968) (questions asking the police informer witness's name and address were precluded); Davis v. Alaska, 415 U.S. 308 (1974) (questions that would have revealed a prosecution witness's juvenile delinquent probationary status were precluded). See also Chambers v. Mississippi, 410 U.S. 284 (1973) (due process).

197. Illinois v. Allen, 397 U.S. 337 (1970).

198. Taylor v. U.S., 414 U.S. 17 (1973). Generally on confrontation, see Westen, The Future of Confrontation, 77 Mich. L. Rev. 1185 (1979).

199. Washington v. Texas, 388 U.S. 14 (1967). Unconstitutional interference with the right to present witnesses was also found when a judge had admonished a putative witness in such terms of intimidation, warning, or threat that he "effectively drove that witness off the stand." Webb v. Texas, 409 U.S. 95 (1972). See also Chambers v. Mississippi, 410 U.S. 284 (1973).

200. Johnson v. Zerbst, 304 U.S. 458 (1938).

201. Powell v. Alabama, 287 U.S. 45 (1932).

202. Betts v. Brady, 316 U.S. 455 (1942). An affluent enough defendant was of course entitled to employ and pay for counsel. Chandler v. Freitag, 348 U.S. 3 (1954).

v. Wainwright burglary case,[203] the principle that Fourteenth Amendment due process, incorporating the Sixth Amendment right to counsel, guaranteed free appointed counsel to indigents. This was a felony case.

In 1972, Argersinger v. Hamlin[204] applied the same point in a misdemeanor case, in a somewhat qualified way: "Absent a knowing and intelligent waiver, no person may be imprisoned for any offense, whether classified as petty misdemeanor or felony, unless he was represented by counsel at his trial." Notice that this ruling is not in terms of a right to counsel for an offense *punishable* by imprisonment. Rather, in an apparent effort to avoid too drastic a drain on funds and personnel, the language here is couched in terms of actual imprisonment. Before the trial, therefore, the judge is required to determine the likelihood of an imprisonment sentence in order to decide whether counsel should be appointed. The Court stuck to its guns in 1979 by a bare majority, by reaffirming *Argersinger* and ruling that a state trial of an indigent defendant without counsel (for a shoplifting offense carrying maximum penalties of a year in jail or $500 fine or both, and for which he was only fined $50) was valid since imprisonment was not imposed.[205]

The right to counsel, though important at the trial stage, accrues at some other stages, too. Under the *Miranda* rule mentioned earlier (at 429-430), which was created to safeguard the self-incrimination privilege rather than as a requirement of the Sixth Amendment, the right of retained or appointed counsel accrues at police interrogation when the suspect is in custody or his freedom is otherwise curtailed significantly. In applying requirements of the Sixth Amendment (and of Fourteenth Amendment due process in a state case), the right is held to accrue at certain "critical" stages, occurring *after* initiation of "adversary judicial criminal proceedings": line-ups;[206]

203. 372 U.S. 335 (1963).

204. 407 U.S. 25 (1972).

205. Scott v. Illinois, 440 U.S. 367 (1979). See Note, 41 U. Pitt. L. Rev. 647 (1980). Rejected by the Court were proposals that the line be drawn at offenses punishable by imprisonment, or be drawn (as in the case of the jury trial right) at offenses punishable by more than six months imprisonment. The National Advisory Commission on Criminal Justice Standards and Goals (in Corrections, 27-28 (1973)) has urged recognition of the right to counsel for all misdemeanants, jailable and otherwise. In the *federal* courts, under Fed. R. Crim. P. 44(a): "Every defendant who is unable to obtain counsel shall be entitled to have counsel assigned to represent him at every stage of the proceedings. . . ." The Court's position in *Argersinger* and *Scott* is similar to that of the American Bar Association Project on Minimum Standards for Criminal Justice, Standards Relating to Providing Defense Services 40 (1968).

206. Kirby v. Illinois, 406 U.S. 682 (1972); U.S. v. Wade, 388 U.S. 218 (1967); Gilbert v. California, 388 U.S. 263 (1967). The Court has read the line-up identification rule narrowly, refusing to apply its principle to a photograph identification

initial appearances before a magistrate in some circumstances;[207] preliminary examinations before a magistrate for determination of probable cause;[208] while in custody, after indictment, with a cell-mate who as government informer was monitoring defendant's conversations;[209] arraignments to receive defendant's plea, though not always;[210] and sentencing.[211] As for appeals, under the Fourteenth Amendment's "equal protection" clause, an indigent defendant in a state case has a right to appointed counsel in the first appeal available as a matter of right,[212] but not for seeking discretionary review in the state appellate courts or in the United States Supreme Court.[213] Finally, the Supreme Court squarely recognized for the first time in 1975 the right of an indigent criminal defendant to refuse appointed counsel and choose

---

session held after indictment. U.S. v. Ash, 413 U.S. 300 (1973). In the *Wade* case, *supra* at 227-228, the Court had indicated inapplicability of the rule to the taking and analyzing of "the accused's fingerprints, blood sample, clothing, hair and the like" because these activities unwitnessed by counsel do not involve the same risks as a suggestive line-up procedure unwitnessed by counsel.

207. White v. Maryland, 373 U.S. 59 (1963). The accused had been asked to enter an informal, non-binding plea at this stage, and the fact that he had pleaded guilty was introduced against him at the trial. Perhaps the initial appearance stage will also be viewed as critical if it is the time when he waived any preliminary examination.

208. Coleman v. Alabama, 399 U.S. 1 (1970). *Grand jury* proceedings do not qualify. The Court stated in 1957 a principle applicable even to retained counsel: that a "witness before a grand jury cannot insist, as a matter of constitutional right, on being represented by his counsel, nor can a witness before other investigatory bodies." In re Groban, 352 U.S. 330, 333 (1957). Even when a grand jury witness was a potential defendant, four out of six Justices who reached the counsel issue found (1) no right to counsel under the Sixth Amendment since no criminal proceedings had yet been instituted against him, and (2) no right to counsel and warnings under the *Miranda* rule, the latter being applicable to the potentially coercive, abuse-prone, police station setting, not to the setting of "courts or other official investigations." U.S. v. Mandujano, 425 U.S. 564, 579 (1976). The witness had no valid objection in this case to the limited right offered him of having his retained counsel available for consultation outside the jury room.

209. U.S. v. Henry, 447 U.S. 264 (1980). Admission in evidence of incriminating statements made to the cell-mate violated this right to counsel. The Court distinguished the government's use of undercover agents to obtain incriminating statements from persons *not in custody* and prior to filing of charges. (See *supra* at n.57.)

210. This is clearly a "critical" stage if he pleaded guilty (and if the law did not allow him to withdraw his guilty plea with no mention of the plea thereafter), but generally not so if he pleaded not guilty and counsel was then appointed for the trial. But even here, circumstances can make arraignment a critical stage, as in the capital case of Hamilton v. Alabama, 368 U.S. 52 (1961). In Alabama, this was the stage at which the defendant had to make any claim to an insanity defense, any "pleas in abatement," and any motions to quash based on invalid drawings of the grand jury.

211. Mempha v. Ray, 389 U.S. 128 (1968). The right accrued even though sentencing had been deferred and then imposed initially at a probation revocation proceeding.

212. Douglas v. California, 372 U.S. 353 (1963).

213. Ross v. Moffit, 417 U.S. 600 (1974).

to be his own trial lawyer.[214] Here, as at other stages of the criminal proceedings, any "waiver" of the right must be "knowing and intelligent."[215]

What about non-criminal proceedings related to criminal cases? At board hearings on the usual type of probation or parole revocation (which have been held *not* part of a "criminal prosecution" under the Sixth Amendment) the indigent has a federal due process right to appointed counsel only if, under the particular facts, he could not get a fair hearing without it[216] — and whether the right to *retained* counsel is any broader was left undecided. In prison disciplinary proceedings, the inmate has no federal constitutional right to either retained or appointed counsel.[217] In post-conviction proceedings, typically habeas corpus, the right to appointed counsel is still unclear. In state juvenile delinquency proceedings, the Fourteenth Amendment due process right to retained counsel and (in the case of parental indigency) to appointed counsel, was announced in 1967.[218]

Some practical limitations on the judicially announced right to appointed counsel have arisen from (1) the varied meanings given by local judges to the *Argersinger* rule — including the disposition of some courts to interpret "indigency" almost in terms of destitution, and to apply in loose fashion the requirements applicable to notice and waiver of the right; (2) the claimed lesser effectiveness of appointed, compared to retained, counsel — stemming partly at least from the fact that most appointed counsel or public defenders are forced to represent clients without the benefit of funds for supportive services like those of investigators or experts; and (3) the claimed inadequacy of supply of public funds and lawyers to fulfill the need.[219]

These supportive services are necessary, an indigent could argue, in order to (a) make the rights to assistance of counsel effective and to

214. Faretta v. California, 422 U.S. 806 (1975).

215. On waiver of right to counsel, see Israel & LaFave, *supra* n.8 at 371-379.

216. Gagnon v. Scarpelli, 441 U.S. 778 (1973); Morrissey v. Brewer, 408 U.S. 471 (1972). The usual type of probation revocation is one in which a sentence had previously been imposed and suspended in favor of probation. The probation and parole board's determination of whether to revoke probation is thus deemed not part of the "criminal prosecution" referred to by the Sixth Amendment.

217. Wolf v. McDonnell, 418 U.S. 539 (1975). This is true though the conduct involved might also be punishable in state criminal proceedings. Baxter v. Palmigiano, 425 U.S. 308 (1976).

218. In re Gault, 387 U.S. 1 (1967).

219. On these points, see Mermin, The Constitutional Right to Counsel In America, 50 Philippine L.J. 430, 435-438 (1975). Further on effectiveness of counsel (which when low enough can be a violation of the counsel right), see Israel & LaFave, *supra* n.8 at 380-391; Schwarzer, Dealing with Incompetent Counsel — The Trial Judge's Role, 93 Harv. L. Rev. 633 (1980); Notes, 93 Harv. L. Rev. 752 (1980), 80 Colum. L. Rev. 1053 (1980), 59 Neb. L. Rev. 1040 (1980); Annot., 2 A.L.R. 4th 27, 807 (1980).

(b) avoid violation of the *equal protection* clause of the Fourteenth Amendment (as well as an equivalent protection against the federal government that has been implied in Fifth Amendment due process). Equal protection was the rationale used in the Supreme Court cases upholding the indigent's right to appointed counsel on first appeal,[220] his right to free transcripts of proceedings for use on appellate review,[221] his right to freedom from certain other costs,[222] and the right not to suffer imprisonment for inability to pay a fine.[223] However, his right to supportive services has not been ruled on by the Supreme Court and is unsettled in lower courts. In many state courts, and in federal courts, the constitutional issue is avoided by statutes or court rules authorizing court appointment of experts, or by judicial practice without specific authorization.[224]

K. Excessive Bail; Excessive Fines; Cruel and Unusual Punishment

According to the Eighth Amendment, "excessive bail shall not be required, nor excessive fines imposed, nor cruel and unusual punishments inflicted." Even with these protections, you will notice, the accused does not receive an absolute constitutional right to bail.[225] Such a right once did exist in England; but by mid-eighteenth century bail was not allowed, according to Blackstone, for offenses of a "very enormous nature." And "[s]ince there were in Blackstone's day about 160 capital crimes, most bailable offenses were minor."[226] At the same time the point was recognized, and embodied in the English Bill of Rights of 1689, that those entitled to bail should not have to provide "excessive" bail. That point is recognized in the Eighth Amendment as well as in state constitutions. Federal statutes have from the beginning recognized a right to bail in non-capital cases[227] and state constitutions have done

220. Douglas v. California, 372 U.S. 352 (1963).

221. Griffin v. Illinois, 351 U.S. 12 (1956); Israel & LaFave, *supra* n.8 at 366-368.

222. This included filing fees for appeals and for post-conviction proceedings, Burns v. Ohio, 360 U.S. 252 (1959); Smith v. Bennett, 365 U.S. 708 (1961).

223. Tate v. Short, 401 U.S. 395 (1971).

224. This is discussed at 368-370 of the second edition, not the third, of Israel & LaFave, *supra* n.8. Another issue is the validity of some state statutes requiring the indigent to reimburse the state at such future time as he can afford to do so. The statutes have been upheld when free from certain discriminations. See Israel & LaFave, *supra* n.8, at 348-349.

225. See Carlson v. Landon, 342 U.S. 524, 545-546 (1952).

226. Fellman, The Defendant's Rights Today 49 (1976).

227. See Stack v. Boyle, 342 U.S. 1, 4 (1951). However, Congress may also provide,

the same (though often excluding *only* those capital cases in which the circumstances suggested that the case against the accused would be a strong one).

When is bail "excessive" under the Eighth Amendment? ". . . The modern practice of requiring a bail bond or the deposit of a sum of money subject to forfeiture serves as additional assurance of the presence of an accused [for trial]. Bail set at a figure higher than an amount reasonably calculated to fulfill this purpose is 'excessive' under the Eighth Amendment."[228] It is known, however, that judges are influenced in setting bail by other factors as well, such as dangerousness of the accused and the seriousness of his crime. That concern has received at least legislative legitimation in some jurisdiction's laws for "preventive detention," as in the District of Columbia law enacted by Congress in 1970.[229] Pointing in the other direction — i.e., away from incarceration — has been the movement for liberalization of bail, represented by Congress's Bail Reform Act of 1966 for the federal courts,[230] as well as the movement for "pre-trial diversion."[231]

---

without violating the Eighth Amendment, that the Attorney General may in his discretion continue in custody without bail certain communist aliens pending final determination of their deportability (in a civil proceeding); the Eighth Amendment does not require bail in all cases "and does not require that bail be allowed under the circumstances of these cases." *Carlson, supra* n.225.

228. Stack v. Boyle, 342 U.S. 1, 5 (1951). The Court also declared that where, as here, the bail has been fixed at "a sum much higher than that usually imposed for offenses with like penalties," there must be "factual showing to justify such action."

229. See D.C. Code, §§23-1321, 23-1322 (Act of July 29, 1970, Pub. L. No. 91-358, §210(a), Title II). The District of Columbia Court of Appeals, upholding the Act, found it unnecessary to decide whether the Act violated any Eighth Amendment bail requirement (though it doubted such violation) since the judge has inherent power to protect future witnesses or jurors from interference or intimidation by the accused, who had been doing just that. The Court further found no violations of due process. Blunt v. U.S., 322 A.2d 579 (D.C. App. 1974); and see the same Court's stronger decision upholding the Act in U.S. v. Edwards, 49 U.S.L.W. 2750, 2753 (1981). On the constitutional issues see Meyer, Constitutionality of Pretrial Detention, 60 Geo. L.J. 1140 and 1382 (1972); Tribe, An Ounce of Detention: Preventive Justice In the World of John Mitchell, 56 Va. L. Rev. 371 (1970).

230. 80 Stat. 214 (1966), 88 Stat. 2086 (1975); 18 U.S.C. §§3146-3156. Under bail liberalization laws, instead of paying a 10% premium to a bondsman, the defendant in several jurisdictions including the federal courts may be released by paying 10% of the bail amount to the court and have it refunded if he appears in court as scheduled. Courts have also in recent years experimented with projects involving pre-trial release of defendants having substantial community ties, exacting no bail at all and only a personal pledge to appear as scheduled. Even where such a bail reform project has existed, about 30% of felony defendants may be unable to meet the court's terms. LaFave, Modern Criminal Law 79 (1978). Generally on bail, see Duke, Bail Reform For the Eighties: A Reply to Senator Kennedy, 49 Fordham L. Rev. 40 (1980); Zeisel, Bail Revisited, 1979 Am. B. Foundation Research J. 769; Thomas, Bail Reform in America (1976); Goldfarb, Ransom: A Critique of the American Bail System (1965).

231. "Diversion" uses a procedure (authorized by statute, court rule, or informal prosecutorial consent) whereby an accused who meets specified criteria has his prosecution suspended for a period and is placed in a community-based rehabilita-

The "excessive fines" portion of the Eighth Amendment has seldom figured in Supreme Court cases. Though federal courts typically have not reviewed criminal sentences, both the "excessive fines" and the "due process" clauses might afford a constitutional basis for review in the extreme case.[232] Still, "[c]ases where reviewing courts have set aside fines on grounds of being excessive have been extremely rare."[233]

Much more prominent in the cases is the "cruel and unusual punishment" clause — which somewhat overlaps the "excessive fines" clause because it is held to apply to imprisonment, fines, and other punishments that are *unusually severe in relation to* the crime committed, as well as to cruel and unusual *forms* of punishment. Examples of the latter would be torture and other forms of unnecessary cruelty,[234] including the "unnecessary and wanton infliction of pain" by a "deliberate indifference to serious medical needs of prisoners."[235] Examples of the former are: (1) punishment for falsification of public records by 15 years' imprisonment at hard labor, with chains at the ankle and wrist, plus a fine of 4,000 pesos, deprivation of political rights, and subjection to police surveillance after sentence completion;[236] (2) inflicting loss of American citizenship as punishment for wartime desertion from the armed forces (not involving desertion to the enemy);[237]

tion program. If the program is unsuccessful, the prosecution is resumed. See Notes, 83 Yale L.J. 827 (1974); 50 Ind. L.J. 783 (1975).

232. See 438-439 *supra* and authorities in nn. 161-163.

233. Fellman, *supra* n.226 at 407.

234. See Wilkerson v. Utah, 99 U.S. 130, 136 (1878) (execution by shooting, upheld); Estelle v. Gamble, 429 U.S. 97, 102 (1976); and the forms and conditions of prison discipline described as cruel and unusual in Hutto v. Finney, 437 U.S. 678, 682-683, 685-687 (1978). (*Cf.* Rhodes v. Chapman, 69 L. Ed. 2d 59 (1981): Putting two inmates in single cell in an otherwise adequate maximum-security state prison was not cruel and unusual punishment.) The *Hutto* opinion states that the cruel and unusual punishment clause prohibits "grossly disproportionate" penalties "as well as" those "that transgress today's 'broad and idealistic concepts of dignity, civilized standards, humanity and decency'" (at 685). Ingraham v. Wright, 430 U.S. 651 (1977), found the Eighth Amendment inapplicable to the paddling form of punishment for school children. The Amendment was held applicable only to criminal cases; state common law and criminal remedies would be applicable to excessive paddling; due process did not require any notice or hearing prior to paddling.

235. Estelle v. Gamble, 429 U.S. 97, 104 (1976). Such injury by federal officials can be redressed by a damage suit based directly on the Eighth Amendment violation, notwithstanding availability of a suit against the federal government itself under the Federal Tort Claims Act. Carlson v. Green, 446 U.S. 14 (1980).

236. Weems v. U.S., 217 U.S. 349 (1910). But in Rummel v. Estelle, 445 U.S. 263 (1980), a 5 to 4 decision ruled that it was not "cruel and unusual" to impose a life sentence, under a state recidivism law, for having been thrice convicted of property-related felonies yielding a total of $229.11 (fraudulent use of credit card; passing forged check; obtaining money by false pretenses).

237. Trop v. Dulles, 357 U.S. 86 (1958). The plurality opinion observed that the meaning of "cruel and unusual punishment" changes with the "evolving standards of decency that mark the progress of a maturing society" (at 101).

and (3) capital punishment for rape of an adult woman by an escapee during commission of other crimes, but not resulting in her death (at least in the absence of aggravating circumstances such as subjecting her to excessive brutality and serious, lasting injury).[238] Still another category of "cruel and unusual punishment" — or perhaps another aspect of the disproportionality category — is the punishment inflicted for mere *status,* e.g., of drug addiction, as distinct from the criminal behavior itself.[239]

Though the death penalty was held disproportionate for certain rape cases, as just described, the death penalty for homicide cases is another matter, as appeared in a series of murder cases in the 1970's in the Supreme Court. The Court ruled in 1972 that the death penalty was cruel and unusual punishment in a case in which sentencing provisions left so much room for discretion that they were administered in an arbitrary and capricious way.[240] After many state legislatures responded by either imposing a *mandatory* death penalty for specified crimes, or establishing certain *standards* as to when the penalty was applicable (e.g., specifying circumstances of aggravation and mitigation), the Court upheld[241] some *standards*-type statutes specifying, or permitting proof of, circumstances of aggravation, and containing other

238. Coker v. Georgia, 433 U.S. 584 (1977).

239. Robinson v. California, 370 U.S. 660 (1962). This case explicitly held the "cruel and unusual punishment" clause applicable to the states through Fourteenth Amendment due process. In Powell v. Texas, 392 U.S. 514 (1968) the Court distinguished *Robinson.* In the words of the plurality opinion, "the present case does not fall within that holding, since appellant was convicted not for being an alcoholic, but for being in public while drunk on a particular occasion. . . . Texas thus has not sought to punish a mere status, as California did in *Robinson*" (at 532).

240. Furman v. Georgia, 408 U.S. 238 (1972).

241. Gregg v. Georgia, 428 U.S. 153 (1976); Proffit v. Florida, 428 U.S. 242 (1976); Jurek v. Texas, 428 U.S. 262 (1976). In a Florida case subsequent to *Proffit* (Gardner v. Florida, 430 U.S. 349 (1977)), it appeared that after a jury recommendation of life imprisonment, the trial judge had decided on the death penalty partly on the basis of a pre-sentence investigation report, a confidential portion of which was not disclosed to or requested by defendant or counsel. In reversing, three Justices thought the procedure as to the pre-sentence report violated due process, two concurred on Eighth Amendment grounds, one concurred without opinion, two continued to believe the death penalty was cruel and unusual *per se* (with one also agreeing with the due process argument), and one dissented. In Lockett v. Ohio, 438 U.S. 586 (1978), and Bell v. Ohio, 438 U.S. 637 (1978), there were many separate views expressed, but most of the Court agreed that the Ohio statute's listing of mitigating factors was defective in not allowing the sentencer to consider the defendant's role being that of aider and abettor rather than participant in the actual killing.

safeguards,[242] but struck down the *mandatory* type.[243] In the latter case, two Justices who thought capital punishment was *per se* cruel and unusual punishment were in the majority with three others who thought standards and safeguards were constitutionally necessary.[244]

242. E.g., the Georgia statute provided for a separate, pre-sentence hearing on the death penalty, in which both evidence and argument would be heard. At least one of ten specified aggravating circumstances must be found to exist beyond a reasonable doubt and be designated in writing before judge or jury may impose death (e.g., murder for profit; prior conviction of violent crime, etc.). An appeal is automatic, with the Georgia Supreme Court determining whether the death penalty was imposed under passion, prejudice, or other arbitrary factor; whether the evidence supported the finding of aggravated circumstances; and whether the penalty went beyond that imposed in similar cases. If that Court affirms, it is to include a reference to the similar cases it considered. However, a 1980 case held that arbitrary and capricious discretion in imposition of sentence was possible under the Georgia court's construction of a statutory standard ("torture, depravity of mind, or an aggravated battery to the victim") in such a way as to let any deliberate, shotgun murder qualify. Godfrey v. Georgia, 446 U.S. 420 (1980).

243. Woodson v. North Carolina, 428 U.S. 280 (1976); Roberts v. Louisiana, 428 U.S. 325 (1976). See also the later case of Roberts v. Louisiana, 431 U.S. 633 (1977).

244. The three Justices thought standards like those of the Georgia law were necessary to avoid arbitrary and capricious imposition, since juries even under a mandatory statute could be expected to exercise discretion, e.g., choose a verdict for a lesser offense when they felt the death penalty would be inappropriate. Also, the Georgia safeguard of meaningful appellate review was lacking here, as a check on the jury's *de facto* discretion. In a 1980 capital case, the Court held that the jury cannot, consistently with due process, be prohibited from considering a verdict of guilt of a lesser, included non-capital offense. (Beck v. Alabama, 447 U.S. 625 (1980)).

For a thorough analysis of death penalty cases and statutes, see Gillers, Deciding Who Dies, 129 U. Pa. L. Rev. 1 (1980). Examples of studies with a more jurisprudential focus are Lempert, Desert and Deterrence: An Assessment of the Moral Bases of the Case for Capital Punishment, 79 Mich. L. Rev. 1177 (1981); Radin, Cruel Punishment and Respect for Persons, 53 S. Calif. L. Rev. 1143 (1980); van den Haag, In Defense of the Death Penalty: A Legal-Political-Moral Analysis, 14 Crim. L. Bull. 51 (1978); Bedau, ed., Capital Punishment in the United States (1976).

Subject Index